The Reformation to the Modern Church

The Reformation to the Modern Church

A Reader in Christian Theology

edited by

Keith D. Stanglin

Fortress Press
Minneapolis

THE REFORMATION TO THE MODERN CHURCH
A Reader in Christian Theology

Cover design: Alisha Lofgren
Cover image: OpenBook/175781110/iStock/Thinkstock

Library of Congress Cataloging-in-Publication Data is available
Print ISBN: 978-1-4514-6551-8
eBook ISBN: 978-1-4514-6976-9

The paper used in this publication meets the minimum requirements of American National Standard for Information Sciences — Permanence of Paper for Printed Library Materials, ANSI Z329.48-1984.

Manufactured in the U.S.A.

Contents

Acknowledgments

In the process of working on a survey text of church history, I could not help but think about the teachers who introduced me to the topic, beginning nearly two decades ago. Clyde Antwine, Don Kinder, John Mark Hicks, Richard Muller, and David Rylaarsdam, in their own unique ways, each reinforced to me the importance of historical perspective in the task of theology and ministry. I am grateful for their examples and for their guidance during my formal training.

Several people have assisted in various ways with the conception and production of this book, and they deserve acknowledgment. Mark Mann, Mark Powell, David Rylaarsdam, John Thompson, and Darren Williamson provided useful feedback toward the end of the difficult task of selection. Kathy Armistead of Abingdon Press provided the critical edition of the Wesley texts with, most importantly, very quick turnaround. Shana Harrington copyedited the entire manuscript and caught some mistakes that my eyes were too tired to find. The staff at Fortress Press is to be thanked for their help along the way, and a few are worthy of mention. Esther Diley acquired and organized the necessary permissions—no small task on a book like this one. Marissa Wold oversaw the book's production. And Will Bergkamp, publisher and managing director deserves special thanks not only for his unwavering support of my idea from its inception but also for his hands-on (in a good way) willingness to offer helpful feedback and prudent advice along the way. Finally, I am grateful to Amanda, Paul, Isaac, and Rachel for their continual flexibility and their permission for me to sit at the computer and work on projects like this one.

I have written and compiled this book for anyone interested in learning more about the "second half" of church history, with the hope that these introductions and selections will benefit readers by opening new horizons for discussion and research. Thus I dedicate this volume to my students who will seek and find this very benefit in it.

Keith Stanglin
Pentecost 2014

Preface

This book is a primary-source reader with excerpts covering from the late medieval period up through the early twenty-first century. It is intended to acquaint students (and anyone interested in intellectual history) with the most influential figures and documents of the past seven hundred years in the Western church. The core curriculum at a number of seminaries and universities surveys the two millennia of "Church History" or "Historical Theology" in the course of two semesters. The division of the two halves tends to settle in the late medieval period leading to the European Reformation. This book is thus meant to be used as a textbook in university, and especially seminary, courses on the Reformation to the modern church—or, practically speaking, the "second half" of church history.

Although there are several primary-source compilations related to church history, I am not aware of any collections that specialize in this time period (from about 1300 to the present). Many anthologies seek to cover the whole of church history. In their attempts to include the whole Christian era, however, their coverage remains too broad and spotty in the second half. Other collections are more narrowly focused on specialized topics, such as the Reformation or American Christianity. In either case, whether the book is too broad or too narrow, instructors of "Church History 2" courses have been forced to supplement such books with extensive readings from the Internet or library reserve. In light of this often frustrating and time-consuming pedagogical challenge, this book seeks to make the correct sources available in one place.

The reading selections have been distributed into nine chapters, each of which begins with an introduction to the period and some of its controversies and closes with suggestions for further secondary-source reading. Each reading selection is also preceded by a brief introduction to set the immediate context. Such compartmentalization, which is helpful for structuring chapters and divisions within a book, should not obscure the complexity of history and especially the tremendous eclecticism and plurality that characterize this whole era. It is a form of evil to pigeonhole thinkers and documents into categories, but it is a necessary evil.

This volume is intended to work in conjunction with a fuller set of lectures and a survey text. Although many surveys of the entire history of the church abound and can be used profitably with the current book, the following recent texts cover roughly the same time period and, without intending to endorse everything about them, are worth noting:

González, Justo L. *The Story of Christianity*, vol. 2, *The Reformation to the Present Day*. 2nd ed. New York: HarperOne, 2010.

Janz, Denis R., ed. *A People's History of Christianity—Student Edition*, vol. 2, *From the Reformation to the 21st Century*. Minneapolis: Fortress Press, 2014.

Woodbridge, John D., and Frank A. James III. *Church History: The Rise and Growth of the Church in Its Cultural, Intellectual, and Political Context*, vol. 2, *From Pre-Reformation to the Present Day*. Grand Rapids, MI: Zondervan, 2013.

At the same time, even though this book works well accompanying a secondary survey text, it may also stand alone as a primer for readers who are unfamiliar with the primary sources and the most important figures and movements in this period of Christian theology. Taken as a whole, the chapter introductions, selection introductions, biographical notices, and primary sources come together to tell some of the most significant aspects of this history.

Reading Primary Sources

Direct interaction with primary sources is indispensable in the study of history. There is no better way to understand the major figures under discussion in a course than to read large chunks of their own writings. The selections that are included are intended not only to inform but also to spark the reader's interest in the whole document from which a selection is taken, or to find other writings of the author and contemporaries. The study of history is incomplete without such reading.

Here are some general methodological guidelines that apply to reading any primary sources, including those collected in this volume.

1. The reader should primarily be attentive to the thesis or central idea of each reading selection. What main point is the author trying to get across?
2. The reader should discern how the author proceeds to ground the thesis. How does the author support the case? What are the arguments? If it is readily available in the editorial note or introduction, the reader should keep in mind the occasion for writing and the intended audience, which help to illuminate the main idea and method of argumentation.
3. The reader should always be on the lookout for any relevant presuppositions, beliefs, values, and themes that illustrate the author's *Sitz im Leben* and that connect with his or her larger corpus and that of his or her contemporaries.
4. Finally, look for the threads of influence that precede the author and for the seeds of theological trajectories that follow. Whom does the author quote or seem to follow, and who later appeals to the author and seems to follow him?

In other words, as in biblical studies—a discipline with which most seminarians have some familiarity—the best way to understand an author is to put one's exegetical skills to work. At the very least, this kind of reading will require annotating one's textbook and perhaps taking separate notes on the readings.

The goals for reading are threefold. As already stated, the primary proximate goal of the reading is to begin to **understand** the authors on their own terms before making any judgments about their orthodoxy or heterodoxy. As Herbert Butterfield wrote, "Real historical understanding is not achieved by the subordination of the past to the present, but rather by our making the past our present and attempting to see life with the eyes of another century than our own."[1] Similarly, Étienne Gilson said, "As a rule it takes much more cleverness to understand a philosophy than to refute it."[2] A good historian is like being a tourist; when one visits another country, one should not deride the people and their customs simply because they are different or prima facie unintelligible.

1. Herbert Butterfield, *The Whig Interpretation of History* (New York: Norton, 1965), 16.
2. Étienne Gilson, *Modern Philosophy: Descartes to Kant* (New York: Random House, 1963), vii.

Instead, one should attempt to understand by means of translation and engagement. Moreover, an understanding of the reading selections should increase the student's grasp of the class lectures, and vice versa. Accurate, descriptive understanding is requisite for and leads to fair **evaluation**, which is the remote goal of the reading.

After understanding and basic evaluation, the question of how the material can **inform one's own faith and practice** in a positive way may be addressed as the ultimate goal—that is, one should ask questions such as these: What can be gained from this historical perspective? What have we learned about ourselves in the process? How does this material inform and influence the theology and controversies of the present day and help the church move forward? Based on our understanding and evaluation, how can we be more faithful disciples, both individually and corporately, leading to the eternal enjoyment of God?

Traditionally, academic courses give more emphasis to the first goal and less attention to the second and third goals. In any case, each of the three goals, though distinct, should never be pursued in isolation from the others.

Selection of Materials

In addition to its unique coverage, it is appropriate here to identify some other characteristics of this book that also shed light on the reason for its reading selections. First, I believe the book should contain just more than enough material for most students to read in a semester of a typical survey course, without being too large and unwieldy. In other words, given that most courses will have at least five hundred pages of secondary source material to work through, the primary source text should equal the length of secondary readings and provide plenty of selections from which instructors may choose. Indeed, since it is impossible to be exhaustive, instructors will surely find occasional readings suited to their purposes to add to those included here.

Second, the reading selections focus on the intellectual and theological development that has taken place in the West from the late medieval to the late modern period. The focus on theology is not intended to deny the importance of social factors; indeed, the brief introductions at the beginning of each section sketch some of the sociopolitical concerns relevant to each period. Because the aim is to shape the book not primarily for modern or social history courses but, rather, for church history courses, the most important *theological* contributions and developments are of chief interest to the intended audience. In sum, I have taken the figures whom I discuss most in my own classroom lectures and have sought salient excerpts from their writings to illustrate what I have to say. Neither do my choices intend to deny the importance of developments in the Eastern churches. The fact remains, however, that theologians in the East since the fourteenth century have not exercised their influence in the West to the degree that most of the writers represented in this book have.

Third, given the constraints of space and the focus on theology, I have attempted to showcase a variety of theological genres and topics. The genres range from polemical to constructive, from academic to devotional, and the readings include excerpts from disputations, letters, sermons, prayers, liturgies, treatises, journal essays, confessions of faith, catechisms, and systematic theologies.

The topics covered are also wide-ranging, though I have highlighted some prominent or controversial topics of each respective period—for example, sacraments and free will in the Reformation and post-Reformation period, epistemology in the Enlightenment, and ethics in the twentieth century. In the broad scope of the period of history covered in this volume, many themes rise to prominence in the theological debates and concerns. Predestination and grace, biblical interpretation, epistemology, the role of women, and sacraments are perennial topics. But none of these debates can ultimately escape the question of religious authority. The rifts that took shape in the late medieval church were motivated by this conundrum, and the fragmentation only increased from there. What are the sources for theology, and what are the criteria for evaluating doctrine? This question of religious authority is of utmost importance. When it is not in the foreground of a theological debate, it lurks in the background. For this reason, many of the selections and chapter introductions will broach the topic of foundations for religious knowledge. If a unifying thread runs through this epoch and through this volume, it is this one.

Finally, emphasis (that is, the greater number of pages) is devoted to figures and documents whose influence and legacy are decisive, or, in the case of the more obscure selections, the documents exemplify the significance of the period and the topic being illustrated. Although some attention is given to late-twentieth-century theology, there is no need to attempt to cover the present-day spectrum of systematic theology or for a historical survey to get into the business of predicting who will be more important in the church's history. Indeed, the closer one gets to the present day, the greater the number of authors are represented, and with generally shorter selections. The premise (to oversimplify a bit) is that, just as the history of philosophy is a series of footnotes to Plato, the second half of church history is in many ways a series of footnotes to Luther. Thus, in order to understand this period, one needs a fairly heavy dose of Erasmus, Luther, Calvin, Trent, and Vatican II. If a reader's interest in Christian theology happens to be limited to a particular modern issue, critical and careful theology still cannot be done without reference to—or at least basic knowledge of—the theology and movements represented by these selections. In the present academic environment, marked as it is by immense diversity and countless trajectories, there is great value in studying the core traditions out of which these movements grow.

The foremost challenge of historiography is selection. It is impossible to tell every story, to examine every important figure, and to read every influential document—especially in one course or one textbook. The omission of worthy candidates is inevitable. Given the criteria for selection I have mentioned and in light of the story I seek to tell, I believe that my selections (and omissions) are justifiable. At the same time, this compilation is nothing if it is not useful to those who employ it in the classroom. Do you have suggestions for how we can make The Reformation to the Modern Church even better? Visit www.fortresspress.com/StanglinBook and click on the feedback tab. We look forward to hearing from you!

Notes and Apparatus

Although in a few places I have made tacit corrections to the texts and have seldom modified the translations based on the original language, in most cases I have left the texts as they are found in the editions cited. This means that, in the case of older translations and original compositions in English (especially before the twentieth century), the reader will find punctuation and spelling that are no longer standard. The reader should resist the sometimes unconscious prejudice that the older style per se somehow reflects less erudition. It does not. For texts composed in a foreign language, I have sought to use what are, to my mind, the best translations.

Except for a very few cases marked with the author's name, the footnotes are all mine. I have not attempted to make a note of every biblical or literary allusion. Rather, I have added a footnote when a word or allusion is not clear, or when an important concept begs to be connected to the larger historical-theological context or to another selection, or, frankly, when I have felt like making a comment or clarifying. In such comments, as in the introductions to each selection and the larger introductions to each chapter, I have tried to keep my preferences to myself and thus allow the reader to evaluate.

Chapter 1
Late Medieval Contexts

The late medieval period has often been portrayed intellectually in the West as a barren wasteland, studied rarely on its own terms but only as a prelude to the Reformation and the Enlightenment. In some real ways, it was not the happiest time in human history, and it was not the golden age of church history. It was a time of deep devotion and piety, of confession and the threat of purgatory. Concern over sin and personal guilt was exacerbated by the arrival of the bubonic plague, which reached Constantinople in 1347 and spread to most of Europe by late 1348. The mortality rate for those infected was around 70 percent, and by the next decade, the "Black Death" had killed about one-third of Europe. The mortality rate among caregiving priests was also high. Along with the famines of the early fourteenth century, these disasters combined to wipe out perhaps two-thirds of Europe's population. Such events shaped the economy, theology, and psyche of Europe in profound ways. Death has always been a necessary feature of human experience, but death—not to mention, the end of the world—seemed a little nearer during the fourteenth century.

Many accounts of the late medieval church have focused on the problems leading to the Reformation—for example, the poor training of clergy, their immorality and frequent absenteeism, as well as the anticlericalism and superstitious piety of the laity. Although these features were present, their prevalence has been exaggerated. Some specific acts of corruption, however, were practiced at the highest levels of the church. The sale of indulgences was a practice open to such abuse. An indulgence is a partial or plenary pardon for temporal punishment of sin still due to someone whose guilt has been forgiven. Sin puts one in debt, and, according to debated biblical passages such as Dan. 4:27 and the venerable tradition it came to reflect, almsgiving was interpreted as one way (from the human side) to redeem or atone for sins. Indulgences, which came to include pardon for people already dead and not personally penitent, became an increasingly common revenue-gathering tactic of the church on the eve of the Reformation. Another well-known abuse was simony, the buying and selling of church offices, which encouraged greed and filled clerical positions with untrained and unqualified men.

The papacy itself was under direct assault. In the high medieval period, especially under Gregory VII (d. 1085) and Innocent III (ca. 1160–1216), the popes exercised their authority successfully by means of discipline and excommunication of both spiritual and political leaders. The papal claims of spiritual and temporal jurisdiction reached their apex under Boniface VIII (ca. 1235–1303), though he was ultimately unable to back them up. There was a growing sense that the papacy was concerned more with worldly matters than with spiritual responsibilities, and that the use or threat of physical force was inconsistent with the papal office. When the papacy moved to Avignon (1302–1378) and later was split between Avignon and Rome and two claimants rivaled for power (1378–1415), it seemed to many that the hierarchical church was in its last throes.

The papacy was weakened, but there was still minimal dissension from the Roman Church in the West. One could not exactly go down the street and start a new church, so some spoke out against

The world as it seemed—with the three continents of Europe, Asia, and Africa—to the cartographer Fra Mauro in 1459.

the immoral practices of the clergy and attempted to reform the church from within. These leaders have generally been known as "forerunners" of the Reformation. One of these forerunners, John Wyclif (ca. 1325–1384), came into open conflict with the Roman Church while he taught at Oxford. Like many reform movements before him, he was known for his emphasis on voluntary poverty and preaching, and like many after him, he opposed the doctrine of transubstantiation and advocated the translation of Scripture. Wyclif was condemned during his life and posthumously at the Council of Constance. His followers, the Lollards, became a kind of reform movement in England for the next century and translated the Latin Vulgate into English.

Although the late medieval era was characterized by struggles that would foreshadow cries for reform and, later, schism, it cannot simply be considered a time of decline and struggle in church and society. Contrary to popular opinion and much of the older scholarship on the period, the Western church witnessed a flowering of scholastic theology during this time. Vibrant, competing schools of thought influenced late medieval theology in a variety of directions. William of Ockham (ca. 1285–1347) was the most prominent nominalist and advocate of the so-called *via moderna*. Other theological luminaries during this period include Thomas Bradwardine (ca. 1295–1349), Gregory of Rimini (d. 1358), and Gabriel Biel (ca. 1420–1495). The *devotio moderna* and its most well-known spokesman, Thomas à Kempis (ca. 1380–1471), inspired a renewal of piety throughout Western Europe. Late medieval Christianity was neither a monolithic system of thought nor a barren wasteland.

This period has also been described as the Renaissance, a rebirth of knowledge facilitated by a return to the classical sources. In the wake of the Crusades and the immigration of Greek speakers fleeing the Turkish conquest of Constantinople (1453), such classical sources became more readily available in the West. More important, the advent of Johann Gutenberg's printing press in the 1450s made the mass production and distribution of books a reality, changing forever the world of scholarship and access to learning. The Renaissance was the age of learned humanists, such as Francesco Petrarch (1304–1374), Niccolò Macchiavelli (1469–1527), and Desiderius Erasmus (ca. 1467–1536). Collectively, the humanistic questioning of authority and philological examination of Scripture would lay the theological foundation for the gradual shift to modernity in Reformation and post-Reformation Europe.

One of the key issues during this whole period, from the time of Boniface VIII to that of Erasmus, was the question of religious authority. As popes struggled to exercise the wide range of authority that some in the office had claimed, and while some were advocating a doctrine of papal infallibility, other theologians were seeking to limit the pope's power, both spiritually and politically. Most theologians and canonists agreed that Scripture was the primary theological norm, but they differed on who or what should be the norm of interpretation. Should the pope, the ecumenical council, or individual scholastic theologians have the final say on biblical interpretation? And—during the papal schism—which pope, or which theologian and school of thought? For a time, the late medieval church was able to embrace the various tensions created by these debates. But the seeds of schism were being sown, and the harvest would prove to be plentiful.

A. Doctrinal Controversies

Selection 1: Pope Boniface VIII, *Unam Sanctam* (1302)

Pope Boniface VIII (ca. 1235–1303) had offended King Philip IV of France, who then cut off French contributions to the Roman Church. On November 18, 1302, Boniface responded to the French king's assertion of power by issuing the bull—that is, an official papal document—*Unam sanctam*. Boniface's argument for supreme papal authority begins with quotations from three authoritative sources: one from the Nicene-Constantinopolitan Creed (381), one from Cyprian of Carthage (d. 258) (*Epistle *73.21), and a few from Scripture. He proceeds to make his case by means of typological exegesis and appeals to traditional teachings of the church. Boniface's defense of the supreme authority of the pope over the state was promptly answered by King Philip, who sent men to plunder the papal palace and abduct Boniface himself, who died a few weeks later. A new precedent was set in the ongoing struggle between church authority and state authority.

We are obliged by faith to believe and hold—and we do firmly believe and sincerely confess—that there is one holy, catholic and apostolic church, and that outside this church there is neither salvation nor remission of sins. . . . In which church there is one Lord, one faith, one baptism. At the time of the flood there was one ark of Noah, symbolizing the one church; this was completed in one cubit and had one, namely Noah, as helmsman and captain; outside which all things on earth, we read, were destroyed.[1] . . . Of this one and only church there is one body and one head—not two heads, like a monster—namely Christ, and Christ's vicar is Peter, and Peter's successor, for the Lord said to Peter himself, "Feed my sheep." "My sheep" he said in general, not these or those sheep; wherefore he is understood to have committed them all to him. Therefore, if the Greeks or others say that they were not committed to Peter and his successors, they necessarily confess that they are not of Christ's sheep, for the Lord says in John, "There is one fold and one shepherd."

And we learn from the words of the gospel that in this church and in her power are two swords, the spiritual and the temporal. For when the apostles said, "Behold here" (that is, in the church, since it was the apostles who spoke) "are two swords"—the Lord did not reply, "It is too much," but "It is enough." Truly he who denies that the temporal sword is in the power of Peter, misunderstands the words of the Lord, "Put up thy sword into the sheath." Both are in the power of the church, the spiritual sword and the material. But the latter is to be used for the church, the former by her; the former by the priest, the latter by kings and captains but at the will and by the permission of the priest. The one sword, then, should be under the other, and temporal authority subject to spiritual. For when the apostle says, "There is no power but of God, and the powers that be ordained of God," they would not be so ordained were not one sword made subject to the other. . . .

Thus, concerning the church and her power, is the prophecy of Jeremiah fulfilled, "See, I have this day set thee over the nations and over the kingdoms," etc. If, therefore, the earthly power err, it shall be judged by the spiritual power; and if a lesser power err, it shall be judged by a greater. But if the supreme power err, it can be judged only by God, not by man; for the testimony of the apostle is "The spiritual man judgeth all things, yet he himself is

1. This typology is loosely based on 1 Pet. 3:18-22.

judged of no man." For this authority, although given to a man and exercised by a man, is not human, but rather divine, given at God's mouth to Peter and established on a rock for him and his successors in him whom he confessed, the Lord saying to Peter himself, "Whatsoever thou shalt bind," etc. Whoever therefore resists this power thus ordained of God, resists the ordinance of God. . . . Furthermore we declare, state, define and pronounce that it is altogether necessary to salvation for every human creature to be subject to the Roman pontiff.

[*Papal Primacy and the Universal Church*, ed. P. Empie and T. A. Murphy (Minneapolis: Augsburg, 1974), 106–7]

Selection 2: *Propositions of Wyclif Condemned* (1382 and 1415) and *The Twelve Conclusions of the Lollards* (1395)

John Wyclif (ca. 1325–1384) was a professor at Oxford University and a pastor in Lutterworth, England. Because of his controversial writings, he was condemned as a heretic and his followers persecuted. The first set of excerpts is from propositions against Wyclif that appeared at a condemnation in London in 1382 and, with numerous additions, at the Council of Constance (posthumously) in 1415. The second document enumerates several beliefs of the early Lollards, the name pejoratively given to Wyclif's followers. Many of the reformist views they advocate would be promoted in the sixteenth-century Reformation.

Over a decade after Constance, in order to reinforce the condemnation, Wyclif's bones were exhumed and burned. The Lollard critique of the church, rejection of transubstantiation, and vernacular translation of Scripture anticipated later reforms; thus Wyclif has been known as the "Morning Star" of the Reformation.

Propositions of Wyclif Condemned

1. That the material substance of bread and the material substance of wine remain in the Sacrament of the altar. . . .

3. That Christ is not in the Sacrament essentially and really, in his own corporeal presence. . . .

30. That the excommunication of the Pope or of any prelate is not to be feared, because it is the censure of antichrist. . . .

42. That it is fatuous to believe in the indulgences of the Pope and the bishops. . . .

The Lollard Conclusions

1. That when the Church of England began to go mad after temporalities, like its great stepmother the Roman Church, and churches were authorized by appropriation in divers places, faith, hope, and charity began to flee from our Church, because pride, with its doleful progeny of moral sins, claimed this under title of truth. This conclusion is general, and proved by experience, custom, and manner or fashion, as you shall afterwards hear.

2. That our usual priesthood which began in Rome, pretended to be of power more lofty than the angels, is not the priesthood which Christ ordained for His apostles. This conclusion is proved because the Roman priesthood is bestowed with signs, rites, and pontifical blessings, of small virtue, nowhere exemplified in Holy Scripture, because the bishop's ordinal and the New Testament scarcely agree, and we cannot see that the Holy Spirit, by reason of any such signs, confers the gift, for He and all His excellent gifts cannot consist in any one with mortal sin. . . .

3. That the law of continence enjoined on priests, which was first ordained to the prejudice of women, brings sodomy into all the Holy Church, but we excuse ourselves by the Bible because the decree says that we should not

mention it, though suspected. Reason and experience prove this conclusion: reason, because the good living of ecclesiastics must have a natural outlet or worse; experience, because the secret proof of such men is that they find delight in women, and when thou hast proved such a man mark him well, because he is one of them. . . .

4. That the pretended miracle of the sacrament of bread drives all men, but a few, to idolatry, because they think that the Body of Christ which is never away from heaven could by power of the priest's word be enclosed essentially in a little bread which they show the people; but God grant that they might be willing to believe what the evangelical doctor[2] says in his Trialogus (iv. 7), that the bread of the altar is habitually the Body of Christ, for we take it that in this way any faithful man and woman can by God's law perform the sacrament of that bread without any such miracle. A final corollary is that although the Body of Christ has been granted eternal joy, the service of Corpus Christi, instituted by Brother Thomas [Aquinas], is not true but is fictitious and full of false miracles. . . .

5. That exorcisms and blessings performed over wine, bread, water and oil, salt, wax, and incense, the stones of the altar, and church walls, over clothing, mitre,[3] cross, and pilgrims' staves, are the genuine performance of necromancy rather than of sacred theology. This conclusion is proved as follows, because by such exorcisms creatures are honoured as being of higher virtue than they are in their own nature, and we do not see any change in any creature which is so exorcized, save by false faith which is the principal characteristic of the Devil's art. A corollary: that if the book of exorcizing holy water, read in church, were entirely trustworthy we think truly that the holy water used in church would be the best medicine for all kinds of illnesses—sores, for instance; whereas we experience the contrary day by day.

6. That king and bishop in one person, prelate and judge in temporal causes, curate and officer in secular office, puts any kingdom beyond good rule. This conclusion is clearly proved because the temporal and spiritual are two halves of the entire Holy Church. And so he who has applied himself to one should not meddle with the other, for no one can serve two masters. It seems that hermaphrodite or ambidexter would be good names for such men of double estate. . . .

7. That special prayers for the souls of the dead offered in our Church, preferring one before another in name, are a false foundation of alms, and for that reason all houses of alms in England have been wrongly founded. This conclusion is proved by two reasons: the one is that meritorious prayer, and of any effect, ought to be a work proceeding from deep charity, and perfect charity leaves out no one, for "Thou shaft love thy neighbour as thyself." And so it is clear to us that the gift of temporal good bestowed on the priesthood and houses of alms is a special incentive to private prayer which is not far from simony. For another reason is that special prayer made for men condemned is very displeasing to God. And although it be doubtful, it is probable to faithful Christian people that founders of a house of alms have for their poisonous endowment passed over for the most part to the broad road. The corollary is: effectual prayer springing from perfect love would in general embrace all whom God would have saved, and would do away with that well-worn way or merchandise in special prayers made for the possessionary mendicants and other hired

2. That is, Wyclif, who, in his book *Trialogus*, described his views of the Eucharist.

3. The mitre is the headdress of a bishop.

priests, who are a people of great burden to the whole realm, kept in idleness: for it has been proved in one book, which the king had, that a hundred houses of alms would suffice in all the realm, and from this would rather accrue possible profit to the temporal estate.

8. That pilgrimages, prayers, and offerings made to blind crosses or roods, and to deaf images of wood or stone, are pretty well akin to idolatry and far from alms, and although these be forbidden and imaginary, a book of error to the lay folk, still the customary image of the Trinity is specially abominable. This conclusion God clearly proves, bidding alms to be done to the needy man because they are the image of God, and more like than wood or stone; for God did not say, "let us make wood or stone in our likeness and image," but man; because the supreme honour which clerks call *latria* appertains to the Godhead only; and the lower honour which clerks call *dulia* appertains to man and angel and to no inferior creature.[4] A corollary is that the service of the cross, performed twice in any year in our church, is full of idolatry, for if that should, so might the nails and lance be so highly honoured; then would the lips of Judas be relics indeed if any were able to possess them. . . .

9. That auricular confession which is said to be so necessary to the salvation of a man, with its pretended power of absolution, exalts the arrogance of priests and gives them opportunity of other secret colloquies which we will not speak of; for both lords and ladies attest that, for fear of their confessors, they dare not speak the truth. And at the time of confession there is a ready occasion or assignation, that is for "wooing," and other secret understandings leading to mortal sins. They themselves say that they are God's representatives to judge of every sin, to pardon and cleanse whomsoever they please. They say that they have the keys of heaven and of hell, and can excommunicate and bless, bind and loose, at their will, so much so that for a drink, or twelve pence, they will sell the blessing of heaven with charter and close warrant sealed with the common seal. This conclusion is so notorious that it needs not any proof. It is a corollary that the pope of Rome, who has given himself out as treasurer of the whole Church, having in charge that worthy jewel of Christ's passion together with the merits of all saints in heaven, whereby he grants pretended indulgence from penalty and guilt, is a treasurer almost devoid of charity, in that he can set free all that are prisoners in hell at his will, and cause that they should never come to that place. But in this any Christian can well see there is much secret falsehood hidden away in our Church.

10. That manslaughter in war, or by pretended law of justice for a temporal cause, without spiritual revelation, is expressly contrary to the New Testament, which indeed is the law of grace and full of mercies. This conclusion is openly proved by the examples of Christ's preaching here on earth, for he specially taught a man to love his enemies, and to show them pity, and not to slay them. The reason is this, that for the most part, when men fight, after the first blow, charity is broken. And whoever dies without charity goes the straight road to hell. . . .

11. That the vow of continence made in our Church by women who are frail and imperfect in nature, is the cause of bringing in the gravest horrible sins possible to human nature, because, although the killing of abortive children before they are baptized and the destruction of nature by drugs are vile sins, yet connexion with themselves or brute beasts of any creature not having life surpasses them in foulness to such an extent as that they should be punished with the pains of hell. The corollary is that, widows and such as take the veil and the ring, being

4. The distinction between *latreia* and *douleia* (in Greek) was dogmatized at the Council of Nicaea II (787).

delicately fed, we could wish that they were given in marriage, because we cannot excuse them from secret sins.

12. That the abundance of unnecessary arts practised in our realm nourishes much sin in waste, profusion, and disguise. This, experience and reason prove in some measure, because nature is sufficient for a man's necessity with few arts. . . .

This is our embassy, which Christ has bidden us fulfil, very necessary for this time for several reasons. And although these matters are briefly noted here they are however set forth at large in another book, and many others besides, at length in our own language, and we wish that these were accessible to all Christian people. We ask God then of His supreme goodness to reform our Church, as being entirely out of joint, to the perfectness of its first beginning.

[*Documents of the Christian Church*, 4th ed., ed. Henry Bettenson and Chris Maunder (Oxford University Press, 2011), 184–90]

Jan Hus at the Council of Constance

Selection 3: Council of Constance (1414–1418)

The Council of Constance met from 1414 until 1418. Its tasks were (a) to put an end to the Great Papal Schism that began in 1378; (b) to deal with the doctrines of dissenters, such as John Wyclif and Jan Hus (ca. 1369–1415) (Hus was burned at the stake at the council itself); and (c) to call for reformation of the church in "head and members." Because this council successfully deposed anti-popes and appointed a new pope (Martin V), it became the paragon of the vibrant but short-lived "conciliar movement," which sought to subject papal authority to that of ecumenical councils. Although the conciliar ideals stated in the early sessions would not officially survive to the end of the council, later reformers would still hope for a council to which the pope would be subject.

Session 5 (6 April 1415)

In the name of the holy and undivided Trinity, Father and Son and holy Spirit. Amen. This holy synod of Constance, which is a general council, for the eradication of the present schism and for bringing unity and reform to God's church in head and members, legitimately assembled in the holy Spirit to the praise of almighty God, ordains, defines, decrees, discerns and declares as follows, in order that this union and reform of God's church may be obtained the more easily, securely, fruitfully and freely.

First it declares that, legitimately assembled in the holy Spirit, constituting a general council and representing the catholic church militant, it has power immediately from Christ; and that everyone of whatever state or dignity, even papal, is bound to obey it in those matters which pertain to the faith, the eradication of the said schism and the general reform of the said church of God in head and members.

Next, it declares that anyone of whatever condition, state or dignity, even papal, who contumaciously refuses to obey the past or future mandates, statutes, ordinances or precepts of this sacred council or of any other legitimately assembled general council, regarding the aforesaid things or matters pertaining to them, shall be subjected to well-deserved penance, unless he repents, and shall be duly punished, even by having recourse, if necessary, to other supports of the law. . . .[5]

5. This is the strongest statement of conciliarism, and the common sentiment it proclaims is far different from the Roman Church's later resting its ultimate authority in the pope (see Selection 96).

Session 12 (29 May 1415)

. . . The said holy synod decrees, determines and ordains for the good of unity in God's church that neither the lord Baldassare de Cossa, recently John XXIII, nor Angelo Correr nor Peter de Luna, called Gregory XII and Benedict XIII by their respective obediences, shall ever be re-elected as pope.[6] If the contrary happens, it is by this very fact null and void. Nobody, of whatever dignity or pre-eminence even if he be emperor, king, cardinal or pontiff, may ever adhere to or obey them or any one of them, contrary to this decree, under pain of eternal damnation and of being a supporter of the said schism. Let those who presume to the contrary, if there are any in the future, also be firmly proceeded against in other ways, even by invoking the secular arm.

Session 39 (9 October 1417)

Since the Roman pontiff exercises such great power among mortals, it is right that he be bound all the more by the incontrovertible bonds of the faith and by the rites that are to be observed regarding the church's sacraments. We therefore decree and ordain, in order that the fullness of the faith may shine in a future Roman pontiff with singular splendour from the earliest moments of his becoming pope, that henceforth whoever is to be elected Roman pontiff shall make the following confession and profession in public, in front of his electors, before his election is published.

In the name of the holy and undivided Trinity, Father and Son and holy Spirit. Amen. In the year of our Lord's nativity one thousand etc., I, N[ame], elected pope, with both heart and mouth confess and profess to almighty God, whose church I undertake with his assistance to govern, and to blessed Peter, prince of the apostles, that as long as I am in this fragile life I will firmly believe and hold the catholic faith, according to the traditions of the apostles, of the general councils and of other holy fathers, . . . and I will preserve this faith unchanged to the last dot and will confirm, defend and preach it to the point of death and the shedding of my blood, and likewise I will follow and observe in every way the rite handed down of the ecclesiastical sacraments of the catholic church. . . .

[*Decrees of the Ecumenical Councils*, ed. Norman P. Tanner, 1:409, 418, 442]

B. Piety

Selection 4: Julian of Norwich, *Showings* (ca. 1393)

Because late medieval women had no official ecclesiastical authority and rarely even* unofficial *teaching authority (Catherine of Siena [ca. 1347–1380] being a notable exception), women often left their mark by describing mystical visions they received directly from God. In* Showings, *or* Revelations of Divine Love, *Julian of Norwich (1342–ca. 1416), an English mystic, recorded sixteen revelations that she received in May 1373, along with her reflections on their meaning.

The Fourth Chapter

And at this, suddenly I saw the red blood running down from under the crown, hot and flowing freely and copiously, a living stream, just as

6. These three men all claimed to be pope simultaneously. The Roman Church officially recognizes Gregory XII, whereas the other two are regarded as anti-popes, whose names (and numbers) were assumed by later popes.

it was at the time when the crown of thorns was pressed on his blessed head.[7] I perceived, truly and powerfully, that it was he who just so, both God and man, himself suffered for me, who showed it to me without any intermediary.

And in the same revelation, suddenly the Trinity filled my heart full of the greatest joy, and I understood that it will be so in heaven without end to all who will come there. For the Trinity is God, God is the Trinity. . . .

I accepted it that at that time our Lord Jesus wanted, out of his courteous love, to show me comfort before my temptations began; for it seemed to me that I might well be tempted by devils, by God's permission and with his protection, before I would die. With this sight of his blessed Passion, with the divinity which I saw in my understanding, I knew well that this was strength enough for me, yes, and for all living creatures who were to be saved, against all the devils of hell and against all their spiritual enemies.

In this he brought our Lady St. Mary to my understanding. I saw her spiritually in her bodily likeness, a simple, humble maiden, young in years, grown a little taller than a child, of the stature which she had when she conceived. Also God showed me part of the wisdom and the truth of her soul, and in this I understood the reverent contemplation with which she beheld her God, who is her Creator, marvelling with great reverence that he was willing to be born of her who was a simple creature created by him. . . . Above her is no created thing, except the blessed humanity of Christ, as I saw.

The Fifth Chapter

At the same time as I saw this sight of the head bleeding, our good Lord showed a spiritual sight of his familiar love. I saw that he is to us everything which is good and comforting for our help. . . .

And in this he showed me something small, no bigger than a hazelnut, lying in the palm of my hand, as it seemed to me, and it was as round as a ball. I looked at it with the eye of my understanding and thought: What can this be? I was amazed that it could last, for I thought that because of its littleness it would suddenly have fallen into nothing. And I was answered in my understanding: It lasts and always will, because God loves it; and thus everything has being through the love of God.

In this little thing I saw three properties. The first is that God made it, the second is that God loves it, the third is that God preserves it. But what did I see in it? It is that God is the Creator and the protector and the lover. For until I am substantially united to him, I can never have perfect rest or true happiness, until, that is, I am so attached to him that there can be no created thing between my God and me.

This little thing which is created seemed to me as if it could have fallen into nothing because of its littleness. We need to have knowledge of this, so that we may delight in despising as nothing everything created, so as to love and have uncreated God. For this is the reason why our hearts and souls are not in perfect ease, because here we seek rest which is so little, in which there is no rest, and we do not know our God who is almighty, all wise and all good, for he is true rest. God wishes to be known, and it pleases him that we should rest in him; for everything which is beneath him is not sufficient for us. . . .[8]

And also our good Lord revealed that it is very greatly pleasing to him that a simple soul should come naked, openly and familiarly. For this is the loving yearning of the soul through

7. Well before Julian, the Western medieval church had developed a piety that focused intensely on the crucified body of Jesus.

8. The language here is Augustinian and reminiscent of the opening paragraph of *Confessions*.

the touch of the Holy Spirit, from the understanding which I have in this revelation: God, of your goodness give me yourself, for you are enough for me, and I can ask for nothing which is less which can pay you full worship. And if I ask anything which is less, always I am in want; but only in you do I have everything.

And these words of the goodness of God are very dear to the soul, and very close to touching our Lord's will, for his goodness fills all his creatures and all his blessed works full, and endlessly overflows in them. For he is everlastingness, and he made us only for himself, and restored us by his precious Passion and always preserves us in his blessed love; and all this is of his goodness.

The Sixth Chapter

This revelation was given to my understanding to teach our souls wisely to adhere to the goodness of God; and in that same time our habits of prayer were brought to my mind, how in our ignorance of love we are accustomed to employ many intermediaries. Then I saw truly that it is more honour to God and more true delight if we faithfully pray to him for his goodness, and adhere to this by grace, with true understanding and steadfast belief, than if we employed all the intermediaries of which a heart may think. . . .

For what I shall say came to my mind at the same time. We pray to God for his holy flesh and for his precious blood, his holy Passion, his precious death and his glorious wounds, for all the blessings of nature and the endless life that we have of all this, it is of the goodness of God. And we pray to him for the love of the sweet mother who bore him, and all the help that we have of her, it is of his goodness. And we pray for his holy Cross on which he died, and all the help and the strength that we have of that Cross, it is of his goodness. And in the same way, all the help that we have from particular saints and from all the blessed company of heaven, the precious love and the holy, endless friendship that we have from them, it is of his goodness. For the intermediaries which the goodness of God has ordained to help us are very lovely and many. Of them the chief and principal intermediary is the blessed nature which he took of the virgin, with all the intermediaries which preceded and followed, which are a part of our redemption and of our endless salvation.

Therefore it pleases him that we seek him and honour him through intermediaries, understanding and knowing that he is the goodness of everything. For the highest form of prayer is to the goodness of God, which comes down to us to our humblest needs. It gives life to our souls and makes them live and grow in grace and virtue. . . .

A man walks upright, and the food in his body is shut in as if in a well-made purse. When the time of his necessity comes, the purse is opened and then shut again, in most seemly fashion. And it is God who does this, as it is shown when he says that he comes down to us in our humblest needs. For he does not despise what he has made, nor does he disdain to serve us in the simplest natural functions of our body, for love of the soul which he created in his own likeness. For as the body is clad in the cloth, and the flesh in the skin, and the bones in the flesh, and the heart in the trunk, so are we, soul and body, clad and enclosed in the goodness of God. . . .

And therefore this lesson of love was revealed, with all that follows, as you will see, for the strength and foundation of everything was revealed in the first vision. For of all things, contemplating and loving the Creator makes the soul to seem less in its own sight, and fills it full with reverent fear and true meekness, and with much love for its fellow Christians.

The Seventh Chapter

And to teach us this, as I understand, our good Lord showed our Lady St. Mary at the same time, that is to signify the exalted wisdom and truth which were hers as she contemplated her Creator. This wisdom and truth showed her in contemplation how great, how exalted, how mighty and how good was her God. . . .

And during all the time that our Lord showed me this spiritual vision which I have now described, I saw the bodily vision of the copious bleeding of the head persist. The great drops of blood fell from beneath the crown like pellets, looking as if they came from the veins, and as they issued they were a brownish red, for the blood was very thick, and as they spread they turned bright red. . . .

The copiousness resembles the drops of water which fall from the eaves of a house after a great shower of rain, falling so thick that no human ingenuity can count them. And in their roundness as they spread over the forehead they were like a herring's scales.

At the time three things occurred to me: The drops were round like pellets as the blood issued, they were round like a herring's scales as they spread, they were like raindrops off a house's eaves, so many that they could not be counted. This vision was living and vivid and hideous and fearful and sweet and lovely; and in all this vision which I saw, what gave me most strength was that our good Lord, who is so to be revered and feared, is so familiar and so courteous, and most of all this filled me full of delight and certainty in my soul.

And so that I might understand this, he showed me this plain example. It is the greatest honour which a majestic king or a great lord can do for a poor servant, to be familiar with him; and especially if he makes this known himself, privately and publicly, with great sincerity and happy mien, this poor creature will think: See, what greater honour and joy could this noble lord give me than to demonstrate to me, who am so little, this wonderful familiarity? . . .

So it is with our Lord Jesus and us, for truly it is the greatest possible joy, as I see it, that he who is highest and mightiest, noblest and most honourable, is lowest and humblest, most familiar and courteous. And verily and truly he will manifest to us all this marvellous joy when we shall see him. . . . For the greatest abundance of joy which we shall have, as I see it, is this wonderful courtesy and familiarity of our Father, who is our Creator, in our Lord Jesus Christ, who is our brother and our saviour. But no man can know this wonderful familiarity in this life, unless by a special revelation from our Lord, or from a great abundance of grace, given within by the Holy Spirit. But faith and belief together with love deserve the reward, and so it is received by grace. For our life is founded on faith with hope and love. This is revealed to whom God wills, and he plainly teaches and expounds and declares it, with many secret details which are a part of our faith and belief, which are to be known to God's glory. And when the revelation, given only for a time, has passed and is hidden, then faith preserves it by the grace of the Holy Spirit to the end of our lives. And so in the revelation there is nothing different from the faith, neither less nor more, as will be seen by our Lord's intention in this same matter, when the whole revelation is completed.

The Eighth Chapter

And as long as I saw this vision of the copious bleeding of the head, I could not stop saying these words: Blessed be the Lord! In this revelation I understood six things. The first is the tokens of his blessed Passion and the plentiful shedding of his precious blood. The second is the virgin who is his beloved mother. The third is the blessed divinity, that always was and is and shall be, almighty, all wisdom and all love. The fourth is everything which he has made, for I know well that heaven and earth and all creation are great, generous and beautiful and good. But the reason why it seemed to my eyes so little was because I saw it in the presence of him who is the Creator. To any soul who sees the Creator of all things, all that is created seems very little. The fifth is that he who created it created everything for love, and by the same love is it preserved, and always will be without end, as has been said already. The sixth is that God is everything which is good, as I see, and the goodness which everything has is God.

God showed me this in the first vision, and he gave me space and time to contemplate it. And then the bodily vision ceased, and the spiritual vision persisted in my understanding. . . .

In all this I was greatly moved in love towards my fellow Christians, that they might all see and know the same as I saw, for I wished it to be a comfort to them, for all this vision was shown for all men.

Then I said to those who were with me: Today is my Doomsday. And I said this because I expected to die; because on the day that a man or a woman dies he receives particular judgment as he will be forever, as I understand. . . .

Everything that I say about me I mean to apply to all my fellow Christians, for I am taught that this is what our Lord intends in this spiritual revelation. And therefore I pray you all for God's sake, and I counsel you for your own profit, that you disregard the wretch to whom it was shown, and that mightily, wisely and meekly you contemplate upon God, who out of his courteous love and his endless goodness was willing to show it generally, to the comfort of us all. . . .

The Ninth Chapter

I am not good because of the revelations, but only if I love God better; and inasmuch as you love God better, it is more to you than to me.[9] I do not say this to those who are wise, because they know it well. But I say it to you who are simple, to give you comfort and strength; for we are all one in love, for truly it was not revealed to me that God loves me better than the humblest soul who is in a state of grace. For I am sure that there are many who never had revelations or visions, but only the common teaching of Holy Church, who love God better than I. If I pay special attention to myself, I am nothing at all; but in general I am, I hope, in the unity of love with all my fellow Christians. For it is in this unity that the life of all men consists who will be saved. For God is everything that is good, as I see; and God has made everything that is made, and God loves everything that he has made. And he who has general love for all his fellow Christians in God has love towards everything that is. For in mankind which will be saved is comprehended all, that is to say all that is made and the maker of all. For God is in man and in God is all. And he who loves thus loves all. And I hope by the grace of God that he who may see it so will be taught the truth and greatly comforted, if he has need of comfort.

I speak of those who will be saved, for at this time God showed me no one else. But in

9. Julian downplays the importance of her visions in comparison with the teaching of the church. Such a sentiment is common among the so-called mystics, challenging the popular dichotomy between (systematic) theology and mysticism.

everything I believe as Holy Church preaches and teaches. For the faith of Holy Church, which I had before I had understanding,[10] and which, as I hope by the grace of God, I intend to preserve whole and to practise, was always in my sight, and I wished and intended never to accept anything which might be contrary to it. And to this end and with this intention I contemplated the revelation with all diligence, for throughout this blessed revelation I contemplated it as God intended.

All this was shown in three parts, that is to say, by bodily vision and by words formed in my understanding and by spiritual vision. But I may not and cannot show the spiritual visions as plainly and fully as I should wish. But I trust in our Lord God almighty that he will, out of his goodness and for love of you, make you accept it more spiritually and more sweetly than I can or may tell it. . . .

The Fifty-Ninth Chapter

And we have all this bliss by mercy and grace, and this kind of bliss we never could have had and known, unless that property of goodness which is in God had been opposed, through which we have this bliss. For wickedness has been suffered to rise in opposition to that goodness; and the goodness of mercy and grace opposed that wickedness, and turned everything to goodness and honour for all who will be saved. For this is that property in God which opposes good to evil. So Jesus Christ, who opposes good to evil, is our true Mother. We have our being from him, where the foundation of motherhood begins, with all the sweet protection of love which endlessly follows.

As truly as God is our Father, so truly is God our Mother, and he revealed that in everything, and especially in these sweet words where he says: I am he; that is to say: I am he, the power and goodness of fatherhood; I am he, the wisdom and the lovingness of motherhood; I am he, the light and the grace which is all blessed love; I am he, the Trinity; I am he, the unity; I am he, the great supreme goodness of every kind of thing; I am he who makes you to love; I am he who makes you to long; I am he, the endless fulfilling of all true desires. For where the soul is highest, noblest, most honourable, still it is lowest, meekest and mildest.

And from this foundation in substance we have all the powers of our sensuality by the gift of nature, and by the help and the furthering of mercy and grace, without which we cannot profit. Our great Father, almighty God, who is being, knows us and loved us before time began. Out of this knowledge, in his most wonderful deep love, by the prescient eternal counsel of all the blessed Trinity, he wanted the second person to become our Mother, our brother and our saviour. From this it follows that as truly as God is our Father, so truly is God our Mother. Our Father wills, our Mother works, our good Lord the Holy Spirit confirms. And therefore it is our part to love our God in whom we have our being, reverently thanking and praising him for our creation, mightily praying to our Mother for mercy and pity, and to our Lord the Holy Spirit for help and grace. For in these three is all our life: nature, mercy and grace, of which we have mildness, patience and pity, and hatred of sin and wickedness; for the virtues must of themselves hate sin and wickedness.

And so Jesus is our true Mother in nature by our first creation, and he is our true Mother in grace by his taking our created nature. All the lovely works and all the sweet loving offices of beloved motherhood are appropriated to the second person, for in him we have this godly

10. That is, prior to the revelations.

will, whole and safe forever, both in nature and in grace, from his own goodness proper to him.

I understand three ways of contemplating motherhood in God. The first is the foundation of our nature's creation; the second is his taking of our nature, where the motherhood of grace begins; the third is the motherhood at work. And in that, by the same grace, everything is penetrated, in length and in breadth, in height and in depth without end; and it is all one love.

[*Julian of Norwich: Showings*, trans. Edmund College and James Walsh, Classics of Western Spirituality (New York: Paulist Press, 1978), 181–92, 295–97]

Selection 5: "Lord, Who Am I?" (early fifteenth century)

The manuscript designated "Beinecke 757" was a typical late medieval devotional book intended to facilitate the daily piety of laypeople. Among the many prayer settings included in its pages, this prayer to be recited before communion serves as a counterexample to the later Protestant caricature that Mass was a rote ceremony in which the status of the worshiper's heart was of no consequence.

Lord, who am I or what kind of person that I should dare come up to your table, I who am about to receive your most sacred body? I know, nevertheless, I know and truly confess that you are able to make me worthy, you who alone can make pure something conceived from impure seed. I beg you all powerful, all sweet, and all holy one, that through the merits of the blessed Virgin Mary and all your elect you may teach me and permit me with such purity of heart and cleanliness of mind, with such devotion and reverence, to come up to so admirable a sacrament, as far as is fitting and expedient.

I implore, that when my heart stirs with the sweetness of your blessed presence, there may be complete cleansing of my spiritual languor, there may be washing away of my sins.[11] May I have constant protection against dangers. May my heart be enflamed with your love. Let my soul taste now how sweet you are, Lord, tasting you so completely that the voluptuousness of the flesh not deceive it.

O delectable bread! O sweetest food! O desirable meal! O sweet feast restoring all things, and in you never failing! May it please you that now, taking you up faithfully, expediently, and purely, my soul the sinner may receive moral virtue from you in this its journey; and thus it may perfect its journey through you and to you without the impediment of Satan. Small is the house of my soul, Lord, whither you may come, and by your grace it may grow larger for you. It is ruined; repair it. It has done many things that offend you.

But to whom except you will I cry? Make me pure by my eyes. Mortify your servants in my members and all lustful actions so that you, king of virgins and lover of chastity, may take up peaceful lodging in my tabernacle. You who, with the Father and the Holy Spirit lives and reigns, God for ever and ever. Amen.

[Trans. Margot Fassler, in *Worship in Medieval and Early Modern Europe: Change and Continuity in Religious Practice*, ed. Karin Maag and John D. Witvliet (Notre Dame: University of Notre Dame Press, 2004), 21–22]

Selection 6: Thomas à Kempis, *Imitation of Christ* (1418)

This anonymous manual of spiritual devotion has traditionally been ascribed to

11. This prayer reflects the intimate connection in the sacrament joining the heart of the worshiper, Christ's bodily presence, and the forgiveness of sins.

Thomas à Kempis (ca. 1380–1471), a Dutch monk belonging to the Brethren of the Common Life. The purpose of the book is to lead believers to perfection by following in the steps of Jesus Christ. The book's simple but profound aphorisms reflect the late medieval piety known as* devotio moderna*, which continues to inspire readers.

Book One: Thoughts Helpful in the Life of the Soul
The First Chapter
Imitating Christ and Despising All Vanities on Earth

"He who follows Me, walks not in darkness," says the Lord (John 8:12). By these words of Christ we are advised to imitate His life and habits, if we wish to be truly enlightened and free from all blindness of heart. Let our chief effort, therefore, be to study the life of Jesus Christ.

The teaching of Christ is more excellent than all the advice of the saints, and he who has His spirit will find in it a hidden manna. Now, there are many who hear the Gospel often but care little for it because they have not the spirit of Christ. Yet whoever wishes to understand fully the words of Christ must try to pattern his whole life on that of Christ.

What good does it do to speak learnedly about the Trinity if, lacking humility, you displease the Trinity? Indeed it is not learning that makes a man holy and just, but a virtuous life makes him pleasing to God. I would rather feel contrition than know how to define it. For what would it profit us to know the whole Bible by heart and the principles of all the philosophers if we live without grace and the love of God? Vanity of vanities and all is vanity, except to love God and serve Him alone.

This is the greatest wisdom—to seek the kingdom of heaven through contempt of the world. It is vanity, therefore, to seek and trust in riches that perish. It is vanity also to court honor and to be puffed up with pride. It is vanity to follow the lusts of the body and to desire things for which severe punishment later must come. It is vanity to wish for long life and to care little about a well-spent life. It is vanity to be concerned with the present only and not to make provision for things to come. It is vanity to love what passes quickly and not to look ahead where eternal joy abides.

Often recall the proverb: "The eye is not satisfied with seeing nor the ear filled with hearing."[12] Try, moreover, to turn your heart from the love of things visible and bring yourself to things invisible. For they who follow their own evil passions stain their consciences and lose the grace of God.

The Second Chapter
Having a Humble Opinion of Self

Every man naturally desires knowledge;[13] but what good is knowledge without fear of God? Indeed a humble rustic who serves God is better than a proud intellectual who neglects his soul to study the course of the stars. He who knows himself well becomes mean in his own eyes and is not happy when praised by men.

If I knew all things in the world and had not charity, what would it profit me before God Who will judge me by my deeds?

Shun too great a desire for knowledge, for in it there is much fretting and delusion. Intellectuals like to appear learned and to be called wise. Yet there are many things the knowledge of which does little or no good to the soul, and he who concerns himself about other things than those which lead to salvation is very unwise.

Many words do not satisfy the soul; but a good life eases the mind and a clean conscience inspires great trust in God.

---

12. Eccles. 1:8.

13. These are the opening words of Aristotle's *Metaphysics*.

The more you know and the better you understand, the more severely will you be judged, unless your life is also the more holy. Do not be proud, therefore, because of your learning or skill. Rather, fear because of the talent given you. If you think you know many things and understand them well enough, realize at the same time that there is much you do not know. Hence, do not affect wisdom, but admit your ignorance. Why prefer yourself to anyone else when many are more learned, more cultured than you?

If you wish to learn and appreciate something worth while, then love to be unknown and considered as nothing. Truly to know and despise self is the best and most perfect counsel. To think of oneself as nothing, and always to think well and highly of others is the best and most perfect wisdom. . . .

The Third Chapter
The Doctrine of Truth

Happy is he to whom truth manifests itself, not in signs and words that fade, but as it actually is. Our opinions, our senses often deceive us and we discern very little.

What good is much discussion of involved and obscure matters when our ignorance of them will not be held against us on Judgment Day? Neglect of things which are profitable and necessary and undue concern with those which are irrelevant and harmful, are great folly.

We have eyes and do not see.

What, therefore, have we to do with questions of philosophy? He to whom the Eternal Word speaks is free from theorizing. For from this Word are all things and of Him all things speak—the Beginning Who also speaks to us. Without this Word no man understands or judges aright. He to whom it becomes everything, who traces all things to it and who sees all things in it, may ease his heart and remain at peace with God.

O God, You Who are the truth, make me one with You in love everlasting. I am often wearied by the many things I hear and read, but in You is all that I long for. Let the learned be still, let all creatures be silent before You; You alone speak to me.

The more recollected a man is, and the more simple of heart he becomes, the easier he understands sublime things, for he receives the light of knowledge from above. The pure, simple, and steadfast spirit is not distracted by many labors, for he does them all for the honor of God. And since he enjoys interior peace he seeks no selfish end in anything. What, indeed, gives more trouble and affliction than uncontrolled desires of the heart?

A good and devout man arranges in his mind the things he has to do, not according to the whims of evil inclination but according to the dictates of right reason. Who is forced to struggle more than he who tries to master himself? This ought to be our purpose, then: to conquer self, to become stronger each day, to advance in virtue.

Every perfection in this life has some imperfection mixed with it and no learning of ours is without some darkness. Humble knowledge of self is a surer path to God than the ardent pursuit of learning. . . .

If men used as much care in uprooting vices and implanting virtues as they do in discussing problems, there would not be so much evil and scandal in the world, or such laxity in religious organizations. On the day of judgment, surely, we shall not be asked what we have read but what we have done; not how well we have spoken but how well we have lived.

Tell me, where now are all the masters and teachers whom you knew so well in life and who were famous for their learning? Others have already taken their places and I know not whether they ever think of their predecessors. During life they seemed to be something; now they are seldom remembered. How quickly the glory of the world passes away! . . .

How many there are who perish because of vain worldly knowledge and too little care for serving God. They became vain in their own conceits because they chose to be great rather than humble.

He is truly great who has great charity. He is truly great who is little in his own eyes and makes nothing of the highest honor. He is truly wise who looks upon all earthly things as folly that he may gain Christ. He who does God's will and renounces his own is truly very learned.

The Fourth Chapter
Prudence in Action

Do not yield to every impulse and suggestion but consider things carefully and patiently in the light of God's will. For very often, sad to say, we are so weak that we believe and speak evil of others rather than good. . . .

Not to act rashly or to cling obstinately to one's opinion, not to believe everything people say or to spread abroad the gossip one has heard, is great wisdom.

Take counsel with a wise and conscientious man. Seek the advice of your betters in preference to following your own inclinations.

A good life makes a man wise according to God and gives him experience in many things, for the more humble he is and the more subject to God, the wiser and the more at peace he will be in all things.

The Fifth Chapter
Reading the Holy Scripture

Truth, not eloquence, is to be sought in reading the Holy Scriptures; and every part must be read in the spirit in which it was written. For in the Scriptures we ought to seek profit rather than polished diction.

Likewise we ought to read simple and devout books as willingly as learned and profound ones. We ought not to be swayed by the authority of the writer, whether he be a great literary light or an insignificant person, but by the love of simple truth. We ought not to ask who is speaking, but mark what is said. Men pass away, but the truth of the Lord remains forever.[14] God speaks to us in many ways without regard for persons.

Our curiosity often impedes our reading of the Scriptures, when we wish to understand and mull over what we ought simply to read and pass by.

If you would profit from it, therefore, read with humility, simplicity, and faith, and never seek a reputation for being learned. Seek willingly and listen attentively to the words of the saints; do not be displeased with the sayings of the ancients, for they were not made without purpose.

The Sixth Chapter
Unbridled Affections

When a man desires a thing too much, he at once becomes ill at ease. A proud and avaricious man never rests, whereas he who is poor and humble of heart lives in a world of peace. . . .

True peace of heart, then, is found in resisting passions, not in satisfying them. There is no peace in the carnal man, in the man given to vain attractions, but there is peace in the fervent and spiritual man.

The Seventh Chapter
Avoiding False Hope and Pride

Vain is the man who puts his trust in men, in created things.

14. Cf. Isa. 40:7-8.

Do not be ashamed to serve others for the love of Jesus Christ and to seem poor in this world. Do not be self-sufficient but place your trust in God. Do what lies in your power and God will aid your good will.[15] Put no trust in your own learning nor in the cunning of any man, but rather in the grace of God Who helps the humble and humbles the proud.

If you have wealth, do not glory in it, nor in friends because they are powerful, but in God Who gives all things and Who desires above all to give Himself. Do not boast of personal stature or of physical beauty, qualities which are marred and destroyed by a little sickness. Do not take pride in your talent or ability, lest you displease God to Whom belongs all the natural gifts that you have.

Do not think yourself better than others lest, perhaps, you be accounted worse before God Who knows what is in man. Do not take pride in your good deeds, for God's judgments differ from those of men and what pleases them often displeases Him. If there is good in you, see more good in others, so that you may remain humble. It does no harm to esteem yourself less than anyone else, but it is very harmful to think yourself better than even one. The humble live in continuous peace, while in the hearts of the proud are envy and frequent anger.

The Eighth Chapter
Shunning Over-Familiarity

Do not open your heart to every man, but discuss your affairs with one who is wise and who fears God. Do not keep company with young people and strangers. Do not fawn upon the rich, and do not be fond of mingling with the great. Associate with the humble and the simple, with the devout and virtuous, and with them speak of edifying things. Be not intimate with any woman, but generally commend all good women to God. Seek only the intimacy of God and of His angels, and avoid the notice of men.

We ought to have charity for all men but familiarity with all is not expedient. Sometimes it happens that a person enjoys a good reputation among those who do not know him, but at the same time is held in slight regard by those who do. . . .

The Ninth Chapter
Obedience and Subjection

It is a very great thing to obey, to live under a superior and not to be one's own master, for it is much safer to be subject than it is to command. Many live in obedience more from necessity than from love. Such become discontented and dejected on the slightest pretext. . . .

Go where you may, you will find no rest except in humble obedience to the rule of authority. Dreams of happiness expected from change and different places have deceived many.

Everyone, it is true, wishes to do as he pleases and is attracted to those who agree with him. But if God be among us, we must at times give up our opinions for the blessings of peace.

Furthermore, who is so wise that he can have full knowledge of everything? Do not trust too much in your own opinions, but be willing to listen to those of others. . . .

The Tenth Chapter
Avoiding Idle Talk

Shun the gossip of men as much as possible, for discussion of worldly affairs, even though sincere, is a great distraction inasmuch as we are quickly ensnared and captivated by vanity.

15. The late medieval maxim "To those who do what is in them God will not deny grace" was a popular saying among some scholastic theologians, such as Gabriel Biel (ca. 1420–1495), but opposed by strict Augustinians. The writer here expresses the sentiment from within an otherwise Augustinian context.

Many a time I wish that I had held my peace and had not associated with men. Why, indeed, do we converse and gossip among ourselves when we so seldom part without a troubled conscience? We do so because we seek comfort from one another's conversation and wish to ease the mind wearied by diverse thoughts. Hence, we talk and think quite fondly of things we like very much or of things we dislike intensely. . . .

Therefore we must watch and pray lest time pass idly.

When the right and opportune moment comes for speaking, say something that will edify.

Bad habits and indifference to spiritual progress do much to remove the guard from the tongue. Devout conversation on spiritual matters, on the contrary, is a great aid to spiritual progress, especially when persons of the same mind and spirit associate together in God.

The Eleventh Chapter
Acquiring Peace and Zeal for Perfection

We should enjoy much peace if we did not concern ourselves with what others say and do, for these are no concern of ours. How can a man who meddles in affairs not his own, who seeks strange distractions, and who is little or seldom inwardly recollected, live long in peace?

Blessed are the simple of heart for they shall enjoy peace in abundance.

Why were some of the saints so perfect and so given to contemplation? Because they tried to mortify entirely in themselves all earthly desires, and thus they were able to attach themselves to God with all their heart and freely to concentrate their innermost thoughts.

We are too occupied with our own whims and fancies, too taken up with passing things. Rarely do we completely conquer even one vice, and we are not inflamed with the desire to improve ourselves day by day; hence, we remain cold and indifferent. . . .

The greatest obstacle, indeed, the only obstacle, is that we are not free from passions and lusts, that we do not try to follow the perfect way of the saints. Thus when we encounter some slight difficulty, we are too easily dejected and turn to human consolations. . . .

If we let our progress in religious life depend on the observance of its externals alone, our devotion will quickly come to an end. Let us, then, lay the ax to the root that we may be freed from our passions and thus have peace of mind.[16]

If we were to uproot only one vice each year, we should soon become perfect. The contrary, however, is often the case—we feel that we were better and purer in the first fervor of our conversion than we are after many years in the practice of our faith. Our fervor and progress ought to increase day by day; yet it is now considered noteworthy if a man can retain even a part of his first fervor.

If we did a little violence to ourselves at the start, we should afterwards be able to do all things with ease and joy. It is hard to break old habits, but harder still to go against our will.

If you do not overcome small, trifling things, how will you overcome the more difficult? Resist temptations in the beginning, and unlearn the evil habit lest perhaps, little by little, it lead to a more evil one.

If you but consider what peace a good life will bring to yourself and what joy it will give to others, I think you will be more concerned about your spiritual progress.

The Twelfth Chapter
The Value of Adversity

It is good for us to have trials and troubles at times, for they often remind us that we are on

16. Cf. Matt. 3:10.

probation and ought not to hope in any worldly thing. It is good for us sometimes to suffer contradiction, to be misjudged by men even though we do well and mean well. These things help us to be humble and shield us from vainglory. . . .

When a man of good will is afflicted, tempted, and tormented by evil thoughts, he realizes clearly that his greatest need is God, without Whom he can do no good. Saddened by his miseries and sufferings, he laments and prays. He wearies of living longer and wishes for death that he might be dissolved and be with Christ. Then he understands fully that perfect security and complete peace cannot be found on earth.

The Thirteenth Chapter
Resisting Temptation

So long as we live in this world we cannot escape suffering and temptation. Whence it is written in Job: "The life of man upon earth is a warfare."[17]. . .

Yet temptations, though troublesome and severe, are often useful to a man, for in them he is humbled, purified, and instructed. The saints all passed through many temptations and trials to profit by them, while those who could not resist became reprobate and fell away. There is no state so holy, no place so secret that temptations and trials will not come. Man is never safe from them as long as he lives, for they come from within us—in sin we were born. When one temptation or trial passes, another comes; we shall always have something to suffer because we have lost the state of original blessedness.

Many people try to escape temptations, only to fall more deeply. We cannot conquer simply by fleeing, but by patience and true humility we become stronger than all our enemies. The man who only shuns temptations outwardly and does not uproot them will make little progress; indeed they will quickly return, more violent than before.

Little by little, in patience and long-suffering you will overcome them, by the help of God rather than by severity and your own rash ways. Often take counsel when tempted; and do not be harsh with others who are tempted, but console them as you yourself would wish to be consoled.

The beginning of all temptation lies in a wavering mind and little trust in God, for as a rudderless ship is driven hither and yon by waves, so a careless and irresolute man is tempted in many ways. Fire tempers iron and temptation steels the just. Often we do not know what we can stand, but temptation shows us what we are.

Above all, we must be especially alert against the beginnings of temptation, for the enemy is more easily conquered if he is refused admittance to the mind and is met beyond the threshold when he knocks.

Someone has said very aptly: "Resist the beginnings; remedies come too late, when by long delay the evil has gained strength."[18] First, a mere thought comes to mind, then strong imagination, followed by pleasure, evil delight, and consent. Thus, because he is not resisted in the beginning, Satan gains full entry. And the longer a man delays in resisting, so much the weaker does he become each day, while the strength of the enemy grows against him.

Some suffer great temptations in the beginning of their conversion, others toward the end, while some are troubled almost constantly throughout their life. Others, again, are tempted but lightly according to the wisdom and justice of Divine Providence Who weighs

17. Job 7:1.

18. Ovid, *Remedia amoris* 91-92.

the status and merit of each and prepares all for the salvation of His elect.

We should not despair, therefore, when we are tempted, but pray to God the more fervently that He may see fit to help us, for according to the word of Paul, He will make issue with temptation that we may be able to bear it.[19] Let us humble our souls under the hand of God in every trial and temptation for He will save and exalt the humble in spirit.

In temptations and trials the progress of a man is measured; in them opportunity for merit and virtue is made more manifest.

When a man is not troubled it is not hard for him to be fervent and devout, but if he bears up patiently in time of adversity, there is hope for great progress.

Some, guarded against great temptations, are frequently overcome by small ones in order that, humbled by their weakness in small trials, they may not presume on their own strength in great ones.

The Fourteenth Chapter
Avoiding Rash Judgment

Turn your attention upon yourself and beware of judging the deeds of other men, for in judging others a man labors vainly, often makes mistakes, and easily sins; whereas, in judging and taking stock of himself he does something that is always profitable.

We frequently judge that things are as we wish them to be, for through personal feeling true perspective is easily lost.

If God were the sole object of our desire, we should not be disturbed so easily by opposition to our opinions. But often something lurks within or happens from without to draw us along with it.

Many, unawares, seek themselves in the things they do. They seem even to enjoy peace of mind when things happen according to their wish and liking, but if otherwise than they desire, they are soon disturbed and saddened. Differences of feeling and opinion often divide friends and acquaintances, even those who are religious and devout.

An old habit is hard to break, and no one is willing to be led farther than he can see.

If you rely more upon your intelligence or industry than upon the virtue of submission to Jesus Christ, you will hardly, and in any case slowly, become an enlightened man. God wants us to be completely subject to Him and, through ardent love, to rise above all human wisdom.

The Fifteenth Chapter
Works Done in Charity

Never do evil for anything in the world, or for the love of any man. For one who is in need, however, a good work may at times be purposely left undone or changed for a better one. This is not the omission of a good deed but rather its improvement.

Without charity external work is of no value, but anything done in charity, be it ever so small and trivial, is entirely fruitful inasmuch as God weighs the love with which a man acts rather than the deed itself.

He does much who loves much. He does much who does a thing well. He does well who serves the common good rather than his own interests.

Now, that which seems to be charity is oftentimes really sensuality, for man's own inclination, his own will, his hope of reward, and his self-interest, are motives seldom absent. On the contrary, he who has true and perfect charity seeks self in nothing, but searches all things for the glory of God. . . .

19. See 1 Cor. 10:13.

If man had but a spark of true charity he would surely sense that all the things of earth are full of vanity!

The Sixteenth Chapter
Bearing with the Faults of Others

Until God ordains otherwise, a man ought to bear patiently whatever he cannot correct in himself and in others. Consider it better thus—perhaps to try your patience and to test you, for without such patience and trial your merits are of little account. Nevertheless, under such difficulties you should pray that God will consent to help you bear them calmly.

If, after being admonished once or twice, a person does not amend, do not argue with him but commit the whole matter to God that His will and honor may be furthered in all His servants, for God knows well how to turn evil to good. Try to bear patiently with the defects and infirmities of others, whatever they may be, because you also have many a fault which others must endure.

If you cannot make yourself what you would wish to be, how can you bend others to your will? We want them to be perfect, yet we do not correct our own faults. We wish them to be severely corrected, yet we will not correct ourselves. Their great liberty displeases us, yet we would not be denied what we ask. We would have them bound by laws, yet we will allow ourselves to be restrained in nothing. Hence, it is clear how seldom we think of others as we do of ourselves.

If all were perfect, what should we have to suffer from others for God's sake? But God has so ordained, that we may learn to bear with one another's burdens,[20] for there is no man without fault, no man without burden, no man sufficient to himself nor wise enough. . . .

20. See Gal. 6:2.

The Seventeenth Chapter
Monastic Life

If you wish peace and concord with others, you must learn to break your will in many things. To live in monasteries or religious communities, to remain there without complaint, and to persevere faithfully till death is no small matter. Blessed indeed is he who there lives a good life and there ends his days in happiness.

A monk in his habit

If you would persevere in seeking perfection, you must consider yourself a pilgrim, an exile on earth.[21] If you would become a religious, you must be content to seem a fool for the sake of Christ. Habit and tonsure change a man but little;[22] it is the change of life, the complete mortification of passions that endow a true religious.

He who seeks anything but God alone and the salvation of his soul will find only trouble and grief, and he who does not try to become the least, the servant of all, cannot remain at peace for long.

You have come to serve, not to rule. You must understand, too, that you have been called to suffer and to work, not to idle and gossip away your time. Here men are tried as gold in a furnace. Here no man can remain unless he desires with all his heart to humble himself before God.

Book Two: The Interior Life
The Sixth Chapter
The Joy of a Good Conscience

The glory of a good man is the testimony of a good conscience. Therefore, keep your conscience good and you will always enjoy happiness, for a good conscience can bear a great deal

21. Cf. 1 Pet. 2:11.

22. That is, the monastic garb and haircut.

and can bring joy even in the midst of adversity. But an evil conscience is ever restive and fearful.

Sweet shall be your rest if your heart does not reproach you.

Do not rejoice unless you have done well. Sinners never experience true interior joy or peace, for "there is no peace to the wicked," says the Lord.[23] Even if they say: "We are at peace, no evil shall befall us and no one dares to hurt us," do not believe them; for the wrath of God will arise quickly, and their deeds will be brought to naught and their thoughts will perish.

To glory in adversity is not hard for the man who loves, for this is to glory in the cross of the Lord. But the glory given or received of men is short lived, and the glory of the world is ever companioned by sorrow. The glory of the good, however, is in their conscience and not in the lips of men, for the joy of the just is from God and in God, and their gladness is founded on truth.

The man who longs for the true, eternal glory does not care for that of time; and he who seeks passing fame or does not in his heart despise it, undoubtedly cares little for the glory of heaven.

He who minds neither praise nor blame possesses great peace of heart and, if his conscience is good, he will easily be contented and at peace.

Praise adds nothing to your holiness, nor does blame take anything from it. You are what you are, and you cannot be said to be better than you are in God's sight. If you consider well what you are within, you will not care what men say about you. They look to appearances but God looks to the heart. They consider the deed but God weighs the motive.

23. Isa. 48:22.

It is characteristic of a humble soul always to do good and to think little of itself. It is a mark of great purity and deep faith to look for no consolation in created things. The man who desires no justification from without has clearly entrusted himself to God: "For not he who commendeth himself is approved," says St. Paul, "but he whom God commendeth."[24]

To walk with God interiorly, to be free from any external affection—this is the state of the inward man.

Book Three: Internal Consolation
The Fifty-Fifth Chapter
The Corruption of Nature and the Efficacy of Divine Grace
The Disciple

O Lord, my God, Who created me to Your own image and likeness, grant me this grace which You have shown to be so great and necessary for salvation, that I may overcome my very evil nature that is drawing me to sin and perdition. For I feel in my flesh the law of sin contradicting the law of my mind and leading me captive to serve sensuality in many things. I cannot resist the passions thereof unless Your most holy grace warmly infused into my heart assist me.

There is need of Your grace, and of great grace, in order to overcome a nature prone to evil from youth. For through the first man, Adam, nature is fallen and weakened by sin, and the punishment of that stain has fallen upon all mankind. Thus nature itself, which You created good and right, is considered a symbol of vice and the weakness of corrupted nature, because when left to itself it tends toward evil and to baser things. The little strength remaining in it is like a spark hidden in ashes. That strength is natural reason which, surrounded by thick darkness, still has the

24. 2 Cor. 10:18.

power of judging good and evil, of seeing the difference between true and false, though it is not able to fulfill all that it approves and does not enjoy the full light of truth or soundness of affection.

Hence it is, my God, that according to the inward man I delight in Your law, knowing that Your command is good, just, and holy, and that it proves the necessity of shunning all evil and sin. But in the flesh I keep the law of sin, obeying sensuality rather than reason. Hence, also, it is that the will to good is present in me, but how to accomplish it I know not. Hence, too, I often propose many good things, but because the grace to help my weakness is lacking, I recoil and give up at the slightest resistance. . . .[25]

How extremely necessary to me, O Lord, Your grace is to begin any good deed, to carry it on and bring it to completion! For without grace I can do nothing, but with its strength I can do all things in You. O Grace truly heavenly, without which our merits are nothing and no gifts of nature are to be esteemed!

Before You, O Lord, no arts or riches, no beauty or strength, no wit or intelligence avail without grace. For the gifts of nature are common to good and bad alike, but the peculiar gift of Your elect is grace or love, and those who are signed with it are held worthy of everlasting life. So excellent is this grace that without it no gift of prophecy or of miracles, no meditation be it ever so exalted, can be considered anything. Not even faith or hope or other virtues are acceptable to You without charity and grace.

O most blessed grace, which makes the poor in spirit rich in virtues, which renders him who is rich in many good things humble of heart, come, descend upon me, fill me quickly with your consolation lest my soul faint with weariness and dryness of mind.

Let me find grace in Your sight, I beg, Lord, for Your grace is enough for me, even though I obtain none of the things which nature desires.[26] If I am tempted and afflicted with many tribulations, I will fear no evils while Your grace is with me. This is my strength. This will give me counsel and help. This is more powerful than all my enemies and wiser than all the wise. . . .

Let Your grace, therefore, go before me and follow me, O Lord, and make me always intent upon good works, through Jesus Christ, Your Son.

The Fifty-Eighth Chapter
High Matters and the Hidden Judgments of God Are Not to Be Scrutinized
The Voice of Christ

My child, beware of discussing high matters and God's hidden judgments—why this person is so forsaken and why that one is favored with so great a grace, or why one man is so afflicted and another so highly exalted. Such things are beyond all human understanding and no reason or disputation can fathom the judgments of God.

When the enemy puts such suggestions in your mind, therefore, or when some curious persons raise questions about them, answer with the prophet: "Thou art just, O Lord, and righteous are Thy judgments"; and this: "The judgments of the Lord are true and wholly righteous."[27] My judgments are to be feared, not discussed, because they are incomprehensible to the understanding of men.

In like manner, do not inquire or dispute about the merits of the saints, as to which is more holy, or which shall be greater in the

25. See Rom. 7:7-25.

26. Cf. 2 Cor. 12:8-9.

27. Ps. 119:137; 19:9.

kingdom of heaven. Such things often breed strife and useless contentions. They nourish pride and vainglory, whence arise envy and quarrels, when one proudly tries to exalt one saint and the other another. A desire to know and pry into such matters brings forth no fruit. . . .

Some are drawn by the ardor of their love with greater affection to these saints or to those, but this affection is human and not divine. I am He who made all the saints. I gave them grace: I brought them to glory. I know the merits of each of them. I came before them in the blessings of My sweetness. I knew My beloved ones before the ages. I chose them out of the world—they did not choose Me. I called them by grace, I drew them on by mercy. I led them safely through various temptations. I poured into them glorious consolations. I gave them perseverance and I crowned their patience. I know the first and the last. I embrace them all with love inestimable. I am to be praised in all My saints. I am to be blessed above all things, and honored in each of those whom I have exalted and predestined so gloriously without any previous merits of their own.

He who despises one of the least of mine, therefore, does no honor to the greatest, for both the small and the great I made. And he who disparages one of the saints disparages Me also and all others in the kingdom of heaven. They are all one through the bond of charity. They have the same thought and the same will, and they mutually love one another; but, what is a much greater thing, they love Me more than themselves or their own merits. Rapt above themselves, and drawn beyond love of self, they are entirely absorbed in love of Me, in Whom they rest. There is nothing that can draw them away or depress them, for they who are filled with eternal truth burn with the fire of unquenchable love.

Therefore, let carnal and sensual men, who know only how to love their own selfish joys, forbear to dispute about the state of God's saints. Such men take away and add according to their own inclinations and not as it pleases the Eternal Truth. . . .

Be careful, then, My child, of treating matters beyond your knowledge out of curiosity. Let it rather be your business and aim to be found, even though the least, in the kingdom of God. . . .

The man who thinks of the greatness of his own sins and the littleness of his virtues, and of the distance between himself and the perfection of the saints, acts much more acceptably to God than the one who argues about who is greater or who is less. It is better to invoke the saints with devout prayers and tears, and with a humble mind to beg their glorious aid, than to search with vain inquisitiveness into their secrets.

The saints are well and perfectly contented if men know how to content themselves and cease their useless discussions. They do not glory in their own merits, for they attribute no good to themselves but all to Me, because out of My infinite charity I gave all to them. They are filled with such love of God and with such overflowing joy, that no glory is wanting to them and they can lack no happiness. All the saints are so much higher in glory as they are more humble in themselves; nearer to Me, and more beloved by Me. . . .

Many ask who is the greater in the kingdom of heaven when they do not know whether they themselves shall be worthy of being numbered among its least. It is a great thing to be even the least in heaven where all are great because all shall be called, and shall be, the children of God. . . .

Woe to those, therefore, who disdain to humble themselves willingly with the little children, for the low gate of the heavenly kingdom will not permit them to enter. Woe also to the rich who have their consolations here, for when the poor enter into God's kingdom, they will stand outside lamenting. Rejoice, you humble, and exult, you poor, for the kingdom of God is yours, if only you walk in the truth.

[*The Imitation of Christ* (Milwaukee: Bruce Publishing Company, 1940; reprint, 1962), 1–24, 62–64, 195–98, 202–7]

C. Desiderius Erasmus of Rotterdam

Biographical Note: Desiderius Erasmus

Desiderius Erasmus of Rotterdam (ca. 1467–1536) was the son of a priest and he spent his early years in a monastery. Here he came under the influence of the Brethren of the Common Life, whose devotio moderna *inspired works such as* The Imitation of Christ.

Erasmus entered the University of Paris to study Greek. He traveled widely throughout the European continent and England. He became a sought-after tutor and a prolific writer. Because of the depth and breadth of his classical learning, he began to distinguish himself as the greatest of the Christian humanists. This erudition is on display in his Adages, *a collection of about eight hundred classical aphorisms and proverbs that he later expanded to three thousand.*

Erasmus's enthusiasm for returning "to the sources" is evident in his many editions of the Greek New Testament, first printed in 1516 in Basel, Switzerland. These Greek texts, which included extensive philological annotations, would become the New Testament of the reformers. His pursuit of the original text led to some noteworthy modifications, none more controversial than his omission of the comma Johanneum *(1 John 5:7), which in the West had become perhaps the greatest proof text for the doctrine of the Trinity. His method inspired the text criticism that would become the heart of modern historical-critical biblical exegesis.*

Erasmus is remembered also for his unflinching wit and satire. He caricatured the worst features of monks, scholastic theologians, and clergy, taking the church establishment to task for its hypocrisy and lack of ethics. Moriae encomium (The Praise of Folly), *a book he dedicated to Sir Thomas More, represents the height of his incisive cultural critique.*

The voluminous literary output of Erasmus includes works of constructive theology and spirituality, which were highly regarded by many of his contemporaries. Although they were kindred spirits in many ways, Martin Luther and Erasmus differed on many issues, especially on the role of the human will in salvation. After Erasmus's Freedom of the Will *(1524) was countered by Luther's* Bondage of the Will *(1525), there was little prospect for cooperation between these two. Erasmus did remain on good terms with many other reformers.*

Erasmus never joined the reform movement or broke with the Roman Church. Yet, because of his anticlericalism and desire to return to a simple, biblical Christian faith, Erasmus had much in common with the reformers. His books were later censured by the Roman Church and universally viewed as supportive of Protestantism. Indeed, though it is an exaggeration and oversimplification, there is a kernel of truth in the old saying that "Erasmus laid the egg and Luther hatched it."

Selection 7: Desiderius Erasmus, a Communicant's Prayer

What tongue or heart could give you the thanks you deserve, Lord Jesus, in return for your indescribable love for us? To redeem the lost human race you condescended to take on human nature and to accept in your person all the harm that attaches to our human condition; and ultimately, as a lamb free from any blemish, you endured the fate of becoming a victim for our sake on the altar of the cross, cancelling out the punishment due for our sins in order to reconcile us to the Father: indeed in life and death you spent, gave, and dedicated yourself totally for us. Nor did your great goodness consider this sufficient, but so that we should never be overtaken by forgetfulness of such great love or begin to lose faith in you, even now as you reign in heaven you continually refresh our souls with the food of your body and gladden our hearts with the sacred cup of your blood. I pray you, let your Spirit purify my heart, so that I do not approach unworthily the heavenly banquet and the table that inspires the angels themselves with awe; but, when I have received you into the recesses of my soul, may I grow strong in you and become more vigorous with an increase of spiritual gifts, so that I may persevere in the blessed company of your mystical body, which you have desired to be as closely united with you as you are with the Father, and bound together by the Holy Spirit, to whom be praise and thanksgiving for ever. Amen.

[*Collected Works of Erasmus*, 69:136]

Selection 8: Desiderius Erasmus, "To the Reader" (1515)

Erasmus's critical edition of the Greek New Testament, entitled* Novum instrumentum, *was published in 1516. The prefatory letter that accompanied it, written in late 1515, describes the aim of the publication—which was solely text critical—as well as some of his methods. His description reflects the growing interest in what would become the full-fledged science of establishing the original text (that is, textual criticism), a discipline that would come to dominate biblical exegesis throughout the modern period.

ERASMUS OF ROTTERDAM TO THE PIOUS READER GREETING

Although I did do so to the best of my ability at the very outset of this work, yet it may be worth while to warn the reader briefly once again both what he ought to expect from these brief notes and what demands I can reasonably make upon him in return. In the first place, what I have written are short annotations, not a commentary, and they are concerned solely with the integrity of the text; so let no one like a selfish guest demand supper in place of a light luncheon, and expect me to give him something different from what I undertook to produce. . . .

I have taken what they call the New Testament and revised it, with all the diligence I could muster and all the accuracy that was appropriate, checking it in the first instance against the true Greek text. For that is, as it were, the fountain-head to which we are not only encouraged to have recourse in any difficulty by the example of eminent divines, but frequently advised to do so by Jerome and Augustine,[28] and so instructed by the actual decrees of the Roman pontiffs. Second, I

28. Augustine (354–430), bishop of Hippo Regius in North Africa, was the most quoted theologian in the medieval and early modern Western church. Jerome (347–420) was perhaps second on the list of most quoted and orthodox of the Western church fathers. Thus, against any potential opposition to his project, Erasmus begins by citing the greatest authorities on his side.

checked it against the tradition of very ancient copies of the Latin version, two of which were made available by that distinguished master of the divine philosophy John Colet, dean of St Paul's in London, in such ancient styles of writing that I had to learn to read them from the beginning, and in order to pick up the rudiments I had to become a schoolboy again. A third was provided by the illustrious lady Margaret, aunt of the emperor Charles; its evidence I have frequently cited in this third edition under the name of the Golden Gospels, because it is entirely clad in gold and finely written in gold letters. After that, I was provided with several manuscripts of remarkable antiquity by the equally ancient and celebrated collegiate church of St Donatian at Bruges. Previously the house of Korssendonk had supplied me with a manuscript very neatly corrected, not to mention some lent me by those excellent scholars the brothers Amerbach. It is not therefore that I have made a certain number of corrections dreamed up out of my own head; I have followed the manuscripts listed, and others like them which it is not so important to name. Finally I have checked by the quotations or corrections or explanations of authors who are fully and universally approved—Origen, Chrysostom, Cyril, Jerome, Ambrose, Hilary, Augustine, Theophylact, Basil, Bede—whose evidence I have adduced on many passages with this in mind, that when the intelligent reader has perceived that in certain definite places my correction and their opinion coincide, he may give me his confidence in other places too, in which probably by chance they have neither supplied a note nor supported me in any other way.

I knew however that it is human nature to object to novelty in everything, but especially in the field of learning, and that most people expect to find the old familiar taste and what they call the traditional flavour; and I also reflected how much easier it is, nowadays especially, to corrupt a sound text than to correct a corrupted one. Consequently, after revising the sacred books I added these pointers (so to call them), partly to explain to the reader's satisfaction why each change was made, or at least to pacify him if he has found something he does not like, for men's temperaments and judgments vary; partly in hopes of preserving my work intact, that it might not be so easy in the future for anyone to spoil a second time what had once been restored with such great exertions. First then, if I found anything damaged by the carelessness or ignorance of scribes or by the injuries of time, I restored the true reading, not haphazardly but after pursuing every available scent. If anything struck me as obscurely expressed, I threw light on it; if as ambiguous or complicated, I explained it; if differences between the copies or alternative punctuations or simply the ambiguity of the language give rise to several meanings, I laid them open in such a way as to show which seemed to me more acceptable, leaving the final decision to the reader. And although I do not willingly disagree with the translator, whoever he was, because his version is traditional and commonly accepted, yet when the facts proclaim that he nodded or was under a delusion, I did not hesitate to make this also clear to the reader: I have championed the truth, but so as to criticize no man. Blunders that were obvious and unnatural I removed, and I followed the rules of correct writing everywhere so far as it was possible to do so, always provided that there was no loss of simplicity. Wherever the idiom of the Greek or its peculiar expression has something about it that helps towards the underlying meaning, I was always ready to demonstrate this and make it visible.

Finally I collected and weighed up the Old Testament evidences, not a few of which are cited either from the Septuagint version or from the Hebrew original, if the form in which they are current differs from their Hebrew source; although this I could not do single-handedly "without my Theseus" as the Greek proverb puts it, for nothing is further from my character and temperament than like Aesop's crow to set myself off with others' plumage.[29] So in this department, when I was first publishing this work,[30] I secured no little help from a man eminent for his knowledge of the three tongues no less than for his piety, which is as much as to say a true theologian, Joannes Oecolampadius of Weinsberg;[31] for I myself had not yet made enough progress in Hebrew to take upon myself the authority to decide.

[*Collected Works of Erasmus*, 3:198–200]

Selection 9: Desiderius Erasmus, *Handbook of a Christian Soldier* (1518)

First written in 1503 and revised in 1518, the **Handbook (Enchiridion)** ***is a prime example of Erasmus's devotional writing. It exhibits the influence of the*** **devotio moderna** ***and is similar in many respects to the*** **Imitation of Christ** ***(see Selection 6). As is the case with most of Erasmus's writings, this book displays his thorough knowledge of the Bible and the Greek and Latin classics. In the midst of the work, he offers twenty-two rules as a guide for living the Christian life. After some selections from the introductory sections, the fifth rule is excerpted, which is to pursue the spirit, not the flesh, a principle that he applies to everything from biblical interpretation to the use of relics.***

The beginning of this wisdom is to know thyself, a saying that antiquity believed to have come down from heaven and that found such acceptance with the great authors that they considered it to be the epitome of all wisdom. But this teaching would have little authority for us if it did not accord with the Scriptures. . . .

What I have said thus far has perhaps been more than sufficient, but in order that you be even more enlightened and self-aware, I should like to touch briefly on the teachings of Origen concerning the division of man. Following Paul he divides man into three parts—spirit, soul, and flesh, which the Apostle associated together when he wrote to the Thessalonians: "May your body, soul, and spirit be kept sound for the coming of our Lord, Jesus Christ." Isaiah, omitting the lower part, mentions two.[32]. . .

As in a republic rent by factions, the soul cannot but attach itself to one of the two sides; solicited on this side and on that, it is free to incline to whichever direction it wishes. If it renounces the flesh and goes over to the side of the spirit, it will itself become spiritual, but if it abandons itself to the cupidities of the flesh, it will degenerate into the body. . . .

Therefore the spirit makes us gods, the flesh makes us brute animals. The soul constitutes us as human beings; the spirit makes us religious, the flesh irreligious, the soul neither the one

29. The point is that Erasmus could not have accomplished this work without help, and he will not pretend that it is all his own. The classical references are typical of Renaissance humanist style in general and of Erasmus's writing in particular.

30. The phrase, "when I was first publishing this work," was added (along with a few other minor phrases) to this preface in the second edition (1519).

31. Johann Oecolampadius (1482–1531) was a humanist theologian. He later became a reformer in Basel and played a prominent role in the *Marburg Colloquy* (see Selection 24).

32. See 1 Thess. 5:23; Isa. 26:9. Erasmus proceeds to quote from Daniel as well.

nor the other. The spirit seeks heavenly things, the flesh seeks pleasure, the soul what is necessary. The spirit elevates us to heaven, the flesh drags us down to hell, the soul has no charge imputed to it. Whatever is carnal is base, whatever is spiritual is perfect, whatever belongs to the soul as life-giving element is in between and indifferent.

Do you wish me to point out to you the distinction between these parts in more concrete language? I shall attempt to do so. You respect your parents; you love your brother; you love your children; you cherish your friend. It is not so much a virtue to do such things as it is unnaturally wicked not to do them. Why would you, a Christian, not do what even pagans do by natural instinct, or even what brute animals do? Whatever comes from nature cannot be ascribed to merit. But if you find yourself in a situation in which you must either neglect your duties to your father, triumph over your affection for your children, disregard the devotion owed to a friend, or offend God, what will you do? Your soul stands at the crossroads. The flesh solicits us on one side, the spirit on the other. The spirit says: "God is to be preferred to one's parent. To the latter you owe merely your body, to God you owe everything." The flesh suggests: "If you do not obey, your father will disinherit you, and people will say that you have no respect for your father. Be practical, think of your reputation. God will either not see it, or will ignore it, or at any rate will easily be appeased." Your soul wavers and vacillates. Whichever way it turns, it will become that which it accedes to. If, in contempt of the spirit, it harkens to the harlot, that is, the flesh, it becomes one with the body. But if, despising the flesh, it is raised up to the spirit, it is transformed into the spirit.

Accustom yourself to this mode of shrewd self-examination. It is a great error of mankind to think that what is merely an instinct of nature is perfect piety. If you are not careful, you can be deceived by certain passions that seem honourable in appearance and are disguised with the mask of virtue. . . .

Many people are attracted or repelled by certain things through natural propensities or traits of character. There are some who are never titillated by the pleasures of the flesh. They should not attribute to their own virtue something that is in itself indifferent. It is a virtue to conquer lust, not simply to be free of it. . . .

Let us add a fifth rule, as a kind of reinforcement to the previous one, that you establish firmly in your mind that perfect piety is the attempt to progress always from visible things, which are usually imperfect or indifferent, to invisible, according to the division of man discussed earlier. This precept is most pertinent to our discussion since it is through neglect or ignorance of it that most Christians are superstitious rather than pious, and except for the name of Christ differ hardly at all from superstitious pagans. Let us imagine, therefore, two worlds, the one merely intelligible, the other visible. The intelligible, which may also be called the angelic, is the one in which God dwells with the blessed spirits, while the visible world comprises the celestial spheres and all that is contained therein. Then there is man, who constitutes, as it were, a third world, participating in the other two, in the visible world through the body, and in the invisible through the soul. Since we are but pilgrims in the visible world, we should never make it our fixed abode, but should relate by a fitting comparison everything that occurs to the senses either to the angelic world or, in more practical terms, to morals and to that part of man that corresponds to the angelic. What the visible sun is here in the visible world the divine mind is in the intelligible world and in that part of you related to it, namely, the spirit. What the moon is here is in that world the assembly of angels and blessed spirits, which they call the church triumphant, and in you it is the spirit. Whatever influence the upper world has over the earth, which lies beneath it, God exercises this same influence over your soul. The sun sets, rises, scorches, becomes temperate, quickens, produces, ripens, attracts, debilitates, cleanses, hardens, softens, illumines, brightens, gladdens. Therefore whatever you observe in it, or rather, whatever you observe in this material world, which is made up of elements, and which some have distinguished from the rest of the universe, and, lastly, whatever you see in the more material part of yourself, learn to refer to God and to the invisible part of yourself. In that way, whatever offers itself to the senses will become for you an occasion for the practice of piety.

As it delights the bodily eye each time this visible sun spreads new light upon the earth, consider for a moment what must be the pleasure of the heavenly spirits, for whom that eternal sun ever rises and never sets; consider what great joy it is for a pure spirit, illumined by divine light. And in response to the promptings of visible creation pray in the words of Paul that "he who commanded light to shine forth from darkness will begin to shine in your heart to illumine the knowledge of the glory of God in the face of Christ Jesus."[33]. . .

Be so convinced of the existence of invisible things that those things that are seen become but mere shadows, which present to the eye only a faint image of invisible realities. Moreover, whatever attracts or repels the senses in material things must be all the more intensely loved or hated by the spirit in the realm of the spirit. A handsome physical appearance is appealing to the eye. Imagine how fair must be the beauty of the soul! A misshapen face is unpleasant to look upon. Consider how odious is a mind defiled by vice. And similarly for the rest. . . .

Therefore let this rule be ever in readiness, that we do not linger over temporal matters at any time, but move on, rising up to the love of spiritual things, which are incomparably better, despising visible things in comparison to those that are invisible. Illness of the body will be easier to bear if you consider it as a physic of the soul. You will be less solicitous about the health of the body if you concentrate your attention on guarding the health of the soul. Death of the body frightens you, but much more to be dreaded is the death of the soul. . . .

This is how we should act in the face of all those things that daily present themselves to our senses and variously influence them according to the diversity of their appearance, producing hope, fear, love, hatred, sorrow, and pleasure. The same rule applies for all literary works, which are made up of a literal sense and a mysterious sense, body and soul, as it were, in which you are to ignore the letter and look rather to the mystery.[34] The writings of all the poets and the Platonist philosophers belong to this category, but especially the sacred Scriptures, which like those images of Silenus mentioned by Alcibiades enclose unadulterated divinity under a lowly and almost ludicrous external appearance. Otherwise, if you were to read the account of creation without recourse to allegory—the formation of the figure of Adam from moist clay and the breathing into it of a soul, the creation of Eve from his rib, the prohibition to eat of the tree, the beguiling serpent, God strolling in the breeze, the guilty pair hiding themselves, the angel placed at the gate of paradise with a flaming sword that revolved in

33. 2 Cor. 4:6.

34. This anthropological analogy applied to Scripture goes back to Origen, *On First Principles* IV.

all directions to prevent their return into the garden, in a word, the whole story of creation—if in all of this you were not to search beneath the surface, I do not see how it is any better than singing of the clay image fashioned by Prometheus, the theft of fire by trickery, and the infusion of life into the clay by means of fire. As a matter of fact, if you read the poetic fable in an allegorical sense, it will be more profitable than the scriptural account if you do not penetrate the outer covering.

The myth of the giants admonishes us that we must not do battle with the forces of heaven, or that we should refrain from those desires from which nature recoils and should set our minds on those things to which our nature is more inclined, provided they are morally acceptable. Thus, do not entangle yourself in marriage if celibacy is more suitable to your character, and conversely, do not vow yourself to celibacy if you seem more adapted to the married state, for whatever you attempt against your natural inclination usually turns out to be unsuccessful. . . .

If you read unallegorically of the infants struggling within the womb, the right of primogeniture sold for a mess of pottage, the fraudulent seizing of a father's blessing ahead of time, David's slaying of Goliath with a sling, and the shaving off of Samson's locks, then it is of no more importance than if you were to read the fiction of the poets. What difference is there whether you read the Book of Kings or the Book of Judges or Livy's history, if in none of them you perceive the allegory? The latter work contains many things that could amend morals,[35] but in the Bible there are some things that are even absurd at first glance and if understood only superficially can be prejudicial to morals. To cite a few examples: David's acts of banditry, his adultery bought at the price of murder, Samson madly in love, the secret intercourse of Lot's daughters with their father, and a thousand other such stories. Therefore you must reject the carnal aspect of the Scriptures, especially the Old Testament, and ferret out the spiritual sense. Manna will taste to you like that which you already have on your palate.

In bringing the mysteries to light you must not follow the conjectures of your own mind, but you must learn the method and the art, so to speak, which was handed down by a writer named Dionysius[36] in his book *De divinis nominibus* and by Augustine in his *De doctrina Christiana.* It was the Apostle Paul who, after Christ, opened up certain sources of allegories. He was followed by Origen, who is by far the predominant figure in this branch of theology. Theologians of the present day either practically despise allegory or treat it very coolly. In the art of subtle distinction they are equal or even superior to ancient commentators, but in the treatment of this subject they cannot even compare with them, for two reasons, as far as I can determine. First, mystical exegesis cannot fail to fall flat if it is not seasoned with the powers of eloquence and a certain gracefulness of style, in which the ancients achieved an excellence that we cannot even approach. The second reason is that they are satisfied with Aristotle alone and banish the Platonists and Pythagoreans from the schools. But Augustine preferred the latter two, not only because many of their ideas are perfectly consistent with our religion, but also because their figurative mode of expression, as I mentioned, and frequent use of allegory are very close to the language of Sacred Scripture. It is no wonder, then, that theological allegories

35. From the opening words of his history of Rome, Livy states the moral goal he has in mind for his readers.

36. (Pseudo-)Dionysius the Areopagite, whose highly influential works were composed around the early sixth century.

were more suitably treated by those who could adorn and enrich arid and tedious subjects through their eloquent command of language, and who, by virtue of their wide learning in all aspects of antiquity, had long since practised in their study of the poets and philosophers the approach that was necessary for the interpretation of the Scriptures. It is their commentaries, therefore, that I wish you to peruse, since I am not training you for scholastic debate, but imparting moral principles.

But if you cannot grasp the mystery, remember none the less that it is there under the surface, and that it is preferable to have hope of understanding what is unknown than to be content with "the letter that kills," and that is true not only of the Old Testament but also of the New. The gospel has its flesh and its spirit. Although the veil was lifted from Moses' face, Paul still "sees in a mirror obscurely," and Christ said in John's Gospel: "The flesh is of no profit, it is the spirit that gives life." I would have had scruples to say: "It is of no profit;" it would have been sufficient to say: "It is of some profit, but the spirit is much more profitable." But Truth itself said: "It is of no profit." Indeed it is of so little profit that according to Paul it is fatal unless it is referred to the spirit. . . .

Perhaps you celebrate the sacrifice of the mass daily, but you live for yourself and are not affected by the misfortunes of your neighbours. Then you are still in the "flesh" of the sacrament. But if in offering sacrifice you are conscious of the meaning of that partaking, namely, that you are one spirit with the spirit of Christ, one body with the body of Christ, a living member of the church; if you love nothing but in Christ, if you consider all your goods to be the common property of all men, if you are afflicted by the misfortunes of others as if they were your own, then you celebrate mass with great profit, since you do so spiritually. . . .

Let what is represented there to the eyes be enacted within you. The death of the Head is represented. Examine yourself in your inmost heart, as they say, to see how close you are to being dead to the world. If you are still subject to anger, ambition, greed, pleasure, and envy, even if you touch the altar, you are still far from the sacrifice. Christ was slain for you; offer these animals to him as sacrificial victims. Sacrifice yourself to him who once immolated himself for you to the Father. If you confide in him without reflecting on these things, God will hate your flabby and gross religion. You were baptized, but do not think that *ipso facto* you became a Christian. . . .

With great veneration you revere the ashes of Paul, which I do not condemn, if your religion is consistent with your devotion. If you venerate mute and dead ashes and ignore his living image still speaking and breathing, as it were, in his writings, is not your religion utterly absurd? . . .

[*Collected Works of Erasmus*, 66:40, 51–53, 65–72]

Selection 10: Desiderius Erasmus, *Julius Excluded from Heaven* (1518)

Pope Julius II

Pope Julius II (r. 1503–1513) won the papacy through bribery and negotiations, and he expanded the papal lands through military campaigns. He is also well known for his patronage of the arts, particularly in commissioning Michelangelo's painting of the ceiling of the Sistine Chapel. After Julius's death, this anonymous dialogue, which was attributed to Erasmus, was printed in 1518, though manuscripts go back at least to 1516. This imaginary dialogue pictures Julius approaching heaven and attempting to

unlock the gates with his key, a symbol of papal authority (cf. Matt. 16:17-19).

Julius: What the devil is this? The doors won't open? Someone must have changed the lock, or at least tampered with it.

Genius:[37] Are you quite sure you haven't brought the wrong key? The key to your treasure-chest won't open this door—and anyway, why didn't you bring both of them with you? The one in your hand is the key of power, not of knowledge.[2]

Julius: This is the only one I've ever had. . . .

Peter: Who are you? What do you want?

Julius: I want you to open the doors, and quickly; if you did your job properly, you'd have come out to meet me—with a solemn procession of angels, too.

Peter: He's domineering enough, anyway! But first of all, tell me who you are.

Julius: As if you can't see that for yourself.

Peter: See for myself? Well, I can see a strange spectacle, or perhaps I should say monster, unlike anything I've ever seen before.

Julius: But I imagine that unless you're quite blind you recognize this key, even if the golden oak isn't familiar; and you can see my triple crown and my robe all glittering with gold and jewels.

Peter: Yes, the silver key is vaguely familiar, but there's only one and it's very different from those which Christ, the true shepherd of the church, entrusted to me long ago. As for that sumptuous crown of yours, why on earth should I recognize it? No barbarian tyrant ever dared wear a thing like that, let alone anyone trying to get in here. I'm certainly not impressed by the robe, because I always scorned gold and jewels and trampled them like so much rubble. But what's this? I see that all your equipment, key, crown, and robe, bears the marks of that villainous huckster and imposter, who had my name but not my nature, Simon, whom I humbled long ago with the aid of Christ.[38]

Julius: Stop this nonsense, if you know what's good for you; for your information, I am Julius, the famous Ligurian; and, unless you've completely forgotten your alphabet, I'm sure you recognize these two letters, P.M.

Peter: I suppose they stand for Pestis Maxima.

Genius: Ha ha ha! Our soothsayer has hit the nail on the head!

Julius: Of course not! Pontifex Maximus.[39]

Peter: Well, you could be thrice Maximus and even greater than Mercurius Trismegistus, but you can't come in here unless you're Optimus,[40] and by that I mean holy.

Julius: Oh, if being called "holy" has anything to do with it, it's most impertinent of you to take so long to open the doors; you may have been merely styled "holy" or "saint" for all these years, but everyone has always called me "most holy." There are thousands of bulls . . .

Genius: "Cock-and-bulls," you might say!

Julius: . . . in which I am many times called "most holy lord"; in fact, I was always referred

37. In ancient pagan Rome, the "genius" was a person's guardian spirit (as in the "genius" of Caesar to which early Christians were obliged to sacrifice); its usage here may carry a pagan connotation.

38. Simon Magus was confronted by Peter in Acts 8. Other, more elaborate traditions were circulated of Peter confronting and humiliating Simon, some of which are recorded in second-century Christian documents.

39. *Pestis maxima* means "the greatest pestilence"; *pontifex maximus*, the pope's title, means "the greatest pontiff."

40. Hermes, or Mercurius, Trismegistus (literally, "thrice greatest") was an otherwise anonymous figure of late antiquity who composed the so-called *Corpus Hermeticum*, a body of mystical writings. *Optimus* means "the best."

to as "his Holiness," not just "holy," so that whatever I fancied doing . . .

Genius: Even when he was drunk!

Julius: . . . people said that "his Holiness, the most holy Lord Julius" had done it.

Peter: Then ask your flatterers to let you into heaven, since they made you "most holy," and let those who gave you "Holiness" grant you bliss as well. Do you really think there's no difference between being holy and being called holy? . . .

Peter: Tell me, when have you acted like an apostle?

Julius: What could be more apostolic than to enlarge the church of Christ? . . .

Peter: How did you enlarge the church, anyway?

Julius: Ah, now you're coming to it: listen. The church, once poor and starving, is now enriched with every possible ornament.

Peter: What ornaments? Warm faith?

Julius: You're talking nonsense again.

Peter: Sacred learning?

Julius: You don't give up, do you?

Peter: Contempt for the world?

Julius: Allow me to explain. I'm talking about real ornaments, not mere words like those.

Peter: What then?

Julius: Royal palaces, the most handsome horses and mules, hordes of servants, well-trained troops, dainty courtiers . . .

Genius: . . . delicious harlots, grovelling pimps . . .

Julius: . . . gold, purple, taxes; in fact, such is the wealth and splendour of the Roman pontiff that, by comparison, any king would seem a poor and insignificant fellow; any man, however ambitious, would admit defeat; any man, however extravagant, would condemn his own frugality; and any rich man—a money-lender, even—would look with envy on our wealth. These, I tell you, are the ornaments that I have protected and increased.

Peter: But tell me, who was the first to burden and defile the church with these ornaments of yours, when Christ intended it to be wholly pure and wholly unencumbered by such things?

Julius: What's that got to do with it? The important thing is that we have them to possess and to enjoy. However, they do say that someone called Constantine transferred the whole majesty of his empire to the Roman pontiff Sylvester, his horses, trappings, chariots, helmet, belt, cloak, guards, swords, golden crowns (very fine gold too), armies, artillery, cities, kingdoms.

Peter: Are there any reliable records of this splendid gift?

Julius: Nothing but one interpolation included among the decretals.[41]

Peter: Perhaps it's all a hoax.

Julius: I sometimes think that myself. What sane man would give up such a magnificent empire, even to his father? But it pleases us greatly to believe it, and we've used threats to impose absolute silence on the snoopers who try to disprove it.

Peter: You still talk of nothing but the world. . . .

Julius: You're only saying that because you begrudge us our glory, realizing how insignificant your pontificate was compared with ours.

Peter: Shameless man, do you dare to compare your glory with mine, although the glory is not mine, but Christ's? First of all, if you will

41. Erasmus is alluding to the *Donation of Constantine*, an alleged fourth-century document in which Constantine grants civil jurisdiction of the Western Roman Empire to the bishop of Rome, Sylvester, and his successors. Some medieval popes appealed to this document to bolster their claims of authority. The Renaissance scholar Lorenzo (Laurentius) Valla (ca. 1407–1457) proved the document to be a later forgery, probably of the eighth century.

allow that Christ is the best and true prince of the church, remember that he gave me the keys of the kingdom in person, that he gave me his sheep to feed, he sealed my faith with his approval. Bribery, fraud, and preoccupation with the things of the world made you pope, if indeed a man like you may be called pope. I won countless thousands of souls for Christ; you led as many to destruction. I was the first to teach Christ to pagan Rome; you have been a teacher of paganism in Christian Rome. I healed the sick with just the shadow of my body, I freed men possessed by devils, I restored the dead to life, and brought abundant blessings to every place I visited. What had your triumphs in common with all this? With one word I was able to consign to Satan anyone I wished: Sapphira and her husband both felt the extent of my power. But whatever power I had, I used for the benefit of all; you benefitted no one, and if you had any power (and even in some cases when you hadn't) you aimed at the general ruin of the world.

Julius: I'm surprised you don't include in your list of glories poverty, vigils, sweat, trials, prison, chains, abuse, stripes, and finally the cross.

Peter: You do well to remind me, for I may more justly be proud of those things than of miracles. Christ commanded us to rejoice and exult because of such things; because of such things he called us blessed. In the same way my former colleague Paul, when boasting of his exploits, does not speak of cities taken by storm, of armies put to the sword, of princes of the world called to arms, of tyrannical splendour, but of shipwrecks, chains, scourges, dangers, snares; this is the true triumph of the apostle, this is the glory of the captain of Christ. He boasts of those he got for Christ, of those he called back from ungodliness, not of how many thousands of ducats he amassed. And now, at last, we celebrate an eternal triumph with Christ and even the wicked follow us with praises; there will be no one who will not revile you, except your own sort and your flatterers. . . .

Julius: Well, if we have no worldly possessions, the common people will take absolutely no notice of us, whereas now they both hate and fear us. What's more, the whole Christian commonwealth would collapse if it couldn't protect itself against the fury of its enemies.

Peter: Not at all: if the common people of Christendom were to see in you the true gifts of Christ, such as holiness of life, sacred learning, fervent charity, prophecy, and miracles, they would recognize your greater detachment from worldly possessions and respect you the more for it. The Christian commonwealth would expand and flourish if the gentiles could admire in it purity of life and contempt for pleasures, wealth, power, and death. At the moment, not only is it confined within a tiny area, but if you examine it carefully, you will find many who are Christians in name only. Tell me: while you were supreme shepherd of the church, did you never reflect upon the way in which the church began, grew, and became established? Was it by wars, wealth, horses? Of course not: it was by suffering, the blood of martyrs (including mine), imprisonment, scourges. You claim that the church has grown, when its servants have to bear the burdens of temporal authority; you call it adorned, when it is sullied by the rewards and delights of the world; you call it well defended, when to further the petty interests of the clergy the entire world is embroiled in disastrous wars; you say that it is flourishing, when it is besotted with worldly pleasures; and that it is calm, because it enjoys its riches, or rather its vices, and no one protests. On these grounds you have imposed upon the princes, and under your tutelage they have learned to call their great robberies and mad battles "the defence of Christ." . . .

Julius: You won't open up then?

Peter: The last person I'd let in is a pestilent fellow like you. In any case, we're all excommunicate, according to you. But would you like some friendly advice? You have a band of energetic followers, an enormous fortune, and you yourself are a great architect; build some new paradise for yourself, but fortify it well to prevent the cacodemons capturing it.

Julius: Never! I shall be true to myself and wait a few months, increasing my army until I can throw you out by force, if you won't surrender. I've no doubt I shall soon be joined by several thousand more soldiers slaughtered in the wars.

Peter: You pestilent fellow! Oh, unhappy church! Hey, Genius, come here; I'd rather talk to you than to that loathsome monster.

Genius: What's up?

Peter: Are the rest of the bishops like him?

Genius: A good many are cast in the same mould, but he's the pacemaker.

Peter: I suppose it was you who incited him to all these crimes?

Genius: Nothing to do with me; in fact, he ran so far ahead that I had trouble keeping up, even with the aid of my wings.

Peter: I'm really not surprised that so few men reach here, when scoundrels like him have seized the helm of the church. However, I may conclude even from all this, that there's some chance of curing the common people, if they will honour this sink of iniquity simply because he bears the title of pope.

[*Collected Works of Erasmus*, 27:168–69, 191–94, 196–97]

Selection 11: Desiderius Erasmus, *On the Freedom of the Will* (1524)

In late December of 1520, Martin Luther published his* Assertion *against the pope's bull of excommunication (see Selection 41). Erasmus regarded Luther's 36th article against free choice as an extreme interpretation out of step with nearly the whole of the Christian tradition. In 1524, Erasmus published this* Diatribe or Discourse on Free Choice *in response to this controversial article of Luther's* Assertion. *Erasmus appealed to the church fathers and medieval scholastics in favor of the human will having some role in the salvation process. Erasmus then dealt with the biblical passages relevant to the topic. Despite Erasmus's reformist tone in other writings, this document is evidence of the distance that remained between his views and those of most reformers. Luther's merciless response to Erasmus in 1525 secured this distance.

Prefatory Observations

In the Name of Jesus.

Among the difficulties, of which not a few crop up in Holy Scripture, there is hardly a more tangled labyrinth than that of "free choice," for it is a subject that has long exercised the minds of philosophers, and also of theologians old and new, in a striking degree, though in my opinion with more labor than fruit.

More recently, however, it has been revived by Carlstadt and Eck, in a fairly moderate debate,[42] and now it has been more violently stirred up by Martin Luther, who has put out an *Assertion* about "free choice" and although he has already been answered by more than one writer, it seemed good to my friends that I should try my hand and see whether, as a result

42. This is the Leipzig Debate of 1519.

of our little set-to, the truth might be made more plain. . . .

And, in fact, so far am I from delighting in "assertions" that I would readily take refuge in the opinion of the Skeptics, wherever this is allowed by the inviolable authority of the Holy Scriptures and by the decrees of the Church, to which I everywhere willingly submit my personal feelings, whether I grasp what it prescribes or not.

Moreover, I prefer this disposition of mine to that with which I see some people endowed who are so uncontrollably attached to their own opinion that they cannot bear anything which dissents from it; but they twist whatever they read in the Scriptures into an assertion of an opinion which they have embraced once for all. They are like young men who love a girl so immoderately that they imagine they see their beloved wherever they turn, or, a much better example, like two combatants who, in the heat of a quarrel, turn whatever is at hand into a missile, whether it be a jug or a dish. I ask you, what sort of sincere judgment can there be when people behave in this way? Who will learn anything fruitful from this sort of discussion—beyond the fact that each leaves the encounter bespattered with the other's filth? There will always be many such, whom the apostle Peter describes as "ignorant and unstable who twist the Scriptures to their own destruction."

As far as I am concerned, I admit that many different views about free choice have been handed down from the ancients about which I have, as yet, no fixed conviction, except that I think there to be a certain power of free choice. For I have read the *Assertion* of Martin Luther, and read it without prejudice, except that I have assumed a certain favor toward him, as an investigator may toward an arraigned prisoner. And yet, although he expounds his case in all its aspects with great ingenuity and fervor of spirit, I must say, quite frankly, that he has not persuaded me.

If anybody ascribes this to my slowness or inexperience, I shall not quarrel with him, provided they allow us slower ones the privilege of learning by meeting those who have received the gift of God in fuller measure, especially since Luther attributes very little importance to scholarship, and most of all to the Spirit, who is wont to instill into the more humble what he denies to the wise. So much for those who shout so loudly that Luther has more learning in his little finger than Erasmus in his whole body, a view that I shall certainly not attempt to refute here. I simply ask from such, however ill-disposed they may be, that if I grant to Luther in this Disputation that he be not weighed down by the prejudgments of doctors, councils, universities, popes, and of the emperor, they will not damage my cause by mere snap judgments.

For even though I believe myself to have mastered Luther's argument, yet I might well be mistaken, and for that reason I play the debater, not the judge; the inquirer, not the dogmatist: ready to learn from anyone if anything truer or more scholarly can be brought. Yet I would willingly persuade the man in the street that in this kind of discussion it is better not to enforce contentions which may the sooner harm Christian concord than advance true religion. . . .

Therefore, in my judgment on this matter of free choice, having learned what is needful to know about this, if we are in the path of true religion, let us go on swiftly to better things, forgetful of the things which are behind, or if we are entangled in sins, let us strive with all our might and have recourse to the remedy of penitence that by all means we may entreat the mercy of the Lord without which no human will or endeavor is effective; and what is evil in us, let us impute to ourselves, and what is good, let us ascribe wholly to divine benevolence, to which we owe our very being, and for the rest, whatever befalls us in this life, whether it be joyful or sad, let us believe it to be sent by him for our salvation, and that no harm can come to us from a God who is by nature just, even if some things happen that seem to us amiss, for none ought to despair of the pardon of a God who is by nature most merciful. This, I say, was in my judgment sufficient for Christian godliness, nor should we through irreverent inquisitiveness rush into those things which are hidden, not to say superfluous: whether God foreknows anything contingently; whether our will accomplishes anything in things pertaining to eternal salvation; whether it simply suffers the action of grace; whether what we do, be it of good or ill, we do by necessity or rather suffer to be done to us. And then there are certain things of which God has willed us to be completely ignorant—such as the hour of death or the Day of Judgment: "It is not for you to know times or seasons which the Father has fixed by his own authority," Acts 1[:7]; and Mark 13[:32]: "But of that day or that hour no one knows, not even the angels in heaven, nor the Son, but only the Father." There are some things which God has willed that we should contemplate, as we venerate himself, in mystic silence; and, moreover, there are many passages in the sacred volumes about which many commentators have made guesses, but no one has finally cleared up their obscurity: as the distinction between the divine persons, the conjunction of the divine and human nature in Christ, the unforgivable sin; yet there are other things which God has willed to be most plainly evident, and such are the precepts for the good life. This is the Word of God, which is not to be bought in the highest heaven, nor in distant lands overseas, but it is close at hand, in our mouth and in our heart. These truths must be learned by all, but the rest are more properly committed to God, and it is more religious to worship them, being unknown, than to discuss them, being insoluble. How many questions, or rather squabbles, have arisen over the distinction of persons, the mode of generation, the distinction between filiation and procession; what a fuss has been raised in the world by the wrangle about the conception of the virgin as Theotokos![43] I ask what profit has there been so far from these laborious inquiries, except that with the loss of harmony we love one another the less, while seeking to be wiser than we need.

Moreover, some things there are of such a kind that, even if they were true and might be known, it would not be proper to prostitute them before common ears. Perhaps it is true, as the Sophists are given to blather, that God, according to his own nature, is not less present in the hole of a beetle (I will not use the more vulgar expression that they are not ashamed to use) than in heaven, and yet this would be unprofitably discussed before the common herd. And that there are three Gods might be said truly according to the rules of dialectic, but would certainly not be spoken before the untutored multitude without great scandal. Even if I were convinced, which is not the case, that this confession which we now use was neither instituted by Christ nor could have been founded by men, and for this reason ought not to be required of any, and further that no satisfaction should be demanded for offenses, yet I should fear to publish this opinion because I see so many mortals who are wonderfully prone to offenses, whom the necessity of confessing either restrains altogether or at least moderates. There are some bodily diseases that are less evil

43. That is, the "God-bearer" (Greek).

to bear than their removal, as though a man were to bathe in the warm blood of murdered babes to avoid leprosy, so there are some errors that it would cause less damage to conceal than to uproot. Paul knew the difference between what things are lawful and what are expedient.[44] It is lawful to speak the truth; it is not expedient to speak the truth to everybody at every time and in every way. If I were convinced that at a certain council some wrong decision or definition had been made, I should have the right to proclaim the truth, but it would not be expedient, lest wicked men be given a handle to scorn the authority of the Fathers, even in those decisions which they have taken in a godly and devout spirit. I would rather say that they took a decision that seemed reasonable from the point of view of their own times which present needs suggest should be repealed.

Let us, therefore, suppose that there is some truth in the doctrine which Wyclif taught and Luther asserted, that whatever is done by us is done not by free choice but by sheer necessity. What could be more useless than to publish this paradox to the world? Again, suppose for a moment that it were true in a certain sense, as Augustine says somewhere, that "God works in us good and evil, and rewards his own good works in us, and punishes his evil works in us"; what a window to impiety would the public avowal of such an opinion open to countless mortals! Especially in view of the slowness of mind of mortal men, their sloth, their malice, and their incurable propensity toward all manner of evil. What weakling will be able to bear the endless and wearisome warfare against his flesh? What evildoer will take pains to correct his life? Who will be able to bring himself to love God with all his heart when He created hell seething with eternal torments in order to punish his own misdeeds in his victims as though he took delight in human torments? For that is how most people will interpret them. For the most part, men are by nature dull-witted and sensual, prone to unbelief, inclined to evil, with a bent to blasphemy, so that there is no need to add fuel to the furnace. And so Paul, as a wise dispenser of the Divine Word, often brings charity to bear, and prefers to follow that which is fitting for one's neighbors rather than the letter of the law: and possesses a wisdom that he speaks among the perfect, but among the weak he reckons to know nothing, save Jesus Christ, and him crucified. Holy Scripture has its own language, adapted to our understanding. There God is angry, grieves, is indignant, rages, threatens, hates, and again has mercy, repents, changes his mind, not that such changes take place in the nature of God, but that to speak thus is suited to our infirmity and slowness. The same prudence I consider befits those who undertake the task of interpreting the Divine Word. Some things for this reason are harmful because they are not expedient, as wine for a fevered patient. Similarly, such matters might allowably have been treated in discussion by the learned world, or even in the theological schools, although I should not think even this to be expedient save with restraint; on the other hand, to debate such fables before the gaze of a mixed multitude seems to me to be not merely useless but even pernicious.

I should, therefore, prefer men to be persuaded not to waste their time and talents in labyrinths of this kind, but to refute or to affirm the views of Luther. My preface would rightly seem too verbose if it were not almost more relevant to the main issue than the disputation itself.

44. See 1 Cor. 6:12.

Introduction to the Disputation

Now, since Luther does not acknowledge the authority of any writer, of however distinguished a reputation, but only listens to the canonical Scriptures, how gladly do I welcome this abridgment of labor, for innumerable Greek and Latin writers treat of free choice, either as a theme or incidentally, so that it would be a great labor to collect out of them what each one has to say either for or against free choice, and to explain the several meanings of each individual opinion, or to resolve or approve their arguments—a tedious and long-winded affair, and as regards Luther and his friends, quite useless, especially as they not only disagree among themselves, but often contradict their own doctrine.

Yet in the meantime let the reader be admonished that if we shall seem to give equal weight with Luther to the testimonies and solid arguments of Holy Scripture, he should also bear constantly in mind so numerous a body of most learned men who have found approval in so many centuries down to our own day, whom not only their skill in divine studies but also godliness of life commend. For some of them gave testimony with their blood to that doctrine of Christ which they defend with their writings; such among the Greeks were Origen, Basil, Chrysostom, Cyril, John of Damascus, Theophylact; among the Latin Fathers, Tertullian, Cyprian, Arnobius, Hilary, Ambrose, Jerome, Augustine, to say nothing meanwhile of Thomas, Scotus, Durandus, Capreolus, Gabriel, Aegidius, Gregory, Alexander, the skill and force of whose dialectic, in my opinion, no one can afford to despise, not to mention the authority of so many universities, councils, and supreme pontiffs.

From the time of the apostles down to the present day, no writer has yet emerged who has totally taken away the power of freedom of choice, save only Manichaeus[45] and John Wyclif. For the authority of Laurentius Valla, who comes nearest to agreement with them, has not much weight among theologians. The doctrine of Manichaeus, indeed, though it has long been exploded and repudiated by common consent of the whole world, yet I am inclined to think less useless to piety than that of Wyclif. For Manichaeus ascribes good and bad works to two natures in man in such a way that we owe good works to God in consequence of our condition, and yet against the power of darkness he leaves cause for imploring the aid of the Creator, that with this aid we may sin more lightly, and more easily do good works. Wyclif, however, ascribes all things to sheer necessity, and what room does he leave either for our prayers or for our endeavors? . . .

Not that, as in human assemblies, I would measure my opinion by the number of votes or the status of the speakers. I know how frequently it happens that the greater part overcomes the better: I know those are not always the best things that are approved by the majority. I know that nothing ever does harm to the investigation of truth, which is added to the industry of one's predecessors. I confess that it is right that the sole authority of Holy Scripture should outweigh all the votes of all mortal men. But the authority of the Scripture is not here in dispute. The same Scriptures are acknowledged and venerated by either side. Our battle is about the meaning of Scripture.

But if in this matter of interpretation some weight is to be given to learning, what minds are sharper and more perceptive than those of the Greeks? Who are more versed in Holy Scripture? Nor among the Latins was insight lacking or skill in interpreting Scripture, for if

45. That is, Mani (ca. 216–ca. 276), the founder of Manichaeism, a gnostic, dualistic sect that combined Persian, Jewish, and Christian elements.

they have yielded pride of place to the Greeks in natural felicity, they have surely been able, building on their achievements, to equal the industry of the Greeks. And if in this point of judgment we have regard rather to holiness of life than to learning, you will see the caliber of the champions in the party that defends free choice; but, as the lawyers say, comparisons are odious! For I should not like to have to compare the heralds of this new gospel with these veterans.

I hear the objection, What need is there of an interpreter when the Scripture itself is crystal clear? But if it is so clear, why have so many outstanding men in so many centuries been blind, and in a matter of such importance, as these would appear? If there is no obscurity in Scripture, what was the need of the work of prophecy in the days of the apostles? You say, "This was the gift of the Spirit." But I have the suspicion that just as the charismata of healings and tongues ceased, this charisma ceased also. And if it did not cease, then one must ask to whom it has been passed on. If to any Tom, Dick, or Harry, all interpretation is uncertain. If to nobody, since even now so many obscurities puzzle learned men, no interpretation will be certain. If to those who have succeeded to the place of the apostles, they will object that for many centuries many have succeeded to the office of the apostles who have nothing of the apostolic Spirit. And yet of these men, other things being equal, it may be concluded as more probable that God has infused his Spirit into those whom he has ordained, just as we may more probably believe grace to be given to the baptized than to the unbaptized. But let us grant, as indeed we must, that it is possible that the Spirit might reveal to a single humble and unlearned man what he has not revealed to the wise and prudent, seeing that Christ thanked his Father for this, that what he had concealed from the wise and prudent, namely, scribes and Pharisees and philosophers, he had revealed to babes, that is, to the simple and foolish according to this world. And perhaps such a fool was Dominic, such was Francis, if it had been permitted to them each to follow his own spirit. But if Paul in his time, in which the gift of the Spirit was in full force, orders spirits to be tested whether they be of God, what ought to be done in this carnal age? How, then, shall we prove the Spirit? By learning? On both sides there are scholars. By holiness of life? On both sides are sinners. On the other hand, there is a whole choir of saints who support free choice. True, they say, but these are only men. But I am now comparing men with men, not men with God. I hear you say, "What has a multitude to do with the meaning of the Spirit?" I reply, "What have a handful?" You say, "What has a miter to do with the understanding of Holy Scripture?" I reply, "What has a sackcloth or a cowl?"[46] You say, "What has the knowledge of philosophy to do with the knowledge of sacred letters?" I reply, "What has ignorance?" You say, "What has an assembled synod to do with the understanding of Scripture, in which it may be that there is nobody who has the Spirit?" I reply, "What, then, of private conventicles of the few, of whom it is much more likely that none has the Spirit?" Paul cries, "Do you wish for proof of Christ who dwells in me?" [2 Cor. 13:3]. The apostles were not believed unless miracles created belief in their doctrine. Now every Tom, Dick, and Harry claims credence who testifies that he has the Spirit of the gospel. . . .

I do not intend this to refer specifically to Luther, whom I do not know personally, and from whose writings I get a mixed impression. I say it rather of certain others better known to

46. The miter is the headdress of a bishop; the cowl, that of a monk.

me who, if there is any controversy concerning the meaning of the Scriptures, when we bring forward the authority of the Early Fathers, chant at once, "Ah! but they were only men." And if you ask them by what argument the true interpretation of Scripture may be known, since both sides are men, they reply, "By the sign of the Spirit." If you ask why the Spirit should rather be absent from those who have illuminated the world by their published miracles than from themselves, they reply as though for thirteen hundred years there had been no gospel in the world. If you seek of them a life worthy of the Spirit, they reply that they are just by faith, not by works. If you look in vain for miracles, they say that the age of miracles is past, and that there is no need of them now that we have so much light in the Scriptures. And if you deny the Scriptures to be clear in such a point about which so many great men have stumbled in darkness, the argument returns full circle.

Moreover, if we grant that he who has the Spirit is sure of the meaning of the Scriptures, how can I be certain of what he finds to be true for himself? What am I to do when many bring diverse interpretations, about which each swears he has the Holy Spirit? And since the Spirit does not furnish the whole truth to anyone, even he who has the Spirit may be mistaken or deceived in some single point. So much for those who so easily reject the interpretation of the Fathers in Holy Scripture and oppose their views to ours as if delivered by an oracle. Finally, even supposing that the Spirit of Christ could have allowed his people to err in trivial matters on which the salvation of men does not greatly depend, how can it be believed that for more than thirteen hundred years he would have concealed the error in his Church and not have found anybody among so many saintly men worthy to be inspired with the knowledge of what these people claim to be the chief doctrine of the whole gospel?

Truly—to conclude this argument—what such people choose to claim for themselves is their own affair. I claim for myself neither learning nor holiness, nor do I trust in my own spirit. I shall merely put forward with simple diligence those considerations which move my mind. If anybody shall try to teach me better, I will not knowingly withstand the truth. If they prefer to rail at one who treats them with courtesy and without invective, rather discoursing than disputing, who will not find them lacking in that spirit of the gospel which is always on their lips? Paul cries, "As for the man who is weak in faith, support him" [Rom. 14:1]. And Christ did not extinguish the smoking flax, while Peter the apostle says, "Always be prepared to make a defense to all who call you to account for the hope that is in you, yet do it with gentleness and reverence" [1 Pet. 3:15]. So that if they reply that Erasmus is an old vessel, and is not capable of the new wine of the Spirit which they offer to the world: if they really rate themselves so highly, let them at least treat us as Christ treated Nicodemus and the apostle [treated] Gamaliel.[47] Although Nicodemus was ignorant, the Lord did not repulse him, because he desired to learn; and the disciples did not reject Gamaliel because he would suspend his judgment until the outcome of the matter should reveal by what spirit it had been done.

Part I. Scripture Passages That Support Free Choice

I have completed half of this book, in which, if I do but persuade the reader that it would be better not to contend too superstitiously about things of this kind, particularly before the multitude, there is no need for the kind of

47. See John 3 and Acts 5.

argument for which I now gird myself, in the hope that truth may everywhere prevail, by comparison of Scriptures, as fire comes from striking flint.

In the first place, it cannot be denied that there are many places in the Holy Scriptures which seem to set forth free choice. On the other hand, others seem to take it wholly away. Yet it is clear that Scripture cannot be in conflict with itself, since the whole proceeds from the same Spirit. First, then, we shall survey those passages which confirm our position; then we shall try to resolve those which seem to make for the opposite point of view. By free choice in this place we mean a power of the human will by which a man can apply himself to the things which lead to eternal salvation, or turn away from them. . . .

Epilogue

. . . One party has made a considerable profit out of confessions and satisfactions, with which they marvelously encumbered the consciences of men, and likewise out of purgatory, concerning which they have asserted certain paradoxes. This fault the other side corrected by saying that confession is an invention of Satan; the most moderate of them say that confession is not compulsory and there is no need of satisfaction for sins, since Christ has paid the penalty for all sins; and finally that there is no purgatory. The one side go so far as to profess that the commands of petty priors are obligatory on pain of hellfire, nor do they hesitate to promise eternal life to him who shall obey. The opposite party meet this extravagance by saying that all the decrees of popes, councils, bishops, are heretical and anti-Christian. Thus one party has enlarged the power of the pontiff beyond all bounds (*"panu hyperbolikos"*[48]), the other speaks openly of him in terms that I would not dare repeat. Again, one party says that the vows of monks and priests are perpetually binding on pain of hellfire, the other says that such vows are thoroughly wicked, that they are not to be undertaken, and if undertaken are not to be kept.

It is from the conflict of such exaggerated views that have been born the thunders and lightnings which now shake the world. And if each side continues to defend bitterly its own exaggerations, I can see such a fight coming as was that between Achilles and Hector whom, since they were both equally ruthless, only death could divide. . . . Pelagius has no doubt attributed too much to free choice, and Scotus quite enough, but Luther first mutilated it by cutting off its right arm; then not content with this he thoroughly cut the throat of free choice and despatched it. I prefer the view of those who do attribute much to free choice, but most to grace.

Nor was it necessary, in avoiding the Scylla of arrogance, that you should be wrecked on the Charybdis of despair or indolence. Nor in mending a dislocated limb need you twist another, but rather put it back into place; nor is it necessary so to fight with an enemy in front that incautiously you receive a wound in the back. The result of this moderation will be the achievement of some good work, albeit imperfect, from which no man can arrogate anything to himself: there will be some merit, but such that the sum *is* owed to God. There is an abundance in human life of weakness, vices, crimes, so that if any man wishes to look at himself he can easily put down his conceit, although we do not assert that man however justified can do nothing but sin, especially since Christ calls him reborn, and Paul, a new creature. Why, you will say, grant anything to free choice? In order to have something to impute justly to the wicked who have voluntarily come short of the

48. Literally, "exceedingly hyperbolically" (Greek).

grace of God, in order that the calumny of cruelty and injustice may be excluded from God, that despair may be kept away from us, that complacency may be excluded also, and that we may be incited to endeavor. For these reasons, almost everyone admits free choice, but as inefficacious apart from the perpetual grace of God, lest we arrogate aught to ourselves. One may object, to what does free choice avail if it accomplishes nothing? I reply, to what does the whole man avail if God so works in him as a potter with clay and just as he could act on a pebble?

[*Luther and Erasmus: Free Will and Salvation*, Library of Christian Classics, trans. and ed. E. Gordon Rupp (Philadelphia: Westminster Press), 35, 37–47, 95–97]

Further Reading

Augustijn, Cornelis. *Erasmus: His Life, Works, and Influence*. Toronto: University of Toronto Press, 1991.

Brady, Thomas A., Jr., et al., eds. *Handbook of European History, 1400–1600: Late Middle Ages, Renaissance, and Reformation*. 2 vols. 1994–95; repr., Grand Rapids, MI: Eerdmans, 1996.

Dykema, Peter A., and Heiko A. Oberman, eds. *Anticlericalism in Late Medieval and Early Modern Europe*. Leiden: Brill, 1993.

Engen, John H. van. *Sisters and Brothers of the Common Life: The Devotio Moderna and the World of the Later Middle Ages*. Philadelphia: University of Pennsylvania Press, 2008.

Hornbeck, J. Patrick, II. *What Is a Lollard? Dissent and Belief in Late Medieval England*. Oxford Theological Monographs. Oxford: Oxford University Press, 2010.

Levy, Ian Christopher. *Holy Scripture and the Quest for Authority at the End of the Middle Ages*. Notre Dame, IN: University of Notre Dame Press, 2012.

Oberman, Heiko A. *The Harvest of Medieval Theology: Gabriel Biel and Late Medieval Nominalism*. 1963; repr., Grand Rapids, MI: Baker Academic, 2000.

Ozment, Steven. *Age of Reform: 1250–1550*. New Haven, CT: Yale University Press, 1980.

Rollo-Koster, Joëlle, and Thomas M. Izbicki, eds. *A Companion to the Great Western Schism (1378–1417)*. Leiden: Brill, 2009.

Chapter 2
Outbreak of Reform

"When Martin Luther nailed his 95 theses to the door of the Castle Church in Wittenberg on October 31, 1517, an era of darkness and superstition came crashing to a close and the enlightened age of the modern church was suddenly and dramatically inaugurated." Although no educated person would describe the events of 1517 and their aftermath quite this simplistically, nevertheless the historiographical inevitability of periodization has often left the impression, especially in popular-level treatments, that the medieval situation drastically and immediately changed with the onset of the Reformation. One result of this mythos is that students tend to expect sixteenth-century Protestants to be more or less modern and therefore tend to read them as such. In fact, these reformers were closer chronologically and intellectually to Thomas Aquinas (1225–1274) than to us. Luther, Calvin, and their contemporaries were medieval men attempting to resolve medieval problems.

The so-called "long sixteenth century" (ca. 1450–ca. 1660) is this transitional period between the medieval and modern world. The century or so before the Reformation raised the social and theological challenges; Luther and his contemporaries simply helped bring the issues to the surface. The sixteenth century proper saw the working out of issues that arose in the late medieval period and led to results that would usher in the modern world, but there is little that is modern about the sixteenth century itself and its reformations.

Reform movements were not unknown in the late medieval period; indeed, the Council of Constance (1414–1418) called for the reformation of the church in head and members. But "grassroots" reform movements were frequently in tension with the established hierarchical church. The mendicant monastic orders, for example, which renounced wealth and took vows of apostolic poverty, were a reaction to and implicit judgment of the church's increasing wealth and power. Even the officially approved movement of the Franciscans could not escape later papal censure. Besides those who operated under the approbation of the Roman Church, there were many reform movements that suffered excommunication and persecution, such as the Waldensians, Lollards, and Hussites.

The sixteenth-century reformations, in the mold of earlier movements, sought to correct perceived doctrinal and moral abuses of the hierarchical church. Like many of their predecessors, their doctrinal questions and reforms were not appreciated but condemned. What separated these reformations (which we can hereafter speak of as "the Reformation") from previous attempts was their ability to do more than merely survive. Whereas earlier movements had been effectively compelled by the threat or execution of church discipline and marginalized even in their homelands, changing social and political realities allowed these sixteenth-century movements to thrive and proliferate openly in northern and western Europe. Increasing loyalty—financial and otherwise—to the emerging nation-states was beginning to supplant primary allegiance to the pope in distant Rome.

An early seventeenth-century portrait depicting the unity of the reformers, including Luther, Zwingli, Calvin, and Bullinger

By the mid-1520s, it was becoming clear to the Roman Church that the reforms were not limited to one man or region but were here to stay. To the political conflicts that were beginning to engulf Europe would now be added increasing religious instability. Peace would still be negotiated and wars fought on political terms and on the basis of political motivations, but now opposing sides within Christian Europe would exploit the new religious divide as means to achieving their goals. An early example of the fragile peace is the Diet (or "meeting") of Speyer in 1526, where it was decided that each region's prince would be free to determine his own region's religion. At the next Diet of Speyer, in 1529, when the Roman Church's bishops and loyal princes decided to reverse the earlier stipulation of tolerance, the followers of Luther submitted a *protestatio*, after which the reformers and their communities have been known as Protestants.

Besides the moral abuses, which the established church was generally willing to acknowledge and condemn, Protestants dissented on the following major points of doctrine:

(1) With regard to *religious authority*, Protestants insisted that primary authority belongs to Scripture alone (*sola Scriptura*), not to the teaching magisterium of the church or the papal office. Some Protestants would give less weight to church tradition than others would, but they all subordinated church teaching to Scripture.

2) With regard to the *doctrine of salvation*, Protestants generally emphasized the assurance of salvation. The sacrament of penance and late medieval system of merits, intended to provide objective assurance, left many consciences in fear of purgatory. Luther himself, knowing he could not live up to God's righteous expectations, feared God's judgments and never felt satisfied after confessing sin.

For the reformers, salvation by grace alone through (or by) faith alone (*sola gratia, sola fide*) meant no more reliance on works of penance and satisfaction, veneration of relics, prayers to saints, and other practices deemed "superstitious." Good works were regarded as the evidence, not the basis, of salvation, and assurance was therefore based on the merit of Christ alone (*solus Christus*).

(3) With regard to the *doctrine of the church*, the sacraments were reduced in number from seven to two, and they were joined with the proclamation of the Word—that is, the Lord's Supper and baptism were viewed not as self-explanatory rituals but as forms that must be accompanied by an intelligible explanation of the gospel.

Finally, although Protestants did not have a uniform church polity, they agreed with one another in rejecting the hierarchical structure of one person holding jurisdiction over the universal church.

Apart from these three contentious areas of doctrine, there was much continuity between Roman Catholic and Protestant theology. But first-generation reformers such as Luther and Zwingli, as well as their Roman Catholic counterparts, emphasized the discontinuities as they sought different resolutions to the same problems.

A. Martin Luther

Biographical Note: Martin Luther

Martin Luther (Luder) (1483–1546) was studying to become a lawyer when his life took a sudden turn. On the night of July 2, 1505, while caught on the road in a storm and after escaping a close encounter with a bolt of lightning, he vowed to devote his life to God and joined the monastery of the Augustinian Hermits. As a monk, Luther could only think of God's righteousness (or justice) in terms of God's harsh judgment. The church's penitential system, which developed in part as a way to achieve an objective personal assurance of salvation, instead added to insecurity with its demand for confession and threat of purgatory. Luther maintained a troubled conscience; in the monastery he experienced the presence of the devil as much as that of Christ.

His abbot was Johann von Staupitz, whom Luther later credited as an influence in his theological turn. It was Staupitz who sent Luther to the Scriptures to find the answers he sought and sent him to Wittenberg to study. Through his study of Paul's Epistle to the Romans, Luther came to understand God's righteousness as God's gift of mercy. The righteousness of Christ is imputed to the sinful believer not because of any merit but because God wills it.

The implications that this realization had for the common theology and practice of the Western church were too serious to ignore. Indeed, Luther's deferential but incessant questioning quickly came to the attention of Pope Leo X, who was determined to silence this apparently insubordinate critic. Luther also refused to back down, insisting, like many medieval theologians before him, that the church's authority and teaching were subordinate to Scripture. After Luther was excommunicated (see Selection 41), the German princes and people rallied to his side, and there was no looking back. The new capability of mass production of books, made possible by the printing press, helped disseminate Luther's thought to a degree that would have been impossible a century earlier.

*Luther was a prolific writer. His early reformist ideas are summed up well in three treatises from 1520—*Address to the Christian Nobility, On the Babylonian Captivity of the Church, *and* On the Freedom of a Christian. *In 1521, Luther began his translation of the Bible from its original languages into German. For the next two and half decades, Luther faithfully lectured at the University of Wittenberg, wrote constructive and polemical theology, and shaped the next generation of reformers in German-speaking lands. Although he was not pleased with the diversity of reform movements that his questioning spawned, most of his contemporaries and all subsequent reformers looked to him as the father of the Protestant Reformation in all its multiplicity.*

Selection 12: Martin Luther, on Prayer

In the past it has happened to us that we did not know how to pray but knew only how to chatter and to read prayers. God pays no attention to this. For no one thinks like this: "Lord, Thou has commanded to pray. Lord, Thou hast promised to hear prayer." Yet these two things will be necessary. Later on one comes and asks for something great for the church, for the ministers of the Word, and for the government. For prayers poured out for many great things give pleasure. Therefore I often pray like this: "Give assistance to the government, be with our brethren, recall those who go astray, strengthen and preserve those who are steadfast. This, Lord, is my prayer. I would not have the courage to pray if Thou hadst not commanded it and hadst not promised to hear."

[*Luther's Works*, 30:324]

Selection 13: Martin Luther, *Disputation against Scholastic Theology* (1517)

A disputation, or set of theses, composed by a professor was meant to be defended before students and interested colleagues in the university setting. The theses are brief and terse, yet they reveal some of Luther's primary concerns about the state of late medieval theology, concerns that would come to fruition in the months and years following this disputation. It is not that Luther had no appreciation for scholasticism or even Aristotle; indeed, he can be found using scholastic method and distinctions, and his right-hand man, Philip Melanchthon (1497–1560), held ongoing lectures on Aristotle's Nicomachean Ethics. ***Luther's contention was that some scholastic theologians had obscured the biblical message about law, suffering, the fallenness of the "natural" will, grace, and the divine will by exalting philosophical content (and Aristotle) above Scripture.***

5. It is false to state that man's inclination is free to choose between either of two opposites. Indeed, the inclination is not free, but captive. This is said in opposition to common opinion. . . .

8. It does not, however, follow that the will is by nature evil, that is, essentially evil, as the Manichaeans maintain. . . .

10. One must concede that the will is not free to strive toward whatever is declared good. This is in opposition to Scotus and Gabriel. . . .[1]

17. Man is by nature unable to want God to be God. Indeed, he himself wants to be God, and does not want God to be God.

18. To love God above all things by nature is a fictitious term, a chimera, as it were. This is contrary to common teaching. . . .

21. No act is done according to nature that is not an act of concupiscence against God.

22. Every act of concupiscence against God is evil and a fornication of the spirit.

23. Nor is it true that an act of concupiscence can be set aright by the virtue of hope. This is in opposition to Gabriel.

24. For hope is not contrary to charity, which seeks and desires only that which is of God.

25. Hope does not grow out of merits, but out of suffering which destroys merits. This is in opposition to the opinion of many. . . .

31. It is said with the idlest demonstrations that the predestined can be damned individually but not collectively. This in opposition to the scholastics. . . .

34. In brief, man by nature has neither correct precept nor good will.

35. It is not true that an invincible ignorance excuses one completely (all scholastics notwithstanding);

36. For ignorance of God and oneself and good work is always invincible to nature.

37. Nature, moreover, inwardly and necessarily glories and takes pride in every work which is apparently and outwardly good.

38. There is no moral virtue without either pride or sorrow, that is, without sin.

39. We are not masters of our actions, from beginning to end, but servants. This in opposition to the philosophers. . . .

1. John Duns Scotus (ca. 1265–1308) and Gabriel Biel (ca. 1420–1495) were scholastic theologians.

41. Virtually the entire *Ethics* of Aristotle is the worst enemy of grace. This in opposition to the scholastics. . . .

43. It is an error to say that no man can become a theologian without Aristotle. This in opposition to common opinion.

44. Indeed, no one can become a theologian unless he becomes one without Aristotle. . . .

49. If a syllogistic form of reasoning holds in divine matters, then the doctrine of the Trinity is demonstrable and not the object of faith. . . .

53. Even the more useful definitions of Aristotle seem to beg the question. . . .

70. A good law will of necessity be bad for the natural will.

71. Law and will are two implacable foes without the grace of God.

72. What the law wants, the will never wants, unless it pretends to want it out of fear or love.

73. The law, as taskmaster of the will, will not be overcome except by the "child, who has been born to us" [Isa. 9:6].

74. The law makes sin abound because it irritates and repels the will [Rom. 7:13]. . . .

79. Condemned are all those who do the works of the law.

80. Blessed are all those who do the works of the grace of God. . . .

83. But even the Decalogue itself and all that can be taught and prescribed inwardly and outwardly is not good law either. . . .

85. Anyone's will would prefer, if it were possible, that there would be no law and to be entirely free. . . .

87. Since the law is good, the will, which is hostile to it, cannot be good.

88. And from this it is clear that everyone's natural will is iniquitous and bad.

89. Grace as a mediator is necessary to reconcile the law with the will. . . .

95. To love God is at the same time to hate oneself and to know nothing but God.

96. We must make our will conform in every respect to the will of God (in opposition to the Cardinal);

97. So that we not only will what God wills, but also ought to will whatever God wills.

In all we wanted to say, we believe we have said nothing that is not in agreement with the Catholic church and the teachers of the church.

[*Luther's Works*, 31:9–16]

Selection 14: Martin Luther, *Ninety-Five Theses* (1517)

On October 31, 1517, Luther publicized this disputation on the topic of indulgences. Along with lectures, disputations were part of the main curriculum of the late medieval university in the disciplines of law, medicine, philosophy, and theology. Luther's posting of these ninety-five propositions, therefore, was not so much an act of defiance as the fulfillment of his duties as a university professor. In a sense, Luther is still quite conservative in this disputation—he does not question the authority of the pope, the existence of purgatory, or the legitimacy of indulgences rightly understood and practiced. Indulgences, he argued, must be accompanied by a penitent heart, and, granting this, they are still inferior to the practice of good works.

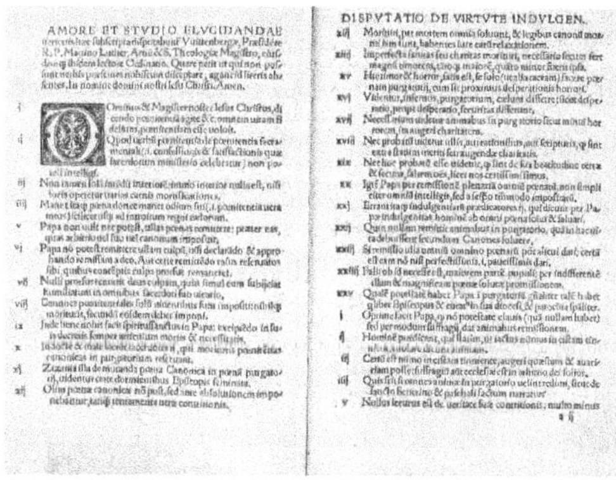
AMORE ET STVDIO ELVCIDANDAE

DISPVTATIO DE VIRTVTE INDVLGEN.

An early Latin printing of the Ninety-Five Theses

Unlike most disputations, this disputation was translated into the vernacular German and distributed far and wide; Luther himself sent it to the archbishop Albert of Mainz. In addition to its primary purpose in the university curriculum, the* Ninety-Five Theses *quickly became a rallying point for questioning church doctrine and later symbolized the beginning of the Protestant Reformation.

Out of love and zeal for truth and the desire to bring it to light, the following theses will be publicly discussed at Wittenberg under the chairmanship of the reverend father Martin Luther, Master of Arts and Sacred Theology and regularly appointed Lecturer on these subjects at that place. He requests that those who cannot be present to debate orally with us will do so by letter.[2]

In the Name of Our Lord Jesus Christ. Amen.

1. When our Lord and Master Jesus Christ said, "Repent" {Matt. 4:17}, he willed the entire life of believers to be one of repentance.

2. This word cannot be understood as referring to the sacrament of penance, that is, confession and satisfaction, as administered by the clergy.

3. Yet it does not mean solely inner repentance; such inner repentance is worthless unless it produces various outward mortifications of the flesh.

4. The penalty of sin remains as long as the hatred of self, that is, true inner repentance, until our entrance into the kingdom of heaven.

5. The pope neither desires nor is able to remit any penalties except those imposed by his own authority or that of the canons.

6. The pope cannot remit any guilt, except by declaring and showing that it has been remitted by God; or, to be sure, by remitting guilt in cases reserved to his judgment. If his right to grant remission in these cases were disregarded, the guilt would certainly remain unforgiven.

7. God remits guilt to no one unless at the same time God humbles believers in all things and makes them submissive to the priest, the divine vicar.

8. The penitential canons are imposed only on the living, and, according to the canons themselves, nothing should be imposed on the dying.

9. Therefore the Holy Spirit through the pope is kind to us insofar as the pope in his decrees always makes exception of the article of death and of necessity.

10. Those priests act ignorantly and wickedly who, in the case of the dying, reserve canonical penalties for purgatory.

11. Those tares of changing the canonical penalty to the penalty of purgatory were evidently sown while the bishops slept {Matt. 13:25}.

12. In former times canonical penalties were imposed, not after, but before absolution, as tests of true contrition.

13. The dying are freed by death from all penalties, are already dead as far as the canon laws are concerned, and have a right to be released from them.

14. Imperfect piety or love on the part of the dying person necessarily brings with it great fear; and the smaller the love, the greater the fear.

15. This fear or horror is sufficient in itself, to say nothing of other things, to constitute the penalty of purgatory, since it is very near the horror of despair.

16. Hell, purgatory, and heaven seem to differ the same as despair, fear, and assurance of salvation.

---

2. The oral, academic disputation did not take place, but the propositions were quickly translated and widely disseminated.

17. It seems as though for the souls in purgatory fear should necessarily decrease and love increase.

18. Furthermore, it does not seem proved, either by reason or Scripture, that souls in purgatory are outside the state of merit, that is, unable to grow in love.

19. Nor does it seem proved that souls in purgatory, at least not all of them, are certain and assured of their own salvation, even if we ourselves may be entirely certain of it.

20. Therefore the pope, when he uses the words "plenary remission of all penalties," does not actually mean "all penalties," but only those imposed by himself.

21. Thus those indulgence preachers are in error when they say that a person is absolved from every penalty and saved by papal indulgences.

22. As a matter of fact, the pope remits to souls in purgatory no penalty which, according to canon law, they should have paid in this life.

23. If remission of all penalties whatsoever could be granted to anyone at all, certainly it would be granted only to the most perfect, that is, to very few.

24. For this reason most people are necessarily deceived by that indiscriminate and high-sounding promise of release from penalty.

25. That power which the pope has in general over purgatory corresponds to the power which any bishop or curate has in a particular way in his own diocese or parish.

26. The pope does very well when he grants remission to souls in purgatory, not by the power of the keys, which he does not have, but by way of intercession for them.

27. They preach only human doctrines who say that as soon as the money clinks into the money chest, the soul flies out of purgatory.

28. It is certain that when money clinks in the money chest, greed and avarice can be increased; but when the church intercedes, the result is in the hands of God alone.

29. Who knows whether all souls in purgatory wish to be redeemed, since we have exceptions in St. Severinus and St. Paschal, as related in a legend.[3]

30. No one is sure of the integrity of his own contrition, much less of having received plenary remission.

31. The one who actually buys indulgences is as rare as the one who is really penitent; indeed, such a person is exceedingly rare.

32. Those who believe that they can be certain of their salvation because they have indulgence letters will be eternally damned, together with their teachers.

33. People must especially be on their guard against those who say that the pope's pardons are that inestimable gift of God by which one is reconciled to God.

34. For the graces of indulgences are concerned only with the penalties of sacramental satisfaction established by man.

35. They who teach that contrition is not necessary on the part of those who intend to buy souls out of purgatory or to buy confessional privileges preach unchristian doctrine.

36. Any truly repentant Christian has a right to full remission of penalty and guilt,[4] even without indulgence letters.

37. Any true Christian, whether living or dead, participates in all the blessings of Christ and the church; and this is granted to the Christian by God, even without indulgence letters.

---

3. The legend holds that Pope Severinus (640) and Pope Paschal I (817–824) preferred to remain in purgatory longer in order to have greater glory in heaven.

4. Theologians distinguished between the guilt (*culpa*) and penalty (*poena*) of sin. Whereas Christ's satisfaction forgave the guilt, certain temporal penalties remained, a sentence that could be carried out in purgatory. Such penalties could be offset by good deeds, such as almsgiving (or purchasing indulgences).

38. Nevertheless, papal remission and blessing are by no means to be disregarded, for they are, as I have said [Thesis 6], the proclamation of the divine remission.

39. It is very difficult, even for the most learned theologians, at one and the same time to commend to the people the bounty of indulgences and the need of true contrition.

40. A Christian who is truly contrite seeks and loves to pay penalties for his sins; the bounty of indulgences, however, relaxes penalties and causes men to hate them—at least it furnishes occasion for hating them.

41. Papal indulgences must be preached with caution, lest people erroneously think that they are preferable to other good works of love.

42. Christians are to be taught that the pope does not intend that the buying of indulgences should in any way be compared with works of mercy.

43. Christians are to be taught that the one who gives to the poor or lends to the needy does a better deed than one who buys indulgences.

44. Because love grows by works of love, a person thereby becomes better. A person does not, however, become better by means of indulgences but is merely freed from penalties.

45. Christians are to be taught that the one who sees a needy person and passes by, yet gives money for indulgences, does not buy papal indulgences but God's wrath.

46. Christians are to be taught that, unless they have more than they need, they must reserve enough for their family needs and by no means squander it on indulgences.

47. Christians are to be taught that the buying of indulgences is a matter of free choice, not commanded.

48. Christians are to be taught that the pope, in granting indulgences, needs and thus desires their devout prayer more than their money.

49. Christians are to be taught that papal indulgences are useful only if they do not put their trust in them, but very harmful if they lose their fear of God because of them.

50. Christians are to be taught that if the pope knew the exactions of the indulgence preachers, he would rather that the basilica of St. Peter were burned to ashes than built up with the skin, flesh, and bones of his sheep.

51. Christians are to be taught that the pope would and should wish to give of his own money, even though he had to sell the basilica of St. Peter, to many of those from whom certain hawkers of indulgences cajole money.

52. It is vain to trust in salvation by indulgence letters, even though the indulgence commissary or even the pope, were to offer his soul as security.

53. They are enemies of Christ and the pope who forbid altogether the preaching of the Word of God in some churches in order that indulgences may be preached in others.

54. Injury is done the Word of God when, in the same sermon, an equal or larger amount of time is devoted to indulgences than to the Word.

55. It is certainly the pope's sentiment that if indulgences, which are a very insignificant thing, are celebrated with one bell, one procession, and one ceremony, then the gospel, which is the very greatest thing, should be preached with a hundred bells, a hundred processions, a hundred ceremonies.

56. The treasures of the church, out of which the pope distributes indulgences, are not sufficiently discussed or known among the people of Christ.

57. That indulgences are not temporal treasures is certainly clear, for many [indulgence] preachers do not distribute them freely but only gather them.

58. Nor are they the merits of Christ and the saints, for, even without the pope, the latter always work grace for the inner man, and the cross, death, and hell for the outer man.

59. St. Laurence said that the poor of the church were the treasures of the church, but he spoke according to the usage of the word in his own time.

60. Without want of consideration we say that the keys of the church, given by the merits of Christ, are that treasure;

61. For it is clear that the pope's power is of itself sufficient for the remission of penalties and cases reserved to him.

62. The true treasure of the church is the most holy gospel of the glory and grace of God.

63. But this treasure is naturally most odious, for it makes the first to be last [Matt. 20:16].

64. On the other hand, the treasure of indulgences is naturally most acceptable, for it makes the last to be first.

65. Therefore the treasures of the gospel are nets with which one formerly fished for men of wealth.

66. The treasures of indulgences are nets with which one now fishes for the wealth of men.

67. The indulgences which the demagogues acclaim as the greatest graces are actually understood to be such only insofar as they promote gain.

68. They are nevertheless in truth the most insignificant graces when compared with the grace of God and the piety of the cross.

69. Bishops and curates are bound to admit the commissaries of papal indulgences with all reverence.

70. But they are much more bound to strain their eyes and ears lest these men preach their own dreams instead of what the pope has commissioned.

71. Let whoever speaks against the truth concerning papal indulgences be anathema and accursed;

72. But let whoever guards against the lust and license of the indulgence preachers be blessed;[5]

73. Just as the pope justly thunders against those who by any means whatsoever contrive harm to the sale of indulgences.

74. But much more does intend to thunder against those who use indulgences as a pretext to contrive harm to holy love and truth.

75. To consider papal indulgences so great that they could absolve a man even if he had done the impossible and had violated the mother of God is madness.

76. We say on the contrary that papal indulgences cannot remove the very least of venial sins as far as guilt is concerned.

77. To say that even St. Peter, if he were now pope, could not grant greater graces is blasphemy against St. Peter and the pope.

78. We say on the contrary that even the present pope, or any pope whatsoever, has greater graces at his disposal, that is, the gospel, spiritual powers, gifts of healing, etc., as it is written in 1 Corinthians 12[:28].

79. To say that the cross emblazoned with the papal coat of arms, and set up by the indulgence preachers, is equal in worth to the cross of Christ is blasphemy.

80. The bishops, curates, and theologians who permit such talk to be spread among the people will have to answer for this.

81. This unbridled preaching of indulgences makes it difficult even for learned people to rescue the reverence which is due the pope from

5. Luther's concern, at this point, is not with the legitimacy of the indulgence but with the greed of the indulgence sellers.

slander or from the shrewd questions of the laity,[6]

82. Such as: "Why does not the pope empty purgatory for the sake of holy love and the dire need of the souls that are there if he redeems an infinite number of souls for the sake of miserable money with which to build a church? The former reasons would be most just; the latter is most trivial."

83. Again, "Why are funeral and anniversary masses for the dead continued and why does he not return or permit the withdrawal of the endowments founded for them, since it is wrong to pray for the redeemed?"

84. Again, "What is this new piety of God and the pope that for a consideration of money they permit a person who is impious and their enemy to buy out of purgatory the pious soul of a friend of God and do not rather, because of the need of that pious and beloved soul, free it for pure love's sake?"

85. Again, "Why are the penitential canons, long since abrogated and dead in actual fact and through disuse, now satisfied by the granting of indulgences as though they were still alive and in force?"

86. Again, "Why does not the pope, whose wealth is today greater than the wealth of the richest Crassus, build this one basilica of St. Peter with his own money rather than with the money of poor believers?"

87. Again, "What does the pope remit or grant to those who by perfect contrition already have a right to full remission and blessings?"

88. Again, "What greater blessing could come to the church than if the pope were to bestow these remissions and blessings on every believer a hundred times a day, as he now does but once?"

6. That is, "learned people" such as Luther, who would like answers to the following questions.

89. "Since the pope seeks the salvation of souls rather than money by his indulgences, why does he suspend the indulgences and pardons previously granted when they have equal efficacy?"

90. To repress these very sharp arguments of the laity by force alone, and not to resolve them by giving reasons, is to expose the church and the pope to the ridicule of their enemies and to make Christians unhappy.

91. If, therefore, indulgences were preached according to the spirit and intention of the pope, all these doubts would be readily resolved. Indeed, they would not exist.

92. Away then with all those prophets who say to the people of Christ, "Peace, peace," and there is no peace! [Jer. 6:14.]

93. Blessed be all those prophets who say to the people of Christ, "Cross, cross," and there is no cross!

94. Christians should be exhorted to be diligent in following Christ, their head, through penalties, death, and hell;

95. And thus be confident of entering into heaven through many tribulations rather than through the false security of peace [Acts 14:22].

[*Luther's Works*, 31:25–33]

Selection 15: Martin Luther, *Preface to the Complete Edition of Luther's Latin Writings* (1545)

Near the end of his life, Luther reflected back on an experience in 1519 that has often been called the Reformation breakthrough. In his study, located in the tower at Wittenberg, he reflected on the significance of "the righteousness of God" in Rom. 1:17. Whereas Luther had previously thought of God's righteousness in the context of divine judgment and wrath, he came to understand justification as the righteousness of Christ imputed to sinners by grace alone through faith

alone. This doctrine of justification would become the genius of the Protestant Reformation.

. . . Meanwhile, I had already during that year [1519] returned to interpret the Psalter anew. I had confidence in the fact that I was more skillful, after I had lectured in the university on St. Paul's epistles to the Romans, to the Galatians, and the one to the Hebrews. I had indeed been captivated with an extraordinary ardor for understanding Paul in the Epistle to the Romans. But until then it was not the cold blood about the heart, but a single word in Chapter 1[:17], "In it the righteousness of God is revealed," that had stood in my way. For I hated that word "righteousness of God," which, according to the use and custom of all the teachers, I had been taught to understand philosophically regarding the formal or active righteousness, as they called it, with which God is righteous and punishes the unrighteous sinner.

Though I lived as a monk without reproach, I felt that I was a sinner before God with an extremely disturbed conscience. I could not believe that he was placated by my satisfaction. I did not love, yes, I hated the righteous God who punishes sinners, and secretly, if not blasphemously, certainly murmuring greatly, I was angry with God, and said, "As if, indeed, it is not enough, that miserable sinners, eternally lost through original sin, are crushed by every kind of calamity by the law of the Decalogue, without having God add pain to pain by the gospel and also by the gospel threatening us with his righteousness and wrath!" Thus I raged with a fierce and troubled conscience. Nevertheless, I beat importunately upon Paul at that place, most ardently desiring to know what St. Paul wanted.

At last, by the mercy of God, meditating day and night, I gave heed to the context of the words, namely, "In it the righteousness of God is revealed, as it is written, 'He who through faith is righteous shall live'." There I began to understand that the righteousness of God is that by which the righteous lives by a gift of God, namely by faith. And this is the meaning: the righteousness of God is revealed by the gospel, namely, the passive righteousness with which merciful God justifies us by faith, as it is written, "He who through faith is righteous shall live." Here I felt that I was altogether born again and had entered paradise itself through open gates. There a totally other face of the entire Scripture showed itself to me. Thereupon I ran through the Scriptures from memory. I also found in other terms an analogy, as, the work of God, that is, what God does in us, the power of God, with which he makes us strong, the wisdom of God, with which he makes us wise, the strength of God, the salvation of God, the glory of God.

And I extolled my sweetest word with a love as great as the hatred with which I had before hated the word "righteousness of God." Thus that place in Paul was for me truly the gate to paradise. Later I read Augustine's *The Spirit and the Letter*, where contrary to hope I found that he, too, interpreted God's righteousness in a similar way, as the righteousness with which God clothes us when he justifies us. Although this was heretofore said imperfectly and he did not explain all things concerning imputation clearly, it nevertheless was pleasing that God's righteousness with which we are justified was taught. Armed more fully with these thoughts, I began a second time to interpret the Psalter. And the work would have grown into a large commentary, if I had not again been compelled to leave the work begun, because Emperor Charles V in the following year [1521] convened the diet at Worms.[7]

---

7. Luther was summoned to Worms to recant his controversial teachings, but, once there, he refused to

I relate these things, good reader, so that, if you are a reader of my puny works, you may keep in mind, that, as I said above, I was all alone and one of those who, as Augustine says of himself, have become proficient by writing and teaching. I was not one of those who from nothing suddenly become the topmost, though they are nothing, neither have labored, nor been tempted, nor become experienced, but have with one look at the Scriptures exhausted their entire spirit.

[*Luther's Works*, 34:336–38]

Selection 16: Martin Luther, *Address to the Christian Nobility of the German Nation* (1520)

In this document, Luther describes three "walls" that the Roman Church has used to protect itself: (1) the superiority of sacred over secular and spiritual distinction between clergy and laity, (2) the papal monopoly on the interpretation of Scripture, and (3) the idea that the pope alone may summon a general church council. After countering these notions, Luther argues that the German princes, though they are laity, are obliged to exercise their spiritual role to guard the health of the church and call a general council to discuss the contemporary matters of controversy. Luther then suggests a number of topics that should be discussed in the council. In the final excerpt, Luther offers his opinion on the problem of begging.

The Romanists have very cleverly built three walls around themselves. Hitherto they have protected themselves by these walls in such a way that no one has been able to reform them. As a result, the whole of Christendom has fallen abominably.

In the first place, when pressed by the temporal power they have made decrees and declared that the temporal power had no jurisdiction over them, but that, on the contrary, the spiritual power is above the temporal. In the second place, when the attempt is made to reprove them with the Scriptures, they raise the objection that only the pope may interpret the Scriptures. In the third place, if threatened with a council, their story is that no one may summon a council but the pope.

In this way they have cunningly stolen our three rods from us, that they may go unpunished. They have ensconced themselves within the safe stronghold of these three walls so that they can practice all the knavery and wickedness which we see today. Even when they have been compelled to hold a council they have weakened its power in advance by putting the princes under oath to let them remain as they were. In addition, they have given the pope full authority over all decisions of a council, so that it is all the same whether there are many councils or no councils. They only deceive us with puppet shows and sham fights. They fear terribly for their skin in a really free council![8] The have so intimidated kings and princes with this technique that they believe it would be an offense against God not to be obedient to the Romanists in all their knavish and ghoulish deceits. . . .

Let us begin by attacking the first wall. It is pure invention that pope, bishops, priests, and monks are called the spiritual estate while princes, lords, artisans, and farmers are called the temporal estate. This is indeed a piece of deceit and hypocrisy. Yet no one need be intimidated by it, and for this reason: all Christians are truly of the spiritual state, and there is no difference among them except that of office.

recant.

8. That is, a council free of papal control, as the Council of Constance (1414–1418) was.

Paul says in I Corinthians 12[:12-13] that we are all one body, yet every member has its own work by which it serves the others. This is because we all have one baptism, one gospel, one faith, and are all Christians alike; for baptism, gospel, and faith alone make us spiritual and a Christian people.

The pope or bishop anoints, shaves heads,[9] ordains, consecrates, and prescribes garb different from that of the laity, but he can never make a man into a Christian or into a spiritual man by so doing. He might well make a man into a hypocrite or a humbug and blockhead, but never a Christian or a spiritual man. As far as that goes, we are all consecrated priests through baptism, as St. Peter says in I Peter 2[:9], "You are a royal priesthood and a priestly realm." The Apocalypse says, "Thou hast made us to be priests and kings by thy blood" [Rev. 5:9-10]. The consecration by pope or bishop would never make a priest, and if we had no higher consecration than that which pope or bishop gives, no one could say mass or preach a sermon or give absolution.

Therefore, when a bishop consecrates it is nothing else than that in the place and stead of the whole community, all of whom have like power, he takes a person and charges him to exercise this power on behalf of the others. It is like ten brothers, all king's sons and equal heirs, choosing one of themselves to rule the inheritance in the interests of all. In one sense they are all kings and of equal power, and yet one of them is charged with the responsibility of ruling. To put it still more clearly: suppose a group of earnest Christian laymen were taken prisoner and set down in a desert without an episcopally ordained priest among them. And suppose they were to come to a common mind there and then in the desert and elect one of their number, whether he were married or not, and charge him to baptize, say mass, pronounce absolution, and preach the gospel. Such a man would be as truly a priest as though he had been ordained by all the bishops and popes in the world. That is why in cases of necessity anyone can baptize and give absolution. This would be impossible if we were not all priests. Through canon law the Romanists have almost destroyed and made unknown the wondrous grace and authority of baptism and justification. In times gone by Christians used to choose their bishops and priests in this way from among their own number, and they were confirmed in their office by the other bishops without all the fuss that goes on nowadays. St. Augustine, Ambrose, and Cyprian each became [a bishop in this way]. . . .[10]

Therefore, just as those who are now called "spiritual," that is, priests, bishops, or popes, are neither different from other Christians nor superior to them, except that they are charged with the administration of the word of God and the sacraments, which is their work and office, so it is with the temporal authorities. They bear the sword and rod in their hand to punish the wicked and protect the good. A cobbler, a smith, a peasant—each has the work and office of his trade, and yet they are all alike consecrated priests and bishops. Further, everyone must benefit and serve every other by means of his own work or office so that in this way many kinds of work may be done for the bodily and spiritual welfare of the community, just as all the members of the body serve one another [1 Cor. 12:14-26]. . . .

So, then, I think this first paper wall is overthrown. Inasmuch as the temporal power has become a member of the Christian body it is a spiritual estate, even though its work is physical. Therefore, its work should extend without

9. That is, the monk's tonsure.

10. Augustine in Hippo, Ambrose (ca. 340–397) in Milan, and Cyprian (ca. 200–258) in Carthage.

hindrance to all the members of the whole body to punish and use force whenever guilt deserves or necessity demands, without regard to whether the culprit is pope, bishop, or priest. Let the Romanists hurl threats and bans about as they like. That is why guilty priests, when they are handed over to secular law, are first deprived of their priestly dignities. This would not be right unless the secular sword previously had had authority over these priests by divine right. Moreover, it is intolerable that in canon law so much importance is attached to the freedom, life, and property of the clergy, as though the laity were not also as spiritual and as good Christians as they, or did not also belong to the church. Why are your life and limb, your property and honor, so cheap and mine not, inasmuch as we are all Christians and have the same baptism, the same faith, the same Spirit and all the rest? If a priest is murdered, the whole country is placed under interdict. Why not when a peasant is murdered? How does this great difference come about between two men who are both Christians? It comes from the laws and fabrications of men. . . .

The second wall is still more loosely built and less substantial. The Romanists want to be the only masters of Holy Scripture, although they never learn a thing from the Bible all their life long. They assume the sole authority for themselves, and, quite unashamed, they play about with words before our very eyes, trying to persuade us that the pope cannot err in matters of faith, regardless of whether he is righteous or wicked.[11] Yet they cannot point to a single letter. This is why so many heretical and un-Christian, even unnatural, ordinances stand in the canon law. But there is no need to talk about these ordinances at present. Since these Romanists think the Holy Spirit never leaves them, no matter how ignorant and wicked they are, they become bold and decree only what they want. And if what they claim were true, why have Holy Scripture at all? Of what use is Scripture? Let us burn the Scripture and be satisfied with the unlearned gentlemen at Rome who possess the Holy Spirit! And yet the Holy Spirit can be possessed only by pious hearts. If I had not read the words with my own eyes, I would not have believed it possible for the devil to have made such stupid claims at Rome, and to have won supporters for them.

But so as not to fight them with mere words, we will quote the Scriptures. St. Paul says in I Corinthians 14[:30], "If something better is revealed to anyone, though he is already sitting and listening to another in God's word, then the one who is speaking shall hold his peace and give place." What would be the point of this commandment if we were compelled to believe only the man who does the talking, or the man who is at the top? Even Christ said in John 6[:45] that all Christians shall be taught by God. If it were to happen that the pope and his cohorts were wicked and not true Christians, were not taught by God and were without understanding, and at the same time some obscure person had a right understanding, why should the people not follow the obscure man? Has the pope not erred many times? Who would help Christendom when the pope erred if we did not have somebody we could trust more than him, somebody who had the Scriptures on his side? . . .

Just think of it! The Romanists must admit that there are among us good Christians who have the true faith, spirit, understanding, word, and mind of Christ. Why, then, should we reject the word and understanding of good Christians and follow the pope, who has neither

11. The doctrine of papal infallibility would not be dogmatized until 1870 (see Selection 96), but it was proposed by some in the medieval period and advocated by some of Luther's opponents.

faith nor the Spirit? To follow the pope would be to deny the whole faith[12] as well as the Christian church. Again, if the article, "I believe in one holy Christian church," is correct, then the pope cannot be the only one who is right. Otherwise, we would have to confess, "I believe in the pope at Rome." This would reduce the Christian church to one man, and be nothing else than a devilish and hellish error.

Besides, if we are all priests, as was said above, and all have one faith, one gospel, one sacrament, why should we not also have the power to test and judge what is right or wrong in matters of faith? What becomes of Paul's words in I Corinthians 2[:15], "A spiritual man judges all things, yet he is judged by no one"? And II Corinthians 4[:13], "We all have one spirit of faith"? Why, then, should not we perceive what is consistent with faith and what is not, just as well as an unbelieving pope does?

We ought to become bold and free on the authority of all these texts, and many others. We ought not to allow the Spirit of freedom (as Paul calls him [2 Cor. 3:17]) to be frightened off by the fabrications of the popes, but we ought to march boldly forward and test all that they do, or leave undone, by our believing understanding of the Scriptures. We must compel the Romanists to follow not their own interpretation but the better one. Long ago Abraham had to listen to Sarah, although she was in more complete subjection to him than we are to anyone on earth [Gen. 21:12]. And Balaam's ass was wiser than the prophet himself [Num. 22:21-35]. If God spoke then through an ass against a prophet, why should he not be able even now to speak through a righteous man against the pope? Similarly, St. Paul rebukes St. Peter as a man in error in Galatians 2[:11-12]. Therefore, it is the duty of every Christian to espouse the cause of the faith, to understand and defend it, and to denounce every error.

The third wall falls of itself when the first two are down. When the pope acts contrary to the Scriptures, it is our duty to stand by the Scriptures, to reprove him and to constrain him, according to the word of Christ, Matthew 18[:15-17], "If your brother sins against you, go and tell it to him, between you and him alone; if he does not listen to you, then take one or two others with you; if he does not listen to them, tell it to the church; if he does not listen to the church, consider him a heathen." Here every member is commanded to care for every other. How much more should we do this when the member that does evil is responsible for the government of the church, and by his evildoing is the cause of much harm and offense to the rest! But if I am to accuse him before the church, I must naturally call the church together.

The Romanists have no basis in Scripture for their claim that the pope alone has the right to call or confirm a council. This is just their own ruling, and it is only valid as long as it is not harmful to Christendom or contrary to the laws of God. Now when the pope deserves punishment, this ruling no longer obtains, for not to punish him by authority of a council is harmful to Christendom.

Thus we read in Acts 15 that it was not St. Peter who called the Apostolic Council but the apostles and elders. If then that right had belonged to St. Peter alone, the council would not have been a Christian council, but a heretical *conciliabulum*.[13] Even the Council of Nicaea, the most famous of all councils, was neither called nor confirmed by the bishop of Rome,

12. Literally, "the creed," that is, the Apostles' Creed, an article of which is mentioned in the following sentence.

13. That is, an unauthorized gathering as opposed to a valid council (*concilium*).

but by the emperor Constantine. Many other emperors after him have done the same, and yet these councils were the most Christian of all. But if the pope alone has the right to convene councils, then these councils would all have been heretical. Further, when I examine the councils the pope did summon, I find that they did nothing of special importance.

Therefore, when necessity demands it, and the pope is an offense to Christendom, the first man who is able should, as a true member of the whole body, do what he can to bring about a truly free council. No one can do this so well as the temporal authorities, especially since they are also fellow-Christians, fellow-priests, fellow-members of the spiritual estate, fellow-lords over all things. Whenever it is necessary or profitable they ought to exercise the office and work which they have received from God over everyone. Would it not be unnatural if a fire broke out in a city and everybody were to stand by and let it burn on and on and consume everything that could burn because nobody had the authority of the mayor, or because, perhaps, the fire broke out in the mayor's house? In such a situation is it not the duty of every citizen to arouse and summon the rest? How much more should this be done in the spiritual city of Christ if a fire of offense breaks out, whether in the papal government, or anywhere else! The same argument holds if an enemy were to attack a city. The man who first roused the others deserves honor and gratitude. Why, then, should he not deserve honor who makes known the presence of the enemy from hell and rouses Christian people and calls them together?

But all their boasting about an authority which dare not be opposed amounts to nothing at all. . . .

21. One of the greatest necessities is the abolition of all begging throughout Christendom. Nobody ought to go begging among Christians. It would even be a very simple matter to make a law to the effect that every city should look after its own poor, if only we had the courage and the intention to do so. No beggar from outside should be allowed into the city whether he might call himself pilgrim or mendicant monk. Every city should support its own poor, and if it was too small, the people in the surrounding villages should also be urged to contribute, since in any case they have to feed so many vagabonds and evil rogues who call themselves mendicants.[14] In this way, too, it could be known who was really poor, and who was not.

There would have to be an overseer or warden who knows all the poor and informs the city council or the clergy what they needed. Or some other better arrangement might be made. As I see it, there is no other business in which so much skullduggery and deceit are practiced as in begging, and yet it could all be easily abolished. Moreover, this unrestricted universal begging is harmful to the common people. I have figured out that each of the five or six mendicant orders visits the same place more than six or seven times every year. In addition to these there are the usual beggars, the "ambassador" beggars, and the panhandlers. This adds up to sixty times a year that a town is laid under tribute! This is over and above what the secular authorities demand in the way of taxes and assessments. All this the Romanist See steals in return for its wares and consumes for no purpose. To me it is one of God's greatest miracles that we can still go on existing and find the wherewithal to support ourselves!

To be sure, some think that if these proposals were adopted the poor would not be so well provided for, that fewer great stone houses and

14. Luther is referring especially to the mendicant orders of monks who take a vow of apostolic poverty and then beg alms. As Luther says, these have "chosen poverty."

monasteries would be built, and fewer so well furnished. I can well believe all this. But none of it is necessary. He who has chosen poverty ought not to be rich. If he wants to be rich, let him put his hand to the plow and seek his fortune from the land. It is enough if the poor are decently cared for so that they do not die of hunger or cold. It is not fitting that one man should live in idleness on another's labor, or be rich and live comfortably at the cost of another's hardship, as it is according to the present perverted custom. St. Paul says, "Whoever will not work shall not eat" [2 Thess. 3:10]. God has not decreed that any man shall live off another man's property, save only the clergy who preach and have a parish to care for, and these should, as St. Paul says in I Corinthians 9[:14], on account of their spiritual labor. And also as Christ says to the apostles, "Every laborer is worthy of his wage" [Luke 10:7].

[*Luther's Works*, 44:126–28, 130–37, 189–91]

Selection 17: Martin Luther, *The Babylonian Captivity of the Church* (1520)

The number and identification of the sacraments had been somewhat fluid until the scholastic period, when Peter Lombard (ca. 1096–1164) identified seven sacraments that were then codified in subsequent church councils. In this treatise, based on the definition of sacrament (a visible sign of invisible grace) and the principle of sola Scriptura, ***Luther deals with all seven ordinances and argues that the number of sacraments should be reduced to two—baptism and communion. His concern with communion is the three "shackles" that the church has placed on it: (1) communion in one kind (withholding the cup), (2) transubstantiation (the dogma that the substance of bread and wine do not remain in the sacrament), and (3) the mass as a continuing sacrifice and work of merit. Luther retained confession of sins as an ordinance, though it is not accompanied by a visible sign and therefore is not strictly a sacrament.***

Jesus

Martin Luther, Augustinian, to his friend, Hermann Tulich,[15] greeting.

Whether I wish it or not, I am compelled to become more learned every day, with so many and such able masters eagerly driving me on and making me work. Some two years ago I wrote on indulgences, but in such a way that I now deeply regret having published that little book. At that time I still clung with a mighty superstition to the tyranny of Rome, and so I held that indulgences should not be altogether rejected, seeing that they were approved by the common consent of so many. No wonder, for at the time I was still engaged singlehanded in this Sisyphean task.[16] Afterwards, thanks to Sylvester,[17] and aided by those friars who so strenuously defended indulgences, I saw that they were nothing but impostures of the Roman flatterers, by which they rob men of their money and their faith in God. Would that I could prevail upon the booksellers and persuade all who have read them to burn the whole of my booklets on indulgences, and instead of all that I have written on this subject adopt this proposition: INDULGENCES ARE WICKED DEVICES OF THE FLATTERERS OF ROME.

Next, Eck and Emser and their fellow-conspirators undertook to instruct me concerning

15. Hermann Tulich was a graduate of Wittenberg and supporter of Luther.

16. In Greek myth, Sisyphus was obliged to spend eternity rolling a boulder up the hill, watching it roll to the bottom, and then beginning the cycle again.

17. Sylvester Prierias (Mazzolini) (1456–1523) was a Dominican theologian who wrote against Luther.

the primacy of the pope.[18] Here too, not to prove ungrateful to such learned men, I acknowledge that I have profited much from their labors. For while I denied the divine authority of the papacy, I still admitted its human authority. But after hearing and reading the super-subtle subtleties of these coxcombs, with which they so adroitly prop up their idol (for my mind is not altogether unteachable in these matters), I now know for certain that the papacy is the kingdom of Babylon and the power of Nimrod, the mighty hunter [Gen. 10:8-9]. Once more, therefore, that all may turn out to my friends' advantage, I beg both the booksellers and my readers that after burning what I have published on this subject they hold this proposition: THE PAPACY IS THE GRAND HUNTING OF THE BISHOP OF ROME. This is proved by the arguments of Eck, Emser, and the Leipzig lecturer on the Scriptures.

Now they are making a game of schooling me concerning communion in both kinds and other weighty subjects: here I must take pains lest I listen in vain to these "eminent teachers" of mine. A certain Italian friar of Cremona has written a "Recantation of Martin Luther before the Holy See," which is not that I revoke anything, as the words declare, but that he revokes me. This is the kind of Latin the Italians are beginning to write nowadays. Another friar, a German of Leipzig, that same lecturer, as you know, on the whole canon of Scripture [Augustinus Alveld] has written against me concerning the sacrament in both kinds and is about to perform, as I understand, still greater and more marvelous things. The Italian [Isidoro Isolani] was canny enough to conceal his name, fearing perhaps the fate of Cajetan[19] and Sylvester. The man of Leipzig, on the other hand, as becomes a fierce and vigorous German, boasts on his ample title page of his name, his life, his sanctity, his learning, his office, his fame, his honor, almost his very clogs. From him I shall doubtless learn a great deal, since he writes his dedicatory epistle to the Son of God himself: so familiar are these saints with Christ who reigns in heaven! . . .

To begin with, I must deny that there are seven sacraments, and for the present maintain that there are but three: baptism, penance, and the bread. All three have been subjected to a miserable captivity by the Roman curia, and the church has been robbed of all her liberty. Yet, if I were to speak according to the usage of the Scriptures, I should have only one single sacrament, but with three sacramental signs, of which I shall treat more fully at the proper time.

Now concerning the sacrament of the bread first of all. . . .

Now there are two passages that do bear very clearly upon this matter: the Gospel narratives of the Lord's Supper and Paul in I Cor. 11. Let us examine these. Matthew [26], Mark [14], and Luke [22] agree that Christ gave the whole sacrament to all his disciples. That Paul delivered both kinds is so certain that no one has ever had the temerity to say otherwise. Add to this that Matt. [26:27] reports that Christ did not say of the bread, "eat of it, all of you," but of the cup, "drink of it, all of you." Mark [14:23] likewise does not say, "they all ate of it," but "they all drank of it." Both attach the note of universality to the cup, not to the bread, as though the Spirit foresaw this schism, by which some would be forbidden to partake of

18. Johann Eck (1486–1543) was professor of theology in Ingolstadt. He faced Luther in the Leipzig Disputation of 1519. Jerome Emser (1477–1527) was a professor in Erfurt. Both men wrote against Luther in the wake of the Leipzig Disputation.

19. Cardinal Cajetan (Thomas de Vio) (1469–1534), Dominican and expert on Thomas Aquinas, faced Luther in Augsburg in 1518.

the cup, which Christ desired should be common to all. How furiously, do you suppose, would they rave against us, if they had found the word "all" attached to the bread instead of to the cup? They would certainly leave us no loophole to escape. They would cry out and brand us as heretics and damn us as schismatics. But now, when the Scripture is on our side and against them, they will not allow themselves to be bound by any force of logic. Men of the most free will they are, even in the things that are God's; they change and change again, and throw everything into confusion. . . .

This is what has prevented me from condemning the Bohemians, who, whether they are wicked men or good, certainly have the word and act of Christ on their side, while we have neither, but only that inane remark of men: "The church has so ordained." It was not the church which ordained these things, but the tyrants of the churches, without the consent of the church, which is the people of God. . . .

The first captivity of this sacrament, therefore, concerns its substance or completeness, which the tyranny of Rome has wrested from us. Not that those who use only one kind sin against Christ, for Christ did not command the use of either kind, but left it to the choice of each individual, when he said: "As often as you do this, do it in remembrance of me" [1 Cor. 11:25]. But they are the sinners, who forbid the giving of both kinds to those who wish to exercise this choice.[20] The fault lies not with the laity, but with the priests. The sacrament does not belong to the priests, but to all men. The priests are not lords, but servants in duty bound to administer both kinds to those who desire them, as often as they desire them. If they wrest this right from the laity and deny it to them by force, they are tyrants; but the laity are without fault, whether they lack one kind or both kinds. In the meantime they must be preserved by their faith and by their desire for the complete sacrament. These same servants are likewise bound to administer baptism and absolution to everyone who seeks them, because he has a right to them; but if they do not administer them, the seeker has the full merit of his faith, while they will be accused before Christ as wicked servants. Thus the holy fathers of old in the desert did not receive the sacrament in any form for many years at a time. . . .

The second captivity of this sacrament is less grievous as far as the conscience is concerned, yet the gravest of dangers threatens the man who would attack it, to say nothing of condemning it. Here I shall be called a Wycliffite and a heretic by six hundred names. But what of it? Since the Roman bishop has ceased to be a bishop and has become a tyrant, I fear none of his decrees; for I know that it is not within his power, nor that of any general council, to make new articles of faith.

Some time ago, when I was drinking in scholastic theology, the learned Cardinal of Cambrai gave me food for thought in his comments on the fourth book of the *Sentences.*[21] He argues with great acumen that to hold that real bread and real wine, and not merely their accidents, are present on the altar, would be much more probable and require fewer superfluous miracles—if only the church had not decreed otherwise. When I learned later what church it was that had decreed this, namely the Thomistic—that is, the Aristotelian church—I grew bolder, and after floating in a sea of doubt, I at

20. The late medieval church offered the bread but withheld the cup from the laity, thus offering communion in "one kind" rather than "both kinds."

21. The Cardinal of Cambrai was Pierre d'Ailly (1350–1420). The *Sentences* of Peter Lombard (ca. 1100–1160) was the primary theology textbook of the late medieval period, and subsequent theologians wrote their own commentaries on the *Sentences*.

last found rest for my conscience in the above view, namely, that it is real bread and real wine, in which Christ's real flesh and real blood are present in no other way and to no less a degree than the others assert them to be under their accidents. I reached this conclusion because I saw that the opinions of the Thomists, whether approved by pope or by council, remain only opinions, and would not become articles of faith even if an angel from heaven were to decree otherwise [Gal. 1:8]. For what is asserted without the Scriptures or proven revelation may be held as an opinion, but need not be believed. But this opinion of Thomas hangs so completely in the air without support of Scripture or reason that it seems to me he knows neither his philosophy nor his logic. For Aristotle speaks of subject and accidents so very differently from St. Thomas that it seems to me this great man is to be pitied not only for attempting to draw his opinions in matters of faith from Aristotle, but also for attempting to base them upon a man whom he did not understand, thus building an unfortunate superstructure upon an unfortunate foundation.

Therefore I permit every man to hold either of these opinions, as he chooses. My one concern at present is to remove all scruples of conscience, so that no one may fear being called a heretic if he believes that real bread and real wine are present on the altar, and that every one may feel at liberty to ponder, hold, and believe either one view or the other without endangering his salvation. However, I shall now set forth my own view.

In the first place, I do not intend to listen or attach the least importance to those who will cry out that this teaching of mine is Wycliffite, Hussite, heretical, and contrary to the decree of the church. No one will do this except those very persons whom I have convicted of manifold heresies in the matter of indulgences, freedom of the will and the grace of God, good works and sins, etc. If Wycliffe was once a heretic, they are heretics ten times over; and it is a pleasure to be blamed and accused by heretics and perverse sophists, since to please them would be the height of impiety. Besides, the only way in which they can prove their opinions and disprove contrary ones is by saying: "That is Wycliffite, Hussite, heretical!" They carry this feeble argument always on the tip of their tongues, and they have nothing else. If you ask for scriptural proof, they say: "This is our opinion, and the church (that is, we ourselves) has decided thus." To such an extent these men, who are reprobate concerning the faith [2 Tim. 3:8] and untrustworthy, have the effrontery to set their own fancies before us in the name of the church as articles of faith. . . .

The third captivity of this sacrament is by far the most wicked abuse of all, in consequence of which there is no opinion more generally held or more firmly believed in the church today than this, that the mass is a good work and a sacrifice. And this abuse has brought an endless host of other abuses in its train, so that the faith of this sacrament has become utterly extinct and the holy sacrament has been turned into mere merchandise, a market, and a profit-making business. Hence participations, brotherhoods, intercessions, merits, anniversaries, memorial days and the like wares are bought and sold, traded and bartered, in the church. On these the priests and monks depend for their entire livelihood. . . .

In the first place, in order that we might safely and happily attain to a true and free knowledge of this sacrament, we must be particularly careful to put aside whatever has been added to its original simple institution by the zeal and devotion of men: such things as vestments, ornaments, chants, prayers, organs, candles, and the whole pageantry of outward things.[83] We must turn our eyes and hearts simply to the institution of Christ and this alone, and set nothing before us but the very word of Christ by which he instituted the sacrament, made it perfect, and committed it to us. For in that word, and in that word alone, reside the power, the nature, and the whole substance of the mass. All the rest is the work of man, added to the word of Christ, and the mass can be held and remain a mass just as well without them. . . .

Let this now suffice for these four sacraments.[22] I know how it will displease those who believe that the number and use of the sacraments are to be learned not from the sacred Scriptures, but from the Roman See. As if the Roman See had given these "sacraments" and had not rather received them from the lecture halls of the universities, to which it is unquestionably indebted for whatever it has. The papal despotism would not have attained its present position, had it not taken over so many things from the universities. For there was scarcely another of the celebrated bishoprics that had so few learned pontiffs as Rome. Only by violence, intrigue, and superstition has she till now prevailed over the rest. For the men who occupied the See a thousand years ago differed so vastly from those who have since come into power, that one is compelled to refuse the name of Roman pontiff to one group or the other.

There are still a few other things which it might seem possible to regard as sacraments; namely, all those things to which a divine promise has been given, such as prayer, the Word, and the cross. For Christ has promised, in many places, that those who pray should be heard; especially in Luke 11[:5-13], where by many parables he invites us to pray. Of the Word he says: "Blessed are those who hear the Word of God and keep it" [Luke 11:28]. And who can count all the times he promises aid and glory to those who are afflicted, suffer, and are cast down? Indeed, who can recount all the promises of God? Why, the whole Scripture is concerned with provoking us to faith; now driving us with commands and threats, now drawing us with promises and consolations. In fact, everything in Scripture is either a command or a promise. The commands humble the proud with their demands, the promises exalt the humble with their forgiveness.

Nevertheless, it has seemed proper to restrict the name of sacrament to those promises which have signs attached to them. The remainder, not being bound to signs, are bare promises. *Hence there are, strictly speaking, but two sacraments in the church of God—baptism and the bread.* For only in these two do we find both the divinely instituted sign and the promise of forgiveness of sins. The sacrament of penance, which I added to these two, lacks the divinely instituted visible sign, and is, as I have said, nothing but a way and a return to baptism. Nor can the scholastics say that their definition fits penance, for they too ascribe to the true sacrament a visible sign, which is to impress upon the senses the form of that which it effects invisibly. But penance or absolution has no such sign. Therefore they are compelled by their own definition either to admit that penance is not a sacrament and thus to reduce their number, or else to bring forth another definition of a sacrament.

Baptism, however, which we have applied to the whole of life, will truly be a sufficient substitute for all the sacraments which we might need as long as we live. And the bread is truly the sacrament of the dying and departing; for in it we commemorate the passing of Christ out of this world, that we may imitate him. Thus we may apportion these two sacraments as

22. In an omitted section, Luther has just discussed confirmation, marriage, ordination, and extreme unction.

follows: baptism may be allotted to the beginning and the entire course of life, while the bread belongs to the end and to death. And the Christian should use them both as long as he is in this mortal frame, until, fully baptized and strengthened, he passes out of this world, and is born into the new eternal life, to eat with Christ in the kingdom of his Father, as he promised at the Last Supper, when he said: "Truly, I say to you, I shall not drink again of this fruit of the vine until it is fulfilled in the kingdom of God" [Matt. 26:29, Mark 14:25, Luke 22:18]. Thus he clearly seems to have instituted the sacrament of the bread with a view to our entrance into the life to come. For then, when the purpose of both sacraments is fulfilled, baptism and bread will cease.

Herewith I conclude this prelude, and freely and gladly offer it to all pious souls who desire to know the genuine sense of the Scriptures and the proper use of the sacraments. For it is a gift of no mean importance, to know the gifts that are given to us, as it is said in I Cor. 2[:12], and what use we ought to make of them. For if we are instructed with this judgment of the spirit, we shall not mistakenly rely on those things which are wrong. These two things our theologians never taught us; indeed, they seem to have taken pains to hide them from us. If I have not taught them, I certainly managed not to conceal them, and have given occasion to others to think out something better. It has at least been my endeavor to set them both forth. Nevertheless, "not all can do all things." To the godless, on the other hand, and those who in obstinate tyranny force on us their own teachings instead of God's, I confidently and freely oppose these pages. I shall be completely indifferent to their senseless fury. Yet I wish even them a right understanding. And I do not despise their efforts; I only distinguish them from what is sound and truly Christian.

I hear a rumor that new bulls and papal maledictions are being prepared against me, in which I am urged to recant or be declared a heretic. If that is true, I desire this little book to be part of the recantation that I shall make; so that the arrogant despots might not complain of having acted in vain. The remainder I will publish very soon; please Christ, it will be such as the Roman See has never seen or heard before. I shall give ample proof of my obedience.[23] In the name of our Lord Jesus Christ. Amen.

[*Luther's Works*, 36:11–13, 18–21, 23, 27–30, 35–36, 123–26]

Selection 18: Martin Luther, *Admonition to Peace concerning the Twelve Articles of the Peasants* (1525)

Many advocates of the German peasants' revolt of 1524–1525 sought an intellectual connection between the uprising and the theological reforms of Luther and others. Indeed, some Roman Catholic opponents of Luther alleged the connection in order to prove that Luther's movement was dangerous and needed to be suppressed. Luther strove to distance himself from this movement, and, in this **Friendly Admonition** ***in response to twelve articles of the peasants, he placed the blame for the imminent revolt both on the peasants and on the princes. The violence that he feared was realized in the later defeat of the peasants.***

The peasants who have now banded together in Swabia have formulated their intolerable grievances against the rulers in twelve articles, and have undertaken to support them with certain passages of Scripture. Now they have published them in printed form. The thing about them

23. The "remainder" was the treatise *Freedom of a Christian*, with a prefatory letter to Pope Leo X.

that pleases me most is that, in the twelfth article, they offer to accept instruction gladly and willingly, if there is need or necessity for it, and are willing to be corrected, to the extent that it can be done by clear, plain, undeniable passages of Scripture. And it is indeed right and proper that no one's conscience should be instructed or corrected except by Holy Scripture.

Now if that is their serious and sincere meaning—and it would not be right for me to interpret it otherwise, because in these articles they come out into the open and do not shy away from the light—then there is good reason to hope that things will be well. Since I have a reputation for being one of those who deal with the Holy Scriptures here on earth, and especially as one whom they mention and call upon by name in the second document, I have all the more courage and confidence in openly publishing my instruction. I do this in a friendly and Christian spirit, as a duty of brotherly love, so that if any misfortune or disaster comes out of this matter, it may not be attributed to me, not will I be blamed before God and men because of my silence. But if this offer of theirs is only pretense and show (without a doubt there are some people like that among them for it is impossible for so big a crowd all to be true Christians and have good intentions; a large part of them must be using the good intentions of the rest for their own selfish purposes and seeking their own advantage) then without doubt it will accomplish very little, or, in fact, it will contribute to their great injury and eternal ruin. . . .

To the Princes and Lords

. . . For you ought to know, dear lords, that God is doing this because this raging of yours cannot, will not, and ought not be endured for long. You must become different men and yield to God's word. If you do not do this amicably and willingly, then you will be compelled to do it by force and destruction. If these peasants do not compel you, others will. Even though you were to defeat them all, they would still not be defeated, for God will raise up others.[24] It is his will to defeat you, and you will be defeated. It is not the peasants, dear lords, who are resisting you; it is God himself, to visit your raging upon you. Some of you have said that you will stake land and people on exterminating the Lutheran teaching. What would you think if you were to turn out to be your own prophets, and your land and people were already at stake? Do not joke with God, dear lords! The Jews, too, said, "We have no king" [John 19:15], and they meant it so seriously that they must be without a king forever.

To make your sin still greater, and guarantee your merciless destruction, some of you are beginning to blame this affair on the gospel and say that it is the fruit of my teaching. Well, well, slander away, dear lords! You did not want to know what I taught or what the gospel is; now the one who will soon teach you is at the door, unless you change your ways. You, and everyone else, must bear witness that I have taught with all quietness, have striven earnestly against rebellion, and have energetically encouraged and exhorted people to obey and respect even you wild and dictatorial tyrants. This rebellion cannot be coming from me. Rather the murder-prophets, who hate me as they hate you, have come among these people and have gone about among them for more than three years, and no one has resisted and fought against them except me.

Therefore, if God intends to punish you and allows the devil through his false prophets to stir up the people against you, and if it is, perhaps, God's will that I shall not be able to

24. Peasants' revolts were not uncommon in the late medieval period.

prevent it any longer, what can I or my gospel do? Not only have we suffered your persecution and murdering and raging; we have also prayed for you and helped to protect and maintain your rule over the common people. If I desired revenge, I could laugh up my sleeve and simply watch what the peasants are doing or even join in with them and help make matters worse; may God keep me from this in the future as he has in the past. . . .

To the Peasants

In the first place, dear brethren, you bear the name of God and call yourselves a "Christian association" or union, and you allege that you want to live and act according to divine law. Now you know that the name, word, and titles of God are not to be assumed idly or in vain, as he says in the second commandment, "Thou shalt not take the name of the Lord your God in vain," and adds, "for the Lord will not hold him guiltless who takes his name in vain" [Deut. 5:11]. Here is a clear, plain text, which applies to you, as to all men. It threatens you, as well as us and all others, with God's wrath without regard to your great numbers, rights, and terror. God is mighty enough and strong enough to punish you as he here threatens if his name is taken in vain, and you know it. So if you take his name in vain, you may expect no good fortune but only trouble. Learn from this how to judge yourselves and accept this friendly warning. It would be a simple thing for God, who once drowned the whole world with a flood [Gen. 7:17-24] and destroyed Sodom with fire [Gen. 19:24-28], to kill or defeat so many thousands of peasants. He is an almighty and terrible God.

Second, it is easy to prove that you are taking God's name in vain and putting it to shame; nor is there any doubt that you will, in the end, encounter all misfortune, unless God is not true. For here is God's word, spoken through the mouth of Christ, "All who take the sword will perish by the sword" [Matt. 26:52]. That means nothing else than that no one, by his own violence, shall arrogate authority to himself; but as Paul says, "Let every person be subject to the governing authorities with fear and reverence" [Rom. 13:1]. . . .

Third, you say that the rulers are wicked and intolerable, for they will not allow us to have the gospel; they oppress us too hard with the burdens they lay on our property, and they are ruining us in body and soul. I answer: The fact that the rulers are wicked and unjust does not excuse disorder and rebellion, for the punishing of wickedness is not the responsibility of everyone, but of the worldly rulers who bear the sword. Thus Paul says in Romans 13[:4] and Peter, in I Peter 3 [2:14], that the rulers are instituted by God for the punishment of the wicked. Then, too, there is the natural law of all the world, which says that no one may sit as judge in his own case or take his own revenge. The proverb is true, "Whoever hits back is in the wrong." Or as it is said, "It takes two to start a fight." The divine law agrees with this, and says, in Deuteronomy 32[:35], "Vengeance is mine; I will repay, says the Lord." Now you cannot deny that your rebellion actually involves you in such a way that you make yourselves your own judges and avenge yourselves. You are quite unwilling to suffer any wrong. That is contrary not only to Christian law and the gospel, but also to natural law and all equity. . . .

On the First Article

"The entire community should have the power and authority to choose and appoint a pastor."[25]

25. This quotation is taken from the Peasants' Articles, followed by Luther's response. The same structure appears below.

This article is just only if it is understood in a Christian sense, even though the chapters indicated in the margin do not support it. If the possessions of the parish come from the rulers and not from the community, then the community cannot give these possessions to one whom they choose, for that would be robbery and theft. If they desire a pastor, let them first humbly ask the rulers to give them one. If the rulers are unwilling, then let them choose their own pastor, and support him out of their own possessions; they should let the rulers keep their property, or else secure it from them in a lawful way. But if the rulers will not tolerate the pastor whom they choose and support, then let him flee to another city, and let any flee with him who want to do as Christ teaches. That is a Christian and evangelical way to choose and have one's own pastor. Whoever does otherwise, acts in an un-Christian manner, and is a robber and brawler.

On the Second Article

The pastor "shall receive out of this tithe . . . ; the remainder shall be distributed to the poor and needy." This article is nothing but theft and highway robbery. They want to appropriate for themselves the tithes, which are not theirs but the rulers' and want to use them to do what they please. Oh, no, dear friends! That is the same as deposing the rulers altogether. Your preface expressly says that no one is to be deprived of what is his. If you want to give gifts and do good, use your own possessions, as the wise man says [Prov. 3:9]. And God says through Isaiah, "I hate the offering that is given out of stolen goods" [Isa. 61:8]. You speak in this article as though you were already lords in the land and had taken all the property of the rulers for your own and would be no one's subjects, and would give nothing. This shows what your intention really is. Stop it, dear sirs, stop it! It will not be you who puts an end to it! The chapters of Scripture which your lying preacher and false prophet has smeared on the margin do not help you at all; they are against you.

On the Third Article

You assert that no one is to be the serf of anyone else, because Christ has made us all free. That is making Christian freedom a completely physical matter. Did not Abraham [Gen. 17:23] and other patriarchs and prophets have slaves? Read what St. Paul teaches about servants, who, at that time, were all slaves. This article, therefore, absolutely contradicts the gospel. It proposes robbery, for it suggests that every man should take his body away from his lord, even though his body is the lord's property. A slave can be a Christian, and have Christian freedom, in the same way that a prisoner or a sick man is a Christian, and yet not free. This article would make all men equal, and turn the spiritual kingdom of Christ into a worldly, external kingdom; and that is impossible. A worldly kingdom cannot exist without an inequality of persons, some being free, some imprisoned, some lords, some subjects, etc.; and St. Paul says in Galatians 5 that in Christ the lord and the servant are equal. . . .

Admonition to Both Rulers and Peasants

Now, dear sirs, there is nothing Christian on either side and nothing Christian is at issue between you; both lords and peasants are discussing questions of justice and injustice in heathen, or worldly, terms. Furthermore, both parties are acting against God and are under his wrath, as you have heard. For God's sake, then, take my advice! Take a hold of these matters properly, with justice and not with force or violence and do not start endless bloodshed in Germany. For because both of you are wrong, and both of you want to avenge and defend yourselves, both of you will destroy yourselves and God will use one rascal to flog another.

Both Scripture and history are against you lords, for both tell how tyrants are punished. Even the heathen poets say that tyrants seldom die a dry death, but are usually slain and perish in their own blood.[26] Because, then, it is an established fact that you rule tyrannically and with rage, prohibit preaching of the gospel, and cheat and oppress the poor, you have no reason to be confident or to hope that you will perish in any other way than your kind have always perished.

Look at all the kingdoms that have come to their end by the sword—Assyria, Persia, Israel, Judah, and Rome. In the end they were all destroyed in the same way they destroyed others. Thus God shows that he is Judge upon earth and that he leaves no wrong unpunished. Therefore nothing is more certain than that this same judgment is breathing down your necks, whether it comes now or later, unless you reform.

Scripture and experience are also against you peasants. They teach that rebellion has never had a good end and that God always keeps his word exactly, "He that takes the sword will perish by the sword" [Matt. 26:52]. You are certainly under the wrath of God, because you are doing wrong by judging your own case and avenging yourselves and are bearing the name Christian unworthily. Even though you win and destroy all the lords, you will finally start tearing the flesh from one another's bones, like wild beasts. For because flesh and blood, not spirit, prevails among you, God will soon send and evil spirit among you, as he did to the men of Shechem and to Abimelech [Judg. 9:22-57]. See the end that finally comes to rebellion in the story of Korah, Numbers 16[:31-35], and of Absalom [2 Sam. 18:14-15], of Sheba [2 Sam. 20:22], Zimri [1 Kgs. 16:18], and others like them. In short, God hates both tyrants and rebels; therefore he sets them against each other, so that both parties perish shamefully, and his wrath and judgment upon the godless are fulfilled.

As I see it, the worst thing about this completely miserable affair is that both sides will sustain irreparable damage; and I would gladly risk my life and even die if I could prevent that from happening. Since neither side fights with a good conscience, but both fight to uphold injustice, it must follow, in the first place, that those who are slain are lost eternally, body and soul, as men who die in their sins, without penitence and without grace, under the wrath of God. Nothing can be done for them. The lords would be fighting to strengthen and maintain their tyranny, their persecution of the gospel, and their unjust oppression of the poor, or else to help that kind of ruler. That is a terrible injustice and is against God. He who commits such a sin must be lost eternally. The peasants, on the other hand, would fight to defend their rebellion and their abuse of the name Christian. Both these things are great sins against God, and he who dies in them or for them must also be lost eternally, and nothing can prevent it.

The second injury is that Germany will be laid waste, and if this bloodshed once starts, it will not stop until everything is destroyed. It is easy to start a fight, but we cannot stop the fighting whenever we want to. What have all these innocent women, children, and old people, whom you fools are drawing with you into such danger, ever done to you? Why do you insist on filling the land with blood and robbery, widows and orphans? Oh, the devil has wicked plans! And God is angry; he threatens to let the devil loose upon us and cool his rage in our blood and souls. Beware, dear sirs, and be

26. This is a saying from Juvenal's *Satires*.

wise! Both of you are equally involved! What good will it do you intentionally to damn yourselves for all eternity and, in addition, to bequeath a desolate, devastated, and bloody land to your descendants, when you still have time to find a better solution by repenting before God, by concluding a friendly agreement, or even by voluntarily suffering for the sake of humanity? You will accomplish nothing[27] through strife and violence.

I, therefore, sincerely advise you to choose certain counts and lords from among the nobility and certain councilmen from the cities and ask them to arbitrate and settle this dispute amicably. You lords, stop being so stubborn! You will finally have to stop being such oppressive tyrants—whether you want to or not. Give these poor people room in which to live and air to breathe. You peasants, let yourselves be instructed and give up the excessive demands of some of your articles. In this way it may be possible to reach a solution of this dispute through human laws and agreements, if not through Christian means.

If you do not follow this advice—God forbid!—I must let you come to blows. But I am innocent of your souls, your blood, or your property. The guilt is yours alone. I have told you that you are both wrong and that what you are fighting for is wrong. You lords are not fighting against Christians—Christians do nothing against you; they prefer to suffer all things—but against outright robbers and defamers of the Christian name. Those of them who die are already condemned eternally. On the other hand, you peasants are not fighting against Christians, but against tyrants, and persecutors of God and man, and murderers of the saints of Christ. Those of them who die are also condemned eternally. There you have God's sure verdict upon both parties. This I know. Do what you please to preserve your bodies and souls, if you will not accept my advice.

I, however, will pray to my God that he will either reconcile you both and bring about an agreement between you, or else graciously prevent things from turning out as you intend. . . .

[*Luther's Works*, 46:17–18, 20–21, 24–25, 37–43]

Selection 19: Martin Luther, *Preface to the Epistles of St. James and St. Jude* (1522; rev. 1546)

For Luther, justification by grace alone through faith alone was the center of the gospel message and the primary criterion of apostolicity and therefore canonicity. Since the Epistle of James seems to contradict this Pauline doctrine, and since it contains no christological reflection, Luther regarded the document as pseudonymous. For other reasons, he also assumed Jude's pseudonymity. Luther's statements about canonicity reflect the patristic and medieval tradition of a somewhat fluid canon and the fact that theologians were quite open about placing some books in the center and others on the margin of the canon. His conclusions about authorship and doctrinal contradiction within the canon helped open the door to later Protestant biblical criticism.

Though this epistle of St. James was rejected by the ancients,[28] I praise it and consider it a good book, because it sets up no doctrines of men but vigorously promulgates the law of God. However, to state my own opinion about it, though without prejudice to anyone, I do not regard it as the writing of an apostle; and my reasons follow.

In the first place it is flatly against St. Paul and all the rest of Scripture in ascribing

27. Luther's original manuscript says "nothing good."

28. Eusebius of Caesarea (ca. 260–ca. 340) includes James and Jude in his list of disputed books.

justification to works [2:24]. It says that Abraham was justified by his works when he offered his son Isaac [2:21]; though in Romans 4[:2-22] St. Paul teaches to the contrary that Abraham was justified apart from works, by his faith alone, before he had offered his son, and proves it by Moses in Genesis 15[:6]. . . .

In the second place its purpose is to teach Christians, but in all this long teaching it does not once mention the Passion, the resurrection, or the Spirit of Christ. He names Christ several times; however he teaches nothing about him, but only speaks of general faith in God. Now it is the office of a true apostle to preach of the Passion and resurrection and office of Christ, and to lay the foundation for faith in him, as Christ himself says in John 15[:27], "You shall bear witness to me." All the genuine sacred books agree in this, that all of them preach in inculcate [*treiben*] Christ. And that is the true test by which to judge all books, when we see whether or not they inculcate Christ. For all the Scriptures show us Christ, Romans 3[:21]; and St. Paul will know nothing but Christ, I Corinthians 2[:2]. Whatever does not teach Christ is not yet apostolic, even though St. Peter or St. Paul does the teaching. Again, whatever preaches Christ would be apostolic, even in Judas, Annas, Pilate, and Herod were doing it.

But this James does nothing more than drive to the law and to its works. Besides, he throws things together so chaotically that it seems to me he must have been some good, pious man, who took a few sayings from the disciples of the apostles and thus tossed them off on paper. Or it may perhaps have been written by someone on the basis of his preaching. He calls the law a "law of liberty" [1:25], though Paul calls it a law of slavery, of wrath, of death, and of sin.

Moreover he cites the sayings of St. Peter [in 5:20]: "Love covers a multitude of sins" [1 Pet. 4:8], and again [in 4:10], "Humble yourselves under the hand of God" [1 Pet. 5:6]; also the saying of St. Paul in Galatians 5[:17], "The Spirit lusteth against envy." And yet, in point of time, St. James was put to death by Herod [Acts 12:2] in Jerusalem, before St. Peter.[29] So it seems that [this author] came along after St. Peter and St. Paul.

In a word, he wanted to guard against those who relied on faith without works, but was unequal to the task. He tries to accomplish by harping on the law what the apostles accomplish by stimulating people to love. Therefore I cannot include him among the chief books, though I would not thereby prevent anyone from including or extolling him as he pleases, for there are otherwise many good sayings in him.

Concerning the epistle of St. Jude, no one can deny that it is an extract or copy of St. Peter's second epistle, so very like it are all the words. He also speaks of the apostles like a disciple who comes long after them [Jude 17] and cites sayings and incidents that are found nowhere else in the Scriptures [Jude 9, 14]. This moved the ancient fathers to exclude this epistle from the main body of the Scriptures. Moreover the Apostle Jude did not go to Greek-speaking lands, but to Persia, as it is said, so that he did not write Greek. Therefore, although I value this book, it is an epistle that need not be counted among the chief books which are supposed to lay the foundations of faith.

[***Luther's Works*, 35:395–98**]

---

29. Luther overlooks the fact that the James to whom the book is traditionally ascribed is not the brother of John and son of Zebedee (Matt. 4:21), later martyred by Herod (Acts 12:2), but the brother of the Lord (Matt. 13:55) who became head of the apostolic church at Jerusalem (Acts 15:13; Gal. 1:19).

Selection 20: Martin Luther, *The German Mass and Order of Service* (1526)

The first completely German worship service was held in Wittenberg on October 29, 1525, and the text for the German mass was printed early in the following year. Luther's German mass was not intended to supplant the Latin mass that was still in use in most German churches but was meant to communicate more effectively to the laity. As Luther says, "What chiefly matters is the teaching and guiding of the people" (*LW *53:80). This principle, along with the complete liturgy in the vernacular, would come to be taken for granted universally in Protestant churches.

Martin Luther's Preface

In the first place, I would kindly and for God's sake request all those who see this order of service or desire to follow it: Do not make it a rigid law to bind or entangle anyone's conscience, but use it in Christian liberty as long, when, where, and how you find it to be practical and useful. For this is being published not as though we meant to lord it over anyone else, or to legislate for him, but because of the widespread demand for German masses and services and the general dissatisfaction and offense that has been caused by the great variety of new masses, for everyone makes his own order of service. Some have the best intentions, but others have no more than an itch to produce something novel so that they might shine before men as leading lights, rather than being ordinary teachers—as is always the case with Christian liberty: very few use it for the glory of God and the good of the neighbor; most use it for their own advantage and pleasure. But while the exercise of this freedom is up to everyone's conscience and must not be cramped or forbidden, nevertheless, we must make sure that freedom shall be and remain a servant of love and of our fellow-man.

Where the people are perplexed and offended by these differences in liturgical usage, however, we are certainly bound to forego our freedom and seek, if possible, to better rather than to offend them by what we do or leave undone. Seeing then that this external order, while it cannot affect the conscience before God, may yet serve the neighbor, we should seek to be of one mind in Christian love, as St. Paul teaches [Rom. 15:5-6; 1 Cor. 1:10; Phil. 2:2]. As far as possible we should observe the same rites and ceremonies, just as all Christians have the same baptism and the same sacrament [of the altar] and no one has received a special one of his own from God. . . .

Concerning the Service

Since the preaching and teaching of God's Word is the most important part of divine service, we have arranged for sermons and lessons as follows: For the holy day or Sunday we retain the customary Epistles and Gospels and have three sermons. At five or six o'clock in the morning a few Psalms are chanted for Matins. A sermon follows on the Epistle of the day, chiefly for the sake of the servants so that they too may be cared for and hear God's Word, since they cannot be present at other sermons. After this an antiphon and the *Te Deum* or the Benedictus, alternately, with an Our Father, collects, and *Benedicamus Domino.* At the mass, at eight or nine o'clock, the sermon is on the Gospel for the day. At Vespers in the afternoon the sermon before the Magnificat takes up the Old Testament chapter by chapter. For the Epistles and Gospels we have retained the customary division according to the church year, because we do not find anything especially reprehensible in this use. And the present situation in Wittenberg is such that many are here who must learn to preach in places where this division is still being observed and may continue in force. Since in this matter we can be of service to others without loss to ourselves, we leave it, but have no objection to others who take up the complete books of the evangelists. This we think provides sufficient preaching and teaching for the lay people. He who desires more will find enough on other days.

Namely, on Monday and Tuesday mornings we have a German lesson on the Ten Commandments, the Creed, Lord's Prayer, baptism, and sacrament, so that these two days preserve and deepen the understanding of the catechism. On Wednesday morning again a German lesson, for which the evangelist Matthew has been appointed so that the day shall be his very own, seeing that he is an excellent evangelist for the instruction of the congregation, records the fine sermon of Christ on the Mount, and strongly urges the exercise of love and good works. But the evangelist John, who so mightily teaches faith, has his own day too, on Saturday afternoon at Vespers, so that two of the evangelists have their own days when they are being read. Thursday and Friday mornings have the weekday lessons from the Epistles of the apostles and the rest of the New Testament assigned to them. Thus enough lessons and sermons have been appointed to give the Word of God free course among us, not to mention the university lectures for scholars.

This is what we do to train the schoolboys in the Bible. Every day of the week they chant a few Psalms in Latin before the lesson,[30] as has been customary at Matins hitherto. For as we stated above, we want to keep the youth well versed in the Latin Bible. After the Psalms, two or three boys in turn read a chapter from the Latin New Testament, depending on the length. Another boy then reads the same chapter in German to familiarize them with it and for the benefit of any layman who might be present and listening. Thereupon they proceed with an antiphon to the German lesson mentioned above. After the lesson the whole congregation sings a German hymn, the Lord's Prayer is said silently, and the pastor or chaplain reads a collect and closes with the *Benedicamus Domino* as usual.

Likewise at Vespers they sing a few of the Vespers Psalms in Latin with an antiphon, as heretofore, followed by a hymn if one is available. Again two or three boys in turn then read a chapter from the Latin Old Testament or half a one, depending on length. Another boy reads the same chapter in German. The Magnificat follows in Latin with an antiphon or hymn, the Lord's Prayer said silently, and the collects with the Benedicamus. This is the daily service throughout the week in cities where there are schools. . . .

This is what I have to say concerning the daily service and instruction in the Word of God, which serves primarily to train the young and challenge the unlearned. For those who itch for new things will soon be sated and tired with it all, as they were heretofore in the Latin service. There was singing and reading in the churches every day, and yet the churches remained deserted and empty. Already they do the same in the German service. Therefore, it is best to plan the services in the interest of the young and such of the unlearned as may happen to come. With the others neither law nor order, neither scolding nor coaxing, will help. Allow them to leave those things in the service alone which they refuse to do willingly and gladly. God is not pleased with unwilling services; they are futile and vain.

But on the festivals, such as Christmas, Easter, Pentecost, St. Michael's, Purification, and the

30. This lesson is from the catechism, the Gospels, and Epistles mentioned in the preceding paragraph.

like, we must continue to use Latin until we have enough German songs. This work is just beginning; not everything has been prepared that is needed. We must arrive at a common standard to assess and control the profusion of orders.

Lent, Palm Sunday, and Holy Week shall be retained, not to force anyone to fast, but to preserve the Passion history and the Gospels appointed for that season. This, however, does not include the Lenten veil,[31] throwing of palms, veiling of pictures, and whatever else there is of such tomfoolery—nor chanting the four Passions, nor preaching on the Passion for eight hours on Good Friday. Holy Week shall be like any other week save that the Passion history be explained every day for an hour throughout the week or on as many days as may be desirable, and that the sacrament be given to everyone who desires it. For among the Christians the whole service should center in the Word and sacrament.

In short, this or any other order shall be so used that whenever it becomes an abuse, it shall be straightway abolished and replaced by another, even as King Hezekiah put away and destroyed the brazen serpent, though God himself had commanded it be made, because the children of Israel made an abuse of it [2 Kgs. 18:4]. For the orders must serve for the promotion of faith and love and not be to the detriment of faith. As soon as they fail to do this, they are invalid, dead and gone; just as a good coin, when counterfeited, is canceled and changed because of the abuse, or as new shoes when they become old and uncomfortable are no longer worn, but thrown away, and new ones bought. An order is an external thing. No matter how good it is, it can be abused. Then it is no longer an order, but a disorder. No order is, therefore, valid in itself—as the popish orders were held to be until now. But the validity, value, power, and virtue of any order is in its proper use. Otherwise it is utterly worthless and good for nothing. God's Spirit and grace be with us all. Amen.

[*Luther's Works*, 53:61, 68–69, 89–90]

31. The Lenten veil was a curtain put in front of the altar to hide it.

Selection 21: Martin Luther, *Table Talk* (first published 1566)

Luther and his wife, the former nun Katherine von Bora, had a family and made their home in what were once the residence halls of a monastery. The Luthers were hospitable and gregarious, and their home often served as a gathering place for Luther and his friends to converse about theology as well as matters of somewhat less importance. As they ate with and listened to Luther, these friends sometimes took notes on these discussions. These more or less random annotations were published as **Table Talk.** ***Although Luther's writings intended for publication are by no means reserved,*** **Table Talk** ***offers a rare glimpse of the more candid exchanges that took place while Luther and his friends sat around his table drinking beer.***

Luther's Own Call to the Ministry

Between November 9 and 30, 1531, No. 113

"Unless those who are in the office of preacher find joy in him who sent them, they will have much trouble. Our Lord God had to ask Moses as many as six times.[32] He also led me into the office in the same way. Had I known about it beforehand, he would have had to take more pains to get me in. Be that as it may, now that I have begun, I intend to perform the duties of the office with his help. On account of the exceedingly great and heavy cares and

32. Cf. Exodus 3–4.

worries connected with it, I would not take the whole world to enter upon this work now. On the other hand, when I regard him who called me, I would not take the whole world not to have begun it. Nor do I wish to have another God. Others before me, like Erasmus, criticized the life that people lived under the papacy, but I never thought I would be able to attack the two pillars on which the papacy rests, the mass and the [monastic] vows, for to do so seemed to me like an attack on God and his creation."

Two Rules for Translating the Bible

Summer or Fall, 1532, No. 312

"In translating the Holy Scriptures I follow two rules:

"First, if some passage is obscure I consider whether it treats of grace or of law, whether wrath or the forgiveness of sin [is contained in it], and with which of these it agrees better. By this procedure I have often understood the most obscure passages. Either the law or the gospel has made them meaningful, for God divides his teaching into law and gospel. The law, moreover, has to do either with civil government or with economic life or with the church. The church is above the earth in heaven, where there is no further division but only a mathematical point, and so principles cannot fail there. This is (and Gerson[33] said it is supreme wisdom) to reduce all things to the first principle, that is, to the most general genus. In theology there are law and gospel, and it must be one or the other. Gerson calls this reduction to the most general genus. So every prophet either threatens and teaches, terrifies and judges things, or makes a promise. Everything ends with this, and it means that God is your gracious Lord. This is my first rule in translation.

33. Jean Gerson (1363–1429) was a leading French theologian and conciliarist at the Council of Constance.

"The second rule is that if the meaning is ambiguous I ask those who have a better knowledge of the language than I have whether the Hebrew words can bear this or that sense which seems to me to be especially fitting. And that is most fitting which is closest to the argument of the book. The Jews go astray so often in the Scriptures because they do not know the [true] contents of the books. But if one knows the contents, that sense ought to be chosen which is nearest to them."

Administration of the Lord's Supper to Convicts

Summer of Fall, 1532, No. 325

When a certain Bohemian said that the sacrament ought not to be given to those who have been convicted of a public crime and have been condemned in a public trial because there is danger that they might not believe, Luther responded, "This doesn't concern the one who administers. His only concern should be that he offer the true Word and the true sacrament. I don't worry about whether he [the communicant] has true faith. I give the sacrament on account of the confession which I have heard, the condition of his heart be what it may. I wager a thousand souls that the absolution and the sacraments are right. I must believe him when he says he is penitent. If he deceives me, he deceives himself. Nevertheless, the sacrament is true and the absolution is true. It is as if I were to give somebody ten pieces of gold and he took them to be only ten coppers. The gold is right in front of his eyes. If he doesn't know what he's taking, the fault is his and the loss is his."

Prenatal Baptisms Are Ridiculed

December, 1532, No. 394

"[According to Aristotle] the whole soul is in each and every part of the body. On this basis they [the papists] baptize a fetus which has not yet been fully brought into the world. Augustine treated of this at great length. If I prick my finger, my whole body feels it. Therefore, when I baptize a finger, I baptize the whole body.

"I don't wish to be baptized thus. But I don't care about the element, whatever one may have. Indeed, it's enough to speak the words. Let the children be committed to our Lord God. The baptism itself is of no concern to me. Besides, the Word is the principal part of baptism. If in an emergency there's no water at hand, it doesn't matter whether water or beer is used."

To Be Glad to Die Is Unnatural

December, 1532, No. 414

"I don't like to see examples of joyful death. On the other hand, I like to see those who tremble and shake and grow pale when they face death and yet get through. It was so with the great saints; they were not glad to die. Fear is something natural because death is a punishment, and therefore something sad. According to the spirit one dies willingly, but according to the flesh the saying applies, 'Another will carry you where you do not wish to go' [John 21:18]. In the Psalms and other histories, as in Jeremiah, one sees how eager men were to escape death. 'Beware,' Jeremiah said, 'or you will bring innocent blood upon yourselves' [Jer. 26:15]. But when Christ said, 'Let this cup pass from me' [Matt. 26:39], the meaning was different, for this was the Same who said, 'I have life and death in my hand' [John 5:21, 24]. We are the ones who drew the bloody sweat from him."

Luther's Estimate of Some Opponents

February, 1533, No. 463

"The papists and I write against each other in different ways.[34] I enter the fray after careful reflection and in a sufficiently hostile frame of mind. For ten years I battled with the devil and established all my positions, and so I knew that they would stand up. But neither Erasmus nor any of the others took the matters seriously. Only Latomus has written excellently against me.[35] Mark this well: Only Latomus wrote against Luther; all the rest, even Erasmus, were croaking toads."

There Are Many Things We Do Not Know

May 12, 1538, No. 3874

Master Philip [Melanchthon] examined a student in Anthony Lauterbach's home. He was a schoolmaster in Stargard, and when he answered thoughtlessly Philip said, "Do not answer so abruptly and burst out so heedlessly, for there are more things we do not know than there are things we know."

Luther remarked in connection with this, "Jonas[36] once claimed that he knew everything in the Holy Scriptures and was angry at me because I didn't let this claim pass unnoticed. But I know there are many things I don't know. I have preached for twenty-five years and still don't understand the verse, 'He who through faith is righteous shall live' [Rom. 1:17]."

Apart from Its Use a Sacrament Is Nothing

June 3, 1539, No. 4634

Then he [Martin Luther] was asked whether the sacraments have a spiritual power in themselves, so that baptism would be consecrated water which by its own strength could wipe out

34. In the presentation of this and other similar documents, it is important to retain their polemical language of "papist" for Roman Catholic in order to reflect accurately the depth of the disputes and not to impose modern sensibilities. At any rate, since Protestants regarded their own movement as "catholic" in the strictest sense, it would have made no sense to refer to their opponents as "Catholics."

35. Jacobus Masson (Latomus) of Louvain wrote against Luther in 1521.

36. Justus Jonas (1493–1555) was Luther's colleague at the University of Wittenberg.

sins, even in case the water were drunk by an ass. He replied, "Because the spiritual power of God doesn't consist of corporeal, inanimate matter, baptism doesn't accomplish anything at all as water existing by itself. But as an action (which would be in its use) baptism has power, so that if anybody sprinkles an infant with water together with a recitation of those words of Christ by which he instituted baptism and promised the forgiveness of sins, that action, and not the water, has divine power. Thus the sacraments are nothing apart from the action and use. Philip Melanchthon [treats] these things."

Luther Rejects the Copernican Cosmology

June 4, 1539, No. 4638

There was mention of a certain new astrologer who wanted to prove that the earth moves and not the sky, the sun, and the moon. This would be as if somebody were riding on a cart or in a ship and imagined that he was standing still while the earth and the trees were moving. [Luther remarked,] "So it goes now. Whoever wants to be clever must agree with nothing that others esteem. He must do something of his own. This is what that fellow does who wishes to turn the whole of astronomy upside down. Even in these things that are thrown into disorder I believe the Holy Scriptures, for Joshua commanded the sun to stand still and not the earth [Josh. 10:12]."

Melanchthon's Gentleness, Luther's Roughness

Between June 11 and 19, 1540, No. 5089

When there was talk about Philip and it was said that he employed the greatest moderation in negotiations pertaining to the gospel, the doctor [Martin Luther] said, "The little fellow is a godly man, and even if he should do wrong, his intention's not bad, but it's because he's taken captive by others. He hasn't accomplished much by his method, and he used bad judgment in dedicating his books.[37]

"I think, when I reflect on the matter, that my way is still the best. I speak right out and scold my opponents like schoolboys. For a knotty stump requires a tough wedge."

[*Luther's Works*, 54:12–13, 42–43, 45, 61, 65, 77, 287, 358–59, 387]

B. Ulrich Zwingli

Biographical Note: Ulrich Zwingli

As a young parish priest in Glarus, Switzerland, Ulrich (or Huldrych) Zwingli (1484–1531) distinguished himself for his powerful preaching and his opposition to the mercenary warfare so common among the Swiss. He imbibed the spirit of Renaissance humanism and was influenced particularly by Erasmus. As a priest in Zurich, beginning in 1519 until his death in 1531, he questioned doctrines related to indulgences and Mariology. Zwingli also advocated practices contrary to the Roman Church, as in his permission of eating meat during Lent and his petition for clerical marriage.

Although they had much in common theologically, Zwingli arrived at his reformist conclusions independently of Luther. Some of these conclusions would prove to be at odds with those of Luther. Zwingli was more adamant than Luther in his adherence to Scripture alone. For example, in the context

37. Melanchthon, as a good humanist, dedicated some of his books to Roman Catholic opponents in hopes of gaining a sympathetic hearing or of winning them over, but it was to no avail.

of worship, Zwingli tended to interpret biblical silence not as permission, but as prohibition, and thus he evidenced a greater inclination toward iconoclasm and a simpler form of worship. Zwingli's sharp separation between the sacramental sign and the thing signified was unprecedented in the history of Christian theology. For these and other reasons, Zwingli shared many affinities with evangelical Anabaptists, though he would later oppose and persecute them for their rejection of infant baptism.

Zwingli met his untimely death on the battlefield as he was serving as chaplain in the Second Battle of Kappel. Through his tireless teaching, preaching, writing, and disputations, Zwingli was instrumental in persuading the magistrates in the German-speaking cantons of Switzerland—especially in Zurich, Bern, and Basel—to back the Reformation. Distinct from the Lutheran trajectory of Protestantism, Zwingli in many ways may be considered the father of what would become Reformed theology.

Selection 22: Ulrich Zwingli, *On Baptism* (1525)

Zwingli was at first impressed by the Zurich Anabaptists' appeal to Scripture in their reform, particularly in their defense of believers' baptism. In 1523, Zwingli even admitted that baptism should normally be preceded by instruction in the Christian faith. By 1524, however, he quickly changed his mind and began to oppose the Anabaptist position, finally declaring it heretical and approving of their execution by drowning.

In this treatise, Zwingli attempted to lay out his positive views of baptism and the use of this word in the New Testament. Church tradition before Zwingli had acknowledged the possibility of salvation apart from water baptism in extreme cases in which a believer died before baptism. But Zwingli's further insistence that salvation has nothing to do with the water ritual, a point he held in common with the Anabaptists, became the dominant view in subsequent Reformed and evangelical Protestant churches.

Now in Scripture the word baptism is used in four different ways.

First, it is used for the immersion in water whereby we are pledged individually to the Christian life.[38] Second, it is used for the inward enlightenment and calling when we know God and cleave to him—that is the baptism of the Spirit.

Third, it is used for the external teaching of salvation and external immersion in water.

Finally it is used for external baptism and internal faith, that is, for the Christian salvation and dispensation as a whole.

Because they do not see clearly these different uses of the term, there are many who fall into strange errors, judging that which they neither know nor understand. We will cite specific texts from Scripture in favour of our view.

1. In John 3 it is written: "And John also was baptizing in Aenon near to Salim, because there was much water there: and they came and were baptized." It is evident that the reference here is simply to water-baptism, for it is pointed out that there was much water there, and the value of this is only for external baptism. And there can be no doubt that those who administer this baptism know very well that they are only baptizing with water.

2. Christ himself speaks of the baptism of the Spirit in Acts 1: "For John truly baptized with water, but ye shall be baptized with the Holy Ghost not many days hence." In this verse Christ stresses that there are two kinds of baptism. John baptized only with water or external teaching. And it is exactly the same today.

38. Indeed, "baptism" literally means immersion.

What men can give is only outward baptism, either by external teaching or pouring or dipping in water. In baptism neither the apostles nor John nor anyone else can do more than give external instruction and immersion in water. Hence the dispute about infant baptism is a dispute only about water-baptism and teaching; are we to baptize infants before we teach them or not? For only God can give the baptism of the Spirit. And that is why Christ at once adds: "But ye shall be baptized with the Holy Ghost." This is the baptism of inward teaching, calling, and cleaving to God. And when he says this, Christ does not repudiate the baptism of John. For the external baptism of John is the same as that of Christ and the apostles, as we shall show later. What Christ says concerning John's baptism may be said of every baptism administered by man. Peter and Paul and James did not administer any baptism but that of water and external teaching. They could not baptize with the Spirit, for God alone baptizes with the Spirit, and he himself chooses how and when and to whom that baptism will be administered.

3. Third, the teaching and baptism of the apostles make it plain that the word "baptism" is used for external teaching and baptism, as may be seen in the words of John himself in John 1: "I baptize with water." For John does not baptize with water only: he teaches as well. But the teaching of John, and also that of the apostles, was only external. It had no power to move the heart. And for that reason it was just as much an external thing as pouring or dipping in water. So then, although John himself says: "I baptize with water," he teaches as well as baptizes, for just before he says: "I am the voice of one crying in the wilderness." And that baptism is used for teaching we see plainly in John 3: "After these things came Jesus into the land of Judaea: and there he tarried with them and baptized." But how did he baptize? Did he do it himself? Immediately following, in John 4, it says: "Though Jesus himself baptized not, but his disciples." But in John 3 it says: "Behold the same baptizeth, and all men come to him." There can be no doubt, then, that in this context the word baptize is expressly used for teach. For as Christ himself said, teaching was his main office, and it is the main office of all apostles, evangelists, bishops and pastors, as Paul says in I Corinthians 1. It was the disciples who baptized with water. And Christ himself knew how he used that baptism to move the heart. Again, it is clear from Matthew 21 that the baptism of John also meant his teaching, for there Christ said to the leaders of the Jews: "I also will ask you one thing: the baptism of John, was it from heaven, or of men?" In this context Christ could not mean only the baptism of water, for in that case it would have been quite right to have replied that it was given him by men. But he asked them concerning his teaching, whether they thought that it was from men or from God. For his adversaries reasoned with themselves, saying, "If we shall say 'From heaven,' he will say, Why did ye not then believe him?" Note that the Jews knew perfectly well that by his baptism he meant his teaching. And baptism is also used for teaching in Acts 19.

4. Fourth, baptism is used for the Christian dispensation and salvation, that is, for the inward faith which saves us, as in I Peter 3: "The like figure whereunto doth now save us . . . even baptism." For neither as water nor as external teaching does baptism save us, but faith.

This division is not my own invention but according to the teaching of Scripture, and those who are not aware whether they are speaking of water-baptism, of baptism as teaching, or of the baptism of the Spirit will fall into serious error. Yet every time that we have tried to make the distinction in our discussions with the Anabaptists and Catabaptists they have answered that they are all the same.[39] They would even have denied the possibility of salvation without water-baptism had we not forcibly restrained them by quoting the words of Christ in John 6: "Verily, verily, I say unto you, he that believeth on me hath everlasting life." Christ himself did not connect salvation with baptism: it is always by faith alone.

We will now show that all the three forms of baptism are given separately.

The disciples gave water-baptism without teaching and without the Spirit. We have seen already in John 4 that when Christ taught but did not baptize it was the disciples who baptized. See too I Corinthians 1: "God (Christ) sent me not to baptize, but to preach the Gospel." On some occasions, then, instruction was given by one and baptism by another. And that some were baptized before they believed we see in John 6, for there can be no doubt that none of those disciples which went away was unbaptized. For as we saw in John 4, "he made and baptized more disciples." But later, in John 6, he upbraided them for their unbelief: "Ye also have seen me and believe not." And finally he said: "There are some of you that believe not." Yet he had permitted them to be baptized. Again, Judas did not believe, as we are told in the same passage: "Have not I chosen you twelve, and one of you is a devil?" But from the verse first quoted it is quite certain that he was baptized, for Christ made many more disciples than John, and he baptized them through his disciples. But those who baptized were not unbaptized themselves. Hence it follows that water-baptism was given even when there was no faith, and it was received even by those who did not believe. The same was true in the case of Simon Magus, concerning whom we are told in Acts 8 that "Simon himself believed also." In this context "believed" must be given the sense of "listened to his message" or "reckoned himself a believer," as Augustine somewhere construes it. For shortly afterwards it became clear that he did not believe. Not that this makes much difference. All that we are trying to prove is that water-baptism is sometimes given even where there is no inward baptism or faith. And unfortunately this is frequently the case at the present time, for many who have no faith allow themselves to be baptized, especially Jews. Yet they are truly baptized with the external baptism of teaching and water. It is evident, then, that the two need not be concurrent: for nothing is more foolish than to say that when a man is baptized he necessarily becomes a believer.

The baptism of teaching was often administered externally when no-one believed or accepted water-baptism. In Acts 18, for example, Paul shook his raiment and excluded the Jews at Corinth because they would not receive Christ. And there are many other cases.

The baptism of the Spirit was also given without the baptism of water. Nicodemus, Joseph of Ramoth and Gamaliel were all believers, but in secret.[40] They were certainly not baptized: otherwise they could not have kept their secret. For baptism is given and received for the sake of fellow-believers, not for a supposed effect in those who receive it. In Acts 10 Cornelius and all who heard Peter received the Holy Spirit before they were baptized. Hence the two baptisms are not always concurrent. Indeed, in the Bible as a whole we find more instances of the Spirit given before water-baptism than after. In one case in particular faith

39. For more on Anabaptists and Catabaptists, see the introduction to chapter 3.

40. See John 19:38-42 and Acts 5:34-39.

was present but not water, and faith was sufficient to save. The thief on the cross believed, and the same day he was with Christ in Paradise, that is, eternal felicity. Now the thief was certainly not baptized with an external baptism. For it is not true that he was baptized in blood, as Jerome asserts in a passage which once misled me. For the thief did not hang there in the cause of God, like the innocents who suffered on behalf of Christ, but because of his act of murder.[41] And Peter says in I Peter 2: "For what glory is it, if, when ye be buffeted for your faults, ye shall take it patiently?"

These passages all serve to show us that in Scripture the word baptism is used in different senses and that there is no salvation in external baptism. We see, then, that water-baptism is a ceremonial sign with which salvation is not indissolubly connected. We have already proved this from the example of the dying thief and others. . . .

[*Zwingli and Bullinger*, 132–36]

Selection 23: Ulrich Zwingli, *Exposition of the Faith* (1531)

Zwingli wrote this Latin treatise in the early summer of 1531, shortly before his death, and it was published by his successor in Zurich, Heinrich Bullinger, in 1536. Zwingli addressed it to the French king, Francis I, in hopes of gaining official sympathy and perhaps even sanction for the emerging Protestant communities in France. To this end, Zwingli provided a concise summary of his faith structured loosely on the Apostles' Creed. In this sense, the Exposition ***functions as an early apology for the Reformed faith in the face of Roman Catholic allegations of heresy.***

41. See Luke 23:40-43.

Preface

Of all the things produced by this tempestuous epoch, there is nothing more useful, most pious king, than dangerous falsehood! For one thing, it is only the good seed of the harvest which the author of evil, the devil, is always attempting to choke (Matt. 13:24f.); for another, the divine husbandman of souls uses wickedness and unbelief to nurture and increase faith and virtue, like the Spartans, who when they had captured a town with much sweat and blood, forbade its utter destruction in order that they might have somewhere to exercise their soldiers in close combat. In the same way, the Lord God allows us too to be threatened in unexpected ways in order that we may be proved usable before him. . . .

I am afraid that by their more than empty and lying insinuations certain faithless persons will attempt to win your clemency. For I know in truth that it can never be exhausted. The more deceitful they are, the more they not only do not reveal but actively defame the truth. And on every possible pretext they charge us with treading religion under foot and despising the holy office and the dignity of kings and magistrates. How little truth there is in all their actions I request your justice to decide when you have heard me expound as best I can the principles of our faith, the laws and customs of our churches, and the respect which we offer to princes.

And nothing is of more concern to a man than to give an account of his faith. For if faith, as the apostle describes it, is the strength and assurance and certainty whereby the soul trusts inflexibly in the unseen God (Heb. 11:1), what man is there so foolish or dullwitted that he cannot explain whether he believes a thing or not? . . .

Concerning God and the things of God this is what we hold:

Of God and the Worship of God

All being is either created or uncreated. God alone is uncreated, for only one thing can be uncreated. . . .

Hence the collapse of all that foolish confidence with which some rely upon most sacred things or the most holy sacraments. For it is in God that we must put our firm and sure trust. If we were to trust in the creature, the creature would have to be the Creator. If we were to trust in the sacraments, the sacraments would have to be God. Not the Eucharist only, but baptism and the laying on of hands would be God. And how absurd that is may be judged not merely by scholars but by all intelligent people. . . .

By this, most gracious king, you will see plainly that we do not disregard or set aside either the saints or the sacraments, as some falsely allege, but rather that we maintain and keep them in their proper place and dignity, thus preventing abuse. We do not dishonour the Mother of God, the Virgin Mary, simply because we do not allow her to be worshipped in the same way as God: for if we tried to attribute to her the dignity and power of the Creator, she herself would not allow such worship. For true piety is the same everywhere and in all men, having its source in one and the self-same Spirit. Hence it is quite unthinkable that any creature should be truly pious and yet allow the worship which is due to God to be paid to it. . . .

The sacraments we esteem and honour as signs and symbols of holy things, but not as though they themselves were the things of which they are the signs. For who is so ignorant as to try to maintain that the sign is the thing which it signifies? If that were the case I would need only to write the word "ape" and your majesty would have before him a real ape.[42] But the sacraments are signs of real things: things which once took place really, literally and naturally they now (as I say) represent and recall and set before our eyes. Please do not misunderstand me, O king. Christ atoned for our sins by his death: and the Lord's Supper is a commemoration of this fact, as he himself said, "This do in remembrance of me." By this commemoration all the benefits which God has displayed in his Son are called to mind. . . .

As the true reverence for the saints and sacraments we transmit and teach that which Christ himself transmitted and taught. "If ye are the children of Abraham," he said (John 8:39), "do the works of Abraham." This is the example which we should follow in respect of all the saints and all holy men. . . . And if they have adorned their religion with holiness of life, we must follow in their steps and attain the same piety and holiness and purity as they did.

Concerning baptism, he says: "Baptize them in the name of the Father, and of the Son, and of the Holy Ghost." Concerning the Supper, he says: "This do in remembrance of me": and by the mouth of Paul: "We are one bread and one body, the whole multitude of believers."[43] Neither in regard to the reverence of the saints nor the institution of the sacraments is it maintained that they have the power and grace which belong to God alone. . . .

We teach therefore that the sacraments should be reverenced as holy things because they signify most holy things, both those which have already happened and those which we ourselves are to produce and do. Thus baptism signifies that Christ has washed us with his blood and also that we are to put on Christ, that is, to follow his example as Paul teaches. Similarly

42. Like words, signs are not to be confused with the real things that they signify. Traditional theology had always distinguished between the sign and the thing signified, but Zwingli presses the distinction to the point of separation.

43. Matt. 28:19; 1 Cor. 11:25; 10:17.

the Supper signifies all the divine favour bestowed upon us in Christ, and also that in thankfulness we are to embrace our brethren with the same love with which Christ has received and redeemed and saved us. The question whether we eat Christ's natural body in the Supper is one which I will discuss more fully later.

To sum up: the source of our religion is to confess that God is the uncreated Creator of all things, and that he alone has power over all things and freely bestows all things. This chief principle of the faith is destroyed by those who ascribe to the creature that which belongs only to the Creator. For in the Creed we confess that we believe in the Creator. Therefore it cannot be the creature in whom we are to believe.

Moreover, we think of God as follows: Since we know that God is the source and Creator of all things, we cannot conceive of anything before or beside him which is not also of him. For if anything could exist which was not of God, God would not be infinite: he would not extend to where that other is, seeing that it exists apart from him. In the Scriptures, as we see, Father, Son, and Holy Ghost are all described as God, but they are not creatures or different gods, but the three are all one, one essence, one *ousia* or existence, one power and might, one knowledge and providence, one goodness and lovingkindness. There are three names or persons, but each and all are one and the self-same God. . . .

Of the Lord Christ

We believe and teach that this Son of God, who is of God, so took to himself the nature of man that his divine nature was not destroyed or changed into that of man: but that each nature is present truly, properly and naturally: his divine nature has not in any way been diminished so as not to be truly, properly and naturally God. Nor has his human nature passed into the divine so that he is not truly, properly and naturally man, except in so far as he is without the propensity to sin. According to his divine nature, in every respect he is God with the Father and the Holy Spirit, not forfeiting any of the divine attributes by the assumption of human weakness. And according to his human nature he is in every way man, having all the properties which belong to the true and proper nature of man save only the propensity of sin, and not lacking any of them by reason of union with the divine nature.

Hence the attitudes and properties of both natures are reflected in all his words and works, so that the pious mind is able to see without difficulty which is to be accredited to each, although everything is rightly ascribed to the one Christ. It is quite correct to say that Christ hungered, for he is both God and man: yet he did not hunger according to his divine nature. . . .

And everywhere we confess that God and Man are one Christ, just as man subsists of a reasonable soul and an earthly body, as St. Athanasius taught. But Christ assumed the nature of man into the hypostasis or person of the Son of God. . . .

We believe that this human nature was received when the Holy Spirit quickened the Virgin, being manifested without any violation of her virginity, that the redeemer and healer of souls might be born into the world of a virgin-mother, he who from all eternity was Lord and God begotten of the Father without mother, to be a holy and spotless sacrifice, to whom the smoke of beast-laden altars ascended in vain. And on his account men should cease from offering up beasts and be moved to offer spiritual sacrifices, seeing that God has himself prepared and offered up for them the sacrifice of his own Son.

We believe that Christ suffered, being nailed to the cross under Pilate the governor. But it was only the man who felt the pangs of suffering, and not God, for God is invisible, and therefore is not subject to any pain, that is, suffering or passion. The cry of pain is this: "My God, my God, why hast thou forsaken me?" But, "Forgive them, for they know not what they do," that is the voice of inviolable deity. . . . [44]

If he had not died and been buried, who would believe that he is very Man? And for the same reason the apostolic Fathers added to the Creed the words, "He descended into hell." They used this expression periphrastically, to signify the reality of his death—for to be numbered amongst those who have descended into hell means to have died—and also to make it clear that the power of his atonement penetrates even to the underworld. . . . On the other hand, if he had not risen again to newness of life, who would have believed that he is very God, having been put to death and being without life or power? . . .

Notice, most courteous sovereign, that the force of the affirmation is in the fact that Christ and all his work is ours. Otherwise it would no more follow to say: Christ rose again, therefore we shall rise, than it would to say: The king has power to pardon the sentenced, therefore everyone has the same power. But the converse is that if Christ is not risen, we shall not rise. For Christ can live and rise of his own power, which we cannot do. There cannot then be any doubt that he allows us and all men to participate in the power of his resurrection. . . .

At this point, most gracious king, I will give my opinion on two further questions:

Of Purgatory

The first is that since Christ did not suffer the pains of hell, as St. Peter teaches in Acts 2, but after his death ascended up into heaven, so we when we are freed from the body shall go up thither without any delay, postponement or renewed affliction if only we have maintained our faith inviolable. Hence those who have held the threat of purgatorial torment over men who are already quite wretched enough without it have been far more concerned to satisfy their own greed than to feed the souls of the faithful.[45]

For first, they utterly invalidate and reject the work of Christ. If Christ died for our sins (as he himself taught, and so too did apostles imbued with his Spirit, and as the doctrine of our religion obliges us to confess, since it tells us that salvation is by the grace and goodness of God), then how can we allow any man to force us to make satisfaction for ourselves? . . .

Second, if Christ does not bear the punishment and penalty incurred by our sins, why did he become man and to what purpose did he suffer? The distinction made by some theologians, that we are redeemed only from guilt and not from punishment, is a frivolous invention, and indeed insulting to God. For no human judge will inflict a penalty where there is no guilt. Once the guilt is pardoned by God, the penalty is also remitted.

Third, inasmuch as Christ himself taught that those who believe in him have eternal life, and that those who believe in him that sent him will not come into condemnation but have already passed from death to life, it is manifest that the period of purgatorial torment laid by the papists upon the souls of those who depart this life is a figment of their own invention.

44. Mark 15:34; Luke 23:34.

45. Rather than providing comfort, as the idea of purgation functions for many today, purgatory was frequently used in this period to frighten people who were already horrified enough of God's judgment.

The Presence of the Body of Christ in the Supper

The second thing which I have undertaken to expound at this point is this, that in the Lord's Supper the natural and essential body of Christ in which he suffered and is now seated in heaven at the right hand of God is not eaten naturally and literally but only spiritually, and that the papist teaching that the body of Christ is eaten in the same form and with the same properties and nature as when he was born and suffered and died is not only presumptuous and foolish but impious and blasphemous.

First, it is quite certain that Christ became a true man consisting of body and soul and in all points like as we are except for the propensity to sin. Hence it follows that all the endowments and properties which belong to our physical nature were most truly present in his body. . . .

It was from these sources that that pillar of theologians, Augustine, drew when he said that the body of Christ has to be in some particular place in heaven by reason of its character as a true body. And again: Seeing that the body of Christ rose from the dead, it is necessarily in one place. . . .

Now for some time there has been bitter contention amongst us as to what the sacraments or signs themselves either do or can do in the Supper. Our adversaries allege that the sacraments give faith, mediate the natural body of Christ, and enable us to eat it as substantially present. But we have good cause to think otherwise.

First, because no external things but only the Holy Spirit can give that faith which is trust in God. The sacraments do give faith, but only historical faith. All celebrations, monuments and statues give historical faith, that is, they remind us of some event, refreshing the memory like the feast of the passover amongst the Hebrews or the remission of debts at Athens, or it may be that they commemorate some victory like the stone at Ebenezer. . . .

Second, we oppose the erroneous teaching of our adversaries when they argue that the natural body of Christ is presented to us in the symbols because that is the force and effect of the words: "This is my body."[46] The argument is met by the words of Christ already adduced, which deny the continued presence of his body in the world. And if that was the force of the words, the body presented would be his passible body. For when he spoke the words he still had a mortal body: hence the disciples partook of his mortal body. For he did not possess two bodies, the one immortal and impassible, the other mortal. And if the apostles ate his mortal body, which do we eat? Naturally, the mortal body. But the body which once was mortal is now immortal and incorruptible. Therefore it follows that if we eat his mortal body he necessarily has a body which is both mortal and immortal. . . . And that is plainly ridiculous. . . .

We believe, then, that as soon as they depart the body the faithful fly away to God, joining themselves to God and enjoying eternal felicity. Therefore, most religious king, if you discharge the office entrusted to you, as David, Hezekiah and Josiah did, you may look forward first to seeing God himself in his very essence and majesty and with all his attributes and powers. . . .

After that you may expect to see the communion and fellowship of all the saints and sages and believers and the steadfast and the brave and the good who have ever lived since the world began. You will see the two Adams, the redeemed and the Redeemer, Abel, Enoch, Noah, Abraham, Isaac, Jacob, Judah, Moses, Joshua, Gideon, Samuel, Phinehas, Elijah, Elisha, Isaiah and the Virgin Mother of God of whom he prophesied, David, Hezekiah, Josiah, the Baptist, Peter, Paul; Hercules too and

46. Matt. 26:26.

Theseus, Socrates, Aristides, Antigonus, Numa, Camillus, the Catos and Scipios;[47] Louis the Pious and your predecessors the Louis, Philips, Pepins and all your ancestors who have departed this life in faith. In short there has not lived a single good man, there has not been a single pious heart or believing soul from the beginning of the world to the end, which you will not see there in the presence of God. . . .

Of the Anabaptists

Now that we have mentioned the Anabaptists, O king, we will briefly describe to you the life and conduct of that sect. They consist for the most part of men of a decadent type, vagrants by necessity, whose trade is the enticement of old women by grandiose speeches on divine things, by which they procure for themselves both a livelihood and also considerable monetary gifts. In all respects they affect the same holiness of life as that which Irenaeus reports concerning the Valentinians and Nazianzus concerning the Eunomians. . . .

Indeed, not a day passes but that they scatter new errors like weeds amongst the good seed of God. And although they have gone out from us because they were not of us, there are still some who ascribe their heresies to us. For that reason we are their most bitter enemies and in all the matters mentioned we take the opposite view. . . .

We do not instigate tumult, nor do we undermine the dignity or laws of magistrates: we are against all failure to redeem promises or to pay debts. Yet we are still accused of these things in some circles, not merely in secret rumour but in public writings. . . .

47. Like many early Christians, Zwingli believed that many pre-Christian pagans, because of their devotion to the Logos, will be among the saved. Hercules is surely one of the more surprising entries in his list.

For that reason I warn your majesty—Do not misunderstand me, for I know that you are surrounded by the most excellent counsellors. Yet it is impossible to take precautions against that which is not foreseen. I know that your advisers could easily provide against the danger if they were aware of it. But as they will not perhaps recognize the peril, I know that you will not take the warning amiss. Therefore seeing that some sparks of the reviving faith have been kindled in your realm, I warn your majesty not to allow the good seed to be choked by the papists, whose power has increased beyond all measure. For in place of that good seed the tares of the Anabaptists will grow up without your being aware of it. And the result will be such general confusion throughout the whole kingdom that it will be extremely difficult to find a remedy. . . .

[*Zwingli and Bullinger*, 245–49, 251–55, 260–61, 275–77]

Selection 24: *Marburg Colloquy* (1529)

Philip of Hesse summoned Luther, Zwingli, Johann Oecolampadius, and other reformers to Marburg in 1529 for the purpose of seeking common ground among the various reformations. The disagreement between Luther and Zwingli on the nature of the eucharistic elements was the primary topic of discussion. Both reformers came to the colloquy with their minds made up. Whereas Luther believed that the true body and blood of the Lord are present with the bread and wine, Zwingli asked how Christ's physical body can be in many places at once.

Seven reports of the colloquy have survived. The discussions, which took place on October 2–3, were mostly amicable, though the disagreement was at times sharp. The theology of the Eucharist, along with its implications concerning the nature of Christ's

incarnation, would remain a key controversy between Lutheran and Reformed churches.

The Report of [Caspar] Hedio
[October 2, 6 a.m.]

Luther, when requested to speak after the close of the chancellor's address, said: Most noble prince, gracious lord! I do not doubt that the colloquy has been planned and arranged with good intentions. Two years ago I rejected it because I knew that enough had been written on both sides and that no further arguments could be presented by either party. Besides, I had made up my mind that I would abide by my opinion until the end of my life. Nor was it my intention to write anything more on the subject. However, when at the Diet of Speyer, my lord, Landgrave Philip, proposed such a colloquy I gave my approval to it; not that I wished to change my conviction of which I am completely sure, but that I might demonstrate the reason for my faith and show where others are in error. But before we can actually begin I want to know about certain opinions that are being put forward by the churches of Zurich, Basel, and Strassburg and which if actually held, would be in error. They concern the Trinity and the person of Christ. For example, they say that the words, "who eats my flesh," refer to the divine nature of Christ; also [they hold a different view] on original sin. Furthermore, they say that I do not understand purgatory correctly; they say the same thing about justification by faith.

Zwingli and *Oecolampadius* replied that they had the correct view in this matter, that they had always taught rightly, and that their books and the church bore witness to this fact. Nevertheless, they desired that first of all there be a discussion of the Lord's Supper for that was why this meeting had been arranged; after this had been finished all the remaining items could readily be discussed.

Luther agreed to this procedure, but protested that he did not agree with the writings of these people. He desired to indicate this disagreement so that people at home might not say that he was not allowed to speak freely. He went on to cite their basic principles:

1) they desire to prove their case by way of logical conclusions;
2) they hold that a body cannot be in two places at the same time and that it cannot be infinite;
3) they appeal to natural reason. . . .

Sunday Afternoon, October 3

Oecolampadius repeated: The body of Christ is not in the sacrament as in a place. Oecolampadius asks in all sincerity: How can he be there as a body?

Luther: At the beginning of our discussion we took Scripture as our basis. Scripture is not against us. You add the fathers; they are not against us either. Among them you have two, Augustine and Fulgentius,[48] on your side; the rest are against you. . . .

Oecolampadius introduces a few passages from Augustine's *On Christian Doctrine* and also from his anti-Manichaean treatises: "The soul is the blood" [cf. Lev. 17:11-14] and "The rock was Christ" [1 Cor. 10:4]. Oecolampadius concedes: [The sacrament] is not a mere sign, but through faith the true body is there.

Luther: Augustine was a young man when he wrote against the Manichaeans and he had no reliable text. "The soul is the blood" [Lev. 17:11]. Again he says, as [he said] earlier: It is necessary to subordinate the teachers to Christ.

48. Fulgentius (468–533) was bishop of Ruspe in North Africa and a follower of Augustine's teachings.

Oecolampadius says that he cannot retract. Oecolampadius brings the matter to a conclusion.

Luther answers: [This is the case] because he cannot agree with our view.

Oecolampadius: Just as our text does not make you give in, so your exposition does not make us give in.

Luther wants to abide by his faith, nor can he yield. He commits us to God and his judgment. Luther then thanks [Oecolampadius] for having carefully explained his views in a friendly manner. He also thanks Zwingli, although he had spoken more sharply. . . .

Oecolampadius begs that the afflicted church be taken into consideration. This is his prayer to God.

Zwingli asks Luther to pardon his harshness, and says that he has always deeply desired his friendship and seeks it even now. Then he added, almost weeping: There are no men, neither in Italy nor in France, whom he would rather see.

Luther says: Pray God that you may come to a right understanding of this matter.

Oecolampadius answers: You, too, should pray for this, for you have the same need.

The Report of [Rudolph] Collin

Before the colloquy began, and as he was about to debate with Zwingli and Oecolampadius, *Luther* had written on his table, "This is my body," in order that he might not allow himself to be diverted from these words. Then in a long speech he testified in advance that he disagreed with the persons of the opposing party and that he would continue to do so, since Christ has said most clear: "Take, eat, this is my body." Here, he said, it must be shown that the body is not the body. He cited the opinion of his opponents, but would allow no questioning on such a clear text. He excluded all rational understanding and common opinion. . . .

Oecolampadius [added]: To believe that Christ is in the bread is an opinion, not faith. It is dangerous to attribute too much to the elements.

Luther: To pick up a piece of straw at the command of the Lord is a spiritual act. He explains the example of the horseshoe at length. One must look not so much upon what is said but, rather, upon who says it. When God says something, we poor, weak humans should listen. . . .

After this argument *Oecolampadius* said: Since we have the spiritual eating, what need is there for bodily eating?

Luther: I care not what is necessary, but since it is written, "Take, eat," etc., it is to be done and to be believed altogether. One must do it. Luther urged this again and again. If he should command me, he said, to eat dung, I should do so, knowing full well that this is salutary for me.

Oecolampadius quotes the passage from the sixth chapter of John: "The flesh is of no avail" [v. 63]. If the flesh, when eaten, is of no avail, but the Spirit is, then we must look to that which is of avail, and pay close attention to the will of God.

Finally both men [Oecolampadius and Luther] testified that they would persevere in their opinion, since neither of the two had convinced the other.

Zwingli begins to accuse Luther of prejudice because he [Luther] testifies that he is unwilling to abandon his view. In the same way Helvidius,[49] with reference to the word "brother," could prove [that Jesus had brothers], since it is clearly

49. Helvidius was a fourth-century theologian who denied the perpetual virginity and came into controversy for suggesting that Jesus' brothers mentioned in the Gospels were the natural sons of Joseph and Mary.

written "his brothers" [John 7:3]. We should compare one passage of Scripture with another. Therefore, if we do not have a passage which says, "This is the figure of my body," we nevertheless have a passage which leads us away from bodily eating. For that reason [it follows] he did not give his body physically in the Supper.

They were of one mind on the cardinal point, namely, the spiritual eating.

Then he [Zwingli] treats the sixth chapter of John, especially these words: "The spirit gives life, the flesh is of no avail" [John 6:63]. He deals with Christ's humanity which suffered; for that was a salutary act. By the logic of his words he proves in a most powerful manner that the flesh which is eaten does not avail in any way. . . .

Luther proves from Scripture against Helvidius that the word "brother" can be used for "cousin." But it cannot be proved that "This is my body" is a trope. If God told me to eat a crabapple, I would eat spiritually. For wherever the word of God is, there is spiritual eating. Therefore, since he added the bodily eating by saying, "This is my body," it is to be believed. By faith we eat this body which is given for us. The mouth receives the body of Christ, the soul believes the words that it is eating the body.

Zwingli: From Scripture it can be proved that the thing signified is often used for the sign; in Ezekiel [5:1ff.], in the "passover" [Exod. 12:27]. Since in passages of Scripture which are uncertain a comparison is demanded, passages similar to them are to be believed.[50]

He accuses Luther of rhetoric and fictitious arguments when the latter says: "If God would command those things or such matters"; for we know that God does not command those things or such matters. The word, he said, is made ambiguous by you.

Words only signify to us the will of God. God does not set before us incomprehensible matters. That Christ is true God and man is not unknown to the believer. We have the example of Mary who asked: "How can this be?" [Luke 1:34]. When she had become more certain through inquiry she then believed. But here in chapter 6 the disciples expressed doubt about the carnal eating because he himself [Christ] taught a spiritual eating. . . .

Luther: The passages from Ezekiel and the "passover" [in Exodus 12] are allegories. But allegory or signification has no meaning in this case. . . .

"Do this," etc. [Luke 22:19]—this word causes the hand of the priest to be the hand of Christ. It is not my mouth, it is not my tongue, but both are Christ's. [This is true] even though I were a knave or rascal. The same applies to baptism. Let us take the example of a prince who defeats the enemy and puts him to flight. In that case the hands of all [the soldiers] are said to be the hands of the prince. "If you will say to this mountain, ['Move hence to yonder place,'] it will move" [Matt. 17:20]. I am not debating whether the "is" may be "signifies," but I am satisfied that Christ says: "This is my body." . . . Therefore, believe the plain words and give glory to God.

Zwingli: We, too, ask you to give glory to God and to stop begging the question. Where do you prove your thesis? I am not going to abandon this passage [from John], which is unassailable and which you treat so lightly. You will have to change your tune.

Luther: You are speaking spitefully.

Zwingli asks whether he believes that Christ in the sixth chapter of John wanted to help the ignorant.

50. The principle of clarifying obscure passages of Scripture by comparison with clearer passages is a traditional rule of premodern exegesis.

Luther: You want to win your case with bold words. "This is a hard saying," etc. [John 6:60]; the Jews are speaking about something which is impossible and absurd. But we will pass over that text because it does not deal with the matter at hand.

Zwingli: No, no, this passage (meaning John 6) is going to break your neck.

Luther: Don't boast too much. You are in Hesse and not in Switzerland. Necks do not break so easily here. On account of this statement other accusations were made and there was much shouting. Yet Luther used a similar phrase in his book *Against the Heavenly Prophets*, where he says: "Let us take the rogue," meaning Karlstadt, "by the throat."

Zwingli apologized for having used an expression common among his people. Recognizing that there were diverse manners of expression, the prince with a nod of his head and an oral statement accepted the excuse.

Zwingli cited Luther's postil in which he had written that Christ had said of himself: "The flesh is of no avail" [John 6: 63]. Then he introduced Melanchthon's remarks about the same passage. That the body is eaten in a bodily way is not established in his statement. When the fathers said that the body of Christ feeds the soul, I understand this to mean the resurrection.

Luther: I do not care what we have written. Prove that "This is my body" is not his body. The body [of Christ] nourishes man's body for eternity. When the mouth receives the body, a person acquires a kind of immortality. For the word on the basis of God's command supplies strength. God says, "Take, do," and so it comes to pass. He speaks and it is done. . . .

The Report of [Andreas] Osiander

. . . When Dr. Stephan (namely, Agricola) of Augsburg, John Brenz of Hall, and I arrived at Marburg on Saturday afternoon and our presence was announced at the court, we were immediately sent for and brought into the prince's chamber where Luther was already debating with Zwingli and Oecolampadius. We were seated with Dr. Martin Luther and Philip Melanchthon in order to listen to the debate and, if necessary, also to take part in it. . . .[51]

Thereafter Luther briefly explained how the opposition had undertaken to prove that the words of Christ, "This is my body . . . this is my blood" [Matt. 26:26ff.], permit and demand an interpretation other than what we believe and teach. When they acknowledged this, Luther continued that he wanted a proof from them, since so far none had been offered. He believed that it could also not be offered in the future. Yet he desired to hear their proof and, wherever he would find it deficient, he would indicate this amicably and briefly. Then, for his own benefit, he wrote the text, "This is my body," etc., on the table with a piece of chalk.

Thereupon Zwingli and Oecolampadius attempted to prove their position with the sacred and divine Scripture and the clear sayings of the fathers. But Luther implored them, rather, to do this in an orderly and kindly way. They should not mingle the two sources, but refrain from mentioning the fathers until the sacred and divine Scripture had first been dealt with. They agreed to this procedure and adhered to it.

Then Zwingli began. He cited the passage from John 6[:63]: "The flesh is of no avail." With it he intended to prove that, since the flesh of Christ is of no avail, Christ did not give it to be eaten. . . .

Zwingli said that it was a disgrace that we upheld, taught, and defended such a difficult

51. Note the first-person usage and perspective of the Lutheran Osiander throughout his report.

article of faith and still were unable and did not wish to cite Scripture in support of it.

At this point Luther removed the velvet cloth and showed him the passage, "This is my body," which he had written for himself on the table with chalk, and said: "Here is our Scripture passage. You have not yet wrested it away from us, as you volunteered to do. We have no need of another passage."

Zwingli asked whether he had no Scripture passage, argument, or testimony other than this one alone.

Luther answered: "Indeed I have others, which you will hear after you have succeeded in taking this one away from me; since I have a sure word of God which no one can wrest from me, why should I let go of it and look about for another? Overthrow this argument, then you can expect to hear what additional arguments I have."

To this extent and no more, Zwingli and Oecolampadius presented testimony from the sacred Scripture; but they went ahead and tried to explore by the use of reason how a body could be in many places or even in no place. Luther did not want to permit this and said: "Reason, philosophy, and mathematics have no place here, for even if we concluded that a body must be only in one place, we would simply be saying that a body must be only in one place according to the common course of nature. However, it could never be the case that God's almighty word would not have the power to do something other than occurs in ordinary nature. Therefore, this approach cannot serve the purpose here."[52] . . .

52. Just as Luther held tenaciously to the one phrase from Jesus, he rejected all attempts to argue from other Scriptures, church fathers, or reason.

The Marburg Articles

. . . *Concerning the Sacrament of the Body and Blood of Christ*

Fifteenth, we all believe and hold concerning the Supper of our dear Lord Jesus Christ that both kinds should be used according to the institution by Christ; [also that the Mass is not a work with which one can secure grace for someone else, whether he is dead or alive;[53]] also that the Sacrament of the Altar is a sacrament of the true body and blood of Jesus Christ and that the spiritual partaking of the same body and blood is especially necessary for every Christian. Similarly, that the use of the sacrament, like the word, has been given and ordained by God Almighty in order that weak consciences may thereby be excited to faith by the Holy Spirit. And although at this time, we have not reached an agreement as to whether the true body and blood of Christ are bodily present in the bread and wine, nevertheless, each side should show Christian love to the other side insofar as conscience will permit, and both sides should diligently pray to Almighty God that through his Spirit he might confirm us in the right understanding. Amen.

Martin Luther
Justus Jonas
Philip Melanchthon
Andreas Osiander
Stephan Agricola
John Brenz
John Oecolampadius
Huldrych Zwingli
Martin Bucer
Caspar Hedio

[***Luther's Works***, **38:15–16, 34–36, 52–57, 63–64, 67, 88–89**]

53. This statement in brackets is added in another manuscript.

C. Family Matters

Selection 25: Katharina Schütz Zell, *Apologia for Master Matthew Zell* (1524)

Katharina Schütz Zell (1498–1562) was a lay reformer who wrote a number of theological works and engaged in correspondence with other reformers. She married Matthew Zell, the main preacher in Strasbourg, on December 2, 1523 (earlier than the public marriage of either Luther or Zwingli), and she remained his faithful companion and coworker until his death. This document is an early example of a layperson's defense of clerical marriage.

They also fight against clerical marriage, which has indeed clear and bright—not faint—grounds in godly scripture, in the Old and New Testaments, so that children and fools can read and understand, as I have shown and proved to the bishop of Strasbourg with a long writing. There I have compared marriage and harlotry with each other according to the teaching of godly scripture.[54] Would to God that the bishop would finally become so angry with me that he would allow everyone to read this writing! However, the reason why (when I would talk about marriage) they remain adamant on this subject is that they [Roman clergy] intend to defy God and to put these scriptural teachings behind them again by force. For this, I must say, they have two reasons.

The first reason is that the pope and bishop and their servants, vicars and their fellows, do not raise so much tax money for harlotry from married people as from harlots and knaves. If a priest has a (legally married) wife, he behaves like any other honorable upright citizen and gives the bishop no tax for it [his married life] because God has given it to him freely. If priests (who are supposed to be celibate) have harlots, they must have their lords' permission and fairly pay them a tax for this permission since they are in feudal relationship to their lords the pope and bishops. . . .

They protect and defend this shame and calumny against all teaching of godly scripture, in which the Holy Spirit strictly banishes harlots and shuts them out of the kingdom of God and forbids that one should either eat or drink with them. As Paul says in the first epistle to the Corinthians in chapters 5 and 6 and to the Ephesians in chapter 5 [1 Cor. 5:1, 11, and 6:15, 18; Eph. 5:3, 5; cf. Lev. 20:10ff.; Isa. 1:21]. But God implanted marriage in all people in the first creation, and no one is to be excused from it except the three kinds of people named in Matthew, chapter 19 [cf. Gen. 2:18, 24; Matt. 19:12]. And marriage also is plainly suitable for priests, as Paul says to Timothy and Titus in his epistles to them [1 Tim. 3:2, 12; Tit. 1:6]. . . .

However, the unchaste "chastity" of celibacy, the sin-flowing harlotry of Sodom and Noah's age,[55] they do not punish and have never punished, but instead they protect it. Indeed, temporal and spiritual authorities have made a covenant together about this to strive powerfully against God. Oh the blindness of the heads of society! How you conspire together! Those who ought to be inclined to all integrity and to give it a helping hand must allow it to be said of them that one has five, six harlots, another seven women in childbed at the same time and nevertheless a pretty prostitute at home and many such like things. It is indeed as Isaiah says, "There is no health from the soles of

54. "Harlotry" here refers to the organized system of taxing clergy who took a concubine.

55. See Gen. 6:1-5; 19:1-9.

the feet to the head" [Isa. 1:6a]. O God, look on this! I know that You are silent so that Your wrath may increase.

Another reason they resist clerical marriage is that, should priests have (legal) wives, they would have to choose one and give up the others. They will not be able to behave as they do with the prostitutes: throwing out one, taking in another. For Paul says, "A bishop should be the husband of one wife" [1 Tim. 3:2]. Therefore they must each live honorably, and if having the same woman does not please the man, he may not exchange her. For in marriage the couple must have and bear many griefs with each other (on which account these priests do not wish to be bound by marriage). Still, one often suffers more from a harlot—he would not suffer half of that from an honest (legal) wife!

However, if they wanted to treat clerical marriage honorably, they would then need to punish adultery in the pulpit more strictly. Otherwise how can they punish it when they are mixed up in it? In such a case (when they are mixed up in it also) the going thing is a mutual blind eye: "If you overlook my fault, I will overlook yours." If, however, a priest had a (legal) wife and then did evil, one would know how to punish him [because he would have a legal means of sexual expression and his violation of that would have no excuse—*trans.*]. But this way the clergy always have an excuse to say nothing else than, "You worldly folk can talk about this easily; you have your wives. So I also am a man; how can I behave like an angel?" and so forth. And that is also true. Oh, then why not leave things the way God made them?! "Let each one have his wife, on account of harlotry" [cf. 1 Cor. 7:2]. Does God not know better than the devil what is good? For the prohibition of marriage comes only from the devil and marriage comes from God, says the Holy Spirit Himself in the epistle to Timothy [1 Tim. 4:3].

Yes, it should be thus, but worldly people cannot bear it—people who have such fornicating priests among them (in their families). When a married couple dies, their legitimate children take the inheritance. If the children are not legitimate, the relations take the inheritance and throw out the bastards; what does it matter to them that the devil carries off the souls of the children? [This is what usually happens to the illegitimate households of fornicating priests, to the destruction of the souls of their children—*trans.*] However, it happens that some harlots and their children provide for themselves well. One sees daily that now a part of them comport themselves like the nobility [maintaining themselves in style on the priests' property—*trans.*], and it is fair that they do this. Also, married priests would have to punish adultery in earnest. As John said, "It is not fitting for you to have seven women in childbed at one time, that is, to live in harlotry, and yet to help to rule the land and people."[56] An adulterous ruler should be set on a gallows and not in a council and should have many stones thrown hard by him (close to him but just missing). Therefore a young fellow once said, when he was being punished for his harlotry, "Should I not do it? My father did it. If he wants to pay me for my harlotry, I would say to him that he should first punish himself."

These are the prejudices of the worldly folk who are against clerical marriage. Part profit from prohibition of clerical marriage, and that comes from their offices and in many other ways. Another part are the priests' friends, fathers, mothers, siblings, aunts, uncles, and so forth; these fear that legitimate wives and children will cut them off from the priests' property and the like. The third part are themselves

56. The "John" here may refer to John the Baptist's rebuke of King Herod, though the narration here is more elaborate than in the Gospels.

involved in harlotry, and they fear they also will be seen to be in the game. Thus it was that finally Sodom and Gomorrah were together consumed in the sulfur and bitumen from heaven. O God, make an end soon! How long must the soul of the righteous Lot be distressed this way? Redeem the upright Lot, as You have spoken through your angel. You have set this biblical account as an example for those in the future who would be godless. For while the righteous person lives righteously among them, he must be distressed from day to day. You know how to redeem the blessed out of temptation but to keep the unrighteous for the day of judgment for punishment [Gen. 6:4-5, 11-12; 19:4-5; Luke 17:27-30; 2 Pet. 2:5-6].

There are still many more things that I will now omit, for people much more clever than I have written enough about them. Among these items is also the service of the saints, about which I must still someday write a little, as Paul bids us in Hebrews in the eleventh, twelfth, and thirteenth chapters to remember the saints.

Should one say to me now, "This is an awkward long excursus; you have indeed quite interrupted and gotten away from your beginning." ANSWER: I know that; it is true. But perhaps it was not done without design. Do you mean that this matter is not my business? Then I say that I see how many souls already belong to the devil and continue so, which was also a reason that I have helped to raise up clerical marriage. With God's help I was also the first woman in Strasbourg who opened the way for clerical marriage, when I was then still not consenting or wishing to marry any man. However, since I saw the great fear and furious opposition to clerical marriage, and also the great harlotry of the clergy, I myself married a priest with the intention of encouraging and making a way for all Christians—as I hope has also happened. Therefore I also made a little book, in which I showed the foundation of my faith and reason for my marriage, because many people had been greatly amazed by my marriage. For no one had in any way been able to perceive in me, by word or deed, that I wanted to be married. Therefore it seemed necessary to me to set out for honest people my apologia and reason for so doing, as Peter teaches us [1 Pet. 3:15].

These reasons also moved my husband (so far as I have experience of him and I can still neither find nor sense anything else in him). He began such a marriage because he wanted very much to raise up God's honor, his own salvation, and that of all his brothers. For I can perceive in him no dishonorableness, no inclination toward lust or other such thing—for I am not gifted with either overwhelming beauty or riches or other virtue that might move one to seek me in marriage! Because of his [Zell's] behavior in teaching and life, he has borne such envy from the godless that it is as if his body and life were given over to the birds in the air and the worms on the earth—to say nothing about what people have done. And so I come again to my beginning, that is, to justify him. Such envy of him is so deeply rooted in the hearts of the godless that if they cannot discredit him in body, soul, and life, they do it through such great devilish lies invented and spoken about him and spread in all lands.

First, it is said that I ran away from him. That needs no reply. The liars must be ashamed of themselves, for I have never been out of Strasbourg for a single day. [That is, they have had me under their eyes all the time and seen that this is not true.—*trans.*]

Next, they have said that he has hanged himself for sorrow that he married me. That needs yet less answer. This lie was started perhaps by a disciple who grew away from him, who is so set against him. Indeed, they would give half their goods if this lie were true!

Third, because he would not be caught in these lies, they found others. They say he took a female citizen into a garden [seduced a woman of Strasbourg—*trans.*]. All that invention did not help them, and they were everywhere found out in their lies, so they have sought another way and invented devilish shameful lies and spread them and said them in all the city of Strasbourg and in the whole land. (1) They say that he treats me so badly, with blows and the like, and has often chased me out. (2) They have shamefully lied that I have found him with the maid, and when I would not tolerate that behavior, he struck me and chased me out of the house. (3) They say that I went weeping to the Ammeister [city official] and stayed away from him [Zell] eight days in my father's house. And more of the same, and still (other) different lies, so that what is said in one place is different from what is said in another. What else should I say about this than that they are children of the devil, who is a liar and works such lies in them [cf. John 8:44]. For without any grounds, only out of what the devil puts in them, they have invented such lies.

For God is my witness—no greater can I have—that I am not lying here.[57] He [Zell] and I have never had a quarter of an hour, that is, in summary, no time at all when we have not been at one. Nor has there been any time when he has done me hurt, great or small, with words or deeds—and, I hope, I have not hurt him either. I know nothing else in this hour than that we would want to satisfy each other in all our intentions insofar as they are godly, and we do that. Also, with regard to the story about the maid: I have no maid, but only an honest little daughter [that is, a young child as a servant], still indeed young and not become cunning, who knows nothing at all of such things, to whom he [Zell] has never said four words so long as she has been in the house. Even if she were already old enough, yet I have found no such wantonness or mischievousness in him that I need have such cares. The servants of the antichrist give him so much to do that he would skip such a thing if it were still in him![58]

In summary, to close with a few words: I do not want to answer about how he kept house before I became his wife. He behaved then just as pope and bishop want: those who forbid the marriage that God commanded and permit harlots whom God forbade. That is also why I married him: having considered his life and that of others, I dared by God's grace and power to try to gain his soul and many others, as I hope I have done for God. But since I became his wife I want to defend him and risk my honor, body, and life for him. I attest that such liars forcibly struggle against him without any reason and lie about him; that these sayings about him that have gone out are altogether lying and invented without any basis in him; and that these lies are also against me and all people. For no one can truthfully chastise him [Zell] before the world; only God can judge the strength of the heart, it cannot be tested by human beings [cf. Acts 15:8 with Luke 24:25 or Rom. 14:4].

God grant that our marriage may thus endure, as it is now, until the end. So I hope it will and may be pleasing to God and useful to both of our souls and advantageous in soul and body to many people. And if it is not useful and

57. Cf. 1 Thess. 2:5, 10.

58. "Antichrist" (1 John 2:18, 22; 4:3; 2 John 7) was a common term that early Protestants used to refer to the Roman pope. It was based on the idea that anyone who sets himself up *anti* (Greek, "in place of") Christ (as in 2 Thess. 2:4), or as the "vicar of Christ," is properly termed "antichrist." Earlier Catholic theologians and even popes, notably including Pope Gregory I the Great (r. 590–604), recognized the same point.

pleasing to the antichrist and his servants, I cannot help that! . . .

[*Church Mother*, trans. and ed. Elsie A. McKee (Chicago: University of Chicago Press, 2006), 73–79]

D. John Calvin

Biographical Note: John Calvin

John Calvin (Jean Cauvin) (1509–1564) was born in Noyon, France. After studying in Paris, in 1528 he began to study law in Orléans and moved back to Paris in 1531. His humanistic interests led him in 1532 to publish his first book, a commentary on the ancient Stoic philosopher Seneca's great work De clementia. *Because it is not a theological treatise, it is difficult to discern Calvin's personal opinions at this time. But by 1533, Calvin had experienced what he called a "sudden conversion," or shift, to reformist ideas. In 1535, having come under increasing religious pressure in France, he fled to Basel, Switzerland.*

While traveling through Geneva on his way to Strasbourg in 1536, he met Guillaume Farel, the reformer of Geneva, who threatened to call down a curse on Calvin if he would not stay in Geneva and help bring reform to the church and city. Farel, who began the reform, saw in Calvin the organizer and thinker he needed to help secure the reform in Geneva. After the reformers had spent two years in Geneva, the city, not yet ready for the reform that Calvin and Farel had in mind and the controversies they would bring, had had its fill of the two. Calvin finally was able to live in Strasbourg, where he continued writing theology and was married. Three years later, in 1541, Geneva called Calvin back, and he returned to stay until his death at age fifty-four.

Modern opinions of Calvin have typically been shaped by timeworn exaggerations and outright misrepresentations of his authority in Geneva. Like most intellectuals of his day, he was no advocate of unbridled religious freedom. Nevertheless, Calvin was not the tyrant and Geneva was not the theocracy that are sometimes depicted.

Calvin's chief task in Geneva was preaching and teaching, which he carried out every Sunday and multiple times throughout every week. He also reformed the church order and liturgy, moderated the Company of Pastors, sought to improve relations with other Swiss cities, and supported the persecuted Protestant churches in France. In the midst of all these tasks, he was an indefatigable writer. He wrote detailed commentaries on nearly every book of the Bible. He wrote apologetic and polemical works, such as Reply to Sadoleto *(1539), which is a defense of the Reformed faith against an archbishop who tried to persuade Geneva to return to the Roman Church. Most famously, he wrote* Institutes of the Christian Religion, *whose final edition appeared in 1559. Although Calvin was born and raised in a Roman Catholic setting and accepted Protestant theology as an adult, he can be considered a second-generation reformer in the sense that he inherited and further systematized many of the ideas of such earlier reformers as Luther and Zwingli. The popular—albeit misleading—use of "Calvinism" as a synonym for "Reformed" theology testifies to the enduring contribution and legacy of Calvin to Protestant theology.*

Selection 26: John Calvin, a Prayer

Grant, Almighty God, as you have deigned to set before our eyes as in a glass that peculiar providence of yours by which you defend your

Church: Grant, that being confirmed by these examples, we may learn to repose entirely upon you. Amid the numerous disturbances by which the world is at this time agitated, may we remain quiet under your protection. May we so commit our safety to you as never to hesitate, whatever may happen, as to our future safety and security. Whatever we may suffer, may it all issue in our salvation, while we are protected by your hand; thus will we call upon your name with sincerity of mind, and you will in return show yourself as our Father in your only-begotten Son. Amen.

[John Calvin, *Commentary on Daniel* 11:11, in loc.]

Selection 27: John Calvin, Preface to *Commentary on Psalms* (1557)

In the preface to his* Commentary on Psalms, *Calvin calls the Psalms "An Anatomy of All the Parts of the Soul," and he sees in David's prayers and struggles a reflection of his own life. This leads to one of the few but also most detailed autobiographical statements by Calvin in all his writings, and it lends contextual understanding to his exegetical method.

The varied and resplendid riches which are contained in this treasury it is no easy matter to express in words; so much so, that I well know that whatever I shall be able to say will be far from approaching the excellence of the subject. But as it is better to give to my readers some taste, however small, of the wonderful advantages they will derive from the study of this book,[59] than to be entirely silent on the point, I may be permitted briefly to advert to a matter, the greatness of which does not admit of being fully unfolded. I have been accustomed to call this book, I think not inappropriately, "An Anatomy of all the Parts of the Soul;" for there is not an emotion of which any one can be conscious that is not here represented as in a mirror. Or rather, the Holy Spirit has here drawn to the life all the griefs, sorrows, fears, doubts, hopes, cares, perplexities, in short, all the distracting emotions with which the minds of men are wont to be agitated. The other parts of Scripture contain the commandments which God enjoined his servants to announce to us. But here the prophets themselves, seeing they are exhibited to us as speaking to God, and laying open all their inmost thoughts and affections, call, or rather draw, each of us to the examination of himself in particular, in order that none of the many infirmities to which we are subject, and of the many vices with which we abound, may remain concealed. It is certainly a rare and singular advantage, when all lurking places are discovered, and the heart is brought into the light, purged from that most baneful infection, hypocrisy. In short, as calling upon God is one of the principal means of securing our safety, and as a better and more unerring rule for guiding us in this exercise cannot be found elsewhere than in The Psalms, it follows, that in proportion to the proficiency which a man shall have attained in understanding them, will be his knowledge of the most important part of celestial doctrine. Genuine and earnest prayer proceeds first from a sense of our need, and next, from faith in the promises of God. It is by perusing these inspired compositions, that men will be most effectually awakened to a sense of their maladies, and, at the same time, instructed in seeking remedies for their cure. In a word, whatever may serve to encourage us when we are about to pray to God, is taught us in this book. And not only are the promises of God presented to us in it, but oftentimes there is exhibited to us one

59. That is, the Psalms.

standing, as it were, amidst the invitations of God on the one hand, and the impediments of the flesh on the other, girding and preparing himself for prayer: thus teaching us, if at any time we are agitated with a variety of doubts, to resist and fight against them, until the soul, freed and disentangled from all these impediments, rise up to God; and not only so, but even when in the midst of doubts, fears, and apprehensions, let us put forth our efforts in prayer until we experience some consolation which may calm and bring contentment to our minds. Although distrust may shut the gate against our prayers, yet we must not allow ourselves to give way, whenever our hearts waver or are agitated with inquietude, but must persevere until faith finally come forth victorious from these conflicts. In many places we may perceive the exercise of the servants of God in prayer so fluctuating, that they are almost overwhelmed by the alternate hope of success and apprehension of failure, and gain the prize only by strenuous exertions. We see on the one hand, the flesh manifesting its infirmity; and on the other, faith putting forth its power; and if it is not so valiant and courageous as might be desired, it is at least prepared to fight until by degrees it acquire perfect strength. But as those things which serve to teach us the true method of praying aright will be found scattered through the whole of this Commentary, I will not now stop to treat of topics which it will be necessary afterwards to repeat, nor detain my readers from proceeding to the work itself. Only it appeared to me to be requisite to show in passing, that this book makes known to us this privilege, which is desirable above all others—that not only is there opened up to us familiar access to God, but also that we have permission and freedom granted us to lay open before him our infirmities, which we would be ashamed to confess before men. Besides, there is also here prescribed to us an infallible rule for directing us with respect to the right manner of offering to God the sacrifice of praise, which he declares to be most precious in his sight, and of the sweetest odour. There is no other book in which there is to be found more express and magnificent commendations, both of the unparalleled liberality of God towards his Church, and of all his works; there is no other book in which there is recorded so many deliverances, nor one in which the evidences and experiences of the fatherly providence and solicitude which God exercises towards us, are celebrated with such splendour of diction, and yet with the strictest adherence to truth; in short, there is no other book in which we are more perfectly taught the right manner of praising God, or in which we are more powerfully stirred up to the performance of this religious exercise. Moreover, although The Psalms are replete with all the precepts which serve to frame our life to every part of holiness, piety, and righteousness, yet they will principally teach and train us to bear the cross; and the bearing of the cross is a genuine proof of our obedience, since by doing this, we renounce the guidance of our own affections, and submit ourselves entirely to God, leaving him to govern us, and to dispose of our life according to his will, so that the afflictions which are the bitterest and most severe to our nature, become sweet to us, because they proceed from him. In one word, not only will we here find general commendations of the goodness of God, which may teach men to repose themselves in him alone, and to seek all their happiness solely in him; and which are intended to teach true believers with their whole hearts confidently to look to him for help in all their necessities; but we will also find that the free remission of sins, which alone reconciles God towards us, and procures for us settled peace with him, is so set forth and magnified, as that here there is nothing wanting which relates to the knowledge of eternal salvation.[60]

Now, if my readers derive any fruit and advantage from the labour which I have bestowed in writing these Commentaries, I would have them to understand that the small measure of experience which I have had by the conflicts with which the Lord has exercised me, has in no ordinary degree assisted me, not only in applying to present use whatever instruction could be gathered from these divine compositions, but also in more easily comprehending the design of each of the writers. And as David holds the principal place among them, it has greatly aided me in understanding more fully the complaints made by him of the internal afflictions which the Church had to sustain through those who gave themselves out to be her members, that I had suffered the same or similar things from the domestic enemies of the Church. For although I follow David at a great distance, and come far short of equalling him; or rather, although in aspiring slowly and with great difficulty to attain to the many virtues in which he excelled, I still feel myself tarnished with the contrary vices; yet if I have any things in common with him, I have no hesitation in comparing myself with him. In reading the instances of his faith, patience, fervour, zeal, and integrity, it has, as it ought, drawn from me unnumbered groans and sighs, that I am so far from approaching them; but it has, notwithstanding, been of very great advantage to me to behold in him as in a mirror, both the commencement of my calling, and the continued course of my function; so that I know the more assuredly, that whatever that most illustrious king and prophet suffered, was exhibited to me by God as an example for imitation.[61] My condition, no doubt, is much inferior to his, and it is unnecessary for me to stay to show this. But as he was taken from the sheepfold, and elevated to the rank of supreme authority; so God having taken me from my originally obscure and humble condition, has reckoned me worthy of being invested with the honourable office of a preacher and minister of the gospel. When I was as yet a very little boy, my father had destined me for the study of theology. But afterwards, when he considered that the legal profession commonly raised those who followed it to wealth, this prospect induced him suddenly to change his purpose. Thus it came to pass, that I was withdrawn from the study of philosophy, and was put to the study of law. To this pursuit I endeavoured faithfully to apply myself, in obedience to the will of my father; but God, by the secret guidance of his providence, at length gave a different direction to my course. And first, since I was too obstinately devoted to the superstitions of Popery to be easily extricated from so profound an abyss of mire, God by a sudden conversion, subdued and brought my mind to a teachable frame, which was more hardened in such matters than might have been expected from one at my early period of life. Having thus received some taste and knowledge of true godliness, I was immediately inflamed with so intense a desire to make progress therein, that although I did not altogether leave off other studies, I yet pursued them with less ardour.

I was quite surprised to find that before a year had elapsed, all who had any desire after purer doctrine were continually coming to me to learn, although I myself was as yet but a

60. Calvin's high praise for the Psalter, as a sort of Old Testament gospel, is typical of other premodern commentators, including Luther. It is also the most quoted book in the New Testament.

61. Calvin regarded David as the author of most of the individual Psalms, but not of every one.

mere novice and tyro.[62] Being of a disposition somewhat unpolished and bashful, which led me always to love the shade and retirement, I then began to seek some secluded corner where I might be withdrawn from the public view; but so far from being able to accomplish the object of my desire, all my retreats were like public schools. In short, whilst my one great object was to live in seclusion without being known, God so led me about through different turnings and changes, that he never permitted me to rest in any place, until, in spite of my natural disposition, he brought me forth to public notice. Leaving my native country, France, I in fact retired into Germany, expressly for the purpose of being able there to enjoy in some obscure corner the repose which I had always desired, and which had been so long denied me. But lo! whilst I lay hidden at Basle, and known only to a few people, many faithful and holy persons were burnt alive in France; and the report of these burnings having reached foreign nations, they excited the strongest disapprobation among a great part of the Germans, whose indignation was kindled against the authors of such tyranny. In order to allay this indignation, certain wicked and lying pamphlets were circulated, stating, that none were treated with such cruelty but Anabaptists and seditious persons, who, by their perverse ravings and false opinions, were overthrowing not only religion but also all civil order. Observing that the object which these instruments of the court aimed at by their disguises, was not only that the disgrace of shedding so much innocent blood might remain buried under the false charges and calumnies which they brought against the holy martyrs after their death, but also, that afterwards they might be able to proceed to the utmost extremity in murdering the poor saints without exciting compassion towards them in the breasts of any, it appeared to me, that unless I opposed them to the utmost of my ability, my silence could not be vindicated from the charge of cowardice and treachery. This was the consideration which induced me to publish my Institute of the Christian Religion. My objects were, first, to prove that these reports were false and calumnious, and thus to vindicate my brethren, whose death was precious in the sight of the Lord; and next, that as the same cruelties might very soon after be exercised against many unhappy individuals, foreign nations might be touched with at least some compassion towards them and solicitude about them. When it was then published, it was not that copious and laboured work which it now is, but only a small treatise containing a summary of the principal truths of the Christian religion, and it was published with no other design than that men might know what was the faith held by those whom I saw basely and wickedly defamed by those flagitious and perfidious flatterers. That my object was not to acquire fame, appeared from this, that immediately after I left Basle, and particularly from the fact that nobody there knew that I was the author.

Wherever else I have gone, I have taken care to conceal that I was the author of that performance; and I had resolved to continue in the same privacy and obscurity, until at length William Farel detained me at Geneva, not so much by counsel and exhortation, as by a dreadful imprecation, which I felt to be as if God had from heaven laid his mighty hand upon me to arrest me. As the most direct road to Strasburg, to which I then intended to retire, was shut up by the wars, I had resolved to pass quickly by Geneva, without staying longer than a single night in that city. A little before this, Popery had been driven from it by the exertions of the excellent person whom I have named, and Peter

62. That is, a "beginner" or a "recruit."

Viret;[63] but matters were not yet brought to a settled state, and the city was divided into unholy and dangerous factions. Then an individual who now basely apostatised and returned to the Papists, discovered me and made me known to others. Upon this, Farel, who burned with an extraordinary zeal to advance the gospel, immediately strained every nerve to detain me. And after having learned that my heart was set upon devoting myself to private studies, for which I wished to keep myself free from other pursuits, and finding that he gained nothing by entreaties, he proceeded to utter an imprecation that God would curse my retirement, and the tranquillity of the studies which I sought, if I should withdraw and refuse to give assistance, when the necessity was so urgent. By this imprecation I was so stricken with terror, that I desisted from the journey which I had undertaken; but sensible of my natural bashfulness and timidity, I would not bring myself under obligation to discharge any particular office. After that, four months had scarcely elapsed, when, on the one hand, the Anabaptists began to assail us, and, on the other, a certain wicked apostate, who being secretly supported by the influence of some of the magistrates of the city, was thus enabled to give us a great deal of trouble. At the same time, a succession of dissensions fell out in the city which strangely afflicted us. Being, as I acknowledge, naturally of a timid, soft, and pusillanimous disposition, I was compelled to encounter these violent tempests as part of my early training; and although I did not sink under them, yet I was not sustained by such greatness of mind, as not to rejoice more than it became me, when, in consequence of certain commotions, I was banished from Geneva.

By this means set at liberty and loosed from the tie of my vocation, I resolved to live in a private station, free from the burden and cares of any public charge, when that most excellent servant of Christ, Martin Bucer, employing a similar kind of remonstrance and protestation as that to which Farel had recourse before, drew me back to a new station. Alarmed by the example of Jonah which he set before me, I still continued in the work of teaching. And although I always continued like myself, studiously avoiding celebrity; yet I was carried, I know not how, as it were by force to the Imperial assemblies, where, willing or unwilling, I was under the necessity of appearing before the eyes of many. Afterwards, when the Lord having compassion on this city, had allayed the hurtful agitations and broils which prevailed in it, and by his wonderful power had defeated both the wicked counsels and the sanguinary attempts of the disturbers of the Republic, necessity was imposed upon me of returning to my former charge, contrary to my desire and inclination. The welfare of this church, it is true, lay so near my heart, that for its sake I would not have hesitated to lay down my life; but my timidity nevertheless suggested to me many reasons for excusing myself from again willingly taking upon my shoulders so heavy a burden. At length, however, a solemn and conscientious regard to my duty, prevailed with me to consent to return to the flock from which I had been torn; but with what grief, tears, great anxiety and distress I did this, the Lord is my best witness, and many godly persons who would have wished to see me delivered from this painful state, had it not been that that which I feared, and which made me give my consent, prevented them and shut their mouths.

Were I to narrate the various conflicts by which the Lord has exercised me since that time, and by what trials he has proved me, it

63. Guillaume Farel (1489–1565) and Pierre Viret (1511–1571) were Calvin's two closest coworkers in the Swiss Reformation, especially in its early years.

would make a long history. But that I may not become tedious to my readers by a waste of words, I shall content myself with repeating briefly what I have touched upon a little before, that in considering the whole course of the life of David, it seemed to me that by his own footsteps he showed me the way, and from this I have experienced no small consolation. As that holy king was harassed by the Philistines and other foreign enemies with continual wars, while he was much more grievously afflicted by the malice and wickedness of some perfidious men amongst his own people, so I can say as to myself, that I have been assailed on all sides, and have scarcely been able to enjoy repose for a single moment, but have always had to sustain some conflict either from enemies without or within the Church. Satan has made many attempts to overthrow the fabric of this Church; and once it came to this, that I, altogether feeble and timorous as I am, was compelled to break and put a stop to his deadly assaults by putting my life in danger, and opposing my person to his blows. Afterwards, for the space of five years, when some wicked libertines were furnished with undue influence, and also some of the common people, corrupted by the allurements and perverse discourse of such persons, desired to obtain the liberty of doing whatever they pleased, without control, I was under the necessity of fighting without ceasing to defend and maintain the discipline of the Church.[64] To these irreligious characters and despisers of the heavenly doctrine, it was a matter of entire indifference, although the Church should sink into ruin, provided they obtained what they sought,—the power of acting just as they pleased. Many, too, harassed by poverty and hunger, and others impelled by insatiable ambition or avarice and a desire of dishonest gain, were become so frantic, that they chose rather, by throwing all things into confusion, to involve themselves and us in one common ruin, than to remain quiet by living peaceably and honestly. During the whole of this lengthened period, I think that there is scarcely any of the weapons which are forged in the workshop of Satan, which has not been employed by them in order to obtain their object. And at length matters had come to such a state, that an end could be put to their machinations in no other way than cutting them off by an ignominious death; which was indeed a painful and pitiable spectacle to me. They no doubt deserved the severest punishment, but I always rather desired that they might live in prosperity, and continue safe and untouched; which would have been the case had they not been altogether incorrigible, and obstinately refused to listen to wholesome admonition.

The trial of these five years was grievous and hard to bear; but I experienced not less excruciating pain from the malignity of those who ceased not to assail myself and my ministry with their envenomed calumnies. A great proportion of them, it is true, are so blinded by a passion for slander and detraction, that to their great disgrace, they betray at once their impudence, while others, however crafty and cunning, cannot so cover or disguise themselves as to escape being shamefully convicted and disgraced; yet when a man has been a hundred times found innocent of a charge brought against him, and when the charge is again repeated without any cause or occasion, it is an indignity hard to bear. Because I affirm and maintain that the world is managed and governed by the secret providence of God, a multitude of presumptuous men rise up against me, and allege that I represent God as the author of sin. This is so foolish a calumny, that it would

64. This reference is to the political opposition in Geneva led by Ami Perrin, who sought to take over the Consistory and its task of church discipline.

of itself quickly come to nothing, did it not meet with persons who have tickled ears, and who take pleasure in feeding upon such discourse. But there are many whose minds are so filled with envy and spleen, or ingratitude, or malignity, that there is no falsehood, however preposterous, yea, even monstrous, which they do not receive, if it is spoken to them. Others endeavour to overthrow God's eternal purpose of predestination, by which he distinguishes between the reprobate and the elect; others take upon them to defend free will; and forthwith many throw themselves into their ranks, not so much through ignorance as by a perversity of zeal which I know not how to characterize. If they were open and avowed enemies, who brought these troubles upon me, the thing might in some way be borne. But that those who shroud themselves under the name of brethren, and not only eat Christ's sacred bread, but also administer it to others, that those, in short, who loudly boast of being preachers of the gospel, should wage such nefarious war against me, how detestable is it?[65] In this matter I may very justly complain with David, "Yea, mine own familiar friend, in whom I trusted, who did eat of my bread, hath lifted up his heel against me," (Ps. xli. 9.) "For it was not an enemy that reproached me; but it was thou, a man mine equal, my guide, and mine acquaintance. We took sweet counsel together, and walked unto the house of God in company," (Ps. lv. 12, 13, 14.) Others circulated ridiculous reports concerning my treasures; others, of the extravagant authority and enormous influence which they say I possess; others speak of my delicacies and magnificence. But when a man is content with scanty food and common clothing, and does not require from the humblest more frugality than he shows and practises himself, shall it be said that such an one is too sumptuous, and lives in too high a style? As to the power and influence of which they envy me, I wish I could discharge this burden upon them; for they estimate my power by the multitude of affairs, and the vast weight of labours with which I am overwhelmed. And if there are some whom I cannot persuade whilst I am alive that I am not rich, my death at length will prove it. I confess, indeed, that I am not poor; for I desire nothing more than what I have. All these are invented stories, and there is no colour whatever for any one of them; but many nevertheless are very easily persuaded of their truth, and applaud them; and the reason is, because the greatest part judge that the only means of cloaking their enormities is to throw all things into disorder, and to confound black and white; and they think that the best and shortest way by which they can obtain full liberty to live with impunity just as they please, is to destroy the authority of Christ's servants.

In addition to these, there are "the hypocritical mockers in feasts," of whom David complains, (Ps. xxxv. 16;) and I mean by these not only lick-dish characters, who seek a meal to fill their belly, but all those who by false reports seek to obtain the favour of the great. Having been long accustomed to swallow such wrongs as these, I have become almost hardened; yet when the insolence of such characters increases, I cannot but sometimes feel my heart wounded with bitter pangs. Nor was it enough that I should be so inhumanly treated by my neighbours. In addition to this, in a distant country towards the frozen ocean, there was raised, I know not how, by the frenzy of a few, a storm which afterwards stirred up against me a vast number of persons, who are too much at leisure, and have nothing to do but by their bickering

65. Indeed, Calvin made many enemies in Geneva, but his emphasis here on the opposition is to highlight the relevance of the Psalms—and David's experiences—to his own life.

to hinder those who are labouring for the edification of the Church. I am still speaking of the internal enemies of the Church—of those who, boasting mightily of the gospel of Christ, nevertheless rush against me with greater impetuosity than against the open adversaries of the Church, because I do not embrace their gross and fictitious notion concerning a carnal way of eating Christ in the sacrament; and of whom I may protest, after the example of David, "I am for peace; but when I speak, they are for war," (Ps. cxx. 7.) Moreover, the cruel ingratitude of all of them is manifest in this, that they scruple not to assail both in flank and rear a man who strenuously exerts himself to maintain a cause which they have in common with him, and whom therefore they ought to aid and succour. Certainly, if such persons were possessed of even a small portion of humanity, the fury of the Papists which is directed against me with such unbridled violence, would appease the most implacable animosity which they may bear towards me. But since the condition of David was such, that though he had deserved well of his own people, he was nevertheless bitterly hated by many without a cause, as he complains in Ps. lxix. 4, "I restored that which I took not away," it afforded me no small consolation when I was groundlessly assailed by the hatred of those who ought to have assisted and solaced me, to conform myself to the example of so great and so excellent a person. This knowledge and experience have been of much service in enabling me to understand The Psalms, so that in my meditations upon them, I did not wander, as it were, in an unknown region.

[*Commentary on the Book of Psalms*, vol. 1, trans. James Anderson (Edinburgh: Calvin Translation Society, 1845), xxxvi–xlviii]

Selection 28: John Calvin, *A Treatise on Relics* (1543)

The ostensible purpose of this French treatise is to offer a brief record of the various relics in a few countries of Europe. The full title is* A Very Useful Account of the Great Profit That Christianity Will Again Receive If It Takes Inventory of All the Sacred Bodies and Relics That Are Located in Italy, France, Germany, Spain, and Other Kingdoms and Countries*. The title is satirical, of course, for the "great profit" that Calvin intends is that people would recognize the deception behind the veneration of relics. Before discussing the specific relics (some of which are excerpted below), Calvin argues that one problem with relics is that they eventually become objects of trust, veneration, and even worship. This claim is part of the Reformed rationale for rejecting icons as well.

This document shows the wit of someone not typically singled out for his humor. More important, it reflects the common Protestant polemic against popular late medieval practices and the attempt by reformers to communicate Reformation principles in the vernacular language. For Calvin, true worship is of the utmost importance, and the veneration of relics undermines it.

Augustine, in his work, entitled, On the Labour of Monks, complaining of certain itinerant impostors, who, as early as his day, plied a vile and sordid traffic, by carrying the relics of martyrs about from place to place, adds, "If, indeed, they are relics of martyrs."[66] By this expression, he intimates the prevalence, even in his day, of abuses and impostures, by which the ignorant populace were cheated into the belief, that bones gathered here and there were those of saints. While the origin of the imposture is

66. Augustine, *On the Work of Monks* 36: "Some hawking about limbs of martyrs, if indeed of martyrs . . ."

thus ancient, there cannot be a doubt that in the long period which has since elapsed, it has exceedingly increased. . . .

But it is not at all necessary to enter into a long discussion of the point, whether or not it is a good thing to have relics merely for preservation, and not for worship; for, as we have said, experience teaches that the one is never separated from the other. Ambrose, indeed, speaking of Helena, (the mother of Constantine,) who had at great labour and expense procured the cross of our Lord, says, that she did not adore the wood, but only the Lord, who had hung upon it.[67] But it is most rare for persons to be at all devoted to relics, without being also polluted by some degree of superstition. I admit that they do not, at the very outset, break out into open idolatry, but that gradually, from one fallacy to another, they move along their downward path, until they at last rush headlong. Indeed, people, calling themselves Christian, have gone to such lengths as to exhibit the madness of idolatry in a degree equal to that of the heathen of old. For they have prostrated themselves, and bent the knee before relics as before God, lighting torches and tapers as in solemn worship, putting confidence in them, and fleeing to them as if they possessed a divine power and grace. If idolatry is just to transfer the honour of God to others, can we deny that this is idolatry? It is no excuse to say it is done through the excessive zeal of rude and ignorant men or old women. The extravagance is of wider extent. It has everywhere prevailed, and been approved even by those who sit holding the reins of government in the Church. Nay, the bones of the dead, and all other sorts of relics, have been placed over the principal altars in the high and lofty place to be adored with greater reverence. . . .

At present, indeed, it is not my design to show what abomination there is in abusing the relics both of Christ and the Saints, in the way in which it has hitherto been done, and is common even in the present day in the greater part of Christendom, for the subject would require a volume to itself. But as it is clear that a great majority of the relics which are exhibited are spurious, being brought forward by certain deceivers, who have impudently imposed on the meanest of the people, it has occurred to me to mention some things which may furnish men of sense with an occasion of thought and reflection. . . .

But in this short treatise, I am not able to accomplish what I particularly desire, for it would be necessary to obtain catalogues from all quarters, that it might be known what relics are said to exist in every separate place, so that they might be compared with each other. In this way it would be made manifest that every Apostle has more than four bodies, and every Saint two or three. The same thing would appear in other instances; in short, when the whole heap was collected, there is no man who would not be amazed at seeing how ridiculously the whole world had been blinded. . . .

Let us begin then with Christ. As his natural body could not be possessed, (though some have found an easy way of fabricating miraculous bodies for him, in whatever numbers, and with whatever frequency they please,) instead of it they have collected six hundred frivolities to compensate for its absence. They have not even allowed the body of Christ to escape entirely, but have managed to retain a portion. For, besides teeth and hair, the monks of Charrox give out that they have the prepuce, that is, the pellicle cut off in his circumcision. And how, pray, did this pellicle come to them? The

67. Ambrose, *On the Death of Theodosius* 46: "She adored the King, not the wood, indeed, because this is an error of the Gentiles and a vanity of the wicked. But she adored Him who hung on the tree . . ."

Evangelist Luke relates that the Lord was circumcised, but it is nowhere said that the skin was preserved for relics. All ancient histories are silent respecting it, and for the space of five hundred years this subject was not once broached in the Christian Church. Where was it lying hid all the time, and how did it so suddenly burst into notice? Moreover, how came it to travel so far as Charrox? But as a proof of its genuineness, they say that some drops of blood fell from it. They, indeed, say this, but they should prove it. It is plainly a mere absurdity. But were we to grant that this pellicle was preserved, and so might be there or elsewhere, what shall we say of the prepuce which is shown at Rome, in the church of Joannes Lateranensis? As it is certain there was only one, it cannot possibly be both at Rome and Charrox. Thus the falsehood becomes manifest. . . .

We come now to the principal relics of our Lord, viz., those connected with his sufferings and death. And, first, let us consider the case of the cross on which he was suspended. I know it is regarded as a certain fact, that Helena, the mother of the Emperor Constantine, discovered it. And I am not ignorant of what ancient Doctors have written, to prove that it undoubtedly was the cross on which our Saviour was crucified. Let all those have their due credit, though it was vain curiosity, or ill-judged religious zeal, that caused Helena to make the search for it. But assuming that her exertions to find out the cross are worthy of all praise, and that our Lord himself, after it was found, miraculously declared that it was truly his cross, let us see how the matter is to be viewed with reference to our own times. The cross which Helena found is said to be still at Jerusalem. And no one calls this in question, though it is plainly inconsistent with ecclesiastical history, which relates that Helena sent part of it to the emperor her son, by whom it was placed on a pillar of porphyry at Constantinople; and that she inclosed the remainder in a silver chest, which she gave to the Bishop of Jerusalem for preservation. Therefore, we must either accuse the history of falsehood, or the things told of the true cross in the present day are utterly vain and frivolous.

Again, let us consider how many fragments of it are scattered up and down over the whole globe. A mere enumeration of those of which I have a catalogue would certainly fill a goodly volume. There is no town, however small, which has not some morsel of it, and this not only in the principal cathedral church of the district, but also in parish churches. There is no abbey so poor as not to have a specimen. In some places, larger fragments exist, as at Paris, in the Holy Chapel, at Poictiers, and at Rome, where a crucifix of tolerable size is said to have been entirely made out of it. In fine, if all the pieces which could be found were collected into a heap, they would form a good ship-load, though the gospel testifies, that a single individual was able to carry it. What effrontery, then, thus to fill the whole world with fragments, which it would take more than three hundred men to carry? But they have fallen upon an explanation, and it is, that how much soever may be cut from it, it never grows less. But this device is too foolish and absurd for the superstitious themselves not easily to see through it. . . .

To proceed in order, we must now consider the case of John the Baptist, who, according to the account given in the Gospel, that is, according to the truth of God, after being beheaded, was buried by his disciples. Theodoret[68] relates that his sepulchre, which was at Sebastia, a town of Syria, was some time afterwards opened by the heathen, who burned the body, and scattered the ashes to the wind. . . . The testimony

68. Theodoret of Cyrrhus (ca. 393–ca. 457).

of ancient history, therefore, is, that the whole body was burned, with the exception of the head, and that all the bones and all the ashes were scattered, except a very small portion, which was carried off by some hermits of Jerusalem. Now, let us see how much is said to be extant. The people of Amiens say that they have the front part of the head; and in the skull exhibited by them a wound appears, which they say Herodias inflicted with a knife. The inhabitants of Joannes Angelicus contradict them, and show the very same part. But the remainder of the head, viz., that reaching from the forehead back to the neck, was formerly in Rhodes, and is now, I think, in Malta; at least the Templars did pretend that it was restored to them by the Turks. The back of the head is at Nevers, and the brain at Novium Rantroviensis. And yet, notwithstanding, part of the head is in the church of Joannes Morienus. Then his jaws are at Besançon, in the church of John the Elder. Another part is at Paris, in the church of Joannes Lateranensis, and the tip of the ear is at Sanflor, in Auvergne, while the forehead and the hair is in St Salvator's, in Spain. At Noyon, also, is a certain portion, which is wont to be exhibited in great state. There is also a part, but I know not what, at Lucca. Is all this true? Go to Rome, and you will hear that the whole head of John is in the monastery of Sylvester. Poets feign that in Spain there once lived a king, named Geryon, who had three heads.[69] If our fabricators of relics could say the same thing of John the Baptist, it would be a great help to their lies. But since there is no room for such a fable, to what excuse will they resort? I am unwilling to press them so far as to ask how his head was cut into such minute portions as to become capable of distribution in so many various places, or how they got it out of Constantinople. I only say that John must have been a monster, or that they are impudent impostors in exhibiting so many fragments of his head. . . .

To draw to a conclusion, I beseech my readers, in the name of God, to give heed to the truth while it lies plainly before them, and recognise how Divine Providence has wonderfully provided, that those who thus wished to mislead the meanest of the people have been so blind that they never thought of using a cloak for their lies, but moving blindfolded, like the Midianites, have set about slaughtering one another. As we see how they are still warring among themselves, and charging each other with falsehood, every man, who is not obstinately determined against the truth, though he may not yet clearly perceive that the worship of any relics, of whatever kind they be, whether genuine or spurious, is execrable idolatry, yet seeing how clear their falsehood is, will have no desire to kiss them any more, and whatever reverence they may have previously inspired, will cease to have any relish for them.

The best thing, indeed, would be, as I mentioned at the outset, if, among us who profess the name of Christ, this heathenish custom were abolished, whether they be relics of Christ or of the saints. In as much as they do degenerate into idols, the pollution and defilement which they occasion ought not on any account to be tolerated in the Church. This we have already demonstrated, both by argument and by the testimony of Scripture. If any one is not satisfied with this, let him look to the manner and practice of the ancient fathers, and conform to their example. . . .

Wherefore, if a complete reformation of this corrupt practice is desired, it will be necessary to begin at the very foundation, and abolish a practice which was at first instituted improperly, and against all reason. But if any one is not able at one step to make such an advance

69. This myth is reported by Hesiod, among others.

towards true understanding, let him at least proceed gradually. And, in the first place, let him open his eyes, and exercise his judgment upon any relics which may be presented to him. No one inclined to make the attempt will find it at all difficult; for among the many transparent lies, such as those to which I have already adverted, where will any relics be found whose genuineness amounts to anything like certainty? Nay, at the very time when this little book was passing through the press, I was informed of a third prepuce, which I had not mentioned, and which is shown at Hildesheim. The number of similar follies is indeed infinite, and a careful inspection would discover more than it is possible to enumerate. Let every one, then, be on his guard, and not allow himself to be led along like an irrational animal, and as if he were incapable of discerning any way or path by which he might be guided safely, I recollect when I was a boy how they were wont to do with the images of our parish. When the feast of Stephen drew near, they adorned them all alike with garlands and necklaces, just decking the murderers who stoned Stephen in the same way as they decked Stephen himself. When the old women saw the murderers thus adorned, they imagined that they were Stephen's companions. Accordingly, every one was presented with his candle. Nay, the same honour was conferred on the devil who contended with Michael, and so on with the rest.[70] And so completely are they all mixed up and huddled together, that it is impossible to have the bones of any martyr without running the risk of worshipping the bones of some thief or robber, or, it may be, the bones of a dog, or a horse, or an ass. Nor can the Virgin Mary's ring, or comb, or girdle, be venerated without the risk of venerating some part of the dress of a strumpet. Let every one, therefore, who is inclined, guard against this risk. Henceforth no man will be able to excuse himself by pretending ignorance.

[*Tracts Relating to the Reformation*, vol. 1, trans. Henry Beveridge (Edinburgh: Calvin Translation Society, 1844), 289, 291, 293–96, 301–2, 321–22, 338–41]

Selection 29: John Calvin, *The Necessity of Reforming the Church* (1543)

Holy Roman Emperor Charles V called an imperial diet in Speyer in February 1544 to deal with the continuing religious disputes. In response to a request from Martin Bucer to assess the status of the disputes, and in preparation for the meeting, Calvin wrote this treatise and addressed it to the emperor. In this document's call for reformation of the church, Calvin emphasizes (and exaggerates) the unity of Protestant thought. He also points out that the Protestants have not created schism but are simply seeking to remain in Christ, and the emperor has a responsibility to help accomplish such reform. For his part, Charles V did attempt to summon a general council of the church but was reproved by the pope.

August Emperor,

This Diet is summoned by you, in order at last to deliberate and decide, along with the Most Illustrious Princes and other Orders of the Empire, upon the means of ameliorating the present condition of the Church, which we all see to be very miserable and almost desperate. Now therefore, while you sit for this consultation, I humbly beg and implore, first of your Imperial Majesty, and at the same time of you also, Most Illustrious Princes and distinguished gentlemen, that you will not decline to read and diligently consider what I have to lay before you. The magnitude and weight of the cause may well incite you to an eagerness to

70. See Acts 7:54-60; Jude 9.

listen. . . . In short, regard this as the common address of all who so earnestly deplore the present corruption of the Church, that they are unable to bear it any longer, and are determined not to rest till they see some amendment. I know with what odious names we are marked down for disgrace; but meanwhile, whatever be the name by which it is thought proper to call us, hear our cause, and after that judge what place we are entitled to hold.

First, then, the question is not whether the Church suffers from many and grievous diseases, for this is admitted even by all moderate judges; but whether the diseases are of a kind whose cure admits of no longer delay, so that it is neither useful nor proper to wait upon too slow remedies.[71] We are accused of rash and impious innovation, for having ventured to propose any change at all in the former state of the Church. What? even if it has been done with good cause and not imperfectly? I hear there are persons who, even in this case, do not hesitate to condemn us; they think us right indeed in desiring amendment, but not right in attempting it. From them, all I would ask at present is that for a little they suspend judgment until I shall have shown from the facts that we have not been prematurely hasty, have attempted nothing rashly, nothing alien to our duty, and have in short done nothing until compelled by the highest necessity. To enable me to prove this, it is necessary to attend to the matters in dispute.

We maintain to start with that, when God raised up Luther and others,[72] who held forth a torch to light us into the way of salvation, and on whose ministry our churches are founded and built, those heads of doctrine in which the truth of our religion, those in which the pure and legitimate worship of God, and those in which the salvation of men are comprehended, were in a great measure obsolete. We maintain that the use of the sacraments was in many ways vitiated and polluted. And we maintain that the government of the Church was converted into a species of horrible and insufferable tyranny. But perhaps these statements have not force enough to move certain individuals until they are better explained. This, therefore, I will do, not as the subject demands, but as far as my ability will permit. Here, however, I have no intention to review and discuss all our controversies; that would require a long discourse, and this is not the place for it. I wish only to demonstrate how just and necessary the causes were which forced us to the changes for which we are blamed.

To accomplish this, I must show that the particular remedies which the Reformers employed were apt and salutary; not here intending to describe the manner in which we proceeded (for this will afterwards be seen), but only to make it manifest that we have had no other end in view than to ameliorate in some degree the very miserable condition of the Church. Our doctrine has been, and is every day, assailed by many cruel calumnies. Some declaim loudly against it in sermons; others attack and ridicule it in their writings. . . .

But I do not wish that all the profit the Church has derived from our labour should avail to mitigate our fault, if in any other respect we have injured her. Therefore let there be an examination of our whole doctrine, of our form of administering the sacraments, and our method of governing the Church; and in none of these three things will it be found that we have made any change in the old form, without

71. All parties agreed that reformation was necessary; what exactly needed reforming, and especially how it would be implemented, were matters of dispute.

72. Even before his death, Luther was seen as the father of the Reformation.

attempting to restore it to the exact standard of the Word of God.

All our controversies concerning doctrine relate either to the legitimate worship of God, or to the ground of salvation. As to the former, certainly we exhort men to worship God in neither a frigid nor a careless manner; and while we point out the way, we neither lose sight of the end, nor omit anything which is relevant to the matter. . . . In short, as God requires us to worship him in a spiritual manner, so we with all zeal urge men to all the spiritual sacrifices which he commends.

Even our enemies cannot deny our assiduity in these exhortations, that men look for the good which they desire from none but God, that they confide in his power, trust in his goodness, depend on his truth, and turn to him with the whole heart, rest on him with full hope, and resort to him in necessity, that is, at every moment, and ascribe to him every good thing enjoyed, and testify to this by expressions of praise. That none may be deterred by difficulty of access, we proclaim that a fountain of all blessings is offered us in Christ, from which we may draw everything needful. . . .

Since, therefore, in our churches, God alone is adored in pure form without superstition, since his goodness, wisdom, power, truth, and other perfections, are there preached more fully than anywhere else, since he is invoked with true faith in the name of Christ, his mercies celebrated with both heart and tongue, and men constantly urged to a simple and sincere obedience; since in short nothing is heard but what tends to promote the sanctification of his name, what cause have those who call themselves Christians to take us up so ill? First, since they love darkness rather than light, they cannot tolerate the sharpness with which we, as in duty bound, rebuke the gross idolatry which is apparent everywhere in the world. . . .

Both sides confess that in the sight of God idolatry is an execrable crime. But when we attack the worship of images, our adversaries immediately take the opposite side, and lend support to the crime which they had with us verbally condemned. . . .

I have not yet adverted to the grosser superstitions, though these cannot be confined to the ignorant, since they are approved by public consent. They adorn their idols now with flowers and chaplets, now with robes, vests, girdles, purses and frivolities of every kind. They light tapers and burn incense before them, and carry them on their shoulders in solemn state. They assemble from long distances to one statue, though they have similar things at home. . . .

But, besides the clear testimonies which occur everywhere in Scripture, we are also supported by the authority of the ancient Church. All the writers of a purer age describe the abuse of images among the Gentiles as not differing from what is seen in the world in the present day; and their observations on the subject are not less applicable to our age than to the persons whom they then censured. . . .

In regard to the worship of God, our adversaries next accuse us, because, in omitting trivialities not only foolish but also tending to hypocrisy, we worship God more simply. That we have in no respect detracted from the spiritual worship of God is attested by fact. Indeed when it had in a great measure sunk into a desuetude, we have reinstated it in its former rights. Let us now see whether they are justly angry with us. In regard to doctrine, I maintain that we make common cause with the prophets. For, next to idolatry, there is nothing for which they rebuke the people more sharply than for falsely imagining that the worship of God consisted in external show. . . .

In inveighing against ceremonies themselves, and also in abrogating a greater part of them, we confess that there is indeed some difference between us and the prophets. They inveighed against their countrymen for confining the worship of God to external ceremonies, which, however, God himself had instituted; we complain that the same honour is paid to frivolities of man's devising. . . .[73]

I am not unaware how difficult it is to persuade the world that God rejects and even abominates everything devised for worship by human reason. The grounds for this error are numerous. "Every one thinks highly of his own," as the old proverb expresses it. Hence the offspring of our own brain delights us more; and besides, as Paul admits (Col. 2:23), this fictitious worship often presents some show of wisdom. Besides, as it has for the most part an external splendour which pleases the eye, it is more agreeable to our carnal nature, than that which alone God requires and approves, but which is less ostentatious. . . .

It is, then, impudent calumny in our enemies to accuse us of alluring men by compliance and indulgence. For were the option given, there is nothing which the carnal man would not prefer to do, rather than consent to worship God as prescribed by our doctrine. It is easy to use the words faith and repentance, but the things are most difficult to perform. Whoever therefore makes the worship of God consist in these by no means loosens the reins of discipline, but compels men to the course which they are most afraid to take. . . .

In prayer we have corrected three things. Discarding the intercession of saints, we have brought men back to Christ, that they might learn both to invoke the Father in his name and trust in him as Mediator; and we have taught them to pray first with firm and solid confidence, and second with understanding also, instead of muttering over confused prayers in an unknown tongue as they did before. Here we are assailed with bitter reproaches for being offensive to the saints, and also for depriving believers of an immense privilege. Both charges we deny. It is no injury to saints not to permit the office of Christ to be attributed to them. There is no honour of which we deprive them, except one improperly and rashly bestowed upon them by human error. I shall mention nothing which may not be expressly pointed out. First, when men are about to pray, they imagine God to be at a great distance, and that they cannot have access to him unless conducted by some patron. Nor is this false opinion current among the rude and unlearned only, but even those who would be thought leaders of the blind entertain it. Then in looking for patrons, every one follows his own fancy. One selects Mary, another Michael, another Peter. Christ they very seldom honour with a place in the list. Indeed there is scarcely one in a hundred who would not be amazed, as at some new prodigy, were he to hear Christ named as an intercessor. Therefore, passing Christ by, they all trust to the patronage of saints. Then superstition creeps in farther and farther, till they invoke the saints promiscuously, just as they do God. I admit, indeed, that when they desire to speak more definitely, all they ask of the saints is to assist them before God with their prayers. But more frequently they lose this distinction, and address and implore at one time God, and at another the saints, just according to the impulse of the moment. Indeed each saint has a peculiar province allotted to him. One gives rain, another fair weather; one delivers from fever, another from shipwreck. But, to say nothing of these profane heathen delusions which everywhere prevail in churches, this one impiety may suffice for all: that, in inviting

73. Calvin and the Reformed were less tolerant of images and ceremonies in worship than were the Lutherans.

intercessors from this quarter and from that, the whole world neglects Christ, whom alone God has set forth, and confides more in the patronage of the saints than in the protection of God. . . .

In condemning the fiction of transubstantiation, and likewise the custom of keeping and carrying about the bread, we were impelled by a stronger necessity. First, it is repugnant to the plain words of Christ; and second, it is abhorrent to the very nature of a sacrament. For there is no sacrament when there is no visible symbol to correspond to the spiritual truth which it represents. . . .

The carrying about of the bread in solemn state, or setting it on an elevated spot to be adored, are corruptions quite alien to the institution of Christ.[74] For in the Supper the Lord sets before us his body and blood, but it is in order that we may eat and drink. . . .

Lastly, we have revived the practice of explaining the doctrine and unfolding the mystery to the people whereas formerly the priest not only used a strange tongue,[75] but muttered in a whisper the words by which he pretended to consecrate the bread and wine. Here our critics have nothing to grumble at, unless it be that we have simply followed the command of Christ. For he did not by a silent exorcism command the bread to become his body, but with a clear voice declared to his apostles that he gave them his body. . . .

[*Calvin: Theological Treatises*, trans. J. K. S. Reid, Library of Christian Classics, vol. 22 (Philadelphia: Westminster Press, 1954), 184–94, 204–5]

74. Calvin is referring to eucharistic processions of the bread, discussed in slightly more detail in Selections 45 and 49.

75. That is, exclusively Latin.

Selection 30: John Calvin, *Institutes of the Christian Religion* (1559)

Calvin's* Institutes *is the most influential and widely known theological treatise from the Reformation. First published in Latin in 1536 as a catechetical tool, it went through four subsequent expansions, with the final and definitive edition appearing in 1559. He also published four French editions along the way, reflecting his intention to make this theology accessible. He designed the* Institutes *not only as an introductory theology text for students and ministers but also as a supplement to his commentaries, which generally stick close to the biblical text and refrain from doctrinal excurses. As a gathering of theological topics, the* Institutes *does not contain the whole of Calvin's thought, but it is an indispensable means for grasping his ideas and their impact in the history of theology.

I.i.1 [*Without knowledge of self there is no knowledge of God*]

Nearly all the wisdom we possess, that is to say, true and sound wisdom, consists of two parts: the knowledge of God and of ourselves.[76] But, while joined by many bonds, which one precedes and brings forth the other is not easy to discern. In the first place, no one can look upon himself without immediately turning his thoughts to the contemplation of God, in whom he "lives and moves" [Acts 17:28]. For, quite clearly, the mighty gifts with which we are endowed are hardly from ourselves; indeed, our very being is nothing but subsistence in the one God. Then, by these benefits shed like dew from heaven upon us, we are led as by rivulets to the spring itself. Indeed, our very poverty

76. Calvin uses *cognitio* and *notitia* interchangeably throughout this section, and they are both translated as "knowledge," but distinct from *sapientia* (wisdom).

better discloses the infinitude of benefits reposing in God. The miserable ruin, into which the rebellion of the first man cast us, especially compels us to look upward. Thus, not only will we, in fasting and hungering, seek thence what we lack; but, in being aroused by fear, we shall learn humility. For, as a veritable world of miseries is to be found in mankind, and we are thereby despoiled of divine raiment, our shameful nakedness exposes a teeming horde of infamies. Each of us must, then, be so stung by the consciousness of his own unhappiness as to attain at least some knowledge of God. Thus, from the feeling of our own ignorance, vanity, poverty, infirmity, and—what is more—depravity and corruption, we recognize that the true light of wisdom, sound virtue, full abundance of every good, and purity of righteousness rest in the Lord alone. To this extent we are prompted by our own ills to contemplate the good things of God; and we cannot seriously aspire to him before we begin to become displeased with ourselves. For what man in all the world would not gladly remain as he is—what man does not remain as he is—so long as he does not know himself, that is, while content with his own gifts, and either ignorant or unmindful of his own misery? Accordingly, the knowledge of ourselves not only arouses us to seek God, but also, as it were, leads us by the hand to find him.

I.i.2 [*Without knowledge of God there is no knowledge of self*]

Again, it is certain that man never achieves a clear knowledge of himself unless he has first looked upon God's face, and then descends from contemplating him to scrutinize himself. For we always seem to ourselves righteous and upright and wise and holy—this pride is innate in all of us—unless by clear proofs we stand convinced of our own unrighteousness, foulness, folly, and impurity. Moreover, we are not thus convinced if we look merely to ourselves and not also to the Lord, who is the sole standard by which this judgment must be measured. For, because all of us are inclined by nature to hypocrisy, a kind of empty image of righteousness in place of righteousness itself abundantly satisfies us. And because nothing appears within or around us that has not been contaminated by great immorality, what is a little less vile pleases us as a thing most pure—so long as we confine our minds within the limits of human corruption. Just so, an eye to which nothing is shown but black objects judges something dirty white or even rather darkly mottled to be whiteness itself. Indeed, we can discern still more clearly from the bodily senses how much we are deluded in estimating the powers of the soul. For if in broad daylight we either look down upon the ground or survey whatever meets our view round about, we seem to ourselves endowed with the strongest and keenest sight; yet when we look up to the sun and gaze straight at it, that power of sight which was particularly strong on earth is at once blunted and confused by a great brilliance, and thus we are compelled to admit that our keenness in looking upon things earthly is sheer dullness when it comes to the sun. So it happens in estimating our spiritual goods. As long as we do not look beyond the earth, being quite content with our own righteousness, wisdom, and virtue, we flatter ourselves most sweetly, and fancy ourselves all but demigods. Suppose we but once begin to raise our thoughts to God, and to ponder his nature, and how completely perfect are his righteousness, wisdom, and power—the straightedge to which we must be shaped. Then, what masquerading earlier as righteousness was pleasing in us will soon grow filthy in its consummate wickedness. What wonderfully impressed us under the name of wisdom will stink in its very foolishness. What wore the face of power will prove itself the most miserable weakness. That is, what in us seems perfection itself corresponds ill to the purity of God.

I.i.3 [*Man before God's majesty*]

Hence that dread and wonder with which Scripture commonly represents the saints as stricken and overcome whenever they felt the presence of God. Thus it comes about that we see men who in his absence normally remained firm and constant, but who, when he manifests his glory, are so shaken and struck dumb as to be laid low by the dread of death—are in fact overwhelmed by it and almost annihilated. As a consequence, we must infer that man is never sufficiently touched and affected by the awareness of his lowly state until he has compared himself with God's majesty. Moreover, we have numerous examples of this consternation both in The Book of Judges and in the Prophets. So frequent was it that this expression was common among God's people: "We shall die, for the Lord has appeared to us" [Judg. 13:22; Isa. 6:5; Ezek. 2:1; 1:28; Judg. 6:22-23; and elsewhere]. The story of Job, in its description of God's wisdom, power, and purity, always expresses a powerful argument that overwhelms men with the realization of their own stupidity, impotence, and corruption [cf. Job 38:1ff.]. And not without cause: for we see how Abraham recognizes more clearly that he is earth and dust [Gen. 18:27] when once he had come nearer to beholding God's glory; and how Elijah, with uncovered face, cannot bear to await his approach, such is the awesomeness of his appearance [I Kgs. 19:13]. And what can man do, who is rottenness itself [Job 13:28] and a worm [Job 7:5; Ps. 22:6], when even the very cherubim must veil their faces out of fear [Isa. 6:2]? It is this indeed of which the prophet Isaiah speaks: "The sun will blush and the moon be confounded when the Lord of Hosts shall reign" [Isa. 24:23]; that is, when he shall bring forth his splendor and cause it to draw nearer, the brightest thing will become darkness before it [Isa. 2:10].

Yet, however the knowledge of God and of ourselves may be mutually connected, the order of right teaching requires that we discuss the former first, then proceed afterward to treat the latter.[77]

I.vi.1 [*God bestows the actual knowledge of himself upon us only in the Scriptures*]

That brightness which is borne in upon the eyes of all men both in heaven and on earth is more than enough to withdraw all support from men's ingratitude—just as God, to involve the human race in the same guilt, sets forth to all without exception his presence portrayed in his creatures. Despite this, it is needful that another and better help be added to direct us aright to the very Creator of the universe. It was not in vain, then, that he added the light of his Word by which to become known unto salvation; and he regarded as worthy of this privilege those whom he pleased to gather more closely and intimately to himself. For because he saw the minds of all men tossed and agitated, after he chose the Jews as his very own flock, he fenced them about that they might not sink into oblivion as others had. With good reason he holds us by the same means in the pure knowledge of himself, since otherwise even those who seem to stand firm before all others would soon melt away. Just as old or bleary-eyed men and those with weak vision, if you thrust before them a most beautiful volume, even if they recognize it to be some

77. The "order of right teaching" reflects Calvin's attention to structure in this basic theology.

sort of writing, yet can scarcely construe two words, but with the aid of spectacles will begin to read distinctly; so Scripture, gathering up the otherwise confused knowledge of God in our minds, having dispersed our dullness, clearly shows us the true God.[78] This, therefore, is a special gift, where God, to instruct the church, not merely uses mute teachers but also opens his own most hallowed lips. Not only does he teach the elect to look upon a god, but also shows himself as the God upon whom they are to look. . . .

I.vi.3 [*Without Scripture we fall into error*]

Suppose we ponder how slippery is the fall of the human mind into forgetfulness of God, how great the tendency to every kind of error, how great the lust to fashion constantly new and artificial religions. Then we may perceive how necessary was such written proof of the heavenly doctrine, that it should neither perish through forgetfulness nor vanish through error nor be corrupted by the audacity of men. It is therefore clear that God has provided the assistance of the Word for the sake of all those to whom he has been pleased to give useful instruction because he foresaw that his likeness imprinted upon the most beautiful form of the universe would be insufficiently effective. Hence, we must strive onward by this straight path if we seriously aspire to the pure contemplation of God. We must come, I say, to the Word, where God is truly and vividly described to us from his works, while these very works are appraised not by our depraved judgment but by the rule of eternal truth. If we turn aside from the Word, as I have just now said, though we may strive with strenuous haste, yet, since we have got off the track, we shall never reach the goal. For we should so reason that the splendor of the divine countenance, which even the apostle calls "unapproachable" [1 Tim. 6:16], is for us like an inexplicable labyrinth unless we are conducted into it by the thread of the Word; so that it is better to limp along this path than to dash with all speed outside it. David very often, therefore, teaching that we ought to banish superstitions from the earth so that pure religion may flourish, represented God as regnant [Pss. 93:1; 96:10; 97:1; 99:1; and the like]. Now he means by the word "regnant" not the power with which he is endowed, and which he exercises in governing the whole of nature, but the doctrine by which he asserts his lawful sovereignty. For errors can never be uprooted from human hearts until true knowledge of God is planted therein.

I.vii.4

. . . Yet they who strive to build up firm faith in Scripture through disputation are doing things backwards. For my part, although I do not excel either in great dexterity or eloquence, if I were struggling against the most crafty sort of despisers of God, who seek to appear shrewd and witty in disparaging Scripture, I am confident it would not be difficult for me to silence their clamorous voices. And if it were a useful labor to refute their cavils, I would with no great trouble shatter the boasts they mutter in their lurking places. But even if anyone clears God's Sacred Word from man's evil speaking, he will not at once imprint upon their hearts that certainty which piety requires. Since for unbelieving men religion seems to stand by opinion alone, they, in order not to believe anything foolishly or lightly, both wish and demand rational proof that Moses and the prophets spoke divinely. But I reply: the testimony of the Spirit is more excellent than all

78. This is one of many passages in which Calvin emphasizes that natural knowledge of God is incomplete without the special revelation of Scripture.

reason. For as God alone is a fit witness of himself in his Word, so also the Word will not find acceptance in men's hearts before it is sealed by the inward testimony of the Spirit. The same Spirit, therefore, who has spoken through the mouths of the prophets must penetrate into our hearts to persuade us that they faithfully proclaimed what had been divinely commanded. Isaiah very aptly expresses this connection in these words: "My Spirit which is in you, and the words that I have put in your mouth, and the mouths of your offspring, shall never fail" [Isa. 59:21]. Some good folk are annoyed that a clear proof is not ready at hand when the impious, unpunished, murmur against God's Word. As if the Spirit were not called both "seal" and "guarantee" [2 Cor. 1:22] for confirming the faith of the godly; because until he illumines their minds, they ever waver among many doubts!

I.xiii.1 [*God's nature is immeasurable and spiritual*]

The Scriptural teaching concerning God's infinite and spiritual essence ought to be enough, not only to banish popular delusions, but also to refute the subtleties of secular philosophy. One of the ancients seems aptly to have remarked, "Whatever we see, and whatever we do not see, is God."[79] According to this, he fancied that divinity was poured out into the various parts of the world. But even if God to keep us sober speaks sparingly of his essence, yet by those two titles that I have used he both banishes stupid imaginings and restrains the boldness of the human mind. Surely, his infinity ought to make us afraid to try to measure him by our own senses. Indeed, his spiritual nature forbids our imagining anything earthly or carnal of him. For the same reason, he quite often assigns to himself a dwelling place in heaven. And yet as he is incomprehensible he also fills the earth itself. But because he sees that our slow minds sink down upon the earth, and rightly, in order to shake off our sluggishness and inertia he raises us above the world. And hence falls to the ground the error of the Manichees, who by postulating two principles made the devil almost equal to God. Undoubtedly this was to wreck God's unity and restrict his infinity. Indeed, that they dared abuse certain testimonies of Scripture was due to base ignorance; just as the error itself sprang from execrable madness. The Anthropomorphites, also, who imagined a corporeal God from the fact that Scripture often ascribes to him a mouth, ears, eyes, hands, and feet, are easily refuted. For who even of slight intelligence does not understand that, as nurses commonly do with infants, God is wont in a measure to "lisp" in speaking to us? Thus such forms of speaking do not so much express clearly what God is like as accommodate the knowledge of him to our slight capacity. To do this he must descend far beneath his loftiness.

II.ii.18 [*The limits of our understanding*]

We must now analyze what human reason can discern with regard to God's Kingdom and to spiritual insight. This spiritual insight consists chiefly in three things: (1) knowing God; (2) knowing his fatherly favor in our behalf, in which our salvation consists; (3) knowing how to frame our life according to the rule of his law. In the first two points—and especially in the second—the greatest geniuses are blinder than moles! Certainly I do not deny that one can read competent and apt statements about God here and there in the philosophers, but these always show a certain giddy imagination. As was stated above, the Lord indeed gave them a slight taste of his divinity that they might not hide their impiety under a cloak of ignorance.

79. Seneca, *Natural Questions*, Prologue I.13.

And sometimes he impelled them to make certain utterances by the confession of which they would themselves be corrected. But they saw things in such a way that their seeing did not direct them to the truth, much less enable them to attain it! They are like a traveler passing through a field at night who in a momentary lightning flash sees far and wide, but the sight vanishes so swiftly that he is plunged again into the darkness of the night before he can take even a step—let alone be directed on his way by its help. Besides, although they may chance to sprinkle their books with droplets of truth, how many monstrous lies defile them! In short, they never even sensed that assurance of God's benevolence toward us (without which man's understanding can only be filled with boundless confusion). Human reason, therefore, neither approaches, nor strives toward, nor even takes a straight aim at, this truth: to understand who the true God is or what sort of God he wishes to be toward us.

III.xxi.1 [*Necessity and beneficial effect of the doctrine of election; danger of curiosity*]

In actual fact, the covenant of life is not preached equally among all men, and among those to whom it is preached, it does not gain the same acceptance either constantly or in equal degree. In this diversity the wonderful depth of God's judgment is made known. For there is no doubt that this variety also serves the decision of God's eternal election. If it is plain that it comes to pass by God's bidding that salvation is freely offered to some while others are barred from access to it, at once great and difficult questions spring up, explicable only when reverent minds regard as settled what they may suitably hold concerning election and predestination. A baffling question this seems to many. For they think nothing more inconsistent than that out of the common multitude of men some should be predestined to salvation, others to destruction.[80] But how mistakenly they entangle themselves will become clear in the following discussion. Besides, in the very darkness that frightens them not only is the usefulness of this doctrine made known but also its very sweet fruit. We shall never be clearly persuaded, as we ought to be, that our salvation flows from the wellspring of God's free mercy until we come to know his eternal election, which illumines God's grace by this contrast: that he does not indiscriminately adopt all into the hope of salvation but gives to some what he denies to others.

How much the ignorance of this principle detracts from God's glory, how much it takes away from true humility, is well known. Yet Paul denies that this which needs so much to be known can be known unless God, utterly disregarding works, chooses those whom he has decreed within himself. "At the present time," he says, "a remnant has been saved according to the election of grace. But if it is by grace, it is no more of works; otherwise grace would no more be grace. But if it is of works, it is no more of grace; otherwise work would not be work." [Rom. 11:5-6.] If—to make it clear that our salvation comes about solely from God's mere generosity—we must be called back to the course of election, those who wish to get rid of all this are obscuring as maliciously as they can what ought to have been gloriously and vociferously proclaimed, and they tear humility up by the very roots. Paul clearly testifies that, when the salvation of a remnant of the people is ascribed to the election of grace,

80. Erasmus may be among the many Roman Catholic opponents of unconditional predestination that Calvin had in mind. See Selection 11. On the later Reformed and Arminian controversy surrounding these same questions, see Selections 55–60.

then only is it acknowledged that God of his mere good pleasure preserves whom he will, and moreover that he pays no reward, since he can owe none.

They who shut the gates that no one may dare seek a taste of this doctrine wrong men no less than God. For neither will anything, else suffice to make us humble as we ought to be nor shall we otherwise sincerely feel how much we are obliged to God. And as Christ teaches, here is our only ground for firmness and confidence: in order to free us of all fear and render us victorious amid so many dangers, snares, and mortal struggles, he promises that whatever the Father has entrusted into his keeping will be safe [John 10:28-29]. From this we infer that all those who do not know that they are God's own will be miserable through constant fear. Hence, those who by being blind to the three benefits we have noted would wish the foundation of our salvation to be removed from our midst, very badly serve the interests of themselves and of all other believers. How is it that the church becomes manifest to us from this, when, as Bernard rightly teaches, "it could not otherwise be found or recognized among creatures, since it lies marvelously hidden . . . both within the bosom of a blessed predestination and within the mass of a miserable condemnation?"[81]

But before I enter into the matter itself, I need to mention by way of preface two kinds of men.

Human curiosity renders the discussion of predestination, already somewhat difficult of itself, very confusing and even dangerous. No restraints can hold it back from wandering in forbidden bypaths and thrusting upward to the heights. If allowed, it will leave no secret to God that it will not search out and unravel. Since we see so many on all sides rushing into this audacity and impudence, among them certain men not otherwise bad, they should in due season be reminded of the measure of their duty in this regard.

First, then, let them remember that when they inquire into predestination they are penetrating the sacred precincts of divine wisdom. If anyone with carefree assurance breaks into this place, he will not succeed in satisfying his curiosity and he will enter a labyrinth from which he can find no exit. For it is not right for man unrestrainedly to search out things that the Lord has willed to be hid in himself, and to unfold from eternity itself the sublimest wisdom, which he would have us revere but not understand that through this also he should fill us with wonder. He has set forth by his Word the secrets of his will that he has decided to reveal to us. These he decided to reveal in so far as he foresaw that they would concern us and benefit us.

III.xxi.2 [*Doctrine of predestination to be sought in Scripture only*]

"We have entered the pathway of faith," says Augustine, "let us hold steadfastly to it. It leads us to the King's chamber, in which are hid all treasures of knowledge and wisdom. For the Lord Christ himself did not bear a grudge against his great and most select disciples when he said: 'I have . . . many things to say to you, but you cannot bear them now' [John 16:12]. We must walk, we must advance, we must grow, that our hearts may be capable of those things which we cannot yet grasp. But if the Last Day finds us advancing, there we shall learn what we could not learn here."[82] If this thought prevails with us, that the Word of the Lord is the sole way that can lead us in our search for all that it is lawful to hold concerning him, and is the sole light to illumine our

81. Bernard of Clairvaux, *Sermons on the Song of Songs* 78.4.

82. Augustine, *John's Gospel* 53.7.

vision of all that we should see of him, it will readily keep and restrain us from all rashness. For we shall know that the moment we exceed the bounds of the Word, our course is outside the pathway and in darkness, and that there we must repeatedly wander, slip, and stumble. Let this, therefore, first of all be before our eyes: to seek any other knowledge of predestination than what the Word of God discloses is not less insane than if one should purpose to walk in a pathless waste [cf. Job 12:24], or to see in darkness. And let us not be ashamed to be ignorant of something in this matter, wherein there is a certain learned ignorance. Rather, let us willingly refrain from inquiring into a kind of knowledge, the ardent desire for which is both foolish and dangerous, nay, even deadly. But if a wanton curiosity agitates us, we shall always do well to oppose to it this restraining thought: just as too much honey is not good, so for the curious the investigation of glory is not turned into glory [Prov. 25:27, cf. Vulgate]. For there is good reason for us to be deterred from this insolence which can only plunge us into ruin.

III.xxi.3 [*The second danger: anxious silence about the doctrine of election*]

There are others who, wishing to cure this evil, all but require that every mention of predestination be buried; indeed, they teach us to avoid any question of it, as we would a reef. Even though their moderation in this matter is rightly to be praised, because they feel that these mysteries ought to be discussed with great soberness, yet because they descend to too low a level, they make little progress with the human understanding, which does not allow itself to be easily restrained. Therefore, to hold to a proper limit in this regard also, we shall have to turn back to the Word of the Lord, in which we have a sure rule for the understanding. For Scripture is the school of the Holy Spirit, in which, as nothing is omitted that is both necessary and useful to know, so nothing is taught but what is expedient to know. Therefore we must guard against depriving believers of anything disclosed about predestination in Scripture, lest we seem either wickedly to defraud them of the blessing of their God or to accuse and scoff at the Holy Spirit for having published what it is in any way profitable to suppress.

Let us, I say, permit the Christian man to open his mind and ears to every utterance of God directed to him, provided it be with such restraint that when the Lord closes his holy lips, he also shall at once close the way to inquiry. The best limit of sobriety for us will be not only to follow God's lead always in learning but, when he sets an end to teaching, to stop trying to be wise. The fact that they fear danger is not sufficiently important that we should on that account turn away our minds from the oracles of God. Solomon's saying is familiar: "It is the glory of God to conceal the word" [Prov. 25:2, Vulgate]. But since piety and common sense show that this is not to be understood indiscriminately of everything, we must seek a distinction, lest under the pretense of modesty and sobriety we are satisfied with brutish ignorance. . . .

III.xxi.4 [*The alleged peril in the doctrine dismissed*]

Profane men, I admit, in the matter of predestination abruptly seize upon something to carp, rail, bark, or scoff at. But if their shamelessness deters us, we shall have to keep secret the chief doctrines of the faith, almost none of which they or their like leave untouched by blasphemy. An obstinate person would be no less insolently puffed up on hearing that within the essence of God there are three Persons than if he were told that God foresaw what would happen to man when he created him. . . .

III.xxi.5 [*Predestination and foreknowledge of God; the election of Israel*]

No one who wishes to be thought religious dares simply deny predestination, by which God adopts some to hope of life, and sentences others to eternal death. But our opponents, especially those who make foreknowledge its cause, envelop it in numerous petty objections. We, indeed, place both doctrines in God, but we say that subjecting one to the other is absurd.

When we attribute foreknowledge to God, we mean that all things always were, and perpetually remain, under his eyes, so that to his knowledge there is nothing future or past, but all things are present. And they are present in such a way that he not only conceives them through ideas, as we have before us those things which our minds remember, but he truly looks upon them and discerns them as things placed before him. And this foreknowledge is extended throughout the universe to every creature. We call predestination God's eternal decree, by which he compacted with himself what he willed to become of each man. For all are not created in equal condition; rather, eternal life is foreordained for some, eternal damnation for others. Therefore, as any man has been created to one or the other of these ends, we speak of him as predestined to life or to death. . . .

III.xxi.6 [*The second stage: election and reprobation of individual Israelites*]

We must now add a second, more limited degree of election, or one in which God's more special grace was evident, that is, when from the same race of Abraham God rejected some but showed that he kept others among his sons by cherishing them in the church. Ishmael had at first obtained equal rank with his brother, Isaac, for in him the spiritual covenant had been equally sealed by the sign of circumcision. Ishmael is cut off; then Esau; afterward, a countless multitude, and well-nigh all Israel. In Isaac the seed was called; the same calling continued in Jacob. God showed a similar example in rejecting Saul. . . .

III.xxiii.7 [*God has also predestined the fall into sin*]

They say it is not stated in so many words that God decreed that Adam should perish for his rebellion. As if, indeed, that very God, who, Scripture proclaims, "does whatever he pleases" [Ps. 115:3], would have created the noblest of his creatures to an uncertain end. . . .

Again I ask: whence does it happen that Adam's fall irremediably involved so many peoples, together with their infant offspring, in eternal death unless because it so pleased God? Here their tongues, otherwise so loquacious, must become mute. The decree is dreadful indeed,[83] I confess. Yet no one can deny that God foreknew what end man was to have before he created him, and consequently foreknew because he so ordained by his decree. If anyone inveighs against God's foreknowledge at this point, he stumbles rashly and heedlessly. What reason is there to accuse the Heavenly Judge because he was not ignorant of what was to happen? If there is any just or manifest complaint, it applies to predestination. And it ought not to seem absurd for me to say that God not only foresaw the fall of the first man, and in him the ruin of his descendants, but also meted it out in accordance with his own decision. For as it pertains to his wisdom to

83. "Decretum quidem horribile." When John Wesley later refers to Calvin's "horrible decree," he is quoting Calvin.

foreknow everything that is to happen, so it pertains to his might to rule and control everything by his hand. And Augustine also skillfully disposes of this question, as of others: "We most wholesomely confess what we most correctly believe, that the God and Lord of all things, who created all things exceedingly good [cf. Gen. 1:31], and foreknew that evil things would rise out of good, and also knew that it pertained to his most omnipotent goodness to bring good out of evil things rather than not to permit evil things to be . . . , so ordained the life of angels and men that in it he might first of all show what free will could do, and then what the blessing of his grace and the verdict of his justice could do."[84]

III.xxiii.10 [*Objection: the doctrine of election leads to the view that God shows partiality toward persons*]

Now the adversaries of God's predestination defame it with a third absurdity. Since we refer solely to the decision of the divine will the release from universal destruction of those whom he accepts as heirs of his Kingdom, from this they conclude that there is with God "partiality toward persons," which Scripture everywhere denies. They further conclude either that Scripture disagrees with itself or that in God's election there is consideration of merits. First, Scripture denies that God shows partiality toward persons in another sense than that in which they judge. For it means by the word "person" not a man but those things in a man which, conspicuous to the eye, customarily either produce favor, grace, and dignity, or arouse hatred, contempt, and disgrace. . . .

Still, the matter can be explained to fuller satisfaction. Do they ask how it happens that of two men indistinguishable in merit, God in his election passes over one but takes the other? I, in turn, ask: "Do they think that there is anything in him who is taken that disposes God to him?" If they admit that there is nothing, as they must, it will follow that God does not consider the man but seeks from his own goodness the reason to do him good. . . .

III.xxiv.8 [*General and special calling*]

The statement of Christ "Many are called but few are chosen" [Matt. 22:14] is, in this manner, very badly understood. Nothing will be ambiguous if we hold fast to what ought to be clear from the foregoing: that there are two kinds of call. There is the general call, by which God invites all equally to himself through the outward preaching of the word—even those to whom he holds it out as a savor of death [cf. 2 Cor. 2:16], and as the occasion for severer condemnation. The other kind of call is special, which he deigns for the most part to give to the believers alone, while by the inward illumination of his Spirit he causes the preached Word to dwell in their hearts. Yet sometimes he also causes those whom he illumines only for a time to partake of it; then he justly forsakes them on account of their ungratefulness and strikes them with even greater blindness.

Now since the Lord saw the gospel published far and wide, held in contempt by many, justly valued by few, he describes God to us in the person of a king, who, in giving a solemn feast, sends his heralds round about to invite a great crowd but can obtain acceptance from very few, for each one claims that something prevents him from coming; hence, since they refuse, he is compelled to call in off the crossroads all met there [Matt. 22:2-9]. Up to this point everyone sees that the parable is to be understood of the outward call. He afterward adds that God acts like a good host, who circulates from table to table, affably greeting his guests. But if he finds one not dressed in a

84. Augustine, *On Rebuke and Grace* 10.27.

wedding garment, he will not allow him, unfitly dressed, to dishonor the festivity of the banquet with his unclean attire [Matt. 22:11-13]. This phrase ought, I admit, to be understood as applying to those who enter the church on profession of faith but not clothed with Christ's sanctification. God will not forever bear such dishonors, even cancers, of his church but as their baseness deserves, will cast them out. . . .

III.xxiv.15 [*Scriptural passages that seem to prove the opposite of the stated doctrine: Ezek. 33:11*]

But our opponents are in the habit of quoting in opposition a few Scripture passages in which God seems to deny that the wicked perish by his ordination, except in so far as by their clamorous protests they of their own accord bring death upon themselves. Let us therefore briefly explain these passages and prove that they do not conflict with the foregoing opinion.

A passage of Ezekiel's is brought forward, that "God does not will the death of the wicked but wills that the wicked turn back and live" [Ezek. 33:11].[85] If it pleases God to extend this to the whole human race, why does he not encourage to repentance the very many whose minds are more amenable to obedience than the minds of those who grow harder and harder at his daily invitations? Among the people of Nineveh [cf. Matt. 12:41] and of Sodom, as Christ testifies, the preaching of the gospel and miracles would have accomplished more than in Judea [Matt. 11:23]. If God wills that all be saved, how does it come to pass that he does not open the door of repentance to the miserable men who would be better prepared to receive grace? Hence we may see that this passage is violently twisted if the will of God, mentioned by the prophet, is opposed to His eternal plan, by which He has distinguished the elect from the reprobate. Now if we are seeking the prophet's true meaning, it is that he would bring the hope of pardon to the penitent only. The gist of it is that God is without doubt ready to forgive, as soon as the sinner is converted. Therefore, in so far as God wills the sinner's repentance, he does not will his death. But experience teaches that God wills the repentance of those whom he invites to himself, in such a way that he does not touch the hearts of all. Yet it is not on that account to be said that he acts deceitfully, for even though only his outward call renders inexcusable those who hear it and do not obey, still it is truly considered evidence of God's grace, by which he reconciles men to himself. Let us therefore regard the prophet's instruction that the death of the sinner is not pleasing to God as designed to assure believers that God is ready to pardon them as soon as they are touched by repentance but to make the wicked feel that their transgression is doubled because they do not respond to God's great kindness and goodness. God's mercy will always, accordingly, go to meet repentance, but all the prophets and all the apostles, as well as Ezekiel himself, clearly teach to whom repentance is given.

[*Institutes of the Christian Religion*, ed. John T. McNeill and trans. Ford Lewis Battles, Library of Christian Classics, vol. 20 (Philadelphia: Westminster Press, 1960), 35–39, 69–70, 72–73, 79–80, 120–21, 277–78, 920–26, 929, 955–56, 958, 974, 982–83]

85. Here and elsewhere in the discussion of this topic, Calvin is referring to, among others, the Dutch Catholic theologian Albert Pighius (ca. 1490–1542).

Further Reading

Gordon, Bruce. *Calvin*. New Haven, CT: Yale University Press, 2009.

Lindberg, Carter. *The European Reformations*. Oxford: Blackwell, 1996.

Muller, Richard A. *The Unaccommodated Calvin: Studies in the Foundation of a Theological Tradition*. Oxford Studies in Historical Theology. New York: Oxford University Press, 2000.

Oberman, Heiko A. *Luther: Man between God and the Devil*. New Haven, CT: Yale University Press, 1989.

Potter, G. R. *Zwingli*. Cambridge: Cambridge University Press, 1976.

Schreiner, Susan E. *Are You Alone Wise? The Search for Certainty in the Early Modern Era*. Oxford Studies in Historical Theology. New York: Oxford University Press, 2011.

Stjerna, Kirsi. *Women and the Reformation*. Oxford: Blackwell, 2009.

Whitford, David, ed. *Reformation and Early Modern Europe: A Guide to Research*. Kirksville, MO: Truman State University Press, 2008.

Chapter 3
Radical Reformation

As reform movements began to take hold in various German-speaking lands, and before the boundaries of discrete Protestant theologies had been drawn, it was an open question as to what extent the ecclesial and doctrinal reforms would be pursued within these movements. As the 1520s progressed, many who were initially supportive of the reformist leadership and principles of Luther and Zwingli became disillusioned by the unwillingness of these same leaders to reform fully or quickly enough. Modern historians have designated these various movements as "radical" in the sense that these reformers intended to return to the roots (Latin, *radices*) of the Christian faith. In most cases, this radical impulse meant a return to the Bible alone, apart from tradition, whereas other reformers were happy to interpret and apply Scripture in the light of the historical tradition of the church. In other cases, there was a reliance on revelation of the Holy Spirit apart from the Word, leading some to prioritize individual revelation above the authority of the Bible.

Besides their consensus that reformers such as Luther and Zwingli had not gone far enough in their reforms, the radical reformers were never a united group with homogeneous doctrine. But one practice almost all radicals opposed was paedobaptism, which in the early sixteenth century was the universal practice of the Western and Eastern churches. When reformers in Zurich came to their understanding of believer's baptism, Zwingli eventually reacted by advocating persecution, a reaction that would be repeated against the radicals many times over for the remainder of the sixteenth century. The majority of both Protestants and Roman Catholics throughout Europe were united in their condemnation of believer's baptism, and they referred to these reformers as "Anabaptists"—that is to say, "re-baptizers" (German, *Wiedertäufer*)—or "Catabaptists" (which implies a disfiguring of baptism).

Anabaptists agreed with Zwingli about the mode of baptism (affusion), and they were in fundamental agreement with his deemphasizing the sacramental efficacy of baptism and the Lord's Supper. The debate concerned the proper candidate for baptism. Thus, when the Anabaptists baptized adult believers who had already been baptized as infants, they did not regard this as re-baptism, but as a declaration that paedobaptism is no genuine baptism at all. This point was not lost on their opponents, who also labeled them "Donatists" after the ancient schismatic heresy that refused to acknowledge the legitimacy of sacraments administered by Catholic bishops.

Along with their almost unanimous rejection of paedobaptism, the majority of radical reformers held to a thoroughgoing nonviolence both in the face of persecution and in the context of war. The individual pacifism was based especially on Jesus' Sermon on the Mount, including the command to turn the other cheek and to love one's enemies. Along with this rationale, their refusal to participate in armed conflict was based on an idea of separation of church and state that was unusual in the premodern world. In addition to pacifism, this separation also meant that most Anabaptists did not seek the support of city magistrates, distinguishing the radicals from the so-called "magisterial" reformations of the Lutheran and Reformed movements. According to these Anabaptists, human authority corrupts the church.

The social implications of these two Anabaptist beliefs (believer's baptism and separation of church and state) were far-reaching. Not to baptize one's infant in the state church (whether Roman or Protestant) and not to take up arms against the invading Muslim Turks were seen as socially subversive and deviant, if not treacherous. Today these views may seem harmless, but then they meant nothing less than the undermining of Christian Europe, the *corpus Christianum*, where everyone in society had been considered a part of the church. Rather, these practices made the church into an exclusively voluntary society, and a portion of society could theoretically be left out of the church. As such, Anabaptists normally emphasized the freedom of the will (in an Erasmian sense) against the unconditional predestination taught by the magisterial reformers. Since the Anabaptists generally did not enjoy state support, and because most were nonresistant, the Anabaptists became an easy and frequent target of persecution by Roman Catholics and Protestants alike.

As if those beliefs were not enough to raise suspicion, a minority of the radicals might be considered extremist in their apocalyptic outlook. To be sure, most sixteenth-century Christians—with their expectations that Christ's literal return was imminent and that biblical, apocalyptic prophecies were being fulfilled in the events of their day—would be viewed as unusually apocalyptic by today's standards. But a few radicals were willing to take social and political action to help bring the prophecies to fulfillment, actions that in turn contradicted the pacifist beliefs of the majority. For example, Thomas Müntzer (1489–1525) participated in the German peasant revolt, which he believed would usher in Christ's second coming.

The burning of Anneken Hendriks, Amsterdam, 1571, from Martyrs' Mirror

Because of the ubiquity and intensity of the persecutions against the radicals, most first-generation Anabaptist leaders did not live long enough to wield a lasting influence through teaching and writing. The earliest major exception to this rule is Menno Simons (1496–1561), a former priest who, after becoming an Anabaptist, brought a stable influence to a group reeling from persecutions and sociopolitical disasters. He traveled primarily in the Low Countries (The Netherlands), establishing and pastoring congregations for twenty-five years, and his followers, the Mennonites, became the most well-known of the Anabaptists.

The whole group of radical reformers is often referred to collectively as "Anabaptists," but George Huntston Williams suggested a typology that classifies the radical reformers into three main groups, based especially on their primary source of religious authority: Anabaptists proper (whose primary appeal was to the New Testament), Spiritualists (who relied on the Holy Spirit), and Evangelical Rationalists (who left comparatively more room for reason). Given that these groups interacted with one another and that many individuals are difficult to place in one category or another, they should not be taken as hard-and-fast boundaries or as an excuse to ignore nuance. Nevertheless, this chapter is ordered accordingly, and its readings reflect the various emphases within this diverse movement.

A. Spiritualists

Selection 31: Andreas Bodenstein von Karlstadt, *Whether One Should Proceed Slowly* (1524)

Andreas Bodenstein von Karlstadt (1486–1541) was Luther's colleague in theology at the University of Wittenberg in the early years of the Reformation. Johann Eck challenged Karlstadt in the Leipzig Debate of 1519, but Luther ended up as Eck's chief opponent in the dispute. While Luther was in hiding at Wartburg Castle in 1521, Karlstadt inspired a radical iconoclasm that Luther then opposed upon his return to Wittenberg. Their theological differences deepened over the years, with Karlstadt emphasizing a kind of mysticism and sanctification with which Luther was uncomfortable.

This treatise,* Whether One Should Proceed Slowly and Avoid Offending the Weak in Matters That Concern God's Will, *was written as a response to Luther's call for patience. A key feature of the radical reform movements, illustrated in this document, was the feeling that Luther, Zwingli, and others were not reforming ecclesiastical abuses and doctrinal errors thoroughly and rapidly enough. In a dire situation, patience is not a virtue.

I, Andreas Karlstadt, wish my especially beloved brother in Christ, Bartel Bach, city secretary of Joachimstal,[1] the art of knowing God through our lord Jesus Christ.

Dear brother, in reply to my description of some changes that have taken place here [i.e., Orlamünde], you wrote me that, as far as you are concerned, you would like to proceed slowly. And through this writing you gave me to understand, without saying it, that one should not proceed quickly or suddenly but slowly in order to avoid offending the weak. You are simply doing what the whole world does now, which is to cry, "The weak, the weak! The sick, the sick! Not so fast! Slowly, slowly!" For this reason I am not angry with you. Nevertheless in this matter you are saying, "Slowly! The sick!," with a great many people. Only you are saying it more politely and with greater sophistication. Accordingly I must tell you that neither in this case nor in other matters concerning God should you regard how the great masses speak or judge. Rather, you should look straight at God's word [i.e., Scripture]. For it has long been clear that the princes, for whom the scribes write, and the great mass of the people have erred formerly and are capable of error. On account of this, God has also ordained what the princes and the whole crowd or ecclesiastical councils should sacrifice because of their ignorance or error (Leviticus 4[:1ff.]). Through this ordinance God clearly shows for all time that all the learned, the princes, and the masses can err and stumble. Therefore God alone has also let it be proclaimed in general and in particular that each one should hasten to righteousness for himself (Exodus 23[:2]) and that no one must follow the masses in deviating from what is right. . . .

In acting one should not have regard for others.

. . . Look, I am asking you whether a son should wait to honor his parents until the weak follow, understand, and want to honor their parents? You would have to reply, "Certainly, those who understand should not rob their parents of their honor, nor wait until all young people follow with understanding and desire." I am asking whether one should wait to stop coveting the goods of other people until others do so? May

1. Bartel Bach was the city secretary of Joachimstal in Bohemia. Ultimately, Karlstadt was unsuccessful in his attempt to win Bach's support.

one steal until the thieves stop stealing? And thus I ask, again and again, in the case of all the commandments, whether it is proper that we wait until others have learned, and have the will to follow us and to do what God wants. . . .

Each community, large or small, should see for itself that it acts righteously and well, and it should wait for no one.

. . . Each community should have its Levite who proclaims to it the covenant of peace and truth. And the father of each household should enjoin, repeat, and explain God's word to his children. From this it follows always that each community and household should pay attention, so that it understands God's commandment and acts accordingly. And God wants us so little to wait until others follow and become pious that he has commanded that the godless be punished just as other vices are punished (Deuteronomy 13 and 17). And in addition he has commanded that whole cities that cultivate their idolatry or do not want to turn to the right path be killed and destroyed.

It is astonishing that our scripturally wise and our rulers punish carnal adultery and allow spiritual adultery to go unpunished. They want to defeat spiritual adultery with their breath and to stave off carnal adultery with swords, iron, fire, and the executioner's wheel. But is this not miserable conduct among Christians? Is it not a devilish thing that they have more regard for, and punish more severely, the dishonoring of man than the dishonoring of God? Moses orders that idolatrous people or spiritual adulterers be killed no less than carnal adulterers. If they looked at their Paul correctly, they would certainly find that Paul did not punish the servants of idols less than the servants of whores. Nor does it have to be true because they want to have it thus, to defend their honor and their reputation. . . .

The beeldenstorm, *or iconoclastic fury, in Antwerp (August 1566)*

Action should promptly and always follow understanding.

. . . Someone could question this as follows: "You want to obligate a servant of God always to act, etc. (Deuteronomy 4 and 11[:1]). There is good reason for this in that it is written, 'You shall always, your whole life long, act according to the law of God' (Tobit 4[:20]). You should always praise God: 'I will always praise God' (Psalm 34[:1]). 'Whoever is a friend always loves his friend' (Proverbs 17[:17]). A friend always shows his love by action, in the manner that Christ says, 'In this they will recognize that you are my disciple, that you love one another' (John 13[:35]). But on the other hand, I also see that it is written, 'Every action has its time' (Ecclesiastes 9[2]). No action can go on forever; it occurs for a time and then stops for a time. Also, God so ordained some commandments that we must keep them at certain times, and not our whole life long or every day, as the Hebrew understanding and you [Karlstadt] want to have it. Namely, God established the Sabbath on the seventh day, the seventh week, the seventh year, the fifteenth year, which came from the number seven. He also established for one time in the year the feast of Passover (Leviticus 25), for one time the feast of the

2. Karlstadt must mean Ecclesiastes 3.

Tabernacles, and the like. They must occur only at one time in the year and not every day."

My answer is that even if such figurative language bound us according to the letter, just as it formerly bound the Jews, nevertheless God's word would endure—namely this: "You should keep God's commandments every day" (Deuteronomy 11[:13]). For these words "every day" means that each person should keep God's commandments according to the time, place, and occasion that God has commanded. There is a time when we should awaken and be busy. There is a time for sleeping. If there are poor people, we should help. If we do not have needy people, our hand may rest. Nonetheless, we must act every day according to God's commandments. We must celebrate every seventh day, etc. We must always come to the assistance of the poor, the destitute, the imprisoned, the naked, and the like. We must forgive the debt of the impoverished if we have such debtors; if we do not have any, then God's law does not bind us. In the same way, the poor [among the Jews] were not obligated to make more expensive sacrifices than the rich. But nevertheless this endures: you should fulfill God's commandments every day. Every day you should actively show your neighbor your love of God and neighbor.

The same is true with respect to the abolition of blasphemous and Christ-blaspheming images [statues and pictures] or Masses. Where we who believe in God rule, and where we find images, we should remove them and deal with them as God commanded. We should also do this for our whole life, or every day. Yes, if we find images in our community—every community in every city—each community is in the same way responsible for distancing itself from images (Deuteronomy 14, 15). This principle must always be right and endure well: You should act every day according to God's commandments, and it is right and good when his commandments are correctly understood. . . .

Offense and love of neighbor are a devilish cloak for every evil.

It is unjust to use the pretext of not offending the weak and of brotherly love, and, under the appearance of not offending and of brotherly love, to practice idolatry. And to allow the Mass and other blasphemies to sprout and bloom. And I will deal with the significance of this issue in a little book that I am writing about giving offense.[3] But on this occasion I want to say that our images are laid out or erected in order to trap and entangle people, and for their ruination, as God has said through Moses and his prophets. In addition, idols are more dangerous in Christendom than whorehouses, and more suitable for committing spiritual adultery than any whore or rogue. Therefore, people do not practice brotherly love who, under the appearance of brotherly love, say that we should maintain idols (which the laity call saints) in the churches, on hills, in valleys, and at crossroads until the weak become strong. For they preach brotherly harm and not brotherly service or love. Such a pretext is nothing but a villain's cloak and a hidden snare for the destruction of poor souls—if God speaks truthfully and Paul teaches correctly. They speak and teach the contrary position in this matter of offending the weak.

We should take such harmful things from the weak, tear them out of their hands, and not pay attention if they cry, scream, or curse about it. The time will come when they who now curse and damn us will thank us. Through an analogy I will show you that he who would break the will of fools with violence would demonstrate toward them the true and best brotherly love. Isaiah says that fools who

3. This book was not published.

maintain idols do not understand their foolishness, and they do not know that they maintain a harmful, foolish thing. I want to say this first. Then I ask this: if I see that a small child has a pointed, sharp knife in his hand and wants to keep it, would I show him brotherly love if I were to allow him to have the harmful knife and have his own way, so that he wounds or kills himself? Or would I show brotherly love when I break his will and take the knife? You must always say that if you take from a child that which would harm him, then you perform a fatherly or brotherly Christian act. For Christ depicted for us genuine Christian and brotherly love in the scriptural passages where he says, "If your hand offends you, cut it off and throw it away" (Matthew 18[:8]). Christ said this in order to point out genuine brotherly love. And Paul agrees with Christ when he speaks about offending.

But if it is true that I am responsible, and that each one is obligated, if he loves God and his neighbor, to take from the foolish their harmful and offensive things without regard for their anger, howls, and curses, then why is there all this talk about brotherly love—that out of brotherly love we should allow idols and other offenses to remain until the weak follow? What they call brotherly love is actually brotherly harm and offense. Their love is like the love of a crazy mother who allows her children to go their own way—and to end on the gallows. Christ never said that we should proceed slowly with offenses if we want to remove them and cast them aside. He says, "Cut it off, chop it down, and throw it away, so that it does not offend you." Moses also says, "Your eye should not spare him, and you should not pity him or conceal him. Instead you should strangle him. Your hand should fall over him first" (Deuteronomy 13[:8-9] and 33[:9], Micah 7[:10]). Moses says this about people who offend. How much more, then, does this language compel the abolition of the offenses through which ignorant souls fall? Such souls have neither flesh nor spirit, neither blood nor breath, and no one may hope for their improvement. About them Moses will always say and cry out, "Spare them not! Kill them! Your hand should be the first!"

Now, whoever wants to add to these words and say that one should proceed slowly, not promptly, and that one should spare the weak and not begin suddenly, this person abuses the words of Christ and Moses. And he adds his own words in opposition to God, and he turns himself into a false Christian and false prophet. Christ says, "If your eye offends you"—that is, if you understand that your eye offends you—"tear it out and throw it away." When does he say, "Go slowly. Do not be too quick" or "Spare the weak"?

Oh, what great and pernicious blindness! If the world knew what harm comes to simple souls from idols and other offenses it would bite its fingers before it tolerated such fraud. But is it not a villain's cloak to preach and promise hellish brotherly harm under the appearance of brotherly love? Oh, devourers of the world! Christ says that it is better for you to chop your hand off, to tear your eye out, and to throw them away than for you to be thrown into the fires of hell with offensive things (Matthew 18[:8]). I have written in great detail about the damage that comes from maintaining devilish saints—i.e., those which our neighbors call saints and we call idols—against the miserable and wretched goat, Emser, but this writing was suppressed on account of the new papists.[4] But those who now read and understand the Bible note well how I have been oppressed by violence, contrary to God.

4. Karlstadt's work was suppressed by his colleagues in Wittenberg, the "new papists."

The devil has thought up this villain's cloak, just as he also invented the lie that "images are the laity's books."[5] For by this means the devil has thievishly robbed God's word of its honor. And he has given this honor to horrible, miserable, blaspheming creatures. And he has compared God's word to idolatrous filth, which God hates and wants us to hate and flee from. It cannot be expressed to what degree God is disgraced by idols and the weak person is destroyed by them. May a patron of idols step up and tell me why the servants of idols have a root that bears gall and wormwood (Exodus 23[:24.], Deuteronomy 29[:16ff.]). If they knew that, they would spit on themselves. (This is said as an aside.) Shame on you, you devastators of Scripture and head-hunters of souls! If as little danger and slight harm arose from idols as you assert, God would not have forbidden them so often through Moses and the prophets. Nor would he have said, "You will destroy yourselves if you make images or any representation," etc. (Deuteronomy 4[:15ff.]). God calls papal sophistry our destruction. But the servants of idols, contrary to God, call it an act of brotherly love. Look there! This is how they understand Paul, who says that the weak—that is, the unwise—perish as food for the idols (1 Corinthians 8[:10-11]).

God ordered the Jews to root out the heathen, their enemies, not in haste or quickly but at a leisurely pace, with measured time. Because of this, it does not follow that therefore Christians should also proceed at a slow, leisurely pace when they abolish offenses. . . .

A special clause follows which refers to the removal of offenses, and it reads thus: "You shall burn images of their gods with fire . . ." etc. (Deuteronomy 7[:25]). It is not written that one should proceed slowly, as asserted above. Rather, you shall ruin them immediately. It is written still more clearly earlier in the above-mentioned seventh chapter, namely, "You shall tear down their altars, destroy their pillars, chop down their leafy trees, and burn their idols" (Deuteronomy 7[:5]). When? Right away, at the time they are to destroy the heathen. Why? So that they do not learn to serve other gods. Or so that the idols do not make them "sin against me," says God (thus Exodus 23[:33]). For it would have contributed to their ruination if they let idols stand. . . .

Now, since God is sufficiently intelligent and adds to his words when and where one should proceed slowly and not suddenly, it is always a great sacrilege of Antichrist to rebuke God's intelligence and to add something to his words. This is especially true when the addition opposes the will of God and damages the soul of one's neighbor. It is a sacrilege to say, "Occasionally one should delay on account of the weak, and proceed slowly," when God has not said that we should proceed slowly or gradually. It is especially sacrilegious when through delay one brings the weak further from the way of truth and into greater error. It is written, "Cursed be he who makes a blind person stray from the path" (Deuteronomy 27[:18]). How much more is he cursed who makes a blind soul err about God's path or word? But each person does this who permits an offense, a mousetrap, or the bait of the devil, to stand in his brother's way. But blessed is he who tears away from his brother what causes his ruination, even against his will, and who grieves for him whom he wishes well, so that he benefits him. Just as a father angers his child, whom he loves, when he takes a sharp knife away from him.

[*The Radical Reformation*, ed. Michael Baylor, 49–50, 52, 57–61, 64–67, 70–71]

5. This was a common and venerable rationale for justifying images, which were thought to help the illiterate understand the history of redemption.

Selection 32: Thomas Müntzer, *Sermon to the Princes* (1524)

Thomas Müntzer viewed the Holy Spirit as the catalyst for a thoroughgoing revolution, and his apocalyptic message became a key inspiration for the German Peasant Revolt of 1524–1525, which he believed would usher in Christ's second coming. This sermon on Daniel 2, preached before Duke John and other magistrates in Allstedt on July 13, 1524, has been called "the high-water mark of torrential Revolutionary Spiritualist counterreformation directed against Luther."[6]

An Exposition of the Second Chapter of Daniel

Firstly. The text of the aforementioned chapter of prophecy of the prophet Daniel will be recounted and translated and thereupon the whole sermon will be set forth in harmony with the text, as follows.

It is known that poor, ailing, disintegrating Christendom can be neither counseled nor aided unless the diligent, untroubled servants of God daily work through the Scriptures, singing, reading, and preaching. But therewith the head of many a pampered priest will continuously have to suffer great blows or [he will] miss out in his handiwork. . . .

Yea, so nicely that the real friends of God are thereby misled; and even with the diligence of the most intense application, they are scarcely able to detect their error, as Matthew (ch. 24:24) clearly shows. This is what the simulated sanctity and the flattering absolution of the godless enemies of God accomplish. . . .

6. George Huntston Williams, *Spiritual and Anabaptist Writers* (Philadelphia: Westminster Press, 1957), 47.

Secondly. . . . Now follows the text [Dan. 2:1-13]: The king Nebuchadnezzar had a dream which is gone from him, etc.

What now should we say to this? It is an unspeakable, indeed uncommon, and odious matter to discuss the dreams of others. The reason is that the whole world has been from the beginning deceived by the interpreters of dreams, as it is written (Deut. 13:2-4; Ecclesiasticus 34:7). Therefore it is shown in this chapter (2) that the king did not wish to believe the clever soothsayers and interpreters of dreams, for he said [vv. 5ff.]: Tell me my dream, *then* the interpretation, otherwise you will be telling me nothing but deception and lies! Then what? They were unable and could not tell him the dream and said: O beloved king, there is not a man upon the earth that can tell thee the dream except the gods who have no fellowship with human beings on the earth. Of course, according to their understanding, they were speaking in a finite rational way. But they had no faith in God; they were, rather, godless hypocrites and flatterers, who there spoke what their masters gladly hear, just as the learned divines now do in our time, who very much like to eat the choice morsels at court. But what is written there in Jeremiah (chs. 5:13; 31 and 8:8f.) is against them. What else is [written] there! The text [of Daniel] says it would have to be men who would have fellowship in heaven! Oh, that is a bitter medicine for the clever! And yet Saint Paul will take it in the same sense in Philippians (ch. 3:20 [—our citizenship in heaven]). Nevertheless such wise men would like to explicate the mystery of God right off. Oh, of such rascals the world has enough, who openly arrogate this to themselves! . . .

Thirdly. . . . Therefore in short it is one's earnest conviction that we must *know*—and not merely be up in the air in our belief—whether what is given us be from God or from the devil or from nature. For if our natural understanding of the same [—what comes from God and what not—] ought to be captured for the service of faith (2 Cor. 10:5), it must arrive at the final degree in [its capacity for] judgment as is shown in Romans (ch. 1:18-23) and Baruch (ch. 3:12-37). Of these judgments one is incapable of proving any in good conscience without God's revelation. For man will clearly discover that he cannot run with his head through heaven but rather that he must first become wholly and utterly a fool (Isa. 29:13f.; 33:18; Obad. 1:8; 1 Cor. 1:18). O what a rare wind that is indeed then for the clever, fleshly, sensual world! Thereupon follow at once the pains like [those of] a woman in travail (Ps. 48:6; John 16:21). Therefore Daniel (ch. 2:17f.), and every single pious person along with him, finds that for him in all circumstances, exactly as for other ordinary people, it is impossible to search out all the things from God. This is what the wise man [the Preacher] means when he says (Eccl. 3:11): He who wishes to search out the majesty of God will be overwhelmed by his splendor. For the more nature gropes after God [to lay hold upon him], the further the operation of the Holy Spirit withdraws itself therefrom, as Ps. 139:6 clearly shows. Indeed if man were only aware of the presumption of the natural light [of reason], without doubt he would not seek improvised help with pilfered [passages of] Scripture, as the learned do with one or two little scraps (Isa. 28:10; Jer. 8:8), but rather he would soon feel the operation of the divine Word spring out of his own heart (John 4:14). Yea, he need not put up with the stagnant water in the well (Jer. 2:13), as our learned men now do. They mix up nature and grace without any distinction. They impede the progress of the Word (Ps. 119:11), which comes forth from the deeps of the soul, as Moses says (Deut. 30:14): The word is not far from thee, behold, it is in thy heart, etc. Now you may ask, How does it then come into the heart? Answer: It comes down from God above in exalted and terrifying astonishment, which I shall let stand as it is [to be discussed] another time.[7] And this astonishment as to whether it be God's word or not, commences when a child is six or seven years old as is signified in Num., ch. 19. Therefore Saint Paul cites Moses (Deut. 30:14) and Isaiah (ch. 65:1) in Rom. 10:8 and 20 and speaks there of the inner Word to be heard in the deeps of the soul through the revelation of God. And what person has not become aware of and receptive to this [Word] through the living testimony of God (Rom. 8:9). He [who has not the Spirit] does not know how to say anything deeply about God, even if he had eaten through a hundred Bibles! From that anybody can well judge how far the world really is from Christian faith. But no one wants to see or hear. . . .

Fourthly. . . . Indeed, it is a [mark of the] truly apostolic, patriarchal, and prophetic spirit to attend upon visions and to attain unto the same in painful tribulation. Therefore it is no wonder that Brother Fattened Swine and Brother Soft Life[8] rejects them (Job 28:12f.). If, however, a person has not hearkened to the clear Word of God in the soul, he must have visions, as when Saint Peter in the Acts of the Apostles failed to understand the law (Lev., ch. 11). He had doubts as to [the ritual cleanness] of food and as to whether to have [table] fellowship with pagans (Acts 10:10ff.). Thereupon God gave him a vision in a flush of emotion. There he saw a linen sheet with four corners let

7. This apparent marginalization of the written word in favor of a direct word from heaven, emphasized throughout this sermon and characteristic of some other Radical Reformers, led to the Anabaptists being labeled as "Schwärmer," fanatics.

8. That is, Martin Luther.

down from heaven to the earth, filled with four-footed animals, and heard a voice from heaven, saying: Kill and eat. Devout Cornelius had something of the same when he did not know how he [as a God fearer] should act (Acts 10:1ff.). Also when Paul came down to Troas, a vision appeared to him in the night. There was a man from Macedonia who stood and besought him, saying: Come over into Macedonia and help us. And after he had seen the vision, immediately we endeavored (says the text: Acts 16:8ff.) to journey toward Macedonia, for we were certain that the Lord had called us thither. Again, when Paul was afraid to preach in Corinth (Acts 18:9f.), the Lord said to him in the night by a vision: Be not afraid, etc. No man shall set on thee to hurt thee, for I have many people in this city, etc. And what need is there to bring forward much testimony from Scripture? It would never be at all possible in these far-flung dangerous matters which rightful preachers, dukes, and princes have [to deal with] that they would on all sides take heed to act securely and blamelessly, if they did not live within the revelation of God, as Aaron heard from Moses (Ex. 4:15), and David from Nathan and Gad (2 Chron. 29:25). For the same reason the beloved apostles were quite accustomed to visions, as the passage in Acts (ch. 12:7-9) demonstrates. When the angel came to Peter and led him out of the prison of Herod, and it seemed to him he was having a vision, he did not know that the angel was carrying out the work of salvation in him. Now if Peter had not been accustomed to visions, how did it happen then that he recognized he was having one? From this now I infer that whoever wishes, by reason of his fleshly judgment, to be utterly hostile about visions [and dreams] without any experience of them, rejecting them all, or [again, whoever] wishes to take them all in without any distinction (because the false dream interpreters have done so much harm to the world through those who think only of their own renown or pleasure)—that surely [*either* extremist] will have a poor run of it and will hurl himself against the Holy Spirit [of these Last Days (Joel 2:28)]. For God speaks clearly, like this text of Daniel, about the [eschatalogical] transformation of the world. He will prepare it in the Last Days in order that his name may be rightly praised. He will free it of its shame, and will pour out his Holy Spirit over all flesh and our sons and daughters shall prophesy and shall have dreams and visions, etc. For if Christendom is not to become apostolic (Acts 2:16ff.) in the way anticipated in Joel, why should one preach at all? To what purpose then the Bible with [its] visions?

It is true, and [I] know it to be true, that the Spirit of God is revealing to many elect, pious persons a decisive, inevitable, imminent reformation [accompanied] by great anguish, andcit must be carried out to completion. Defend oneself against it as one may, the prophecy of Daniel remains unweakened, even if no one believes it, as also Paul says to the Romans (ch. 3:3). This passage of Daniel is thus as clear as the sun, and the process of ending the fifth monarchy of the world is in full swing. . . .

[*Spiritual and Anabaptist Writers*, 49–50, 55–58, 61–63]

B. Anabaptists

Selection 33: Conrad Grebel, *Letter to Thomas Müntzer* (1524)

Conrad Grebel (ca. 1498–1526) initially was a supporter of Zwingli in Zurich. But after their growing estrangement, Grebel, along with other companions, addressed this letter to Müntzer on September 5, 1524, to find out

what his Swiss group might have in common with Müntzer and his program. Besides their mutual frustration with the slow reform of Luther and others, the Swiss group turned out to have little in common with Müntzer.

To the sincere and true proclaimer of the gospel, Thomas Müntzer at Allstedt in the Hartz, our true and beloved brother with us in Christ: May peace, grace, and mercy from God, our Father, and Jesus Christ, our Lord, be with us all. Amen.

Dear Brother Thomas:

. . . Just as our forebears fell away from the true God and from the one true, common, divine Word, from the divine institutions, from Christian love and life, and lived without God's law and gospel in human, useless, unchristian customs and ceremonies, and expected to attain salvation therein, yet fell far short of it, as the evangelical preachers have declared, and to some extent are still declaring, so today too every man wants to be saved by superficial faith, without fruits of faith, without baptism of trial and probation, without love and hope, without right Christian practices, and wants to persist in all the old manner of personal vices, and in the common ritualistic and anti-Christian customs of baptism and of the Lord's Supper, in disrespect for the divine Word and in respect for the word of the pope and of the antipapal preachers, which yet is not equal to the divine Word nor in harmony with it. In respecting persons and in manifold seduction there is grosser and more pernicious error now than ever has been since the beginning of the world. . . .

While we were marking and deploring these facts, thy book against false faith and baptism was brought to us,[9] and we were more fully informed and confirmed, and it rejoiced us wonderfully that we found one who was of the same Christian mind with us and dared to show the evangelical preachers their lack, how that in all the chief points they falsely forbear and act and set their own opinions, and even those of Antichrist, above God and against God, as befits not the ambassadors of God to act and preach. Therefore we beg and admonish thee as a brother by the name, the power, the word, the spirit, and the salvation, which has come to all Christians through Jesus Christ our Master and Saviour *(seligmacher),* that thou wilt take earnest heed to preach only the divine Word without fear, to set up and guard only divine institutions, to esteem as good and right only what may be found in pure and clear Scripture, to reject, hate, and curse all devices, words, customs, and opinions of men, including thy own.

(1.) We understand and have seen that thou hast translated the Mass into German and hast introduced new German hymns. That cannot be for the good, since we find nothing taught in the New Testament about singing, no example of it. Paul scolds the learned among the Corinthians more than he praises them, because they mumbled in meeting as if they sang, just as the Jews and the Italians chant their words song-fashion. (2.) Since singing in Latin grew up without divine instruction and apostolic example and custom, without producing good or edifying, it will still less edify in German and will create a faith of outward appearance only. (3.) Paul very clearly forbids singing in Eph. 5:19 and Col. 3:16 since he says and teaches that they are to speak to one another and teach one another with psalms and spiritual songs, and if anyone would sing, he should sing and give thanks in his heart. (4.) Whatever we are not taught by clear passages or examples must

9. Müntzer's book is *Protestation odder Empietung . . .unnd tzum Anfang von dem rechten Christen glawben, unnd der Tawffe* (Protestation or proposition about the beginning of true Christian faith and baptism) (1524).

be regarded as forbidden, just as if it were written: "This do not; sing not."[10] (5.) Christ in the Old and especially in the New Testament bids his messengers *(botten)* simply proclaim the word. Paul too says that the word of Christ profits us, not the song. Whoever sings poorly gets vexation by it; whoever can sing well gets conceit. (6.) We must not follow our notions; we must add nothing to the word and take nothing from it. (7.) If thou wilt abolish the Mass, it cannot be accomplished with German chants, which is thy suggestion perhaps, or comes from Luther. (8.) It must be rooted up by the word and command of Christ. (9.) For it is not planted by God. (10.) The Supper of fellowship Christ did institute and plant. (11.) The words found in Matt., ch. 26, Mark, ch. 14, Luke, ch. 22, and 1 Cor., ch. 11, alone are to be used, no more, no less. [12.] The server from out of the congregation should pronounce them from one of the Evangelists or from Paul. (13.) They are the words of the instituted meal of fellowship, not words of consecration. (14.) Ordinary bread ought to be used, without idols and additions. (15.) For [the latter] creates an external reverence and veneration of the bread, and a turning away from the inward. An ordinary drinking vessel too ought to be used. (16.) This would do away with the adoration and bring true understanding and appreciation of the Supper, since the bread is nought but bread. In faith, it is the body of Christ and the incorporation with Christ and the brethren. But one must eat and drink in the Spirit and love, as John shows in ch. 6 and the other passages, Paul in 1 Cor., chs. 10 and 11, and as is clearly learned in Acts, ch. 2. (17.) Although it is simply bread, yet if faith and brotherly love precede it, it is to be received with joy, since, when it is used in the church, it is to show us that we are truly one bread and one body, and that we are and wish to be true brethren with one another, etc. (18.) But if one is found who will not live the brotherly life, he eats unto condemnation, since he eats it without discerning, like any other meal, and dishonors love, which is the inner bond, and the bread, which is the outer bond. (19.) For also it does not call to his mind Christ's body and blood, the covenant of the cross, nor that he should be willing to live and suffer for the sake of Christ and the brethren, of the head and the members. (20.) Also it ought not to be administered by thee. That was the beginning of the Mass that only a few would partake, for the Supper is an expression of fellowship, not a Mass and sacrament. Therefore none is to receive it alone, neither on his deathbed nor otherwise. Neither is the bread to be locked away, etc., for the use of a single person, since no one should take for himself alone the bread of those in unity, unless he is not one with himself—which no one is, etc. (21.) Neither is it to be used in "temples" according to all Scripture and example, since that creates a false reverence. (22.) It should be used much and often. (23.) It should not be used without the rule of Christ in Matt. 18:15-18, otherwise it is not the Lord's Supper, for without that rule every man will run after the externals. The inner matter, love, is passed by, if brethren and false brethren approach or eat it [together]. (24.) If ever thou desirest to serve it, we should wish that it would be done without priestly garment and vestment of the Mass, without singing, without addition. (25.) As for the time, we know that Christ gave it to the apostles at supper and that the Corinthians had the same usage. We fix no definite time with us, etc.

Let this suffice, since thou art much better instructed about the Lord's Supper, and we only

10. In general, the Radical Reformers interpreted biblical silence regarding worship practices to be prohibitive, whereas Luther generally interpreted the silence as permissive.

state things as we understand them. If we are not in the right, teach us better. And do thou drop singing and the Mass, and act in all things only according to the Word, and bring forth and establish by the Word the usages of the apostles. If that cannot be done, it would be better to leave all things in Latin and unaltered and mediated [by a priest]. If the right cannot be established, do not then administer according to thy *own* or the priestly usage of Antichrist. And at least teach how it ought to be, as Christ does in John, ch. 6, and teaches how we must eat and drink his flesh and blood, and takes no heed of backsliding and anti-Christian caution, of which the most learned and foremost evangelical preachers have made a veritable idol and propagated it in all the world.[11] It is much better that a few be rightly taught through the Word of God, believing and walking aright in virtues and practices, than that many believe falsely and deceitfully through adulterated doctrine. . . .

On the matter of baptism thy book pleases us well, and we desire to be further instructed by thee. We understand that even an adult is not to be baptized without Christ's rule of binding and loosing. The Scripture describes baptism for us thus, that it signifies that, by faith and the blood of Christ, sins have been washed away for him who is baptized, changes his mind, and believes before and after; that it signifies that a man is dead and ought to be dead to sin and walks in newness of life and spirit, and that he shall certainly be saved if, according to this meaning, by inner baptism he lives his faith; so that the water does not confirm or increase faith, as the scholars at Wittenberg say, and [does not] give very great comfort [nor] is it the final refuge on the deathbed. Also baptism does not save, as Augustine, Tertullian, Theophylact, and Cyprian have taught, dishonoring faith and the suffering of Christ in the case of the old and adult, and dishonoring the suffering of Christ in the case of the unbaptized infants. We hold (according to the following passages: Gen. 8:21; Deut. 1:39; 30:6; 31:13; and 1 Cor. 14:20; Wisdom of Solomon 12:19; 1 Peter 2:2; Rom., chs. 1; 2; 7; 10 [allusions uncertain]; Matt. 18:1-6; 19:13-15; Mark 9:33-47; 10:13-16; Luke 18:15-17; etc.) that all children who have not yet come to the discernment of the knowledge of good and evil, and have not yet eaten of the tree of knowledge, that they are surely saved by the suffering of Christ, the new Adam, who has restored their vitiated life, because they would have been subject to death and condemnation only if Christ had not suffered; but they're not yet grown up to the infirmity of our broken nature—unless, indeed, it can be proved that Christ did not suffer for children. . . .

God be with us.

Whatever we have not understood correctly, inform and instruct us.

Given at Zurich on the fifth day of September in the year 1524.

Conrad Grebel, Andrew Castelberg, Felix Mantz, John Ockenfuss, Bartholomew Pur, Henry Aberli, and other brethren of thine in Christ, if God will, who have written this to thee, wish for thee and us all and all thy flock till further message and true word of God, true faith, love, and hope with all peace and grace from God through Jesus Christ. Amen.

I, C. Grebel, meant to write to Luther in the name of all of us, and to exhort him to cease from his [policy of] caution, which he uses without [authority of] Scripture and which he established in the world, and others after him. But my affliction and time would not permit. Do it according to your duty, etc.

11. See Karlstadt's denunciation of this kind of caution (Selection 31).

Postscript or Second Letter

Dearly beloved Brother Thomas:

When I had subscribed all our names in a hurry and had thought this messenger would not wait until we wrote to Luther too, he had to bide and wait on account of rain. So I wrote to Luther too, on behalf of my brethren and thine, and have exhorted him to cease from the false sparing of the weak, who are [really] themselves. Andrew Castelberg has written to Carlstadt. Meanwhile there has come here to Hans Hujuff of Halle, our fellow citizen and brother, who recently visited thee, a letter and shameful tract by Luther, which no man ought to write who wants to be first fruits like the apostles. Paul teaches differently: *porro servum Domini,* etc.[12] I see that he wants to have thee outlawed and deliver thee to the prince to whom he has tied his gospel, even as Aaron had to hold Moses as a god. . . .

[*Spiritual and Anabaptist Writers*, 73–77, 80–83]

Selection 34: Balthasar Hubmaier, *Freedom of Will* (1527)

Balthasar Hubmaier (ca. 1480–1528), onetime protégé of Johann Eck, was a minister and writer who, after joining the Anabaptists in 1525, became the foremost academic theologian of the early radical movements. He advocated persuasion instead of religious coercion in his work **On Heretics and Those Who Burn Them** ***(1524). Nevertheless, for his beliefs and teachings, he was arrested and burned at the stake and his wife drowned in Vienna in March 1528. He concluded his treatises with his motto: "Truth is immortal."***

12. That is, "but the servant of the Lord. . . ." Cf. 2 Tim. 2:24.

In this treatise, Hubmaier engages the controversial issue of free will. It was written in two parts (April 1 and May 20, 1527). The first section deals more with strictly theological issues, and the second with biblical texts. The influence of Erasmus's treatise on the same topic can be detected in the content and even the order of presentation. Although Hubmaier's theological sophistication was unusual among the early Anabaptists, his position on the topic of free will is typical of the radical movements.

To the majestic, highborn prince and lord, Lord George, Margrave at Branndenburg, ...

Although for several years great earnestness and diligence has been expended so that the gospel was preached to all creatures, I, nevertheless, unfortunately, find many people who to this point have learned and grasped no more than two pieces from all the preaching. First, one says: "We believe; faith saves us." Second, "We can do nothing good. God works in us the desire and the doing. We have no free will." Now, however, such remarks are only half-truths from which one can conclude no more than half-judgments. Whoever makes a whole judgment and does not lay the counter-Scriptures on the same scale next to it, to him a half-truth is more damaging than a whole lie. For when the half-truth is believed and sold under the appearance of a whole truth, then all sects, quarrels, and heresies result. They are only doing patchwork with the Scripture, not comparing opposing Scriptures and uniting both into a whole judgment.[13] Whoever does not divide the judgment in the Scripture in such a way eats of the unclean animals who do not part their hooves, Lev. 11:4. Indeed, under the cover of these aforementioned half-truths all kinds of

13. The assumption of the unity of Scripture was a basic hermeneutical principle in premodern biblical exegesis.

evil, disloyalty, and unrighteousness have fully and totally gotten the upper hand. Now all carelessness and impudence hang in the balance. There sit unfaithfulness and falsehood in their splendid throne, ruling and triumphing mightily in all things. No longer does any Christian work shine forth among all people. Brotherly love is extinguished in all hearts; and it has come to pass, as the prophet says, that truth has fallen to the ground in the streets and righteousness cannot enter anywhere, Isa. 59:14. Wisdom calls aloud and no one wants to hear her, Prov. 1:20. For it has come about (may it be faithfully lamented to God) that the world is now more evil than a thousand years ago, as all histories prove. All this happens, as painful as it is to say it, under the appearance of the gospel. For as soon as one says to them, "It is written: leave evil and do good," Ps. 37:27, they answer: "We can do no good. Everything happens out of the providence of God and from necessity." They imagine that by that they are permitted to sin. If one says further: "It is written: 'Whoever does evil will go into the eternal fire,'" John 5:29; Matt. 25:41, immediately they find a fan of fig leaves with which to cover their vices and they say: "Faith alone saves us and not our works." Yes, I have heard of many people who have not prayed, fasted, nor given alms for a long time, for their priests say that their works are of no value before God, wherefore they straightway neglect them. These are the half-truths under which we, as under the form of angels, protect all license of the flesh and blame all our sin and guilt on God, as Adam did on his Eve and Eve on the snake, Gen. 3:12. Yes, God must be responsible for all our vices, which is the greatest blasphemy on earth. . . .

The human being is a corporal and rational creature, created by God as body, spirit, and soul, Gen. 2:7. These three elements are found essentially and in varying ways in every human being, as the Scripture thoroughly proves.[14] When the Lord God made the human being out of the dust from the earth, he blew a living breath into his face and thus the human being became a living soul, Gen. 2:7. Here Moses points to three things with distinct names. First, the flesh or the body is made out of the earth, which clod of earth or lump of clay, *aphar* and *erets* in the Hebrew, is translated in German as "dust," "ashes," or "mud taken from the earth." Second, notice the living breath, *neshamah* in the Hebrew, translated as "blowing on," "breathing on," "blowing upon," or "spirit." Third, the soul, called *nephesh,* is expressed separately; it is that which makes the body alive. Saint Paul mentioned these three essential substances quite clearly also with special and distinctive Greek names in writing to the Thessalonians: *pneuma, psyche,* and *soma*; in Latin: *spiritus, anima, corpus*; in German: *Geist, Seel, Leib.* He said: "May he, the God of peace, sanctify you through and through and preserve your whole spirit, soul, and body without fault until our Lord Jesus Christ returns," 1 Thess. 5:23. . . . Here, Christian reader, you see bright and clear that these three special and essential substances—soul, spirit, and body—are made and unified in every human being according to the image of the Holy Trinity.

Now since with scriptural authority no one can deny these three essential things, substances, or essences, it follows that one must confess also three kinds of will in human beings, namely, the will of the flesh, the will of the soul, and the will of the spirit. However, so that I might teach in clear writing the different

14. Not only does Scripture use this language of a tripartite anthropology, but it is present in Platonism and Christian tradition, notably in Origen as well as Erasmus, the more immediate influence on Hubmaier (see Selection 9).

divisions of these three wills, the Spirit of God speaks in John 1:13 of the will of the flesh, which does not want to suffer; the will of the soul, willing to suffer, but due to the flesh seeks not to; and the will of the spirit which strongly desires to suffer (cf. John 1:13). In order that I might teach with clear writing the different divisions of these three wills, the Spirit of God through the disciple whom Christ especially loved, speaks these words of the true and eternal light which became human and came to his own and his own did not accept him. To as many as accepted him, he gave the power to become God's children. Yes, to those who believe in his name, who are born not of blood, nor out of the will of the flesh nor out of the will of man (thus is the soul called in Scripture) but out of God, John 1:13; 1 Sam. 10. Now we are once born, but in original sin and wrath, as Paul laments to the Romans and Ephesians, also David, Job and Jeremiah, Rom. 7:5; Eph. 2:3; Ps. 51:7; Job 3:1. Accordingly we must be born again or we cannot see the kingdom of God, nor enter it. We must be born of water and Spirit, that is, through the Word of God, which is water to all who thirst for salvation, which Word is made alive in us through the Spirit of God, without whose working it is a killing letter, Jer. 20:14; John 3:5, 4:14, 7:48; 2 Cor. 3:6; Rom. 8:13; Ps. 51:12; Deut. 8:3; Matt. 4:4. The same helps our spirit, bears witness to it, and strengthens it in the battle and strife against the flesh, sin, world, death, devil, and hell. To this end every word that proceeds out of the mouth of God helps the spirit so that the flesh with its evil will and lusts can nowhere flee, hide, or cover itself. It finds outwardly neither rest nor respite before the preached Word of God whose sound goes throughout the whole world, nor internally in the spirit for it is everywhere convicted Ps. 19:5; Mark 16:15; Acts 1:8; Rom. 10:18; Rom. 2:15. Since all testimony is proved in the mouth of two or three witnesses, thence comes the conscience and the gnawing worm into the heart of the human being.

That is the true rebirth of which Christ speaks in John 3:3, whereby our Adam, who had become a woman and an Eve through the Fall, now again becomes a man; and the soul, which had become flesh, now again becomes spirit. . . .

It is to be noted that the human being should be considered in three states or forms: first, how he had been before the Fall of Adam; second, how he became after the Fall; third, how he is after the restoration.

How the Human Being Was Before the Fall of Adam

Before the transgression of Adam all three substances in the human being—flesh, soul, and spirit—were good, Gen. 1:31. For God considered all the things which he had made and they were very good—indeed, especially the human being made in the image of God, Gen. 1:31. The three substances were also wholly free to choose good or evil, life or death, heaven or hell. Thus they were originally made good and free also in the recognition, in the capability, and performance of good and evil by God, as the Scripture itself testifies and says: "God made the human being from the beginning and left him free in the power of his own counsel," Ecclesiasticus 15:14ff. He gave him the commandments and the law and said: "If you will to keep the commandments" (God says: If you, man, will, it is given to you to keep the commandments), "then they will preserve you." He has set water and fire before you (note: you); you have only to stretch out your hand to the one you want. Before the human being are life and death, good and evil; whatever pleases him (yes, him) is given to him. Here the Scripture[15] clearly and plainly shows us that the human being originally, in body, soul, and spirit, was given a free will to will and to perform good or evil. However, after the transgression of Adam, it has become otherwise for him.

How the Human Being Has Become After the Fall of Adam Concerning the Flesh

After our first father Adam transgressed the commandment of God by his disobedience, he lost this freedom for himself and all his descendants. Likewise, if a nobleman receives a fief from a king and if he acts against the king, the king will take this fief from the nobleman and all his heirs, for they must all carry the guilt of their forefather. Thus the flesh has irretrievably lost its goodness and freedom through the Fall of Adam and has become entirely and wholly worthless and hopeless unto death. It is not able or capable of anything other than sin, striving against God and being the enemy of his commandments. . . .

Concerning the Spirit

The spirit of the human being, however, has before, during, and after the Fall remained upright, whole, and good. For it has neither with counsel nor deed, will nor action, been disobedient in any way in allowing the flesh to eat the forbidden fruit. Indeed, like a prisoner in the body, it had to eat against its will. However, the guilt was not its own, but that of the flesh and the soul, which also became flesh. This wholeness and uprightness of the spirit Saint Paul already demonstrates clearly in writing to the Thessalonians: "And may your whole spirit and soul and body be held blameless until the coming of our Lord Jesus Christ," 1 Thess. 5:23. He says, "Your whole spirit" and not "your whole soul," or "your whole body." For what has once disintegrated and been shattered is no longer whole. . . .

Concerning the Soul

However, the soul, the third part of the human being, has through this disobedience of Adam been wounded in the will in such a way and become sick unto death so that it can on its own choose nothing good. Nor can it refuse evil since it has lost the knowledge of good and evil. Gen. 2; 3. There is nothing left to it but to sin and to die. Yes, as far as doing good goes, the soul has become entirely powerless and ineffective, Rom. 7. Only the flesh can act, without which the soul is outwardly able to do nothing, for the flesh is its instrument. Since, however, the instrument is incapable of doing anything, how can anything good be done with it, even if the soul gladly wanted to and made every effort. Nevertheless this Fall of the soul is reparable through the Word of God, Ps. 119:7. . . .[16]

That, however, this Fall of the soul is also reparable and harmless here on earth, while that of the flesh irreparable and even deadly, is due to the following: Adam, a figure of the soul—as Eve is a figure of the flesh—would have preferred not to eat of the forbidden tree, 1 Tim. 2:14. He was not seduced by the snake but Eve was, Gen. 3:6. Adam knew well that the word of the serpent contradicted the Word of God. Nevertheless, he willed to eat of this fruit against his own conscience in order not to grieve or anger his rib and flesh, Eve. He would have preferred not to do it. Thus, since he was more obedient to his Eve than to God, he lost

15. Hubmaier considers Ecclesiasticus (that is, the Wisdom of Ben-Sira), part of the so-called Apocrypha, to be Scripture.

16. It is typical, especially after Augustine, to distinguish human nature before the fall, after the fall, and after regeneration. It is less common to distinguish effects peculiar to each part of the human nature, as Hubmaier does here.

the knowledge of good and evil. So he cannot will or choose good, nor can he not will or flee something evil, for he does not know what is truly good or evil before God, Ps. 14:3; 32:5; 53:2. Nothing tastes good to him but that which tastes and seems good to his Eve, that is, his flesh. For he has lost the right sense of taste.

A parable: a wounded or feverish person neither wants nor likes to eat or drink something good and healthy. Only cold water and harmful food taste good to him. That happens because his healthy nature and whole constitution have been disordered by sickness, for he has lost the right and healthy taste of knowledge. He has an embittered tongue so that he judges to be good what is harmful to him and to be evil what is useful. Just so is it with our soul after the transgression of Adam. As soon as he ate from the tree of the knowledge: of good and evil, from that hour on he lost the taste of the knowledge of good and evil so that he can neither know nor judge what is right, good, or evil before God, what righteousness is sufficient before God, or what works are pleasing to God; all this even though he would gladly do right according to the spirit. This desire is still present today in all people, in Jews and heathen, as Paul writes to the Romans, Rom. 2:14. Indeed, if one is blind, he would gladly see.

If one is lame, then he would gladly go upright. Has one fallen among murderers, wounded and half dead, then he would gladly be whole again. However, as to the right way, truth, and means for coming to this health of the soul, all err who are not instructed by the Word of God. From this now follow all deviations, false doctrine, error, idolatry, and heresy, Ps. 119:11. . . .

In summary: Here you see, reader, how God created the human being so free that he was at first able without new grace to remain in his inborn innocence and righteousness unto eternal life. He could also forfeit this grace through disobedience, which is what happened. As a result, through the Fall, grace and freedom have been darkened and lost to such a degree that the human being does not know any longer what is good or evil without a special and new grace of God. How can one will to do good and avoid evil if one cannot will anything good, unless one has recognized it beforehand. However, after the restoration, the human being has acquired and again received such grace, health, and freedom through the merits of our Lord Jesus Christ that one can now again will the good and do it, indeed against the nature and will of the flesh in which there is nothing good.

In the third place: since free will in the human being is nothing other than a power, force, energy, or adroitness of the soul to will or not will something, to choose or flee, to accept or to reject good or evil, according to the will of God, or according to the will of the flesh, which fleshly will and potentiality should more exactly be called an impotence rather than a power or energy. But the soul, through the eating of the forbidden tree lost the recognition of good and evil in the sight of God, which knowledge it certainly had before the Fall, as far as it was necessary and sufficient for a human creature to know. Therefore that same tree was called a tree of the knowledge of good and evil from which God forbade Adam to eat, Gen. 2:17, that is, to desire, know, and experience more than is necessary for a human being. For Eve wanted also to know everything that God knows, as promised to her by the crafty serpent. "On the day they eat thereof, their eyes will open and they will become as gods, knowing good and evil," Gen. 3:5. Accordingly they were rightly removed and robbed of this knowledge of good and evil by God and have become as a horse and a mule in whom there is no understanding.[17] . . .

For that is the grace and favor of God which he bears to us and with which he embraces us: that power which he offers us through his preached Word, so that we—it lies now in our power—can become children of God, also desire and complete his fatherly will and please him, John 1:12; Rev. 3:20.

Grace comes to us, not out of us, so that no one boasts in himself but in the merits of our Lord Jesus Christ, 1 Cor. 1:4. For our flesh and blood cannot reach such sonship out of their own power, John 1:12; Matt. 16:17; 1 Cor. 15:50.

Since, however, this sonship is offered to all people equally, for the seed of the divine Word falls equally in four kinds of earth, it follows that we have the equal power to accept the seed and to bear fruit, John 1:12; Matt. 28:19; Mark 16:15; Matt. 13:3ff.; Mark 4:3ff. If we do not do that, then it is not God who is guilty, or his seed, but the evil of] the earth, that is, we ourselves. . . .

"Like the division of the water, so is the heart of the king in the hand of the Lord," Proverbs 21:1.

Here my friend Zophar is of the opinion that what the king does he does out of necessity, for his heart is not in his own power but in the hand of the Lord. I am most amazed that he and others of my friends cite such Scriptures which do not serve them at all. For it is well known that Solomon here masters and kills the wrath and anger of the queen, teaching her to be merciful and mild, for, as the general proverb states, if they want to tyrannize too strongly then Jesus will appear to them on the way and knock them down himself, as it happened also to Paul and the prophet Balaam, Acts 9:4; Num. 22:21ff. Therefore, however, freedom of the will is not taken away from all people or in all things. For the exceptional case does not rob the general truth of the Scriptures.

"Without me you can do nothing," John 15:5.

Yes, it is so, dear friend, that without God we do not know what is good; how then could we do it without him, for our spirit is imprisoned, our soul wounded, our body killed, Gen. 2; 3. But if we remain in the vine, that is, in the knowledge of his divine Word, the same will teach us what we will, should do, and are able to do, John 15:5ff. . . .

[*Balthasar Hubmaier: Theologian of Anabaptism*, trans. Pipkin and Yoder (Scottdale, PA: Herald Press, 1989), 427–36, 443, 468, 486–87]

Selection 35: *Schleitheim Confession* (1527)

Michael Sattler (ca. 1490–1527) presided over a meeting of Anabaptists at Schleitheim on February 24, 1527. The group, with Sattler as the primary author, drew up seven articles distinct to their movement. This document summarizes their rationale for rejecting infant baptism, adhering to pacifism, and refusing to participate in civil government and court proceedings. Paedobaptism was seen as a papal innovation. War was thought to be forbidden by Christ's teaching in the Sermon on the Mount and, like other practices eschewed by the Anabaptists, driven by nothing but worldly concerns. Particularly on these distinctive Anabaptist beliefs, this document is succinct but representative of Anabaptist teaching.

The articles we have dealt with, and in which we have been united, are these: baptism, ban, the breaking of bread, separation from abomination, shepherds in the congregation, the sword, the oath.

17. Cf. Ps. 32:9.

i. Notice concerning baptism. Baptism shall be given to all those who have been taught repentance and the amendment of life and [who] believe truly that their sins are taken away through Christ, and to all those who desire to walk in the resurrection of Jesus Christ and be buried with him in death, so that they might rise with him; to all those who with such an understanding themselves desire and request it from us; hereby is excluded all infant baptism, the greatest and first abomination of the pope. For this you have the reasons and the testimony of the writings and the practice of the apostles. We wish simply yet resolutely and with assurance to hold to the same.

ii. We have been united as follows concerning the ban.[18] The ban shall be employed with all these who have given themselves over to the Lord, to walk after [him] in his commandments; those who have been baptized into the one body of Christ, and let themselves be called brothers or sisters, and still somehow slip and fall into error and sin, being inadvertently overtaken. The same [shall] be warned twice privately and the third time be publicly admonished before the entire congregation according to the command of Christ (Matthew 18). But this shall be done according to the ordering of the Spirit of God before the breaking of bread, so that we may all in one spirit and in one love break and eat from one bread and drink from one cup.

iii. Concerning the breaking of bread, we have become one and agree thus: all those who desire to break the one bread in remembrance of the broken body of Christ and all those who wish to drink of one drink in remembrance of the shed blood of Christ, they must beforehand be united in the one body of Christ, that is, the congregation of God, whose head is Christ, and that by baptism. For as Paul indicates, we cannot be partakers at the same time of the table of the Lord and the table of devils.[19] Nor can we at the same time partake and drink of the cup of the Lord and the cup of devils. That is: all those who have fellowship with the dead works of darkness have no part in the light. Thus all who follow the devil and the world, have no part with those who have been called out of the world unto God. All those who lie in evil have no part in the good. . . .

iv. We have been united concerning the separation that shall take place from the evil and the wickedness which the devil has planted in the world, simply in this: that we have no fellowship with them, and do not run with them in the confusion of their abomination. So it is; since all who have not entered into the obedience of faith and have not united themselves with God so that they will to do his will, are a great abomination before God; therefore nothing else can or really will grow or spring forth from them than abominable things. Now there is nothing else in the world and all creation than good or evil, believing and unbelieving, darkness and light, the world and those who are [come] out of the world, God's temple and idols, Christ and Belial, and none will have part with the other. . . .

Further, [the Lord] admonishes us therefore to go out from Babylon and from the earthly Egypt, that we may not be partakers in their torment and suffering, which the Lord will bring upon them. . . .

Thereby shall also fall away from us the diabolical weapons of violence—such as sword, armor, and the like, and all of their use to protect friends or against enemies—by virtue of the word of Christ: "you shall not resist evil."

v. We have been united as follows concerning shepherds in the church of God. The

18. That is, church discipline, which bans from fellowship.

19. See 1 Cor. 10:21.

shepherd in the church shall be a person according to the rule of Paul, fully and completely, who has a good report of those who are outside the faith.[20] The office of such a person shall be to read and exhort and teach, warn, admonish, or ban in the congregation, and properly to preside among the sisters and brothers in prayer, and in the breaking of the bread, and in all things to take care of the body of Christ, that it may be built up and developed, so that the name of God might be praised and honored through us, and the mouth of the mocker be stopped.

He shall be supported, wherein he has need, by the congregation which has chosen him, so that he who serves the gospel can also live therefrom, as the Lord has ordered. But should a shepherd do something worthy of reprimand, nothing shall be done with him without the voice of two or three witnesses. If they sin they shall be publicly reprimanded, so that others might fear. . . .

vi. We have been united as follows concerning the sword. The sword is an ordering of God outside the perfection of Christ. It punishes and kills the wicked, and guards and protects the good. In the law the sword is established over the wicked for punishment and for death, and the secular rulers are established to wield the same. . . .

Now many, who do not understand Christ's will for us, will ask whether a Christian may or should use the sword against the wicked for the protection and defense of the good, or for the sake of love.

The answer is unanimously revealed: Christ teaches and commands us to learn from him, for he is meek and lowly of heart, and thus we shall find rest for our souls. Now Christ says to the woman who was taken in adultery, not that she should be stoned according to the law of his Father (and yet he says, "What the Father commanded me, that I do"), but with mercy and forgiveness and the warning to sin no more, says: "Go, sin no more." Exactly thus should we also proceed, according to the rule of the ban.

Second, is asked concerning the sword whether a Christian shall pass sentence in disputes and strife about worldly matters, such as the unbelievers have with one another. The answer: Christ did not wish to decide or pass judgment between brother and brother concerning inheritance, but refused to do so. So should we also do.

Third, is asked concerning the sword whether the Christian should be a magistrate if he is chosen thereto. This is answered thus: Christ was to be made king, but he fled and did not discern the ordinance of his Father. Thus we should also do as he did and follow after him, and we shall not walk in darkness. For he himself says: "Whoever would come after me, let him deny himself and take up his cross and follow me." He himself further forbids the violence of the sword when he says, "The princes of this world lord it over them etc., but among you it shall not be so." Further Paul says: "Whom God has foreknown, the same he has also predestined to be conformed to the image of his Son," etc. Peter also says: "Christ has suffered (not ruled) and has left us an example, that you should follow after in his steps."

Lastly one can see in the following points that it does not befit a Christian to be a magistrate: the rule of the government is according to the flesh, that of the Christians according to the spirit. Their houses and dwelling remain in this world; that of the Christians is in heaven. Their citizenship is in this world; that of the Christians is in heaven. The weapons of their battle and warfare are carnal and only against the flesh, but the weapons of Christians are spiritual, against the fortification of the devil.

20. See 1 Tim. 3:7.

The worldly are armed with steel and iron, but Christians are armed with the armor of God, with truth, righteousness, peace, faith, salvation, and with the Word of God. In sum: as Christ our Head is minded, so also must be minded the members of the body of Christ through him, so that there be no division in the body, through which it would be destroyed. Since then Christ is as is written of him, so must his members also be the same, so that his body may remain whole and unified for its own advancement and upbuilding. For any kingdom which is divided within itself will be destroyed.

vii. We have been united as follows concerning the oath. The oath is a confirmation among those who are quarreling or making promises. In the law it is commanded that it should be done only in the name of God, truthfully and not falsely. Christ, who teaches the perfection of the law, forbids his [followers] all swearing, whether true or false; neither by heaven nor by earth, neither by Jerusalem nor by our head; and that for the reason which he goes on to give: "For you cannot make one hair white or black." You see, thereby all swearing is forbidden. We cannot perform what is promised in swearing, for we are not able to change the smallest part of ourselves.

Now there are some who do not believe the simple commandment of God and who say, "But God swore by himself to Abraham, because he was God (as he promised him that he would do good to him and would be his God if he kept his commandments). Why then should I not swear if I promise something to someone?" The answer: hear what Scripture says. "God, since he wished to prove over-abundantly to the heirs of his promise that his will did not change, inserted an oath so that by two immutable things we might have a stronger consolation (for it is impossible that God should lie)." Notice the meaning of the passage: God has the power to do what he forbids you, for everything is possible to him. God swore an oath to Abraham, Scripture says, in order to prove that his counsel is immutable. That means: no one can withstand and thwart his will; thus he can keep his oath. But we cannot, as Christ said above, hold or perform our oath; therefore we should not swear. . . .

Others say, if it is then wrong to use God for truth, then the apostles Peter and Paul also swore. Answer: Peter and Paul only testify to that which God promised Abraham, whom we long after have received. But when one testifies, one testifies concerning that which is present, whether it be good or evil. Thus Simeon spoke of Christ to Mary and testified: "Behold: this one is ordained for the falling and rising of many in Israel and to be a sign which will be spoken against."

Christ taught us similarly when he says: Your speech shall be yea, yea; and nay, nay; for what is more than that comes of evil. He says, your speech or your word shall be yes and no, so that no one might understand that he had permitted it.[21] Christ is simply yea and nay, and all those who seek him simply will understand his Word. Amen.

[*The Legacy of Michael Sattler* (Scottdale, PA: Herald Press, 1973), 36–42]

Selection 36: Menno Simons, *Christian Baptism* (1539)

Menno Simons here explains the Anabaptist position on their most controversial doctrine. Like Zwingli, Menno rejects the notion that salvation is tied to the external rite of

21. See Matt. 5:37.

baptism. Unlike Zwingli, however, Menno denies that infants are the proper candidates for baptism. Toward the document's end, he pleads for toleration.

Beloved readers, in our first publication concerning baptism[22] we have with Christian truth satisfied the desire of every pious Christian. Yet there are some frivolous, rebellious, and carnal persons who, without cause and Scripture, and in every respect without the fear of God, teach, write, admonish, and cry out against us, saying, It is heresy and deceit; for it is written and taught contrary to the learned, and against the doctrine of the holy, Christian church. . . .

[I.] Explanation of Christian Baptism

Hear ye now, O illustrious, noble, wise lords and princes! Listen, all judges of the land, where the sword of God is given to the destruction of evildoers, to the protection of the good, and to the punishment of the wicked. Hear, ye wise and prudent who think that you bear the vessels of the Lord. Hear all ye people of whatever state, condition, trade, or class, who call yourselves Christian, and who boast of His bitter death and precious blood.

[A. Baptism Occasions Our Being Persecuted]

Since we, for the sake of baptism, are so miserably abused, slandered, and persecuted by all men, and since we are ever suspicioned because of the ungodly sects (which are to you very harmful, perilous, and abominable, as may be plainly seen); therefore we say and testify in Christ Jesus, before God, before His holy angels, before you, and before the whole world that we are driven only by a God-fearing faith which we have in the Word of God to baptize and to be baptized, and by nothing else; nor will it be found otherwise, neither in this life, nor in death, nor in the last judgment of God.

My dear sirs, we seek nothing in this baptism other than to obey our beloved Lord Jesus Christ, who has taught and commanded us this with His own blessed mouth. Matt. 28:19; Mark 16:16. . . .

How could Abraham, Isaac, and Jacob together with all the dear fathers and patriarchs have obtained the comforting promise of God, if they had not done, be it ever so little, that which God had commanded them through His holy Word? But they heard the Word of God, firmly believed and carefully obeyed it; and therefore they became joint heirs of righteousness. Heb. 11:8.

On the other hand, however, all those who did not obey God undoubtedly have had to bear the punishment of the Lord, such as Adam and Eve; Nadab and Abihu; Korah, Dathan, and Abiram; as Saul; as the man of God who reproved Jeroboam the king for his idolatry and was deceived by the old prophet in Bethel, and other instances which may be read of in Moses and other Scriptural writings.

Since we are so sadly opposed by all men in regard to our doctrine and practice of Christian baptism, and since they do not realize that their opposition tends to eternal death, for they oppose Christ and His Word; therefore I will again briefly show from God's Word to them and all persons who shall read, see, or hear these my writings, how wonderfully, powerfully; nay, how incontrovertibly this our doctrine and practice is contained and founded on the holy Gospel of Jesus Christ—although we have fully shown and proved this before in our writings on baptism.

22. It is not clear whether Menno is referring to a now unknown writing or to a known document that also discusses baptism.

[B. Why We Practice Believer's Baptism]

Beloved, that our faith accepts this baptism under such a heavy cross and distress is because it is driven to it by three considerations. First because of the divine commandment of our beloved Lord Jesus Christ, a commandment which can never be broken. Second, because of the teachings of the holy apostles. Third, because of the practice of these same apostles. . . .

[III.] The Teachings of the Holy Apostles Concerning Baptism by Water

We are urged by the pure, chaste teaching of the holy apostle diligently to teach and accept this Christian baptism. First, because it is written, Now when they heard this, they were pricked in their hearts, and said unto Peter, Men and brethren, what shall we do? Then Peter said unto them, Repent and be baptized, every one of you, in the name of Jesus Christ for the remission of sins, and ye shall receive the gift of the Holy Ghost. Acts 2:37, 38.

Dearest friends, impress this upon yourselves both now and all the days of your lives, not only concerning baptism, but concerning all doctrine you may hear, lest you be deceived by false teachers. Namely, that even as all the true prophets of God, who were between Moses and Christ, conformed their teachings to the doctrine of Moses, so the holy apostles have conformed their teaching to the doctrine of Christ Jesus, as He had commanded them, saying, Teaching them to observe all things whatsoever I have commanded you. Matt. 28:20.

Therefore consider and ponder well that which shall be taught you by the grace of the Lord, from the Word of God, and you will perceive from the words of Peter how the words of Jesus to Nicodemus, concerning the new birth, should be understood: Verily, verily, I say unto thee, Except a man be born of water and of the Spirit, he cannot enter into the kingdom of God. John 3:5. Dear brethren, the new birth is effected by the Word of God. I Pet. 1:3; Jas. 1:19. . . .

Observe, my elect brethren, how harmonious are both Master and disciples in their teaching, namely, first the birth from above, by which we become children of God (John 1:14); and then the water, by which the obedience of the children of God is signified. Third, the communion of the Holy Ghost, by which we are assured in our hearts of the grace of God, of the remission of sins, and of everlasting life through Christ Jesus our Lord.

Inasmuch as the holy Peter, who is the apostle of God, a true witness sent by Jesus Christ with the words of everlasting life, and who was enlightened and taught by the Holy Ghost, has thus taught and commanded us, namely, that we shall have ourselves baptized, seeing that we believe according to the commandment of the Lord; and in the name of Christ for the remission of sins: therefore we must receive this baptism, even as it is commanded us in the holy Scriptures. Otherwise we cannot obtain remission of our sins nor the Holy Ghost. For who has ever received remission of sins contrary to the Word of God? Surely we cannot take the remission of sins and the Holy Ghost from God as by force. . . .

Here it avails nothing that some teach and say, contrary to the holy Scriptures, that the little children are born of Adam, with a sinful or wicked nature, and that therefore they should be washed of their original guilt and sin by baptism. To teach and believe thus, my brethren, is first of all a dangerous idolatry and an abominable blasphemy against the blood of Christ. There is no remedy in heaven nor on earth for our sins, whether original or actual other than the blood of Christ, as we have shown in our first writings. I Pet. 1:19; I John 1:7; Eph. 1:7. If we ascribe the remission of sins to baptism and not to the blood of Christ, then we mold a golden calf and place it in the stead of Christ. . . .

Those who believe receive remission of sins, not through baptism but in baptism, and in this manner. Since they now sincerely believe the blessed Gospel of Jesus Christ which has been preached and taught to them, the glad tidings of grace; namely, of the remission of sin, of grace, of peace, of favor, of mercy, and of eternal life through Jesus Christ our Lord; so they become a new mind, deny themselves, bitterly lament their old corrupted life, and look diligently to the Word of God, who has shown them such great love, to fulfill all that which He has taught and commanded them in His holy Gospel; trusting firmly in the word of grace, in the remission of their sins through the crimson blood and through the merits of our beloved Lord Jesus Christ. . . .

Observe, dear friends, here is the whole matter. We are not cleansed by the washing of the water, but by the Word of the Lord, as the holy Paul clearly teaches us in the before-mentioned words. . . .

Brethren, judge rightly and do not deceive your souls. We know that they say infants are cleansed of their original sin, and that therefore their baptism is not in vain. To this we reply with the Word of God: that such belief is an abominable idolatry, for only the blood of Christ avails, and not the outward baptism, as has been shown above.

In the second place they say that thereby they are accepted into the covenant of God. And we reply, that is not because of baptism, but only through the gracious election of grace (Eph. 1:6); for it is grace and not merit (Rom. 11:6).

In the third place they say that children should be baptized in order that they might the better be trained in the Word of God and His commandments. We reply that we desire to know where such is expressed and written in the holy Scriptures. . . .[23]

Because this infant baptism is nowhere commanded nor implied in the divine Word, therefore we testify before you and all the world that we have no regard for it, but believe and proclaim it to be idolatrous, useless, and empty, and we do this, not only with words, but also at the cost of our lives, as has been proved by events in many Germanic lands. The reason is this. It is administered without the Word and commandment of God; righteousness is sought therein; and because of this infant baptism the true baptism of Jesus Christ, that is, believer's baptism, is so lamentably rejected and trampled upon by all men as an heretical baptism, as far as the name of Christ is mentioned. . . .

O Lord and Father, how very broad, soft, and pleasing to the flesh is the entrance into this miserable, carnal church; for in her this takes place, no matter who or what or how he is. It is all right if he has only been exorcised before a font, and washed and baptized by a magic-dealing idolater. But how wonderfully narrow, O Lord, is Thy way, and how very strait is the gate which leadeth into Thy poor and holy church.[24] So narrow that on its doorposts are made to hang gold and goods, flesh and blood, all the lust and inclinations of those who desire and sincerely seek to enter in at this narrow gate; and so by Thy grace to rest and remain forever in Thy holy church. . . .

Since then an unbelieving man cannot be surety before God for the faith of another, nor teach him faith, nor intercede for it, therefore (even if the institution of godfathers were

23. The devotion to the Bible as the only source of doctrine and practice is reflected clearly in Menno's argument against infant baptism.

24. See Matt. 7:13-14.

founded on the ordinance of God, which however it is not) it must be acknowledged and admitted that the practice of godfathers in infant baptism is entirely vain, useless, and empty. I will leave it to every intelligent Christian to judge what kind of faith there is in the godfathers themselves.

I know that I will be asked if there are no good, believing godfathers who with good consciences can present the children for baptism. To this I answer quite unequivocally: No. For in the first place, it is human righteousness, contrary to the Word of God and without the ordinance of Christ; and therefore it cannot be practiced with a good conscience. In the second place, I admit that there are godfathers who are honorable and virtuous, but truly I do not know that they believe correctly; for if they did, it would be impossible for them ever to be led to practice such abominable shame with infants, without the Word of Christ. . . .

And so you have presented to you, first, the parents of whom the children are born, with their unbelief and carnal life; secondly, the godfathers, together with their abuses, unbelief, and evil fruits, those who present the children at the font for baptism and answer for their confession; and thirdly, the teachers or baptizers together with their calling, doctrine, idolatry, unbelief, and ungodly works, who baptize the infants as they say, to cleanse and wash them of their original sin. And now all three of these, namely, parents, godfathers, and baptizers, do not themselves know in their hearts either knowledge or faith, or truth, or love, or fear of God, or Gospel, or Christian fruits, or obedience, or remission of sins, or peace of mind, or prayer, or promise, or God, or Christ, or Spirit, or eternal life; but are only Christian in name and boast. These presume to make a Christian out of a child just born, which can neither stand nor walk, hear nor speak, understand nor comprehend, for lack of understanding, as irrational as the animals, unable to distinguish between good and bad, without the Word and without faith, by no other means than by crucifixes, breathings, by salt, oil, chrisms, candles, cloths, empty questions and answers, blessings, exorcisms, baptizings, offerings, and such like abominations. And when this loquacious, idolatrous sham has been practiced upon the infants, then they are Christian people as the nurses tell the mother after these things have been performed saying, We have received from you a heathen but a Christian we return and deliver to you again. . . .

Inasmuch as Christ Jesus has commanded but one baptism, namely, believer's baptism, and since the apostles have taught and practiced it; therefore those who defend infant baptism must consent and admit, driven by the Word of God, that infant baptism is not by the commandment of Christ, not by the teaching and practice of the holy apostles, but by the doctrine of Antichrist and by the practice of his preachers. . . .

Yet you should know and acknowledge, O dear noble, illustrious lords, ye judges and officers of the law, that as often as you take, condemn, and put to the sword such people, that you thrust your tyrannical sword into the blessed flesh of the Lord Jesus Christ, that you break the bones of His holy body, for they are flesh of His flesh and bone of His bone. Eph. 5:30. . . .

Why? Because they have by the operation of their faith and led by the Holy Spirit heartily committed themselves to the service of our beloved Lord Jesus Christ. They do not live any more according to their lusts but in conformity to the will of God alone as indicated in His holy, blessed Word. . . .

Therefore we pray you, as our beloved and gracious rulers according to the flesh, by the mercy of God, to consider and realize if there be reasonableness in you, in what great anxiety and anguish we poor, miserable people are placed. If we abandon Christ Jesus and His holy Word, we fall into the wrath of God. And if we remain firm in His holy Word, then we are put to your cruel sword. O Lord, if it were true that this vast church were Thy holy church, bride, and body as they boast it to be, then we might truthfully assert that Thou art the prince, bridegroom, and head of an abominable, detestable band of murderers who seek after the innocent blood of those who sincerely seek, fear, love, and serve God. . . .

[*The Complete Writings of Menno Simons*, trans. Leonard Verduin and ed. J. C. Wenger (Scottdale, PA: Herald Press), 231, 236–37, 243–45, 249, 252, 254, 256–57, 276, 285]

Selection 37: *The Trial and Martyrdom of Michael Sattler* (1527)

Four accounts of Michael Sattler's trial and martyrdom are extant. After his arrest by Austrian authorities, Sattler was brought to trial on May 17, 1527. He was killed three or four days later, and then his wife was drowned two days after his death.

After many legal transactions on the day of his departure from this world, the articles against him being many, Michael Sattler . . . requested that they might once more be read to him and that he might again be heard upon them. This the bailiff, as the attorney [for the defense] of his lord [the emperor], opposed and would not consent to it. Michael Sattler then requested a ruling. After a consultation, the judges returned as their answer that, if his opponents would allow it, they, the judges, would consent. Thereupon the town clerk of Ensisheim,[25] as the spokesman of the said attorney, spoke thus: "Prudent, honorable, and wise lords, he has boasted of the Holy Spirit. Now if his boast is true, it seems to me, it is unnecessary to grant him this; for, if he has the Holy Spirit, as he boasts, the same will tell him what has been done here." To this Michael Sattler replied: "You servants of God, I hope my request will not be denied, for the said articles are as yet unclear to me [because of their number]." The town clerk responded: "Prudent, honorable, and wise lords, though we are not bound to do this, yet in order to give satisfaction, we will grant him his request that it may not be thought that injustice is being done him in his heresy or that we desire to abridge him of his rights. Hence let the articles be read to him again." [The charges are omitted here; Sattler answers them below.]

Thereupon Michael Sattler requested permission to confer with his brethren and sisters, which was granted him. Having conferred with them for a little while, he began and undauntedly answered as follows: "In regard to the articles relating to me and my brethren and sisters, hear this brief answer:

"First, that we have acted contrary to the imperial mandate, we do not admit. For the same says that the Lutheran doctrine and delusion is not to be adhered to, but only the gospel and the Word of God. This we have kept. For I am not aware that we have acted contrary to the gospel and the Word of God. I appeal to the words of Christ.

"Secondly, that the real body of Christ the Lord is not present in the sacrament, we admit. For the Scripture says: Christ ascended into heaven and sitteth on the right hand of his heavenly Father, whence he shall come to judge

25. Ensisheim, today in Alsace, northeastern France, was the seat of the Austrian government in that region. Its town clerk was Eberhard Hofmann.

the quick and the dead,[26] from which it follows that, if he is in heaven and not in the bread, he may not be eaten bodily.

"Thirdly, as to baptism we say infant baptism is of no avail to salvation. For it is written [Rom. 1:17] that we live by faith alone. Again [Mark 16:16]: He that believeth and is baptized shall be saved. Peter says the same [1 Pet. 3:21]: Which doth also now save you in baptism (which is signified by that [ark of Noah]), not the putting away of the filth of the flesh but rather the covenant of a good conscience with God by the resurrection of Jesus Christ.

"Fourthly, we have not rejected the oil [of extreme unction]. For it is a creature of God, and what God has made is good and not to be refused, but that the pope, bishops, monks, and priests can make it better we do not believe; for the pope never made anything good. That of which the Epistle of James [5:14] speaks is not the pope's oil.

"Fifthly, we have not insulted the mother of God and the saints. For the mother of Christ is to be blessed among all women because unto her was accorded the favor of giving birth to the Savior of the whole world. But that she is a mediatrix and advocatess—of this the Scriptures know nothing, for she must with us await the judgment. Paul said to Timothy [1 Tim. 2:5]: Christ is our mediator and advocate with God. As regards the saints, we say that we who live and believe are the saints, which I prove by the epistles of Paul to the Romans [1:7], the Corinthians [1 Cor. 1:2], the Ephesians [1:1], and other places where he always writes "to the beloved saints." Hence, we who believe are the saints, but those who have died in the faith we regard as the blessed.

"Sixthly, we hold that we are not to swear before the authorities, for the Lord says [Matt. 5:34-37]: Swear not, but let your communication be, Yea, yea; nay, nay.

"Seventhly, when God called me to testify of his Word and I had read Paul and also considered the unchristian and perilous state in which I was, beholding the pomp, pride, usury, and great whoredom of the monks and priests, I went and took unto me a wife, according to the command of God; for Paul well prophesies concerning this to Timothy [1 Tim. 4:3]: In the latter time it shall come to pass that men shall forbid to marry and command to abstain from meats which God hath created to be received with thanksgiving.

"Eighthly, if the Turks should come, we ought not to resist them. For it is written [Matt. 5:21]: Thou shalt not kill. We must not defend ourselves against the Turks and others of our persecutors, but are to beseech God with earnest prayer to repel and resist them. But that I said that, if warring were right, I would rather take the field against so-called Christians who persecute, capture, and kill pious Christians than against the Turks was for the following reason. The Turk is a true Turk, knows nothing of the Christian faith, and is a Turk after the flesh. But you who would be Christians and who make your boast of Christ persecute the pious witnesses of Christ and are Turks after the spirit!

"In conclusion, ministers of God, I admonish you to consider the end for which God has appointed you, to punish the evil and to defend and protect the pious. Whereas, then, we have not acted contrary to God and the gospel, you will find that neither I nor my brethren and sisters have offended in word or deed against any authority. Therefore, ministers of God, if you have neither heard nor read the Word of God, send for the most learned men and for the sacred books of the Bible in whatsoever language they may be and let them confer with us

26. These phrases are in various passages of Scripture, but this is a direct quotation of the Apostles' Creed.

in the Word of God. If they prove to us with the Holy Scriptures that we err and are in the wrong, we will gladly desist and recant and also willingly suffer the sentence and punishment for that of which we have been accused; but if no error is proven to us, I hope to God that you will be converted and receive instruction."

Upon this speech the judges laughed and put their heads together, and the town clerk of Ensisheim said: "Yes, you infamous, desperate rascal of a monk, should we dispute with you? The hangman will dispute with you, I assure you!"

Michael said: "God's will be done."

The town clerk said: "It were well if you had never been born."

Michael replied: "God knows what is good."

The town clerk: "You archheretic, you have seduced pious people. If they would only now forsake their error and commit themselves to grace!"

Michael: "Grace is with God alone."

One of the prisoners also said: "We must not depart from the truth."

The town clerk: "Yes, you desperate villain, you archheretic, I say, if there were no hangman here, I would hang you myself and be doing God a service thereby."

Michael: "God will judge aright." Thereupon the town clerk said a few words to him in Latin, what, we do not know. Michael Sattler answered him, *Judica.*[27]

The town clerk then admonished the judges and said: "He will not cease from this chatter anyway. Therefore, my Lord Judge, you may proceed with the sentence. I call for a decision of the court."

The judge asked Michael Sattler whether he too committed it to the court. He replied: "Ministers of God, I am not sent to judge the Word of God. We are sent to testify and hence cannot consent to any adjudication, since we have no command from God concerning it. But we are not for that reason removed from being judged and we are ready to suffer and to await what God is planning to do with us. We will continue in our faith in Christ so long as we have breath in us, unless we be dissuaded from it by the Scriptures."

The town clerk said: "The hangman will instruct you; he will dispute with you, archheretic."

Michael: "I appeal to the Scriptures."

Then the judges arose and went into another room where they remained for an hour and a half and determined on the sentence. In the meantime some [of the soldiers] in the room treated Michael Sattler most unmercifully, heaping reproach upon him. One of them said: "What have you in prospect for yourself and the others that you have so seduced them?" With this he also drew a sword which lay upon the table, saying: "See, with this they will dispute with you." But Michael did not answer upon a single word concerning himself but willingly endured it all. One of the prisoners said: "We must not cast pearls before swine." Being also asked why he had not remained a lord in the convent, Michael answered: "According to the flesh I was a lord, but it is better as it is." He did not say more than what is recorded here, and this he spoke fearlessly.

The judges having returned to the room, the sentence was read. It was as follows: "In the case of the attorney of His Imperial Majesty vs. Michael Sattler, judgment is passed that Michael Sattler shall be delivered to the executioner, who shall lead him to the place of execution and cut out his tongue, then forge him fast to a wagon and thereon with red-hot tongs twice tear pieces from his body; and after he has been brought outside the gate, he shall be plied five times more in the same manner. . . ."

27. That is, "Give judgment."

After this had been done in the manner prescribed, he was burned to ashes as a heretic. His fellow brethren were executed with the sword, and the sisters drowned. His wife, also after being subjected to many entreaties, admonitions, and threats, under which she remained steadfast, was drowned a few days afterward. Done the 21st day of May, A.D. 1527.[28]

[*Spiritual and Anabaptist Writers*, 138–44]

Selection 38: Janneken van Munstdorp, "Testament" (1573)

In order to keep the Low Countries in check, Philip II sent the notorious Duke of Alba to govern the region, and he did so with a heavy hand, executing thousands who would not confess the Roman Catholic faith. As had been the case since the 1520s, the Anabaptists, despised by most Catholics and Protestants, remained easy targets due to their nonresistance.

Janneken van Munstdorp (d. 1573), a Flemish Anabaptist who lived near Antwerp, was one of the many martyrs who died for her faith and was celebrated in the **Martyrs' Mirror*****, a collection of Anabaptist firsthand reports and martyrologies from the sixteenth century. Munstdorp was arrested with her husband of six months, Hans, who was quickly executed. Janneken, however, carrying their first child, was allowed to deliver her baby in prison and give the child to her friends. A few weeks before she was burned at the stake, she wrote this testimony to her then one-month-old daughter, to whom she passed on her own name, Janneken.***

Testament written by Janneken, while in prison at Antwerp, addressed to her daughter, A. D. 1573.

May the true love of God, and the wisdom of the Father, strengthen you in every virtue, my dearest child. May the God of heaven and of earth, the God of Abraham, of Isaac, and of Jacob, the Lord of Israel, preserve you in every virtue and strengthen your understanding in his truth. I commend you, my dear infant, to God. . . .

But since the Lord has so ordained it, that I must leave you here, deprived of both father and mother, I will therefore commend you to the Lord, to do with you what seems meet in his sight; he will provide for you, if you only fear God, for he is a father to the orphan and a protector to the widow.

I, your dear mother, in prison, cannot help or provide for you, because I had to leave your father for the Lord's sake, with whom I lived but six months. Then we were both apprehended and separated, because we sought to work out our souls' salvation. They took him from me, and I knew not whether I was *encient*[29] (pregnant) or not; I had yet to remain in prison and see him go on before, which caused me great distress. But after patiently spending my time solitarily, and carrying you nine months under my breasts, I bore you, after many excruciating throes; they then took me away from you, and I am now waiting here every morning to meet death, and will soon follow your dear father. Hence, I write this to you as a memento of your dear mother.

Since I have been condemned to die, and have to leave you here, I take this method to remind you, that, if you come to the years of discretion, you would fear and serve God diligently; examine and learn why and for whose sake we both were put to death, and be not ashamed to confess us before the world—for we did not suffer as evil-doers.[30] Therefore, be not

28. Sattler was executed on May 20 or May 21, 1527.

29. From the French loanword *enceinte* ("pregnant").

30. See 1 Pet. 2:20; 4:15-16.

ashamed of us, for it is the way in which the prophets and apostles had to go before us—for there is no other way in which we can be saved.

Therefore, my dear one, for whom I had great sorrow and anxiety of mind, if you attain the years of discretion examine well into this way, although you may expect much tribulation and affliction on it and be exposed to many imminent dangers, as we may see and read if we examine the scriptures—for they mention many of the sufferings of Christ in this way: but the world seek to be free from all these, by turning the back upon Christ. But, my dear child, if we desire to reign with Christ we must also suffer with him—we must bear the cross—and this is the cross that Christ would have us to bear, namely: that we should walk in his footsteps, and help to bear his reproach; for Christ himself declares: *Ye shall be hated and persecuted for my name's sake*![31] . . .

Now I have to forsake all this for the Lord, which the world is not worthy to suffer—for had we remained in the world, we need not have done all this; for when we agreed with the world, committed idolatry and all manner of unrighteousness, the world was then perfectly satisfied with us: but, because we sought to fear God and to avoid such an ungodly course of life, knowing that God could not thus approbate our conduct, we immediately strove to avoid such things, and are turned from idols to the living God, and sought to live a life of faith, in all quietness; because we did so, the world immediately molested us, persecuted us unto death, and we had to be a prey for every one and become an open spectacle to all the world.

They seek to murder and burn us—we are driven from pillar to post, and exposed at stakes—and our flesh they give to worms to feed upon: therefore, my dear child, is fulfilled in your father and mother, what was foretold that should befall us. But not everyone is chosen to suffer, nor need all anticipate to suffer—but the Lord has chosen us to suffer; so, then, if you arrive at the years of understanding, follow the example of your father and mother. This I desire of you, for you are yet quite young. I wrote this when you were but one month old; and since I am soon, by the help of the Lord, to make my sacrifice, I leave this to you that you might do what I desire of you, and always cleave to those who fear God, and not look upon the vain things of this world—upon the multitude who are on the downward road to ruin, which leads to hell. . . .

I would further entreat, always live honestly when you have come to the years of understanding, so that none will have cause of complaint towards you. Be always faithful and true, and take advantage of none; always keep your hands pure, and always be willing to work with your own hands, for Paul says: He that will not work shall not eat; and Peter says: He that would live long and see good days, must keep his tongue from speaking evil.

Therefore, my dear Janneken, do not accustom yourself to evil speaking; do not indulge in vain and vulgar conversation, nor tell falsehoods, for liars shall not inherit the kingdom of Heaven—for it is written: A lying mouth kills the soil. Therefore, be careful to avoid all such things, and do not run about in the streets like other ill-bred children; rather take your book and read, and seek what will promote your salvation.

Be subject to those with whom you may live: if they speak ill of those who give you bread, do you speak well of them, and be always doing something. Do not exalt yourself, but compare yourself with the humble; always honor seniors, wherever you may be.

I will leave you. If it should have pleased the Lord to continue me with you to raise you, I

31. See Matt. 10:22; 24:9.

would have spared no pains to do so; but it appears it is not the will of the Lord to do so. . . .

My dear child, if it were not so, still I know that he is faithful and true. Therefore, my dear, be content. Though you be deprived of father and mother, remember that you have a Father in heaven, who will, undoubtedly, provide for you. . . .

The prophets and apostles have set us an example, by walking in the same road before us—nor did Christ, for our sakes, shun himself, but suffered death for us, and how should he not then give us all things? Therefore I entreat you, my dear, strive to walk in this way—for this is the only way to life; there is no other way whereby men can be saved than through Jesus Christ, as Paul says: Other foundation cannot be laid than that which is laid, which is Jesus Christ, through whose streams we are healed and through whose blood we are purchased—for we are not purchased with silver or gold, but with the precious shed blood of Christ, and he has called us as the first begotten of Christ.

All those who have died to sin and have reformed, and have risen with Christ into a new life, so that they do not live any more to themselves but belong to the Lord, and whether they live or die, live and die to the Lord. These, then, do belong to the Lord—they are his own: for, my dear, what shall the death of Christ avail those who still live in sin, and do not repent of their ungodly life in which they live, such as drunkards, murderers, fornicators, idolaters, liars, backbiters, who cannot please God? Their works are only of the devil. . . .

We can merit nothing—we must be saved by grace: therefore, always fear God, for the fear of the Lord is the beginning of wisdom; and he that fears the Lord will do right—he shall prosper in this world and the world to come. Always cleave to those who fear the Lord sincerely. Do not conform to this world, and do not lead a dissolute life—for the world and all in it will perish. Have no communion with the unfruitful works of darkness, but rather much more reprove them; and be renewed in life, so that you may proclaim the virtues to which God has called you.

Ah! my most beloved, that you might learn to know the truth when you grow up, and follow your dear father and mother, who have gone on before you; for your dear father testified with his own blood that this is the truth, and I trust to seal it with my blood, although flesh and blood must remain suspended to posts and stakes, inasmuch as I assuredly know we shall meet again. Follow us, my dear, so that you may come there also, when we shall see each other again; then will the Lord say to you: Come thou blessed of my Father, inherit the kingdom prepared for you from the foundation of the world.

Then we shall not be deprived of our joy. If they have separated us here, and we had to leave you, I am, nevertheless, persuaded that it was the will of the Lord; for if it had pleased the Lord, he might have ordered it otherwise. Therefore, remain satisfied he knows what he intends with you, because I have to leave you.

Drowning of Anneken Jans, Rotterdam, 1539, from Martyrs' Mirror

Always act honorably, and be complaisant towards every one. When you are grown, let your discretion be manifest to all men.

I leave you among my friends, and hope that my father and step-mother, my brothers and sisters, will do much for your comfort as long as they live: obey them in all things not contrary to the will of God. All that I am to receive, thirty guilders, I bequeath to you; if there should be any more, I bequeath the same—but whether there will be I know not, for I have been confined a long time in this place, and I know not what the expenses may be; but I trust that my sister Grietjen will do the best in this matter. I do not know what is coming to you from your father, for I know very little about his parent's circumstances, because they live far from home. . . .

Now, my dear Janneken, you who are yet so very young and little, I leave you this letter, and a gold *real* which I had with me in prison[32]; these things I leave you, as a *testament* and as a *memento*. Read this letter carefully when you arrive at years of understanding, and preserve it as long as you live, in remembrance of me and your father, so that you may be edified by it. I bid you good night, and kiss you cordially with the kiss of peace. Follow me and your father, and be not ashamed to confess us before the world—for we are not ashamed to confess our father before the world, and this adulterous generation: hence, I entreat you not to be ashamed to confess our faith, for it is the true evangelical faith—there will never be any other.

Rejoice, that we did not die as evil-doers. Should they attempt to put you to death, do not be deterred from fearing God; for if you strive to do good, none can prevent you from fearing God. Seek peace, and follow after it—then you shall receive the crown of life. May you receive this crown, and may the despised Jesus be your bridegroom; this is my sincere prayer. Always remember your father, and your mother, who wrote this with her own hand for your edification. Always keep this gold real with you, and this letter as an everlasting testament. I bid you good night. I trust to seal this letter with my own blood, at the stake.

I now commend you to the Lord, and the word of his grace. I expect to meet you. Follow me, my dear child. Farewell.

Written August 10th, A. D. 1573, at Antwerp.

This is the testament that I wrote in prison for my daughter Janneken, whom I bore and brought forth in these bonds.

By me, your dear mother,

Janneken Munstdorp,

A prisoner for the sake of the Lord.

[Thieleman J. van Braght, *The Bloody Theatre, or Martyrs' Mirror, of the Defenceless Christians*, trans. I. Daniel Rupp (Lancaster, PA: David Miller, 1837), 895–98]

C. Evangelical Rationalists

Selection 39: *The Racovian Catechism* (1605)

One radical wing of the Reformation is the so-called Evangelical Rationalists, who, on the basis of the Bible and rationalistic principles, came to question and reject the preexistence and divinity of Jesus Christ (and, thus, the doctrine of the Trinity) as well as the satisfaction theory of atonement. Their teachings were represented famously by the anti-Trinitarian Fausto Sozzini (Faustus Socinus) (1539–1604), an Italian who fled to Poland, whose followers there became

32. A Spanish "real" was a coin worth less than a Dutch guilder.

known as the Minor Reformed Church or Polish Brethren.

The Racovian Catechism—*drawn up by some Polish Brethren and named after their headquarters in Raków, Poland—is a basic statement of Socinian theology. It discusses the Scriptures, salvation, and the doctrines of God and Christ. It was composed in Polish and translated into German, Latin, and English. In its own day, in most places, the catechism made its way to the burn pile. But its distinct teachings foreshadow the Unitarian movement and what would become liberal Protestant theology.*

[Question:] What are the things relating to the nature of God, the knowledge of which is necessary to salvation?

[Answer:] They are the following:—first, That God is; secondly, That he is one only; thirdly, That he is eternal; and fourthly, That he is perfectly just, wise, and powerful.

[Q:] What is it to know that God is?

[A:] It is to know, and be firmly convinced, that there actually exists a Being who possesses supreme dominion over all things.

[Q:] What is it to know that God is one only?

[A:] This you may of yourself easily understand—that there cannot be more beings than one who possess supreme dominion over all things.

[Q:] But do not the Scriptures teach that there are "many Gods?"[33]

[A:] Though they do indeed assert this, yet it is not in that sense in which they proclaim and declare that there is one only God,—namely, he who possesses supreme dominion, derived from no other being, and consequently circumscribed by no limits. But by Gods they mean to designate those who received what divinity they had from that one God, upon whom, as their head, they depended: thus in the following passages, Psalm lxxxii. 1 and 6: "God standeth in the congregation of the mighty; he judgeth among the Gods." "I have said ye are Gods, and all of you are children of the Most High." John x. 34, 35: "Is it not written in your law, I said ye are Gods?" . . .

[Q:] But why do the Scriptures thus speak?

[A:] Because that he alone has dominion of himself, and is the head of all things; while all other beings are dependent upon him, and exercise their derived dominion solely through his kindness: on which accounts, also, it is stated that he is the "only wise God," "who alone hath immortality," and that "there is none good but he." Rom. xvi. 27. Jude 25. 1 Tim. vi. 16. Matt. xix. 17. . . .

[Q:] How do you prove the second particular, that God is one, to be necessary to salvation?

[A:] Unless we believe God to be but one, we shall be led to worship more Gods; which, as I shall show hereafter, is contrary to the way of salvation. For if God be not one only, we cannot love him with "*all* our heart, and soul, and strength." On which account the Scriptures frequently admonish us of this truth, that God is one. . . .

[Q:] You have explained to me what things are necessary to be known concerning the attributes of God, in order to salvation: state, in the next place, what those are which you deem eminently conducive to the same end?

[A:] The principal thing is to guard against falling into the common error, wherein it is maintained, with palpable contradiction, that there is in God only *one* essence, but that he has three persons.

[Q:] Prove to me that in the one essence of God, there is but one Person?

[A:] This indeed may be seen from hence, that the essence of God is one, not in kind but

33. See 1 Cor. 8:5.

in number. Wherefore it cannot, in any way, contain a plurality of persons, since a person is nothing else than an individual intelligent essence. Wherever, then, there exist three numerical persons, there must necessarily, in like manner, be reckoned three individual essences; for in the same sense in which it is affirmed that there is one numerical essence, it must be held that there is also one numerical person.

[Q:] Who is this one divine Person?

[A:] The Father of our Lord Jesus Christ.

[Q:] How do you prove this?

[A:] By most decisive testimonies of Scripture:[34]—thus Jesus says (John xvii. 3) "This is life eternal, that they might know *Thee*, (the Father) *the only true God*." The apostle Paul writes to the Corinthians (1 Cor. viii. 6), "To us there is but *one God, the Father*, of whom are all things:"—and again, in addressing the Ephesians (chap. iv. 6), he says, "There is—*one God and Father of all*; who is above all, and through all, and in you all."

[Q:] How happens it, then, that Christians commonly maintain, that, with the Father,—the Son and the Holy Spirit are persons in one and the same Deity?

[A:] In this they lamentably err—deducing their arguments from passages of Scripture ill understood.

[Q:] What are the arguments by which they endeavour to support their opinion?

[A:] The principal are these: first, they affirm, that in the Scriptures, not only the Father, but the Son also, and the Holy Spirit, are severally called and shown to be God; and, since the same Scriptures assert that God is only one, they infer that these three compose that one God.

[Q:] How can this argument be invalidated?

[A:] I will reply to this question, first, as it respects the Son, and afterwards as it relates to the Holy Spirit.

[Q:] What answer do you make in respect to the Son?

[A:] The term *God* is employed in the Scriptures chiefly in two senses. The former of these is, when it designates Him who so rules and presides over all things in heaven and on earth, that he acknowledges no superior; and is in such respects the author and head of all things, that he depends upon no other being, and possesses power which is absolutely infinite: and in this sense the Scriptures assert that God is One. The latter sense is, when it denotes a Being, who has received from that one God some kind of superior authority either in heaven, or on earth among men, or power superior to all things human, or authority to sit in judgement upon other men; and is thus rendered in some sense, a partaker of the Deity of the one God.[35] Hence it is that in the Scriptures the one God is styled the "God of Gods," Psalm cxxxvi. 2; and it is in this latter sense that the Son of God is called God in some passages of Scripture.

[Q:] Whence do you prove that the Son of God is in this latter sense called God in the Scriptures?

[A:] From those words of the Son of God himself, (John x. 35, 36) "If he" (David) "called them Gods, (that is, Psalm lxxxii. 6, "ye are Gods") unto whom the word of God came, and the Scripture cannot be broken; say ye of him, whom the Father hath sanctified and sent into the world, Thou blasphemest, because I said, I am the Son of God?" Christ most clearly intimates in these words that the title God is applied in the Scriptures to those who are greatly inferior to the one God; that is, to the

34. Note well the thoroughly biblical case being made to overturn historic Christian teaching on the Trinity, which was also based on biblical interpretation.

35. Cf. 2 Pet. 1:4.

rulers and judges of the people: and tacitly implies that he was himself for this reason the Son of God, that is, peculiarly, being not inferior to any one of those persons whom God had honoured with the title of Gods, but rather greatly the superior of them all; and was on this very account God,—that the "Father had sanctified him, and sent him into the world:" which cause, and the whole of this reasoning of Christ, are accommodated to the latter, and not to the former signification of the term God.

[Q:] What reply do you make respecting the Holy Spirit?

[A:] The Holy Spirit is never expressly called God in the Scriptures. Nor is it to be inferred that it is itself God, or a person of the Divinity, because in some places those things are attributed to it which belong to God: but this proceeds from a very different cause, as you shall hear in its proper place.

[Q:] What is the second argument whereby it is attempted to be proved that these three persons are united in one Deity?

[A:] This argument is drawn from those passages of Scripture wherein the Father, Son, and Holy Spirit are, on some account, joined together.

[Q:] Which are those passages?

[A:] The first is the command of Jesus (Matthew xxviii. 19), to baptize "in the name of the Father, the Son, and the Holy Spirit." The second is comprised in the address of Paul to the Corinthians (1 Corinth. xii. 4-6), "There are diversities of gifts, but the same Spirit: and there are differences of administrations, but the same Lord: and there are diversities of operations, but it is the same God which worketh all in all." The third is found in the First Epistle of John, chap. v. 7, "There are three that bear record in heaven, the Father, the Word, and the Holy Spirit, and these three are one."

[Q:] What ought we to think of these testimonies?

[A:] I answer generally in respect to them, that they only prove the existence of the Father, Son, and Holy Spirit, and that they are associated in divine things; which I not only admit, but also constantly declare; insomuch that I pronounce that person to be no Christian who either does not know or does not believe this. It is evident, nevertheless, that these testimonies do not prove the matter in dispute; namely, that the Father, Son, and Holy Spirit, are three persons in the one essence of God.

[Q:] It does, however, seem as if it might be inferred, from the kind of union affirmed of these three in the cited passages, that they are three persons in one divine essence?

[A:] By no means. For, in respect to the first, the baptismal command, although the Father, Son, and Holy Spirit, are so associated together that we are to be baptized in their joint names, yet it cannot be hence proved that they are persons in one divine essence. For it is not at all unusual in the Scriptures, in other cases equally with the ordinance of baptism, to join with God, in religious matters, both persons and things which in no way pertain to the divine essence. Of *persons*, you have an example in the First Book of Samuel (chap. xii. 18), where it is said that "all the people greatly feared the Lord, *and Samuel*."—So also Exodus xiv.31, "And the people feared the Lord, and believed the Lord *and his servant Moses*."—Of *things*, we have an instance in Acts xx. 32; where Paul, addressing the Ephesians, says, "I commend you to God, *and to the word of his grace*." Things are also joined with Christ (Ephes. vi. 10), "Be strong in the Lord, *and in the power of his might*." And in the Book of Revelation (chap. iii. 12), things are joined to God and Christ: "I will write upon him the name of my God, *and the name of the city of my God, which is New Jerusalem*, which cometh down out of heaven from my God; and I will write upon him my new name."

[Q:] But it is maintained, that he must necessarily be God, in whose name we are baptized?

[A:] Those who hold this opinion egregiously err: for we read (1 Cor. x. 2) that the Israelites "were all baptized *unto Moses* in the cloud and in the sea:" Acts xix. 3, that some were baptized "*unto John's baptism*:" and Rom. vi. 3, that Christians are "baptized *into the death of Christ*:"—though Moses was not God, and though neither the baptism of John nor the death of Christ, was even a person, much less God.

[Q:] But to be baptized into any one's *name*, seems to be a very different thing from being baptized into any person or thing?

[A:] Not at all: for agreeably to the import of the Hebrew idiom, both phrases are well known to have the same meaning, as may be seen in this very case. For what is stated in Acts ii. 38, of converts being "baptized in the name of Jesus Christ," is in other places (Rom. vi. 3; Gal. iii. 27) expressed more briefly by being "baptized into Jesus Christ."

[Q:] But why does Christ speak in this manner of the Holy Spirit, if it be not a person?

[A:] Because he connects the Holy Spirit with the Father and himself, as a kind of celestial teacher and master, by whose inspiration and power his doctrine would be promulgated in the world.

[Q:] What reply do you make to the second cited testimony, wherein the apostle Paul seems to ascribe divine operations to the Holy Spirit, equally with the Father and the Son?

[A:] Although divine operations are here attributed to God, to the Lord, (who is Christ,) and also to the Holy Spirit, it cannot be hence proved that these three are the one God. Indeed the direct contrary is to be inferred from the passage; since the Lord, (that is Christ,) and the Holy Spirit, are most clearly distinguished by the apostle from the one God. The Lord, (or Christ,) and the Holy Spirit, are mentioned conjointly with God on this account,—because the former is the person by whose instrumentality God operates all the effects which are there referred to; and the latter the virtue or energy of God, by the communication of which all those operations are performed.[36]

[Q:] What answer do you make to the third testimony quoted from the First Epistle of John, respecting the three heavenly witnesses?

[A:] I observe, first, that since it is known that these words are wanting in most of the older Greek copies,[37] and also in the Syriac, Arabic, Aethiopic, and the more ancient Latin versions, as the principal persons even among our adversaries have themselves shown, nothing certain can be concluded from them. There are, besides, some persons who deem the genuineness of the passage suspicious;—that is to say, Erasmus, Beza, Franc. Lucas, and the Louvain divines. On this account Luther could not venture to admit the words; and his colleague Bugenhagius, in his Commentary on John, warned all printers against inserting them in the text. Besides, the principal Fathers among the advocates of the doctrine of the Trinity, whose names may be seen in the editions of Louvain, of Beza, Serarius, and Pelargus, do not acknowledge them.[38] They do not agree with

36. The Spirit, as the power or "energy" of God, is treated as an impersonal force.

37. Erasmus's first edition of the Greek New Testament (1516) did not include this long reading in 1 John 5:7, but he placed it in subsequent editions because some late Greek manuscripts that contained the phrase in question were presented to him. All text critics recognize the Trinitarian allusion as a late addition in Latin.

38. As the writer here admits, the early church fathers were perfectly capable of advocating the doctrine of the Trinity without the aid of the longer 1 John 5:7. Only later—after theologians had come to rely on the long reading as a proof text for Trinitarianism—did its omission present a theological challenge.

the preceding context. And Grotius asserts that they are wholly wanting in a very ancient manuscript which was transmitted by the patriarch Cyrillus to the king of Great Britain.—I observe in the next place, that even if the passage were found in the authentic Scriptures, it could not be proved from it that there are three persons in one God. . . .

[*The Racovian Catechism, with Notes and Illustrations*, trans. Thomas Rees (London: For Longman, Hurst, Rees, Orme, and Brown, 1818), 26–27, 29, 33–41]

Further Reading

Estep, W. R. *The Anabaptist Story: An Introduction to Sixteenth-Century Anabaptism.* 3rd ed. Grand Rapids, MI: Eerdmans, 1996.

Rempel, John D. *The Lord's Supper in Anabaptism: A Study in the Christology of Balthasar Hubmaier, Pilgram Marpeck, and Dirk Philips.* Waterloo: Herald, 1993.

Snyder, C. Arnold. *Anabaptist History and Theology: An Introduction.* Kitchener, ON: Pandora Press, 1996.

Stayer, James. *Anabaptists and the Sword.* Lawrence, KS: Coronado, 1972.

Verduin, Leonard. *The Reformers and Their Stepchildren.* Grand Rapids, MI: Eerdmans, 1964.

Williams, George Huntston. *The Radical Reformation.* 3rd ed. Sixteenth Century Essays and Studies, 15. Kirksville, MO: Truman State University Press, 2000.

Chapter 4
Roman Catholic (Counter-)Reformation

The sixteenth-century development within the churches in fellowship with the bishop of Rome has traditionally been known as the "Counter-Reformation." This designation is accurate to the extent that these changes indeed were a response to the Protestant Reformation. At the same time, because the roots of much of the Catholic reform can be found prior to the sixteenth century, the Catholic Reformation cannot be characterized as merely reactionary or "counter" to the Protestants. Reformation, especially moral reformation of the clergy, had been a common cry within the late medieval Western Church.

The same diversity within the late medieval Western Church that produced the Protestant Reformation also led to reform within the Roman Church. An exemplary figure during this period was Francisco Ximénez de Cisneros (1436–1517), the confessor of Queen Isabella of Spain. He became the archbishop of Toledo and a cardinal. Cisneros worked with Isabella for moral reform and sponsored the publication of the Complutensian Polyglot, a Bible printed in Greek and Latin (and Hebrew added in the Old Testament). Well into the sixteenth century, there were several reform-minded bishops and cardinals who promoted widespread study of the Bible and even advocated an almost Lutheran doctrine of justification by grace through faith. Formal discussions took place between Protestant and Roman Catholic clergy in an attempt to reach compromise, perhaps most famously at the Colloquy of Regensburg in 1541. At the same time, there was the dominant stream that supported moral reform but, from the very beginning, staunchly resisted the Protestant calls for a new doctrinal direction.

The sixteenth century also saw the rise of new monastic orders. The Jesuit order, founded in 1540 by Ignatius of Loyola (1491–1556), became immensely influential during the Catholic Reformation and has remained a steady, if sometimes controversial, influence ever since. Teresa of Ávila (1515–1582) and John of the Cross (1542–1591) also worked to establish female and male houses of the Discalced Carmelites.

The Council of Trent (1545–1563) was the most significant event in Roman Catholicism until the Second Vatican Council in the 1960s. The council defined many doctrines and practices that had long been recognized, and it reaffirmed others that had been defined in previous councils and decrees. In the process of reaching many controversial conclusions against the Protestants, Trent also declared that doctrinal truth is founded equally on written and unwritten traditions, that is, on Scripture and the teaching magisterium of the church. The Profession of the Tridentine Faith (1564) obliges acknowledgment of the "holy, catholic, and apostolic Roman Church" as the mother and master of all churches, swearing of true obedience to the Roman pontiff, and affirmation of all the anathemas declared in the council against Protestants. This confession of faith, along with the canons and decrees of Trent, further alienated the Protestants and their concerns, completing the schism that had loomed for several decades and in turn generating more Protestant reactions. The Jesuit cardinal Robert Bellarmine (1542–1621) would become the era's most formidable anti-Protestant polemicist; he, along with other scholastic Catholic theologians, helped spur the Protestants to new heights of scholastic theology in a more substantive articulation and defense of their own faith. By the 1570s, the Catholic Reformation and call to action had effectively stopped the further spread of Protestantism into new European lands.

The reality that neither side of this new Western schism would retreat or give in to the other had profound social effects. With the disintegration of the *corpus Christianum*—the ideal of one "Christian body" unified under one pope and one emperor—came the subsequent question of how these competing religious bodies could coexist. First of all, there was a contest throughout Europe for the hearts and minds of the magistrates and their citizens, as Protestant clergy sought to persuade cities and kingdoms from the top down and the bottom up. Protestants had their share of success in northern and western Europe but were rejected by the magistracy and made little headway with the populace of southern Europe. France, for example, was a key battleground that boasted a strong minority of Reformed churches but eventually adhered to its Roman Catholic heritage and fiercely persecuted the Protestant Huguenots. After the region's religion was established, there was the issue of the reality of life for such minorities living in various realms where one interpretation of the faith dominated, but did not eliminate, others. Much of Europe was as xenophobic at the end of the sixteenth century as it was at the beginning, and perhaps less tolerant and more suspicious of these different interpretations of the same Christian faith. This phenomenon can be seen with particular clarity in England, whose comparatively stable monarchy presided over a series of official religious shifts within England's relatively well-defined borders and population. A certain level of intolerance from the Established Church drove dissenters out of the country or underground, enacting policies that would eventually affect the religious landscape as far away as the New World.

A. Responses to Luther

Selection 40: Johann Tetzel, *Rebuttal to Luther's Sermon on Indulgences* (1518)

Johann Tetzel (1460–1519), a German Dominican, was a popular preacher of indulgences. His claim that indulgences could positively affect the deceased in purgatory drew the attention of Martin Luther (see Selection 14). This sermon given in German by Tetzel, published only six months after Luther's **Ninety-Five Theses,** ***is a rebuttal to Luther's German sermon on the same topic of indulgences. Tetzel quotes and replies to twenty "erroneous articles" of Luther, four of which are excerpted here.***

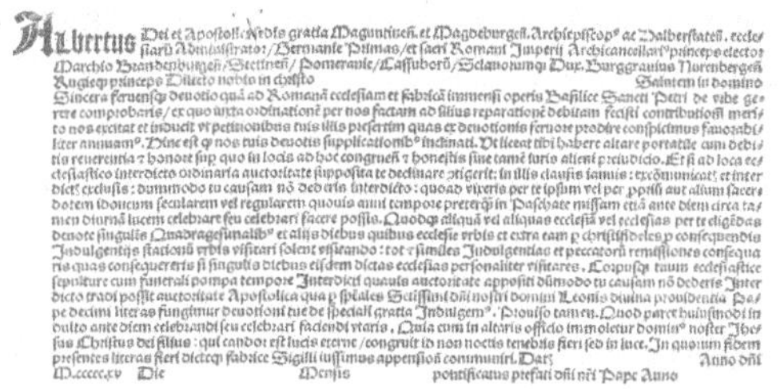

An (unused) indulgence, 1515

XVI.

The sixteenth erroneous article reads as follows:

[Luther:] "Sixteenth, far better is the good work shown a needy person than that given to a building. It is also far better than the indulgence granted for it. For as it is said: 'Better is a good work done than much remitted.' The indulgence, however, is the remittance of many good works, or else nothing is remitted. . . .

"If you then declare, 'Then I will never more buy an indulgence,' I reply, 'I have already said earlier that my will, desire, request, and advice is that no one seek an indulgence. Let lazy and sleepy Christians buy indulgences. You go your own way.' "[1]

[Tetzel:] It is rebutted in Christian manner thusly: First, it is unfounded and entirely obscure, since it considers one matter and leaves the other matter unmentioned. For giving alms to a poor person is more beneficial for the earning of salvation, yet buying a plenary—or indeed any indulgence—is more beneficial for the speedier satisfaction of punishment due to sin. Further, everyone should know that buying an indulgence is also a work of mercy. For whoever buys an indulgence takes pity on his soul and makes himself well-pleasing to God thereby. . . .

This article also implies that people are given true teaching in the erroneous sermon.

That corresponds not at all with the truth. Rather, it "is wished, implored, and advised" in this article "that no one should buy an indulgence," advice which is detrimental to salvation. The article says further that only "lazy and sleepy Christians" should purchase an indulgence, which cruelly misleads Christianity. Consider that a person does himself much more good in purchasing the indulgence he needs, than in giving alms to a poor person who is not in a state of utmost need. For the alms or the good work with which someone is earning the indulgence functions just as meritoriously toward eternal life, since it is done for the love of God, as do the alms given to a poor person. . . .

XVIII.

The eighteenth erroneous article reads as follows:

[Luther:] "Eighteenth, whether souls are drawn out of purgatory by indulgences, I do not know. Still, I do not believe so, although

1. The quotation at the beginning of each article is taken from Martin Luther, *Ein Sermon von Ablass und Gnade* (*A Sermon on Indulgence and Grace*) (1518).

various modern scholars say so. But it is impossible for them to prove it, and furthermore, the Church has not yet come to a conclusion. Therefore, for greater certainty it is better that you pray for them and labor for them. For this is more proven and is certain."

[Tetzel:] It is refuted thusly in Christian manner: First, it is full of malicious guile, when it claims that the Church has not concluded that souls can be delivered from purgatory through indulgences. For the tradition of the Roman Church does maintain that souls are delivered from purgatory by an indulgence. . . .

Now indulgences also concern faith, for whoever does not believe that the pope can grant indulgences and plenary indulgences to the living and the dead—as long as they remain in God's love—that person maintains that the pope has not received complete authority from the Lord Christ over Christian believers, which contradicts sacred canon law. . . .

XIX.

The nineteenth erroneous article reads as follows:

[Luther:] "Nineteenth, in these points I have no doubts and they are sufficiently grounded in Scripture. Therefore, you should also have no doubt and let the Scholastic Doctors remain Scholastics. Taken all together they are not enough with their opinions to substantiate a sermon."

[Tetzel:] It is refuted in Christian manner accordingly: First, this article and all the articles cited are totally ungrounded in Scripture. For the articles contradict the practice of the holy Roman Church and the teaching of all modern, venerable Christian teachers. . . .

This article also states, "One should let the "*Doctores Scholasticos*"[2] remain "Scholastics," for taken all together, they with their opinions are unable to substantiate a sermon." [And further,] ignorant people hold this opinion of the venerable scholastic doctors, for these venerable "*Doctores*" uncover and oppose all new errors. Therefore, wrong-thinking people deride them. However, the holy Roman Church together with the whole community of sacred Christendom are in unanimous agreement that the revered venerable "*Doctores Scholasticos*" buttress the holy Christian faith against the heretics with their truly salvific teaching based on solid Christian doctrine. And what is more, they are certainly able to preach a sermon! Thus this article makes sport of them quite unfairly and shamefully and contrary to all reason and truth. . . .

XX.

The twentieth erroneous article reads as follows:

[Luther:] "Twentieth, whether some people reproach me as a heretic (for such a truth is quite injurious for their money boxes), I pay little heed to such babblings inasmuch as no one does so except some muddled brains who have never sniffed a Bible, have never read the Christian teachers, have never understood their own teachers but rather are decaying in their riddled and fragmented opinions. For if they had understood them, they would know that they should defame no one without hearing and challenging him. Nonetheless, may God give them and us right understanding. Amen."

[Tetzel:] It is refuted in a Christian and well-grounded manner: First, it is totally erroneous, and it requires no riddled brain to know who is a heretic. Therefore I, Brother Johann Tetzel, Order of Preachers, am forced to leave out several other teachings and positions here, which I intend, with God's help, to discuss and prove correct in a Christian manner at the

2. That is, "Scholastic Doctors."

respected University of Frankfurt an der Oder on a date to be arranged. . . .

From all this it will also become clear who "has a confused brain, who has never sniffed a Bible, never read the Christian masters, has never understood his own teachers." Therefore, I offer all of this rebuttal and my position that I have written regarding these matters for the consideration and judgment of His Holiness the Pope, the holy Roman Church, all trustworthy

Christian universities, and doctors with sure trust in the truth, with the commitment to suffer whatever they judge just, [if any of it be heretical], be it through imprisonment, the stocks, drowning, or burning at the stake.

I write this as true Christian fraternal admonition, so that from now on no one should believe the sermon on the twenty erroneous articles nor the theses that begin, *"Dominus et Magister noster Jhesus Christus dicendo penitentiam agite etc.,"* and end, *"Ac sic magis per multas tribulationes intrare celum etc.,"*[3] [that is to say], unless their author were to submit to the consideration and judgment of His Papal Holiness, the holy Roman Church, and all trustworthy Christian universities and shall have proven such submission through his actions. For I am confident that without such submission, the sermon on the twenty articles and the recently mentioned theses would be neither sermon nor redemptive doctrine but rather a seduction and a perversion of the people. For Christ himself says, "Whoever hears not the Church, that one shall be to you as a gentile and a publican." [Matthew 18:17] . . .

Submitted for the praise of God, for the salvation of humankind, and to the honor of the holy Papal See.

[*Rebuttal to Luther's Sermon on Indulgences*, trans. Dewey Weiss Kramer (Atlanta: Pitts Theology Library, 2012), 26–29, 30–32]

3. This is a reference to Luther's *Ninety-five Theses on Indulgences* (1517) (see Selection 14).

Selection 41: Pope Leo X, *Exsurge Domine* (1520)

On June 15, 1520, Pope Leo X issued this bull giving Luther sixty days to recant before being excommunicated. Luther received the text several weeks later and responded to it in writing and by publicly burning it. The excommunication was final on January 3, 1521, thus sealing the rift between Luther and the papacy.

Arise O Lord and judge thy cause. . . . Arise O Peter, and in the name of the pastoral charge committed to thee from on high, put forth thy strength in the cause of the holy Roman Church, the mother of all churches, the mistress of the faith. . . . Arise thou also, O Paul, we beg thee, who hast enlightened her with thy teaching. . . . In a word, let every saint arise and the whole remaining universal church. . . . Let intercession be made to almighty God, that his sheep may be purged of their errors and every heresy be expelled from the confines of the faithful, and that God may deign to preserve the peace and unity of his holy church. . . .

For some time we have been hearing of, or rather, alas!, seeing and reading with our own eyes, many different errors which, although in part condemned aforetimes by councils and decisions of our predecessors . . . have been stirred up afresh, and latterly . . . sown abroad in the renowned nation of Germany. . . . We cannot, in view of our pastoral office, laid on us by divine grace, any longer tolerate the poisonous virus of these errors. . . .[4]

[*Martin Luther*, ed. E.G. Rupp and B. Drewery (New York: St. Martin's, 1970), 36–40]

4. In Leo's text, a list of forty-one alleged errors of Luther follows.

B. Roman Catholic Spirituality

Biographical Note: Ignatius of Loyola

Iñigo (Ignatius) López de Loyola (1491–1556) was born into a noble family at the castle of Loyola, located in the Basque country of northern Spain. In 1517, following the path typical of his ancestors, he began a military career. But it was to be short-lived. In 1521, during the siege of Pamplona, Ignatius was injured by a cannonball while he was defending the city. His right leg was completely broken and his left leg badly wounded. The period of recovery in his brother's house afforded a time of contemplation and self-examination (see Selection 42), including receiving a vision of the virgin Mary with her child.

After this turning point at which he devoted himself to the work of God, Ignatius traveled widely (even visiting Jerusalem) before arriving in Venice in 1535. In 1537, he and six of his friends were ordained as priests. What would become the Jesuit order began as an informal group of ten friends carrying on their ministries. Ignatius eventually moved to Rome, where his ministry made a direct impression on the pope. For his impact on reform within the Roman Church, Ignatius is often regarded as the Roman Catholic counterpart to Martin Luther.

On September 27, 1540, Pope Paul III officially approved of Ignatius's new order, Societas Iesu *(the Society of Jesus). The Jesuits were founded for "the defense and propagation of the faith" and in order to inspire religious fervor. The order quickly spread throughout southern Europe, into Protestant territories, and as far as India. Their unofficial motto became* ad maiorem Dei gloriam *("for the greater glory of God").*

An early Jesuit seal

As the Jesuits commonly put it, their purpose was "to help souls" by means of their ministries of the Word, the sacraments, and works of mercy. The ministry of the Word—which included all preaching, lecturing (distinct from sermons), catechetical teaching, publication, and mission—took precedence especially in the face of the Protestant critique of lack of preaching and teaching in the church. All of these ministries were anticipated by the work of Ignatius and his companions prior to 1540, and they continued under his leadership until his death in 1556. Among these ministries, the Jesuit order is probably best known for their work in education and evangelism. In the sixteenth century, they were largely responsible for the intellectual Renaissance of scholastic philosophy that even influenced Protestants, and they led the way for missions in the New World and elsewhere.

Selection 42: Ignatius of Loyola, *Autobiography* (1555)

Between 1553 and 1555, Ignatius of Loyola dictated his Autobiography, *which provides a firsthand account of his spiritual life, writ-*

ten in third-person narration. This selection begins where the autobiography begins—with his battle wound in 1521 and the period of recovery during which he immersed himself in reading the Bible, the life of Jesus, and the lives of the saints. As hard as it is to resist comparing the despair of Ignatius to that of his older contemporary Martin Luther, one is likewise compelled to note the contrast in their solutions. Whereas Luther discovered God's assuring grace apart from good works, Ignatius sought God's grace in his resolution to do good works. Each event, in some ways a caricature, is indicative of the trajectory of the two competing positions on justification in the sixteenth-century Western Church.

Chapter I

Until the age of twenty-six he was a man given over to vanities of the world; with a great and vain desire to win fame he delighted especially in the exercise of arms.[5] Once when he was in a fortress that the French were attacking, although all the others saw clearly that they could not defend themselves and were of the opinion that they should surrender provided their lives were spared, he gave so many reasons to the commander that he persuaded him at last to defend it; this was contrary to the views of all the knights, but they were encouraged by his valor and energy. When the day arrived on which the bombardment was expected, he confessed to one of his companions in arms. After the bombardment had lasted a good while, a shot hit him in the leg, breaking it completely; since the ball passed through both legs, the other one was also badly damaged.

When he fell, the defenders of the fortress surrendered immediately to the French who, having taken possession of it, treated the wounded man very well, with courtesy and kindness. After he had been in Pamplona for twelve or fifteen days, they carried him on a litter to his own country where he was very ill. All the doctors and surgeons who were summoned from many places decided that the leg ought to be broken again and the bones reset because they had been badly set the first time or had been broken on the road and were out of place and could not heal. This butchery was done again; during it, as in all the others he suffered before or since, he never spoke a word nor showed any sign of pain other than to clench his fists.

Yet he continued to get worse, not being able to eat and showing the other indications that are usually signs of death. When the feast of St. John came, because the doctors had very little confidence in his health, he was advised to confess; he received the sacraments on the vigil of Sts. Peter and Paul. The doctors said that if he did not feel better by midnight, he could consider himself dead. As the sick man had devotion to St. Peter, Our Lord willed that he should begin to improve that very midnight. His improvement proceeded so quickly that some days later it was decided that he was out of danger of death.

As his bones knit together, one bone below the knee remained on top of another, shortening his leg. The bone protruded so much that it was an ugly sight. He was unable to abide it because he was determined to follow the world and he thought that it would deform him; he asked the surgeons if it could be cut away. They said that indeed it could be cut away, but that the pain would be greater than all those that he had suffered, because it was already healed and it would take some time to cut it. Yet he was

5. Ignatius seems to be mistaken about his age; he was probably twenty-nine or thirty. The event described in the next sentence, the attack on Pamplona, occurred in May 1521.

determined to make himself a martyr to his own pleasure. His older brother was astounded and said that he himself would not dare to suffer such pain, but the wounded man endured it with his customary patience.

After the flesh and excess bone were cut away, means were taken so the leg would not be so short; many ointments were applied to it, and, as it was stretched continually with instruments, he suffered martyrdom for many days. But Our Lord was restoring his health, and he was getting well. In everything else he was healthy except that he could not stand easily on his leg and had to stay in bed. As he was much given to reading worldly and fictitious books, usually called books of chivalry, when he felt better he asked to be given some of them to pass the time. But in that house none of those that he usually read could be found, so they gave him a Life of Christ and a book of the lives of the saints in Spanish.

As he read them over many times, he became rather fond of what he found written there. Putting his reading aside, he sometimes stopped to think about the things he had read and at other times about the things of the world that he used to think about before. Of the many vain things that presented themselves to him, one took such a hold on his heart that he was absorbed in thinking about it for two or three or four hours without *realizing* it: he imagined what he would do in the service of a certain lady, the means he would take so he could go to the country where she lived, the verses, the words he would say to her, the deeds of arms he would do in her service. He became so conceited with this that he did not consider how impossible it would be because the lady was not of the lower nobility nor a countess nor a duchess, but her station was higher than any of these.

Nevertheless, Our Lord assisted him, causing other thoughts that arose from the things he read to follow these. While reading the life of Our Lord and of the saints, he stopped to think, reasoning within himself, "What if I should do what St. Francis did, what St. Dominic did?" . . .

From this reading he obtained not a little insight, and he began to think more earnestly about his past life and about the great need he had to do penance for it. At this point the desire to imitate the saints came to him, though he gave no thought to the circumstances, but only promised with God's grace to do as they had done. All he wanted to do was to go to Jerusalem as soon as he recovered, as mentioned above, performing all the disciplines and abstinences which a generous soul, inflamed by God, usually wants to do.

And so he began to forget the thoughts of the past with these holy desires he had, and they were confirmed by a vision in this manner. One night while he was awake, he saw clearly an image of Our Lady with the holy child Jesus. From this sight he received for a considerable time very great consolation, and he was left with such loathing for his whole past life and especially for the things of the flesh, that it seemed that all the fantasies he had previously pictured in his mind were driven from it. Thus from that hour until August 1553 when this was written, he never gave the slightest consent to the things of the flesh. For this reason the vision may be considered the work of God, although he did not dare to claim it nor to say more than to affirm the above. . . .

Chapter III

. . . He persevered in his seven hours of prayer on his knees, getting up continually at midnight and doing all the other exercises already mentioned. But he found no cure for his scruples in any of them; many months had now passed since they had begun to torment him.

Once when he was very upset by them he began to pray with such fervor that he shouted out loud to God, saying, "Help me, Lord, for I find no remedy among men nor in any creature, yet if I thought I could find it, no labor would be too great for me. Show me, O Lord, where I may find it; even though I should have to follow a little dog so he could help me, I would do it."

While he had these thoughts, the temptation often came over him with great force to throw himself into a large hole in his room next to the place where he was praying. But realizing that it was a sin to kill oneself, he shouted again, "Lord, I will do nothing to offend you," repeating these words many times, as well as the previous ones. . . .

This happened one Sunday after he had received communion; he persevered the whole week without putting anything into his mouth nor ceasing to do his usual exercises, even going to divine office and saying his prayers on his knees, even at midnight and so forth. But when the next Sunday came and he had to go to confession, because he used to tell his confessor in very great detail what he had done, he also told him how he had eaten nothing during that week. His confessor ordered him to break off his abstinence; though he still felt strong he obeyed his confessor and that day and the next felt free from scruples. But on the third day, which was Tuesday, while at prayer he began to remember his sins one by one, and he went on thinking about one sin after the other out of his past and felt he was required to confess them again. But after these thoughts, disgust for the life he led and the desire to give it up came over him. In this way the Lord wished to awaken him as if from a dream. From the lessons God had given him he now had some experience of the diversity of spirits, and he began to wonder about the means by which that spirit had come. He decided very clearly, therefore, not to confess anything from the past anymore; from that day forward he remained free of those scruples and held it for certain that Our Lord through his mercy had wished to deliver him. . . .

[*The Autobiography of St. Ignatius Loyola with Related Documents*, trans. Joseph F. O'Callaghan (Fordham University Press, 1992), 21–25, 35–36]

Selection 43: Ignatius of Loyola, *Spiritual Exercises* (1548)

The basis for the **Spiritual Exercises** ***was developed the next year after Ignatius's injury, during an intense period of prayer and self-mortification. The book, which was under revision until its publication in 1548, contains pieces from a variety of literary genres. As its title indicates, the whole work is intended as a method to be experienced, not simply a text to be read. This excerpt from the*** **Rules for Thinking with the Church,** ***included in the*** **Exercises,** ***shows how Jesuits were to be completely submissive to the hierarchical church.***

Introductory Observations

By the term "Spiritual Exercises" is meant every method of examination of conscience, of meditation, of contemplation, of vocal and mental prayer, and of other spiritual activities that will be mentioned later. For just as taking a walk, journeying on foot, and running are bodily exercises, so we call spiritual exercises every way of preparing and disposing the soul to rid itself of all inordinate attachments, and, after their removal, of seeking and finding the will of God in the disposition of our life for the salvation of our soul. . . .

First Principle and Foundation

Man is created to praise, reverence, and serve God our Lord, and by this means to save his soul.

The other things on the face of the earth are created for man to help him in attaining the end for which he is created. . . .

Rules for Thinking with the Church

The following rules should be observed to foster the true attitude of mind we ought to have in the church militant. . . .

4. We must praise highly religious life, virginity, and continence; and matrimony ought not be praised as much as any of these. . . .

9. Finally, we must praise all the commandments of the church, and be on the alert to find reasons to defend them, and by no means in order to criticize them. . . .[6]

13. If we wish to proceed securely in all things, we must hold fast to the following principle: What seems to me white, I will believe black if the hierarchical church so defines. For I must be convinced that in Christ our Lord, the bridegroom, and in his spouse the church, only one Spirit holds sway, which governs and rules for the salvation of souls. For it is by the same Spirit and Lord who gave the Ten Commandments that our holy mother church is ruled and governed. . . .

15. We should not make it a habit of speaking much of predestination. If somehow at times it comes to be spoken of, it must be done in such a way that the people are not led into any error. They are at times misled, so that they say: "Whether I shall be saved or lost, has already been determined, and this cannot be changed whether my actions are good or bad." So they become indolent and neglect the works that are conducive to the salvation and spiritual progress of their souls.

16. In the same way, much caution is necessary, lest by much talk about faith, and much insistence on it without any distinctions or explanations, occasion be given to the people, whether before or after they have faith informed by charity, to become slothful and lazy in good works.

17. Likewise we ought not to speak of grace at such length and with such emphasis that the poison of doing away with liberty is engendered.

Hence, as far as is possible with the help of God, one may speak of faith and grace that the divine majesty may be praised. But let it not be done in such a way, above all not in times which are as dangerous as ours, that works and free will suffer harm, or that they are considered of no value.[7]

18. Though the zealous service of God our Lord out of pure love should be esteemed above all, we ought also to praise highly the fear of the divine majesty. For not only filial fear but also servile fear is pious and very holy. When nothing higher or more useful is attained, it is very helpful for rising from mortal sin, and once this is accomplished, one may easily advance to filial fear, which is wholly pleasing and agreeable to God our Lord since it is inseparably associated with the love of him.

[*The Spiritual Exercises of St. Ignatius*, ed. Louis J. Puhl (Chicago: Loyola University Press, 1951), 1, 12, 157–61]

Selection 44: Teresa of Ávila, *The Book of Her Life* (1562)

Teresa of Ávila (1515–1582) became a Carmelite nun in 1535, but her increase in devotion occurred around

6. Contrast this sentiment with Luther's method of questioning the commandments of the church in Selection 14, *95 Theses*, theses 81–91.

7. In these rules, Ignatius reflects the common Catholic concern that the Protestants emphasize grace and faith to the exclusion of free will and good works.

1555 while she was praying before an image of the suffering Christ. She founded her own Carmelite house in 1562 that would follow the order's primitive rule, which became known as the "Discalced" (barefoot) Carmelites. In 1970, Teresa became the first woman to be officially declared a Doctor of the Church.

This excerpt from her autobiography discusses the beginning stages of prayer on the way to mystical union. The final excerpt describes her most famous ecstatic vision.

Chapter 11

3. What a charming way to seek the love of God! And then we desire it with our hands full, as they say. We have our attachments since we do not strive to direct our desires to a good effect and raise them up from the earth completely; but to have many spiritual consolations along with attachments is incongruous, nor does it seem to me that the two can get along together. Since we do not succeed in giving up everything at once, this treasure as a result is not given to us all at once. May it please the Lord that drop by drop He may give it to us, even though it cost us all the trials in the world. . . .

6. I shall have to make use of some comparison, although I should like to excuse myself from this since I am a woman and write simply what they ordered me to write. But these spiritual matters for anyone who like myself has not gone through studies are so difficult to explain. I shall have to find some mode of explaining myself, and it may be less often that I hit upon a good comparison. Seeing so much stupidity will provide some recreation for your Reverence.

It seems now to me that I read or heard of this comparison—for since I have a bad memory, I don't know where or for what reason it was used, but it will be all right for my purposes. Beginners must realize that in order to give delight to the Lord they are starting to cultivate a garden on very barren soil, full of abominable weeds. His Majesty pulls up the weeds and plants good seed. Now let us keep in mind that all of this is already done by the time a soul is determined to practice prayer and has begun to make use of it. And with the help of God we must strive like good gardeners to get these plants to grow and take pains to water them so that they don't wither but come to bud and flower and give forth a most pleasant fragrance to provide refreshment for this Lord of ours. Then He will often come to take delight in this garden and find His joy among these virtues. . . .

Chapter 29

13. The Lord wanted me while in this state [of rapture] to see sometimes the following vision:[8] I saw close to me toward my left side an angel in bodily form. I don't usually see angels in bodily form except on rare occasions; although many times angels appear to me, but without my seeing them, as in the intellectual vision I spoke about before. This time, though, the Lord desired that I see the vision in the following way: the angel was not large but small; he was very beautiful, and his face was so aflame that he seemed to be one of those very sublime angels that appear to be all afire. They must belong to those they call the cherubim, for they didn't tell me their names. But I see clearly that in heaven there is so much difference between some angels and others and between these latter and still others that I wouldn't know how to explain it. I saw in his hands a large golden dart and at the end of the iron tip there appeared to be a little fire. It seemed to me this angel plunged the dart several times into my heart

8. According to Teresa, this rapture, or mystical union with God, is the final stage of prayer.

and that it reached deep within me. When he drew it out, I thought he was carrying off with him the deepest part of me; and he left me all on fire with great love of God. The pain was so great that it made me moan, and the sweetness this greatest pain caused me was so superabundant that there is no desire capable of taking it away; nor is the soul content with less than God. The pain is not bodily but spiritual, although the body doesn't fail to share in some of it, and even a great deal. The loving exchange that takes place between the soul and God is so sweet that I beg Him in His goodness to give a taste of this love to anyone who thinks I am lying. . . .

[*The Collected Works of St. Teresa of Avila*, vol. 1, trans. K. Kavanaugh and O. Rodriguez (Washington, DC: ICS Publications, 1976), 111–13, 252]

C. Roman Catholic Confessionalization

Selection 45: Council of Trent (1545–1563)

The Council of Trent (1545–1547, 1551–1552, 1562–1563), regarded by the Roman Catholic Church as the nineteenth ecumenical council, gathered to consider the new doctrinal challenges of the Protestants. The council affirmed the normative equality of Scripture and church teaching, accepted the Greek books (or Apocrypha) of the Old Testament into the canon of Scripture, and countered Protestant interpretations of doctrines such as justification, sacraments, and Eucharist. Trent also decreed that theological publications would be subject to episcopal approval.

The Council of Trent helped seal the schism in the Western Church that began with the conflict between Luther and Pope Leo X. Trent was the conciliar and official endorsement of a certain medieval thread of doctrinal development that, from the Protestant perspective, was characterized by a set of unwarranted innovations. As a codification of Roman Catholic "Reformation," the Tridentine decrees and canons embodied an anti-Protestant confessionalization that endured for four centuries, until Vatican II in the 1960s.

SESSION 4 (8 April 1546)
Decree concerning the Canonical Scriptures

The sacred and holy, ecumenical, and general Synod of Trent,—lawfully assembled in the Holy Ghost, the same three legates of the Apostolic See presiding therein,—keeping this always in view, that, errors being removed, the purity itself of the Gospel be preserved in the Church; which (Gospel), before promised through the prophets in the holy Scriptures, our Lord Jesus Christ, the Son of God, first promulgated with His own mouth, and then commanded to be preached by His Apostles to every creature, as the fountain of all, both saving truth, and moral discipline; and seeing clearly that this truth and discipline are contained in the written books, and the unwritten traditions which, received by the Apostles from the mouth of Christ himself, or from the Apostles themselves, the Holy Ghost dictating, have come down even unto us, transmitted as it were from hand to hand: [the Synod] following the examples of the orthodox Fathers, receives and venerates with an equal affection of piety and reverence, all the books both of the Old and of the New Testament—seeing that one God is the author of both—as also the said traditions, as well those appertaining to faith as to morals, as having been dictated, either by Christ's own word of mouth, or by the Holy Ghost, and preserved in the Catholic Church by a continuous succession.

And it has thought it meet that a list of the sacred books be inserted in this decree, lest a doubt may arise in any one's mind, which are the books that are received by this Synod. They are as set down here below: of the Old Testament: the five books of Moses, to wit, Genesis, Exodus, Leviticus, Numbers, Deuteronomy; Joshua, Judges, Ruth, four books of Kings, two of Paralipomenon, the first book of Esdras, and the second which is entitled Nehemiah; Tobit, Judith, Esther, Job, the Davidical Psalter, consisting of a hundred and fifty psalms; the Proverbs, Ecclesiastes, the Canticle of Canticles, Wisdom, Ecclesiasticus, Isaiah, Jeremiah, with Baruch; Ezekiel, Daniel; the twelve minor prophets, to wit, Hosea, Joel, Amos, Obadiah, Jonah, Micah, Nahum, Habakkuk, Zephaniah, Haggai, Zechariah, Malachi; two books of the Maccabees, the first and the second. Of the New Testament: the four Gospels, according to Matthew, Mark, Luke, and John; the Acts of the Apostles written by Luke the Evangelist; fourteen epistles of Paul the apostle, (one) to the Romans, two to the Corinthians, (one) to the Galatians, to the Ephesians, to the Philippians, to the Colossians, two to the Thessalonians, two to Timothy, (one) to Titus, to Philemon, to the Hebrews; two of Peter the apostle, three of John the apostle, one of the apostle James, one of Jude the apostle, and the Apocalypse of John the apostle.

But if any one receive not, as sacred and canonical, the said books entire with all their parts, as they have been used to be read in the Catholic Church, and as they are contained in the old Latin vulgate edition; and knowingly and deliberately contemn the traditions aforesaid; let him be anathema. Let all, therefore, understand, in what order, and in what manner, the said Synod, after having laid the foundation of the Confession of faith, will proceed, and what testimonies and authorities it will mainly use in confirming dogmas, and in restoring morals in the Church.[9]

SESSION 6 (13 January 1547)
Canons on Justification

Canon I.—If any one saith, that man may be justified before God by his own works, whether done through the teaching of human nature, or that of the law, without the grace of God through Jesus Christ: let him be anathema.

Canon II.—If any one saith, that the grace of God, through Jesus Christ, is given only for this, that man may be able more easily to live justly, and to merit eternal life, as if, by free-will without grace, he were able to do both, though hardly indeed and with difficulty: let him be anathema.

Canon III.—If any one saith, that without the prevenient inspiration of the Holy Ghost, and without his help, man can believe, hope, love, or be penitent as he ought, so that the grace of Justification may be bestowed upon him: let him be anathema.

Canon IV.—If any one saith, that man's free-will moved and excited by God, by assenting to God exciting and calling, nowise cooperates towards disposing and preparing itself for obtaining the grace of Justification; that it can not refuse its consent, if it would, but that, as something inanimate, it does nothing whatever and is merely passive: let him be anathema.

9. In the ongoing question about religious authority, the Roman Church here defines more precisely the extent of the written canon, which, especially in the case of the Old Testament, had remained somewhat fluid since the patristic period.

Canon V.—If any one saith, that, since Adam's sin, the free-will of man is lost and extinguished; or, that it is a thing with only a name, yea a name without a reality, a figment, in fine, introduced into the Church by Satan: let him be anathema.

Canon VI.—If any one saith, that it is not in man's power to make his ways evil, but that the works that are evil God worketh as well as those that are good, not permissively only, but properly, and of himself, in such wise that the treason of Judas is no less his own proper work than the vocation of Paul: let him be anathema.

Canon VII.—If any one saith, that all works done before Justification, in whatsoever way they be done, are truly sins, or merit the hatred of God; or that the more earnestly one strives to dispose himself for grace, the more grievously he sins: let him be anathema.

Canon VIII.—If any one saith, that the fear of hell,—whereby, by grieving for our sins, we flee unto the mercy of God, or refrain from sinning,—is a sin, or makes sinners worse: let him be anathema.

Canon IX.—If any one saith, that by faith alone the impious is justified, in such wise as to mean, that nothing else is required to cooperate in order to the obtaining the grace of Justification, and that it is not in any way necessary, that he be prepared and disposed by the movement of his own will: let him be anathema.

Canon X.—If any one saith, that men are just without the justice of Christ, whereby he merited for us to be justified; or that it is by that justice itself that they are formally just: let him be anathema.

Canon XI.—If any one saith, that men are justified, either by the sole imputation of the justice of Christ, or by the sole remission of sins, to the exclusion of the grace and *the charity which is poured forth in their hearts by the Holy Ghost*,[10] and is inherent in them; or even that the grace, whereby we are justified, is only the favor of God: let him be anathema.

Canon XII.—If any one saith, that justifying faith is nothing else but confidence in the divine mercy which remits sins for Christ's sake; or, that this confidence alone is that whereby we are justified: let him be anathema.

Canon XIII.—If any one saith, that it is necessary for every one, for the obtaining the remission of sins, that he believe for certain, and without any wavering arising from his own infirmity and indisposition, that his sins are forgiven him: let him be anathema.

Canon XIV.—If any one saith, that man is truly absolved from his sins and justified, because that he assuredly believed himself absolved and justified; or, that no one is truly justified but he who believes himself justified; and that, by this faith alone, absolution and justification are effected: let him be anathema.

Canon XV.—If any one saith, that a man, who is born again and justified, is bound of faith to believe that he is assuredly in the number of the predestinate: let him be anathema.

Canon XVI.—If any one saith, that he will for certain, of an absolute and infallible certainty, have that great gift of perseverance unto the end,—unless he have learned this by special revelation: let him be anathema.

Canon XVII.—If any one saith, that the grace of Justification is only attained to by those who are predestined unto life; but that all others who are called, are called indeed, but receive not grace, as being, by the divine power, predestined unto evil: let him be anathema.

Canon XVIII.—If any one saith, that the commandments of God are, even for one that is justified and constituted in grace, impossible to keep: let him be anathema.

10. Rom. 5:5.

Canon XIX.—If any one saith, that nothing besides faith is commanded in the Gospel; that other things are indifferent, neither commanded nor prohibited, but free; or, that the ten commandments nowise appertain to Christians: let him be anathema.

Canon XX.—If any one saith, that the man who is justified and how perfect soever, is not bound to observe the commandments of God and of the Church, but only to believe; as if indeed the Gospel were a bare and absolute promise of eternal life, without the condition of observing the commandments: let him be anathema.

Canon XXI.—If any one saith, that Christ Jesus was given of God to men, as a redeemer in whom to trust, and not also as a legislator whom to obey: let him be anathema.

Canon XXII.—If any one saith, that the justified, either is able to persevere, without the special help of God, in the justice received; or that, with that help, he is not able: let him be anathema.

Canon XXIII.—If any one saith, that a man once justified can sin no more, nor lose grace, and that therefore he that falls and sins was never truly justified; or, on the other hand, that he is able, during his whole life, to avoid all sins, even those that are venial,—except by a special privilege from God, as the Church holds in regard of the Blessed Virgin: let him be anathema.

Canon XXIV.—If any one saith, that the justice received is not preserved and also increased before God through good works; but that the said works are merely the fruits and signs of Justification obtained, but not a cause of the increase thereof: let him be anathema.

Canon XXV.—If any one saith, that, in every good work, the just sins venially at least, or—which is more intolerable still—mortally, and consequently deserves eternal punishments; and that for this cause only he is not damned, that God does not impute those works unto damnation: let him be anathema.

Canon XXVI.—If any one saith, that the just ought not, for their good works done in God,[11] to expect and hope for an eternal recompense from God, through his mercy and the merit of Jesus Christ, if so be that they persevere to the end in well doing and in keeping the divine commandments: let him be anathema.

Canon XXVII.—If any one saith, that there is no mortal sin but that of infidelity; or, that grace once received is not lost by any other sin, however grievous and enormous, save by that of infidelity: let him be anathema.

Canon XXVIII.—If any one saith, that, grace being lost through sin, faith also is always lost with it; or, that the faith which remains, though it be not a lively faith, is not a true faith; or, that he who has faith without charity is not a Christian: let him be anathema.

Canon XXIX.—If any one saith, that he who has fallen after baptism is not able by the grace of God to rise again; or, that he is able indeed to recover the justice which he has lost, but by faith alone without the sacrament of Penance, contrary to what the holy Roman and universal Church—instructed by Christ and his Apostles—has hitherto professed, observed, and taught: let him be anathema.

Canon XXX.—If any one saith, that, after the grace of Justification has been received, to every penitent sinner the guilt is remitted, and the debt of eternal punishment is blotted out in such wise that there remains not any debt of temporal punishment to be discharged either in this world, or in the next in Purgatory, before the entrance to the kingdom of heaven can be opened [to him]: let him be anathema.

Canon XXXI.—If any one saith, that the justified sins when he performs good works

11. See John 3:21.

with a view to an eternal recompense: let him be anathema.

Canon XXXII.—If any one saith, that the good works of one that is justified are in such manner the gifts of God, that they are not also the good merits of him that is justified; or, that the said justified, by the good works which he performs through the grace of God and the merit of Jesus Christ, whose living member he is, does not truly merit increase of grace, eternal life, and the attainment of that eternal life,—if so be, however, that he depart in grace,—and also an increase of glory: let him be anathema.

Canon XXXIII.—If any one saith, that, by the Catholic doctrine touching Justification, by this holy Synod set forth in this present decree, the glory of God, or the merits of our Lord Jesus Christ are in any way derogated from, and not rather that the truth of our faith, and the glory in fine of God and of Jesus Christ are rendered [more] illustrious: let him be anathema.

SESSION 13 (11 October 1551)
Decree concerning the Most Holy Sacrament of the Eucharist

Chapter V: On the worship and veneration to be shown to this most holy sacrament

Wherefore, there is no room left for doubt, that all the faithful of Christ may, according to the custom ever received in the Catholic Church, render in veneration the worship of latria,[12] which is due to the true God, to this most holy sacrament. For not therefore is it the less to be adored on this account, that it was instituted by Christ, the Lord, in order to be received; for we believe that same God to be present therein, of whom the eternal Father, when introducing him into the world, says: *And let all the angels of God adore him;* whom the Magi, *falling down, adored;* who, in fine, as the Scripture testifies, was adored by the apostles in Galilee.

The holy Synod declares, moreover, that very piously and religiously was this custom introduced into the Church, that this sublime and venerable sacrament be, with special veneration and solemnity, celebrated, every year, on a certain day, and that a festival; and that it be borne reverently and with honor in processions through the streets and public places. For it is most just that there be certain appointed holy days, whereon all Christians may, with a special and unusual demonstration, testify that their minds are grateful and thankful to their common Lord and Redeemer for so ineffable and truly divine a benefit, whereby the victory and triumph of his death are represented. And so indeed did it behoove victorious truth to celebrate a triumph over falsehood and heresy, that thus her adversaries, at the sight of so much splendor, and in the midst of so great joy of the universal Church, may either *pine away* weakened and broken; or, touched with shame and confounded, at length repent.

A Corpus Christi procession of the sacrament

12. *Latreia* is the Greek word for "worship," and, according to the seventh ecumenical council (Nicaea II in 787), *latreia* is the true adoration due to God alone, distinct from *douleia*, the veneration due to icons. Here, the highest degree of worship is reserved for the eucharistic elements in procession. See also Canon VI below. This claim helps explain the strong reaction of the Protestant opponents.

Canons on the Most Holy Sacrament of the Eucharist

Canon I.—If any one denieth, that, in the sacrament of the most holy Eucharist, are contained truly, really, and substantially, the body and blood together with the soul and divinity of our Lord Jesus Christ, and consequently the whole Christ; but saith that he is only therein as in a sign, or in figure, or virtue: let him be anathema.

Canon II.—If any one saith, that, in the sacred and holy sacrament of the Eucharist, the substance of the bread and wine remains conjointly with the body and blood of our Lord Jesus Christ, and denieth that wonderful and singular conversion of the whole substance of the bread into the body, and of the whole substance of the wine into the blood—the species only of the bread and wine remaining—which conversion indeed the Catholic Church most aptly calls Transubstantiation: let him be anathema.

Canon III.—If any one denieth, that, in the venerable sacrament of the Eucharist, the whole Christ is contained under each species, and under every part of each species, when separated: let him be anathema.

Canon IV.—If any one saith, that, after the consecration is completed, the body and blood of our Lord Jesus Christ are not in the admirable sacrament of the Eucharist, but [are there] only during the use, whilst it is being taken, and not either before or after; and that, in the hosts, or consecrated particles, which are reserved or which remain after communion, the true body of the Lord remaineth not: let him be anathema.

Canon V.—If any one saith, either that the principal fruit of the most holy Eucharist is the remission of sins, or that other effects do not result therefrom: let him be anathema.

Canon VI.—If any one saith, that, in the holy sacrament of the Eucharist, Christ, the only-begotten Son of God, is not to be adored with the worship, even external of latria; and is, consequently, neither to be venerated with a special festive solemnity, nor to be solemnly borne about in procession, according to the laudable and universal rite and custom of holy Church; or, is not to be proposed publicly to the people to be adored, and that the adorers thereof are idolaters: let him be anathema.

Canon VII.—If any one saith, that it is not lawful for the sacred Eucharist to be reserved in the *sacrarium*,[13] but that, immediately after consecration, it must necessarily be distributed amongst those present; or, that it is not lawful that it be carried with honor to the sick: let him be anathema.

Canon VIII.—If any one saith, that Christ, given in the Eucharist, is eaten spiritually only, and not also sacramentally and really: let him be anathema.

Canon IX.—If any one denieth, that all and each of Christ's faithful of both sexes are bound, when they have attained to years of discretion, to communicate every year, at least at Easter, in accordance with the precept of holy Mother Church: let him be anathema.

Canon X.—If any one saith, that it is not lawful for the celebrating priest to communicate himself: let him be anathema.

Canon XI.—If any one saith, that faith alone is a sufficient preparation for receiving the sacrament of the most holy Eucharist: let him be anathema. And for fear lest so great a sacrament may be received unworthily, and so unto death and condemnation, this holy Synod ordains and declares, that sacramental confession, when a confessor may be had, is of necessity to be made beforehand, by those whose conscience is burthened with mortal sin, how contrite even soever they may think themselves. But if any one shall presume to teach, preach, or

13. That is, a sacred place within the church building.

obstinately to assert, or even in public disputation to defend the contrary, he shall be thereupon excommunicated.

SESSION 14 (25 November 1551)
Canons on the Most Holy Sacrament of Penance

Canon I.—If any one saith, that in the Catholic Church Penance is not truly and properly a sacrament, instituted by Christ our Lord for reconciling the faithful unto God, as often as they fall into sin after baptism: let him be anathema.

Canon II.—If any one, confounding the sacraments, saith that baptism is itself the sacrament of Penance, as though these two sacraments were not distinct, and that therefore Penance is not rightly called a second plank after shipwreck: let him be anathema.

Canon III.—If any one saith, that those words of the Lord the Saviour, *Receive ye the Holy Ghost, whose sins you shall forgive, they are forgiven them, and whose sins you shall retain, they are retained*, are not to be understood of the power of forgiving and of retaining sins in the sacrament of Penance, as the Catholic Church has always from the beginning understood them; but wrests them, contrary to the institution of this sacrament, to the power of preaching the gospel: let him be anathema.

Canon IV.—If any one denieth, that, for the entire and perfect remission of sins, there are required three acts in the penitent, which are as it were the matter of the sacrament of Penance, to wit, contrition, confession, and satisfaction, which are called the three parts of penance; or saith that there are two parts only of penance, to wit, the terrors with which the conscience is smitten upon being convinced of sin, and the faith, generated by the gospel, or by the absolution, whereby one believes that his sins are forgiven him through Christ: let him be anathema.

Canon V.—If any one saith, that the contrition which is acquired by means of the examination, collection, and detestation of sins,—whereby one *thinks over his years in the bitterness of his soul*,[14] by pondering on the grievousness, the multitude, the filthiness of his sins, the loss of eternal blessedness, and the eternal damnation which he has incurred, having therewith the purpose of a better life,—is not a true and profitable sorrow, does not prepare for grace, but makes a man a hypocrite and a greater sinner; in fine, that this [contrition] is a forced and not free and voluntary sorrow: let him be anathema.

Canon VI.—If any one denieth, either that sacramental confession was instituted, or is necessary to salvation, of divine right; or saith, that the manner of confessing secretly to a priest alone, which the Church hath ever observed from the beginning, and doth observe, is alien from the institution and command of Christ, and is a human invention: let him be anathema.

Canon VII.—If any one saith, that, in the sacrament of Penance, it is not necessary, of divine right, for the remission of sins, to confess all and singular the mortal sins which after due and diligent previous meditation are remembered, even those [mortal sins] which are secret, and those which are opposed to the two last commandments of the Decalogue, as also the circumstances which change the species of a sin; but [saith] that such confession is only useful to instruct and console the penitent, and that it was of old only observed in order to impose a canonical satisfaction; or saith that they, who strive to confess all their sins, wish to leave nothing to the divine mercy to pardon; or, finally, that it is not lawful to confess venial sins: let him be anathema.

Canon VIII.—If any one saith, that the confession of all sins, such as it is observed in the Church, is impossible, and is a human tradition

14. Isa. 38:15.

to be abolished by the godly; or that all and each of the faithful of Christ, of either sex, are not obliged thereunto once a year, conformably to the constitution of the great Council of Lateran, and that, for this cause, the faithful of Christ are to be persuaded not to confess during Lent: let him be anathema.

Canon IX.—If any one saith, that the sacramental absolution of the priest is not a judicial act, but a bare ministry of pronouncing and declaring sins to be forgiven to him who confesses; provided only he believe himself to be absolved, or [even though] the priest absolve not in earnest, but in joke; or saith, that the confession of the penitent is not required, in order that the priest may be able to absolve him: let him be anathema.

Canon X.—If any one saith, that priests, who are in mortal sin, have not the power of binding and loosing; or, that not priests alone are the ministers of absolution, but that, to all and each of the faithful of Christ is it said: *Whatsoever you shall bind upon earth shall be bound also in heaven; and whatsoever you shall loose upon earth, shall be loosed also in heaven; and, whose sins you shall forgive, they are forgiven them; and whose sins you shall retain, they are retained*;[15] by virtue of which words every one is able to absolve from sins, to wit, from public sins by reproof only, provided he who is reproved yield thereto, and from secret sins by a voluntary confession: let him be anathema.

Canon XI.—If any one saith, that bishops have not the right of reserving cases to themselves, except as regards external polity, and that therefore the reservation of cases hinders not, but that a priest may truly absolve from reserved cases: let him be anathema.

Canon XII.—If any one saith, that God always remits the whole punishment together with the guilt, and that the satisfaction of penitents is no other than the faith whereby they apprehend that Christ has satisfied for them: let him be anathema.

Canon XIII.—If any one saith, that satisfaction for sins, as to their temporal punishment, is nowise made to God, through the merits of Jesus Christ, by the punishments inflicted by him, and patiently borne, or by those enjoined by the priest, nor even by those voluntarily undertaken, as by fastings, prayers, alms-deeds, or by other works also of piety; and that, therefore, the best penance is merely a new life: let him be anathema.

Canon XIV.—If any one saith, that the satisfactions, by which penitents redeem their sins through Jesus Christ, are not a worship of God, but traditions of men, which obscure the doctrine of grace, and the true worship of God, and the benefit itself of the death of Christ: let him be anathema.

Canon XV.—If any one saith, that the keys are given to the Church, only *to loose*, not also *to bind;* and that, therefore, priests act contrary to the purpose of the keys, and contrary to the institution of Christ, when they impose punishments on those who confess; and that it is a fiction, that, after the eternal punishment has, by virtue of the keys, been removed, there remains for the most part a temporal punishment to be discharged: let him be anathema.

SESSION 22 (17 September 1562)
Doctrine on the Sacrifice of the Mass
Chapter 1

Forasmuch as, under the former Testament, according to the testimony of the Apostle Paul, there was no *perfection, because of the weakness of the Levitical priesthood;* there was need, God, the Father of mercies, so ordaining, that *another priest should rise, according to the order of Melchisedech*, our Lord Jesus Christ, who might consummate, and lead to what is perfect, as many

15. Matt. 18:18; John 20:23.

as were to be sanctified. He, therefore, our God and Lord, though he was about to offer himself once on the altar of the cross unto God the Father, *by means of his death*, there to operate *an eternal redemption;* nevertheless, because that his priesthood was not to be extinguished by his death, in the Last Supper, on the night in which he was betrayed,—that he might leave, to his own beloved Spouse the Church, a visible sacrifice, such as the nature of man requires, whereby that bloody sacrifice, once to be accomplished on the cross, might be represented, and the memory thereof remain even unto the end of the world, and its salutary virtue be applied to the remission of those sins which we daily commit,—declaring himself constituted *a priest forever, according to the order of Melchisedech*, he offered up to God the Father his own body and blood under the species of bread and wine; and, under the symbols of those same things, he delivered [his own body and blood] to be received by his apostles, whom he then constituted priests of the New Testament; and by those words, *Do this in commemoration of me*, he commanded them and their successors in the priesthood to offer [them]; even as the Catholic Church has always understood and taught. For, having celebrated the ancient Passover, which the multitude of the children of Israel immolated in memory of their going out of Egypt, he instituted the new Passover [to wit], himself to be immolated, under visible signs, by the Church through [the ministry of] priests, in memory of his own passage from this world unto the Father, when by the effusion of his own blood he redeemed us, *and delivered us from the power of darkness, and translated us into his kingdom.* And this is indeed that clean oblation, which can not be defiled by any unworthiness, or malice of those that offer [it]; which the Lord foretold by Malachi was to be *offered in every place, clean to his name, which was to be great amongst the Gentiles;*[16] and which the Apostle Paul, writing to the Corinthians, has not obscurely indicated, when he says, that they who are defiled by *the participation of the table of devils, can not be partakers of the table of the Lord;* by *the table*, meaning in both places the altar. This, in fine, is that oblation which was prefigured by various types of sacrifices, during the period of nature, and of the law; inasmuch as it comprises all the good things signified by those sacrifices, as being the consummation and perfection of them all.

[*The Creeds of Christendom*, vol. 2, ed. Philip Schaff (repr. Grand Rapids, MI: Baker, 1998), 79–82, 110–18, 131–32, 136–39, 163–69, 176–78]

Selection 46: *The Injunctions of Queen Mary* (1554)

After thoroughgoing reform in the Church of England was enacted under King Edward VI (r. 1547–1553), his successor Queen Mary Tudor (r. 1553–1558) steered the church back to Roman Catholicism. Although the* Marian Injunctions *did not outlast her short reign, they reflect her effort to reverse the advance of Protestant theology and practice. This temporary persecution of Protestants earned her the nickname "Bloody Mary."

4. Item, that every bishop and his officers, with all other persons aforesaid, have a vigilant eye, and use special diligence and foresight, that no person be admitted or received to any ecclesiastical function, benefice, or office, being a sacramentary,[17] infected or defamed with any notable kind of heresy or other great crime; and

16. Mal. 1:11 was frequently read in the early church in the context of the Lord's Supper.

17. That is, someone holding a Reformed (and especially Zwinglian) view that rejects the bodily presence of Christ in the Eucharist.

that the said bishop do stay, and cause to be stayed, as much as lieth in him, that benefices and ecclesiastical promotions do not notably decay, or take hindrance, by passing or confirming of unreasonable leases. . . .

7. Item, that every bishop, and all the other persons aforesaid, proceeding summarily, and with all celerity and speed, may and shall deprive, or declare deprived, and amove, according to their learning and discretion, all such persons from their benefices and ecclesiastical promotions, who, contrary to the state of their order and the laudable custom of the Church, have married and used women as their wives, or otherwise notably and slanderously disordered or abused themselves; sequestering also, during the said process, the fruits and profits of the said benefices and ecclesiastical promotions. . . .

11. Item, that all and all manner of processions of the Church be used, frequented, and continued after the old order of the Church, in the Latin tongue. . . .

15. Item, touching such persons as were heretofore promoted to any orders after the new sort and fashion of order, considering they were not ordered in very deed, the bishop of the diocese finding otherwise sufficiency and ability in those men, may supply that thing which wanted in them before; and then, according to his discretion, admit them to minister.

[*Documents Illustrative of English Church History*, ed. Henry Gee and William John Hardy (London: Macmillan, 1914), 380–83]

Further Reading

Bagchi, David V. N. *Luther's Earliest Opponents: Catholic Controversialists 1518–1525*. Minneapolis: Fortress Press, 1991.

Bireley, Robert. *The Refashioning of Catholicism, 1450–1700: A Reassessment of the Counter-Reformation*. Washington, D. C.: The Catholic University of America Press, 1999.

Idigoras, J. Ignacio Tellechea. *Ignatius of Loyola: The Pilgrim Saint*. Trans. Cornelius Michael Buckley. Chicago: Loyola University Press, 1994.

O'Malley, John W. *The First Jesuits*. Cambridge, MA: Harvard University Press, 1993.

———. *Trent: What Happened at the Council*. Cambridge, MA: Belknap Press of Harvard University Press, 2013.

———, ed. *Catholicism in Early Modern Europe: A Guide to Research*. St. Louis: Center for Reformation Research, 1988.

Chapter 5
Protestant Codifiers and Confessionalization

Reformist ideas caught on in many cities and spread like wildfire throughout northern and western Europe. Differences with the doctrines and practices of the Roman Church proved to be too deep for many reform-minded groups to remain in fellowship with Rome and its pope. In the 1520s and 1530s, it was not clear either that Protestant churches would survive or that reconciliation between them and the pope would be impossible. Yet the lines were quickly and sharply drawn that would lead to what we now call Roman Catholic and Protestant communions.

The relationships among Protestants were not so well defined, and ecclesiastical affiliations remained blurry into the second half of the sixteenth century. Protestant attempts to clarify these relationships sometimes forged much-needed unity but at other times tended to bring disunity to the reform movements. For example, the meeting of Luther and Zwingli in 1529 at the Marburg Colloquy was an early indication of just where the doctrinal boundaries were beginning to crystallize and would remain between Lutheran and Reformed Churches.

Real change happened during what has become known as the period of "confessionalization," from the Peace of Augsburg to the Peace of Westphalia (1555–1648). Especially during this period, Europe's unified Christian body was breaking down into various confessional identities and regions, affecting religious and political realities. These divisions were codified in more systematic presentations of doctrine and especially in "confessions" of faith. These confessions functioned to unify faith communities and to catechize the members, educating them in what was swiftly becoming a pluralistic environment with options. During this period, Protestant churches began forging their respective identities not only vis-à-vis the Roman Church—which had defined its position at Trent—but also in contrast with fellow Protestants. Subscription to these various confessional formulae marks the beginning of denominationalism in the West.

The Reformed Churches, led in the first generation by Zwingli, Johannes Oecolampadius (1482–1531), and Martin Bucer (1491–1551), found a powerful voice in John Calvin (1509–1564). Calvin, along with other such other second-generation reformers as Heinrich Bullinger (1504–1575), Wolfgang Musculus (1497–1563), and Peter Martyr Vermigli (1499–1562), began to codify Reformed thought as a distinct theological option. Calvin was never the lone voice of the Reformed tradition, but history has regarded him as this tradition's foremost spokesman. The Church of England, heavily influenced by Continental Reformed theology, was guided through its early years of reform primarily by the Archbishop of Canterbury, Thomas Cranmer (1489–1556), who was executed under the Catholic Queen Mary. The Protestant future of the Church, however, was stabilized under the long reign of Queen Elizabeth.

After Luther's death, the Lutheran Reformation did not have as many talented, internationally influential leaders as the Reformed Churches had. The chief exception to this generalization is Philipp Melanchthon (1497–1560), the younger contemporary and friend of Luther in Wittenberg.

Melanchthon was the primary author of the Augsburg Confession in 1530, and he aimed to be a moderating and irenic factor within Lutheranism. The "Philippists" who followed Melanchthon's lead in the midsixteenth century were opposed by the "Gnesio-" (that is, *genuine*) Lutherans, led by Matthias Flacius Illyricus (1520–1575). Against the later Melanchthon, the Gnesio-Lutherans held to a very strict doctrine of unconditional predestination, accusing the Philippists of synergism and semi-Pelagianism (neologisms coined in Protestant debates). But to the Philippists, Flacius approached Manichaeism when he suggested that sin is a substance. The greatest mediating influence in the Lutheran debates was Martin Chemnitz (1522–1586), who wrote, among other theological works, an extensive critique of the Council of Trent. The Formula of Concord (1577), largely due to Chemnitz's labor and influence, united the Lutheran factions. So instrumental was Martin Chemnitz to the harmony and systematizing of Lutheranism that an old saying claims, "If the second Martin had not come, the first Martin would scarcely have endured."

The revolutionary character of the early Reformation predictably settled into the post-Reformation impulse to secure its results. The distinctive ecclesiastical identities, shaped by the theologians and confessional documents, gave rise to Protestant orthodoxies that needed to be elaborated and defended against Roman Catholic and other Protestant opponents. The late sixteenth century witnessed the proliferation of Protestant universities and, within such academic settings, the thriving of Protestant scholasticism as a means of articulating these emerging theological trajectories. Scholastic method enabled Protestant theologians to meet their Roman Catholic counterparts with comparable academic weapons.

The Arminian controversy in The Netherlands serves as a typical illustration and reflection of the complex convergence of challenges throughout Europe during this period, including the use and authority of these new confessions of faith and their relationship to the Bible, the roles of church and state, religious toleration, the realities of ongoing war, and the controversy over predestination, a doctrine that caused furious debate within most confessional groups, including Roman Catholics, Lutherans, Anglicans, and the Reformed. The dispute over predestination and related topics, particularly as carried out in the Arminian context, would reverberate through and shape Protestant evangelicalism for the next four centuries.

A. Reformed

Selection 47: Guido de Brès, *Belgic Confession* (1561; rev. 1619)

Guido de Brès (1522–1567) composed the Belgic Confession for use in the French-speaking churches of the southern Low Countries. As an objection to Roman Catholic persecution of Protestants in The Netherlands, it was written to show that Reformed Christians were orthodox in their beliefs and practices and posed no threat to the social order. De Brès himself was martyred in 1567. His confession, which was revised at the Synod of Dordt in 1619, was readily received and, along with the Heidelberg Catechism *(see Selection 48) and the* Canons of the Synod of Dordt *(see Selection 60), it has been used as a standard in many Reformed Churches since 1571.*

Besides reflecting this stage of Reformed theology in the second generation of the Reformation, the Belgic Confession is also notable as one of the earliest Protestant statements positively to exclude the so-called Apocrypha from the Old Testament canon (articles 4 and 6). However, in line with most early Protestant sentiment, it still encourages Christians to "read these books and learn from them."

Article 1: The Only God

We all believe in our hearts and confess with our mouths that there is a single and simple spiritual being, whom we call God—eternal, incomprehensible, invisible, unchangeable, infinite, almighty; completely wise, just, and good, and the overflowing source of all good.

Article 2: The Means by Which We Know God

We know him by two means: First, by the creation, preservation, and government of the universe, since that universe is before our eyes like a beautiful book in which all creatures, great and small, are as letters to make us ponder the invisible things of God: his eternal power and his divinity, as the apostle Paul says in Romans 1:20. All these things are enough to convict men and to leave them without excuse.

Second, he makes himself known to us more openly by his holy and divine Word, as much as we need in this life, for his glory and for the salvation of his own.[1]

Article 3: The Written Word of God

We confess that this Word of God was not sent nor delivered by the will of men, but that holy men of God spoke, being moved by the Holy Spirit, as Peter says [2 Pet. 1:21]. Afterwards our God—because of the special care he has for us and our salvation—commanded his servants, the prophets and apostles, to commit this revealed Word to writing. He himself wrote with his own finger the two tables of the law. Therefore we call such writings holy and divine Scriptures.

Article 4: The Canonical Books

. . . In the church of God the list is as follows:

In the Old Testament, the five books of Moses—Genesis, Exodus, Leviticus, Numbers, Deuteronomy; the books of Joshua, Judges, and Ruth; the two books of Samuel, and two of Kings; the two books of Chronicles, called Paralipomenon; the first book of Ezra; Nehemiah, Esther, Job; the Psalms of David; the three books of Solomon—Proverbs, Ecclesiastes, and the Song; the four major prophets—Isaiah,

1. These two means of knowledge are also known as general revelation and special revelation, respectively.

Jeremiah,[2] Ezekiel, Daniel; and then the other twelve minor prophets—Hosea, Joel, Amos, Obadiah, Jonah, Micah, Nahum, Habakkuk, Zephaniah, Haggai, Zechariah, Malachi.

In the New Testament, the four gospels—Matthew, Mark, Luke, and John; the Acts of the Apostles; the fourteen letters of Paul—to the Romans; the two letters to the Corinthians; to the Galatians, Ephesians, Philippians, and Colossians; the two letters to the Thessalonians; the two letters to Timothy; to Titus, Philemon, and to the Hebrews; the seven letters of the other apostles—one of James; two of Peter; three of John; one of Jude; and the Revelation of the apostle John.

Article 5: The Authority of Scripture

We receive all these books and these only as holy and canonical, for the regulating, founding, and establishing of our faith. And we believe without a doubt all things contained in them—not so much because the church receives and approves them as such but above all because the Holy Spirit testifies in our hearts that they are from God, and also because they prove themselves to be from God. For even the blind themselves are able to see that the things predicted in them do happen.

Article 6: The Difference Between Canonical and Apocryphal Books

We distinguish between these holy books and the apocryphal ones, which are the third and fourth books of Esdras; the books of Tobit, Judith, Wisdom, Jesus Sirach, Baruch; what was added to the Story of Esther; the Song of the Three Children in the Furnace; the Story of Susannah; the Story of Bell and the Dragon; the Prayer of Manasseh; and the two books of Maccabees. The church may certainly read these books and learn from them as far as they agree with the canonical books. But they do not have such power and virtue that one could confirm from their testimony any point of faith or of the Christian religion. Much less can they detract from the authority of the other holy books.

Article 7: The Sufficiency of Scripture

We believe that this Holy Scripture contains the will of God completely and that everything one must believe to be saved is sufficiently taught in it. For since the entire manner of service which God requires of us is described in it at great length, no one—even an apostle or an angel from heaven, as Paul says [Gal. 1:8]—ought to teach other than what the Holy Scriptures have already taught us. For since it is forbidden to add to or subtract from the Word of God [Deut. 12:32; Rev. 22:18-19], this plainly demonstrates that the teaching is perfect and complete in all respects. Therefore we must not consider human writings—no matter how holy their authors may have been—equal to the divine writings; nor may we put custom, nor the majority, nor age, nor the passage of time or persons, nor councils, decrees, or official decisions above the truth of God, for truth is above everything else. For all human beings are liars by nature and more vain than vanity itself. Therefore we reject with all our hearts everything that does not agree with this infallible rule, as we are taught to do by the apostles when they say, "Test the spirits to see if they are of God" [1 John 4:1], and also, "If anyone comes to you and does not bring this teaching, do not receive him into your house" [2 John 10].

Article 8: The Trinity

In keeping with this truth and Word of God we believe in one God, who is one single essence, in whom there are three persons, really, truly,

2. "Jeremiah" includes both the prophetic book and Lamentations.

and eternally distinct according to their incommunicable properties—namely, Father, Son, and Holy Spirit. The Father is the cause, origin, and source of all things, visible as well as invisible. The Son is the Word, the Wisdom, and the image of the Father. The Holy Spirit is the eternal power and might, proceeding from the Father and the Son.[3] Nevertheless, this distinction does not divide God into three, since Scripture teaches us that the Father, the Son, and the Holy Spirit each has his own subsistence distinguished by characteristics—yet in such a way that these three persons are only one God. It is evident then that the Father is not the Son and that the Son is not the Father, and that likewise the Holy Spirit is neither the Father nor the Son. Nevertheless, these persons, thus distinct, are neither divided nor fused or mixed together. For the Father did not take on flesh, nor did the Spirit, but only the Son. The Father was never without his Son, nor without his Holy Spirit, since all these are equal from eternity, in one and the same essence. There is neither a first nor a last, for all three are one in truth and power, in goodness and mercy. . . .

Article 13: The Doctrine of God's Providence

We believe that this good God, after he created all things, did not abandon them to chance or fortune but leads and governs them according to his holy will, in such a way that nothing happens in this world without his orderly arrangement. Yet God is not the author of, nor can he be charged with, the sin that occurs. . . .

This doctrine gives us unspeakable comfort since it teaches us that nothing can happen to us by chance but only by the arrangement of our gracious heavenly Father. He watches over us with fatherly care, keeping all creatures under his control, so that not one of the hairs on our heads (for they are all numbered) nor even a little bird can fall to the ground [Matt. 10:29-30] without the will of our Father. In this thought we rest, knowing that he holds in check the devils and all our enemies, who cannot hurt us without his permission and will. . . .

Article 14: The Creation and Fall of Man

We believe that God created man from the dust of the earth and made and formed him in his image and likeness—good, just, and holy; able by his own will to conform in all things to the will of God. But when he was in honor he did not understand it [Ps. 49:20] and did not recognize his excellence. But he subjected himself willingly to sin and consequently to death and the curse, lending his ear to the word of the devil. For he transgressed the commandment of life, which he had received, and by his sin he separated himself from God, who was his true life, having corrupted his entire nature. So he made himself guilty and subject to physical and spiritual death, having become wicked, perverse, and corrupt in all his ways. He lost all his excellent gifts which he had received from God, and he retained none of them except for small traces which are enough to make him inexcusable. Moreover, all the light in us is turned to darkness, as the Scripture teaches us: "The light shone in the darkness, and the darkness did not receive it" [John 1:5]. Here John calls men "darkness." . . .

Article 15: The Doctrine of Original Sin

We believe that by the disobedience of Adam original sin has been spread through the whole human race. It is a corruption of all nature—an inherited depravity which even infects small infants in their mother's womb, and the root which produces in man every sort of sin. It is therefore so vile and enormous in God's sight

3. The affirmation of the "filioque" clause ("and the Son"), added to the Western version of the Nicene-Constantinopolitan Symbol, is typical among Protestants.

that it is enough to condemn the human race, and it is not abolished or wholly uprooted even by baptism, seeing that sin constantly boils forth as though from a contaminated spring. Nevertheless, it is not imputed to God's children for their condemnation but is forgiven by his grace and mercy—not to put them to sleep but so that the awareness of this corruption might often make believers groan as they long to be set free from the "body of this death" [Rom. 7:24]. Therefore we reject the error of the Pelagians who say that this sin is nothing else than a matter of imitation.

Article 16: The Doctrine of Election

We believe that—all Adam's descendants having thus fallen into perdition and ruin by the sin of the first man—God showed himself to be as he is: merciful and just. He is merciful in withdrawing and saving from this perdition those whom he, in his eternal and unchangeable counsel, has elected and chosen in Jesus Christ our Lord by his pure goodness, without any consideration of their works. He is just in leaving the others in their ruin and fall into which they plunged themselves. . . .

Article 36: The Civil Government

We believe that because of the depravity of the human race our good God has ordained kings, princes, and civil officers. He wants the world to be governed by laws and policies so that human lawlessness may be restrained and that everything may be conducted in good order among human beings. For that purpose he has placed the sword in the hands of the government, to punish evil people and protect the good. And the government's task is not limited to caring for and watching over the public domain but extends also to upholding the sacred ministry, with a view to removing and destroying all idolatry and false worship of the Antichrist; to promoting the kingdom of Jesus Christ; and to furthering the preaching of the gospel everywhere; to the end that God may be honored and served by everyone, as he requires in his Word. . . .

And on this matter we denounce the Anabaptists, other anarchists, and in general all those who want to reject the authorities and civil officers and to subvert justice by introducing common ownership of goods and corrupting the moral order that God has established among human beings. . . .[4]

[*Belgic Confession* (Grand Rapids, MI: Faith Alive, 1985), 1–6, 11–15, 37–38]

Selection 48: *Heidelberg Catechism* (1563)

In response to a perceived lack of lay education and involvement in the one catholic faith, reformers stressed the need for all believers to add knowledge to their faith. Catechisms were produced in order to instruct believers in the basic principles of the faith and to reiterate the distinctive emphases of the Reformation. Not only was the Reformation a catechetical movement—with its stress on lay education—but it was also biblical and polemical. The reference in Q&A 80 to the Roman Mass as "an accursed idolatry" was not present in the first edition but was quickly added under pressure from Frederick III (Elector Palatine). All these characteristics are reflected in the Heidelberg Catechism, written primarily by Zacharias Ursinus (1534–1583) for the Reformed Churches in German-speaking lands.

4. In recent editions designed for confessional subscription, the last two sentences of Article 36 included here have been stricken from the body of the text and placed in footnotes.

1. Q[uestion]. What is your only comfort in life and in death?

A[nswer]. That I am not my own, but belong—body and soul, in life and in death—to my faithful Savior, Jesus Christ. He has fully paid for all my sins with his precious blood, and has set me free from the tyranny of the devil. He also watches over me in such a way that not a hair can fall from my head without the will of my Father in heaven; in fact, all things must work together for my salvation. Because I belong to him, Christ, by his Holy Spirit, assures me of eternal life and makes me wholeheartedly willing and ready from now on to live for him.

2. Q. What must you know to live and die in the joy of this comfort?

A. Three things: first, how great my sin and misery are; second, how I am set free from all my sins and misery; third, how I am to thank God for such deliverance. . . .[5]

75. Q. How does the holy supper remind and assure you that you share in Christ's one sacrifice on the cross and in all his benefits?

A. In this way: Christ has commanded me and all believers to eat this broken bread and to drink this cup in remembrance of him. With this command come these promises: First, as surely as I see with my eyes the bread of the Lord broken for me and the cup shared with me, so surely his body was offered and broken for me and his blood poured out for me on the cross. Second, as surely as I receive from the hand of the one who serves, and taste with my mouth the bread and cup of the Lord, given me as sure signs of Christ's body and blood, so surely he nourishes and refreshes my soul for eternal life with his crucified body and poured-out blood.

76. Q. What does it mean to eat the crucified body of Christ and to drink his poured-out blood?

A. It means to accept with a believing heart the entire suffering and death of Christ and thereby to receive forgiveness of sins and eternal life. But it means more. Through the Holy Spirit, who lives both in Christ and in us, we are united more and more to Christ's blessed body. And so, although he is in heaven and we are on earth, we are flesh of his flesh and bone of his bone. And we forever live on and are governed by one Spirit, as the members of our body are by one soul. . . .

78. Q. Do the bread and wine become the real body and blood of Christ?

A. No. Just as the water of baptism is not changed into Christ's blood and does not itself wash away sins but is simply a divine sign and assurance of these things, so too the holy bread of the Lord's Supper does not become the actual body of Christ, even though it is called the body of Christ in keeping with the nature and language of sacraments.

79. Q. Why then does Christ call the bread his body and the cup his blood, or the new covenant in his blood, and Paul use the words, a sharing in Christ's body and blood?

A. Christ has good reason for these words. He wants to teach us that just as bread and wine nourish the temporal life, so too his crucified body and poured-out blood are the true food and drink of our souls for eternal life. But more important, he wants to assure us, by this visible sign and pledge, that we, through the

5. This answer provides the structure for the three main sections of the catechism: Misery (Part 1), Deliverance (Part 2), and Gratitude (Part 3).

Holy Spirit's work, share in his true body and blood as surely as our mouths receive these holy signs in his remembrance, and that all of his suffering and obedience are as definitely ours as if we personally had suffered and made satisfaction for our sins.

80. Q. How does the Lord's Supper differ from the Roman Catholic Mass?

A. The Lord's Supper declares to us that all our sins are completely forgiven through the one sacrifice of Jesus Christ, which he himself accomplished on the cross once for all. It also declares to us that the Holy Spirit grafts us into Christ, who with his true body is now in heaven at the right hand of the Father where he wants us to worship him. But the Mass teaches that the living and the dead do not have their sins forgiven through the suffering of Christ unless Christ is still offered for them daily by the priests. It also teaches that Christ is bodily present under the form of bread and wine where Christ is therefore to be worshiped. Thus the Mass is basically nothing but a denial of the one sacrifice and suffering of Jesus Christ and a condemnable idolatry.[6]

81. Q. Who should come to the Lord's table?

A. Those who are displeased with themselves because of their sins, but who nevertheless trust that their sins are pardoned and that their remaining weakness is covered by the suffering and death of Christ, and who also desire more and more to strengthen their faith and to lead a better life. Hypocrites and those who are unrepentant, however, eat and drink judgment on themselves.

82. Q. Should those be admitted to the Lord's Supper who show by what they profess and how they live that they are unbelieving and ungodly?

A. No, that would dishonor God's covenant and bring down God's wrath upon the entire congregation. Therefore, according to the instruction of Christ and his apostles, the Christian church is duty-bound to exclude such people, by the official use of the keys of the kingdom, until they reform their lives.

83. Q. What are the keys of the kingdom?

A. The preaching of the holy gospel and Christian discipline toward repentance. Both of them open the kingdom of heaven to believers and close it to unbelievers.

84. Q. How does preaching the holy gospel open and close the kingdom of heaven?

A. According to the command of Christ: The kingdom of heaven is opened by proclaiming and publicly declaring to all believers, each and every one, that, as often as they accept the gospel promise in true faith, God, because of Christ's merit, truly forgives all their sins. The kingdom of heaven is closed, however, by proclaiming and publicly declaring to unbelievers and hypocrites that, as long as they do not repent, the wrath of God and eternal condemnation rest on them. God's judgment, both in this life and in the life to come, is based on this gospel testimony.

85. Q. How is the kingdom of heaven closed and opened by Christian discipline?

6. The first edition of the catechism did not include Q&A 80. It was added to the second edition, and the language of "condemnable idolatry" was added to the third edition. It is a direct response to the canons and decrees of the Council of Trent on the Mass (see Selection 45). The polemical, final three sentences of the answer are often set off from the main text in brackets in modern editions.

A. According to the command of Christ: Those who, though called Christians, profess unchristian teachings or live unchristian lives, and who after repeated personal and loving admonitions, refuse to abandon their errors and evil ways, and who after being reported to the church, that is, to those ordained by the church for that purpose, fail to respond also to the church's admonitions—such persons the church excludes from the Christian community by withholding the sacraments from them, and God also excludes them from the kingdom of Christ.

Such persons, when promising and demonstrating genuine reform, are received again as members of Christ and of his church.[7]

[*Heidelberg Catechism* (Grand Rapids, MI: Faith Alive, 2013), 1–2, 26–31]

Selection 49: Zacharias Ursinus, *Commentary on the Heidelberg Catechism* (1584)

Ursinus, professor at Heidelberg and the primary author of the Heidelberg Catechism *(see Selection 48), delivered his ongoing lectures on the* Catechism, *gathered and published posthumously as* Doctrinae Christianae compendium (A Compendium of Christian Doctrine). *This selection provides an example of the authorial intention, doctrinal formulae, and polemical theology behind the simple questions and answers that appear in the* Catechism *intended for the laity. The interpretation and binding force of the emerging confessions and catechisms became topics for conversation and heated debate during this period of Protestant scholasticism. In this excerpt on the Lord's Supper (specifically, from his exposition of Q&A 78 and 80), Ursinus distinguishes the Reformed view from the Lutheran and also explains the strong language of the* Catechism *directed against the Roman Mass.*

Question 78: Do the bread and wine become the real body and blood of Christ?

Exposition
The Arguments Drawn from the Analogy, or Correspondence of the Articles of Our Faith

From the article of Christ's ascension. . . .[8] Here, however, two things must be observed: 1. The argument which we draw from the article of Christ's ascension, does not remove his body from the supper, as some slanderously say of us; but only from the bread; for the distance between heaven and earth, whilst it makes it impossible that Christ's body should exist in heaven, and be in the bread at the same time, does not stand in the way of his presence in the supper to be eaten spiritually by faith. Our faith in the promise joined to the bread and wine, beholds and embraces the body and blood of Christ, and all his benefits as most truly present in the supper. 2. The argument here deduced from the two articles of faith alluded to, overthrows the conceit of Christ's corporal presence in the bread; for if the human nature of Christ might be everywhere, or present at the same time in many places, his ascension would not prevent its being both in heaven and in the bread at one and the same time. But as the human nature of Christ is finite, and not present in many, nor in all places, it follows

7. Among Protestants, the Radical Reformers were the first to give strong emphasis to church discipline. It quickly became a mark of the church among the Reformed.

8. In the larger context, Ursinus is defending the spiritual presence of Christ in the Eucharist on the basis of several different articles contained in the Apostles' Creed.

that the argument which we deduce from his ascension into heaven is irresistible. For as the consequence which naturally follows from the property of Christ's human nature, in respect to the first celebration of the supper, which we may thus state: The body of Christ sat at the table; therefore it was not in the bread, nor in the mouths of his disciples: as this consequence is legitimate and irresistible, so it is a proper consequence which we draw from the truth of the ascension of Christ into heaven, when we thus reason: The body of Christ is in heaven; therefore it is not in the bread, nor anywhere else upon the earth. . . .

To this it is objected as follows: The Scriptures attribute to the body of Christ many properties and prerogatives which are beyond and above nature, which our bodies do not possess, such as to walk upon the water, to be transfigured, to be carried up into heaven, to pass through a rock and closed doors, to be personally united to Deity, to be made a sacrifice for sin, etc. Therefore it is not absurd to say, that it is present at the same time in heaven and in the bread, or that it possesses ubiquity itself. Ans[wer]. The antecedent has falsehood mingled with what is true. The Scriptures nowhere affirm that the body of Christ passed through a rock, and doors that were closed. Hence we deny it. The other things which are enumerated are, indeed, spoken of in the Scriptures, but they are such things as may be found in connection with a nature that is truly human; for Peter also walked upon the water; and we shall also be transformed and ascend into heaven. But the ubiquity or presence of Christ's flesh, in many places at the same time, is never affirmed in the Scriptures. . . .

Concerning Consubstantiation

The Papists, from what we have said, imagined that two great miracles were wrought in the eucharist by virtue of the consecration of the elements; the changing of the substance of the bread and wine into the body and blood of Christ, and the subsistence of the accidents of the bread and wine, independent of any subject; both of which may easily be refuted; for the former evidently contradicts the analogy of the entire Christian faith, whilst the latter is at war with all sound philosophy. And, as to that virtue which there is in the act of consecration, of which they make so much account, it is nothing more than a magical device of the devil and of human ingenuity.

When some of the ancient Doctors perceived these absurdities, they rejected the doctrine of transubstantiation, and coined that of consubstantiation, which teaches the co-existence of two substances in the same place, or the presence of the body and blood of Christ, not under the forms of bread and wine, but in, or under the bread and wine itself. These persons maintained that the signs were not transubstantiated, or changed as to their substance; but that they were consubstantiated, by which they meant, that the bread and wine remained; but that the body and blood of Christ were substantially present *with*, *in*, and *under* the bread and wine, and eaten and drunk with the mouth. . . .

At length Luther, falling in with the opinion of this cardinal of Cambrai,[9] as he himself testifies, did not at first regard it as an article of faith, to believe that the substance of the bread remains, or does not remain with the body of Christ, but maintained that either view might be held without subjecting their advocates to the charge of heresy. Subsequently, however, it seemed more probable to him that the bread should remain, and that the body of Christ should be present *in*, *with*, and *under* the bread. This is now the generally received opinion of those who call themselves Lutherans. . . .

9. That is, Pierre d'Ailly (1350–1420).

For instead of the absurd miracle of the Papists, in regard to the subsistence of the accidents of the bread and wine, independent of any subject, they imagine another still more absurd, viz: the penetration of two bodies; so that they may be said to have wandered farther, than the Papists themselves from the words of Christ, whether we regard the letter or sense of the words. For the words, if taken literally, must be thus understood: *This*, that is, *this bread, is my body*; and if we have respect to the sense, or true meaning of the words, it must be: *This visible bread which is broken and given is my true and essential body given for you. . . .*

Question 80: How does the Lord's Supper differ from the Popish Mass?

Exposition

. . . We may now, from what has been said, perceive the difference between the Lord's supper and the Popish mass; which difference is so great as to require that the mass be wholly abolished. The Catechism points out three things in which the Lord's supper and the Popish mass chiefly differ from each other:

1. The Lord's supper testifies to us that we have a free pardon of all sin, by the only sacrifice of Jesus Christ, which he himself has once accomplished on the cross, according as it is said . . . (1 Cor. 11. Heb. 7:27; 9:12, 26; 10:10, 12, 14.)

The mass, on the other hand, teaches that the living and the dead have not the pardon of sins through the sufferings of Christ, unless Christ is also daily offered for them by the priests. Their Canon, which they call the less, thus teaches in reference to this subject: "*Holy Father, Almighty and Eternal God, receive this immaculate host, which I, thine unworthy servant, offer unto thee, the living and true God, for my innumerable sins, offences, and neglects, and for all round about me; yea, and for all faithful Christians, living and dead, that it may result in salvation to me and them unto everlasting life.*" Their greater Canon has the following: "*Remember, Lord, thy servants and handmaidens N{ame} N{ame}, and all round about me, whose faith and acknowledged devotion are known unto thee, for whom we offer unto thee, or who present unto thee this sacrifice of praise for themselves and for all theirs, for the redemption of their souls, for the hope of their salvation and preservation*," etc. What need was there that Christ should offer himself, if the oblation of a sacrificing priest might avail for the redemption of souls?

2. The Lord's supper testifies to us according to the articles of our faith, that Christ, as to his human nature, is now in heaven at the right hand of the Father, and not concealed under the accidents of the bread and wine; but that he exhibits to us in the Supper his body and blood, to be eaten and drunk by faith, and engrafts us into himself by the Holy Ghost, that we may abide in him, and have him abide in us, as it is said: "He that is joined to the Lord, is one Spirit." "The bread which we break, is it not the communion of the body of Christ?" "We have such an High Priest, who is set on the right hand of the throne of the Majesty in the heavens." "For if he were on earth, he should not be a priest." (1 Cor. 6:17; 10:16. Heb. 8:1, 4.)

The mass teaches, on the other hand, that the bread and wine, by virtue of the consecration, are changed into the body and blood of Christ, and that his body and blood, in the act of consecration, are brought down from heaven; that they are concealed, after a bodily manner, under the forms of bread and wine; that they are really handled by the hands of the minister, carried about, and eaten and received with the mouth by the communicants. These figments of the brain are opposed to the incarnation, the ascension, the intercession, and return of Christ to judgment; all of which are important articles of our faith, and also to the nature of sacraments, in which the signs must necessarily remain, and not lose their nature, as we have already demonstrated.

3. The Lord's supper teaches that Christ is to be worshipped by us in heaven at the right hand of the Father: for it does not overthrow, but establishes the articles of our faith, and the doctrine of the whole gospel, which teaches that Christ is to be sought and worshipped *above*. "Seek those things which are *above, where* Christ sitteth on the right hand of God." (Col. 3:1.) Stephen, when he was stoned, saw Christ and worshipped him *above*, standing at the right of God. (Acts 7:55.) The ancient church also sang in her service, or liturgy, *sursum corda habemus ad Dominum*, we lift up our hearts unto the Lord.[10]

The mass teaches, on the other hand, that Christ is to be worshipped in the bread, which worship is, without doubt, idolatrous. For to worship Christ in the bread, is to direct our worship in soul, mind, thought, and as much as may be, in the motion or gesture of the body, to the place where the bread is, and looking thither, pay homage and reverence to Christ, as though he were there more especially than elsewhere. . . . Hence we must abolish and hold in abhorrence the wicked device of the corporal presence of Christ in the bread, which is the foundation of the idolatrous worship of the Papists: for as long as Christ's bodily presence in the bread is retained, whether it be by tran- or consubstantiation, so long the Popish worship will remain. For as in former times, before the ascension of Christ into heaven, it was not only lawful, but even necessary to worship Christ in whatever place he was; so now, if he is in the bread, he must be worshipped in the bread, whether we see him or not. Yea, we ought rather to believe the word of God, than any of our senses, if it taught any such thing. But if, on the other hand, we reject the corporal presence of Christ in the bread, we also abolish, by the command of God himself, this shameful worship which the Papists are wont to bestow upon the body of Christ, which they say lies concealed under the forms of bread and wine.

10. This call and response in the eucharistic liturgy appear as early as Hippolytus's *Apostolic Tradition* (ca. 215).

[*The Commentary of Dr. Zacharias Ursinus on the Heidelberg Catechism*, trans. G. W. Williard, 3rd ed. (Cincinnati: T. P. Bucher, [1851]), 396–98, 409–10, 418–20]

Selection 50: Heinrich Bullinger, *Second Helvetic Confession* (1566)

Heinrich Bullinger (1504–1575) began his ministerial career as a Catholic teacher in Switzerland who introduced humanist and reformist ideas to his monastery. He eventually became the successor to Zwingli's ministry in Zurich. His Helvetic (that is, Swiss) confessions won broad acceptance among the Swiss Protestant Churches.

Chapter 9: Of Free Will, and Thus of Human Powers

[1.] In this matter, which has always produced many conflicts in the church, we teach that a threefold condition or state of man is to be considered. [2.] *What Man Was Before the Fall.* There is the state in which man was in the beginning before the fall, namely, upright and free, so that he could either continue in goodness or decline toward evil. However, he declined to evil, and has involved himself and the whole human race in sin and death, as has been said already. *What Man Was After the Fall.* Then we are to consider what man was after the fall. To be sure, his reason was not taken from him, nor was he deprived of will, and he was not entirely changed into a stone or a tree. But they were so altered and weakened that they no longer can do what they could before the fall. For the understanding is darkened, and the will which was free has become an enslaved will. [3.] Now it serves sin, not unwillingly but willingly. And indeed, it is called a will, not an unwilling.

Man Does Evil by His Own Free Will. Therefore, in regard to evil or sin, man is not forced by God or by the devil but does evil by his own free will, and in this respect he has a most free will. But when we frequently see that the worst crimes and designs of men are prevented by God from reaching their purpose, this does nor rake away man's freedom in doing evil, but God by his own power prevents what man freely planned otherwise. . . .

[4.] *Man Is Not Capable of Good per se.* In regard to goodness and virtue man's reason does not judge rightly of itself concerning divine things. For the evangelical and apostolic Scripture requires regeneration of whoever among us wishes to be saved. Hence our first birth from Adam contributes nothing to our salvation. Paul says: "The unspiritual man does not receive the gifts of the Spirit of God," etc.[11] And in another place he denies that we of ourselves are capable of thinking anything good. [5.] Now it is known that the mind or intellect is the guide of the will, and when the guide is blind, it is obvious how far the will reaches. Wherefore, man not yet regenerate has no free will for good, no strength to perform what is good. . . . [6.] Yet in regard to earthly things, fallen man is not entirely lacking in understanding.

Understanding of the Arts. For God in his mercy has permitted the powers of the intellect to remain, though differing greatly from what was in man before the fall. God commands us to cultivate our natural talents, and meanwhile adds both gifts and success. And it is obvious that we make no progress in all the arts without God's blessing. In any case, Scripture refers all the arts to God; and, indeed, the heathen trace the origin of the arts to the gods who invented them.

[7.] *Of What Kind Are the Powers of the Regenerate, and in What Way Their Wills Are Free.* Finally, we must see whether the regenerate have free wills, and to what extent. In regeneration the understanding is illumined by the Holy Spirit in order that it may understand both the mysteries and the will of God. And the will itself is not only changed by the Spirit, but it is also equipped with faculties so that it wills and is able to do the good of its own accord. . . .

[8.] *The Regenerate Work Not Only Passively but Actively.* However, in this connection we teach that there are two things to be observed: First, that the regenerate, in choosing and doing good, work not only passively but actively, for they are moved by God that they may do themselves what they do. For Augustine rightly adduces the saying that "God is said to be our helper. But no one can be helped unless he does something." The Manichaeans robbed man of all activity and made him like a stone or block of wood.

[9.] *The Free Will Is Weak in the Regenerate.* Secondly, in the regenerate a weakness remains. For since sin dwells in us, and in the regenerate the flesh struggles against the Spirit till the end of our lives, they do not easily accomplish in all things what they had planned. These things are confirmed by the apostle in Romans 7, and Galatians 5. [10.] Therefore that free will is weak in us on account of the remnants of the old Adam and of innate human corruption remaining in us until the end of our lives. Meanwhile, since the power of the flesh and the remnants of the old man are not so efficacious

11. 1 Cor. 2:14.

that they wholly extinguish the work of the Spirit, for that reason the faithful are said to be free, yet so that they acknowledge their infirmity and do not glory at all in their free will. . . .

[11.] *In External Things There Is Liberty.* Moreover, no one denies that in external things both the regenerate and the unregenerate enjoy free will. For man has in common with other living creatures (to which he is not inferior) this nature to will some things and not to will others. Thus he is able to speak or to keep silent, to go out of his house or to remain at home, etc. . . .

[12.] *Heresies.* In this matter we condemn the Manichaeans, who deny that the beginning of evil was for man [created] good, from his free will. We also condemn the Pelagians, who assert that an evil man has sufficient free will to do the good that is commanded. Both are refuted by Holy Scripture. . . .

Chapter 10. Of the Predestination of God and the Election of the Saints

[1.] *God Has Elected Us out of Grace.* From eternity God has freely, and of his mere grace, without any respect to men, predestinated or elected the saints whom he wills to save in Christ, according to the saying of the apostle, "God chose us in him before the foundation of the world." And again: "Who saved us and called us with a holy calling, not in virtue of our works but in virtue of his own purpose and the grace which he gave us in Christ Jesus ages ago, and now has manifested through the appearing of our Savior Christ Jesus."[12]

[2.] *We Are Elected or Predestinated in Christ.* Therefore, although not on account of any merit of ours, God has elected us, not directly, but in Christ, and on account of Christ, in order that those who are now engrafted into Christ by faith might also be elected. But those who were outside Christ were rejected, according to the words of the apostle, "Examine yourselves, to see whether you are holding to your faith. Test yourselves. Do you not realize that Jesus Christ is in you?—unless indeed you fail to meet the test!"[13]

[3.] *We Are Elected for a Definite Purpose.* Finally, the saints are chosen by God for a definite purpose, which the apostle himself explains when he says, "He chose us in him for adoption that we should be holy and blameless before him in love. He destined us for adoption to be his sons through Jesus Christ that they should be to the praise of the glory of his grace."

[4.] *We Are to Have a Good Hope for All.* And although God knows who are his, and here and there mention is made of the small number of elect, yet we must hope well of all, and not rashly judge any man to be a reprobate. For Paul says to the Philippians, "I thank my God for you all" (now he speaks of the whole church in Philippi), "because of your fellowship in the gospel, being persuaded that he who began a good work in you will bring it to completion at the day of Jesus Christ. It is also right that I have this opinion of you all."

[5.] *Whether Few Are Elect.* And when the Lord was asked whether there were few that should be saved, he does not answer and tell them that few or many should be saved or damned, but rather he exhorts every man to "strive to enter by the narrow door": as if he should say, It is not for you curiously to inquire about these matters, but rather to endeavor that you may enter into heaven by the straight way.

[6.] *What in This Matter Is to Be Condemned.* Therefore we do not approve of the impious speeches of some who say, "Few are chosen, and since I do not know whether I am among the number of the few, I will enjoy myself." Others say, "If I am predestinated and elected by God,

12. Eph. 1:4; 2 Tim. 1:9-10.

13. 2 Cor. 13:5.

nothing can hinder me from salvation, which is already certainly appointed for me, no matter what I do. But if I am in the number of the reprobate, no faith or repentance will help me, since the decree of God cannot be changed. Therefore all doctrines and admonitions are useless." Now the saying of the apostle contradicts these men: "The Lord's servant must be ready to teach, instructing those who oppose him, so that if God should grant that they repent to know the truth, they may recover from the snare of the devil, after being held captive by him to do his will."[14]

[7.] *Admonitions Are Not in Vain Because Salvation Proceeds from Election.* Augustine also shows that both the grace of free election and predestination, and also salutary admonitions and doctrines, are to be preached (*Liber de Dono Perseverantiae,* cap. *14ff.).*

Whether We Are Elected. We therefore find fault with those who outside of Christ ask whether they are elected. And what has God decreed concerning them before all eternity? [8.] For the preaching of the gospel is to be heard, and it is to be believed; and it is to be held as beyond doubt that if you believe and are in Christ, you are elected. For the Father has revealed unto us in Christ the eternal purpose of his predestination, as I have just now shown from the apostle in 2 Timothy 1. This is therefore above all to be taught and considered, what great love of the Father toward us is revealed to us in Christ. . . .

[9.] Let Christ, therefore be the looking glass, in whom we may contemplate our predestination. We shall have a sufficiently clear and sure testimony that we are inscribed in the book of life if we have fellowship with Christ, and he is ours and we are his in true faith.

Temptation in Regard to Predestination. In the temptation in regard to predestination, than which there is scarcely any other more dangerous, we are comforted in the fact that God's promises apply to all the faithful, for he says: "Ask, and everyone who seeks, shall receive." [10.] This finally we pray, with the whole church of God, "Our Father who art in heaven," both because by baptism we are engrafted into the body of Christ, and we are often fed in his church with his flesh and blood unto life eternal. Thereby, being strengthened, we are commanded to work out our salvation with fear and trembling, according to the precept of Paul.

[*Creeds and Confessions of Faith in the Christian Tradition*, ed. Jaroslav Pelikan and Valerie Hotchkiss, 2:471–75]

14. 2 Tim. 2:24-26.

B. Anglican

Selection 51: *Thirty-Nine Articles* (1563)

The Thirty-Nine Articles *are included in the* Book of Common Prayer *of the Church of England, which was itself first issued in 1549. The* Articles *remain the only prescribed confessional document in the established church, although the twenty-one sermons in the* Book of Homilies *have held an important but subordinate status since their revised publication in 1571. The stated purpose of the* Articles *is to establish consensus in the church and to avoid diversity of opinions on the considered topics.*

As early as 1536, the Ten Articles *had been issued for the Church of England under King Henry VIII. But the immediate history of the* Thirty-Nine Articles *goes back to the* Forty-Two Articles *(1553) written by Archbishop of Canterbury Thomas Cranmer (1489–1556). Finally revised under Archbishop Matthew Parker (1504–1575) in 1563, the* Thirty-Nine Articles *possess a decidedly Reformed character. The one*

statement on predestination, however, is ambiguous enough to allow for the doctrine of conditional election.

Articles whereupon it was agreed by the archbishops and bishops of both provinces and the whole clergy, in the convocation holden at London in the year of our Lord God 1562,[15] according to the computation of the Church of England, for the avoiding of the diversities of opinions, and for the establishing of consent touching true religion.

1. Of Faith in the Holy Trinity

There is but one living and true God, everlasting, without body, parts or passions, of infinite power, wisdom and goodness, the maker and preserver of all things both visible and invisible. And in unity of this Godhead there be three persons, of one substance, power and eternity, the Father, the Son, and the Holy Spirit.

2. That of the Word or Son of God, Which Was Made Very Man

The Son, which is the Word of the Father, begotten from everlasting of the Father, the very and eternal God, of one substance with the Father, took man's nature in the womb of the Blessed Virgin, of her substance: so that two whole and perfect natures, that is to say the godhead and manhood, were joined together in one person, never to be divided, whereof is one Christ, very God and very man, who truly suffered, was crucified, dead, and buried, to reconcile his Father to us and to be a sacrifice not only for original guilt but also for all actual sins of men.

3. Of the Going Down of Christ into Hell

As Christ died for us, and was buried, so also it is to be believed, that he went down into hell.

4. Of the Resurrection of Christ

Christ did truly arise again from death, and took again his body, with flesh, bones, and all things appertaining to the perfection of man's nature, wherewith he ascended into heaven, and there sitteth, until he return to judge all men at the last day.

5. Of the Holy Spirit

The Holy Spirit, proceeding from the Father and the Son, is of one substance, majesty and glory with the Father and the Son, very and eternal God.

6. Of the Sufficiency of the Holy Scriptures for Salvation

. . . In the name of Holy Scripture we do understand those canonical books of the Old and New Testament, of whose authority was never any doubt in the church. . . .[16]

7. Of the Old Testament

The Old Testament is not contrary to the New, for both in the Old and New Testament everlasting life is offered to mankind by Christ, who is the only Mediator between God and man, being both God and man. Wherefore they are not to be heard which feign that the old Fathers did look only for transitory promises. Although the law given from God by Moses, as touching ceremonies and rites, do not bind Christian men, nor the civil precepts thereof, ought of necessity to be received in any commonwealth; yet notwithstanding, no Christian man whatsoever is free from the obedience of the commandments which are called moral.

8. Of the Three Creeds

The three creeds, Nicene Creed, Athanasius' Creed, and that which is commonly called the Apostles' Creed, ought thoroughly to be received and believed, for they may be proved by most certain warrants of Holy Scripture.

9. Of Original, or Birth Sin

Original sin standeth not in the following of Adam, as the Pelagians do vainly talk, but it is

15. That is, 1563 (new style).

16. Article 6 then provides a list of books that excludes the so-called Old Testament Apocrypha from the canon.

the fault and corruption of the nature of every man, that naturally is engendered of the off-spring of Adam, whereby man is very far gone from original righteousness, and is of his own nature inclined to evil, so that the flesh lusteth always contrary to the spirit, and therefore in every person born into this world, it deserveth God's wrath and damnation. And this infection of nature doth remain, yea in them that are regenerated, whereby the lust of the flesh, called in Greek *phronema sarkos,* which some do expound the wisdom, some sensuality, some the affection, and some the desire of the flesh, is not subject to the law of God. And although there is no condemnation for them that believe and are baptized, yet the apostle doth confess that concupiscence and lust hath of itself the nature of sin.

10. Of Free Will

The condition of man after the fall of Adam is such that he cannot turn and prepare himself by his own natural strength and good works to faith and calling upon God; wherefore we have no power to do good works pleasant and acceptable to God, without the grace of God preventing us, that we may have a good will, and working with us, when we have that good will.

11. Of the Justification of Man

We are accounted righteous before God only for the merit of our Lord and Savior Jesus Christ by faith, and not for our own works or deservings. Wherefore, that we are justified by faith only, is a most wholesome doctrine, and very full of comfort, as more largely is expressed in the Homily of Justification.

12. Of Good Works

Albeit that good works, which are the fruits of faith, and follow after justification, cannot put away our sins, and endure the severity of God's judgment; yet are they pleasing and acceptable to God in Christ, and do spring out necessarily of a true and lively faith, insomuch that by them a lively faith may be as evidently known, as a tree discerned by the fruit.

13. Of Works before Justification

Works done before the grace of Christ, and the inspiration of his Spirit, are not pleasant to God, forasmuch as they spring not of faith in Jesus Christ, neither do they make men meet to receive grace, or as the school authors say, deserve grace of congruity; yet rather for that they are not done as God hath willed and commanded them to be done, we doubt not but they have the nature of sin.

14. Of Works of Supererogation

Voluntary works besides, over and above God's commandments, which they call works of super-erogation, cannot be taught without arrogance and impiety. For by them men do declare that they do not only render unto God as much as they are bound to do, but that they do more for his sake than of bounden duty is required; whereas Christ saith plainly: "When ye have done all that are commanded to you, say: We be unprofitable servants."[17]

15. Of Christ Alone without Sin

Christ in the truth of our nature, was made like unto us in all things, sin only except, from which he was clearly void, both in his flesh and in his spirit. He came to be the lamb without spot, who by the sacrifice of himself once made, should take away the sins of the world; and sin, as St. John saith, was not in him. But all we the rest, although baptized and born again in Christ, yet offend in many things, and if we say we have no sin, we deceive ourselves and the truth is not in us.

16. Of Sin after Baptism

Not every deadly sin willingly committed after baptism is sin against the Holy Spirit, and unpardonable. Wherefore the grant of repentance is not to be denied to such as fall into sin after baptism. After we have received the Holy

17. See Luke 17:10.

Spirit, we may depart from grace given and fall into sin, and by the grace of God we may arise again and amend our lives. And therefore they are to be condemned, which say they can no more sin as long as they live here, or deny the place of forgiveness to such as truly repent.

17. Of Predestination and Election

Predestination to life is the everlasting purpose of God, whereby before the foundations of the world were laid, he hath constantly decreed by his counsel secret to us, to deliver from curse and damnation those whom he hath chosen in Christ out of mankind, and to bring them by Christ to everlasting salvation, as vessels made to honor. Wherefore they which be imbued with so excellent a benefit of God be called according to God's purpose by his Spirit, working in due season; they through grace obey the calling; they be justified freely; they be made sons of God by adoption; they be made like the image of his only-begotten Son Jesus Christ; they walk religiously in good works and at length by God's mercy, they attain to everlasting felicity.

As the godly consideration of predestination, and our election in Christ is full of sweet, pleasant and unspeakable comfort to godly persons, and such as feel in themselves the working of the spirit of Christ, mortifying the works of the flesh and their earthly members, and drawing up their mind to high and heavenly things, as well because it doth greatly establish and confirm their faith of eternal salvation to be enjoyed through Christ, as because it doth fervently kindle their love toward God; so for curious and carnal persons, lacking the spirit of Christ, to have continually before their eyes the sentence of God's predestination, is a most dangerous downfall, whereby the devil doth thrust them either into desperation, or into recklessness of most unclean living, no less perilous than desperation. . . .

18. Of Obtaining Eternal Salvation, Only by the Name of Christ

They also are to be had accursed that presume to say that every man shall be saved by the law or sect which he professeth, so that he be diligent to frame his life according to that law, and the light of nature. For Holy Scripture doth set out unto us only the name of Jesus Christ, whereby men must be saved.

19. Of the Church

The visible church of Christ is a congregation of faithful men in which the pure Word of God is preached and the sacraments be duly administered, according to Christ's ordinance in all those things that of necessity are requisite to the same.

As the church of Jerusalem, Alexandria, and Antioch have erred, so also the church of Rome hath erred, not only in their living and manner of ceremonies, but also in matters of faith.

20. Of the Authority of the Church

The church hath power to decree rites and ceremonies, and authority in controversies of faith; and yet it is not lawful for the church to ordain anything that is contrary to God's Word written, neither may it so expound one place of Scripture that it is repugnant to another. Wherefore, although the church be a witness and a keeper of Holy Writ; yet as it ought not to decree anything against the same, so besides the same, ought it not to enforce anything to be believed for necessity of salvation.

21. Of the Authority of General Councils

General councils may not be gathered together without the commandment and will of princes. And when they be gathered together, forasmuch as they shall be an assembly of men, whereof all be not governed with the Spirit and Word of God, they may err, and sometimes have erred, even in things pertaining unto God. Wherefore things ordained by them as necessary to salvation have neither strength nor authority, unless it may be declared that they be taken out of Holy Scripture.

22. Of Purgatory

The Romish doctrine concerning purgatory, pardons, worshiping and adoration as well of images as of relics, and also invocation of saints, is a fond[18] thing vainly invented, and grounded upon no warranty of Scripture, but rather repugnant to the Word of God.

23. Of Ministering in the Congregation

It is not lawful for any man to take upon him the office of public preaching, or ministering the sacraments in the congregation, before he be lawfully called and sent to execute the same. And those we ought to judge lawfully called to this work by men, who have public authority given unto them in the congregation, to call and send ministers into the Lord's vineyard.

24. Of Speaking in the Congregation in Such a Tongue as the People Understandeth

It is a thing plainly repugnant to the Word of God and the custom of the primitive church to have public prayer in the church, or to minister the sacraments in a tongue not understanded of the people.

25. Of the Sacraments

. . . There are two sacraments ordained of Christ our Lord in the gospel, that is to say, baptism and the supper of the Lord. . . .[19]

26. Of the Unworthiness of the Ministers, Which Hinders Not the Effect of the Sacraments

Although in the visible church the evil be ever mingled with the good, and sometime the evil have chief authority in the ministration of the Word and sacraments; yet forasmuch as they do not the same in their own name but in Christ's, and do minister by his commission and authority; we may use their ministry both in hearing the Word of God, and in the receiving of the sacraments. Neither is the effect of Christ's ordinances taken away by their wickedness, nor the grace of God's gifts diminished from such as by faith and rightly do receive the sacraments ministered unto them, which be effectual because of Christ's institution and promise, although they be ministered by evil men. Nevertheless it appertaineth to the discipline of the church, that inquiry be made of evil ministers, and that they be accused by those that have knowledge of their offenses, and finally, being found guilty by just judgment, be deposed.

27. Of Baptism

Baptism is not only a sign of profession and mark of difference, whereby Christian men are discerned from other that be not christened; but is also a sign of regeneration or new birth, whereby as by an instrument, they that receive baptism rightly are grafted into the church; the promises of the forgiveness of sin, and of our adoption to be the sons of God, by the Holy Spirit, are visibly signed and sealed; faith is confirmed; and grace increased by virtue of prayer unto God. The baptism of young children is in any wise to be retained in the church as most agreeable with the institution of Christ.

28. Of the Lord's Supper

. . . The body of Christ is given, taken, and eaten in the supper only after an heavenly and spiritual manner; and the mean whereby the body of Christ is received and eaten in the supper is faith. . . .

29. Of the Wicked Which Do Not Eat the Body of Christ in the Use of the Lord's Supper

The wicked, and such as be void of a lively faith, although they do carnally and visibly press with their teeth, as St. Augustine saith,

18. That is, futile.

19. Article 25 proceeds to exclude the other five sacraments of the Roman Catholic Church.

the sacrament of the body and blood of Christ; yet in no wise are they partakers of Christ, but rather to their condemnation do eat and drink the sign or sacrament of so great a thing.

30. Of Both Kinds

The cup of the Lord is not to be denied to the laypeople. For both the parts of the Lord's sacrament, by Christ's ordinance and commandment, ought to be ministered to all Christian men alike.

31. Of the One Oblation of Christ Finished upon the Cross

The offering of Christ once made, is the perfect redemption, propitiation, and satisfaction for all the sins of the whole world, both original and actual, and there is none other satisfaction for sin but that alone. Wherefore the sacrifices of masses, in the which it was commonly said that the priests did offer Christ for the quick and the dead, to have remission of pain or guilt, were blasphemous fables and dangerous deceits.

32. Of the Marriage of Priests

Bishops, priests, and deacons are not commanded by God's law to vow the estate of single life or to abstain from marriage. Therefore it is lawful also for them, as for all other Christian men, to marry at their own discretion, as they shall judge the same to serve better godliness.

33. Of Excommunicate Persons, How They Are to Be Avoided

That person, which by open denunciation of the church is rightly cut off from the unity of the church and excommunicated, ought to be taken of the whole multitude of the faithful as an heathen and publican, until he be openly reconciled by penance, and received into the Church by a judge that hath authority thereto.

34. Of the Traditions of the Church

It is not necessary that traditions and ceremonies be in all places one or utterly like, for at all times they have been diverse, and may be changed according to the diversity of countries, times, and men's manners, so that nothing be ordained against God's Word.

Whosoever through his private judgment willingly and purposely doth openly break the traditions and ceremonies of the church, which be not repugnant to the Word of God and be ordained and approved by common authority, ought to be rebuked openly, that other may fear to do the like, as he that offendeth against the common order of the church and hurteth the authority of the magistrate, and woundeth the consciences of the weak brethren. . . .

35. Of Homilies

The second Book of Homilies, the several titles whereof we have joined under this Article, doth contain a godly and wholesome doctrine, and necessary for these times, as doth the former Book of Homilies, which were set forth in the time of King Edward the Sixth; and therefore we judge them to be read in churches by the ministers diligently and distinctly, that they may be understanded of the people. . . .[20]

36. Of Consecration of Bishops and Ministers

The book of consecration of archbishops and bishops, and ordering of priests and deacons, lately set forth in the time of Edward the Sixth, and confirmed at the same time by authority of Parliament, doth contain all things necessary to such consecration and ordering; neither hath it anything that of itself is superstitious or ungodly. And therefore, whosoever are consecrate or ordered according to the rites of that book, since the second year of the aforenamed King Edward, unto this time, or hereafter shall be consecrated or ordered according to the same rites we decree all such to be rightly, orderly, and lawfully consecrated and ordered.

20. A list of homily titles follows.

37. Of the Civil Magistrates

. . . Where we attribute to the Queen's Majesty the chief government, by which titles we under-stand the minds of some slanderous folk to be offended; we give not to our princes the ministering either of God's Word or of sacraments, the which thing the injunctions also lately set forth by Elizabeth our queen doth most plainly testify; but that only prerogative which we see to have been given always to all godly princes in Holy Scriptures by God himself, that is, that they should rule all estates and degrees committed to their charge by God, whether they be ecclesiastical or temporal, and restrain with the civil sword the stubborn and evildoers.

The bishop of Rome hath no jurisdiction in this realm of England.

The laws of the realm may punish Christian men with death for heinous and grievous offenses. It is lawful for Christian men, at the commandment of the magistrate, to wear weapons and to serve in the wars.

38. Of Christian Men's Goods, Which Are Not Common

The riches and goods of Christians are not common, as touching the right title and possession of the same, as certain Anabaptists do falsely boast; notwithstanding, every man ought of such things as he possesseth, liberally to give alms to the poor, according to his ability.

39. Of a Christian Man's Oath

As we confess that vain and rash swearing is forbidden Christian men by our Lord Jesus Christ, and James his apostle; so we judge that Christian religion doth not prohibit, but that a man may swear when the magistrate requireth, in a cause of faith and charity, so it be done, according to the prophet's teaching, in justice, judgment, and truth.

The Ratification

These Articles of the Christian faith, containing in all nineteen pages in the original, which is kept by the most reverend father in Christ, Matthew Archbishop of Canterbury, Primate of all England and Metropolitan, the archbishops and bishops of each province of the realm of England, gathered lawfully in the holy provincial synod, receive with one voice and confess, and by the subscription of their own hands approve as true and orthodox, the twenty-ninth day of the month of January, in the year of our Lord, according to the reckoning of the Church of England, one thousand five hundred and sixty-two.[21] And the whole clergy of the lower house has likewise received and confessed them with one voice, as is clear from the subscriptions of their own hands, which subscriptions the clergy have presented and deposited with the same most reverend archbishop of Canterbury, the fifth day of February in the aforesaid year.

[*Documents of the English Reformation*, ed. Gerald Bray (Minneapolis: Fortress Press, 1994), 285–311]

Selection 52: John Jewel, *An Apology for the Church of England* (1562)

John Jewel (1522–1571) became bishop of Salisbury in 1560. Written only four years after Elizabeth's accession to the throne and the reestablishment of English Protestantism, the* Apology *was a defense against Roman Catholic accusations of heresy and a positive statement of the Anglican faith.

It has been an old complaint, even from the time of the patriarchs and prophets, which is fully confirmed by the writers of all ages, that Truth is considered a mere stranger upon earth,

21. That is, 1563 (new style).

and generally exposed to the enmity and persecution of the ignorant.

Although this may appear incredible to some, who have not given the subject due consideration, more especially since man, uninfluenced by the instruction of a master, is naturally anxious to discover truth; and Christ himself, our Saviour, when on earth, was desirous of being distinguished by that appellation as most expressive of his divine attributes: yet we, who are well acquainted with the Scriptures, and have both read and seen what hath happened to men of piety in all ages; to the prophets, apostles, holy martyrs, and to Christ himself: with what insults, revilings, and indignities they have been persecuted for the sake of truth alone: we (I say) find nothing new or incredible in this, but consider it as a thing well known, and commonly practised in all ages. On the contrary, it would appear much more worthy our admiration if the Devil, who is the father of lies, and the enemy of all truth, should now on a sudden change his nature, and hope to suppress truth by any other means than falsehood; or undertake now to establish his kingdom by any other arts than those which he has practised from the first. For whether we consider Religion in its rise, progress, or reformation, we shall scarcely find a single period on record, wherein virtue and truth were not subjected to every species of reproach and persecution. For the Devil clearly perceives, that whilst truth prevails, his dominion cannot be maintained. . . .

At this very hour, they every where loudly assert that we are all heretics, that we have forsaken the true faith, that we have destroyed the unity of the church by new systems, and impious doctrines. . . .

With respect to their accusations against us, many of them are totally false; many condemned by the very persons who uttered them; others, notwithstanding their absolute falsehood, by an artful and plausible gloss of language, exhibit a certain shew and appearance of truth, which may easily deceive a careless and inattentive reader; and some are of such a nature, that, far from attempting to refute them, we ought boldly to declare that they are founded on the basis of truth and reason. . . .

But since the eyes of nearly the whole world are now opened to see the truth, it may appear that enough has been already said on our part; and that when facts speak so plainly for themselves, a laboured defence is unnecessary, especially since during the last twenty years so many thousands of our brethren, in the midst of the most exquisite tortures, have borne testimony to the truth, and all the attempts of princes and potentates to arrest the progress of the Gospel, have been entirely defeated: for if the Popes themselves were either willing or able to consider the matter dispassionately, and examine the rise and progress of our religion; how the decay of their influence has gradually proceeded, without any appearance of human opposition; and on the contrary, how our doctrines have increased, and by degrees, been propagated through all countries, and now finally obtained admission into the palaces of monarchs, against the inveterate hostility of so many emperors, kings, popes, nay, of almost the entire world; these circumstances alone, would afford sufficient proof that God himself is on our side; that heaven interposes to defeat their attempts, and that such is the force of truth, that no human efforts, nor even the gates of hell itself can prevail against it. For it cannot be attributed to infatuation or madness, that so many free cities, so many kings, so many princes, have deserted the See of Rome, and preferred the Gospel of Christ.

And although the popes hitherto may not have been able to pay serious attention to these affairs, or if their minds are at this time perplexed and harassed with other interests, and they think it derogatory to the papal dignity to waste a moment's thought on a subject of such trifling importance; is this any reason why our cause should suffer in the public estimation? Or, if they will shut their eyes, and close their hearts, against the acknowledgment of truth, are we to be considered as heretics, because we obey not their will and pleasure? And if Pope Pius[22] were the man (we do not say that he so earnestly wishes to be thought) but if he were indeed a person who would consider us as his brethren, or even as men, he would first diligently have examined our arguments, and what might be urged either for or against us; and not, blinded by prejudice, so rashly have condemned unheard so large a portion of the world, so many states, kings, and princes, in that Bull whereby he lately pretended to convene a council.[23]

But lest, when we are in this public manner stigmatized by him, our silence should be construed as an admission of our guilt, especially since we are not allowed an audience in the public assembly of the general Council, wherein none are suffered to give their votes, or declare their opinions, but the avowed admirers and sworn advocates of the Roman See; (for of this we had too great an experience in the last council of Trent, when the ambassadors and divines of the German princes and free cities were totally excluded from every convention: nor can we forget that Julius the third, ten years previously, took special care by his rescript to prevent any of our party being heard before the Council, unless perchance some one could be found who would openly recant, and change his opinions) for this reason, we have thought proper to make a written profession of our Faith, and fairly and openly to reply to the objections publicly advanced against us: that the whole world may see the foundation of those Articles of Belief, which so many excellent men have valued above their lives, and that all mankind may thoroughly understand the nature, disposition, and religious sentiments of those persons whom the Roman Pontiff, without suffering them to be heard in their defence, in defiance of law and precedent, has rashly and inconsiderately condemned as heretics, on the bare report of some difference existing between them on certain points of religion. . . .

Now, if we prove, and that not obscurely and craftily, but in good faith before God, truly, ingenuously, clearly, and evidently, that the most holy gospel, the ancient bishops, and primitive church, agree with us; and that we have not without reason renounced the Popish tenets, and returned to the apostles, and to the ancient catholic fathers; and if those very persons who detest our doctrine, and pride themselves in the name of Catholics, shall be clearly convinced that all these titles of antiquity, of which they so immoderately boast, belong not to them; and that there is more strength in our cause than they have been willing to allow; then we devoutly hope, that not one of them will be so careless of his Salvation, as not duly and pain fully to deliberate, to which party he ought to belong. Undoubtedly, if a man hath not hardened his heart, and stopped his ear against conviction, he will never regret the attentive perusal of our defence, and the having considered how far our profession of Faith is conformable to the Christian religion.

With respect to the charge of HERESY, which is made against us, it is a crime so

22. Pope Pius IV (1499–1565) presided over the final sessions of the Council of Trent.

23. When Jewel wrote these words, the bull had already been issued (November 1560) to reconvene the Council of Trent, but he may not have been aware that the council had in fact reconvened (January 1562).

heinous, that it ought not to be believed of any Christian, unless established by the clearest evidence, and as it were, seen with the eyes, and handled with the hands; for heresy is the renunciation of our salvation, the rejection of the grace of God, a separation from the body and spirit of Christ. But this has ever been an invariable custom, both with them and their fathers, to condemn as sectarians, and promoters of heresy and schism, all who presumed to complain of their errors, and desired a reformation in religion. For no other reason was Christ himself called a Samaritan, but because he was thought to have fallen off to some new religion, and to have been the founder of a new sect: and Paul, the Apostle of Jesus was summoned to appear before the judges, and defend himself against a charge of heresy; whereupon he replied, "I confess unto thee, that after the way which they call heresy, so worship I the God of my fathers, believing all things which are written in the law and the prophets." . . .

[Jewel proceeds in the second chapter to summarize the alleged "heresies" of the Church of England.]

These are the frightful heresies under colour of which a great part of the world is at this day condemned by the Pope without a trial. The attack should rather have been commenced against Christ, against the Apostles, against the holy Fathers; for with them have these doctrines originated, by them have they been sanctioned and established. . . .[24]

[*An Apology for the Church of England*, trans. Stephen Isaacson, 2nd ed. (London: John Hearne, 1829), 1–3, 7, 9, 12–19, 56]

24. Throughout his book, Jewel articulates the common Protestant claim that they, not the Roman Church, are the true heirs of the apostolic and early church.

Selection 53: *Act against Recusants* (1593)

Mary's successor, Queen Elizabeth (r. 1558–1603), brought the Church of England back to its Protestant commitments, and for her efforts she was excommunicated by the pope in 1570. Roman Catholic recusants—that is, those who refused to attend the services of the established church—had an ongoing presence in England, always hoping for another reversal under the next monarch. The 1593 **Act against Recusants** ***represents the culmination of legislation against Roman Catholics under Elizabeth.***

Recusancy was often viewed as a lack of patriotism or with suspicion of treachery. Because England was in an intermittent war with Spain, which was staunchly Roman Catholic, any devotees of the pope or any Protestants who sympathized with aspects of Roman Catholic theology could be seen as traitors. The influx of Jesuits into England around 1580 only increased the tension. This context is necessary for understanding the strong language and why political overtones often accompanied religious allegiances during this period in Europe.

For the better discovering and avoiding of all such traitorous and most dangerous conspiracies and attempts as are daily devised and practised against our most gracious sovereign lady the queen's majesty and the happy estate of this commonweal, by sundry wicked and seditious persons, who, terming themselves Catholics, and being indeed spies and intelligencers, not only for her majesty's foreign enemies, but also for rebellious and traitorous subjects born within her highness's realms and dominions, and hiding their most detestable and devilish purposes under a false pretext of religion and conscience, do secretly wander and shift from place to place within this realm, to corrupt and seduce her majesty's subjects, and to stir them to sedition and rebellion: . . .

And also that every person being above the age of sixteen years, born within any her majesty's realms or dominions, or made denizen, and having, or which hereafter shall have, any certain place of dwelling and abode within this realm, which, being then a popish recusant, shall at any time hereafter be lawfully convicted for not repairing to some church, chapel, or usual place of common prayer, to hear divine service there, but forbearing the same contrary to the said laws and statutes, and being within this realm at the time that they shall be convicted, shall within forty days next after the same conviction (if they be not restrained or stayed by imprisonment or otherwise, as is aforesaid, and in such cases of restraint and stay, then within twenty days next after they shall be enlarged of such imprisonment or restraint, and shall be able to travel) repair to their place of usual dwelling and abode, and shall not at any time after pass or remove above five miles from thence; upon pain that every person and persons that shall offend against the tenor and intent of this Act in anything before mentioned, shall lose and forfeit all his and their goods and chattels, and shall also forfeit to the queen's majesty all the lands, tenements, and hereditaments, and all the rents and annuities of every such person so doing or offending, during the life of the same offender. . . .

Provided always, and be it further enacted by the authority aforesaid, that all such persons as by the intent and true meaning of this Act are to make their repair to their place of dwelling and abode, or to the place where they were born, or where their father or mother shall be dwelling, and not to remove or pass above five miles from thence as is aforesaid, shall within twenty days next after their coming to any of the said places (as the case shall happen) notify their coming thither, and present themselves, and deliver their true names in writing, to the minister or curate of the same parish, and to the constable, headborough, or tithingman of the town,[25] and thereupon the said minister or curate shall presently enter the same into a book to be kept in every parish for that purpose. . . .

And to the end that the realm be not pestered and overcharged with the multitude of such seditious and dangerous people as is aforesaid, who, having little or no ability to answer or satisfy any competent penalty for their contempt and disobedience of the said laws and statutes, and being committed to prison for the same, do live for the most part in better case there, than they could if they were abroad at their own liberty; the Lords spiritual and temporal, and the Commons, in this present Parliament assembled, do most humbly and instantly beseech the queen's majesty, that it may be further enacted, that if any such person or persons, being a popish recusant . . . shall not within the time before in this Act in that behalf limited and appointed, repair to their place of usual dwelling and abode, . . . and shall not within three months next after such person shall be apprehended or taken for offending as is aforesaid, conform themselves to the obedience of the laws and statutes of this realm, in coming usually to the church to hear divine service, and in making such public confession and submission, as hereafter in this Act is appointed and expressed, being thereunto required by the bishop of the diocese, or any justice of the peace of the county where the same person shall happen to be, or by the minister or curate of the parish; that in every such case every such offender, being thereunto warned or required by any two justices of the peace or coroner of

25. Constables, headboroughs, and tithingmen were peace, or law enforcement, officers.

the same county where such offenders shall then be, shall upon his and their corporal oath before any two justices of the peace, or coroner of the same county, abjure this realm of England, and all other the queen's majesty's dominions for ever. . . .

And if any such offender, which by the tenor and intent of this Act is to be abjured as is aforesaid, shall refuse to make such abjuration as is aforesaid, or after such abjuration made shall not go to such haven, and within such time as is before appointed, and from thence depart out of this realm, according to this present Act, or after such his departure shall return or come again into any her majesty's realms or dominions, without her majesty's special licence in that behalf first had and obtained; that then, in every such case, the person so offending shall be adjudged a felon, and shall suffer and lose as in case of felony without benefit of clergy.

And be it further enacted and ordained by the authority aforesaid, that if any person which shall be suspected to be a Jesuit, seminary or massing priest, being examined by any person having lawful authority in that behalf to examine such person which shall be so suspected, shall refuse to answer directly and truly whether he be a Jesuit, or a seminary or massing priest, as is aforesaid, every such person so refusing to answer shall for his disobedience and contempt in that behalf, be committed to prison by such as shall examine him as is aforesaid, and thereupon shall remain and continue in prison without bail or mainprize, until he shall make direct and true answer to the said questions whereupon he shall be so examined. . . .

And furthermore be it enacted by the authority of this present Parliament, that if any person, or persons, that shall at any time hereafter offend against this Act, shall before he or they shall be thereof convicted come to some parish church on some Sunday or other festival day, and then and there hear divine service, and at service-time, before the sermon, or reading of the gospel, make public and open submission and declaration of his and their conformity to her majesty's laws and statutes, as hereafter in this Act is declared and appointed; that then the same offender shall thereupon be clearly discharged of and from all and every pains and forfeitures inflicted or imposed by this Act for any of the said offences in this Act contained: the same submission to be made as hereafter follows, that is to say:

"I, *A. B.*, do humbly confess and acknowledge, that I have grievously offended God in contemning her majesty's godly and lawful government and authority, by absenting myself from church, and from hearing divine service, contrary to the godly laws and statutes of this realm: and I am heartily sorry for the same, and do acknowledge and testify in my conscience, that the bishop or see of Rome has not, nor ought to have, any power or authority over her majesty, or within any her majesty's realms or dominions: and I do promise and protest, without any dissimulation, or any colour or means of any dispensation, that from henceforth I will from time to time obey and perform her majesty's laws and statutes, in repairing to the church, and hearing divine service, and do my uttermost endeavour to maintain and defend the same." . . .

Provided nevertheless, that if any such offender, after such submission made as is aforesaid, shall afterwards fall into, relapse, or eftsoons[26] become a recusant, in not repairing to church to hear divine service, but shall forbear the same, contrary to the laws and statutes in that behalf made and provided; that then every such offender shall lose all such benefit as he or she might otherwise, by virtue of this Act, have

26. That is, "a second time" or "soon afterward."

or enjoy by reason of their said submission; and shall thereupon stand and remain in such plight, condition, and degree, to all intents, as though such submission had never been made. . . .

[*Documents Illustrative of English Church History*, ed. Henry Gee and William John Hardy (London: Macmillan, 1914), 499–507]

C. Lutheran

Title page of the Book of Concord *(1580)"*

Selection 54: *Formula of Concord* (1577)

In the wake of theological controversy within the Lutheran camp, especially between the Philippists (followers of Philip Melanchthon [1497–1560]) and the Gnesio-Lutherans (the "genuine" Lutherans, influenced especially by Matthias Flacius Illyricus [1520–1575]), the* Formula of Concord *was an attempt to resolve the differences and state the terms of agreement. As with earlier Reformed confessions, it solidified many doctrinal issues and helped to create a Lutheran orthodoxy. The* Formula *was collected with other earlier works to form the primary confessional document of the Lutheran Church, the* Book of Concord, *first published in 1580.

Art. II. Concerning the Free Will

Status controversiae[27]
The Chief Question in This Dispute

Because the human will is found in four dissimilar situations (1. before the fall; 2. after the fall; 3. after new birth; 4. after the resurrection of the flesh), the primary question concerns only the human will and capacity in the second situation: what kind of powers do human beings have after the fall of our first parents, before rebirth, on their own, in spiritual matters? Are they able, with their own powers, before they receive new birth through God's Spirit, to dispose themselves favorably toward God's grace and to prepare themselves to accept the grace offered by the Holy Spirit in the Word and the holy sacraments, or not?

Affirmative Theses
The Pure Teaching concerning This Article on the Basis of God's Word

1. On this article it is our teaching, faith, and confession that human reason and understanding are blind in spiritual matters and understand nothing on the basis of their own powers, as it is written, "Those who are natural do not receive the gifts of God's Spirit, for they are foolishness to them and they are unable to understand them" [1 Cor. 2:14] when they are asked about spiritual matters.

2. Likewise, we believe, teach, and confess that the unregenerated human will is not only turned away from God but has also become God's enemy, that it has only the desire and will to do evil and whatever is opposed to God, as it is written, "The inclination of the human heart is evil from youth" [Gen. 8:21]. Likewise, "The mind that is set on the flesh is hostile to God; it does not submit to God's law—indeed, it cannot" [Rom. 8:7]. . . .

3. However, God the Holy Spirit does not effect conversion without means, but he uses the preaching and the hearing of God's Word to accomplish it, as it is written (Rom. 1[:16]), the gospel is a "power of God" to save. Likewise, faith comes from hearing God's Word

27. That is, "the state of the controversy."

(Rom. 10[:17]). And it is God's will that people hear his Word and not plug their ears. . . .

Negative Theses
Contrary False Teaching

Therefore, we reject and condemn all the following errors as contrary to the guiding principle of God's Word:

1. The mad invention of the philosophers who are called Stoics, as well as the Manichaeans, who taught that everything that happens has to happen just so and could not happen in any other way, and that people do everything that they do, even in external things, under coercion and that they are coerced to do evil works and deeds, such as fornication, robbery, murder, thievery, and the like.

2. We also reject the error of the crass Pelagians, who taught that human beings could convert themselves to God, believe the gospel, be obedient to God's law with their whole hearts, and thus merit forgiveness of sins and eternal life out of their own powers apart from the grace of the Holy Spirit.

3. We also reject the error of the Semi-Pelagians, who teach that human beings can initiate their conversion by means of their own powers, but cannot complete it without the grace of the Holy Spirit.[28]

4. Likewise, the teaching that, although human beings are too weak to initiate conversion with their free will before rebirth, and thus convert themselves to God on the basis of their own natural powers and be obedient to God's law with their whole hearts, nonetheless, once the Holy Spirit has made a beginning through the preaching of the Word and in it has offered his grace, the human will is able out of its own natural powers to a certain degree, even though small and feeble, to do something, to help and cooperate, to dispose and prepare itself for grace, to grasp this grace, to accept it, and to believe the gospel.

5. Likewise, that the human being, after rebirth, can keep God's law perfectly and fulfill it completely, and that this fulfilling of the law constitutes our righteousness before God, with which we merit eternal life.

6. Likewise, we also reject and condemn the error of the Enthusiasts, who contrive the idea that God draws people to himself, enlightens them, makes them righteous, and saves them without means, without the hearing of God's Word, even without the use of the holy sacraments.

7. Likewise, that in conversion and new birth God completely destroys the substance and essence of the old creature, especially the rational soul, and creates a new essence of the soul out of nothing.

8. Likewise, when this wording is used without explanation: that the human will resists the Holy Spirit before, in, and after conversion, and that the Holy Spirit is given to those who intentionally and stubbornly resist him. For, as Augustine says, in conversion God makes willing people out of the unwilling and dwells in the willing.

Some ancient and modern teachers of the church have used expressions such as, "Deus trahit, sed volentem trahit," that is, "God draws, but he draws those who are willing"; and "Hominis voluntas in conversione non est otiosa, sed agit aliquid," that is, "The human will is not idle in conversion but also is doing something." Because such expressions have been introduced as confirmation of the natural

28. "Semi-Pelagianism" was a recently invented pejorative term originally used by Protestants to describe the synergism of fellow Protestants and Roman Catholics, to distinguish such synergism in salvation from full-blown Augustinianism or Pelagianism, but also to associate the view more with the latter. The term was later applied to the fifth- and sixth-century controversies treated at the Council of Orange in 529.

free will in conversion contrary to the teaching of God's grace, we hold that these expressions do not correspond to the form of sound teaching, and therefore it is proper to avoid them when speaking of conversion to God.

On the other hand, it is correct to say that in conversion God changes recalcitrant, unwilling people into willing people through the drawing power of the Holy Spirit, and that after this conversion the reborn human will is not idle in the daily exercise of repentance, but cooperates in all the works of the Holy Spirit which he performs through us.

9. Likewise, when Dr. Luther wrote that the human will conducts itself *pure passive* (that is, that it does absolutely nothing at all), that must be understood *respectu divinae gratiae in accendendis novis motibus*,[29] that is, insofar as God's Spirit takes hold of the human will through the Word that is heard or through the use of the holy sacraments and effects new birth and conversion. For when the Holy Spirit has effected and accomplished new birth and conversion and has altered and renewed the human will solely through his divine power and activity, then the new human will is an instrument and tool of God the Holy Spirit, in that the will not only accepts grace but also cooperates with the Holy Spirit in the works that proceed from it.

Therefore, before the conversion of the human being there are only two efficient causes, the Holy Spirit and God's Word as the instrument of the Holy Spirit, through which he effects conversion; the human creature must hear this Word, but cannot believe and accept it on the basis of its own powers but only through the grace and action of God the Holy Spirit.

29. That is, "purely passively" and "with respect to divine grace in the kindling of new movements."

Art. VII. Concerning the Holy Supper of Christ

Although those who teach Zwinglian doctrine are not to be counted among the theologians of the Augsburg Confession—since they separated themselves from this confession immediately, at the time it was presented—we, nonetheless, want to report on this controversy because they are insinuating themselves and spreading their error under the name of this Christian confession.

Status controversiae
The Chief Issue between Us and the Teaching of the Sacramentarians on This Article

In the Holy Supper are the true body and blood of our Lord Jesus Christ truly and essentially present, distributed with the bread and wine, and received by mouth by all those who avail themselves of the sacrament—whether they are worthy or unworthy, godly or ungodly, believers or unbelievers—to bring believers comfort and life and to bring judgment upon unbelievers?

The sacramentarians say no; we say yes.

To explain this controversy, it must first of all be noted that there are two kinds of sacramentarians. These are the crude sacramentarians, who state in plain language what they believe in their hearts: that in the Holy Supper there is nothing more than bread and wine present, nothing more distributed and received with the mouth. Then there are the cunning sacramentarians, the most dangerous kind, who in part appear to use our language and who pretend that they also believe in a true presence of the true, essential, living body and blood of Christ in the Holy Supper, but that this takes place spiritually, through faith. Yet, under the guise of such plausible words, they retain the former, crude opinion, that nothing more than bread and wine is present in the Holy Supper and received there by mouth.

For "spiritually" means to them nothing other than "the spirit of Christ" that is present, or "the power of the absent body of Christ and his merit." The body of Christ, according to this opinion, is, however, in no way or form present, but it is only up there in the highest heaven; to this body we lift ourselves into heaven through the thoughts of our faith. There we should seek his body and blood, but never in the bread and wine of the Supper.

Affirmative Theses

The Confession of Pure Teaching concerning the Holy Supper, against the Sacramentarians.

1. We believe, teach, and confess that in the Holy Supper the body and blood of Christ are truly and essentially present, truly distributed and received with the bread and wine.

2. We believe, teach, and confess that the words of the testament of Christ are not to be understood in any other way than the way they literally sound, that is, not that the bread symbolizes the absent body and the wine the absent blood of Christ, but that they are truly the true body and blood of Christ because of the sacramental union.

3. Concerning the consecration, we believe, teach, and confess that neither human effort nor the recitation of the minister effect this presence of the body and blood of Christ in the Holy Supper, but that it is to be attributed solely and alone to the almighty power of our Lord Jesus Christ.

4. In addition, we believe, teach, and hold with one accord that in the use of the Holy Supper the words of Christ's institution may under no circumstances be omitted but must be spoken publicly, as it is written, "The cup of blessing that we bless . . ." (1 Cor. 11 [10:16]). This blessing takes place through the pronouncement of the words of Christ.

5. The reasons for our position against the sacramentarians on this matter are those which Dr. Luther set forth in his *Great Confession*: "The first [reason for this position] is this article of our faith, that Jesus Christ is true, essential, natural, complete God and human being in one person, undivided and inseparable. The second, that the right hand of God is everything." . . . "The third, that the Word of God is not false or deceitful. The fourth that God has and knows various ways to be present at a certain place, not only the single one . . . , which the philosophers call 'local' " or spatial.

6. We believe, teach, and confess that the body and blood of Christ are received not only spiritually through faith but also orally with the bread and wine, though not in Capernaitic fashion but rather in a supernatural, heavenly way because of the sacramental union of the elements.[30] The words of Christ clearly demonstrate this, when Christ said, "take, eat, and drink," and the apostles did this. For it is written, "and they all drank from it" (Mark 14[:23]). . . .

7. We believe, teach, and confess that not only those who truly believe and are worthy, but also the unworthy and unbelievers receive the true body and blood of Christ, though they do not receive life and comfort, but rather judgment and damnation, if they do not turn and repent.

For though they reject Christ as a savior, they still must, against their will, accept him as a harsh judge, who is just as much present to exercise and visit judgment upon unrepentant guests as he is to bestow life and comfort upon

---

30. "Capernaitic" refers to a crass, merely physical consuming of flesh and blood, of which Reformed opponents accused the Lutherans. The term is based on the misunderstanding of Jesus' words at the synagogue in Capernaum (John 6:51-59). See further below in this same selection.

the hearts of those who truly believe and are worthy guests.

8. We believe, teach, and confess that there is only one kind of unworthy guest, those who do not believe. Of them it is written, "Those who do not believe are condemned already" [John 3:18]. The unworthy use of the holy sacrament increases, magnifies, and aggravates this condemnation (1 Cor. 11[:27, 29]).

9. We believe, teach, and confess that no genuine believers—no matter how weak—as long as they retain a living faith, receive the Holy Supper as condemnation. For Christ instituted this supper particularly for Christians who are weak in faith but repentant, to comfort them and to strengthen their weak faith.

10. We believe, teach, and confess that the entire worthiness of the guests at the table of this heavenly meal is and consists alone in the most holy obedience and perfect merit of Christ. We make his obedience and merit our own through true faith, concerning which we receive assurance through the sacrament. Worthiness consists in no way in our own virtues, or in internal or external preparations.

Negative Theses

The Contrary, Condemned Teaching of the Sacramentarians

On the other hand, we unanimously reject and condemn all the following erroneous articles, which oppose and are contrary to the teaching presented here, the simple belief and confession regarding the Supper of Christ:

1. The papal transubstantiation, when it is taught in the papacy that bread and wine in the Holy Supper lose their substance and natural essence and thus cease to exist, in such a way that the bread is transformed into the body of Christ and only its outward form remains.

2. The papal sacrifice of the Mass for the sins of the living and the dead.

3. That the laity are given only one of the sacramental elements and that against the clear words of the testament of Christ the chalice is kept from them and they are robbed of the blood of Christ.

4. When it is taught that the words of Christ's testament ought not to be understood or believed simply as they sound, but that they are an obscure expression, the meaning of which must be sought in other passages.

5. That the body of Christ in the holy sacrament is not received orally with the bread, but only bread and wine are received by mouth; the body of Christ, however, is received only spiritually, through faith.

6. That the bread and wine in the Holy Supper are no more than distinguishing marks, through which Christians recognize each other.

7. That the bread and wine are only representations, similes, and symbols of the far-distant body and blood of Christ.

8. That the bread and wine are no more than a reminder, a seal, or a guarantee, through which we are assured that when faith soars into heaven, it will participate there in the body and blood of Christ as truly as we eat and drink bread and wine in the Supper.

9. That the assurance and confirmation of our faith in the Holy Supper take place only through the outward signs of bread and wine, and not through the true body and blood of Christ present there.

10. That in the Holy Supper only the power, effect, or merit of the absent body and blood of Christ are distributed.

11. That the body of Christ is enclosed in heaven, so that it can in no way be present at the same time in many or all places on earth where his Holy Supper is being conducted.

12. That Christ could not have promised the essential presence of his body and blood in the Holy Supper, nor could he make that possible,

because the nature and characteristics of the assumed human nature would not permit or allow that.[31]

13. That God, even on the basis of his total omnipotence (a dreadful statement!), cannot possibly make his body to be essentially present in more than one place at one particular time.

14. That not the almighty words of the testament of Christ, but rather faith, effects and creates the presence of the body and blood of Christ in the Holy Supper.

15. That believers should not look for the body of Christ in the bread and wine of the Holy Supper but should instead lift their eyes from the bread to heaven and look there for the body of Christ.

16. That unbelieving, unrepentant Christians do not receive the true body and blood of Christ in the Holy Supper but only the bread and wine.

17. That the worthiness of the guests at this heavenly meal consists not only in true faith in Christ but indeed also in people's outward preparation.

18. That those who truly believe, who have and retain a true, living, pure faith in Christ, can receive this sacrament to their judgment, simply because they are still imperfect in their outward way of life.

19. That the outward, visible elements of bread and wine in the holy sacrament should be adored.

20. Likewise, we commend to the proper judgment of God all impudent, sarcastic, blasphemous questions and expressions, which we will not recite for the sake of propriety and which the sacramentarians utter in a crude, carnal, Capernaitic, and detestable manner, blasphemously, and with great offense concerning the supernatural, celestial mysteries of this sacrament.

21. We also hereby completely condemn the Capernaitic eating of the body of Christ. It suggests that his flesh is chewed up with the teeth and digested like other food. The sacramentarians maliciously attribute this view to us against the witness of their own conscience, despite our many protests. In this way they make our teaching detestable among their hearers. On the contrary, on the basis of the simple words of Christ's testament, we hold and teach the true, but supernatural, eating of the body of Christ and the drinking of his blood. Human reason and understanding cannot grasp this, but our understanding must be taken captive by obedience to Christ here as in all other articles of faith. Such a mystery cannot be grasped except by faith and is revealed alone in the Word.

Art. XI. Concerning the Eternal Predestination and Election of God

On this article there has been no public conflict among the theologians of the Augsburg Confession. However, because it is an article of comfort when properly treated, it is also explained in this document so that no offensive dispute may arise in the future.

Affirmative Theses

The Pure, True Teaching concerning This Article

1. First of all, the difference between *praescientia* and *praedestinatio*,[32] that is, between God's foreknowledge and his eternal election, must be carefully noted.

2. God's foreknowledge is nothing else than that God knows all things before they happen, as it is written, "God in heaven reveals mysteries. He has disclosed to King Nebuchadnezzar

31. The Lutheran view of the *communicatio idiomatum* (communication of attributes) affirms that the divine attribute of omnipresence can be communicated to the human nature of Jesus Christ.

32. Literally, "foreknowledge" and "predestination."

what will happen in future times" (Dan. 2[:28]).

3. This foreknowledge extends equally over godly people and evil people, but it is not a cause of evil. It is not the cause of sins, when people act wrongly (sin proceeds originally from the devil and the wicked, perverted human will), nor of human corruption, for which people are responsible themselves. Instead, God's foreknowledge provides order in the midst of evil and sets limits to it. It determines how long evil can continue and determines also that everything, even if it is evil in itself, serves the welfare of God's elect.

4. *Praedestinatio*, however, or God's eternal election, extends only to the righteous, God-pleasing children of God.[33] It is a cause of their salvation, which God brings about. He has arranged everything that belongs to it. Our salvation is so firmly grounded on it [cf. John 10:26-29] that "the gates of hell will not prevail against it" [Matt. 16:18].

5. This election is not to be probed in the secret counsel of God but rather is to be sought in the Word, where it has also been revealed.

6. However, the Word of God leads us to Christ, who is the "Book of Life" [Phil. 4:3; Rev. 3:5], in whom are inscribed and chosen all who shall be eternally saved, as it is written, "He chose us in Christ before the foundation of the world" [Eph. 1:4].

7. This Christ calls all sinners to himself and promises them refreshment. He is utterly serious in his desire that all people should come to him and seek help for themselves [cf. Matt. 11:28; 1 Tim. 2:4]. He offers himself to them in the Word. He desires them to hear the Word and not to plug their ears or despise his Word. To this end he promises the power and activity of the Holy Spirit, divine assistance in remaining faithful and attaining eternal salvation.

8. Therefore we are to make judgments regarding our election to eternal life neither on the basis of reason nor on the basis of God's law. Such a course of action would lead us either into a wild, irresponsible, Epicurean life, or into despair—and would awaken harmful thoughts in human hearts. Whenever people follow their reason, they can hardly escape such reflections as these: "As long as God has chosen me for salvation, I cannot be condemned no matter what I do!" or, "I have not been chosen for eternal life, so it does not help when I do good; everything is really in vain."

9. Instead, the true meaning of election must be learned from the holy gospel of Christ. It clearly states, "God imprisoned all in unbelief that he may be merciful to all," and that he wants no one to be lost but rather that everyone repent and believe on the Lord Christ [Rom. 11:32; 1 Tim. 2:4; cf. Ezek. 33:11; 18:23].

10. This teaching is useful and comforting for all those who are concerned about the revealed will of God and follow the order which St. Paul observed in the Epistle to the Romans. There he first of all points people to repentance, acknowledgement of their sins, and then to faith in Christ and obedience to God before he speaks of the mystery of God's eternal election.

11. That "many are called and few are chosen" [Matt. 20:16] does not mean that God does not want to save everyone. Instead, the reason for condemnation lies in their not hearing God's Word at all or arrogantly despising it, plugging their ears and their hearts, and thus blocking the Holy Spirit's ordinary path, so that he cannot carry out his work in them; or if they have given it a hearing, they cast it to the wind and pay no attention to it. Then the fault lies not with God and his election but

33. *Predestination* is used here, consistent with Thomas Aquinas and other theologians, to refer to election only. Reformed scholasticism tended to use the term to speak of the decrees of both election and reprobation.

with their own wickedness [cf. 2 Pet. 2:9-15; Luke 11:47-52; Heb. 12:15-17, 25].

12. A Christian should only think about the article of God's eternal election to the extent that it is revealed in God's Word. The Word holds Christ before our eyes as the "Book of Life," which he opens and reveals for us through the preaching of the holy gospel, as it is written, "Those whom he has chosen, he also called" [Rom. 8:30]. In Christ we are to seek the Father's eternal election. . . .

13. Along with this we should strive as diligently as possible to live according to God's will and to "confirm our calling," as Saint Peter admonishes [2 Pet. 1:10]. We should especially abide by the revealed Word that cannot and will not fail us.

14. This short explanation of God's eternal election gives God his honor fully and completely. On the basis of his pure mercy alone, without any merit of ours at all, he saves us "according to the purpose of his will" [Eph. 1:11]. In addition, no one is given reason either for faintheartedness or for a reckless, wild life.

Antitheses or Negative Theses

False Teaching regarding This Article

Accordingly, we believe and maintain that those who present the teaching of God's gracious election to eternal life either in such a way that troubled Christians cannot find comfort in it but are driven to faintheartedness or despair, or in such a way that the impenitent are strengthened in their arrogance,[34] are not preaching this teaching according to the Word and will of God but rather according to their own reason, and at the instigation of the accursed devil, because (as the Apostle testifies) "whatever was written was written for our instruction, so that by steadfastness and by the comfort of the Scriptures we might have hope" [Rom. 15:4]. Therefore, we reject the following errors:

1. When it is taught that God does not want all people to repent and believe the gospel.

2. Likewise, that when God calls us to himself, he does not seriously intend that all people should come to him.

3. Likewise, that God does not desire that everyone should be saved, but rather that without regard to their sins—only because of God's naked decision, intention, and will—some are designated for damnation, so that there is no way that they could be saved.

4. Likewise, that the cause of God's election does not lie exclusively in God's mercy and the most holy merit of Christ but that there is also a cause in us, because of which God has chosen for us eternal life.

These are blasphemous, horrible, and erroneous teachings, which take away from Christians all the comfort that they have in the holy gospel and in the use of the holy sacraments. Therefore, these errors dare not be tolerated in the church of God.

[*The Book of Concord: The Confessions of the Evangelical Lutheran Church*, ed. Robert Kolb and Timothy Wengert, trans. Charles Arand (Minneapolis: Augsburg Fortress, 2000), 491–94, 503–8, 517–19]

D. The Arminian Controversy

Selection 55: *Lambeth Articles* (1595)

Peter Baro (1534–1599), Lady Margaret Professor of Divinity at Cambridge since 1574, came into controversy for his doctrine of conditional predestination. At the climax of this particular dispute in 1595, the* Lambeth Articles *were drafted by his opponents

34. These twin dangers of despair and security were ubiquitously addressed in discussions of predestination.

as a rule for teaching at Cambridge. Although they never attained confessional status in the Church of England, they reflect the increasing influence of Continental Reformed theology in England and the attempt by some leading theologians to exclude what would later become known as "Arminianism," which is not directly excluded in the Thirty-Nine Articles. *In the end, however, even Peter Baro could interpret the Lambeth Articles to be consistent with conditional predestination.*

1. God from eternity hath predestinated certain men unto life; certain men he hath reprobated.

2. The moving or efficient cause of predestination unto life is not the foresight of faith, or of perseverance, or of good works, or of any thing that is in the person predestinated, but only the good will and pleasure of God.[35]

3. There is predetermined a certain number of the predestinate, which can neither be augmented nor diminished.

4. Those who are not predestinated to salvation shall be necessarily damned for their sins.

5. A true, living, and justifying faith, and the Spirit of God sanctifying, is not extinguished, falleth not away; it vanisheth not away in the elect, either finally or totally.

6. A man truly faithful, that is, such a one who is endued with a justifying faith, is certain, with the full assurance of faith, of the remission of his sins and of his everlasting salvation by Christ.

7. Saving grace is not given, is not granted, is not communicated to all men, by which they may be saved if they will.

8. No man can come unto Christ unless it shall be given unto him, and unless the Father shall draw him; and all men are not drawn by the Father, that they may come to the Son.

9. It is not in the will or power of every one to be saved.

[*The Creeds of Christendom*, vol. 3, ed. Philip Schaff (repr., Grand Rapids, MI: Baker, 1998), 523–24]

35. Peter Baro understood the "good pleasure (*beneplacitum*) of God" to be God's good will favorably disposed toward all people.

Biographical Note: Jacob Arminius

Jacob Arminius (Harmenszoon) (1559–1609) was born and raised in the Dutch town of Oudewater. His father died probably before he was born, so his early education was provided by the patronage of others. As an adolescent, he studied in Utrecht and then Marburg. While he was away in Marburg, his mother, siblings, and much of his extended family were killed in the Spanish massacre at Oudewater in 1575. He later finished his education at Leiden, Basel, and finally Geneva, where he studied under Calvin's successor Theodore Beza (1519–1605).

Arminius moved from Geneva to Amsterdam in 1587, where he was ordained in 1588 in the city's Old Church (Oude Kerk). Arminius came into controversy in the early 1590s as he preached through the Epistle to the Romans. As a result of interpreting Romans 7 as a not yet regenerate person struggling with sin, he was accused of having an overly optimistic anthropology. And in his interpretation of Romans 9, he taught that predestination to salvation or condemnation is conditional upon one's faith or unbelief; predestination is not an absolute, unconditional predetermination of God.

His otherwise uneventful and fruitful ministry in Amsterdam came to a close in 1603 when he was appointed as full professor of theology at Leiden University. His faculty colleagues in theology opposed his views on grace, predestination, and related doc-

trines, and the controversy within the theological college erupted in late 1604. Gradually, the debates spilled into the churches, and Arminius became the object of increasing suspicion among his theological opponents. The Dutch magistrates intervened in a vain attempt to quell the controversies, which by 1609 were threatening to divide the Reformed Church. Due to severe illness, Arminius had to leave one of these conferences prematurely in August 1609. He returned home to Leiden, where he died on October 19, 1609.

Like most theologians in his day, Arminius did not want to be known as an innovator. In fact, most of what he taught was unoriginal to him. What makes him stand out in the history of theology is the new context in which he forged his theology. As a minister and professor in the Reformed tradition, he learned from and contributed to what was becoming Reformed orthodoxy and scholasticism. But he also broke from that tradition in profound ways, emphasizing conditional predestination, resistible grace that cooperates with human nature, and God's commitment to communicating his goodness and love to creation. In doing so, Arminius was willing to appropriate concepts not only from the early church but also from contemporary Roman Catholic Jesuit theology (for example, the doctrine of divine middle knowledge). Although Arminius's thought was often oversimplified and lost in later controversies, the legacy of "Arminianism" has made a lasting impact in Protestant and evangelical churches.

Selection 56: Jacob Arminius, a Prayer from His Deathbed

Lord Jesus, faithful and merciful high priest—you who were willing to be tempted as we are in all things without sin, so that, being taught by such experience how painful a thing it is to obey God in sufferings, you can be affected with the sense of our infirmities—have mercy on me; help me your servant who is lying ill and oppressed with so many maladies. God of my salvation, render my soul fit for your heavenly kingdom, indeed my body for the resurrection.

[*The Works of James Arminius*, 3 vols., London ed., trans. James Nichols and William Nichols (London, 1825–1875), vol. 1, 44–45]

Selection 57: Jacob Arminius, *Apology or Defense of Arminius against Thirty-one Articles* (1608)

In 1608, a document was circulated by Arminius's opponents in and around Amsterdam that contained thirty-one theological theses allegedly representing the thought of Arminius and a Leiden minister, Adrian van den Borre. Arminius responded to each of the thirty-one articles in this Apologia, *which reflects, among other things, his views on religious authority and his frustration with his opponents.*

Article XXVII. (VII.) *Faith is not the pure gift of God, but depends partly on the grace of God, and partly on the powers of Free Will; that, if a man will, he may believe or not believe.*

Answer.

I never said this, I never thought of saying it, and, relying on God's grace, I never will enunciate my sentiments on matters of this description in a manner thus desperate and confused. I simply affirm, that this enunciation is false, "Faith is not the pure gift of God;" that this is likewise false, if taken according to the rigour of the words, "Faith depends partly on the grace of God, and partly on the powers of Free Will;" and that this is also false when thus enunciated, "If a man will, he can believe or not believe." If they suppose, that I hold some opinions from which these assertions may by good consequence be deduced, why do they not quote my words? It is a species of injustice to attach to any person those consequences, which one may frame out of his words, as if they were his sentiments: But the injustice is still more flagrant, if those conclusions cannot by good consequence be deduced from what he has said. Let my brethren, therefore, make the experiment, whether they can deduce such consectaries as these, from the things which I teach; but let the experiment be made in my company, and not by themselves in their own circle: For that sport will be vain, equally void of profit or of victory; as boys sometimes feel, when they play alone at chess with their own dice.

For the proper explanation of this matter, a discussion *on the Concurrence and Agreement of Divine Grace and of Free Will, or of the human Will,* would be required; but because this would be a labour much too prolix, I shall not now make the attempt. To explain the matter I will employ a *simile,* which yet, I confess, is very *dissimilar;* but its dissimilitude is greatly in favour of my sentiments. A rich man bestows, on a poor and famishing beggar, alms by which he may be able to maintain himself and his family. Does it cease to be a pure gift, because the beggar extends his hand to receive it? Can it be said with propriety, that "the alms depended partly on *the liberality* of the Donor, and partly on *the liberty* of the Receiver," though the latter would not have possessed the alms unless he had received it by stretching out his hand? Can it be correctly said, *because the beggar is always prepared to receive,* that "he can have the alms, or not have it, just as he pleases?" If these assertions cannot be truly made about a beggar who receives alms, how much less can they be made about the gift of faith, for the receiving of which far more acts of Divine Grace are required! This is the question which it will be requisite to discuss, "What acts of Divine Grace are required to produce faith in man?" If I omit any act which is necessary, or which concurs, [in the production of faith,] let it be demonstrated from the Scriptures, and I will add it to the rest.

It is not our wish to do the least injury to Divine Grace, by taking from it any thing that belongs to it: But let my brethren take care, that they themselves neither inflict an injury on Divine Justice, by attributing that to it which it refuses; nor on Divine Grace, by transforming it into something else, which cannot be called *Grace.* That I may in one word intimate what they must prove, such a transformation they effect when they represent "the sufficient and efficacious grace, which is necessary to salvation, to be irresistible," or as acting with such potency that it cannot be resisted by any free creature.

A spotprent *mocking Arminius*

Article XXVIII. (VIII.) *The grace sufficient for salvation is conferred on the Elect, and on the Non-elect; that, if they will, they may believe or not believe, may be saved or not saved.*

Answer.

Our brethren here also manifest the same negligence. They take no pains to know what my sentiments are; they are not careful in examining what truth there is in my opinions; and they exercise no discretion about the words in which they enunciate my sentiments and their own. They know that I use the word "Election" in two senses: (i.) For the decree by which God resolves to justify believers and to condemn unbelievers, and which is called by the Apostle, "the purpose of God according to election:" (Rom. ix, 11)—(ii.) And for the decree by which He resolves to elect these or those nations and men with the design of communicating to them the means of faith, but to pass by other nations and men. Yet, without this distinction, they fasten these sentiments on me; when, by its aid, I am enabled to affirm, not only, "Sufficient Grace is conferred on, or rather *is offered* to, the Elect and the Non-elect;" but also, "Sufficient Grace is not offered to any except the Elect."—(i.) "It is offered to the Elect and the Non-elect," because it is offered to unbelievers, whether they will afterwards believe or not believe.—(ii.) "It is offered to none except the Elect," because, by that very thing which is offered to them, they cease to be of the number of those of whom it is said, "He suffered them to walk in their own ways;" (Acts xiv, 16;) and, "He hath not dealt so with any nation." (Psalm cxlvii, 20.) And who shall compel me to use words of their prescribing, unless proof be brought from Scripture that the words are to be thus and in no other way received?

To the whole together I reply, that nothing is declared in these words, in whatever manner they may be understood, which St. Augustine himself and his followers would not willingly have acknowledged as true: I say, in these words are enunciated the very sentiments of St. Augustine; yet he was the chief champion against the Pelagian heresy, being accounted in that age its most successful combatant. For in his Treatise *On Nature and Grace,* (c. 67,) St. Augustine speaks thus: "Since He is everywhere present, who, by many methods through the creature that is subservient to Him as his Lord, can call him who is averse, can teach a believer, can comfort him who hopes, can exhort the diligent man, can aid him who strives, and can lend an attentive ear to him who deprecates; it is not imputed to thee as a fault, that thou art unwillingly ignorant, but that thou neglectest to enquire after that of which thou art ignorant; not that thou dost not collect and bind together the shattered and wounded members, but that thou despisest Him who is willing to heal thee." The Book entitled *The Vocation of the Gentiles*, which is attributed with a greater semblance of probability to Prosper, than to St. Ambrose,[36] has the following passage: "On all men has always been bestowed some measure of heavenly doctrine, which, though it was of more sparing and hidden grace, was yet sufficient, as the Lord has judged, to serve some men for a remedy, and all men for a testimony." *(Lib.* 2. c. 5.) In the commencement of the Ninth Chapter of the same book, he explains the whole matter by saying: "The Grace of God has indeed *{principaliter}* the decided pre-eminence in our justifications, persuading us by exhortations, admonishing us by examples, affrighting us by dangers, exciting us by miracles, by giving understanding, by inspiring counsel, and by illuminating the heart itself and imbuing it with the affections of faith. But

36. Prosper of Aquitaine (ca. 390–ca. 463), not Ambrose of Milan, was indeed the author of the named treatise.

the will of man is likewise subjoined to it and is united with it, which has been excited to this by the before-mentioned succours,—that it may co-operate in the Divine work within itself, and may begin *{exercere ad meritum}* to follow after the reward which, by the heavenly seed, it has conceived for the object of its desire, ascribing the failure to its own mutability, and the success (if the issue be prosperous) to the aid of grace. This aid is afforded to all men, by innumerable methods both secret and manifest; and the rejection of this assistance by many persons, is to be ascribed to their negligence; but its reception by many persons, is both of Divine Grace and of the human will."

I do not produce these passages, as if I thought that either my brethren or I must abide by the sentiments of the Fathers, but only for the purpose of removing from myself the crime of Pelagianism in this matter.

Article XXIX. (IX.) *Believers can perfectly fulfil the Law, and live in the world without sin.*

Answer.

This is what I never said. But when a certain person once, in a public disputation on the *Baptism of Infants,* was endeavouring by a long digression to bring me to the point—either to declare that believers could perfectly fulfil the law of God,—or that they could not,—I declined an answer, but quoted the opinion of St. Augustine, from the Second Book of his Treatise *On the Demerits and Remission of Sins, against the Pelagians.* That passage I will here transcribe, that I may defend myself against the charge of Pelagianism; because I perceive, that the men with whom I have to do consider even these sentiments to be Pelagian, though they can on no account whatever be reckoned such.

St. Augustine says: "We must not instantly with an incautious rashness oppose those who assert, that it is possible for man to be in this life without sin. For if we deny the possibility of this, we shall derogate both from *the free will of man,* which desires to be in such a perfect state by willing it; and from *the Power or Mercy of God,* who effects it by the assistance which He affords." . . .

I do not oppose this opinion of St. Augustine; but I do not enter into a contest about any part of the whole matter. For I think the time may be far more happily and usefully employed in prayers to obtain what is lacking in each of us, and in serious admonitions that every one endeavour to proceed and to press forward towards the mark of Perfection, than when spent in such disputations.

But my brethren will say, that in the 114th Question of our Catechism[37] this very subject is treated, and that it is there asked, "Can those persons who are converted to God, perfectly observe the Divine Commands?" The answer subjoined is, *{minime,}* "By no means."—To this observation I reply, that I do not say any thing against it; but that the reason of the negative answer is about *the act,* when the question itself is about *the possibility;* and that therefore, from this, nothing is proved. It is also well known, that this answer had been rejected by some persons; and that it was only by the intervention of the brethren, who added an explanation to it, that it afterwards obtained the approbation of the same individuals. But I shall be perfectly willing to enter into a conference with my brethren about this matter, whenever it shall be convenient; and I hope we shall easily agree in opinion.

Article XXX. (X.) *It may admit of Discussion, whether Semi-Pelagianism is not real Christianity.*

37. That is, the *Heidelberg Catechism,* the German Reformed document that had become regulative in the Dutch Reformed Church (see Selection 48).

Answer.

In a certain Lecture I said, that it would be easy, under the pretext of Pelagianism, to condemn all those things of which we do not approve, if we may invent *half* [*semi*], *quarter, three quarters, four fifths-Pelagianism,* and so upwards: And I added, that it might admit of discussion, *whether Semi-Pelagianism is not real Christianity.* By these remarks it was not my wish to patronize Pelagian doctrine; but I was desirous to intimate, that something might be accounted as Semi-Pelagianism which does not depart from the truth of Christian doctrine. For as, when a departure is once made from the Truth, the descent towards falsehood becomes more and more rapid; so, by receding from falsehood, it is possible for men to arrive at truth, which is often accustomed to stand as *the mean* between two extremes of falsehood. Such indeed is the state of the matter in Pelagianism and Manicheism: If any man can enter on a middle way between these two heresies, he will be a true Catholic, neither inflicting an injury on Grace as the Pelagians do, nor on Free Will as do the Manichees. Let the Refutations be perused which St. Augustine wrote against both these heresies, and it will appear that he makes this very acknowledgment.[38] For this reason it has happened, that, for the sake of confirming their different opinions, St. Augustine's words, when writing against the Manichees, have been frequently quoted by the Pelagians; and those which he wrote against the Pelagians, have been quoted by the Manichees.

This therefore is what I intended to convey; and that my brethren may understand my meaning, I declare openly, "that it will be quite as easy a task for me to convict the sentiments of some among them of Manicheism, and even of Stoicism, as they will be really capable of convicting others of Pelagianism, whom they suspect of holding that error." But I wish us all to abstain from odious names of this description, as they are employed without producing any benefit. For he who is accused will either deny, that his sentiments are the same as those of Pelagius; or, if he acknowledges the existence of a similarity, he will say that Pelagius was wrongly condemned by the Church. It would be better then to omit these epithets, and to confer solely about the matter itself; unless, approaching to the opinion of the Papists, we hold that what has once been determined by the Church cannot be drawn into controversy.

Article XXXI. (XI.) *It is not correctly said in the Catechism, that "God is angry with us for* [innata] *birth-sins;" because original sin is a punishment: But whatever is a punishment is not properly a sin.*

Answer.

Nearly two months ago, a certain Minister of God's Word came to me, desirous, as he declared, to confer with me about the opinion which I held concerning the Catechism and Dutch Confession being subjected to examination in our National Synod.[39] On this subject we had some conversation together, and I concluded the expression of my opinion with this syllogism: "Every human writing which is not *autopiston* [in itself entitled to implicit credit], not authentic, and not Divine, may be examined, and indeed ought to be; when it can be done in order, and after a legitimate manner, that is, in a Synod, to which [the consideration of] these writings belongs. But such productions are the Catechism and our Confession:—*Therefore* they

38. Along with Donatism, Manichaeism and Pelagianism were the defining controversies of Augustine's career.

39. The *Belgic Confession* (see Selection 47) and the *Heidelberg Catechism* were to be topics for discussion at a Dutch national synod, or council, but did not occur until a decade after Arminius's death at the Synod of Dordt (see Selection 60).

may and ought to be subjected to examination." When he had wearied himself in opposing a few things to this syllogism, which I soon dispersed by the clearest light of truth, he began to inquire what [objections] they were which I had against the Confession and Catechism; I replied, that I had nothing against those formularies, for that would be an act of prejudging which I would not take upon myself; but that there were matters in those two productions, about which it was my wish to confer in a legitimate and orderly manner, with my brethren at their own time, in a Synod, whether on every point they be agreeable to the scriptures, or whether they dissent in any respect from them: For this purpose, that if, after a serious and strict examination, they be found to agree with the Scriptures, they may be approved and confirmed by recent and fresh sanctions; or that, if found to dissent from them, they may be corrected as commodiously as possible.

He became urgent with me, therefore, and requested that I would disclose to him those points about which I was desirous to confer; and he declared, that he asked this favour for no other reason than that he might be able himself to think seriously about them. Unwilling positively to deny this his request, I began to produce some parts of the Confession, and especially the Fourteenth Article. But he said, "that he made small account of this, because he thought something might easily be discovered in the Confession, which did not perfectly and in every respect correspond with the Scriptures, at least with regard to its phraseology, for it was the composition of only a few persons, and in fact was written in the earliest times [of the Dutch Reformation]; and that he perceived very little danger in the Confession being corrected in some passages, since it was not much in use among the people."[40]

But when he began to be still more urgent concerning the Catechism, desirous in that particular likewise to gratify him, I adduced some passages, and, among others, the Answer to the Tenth Question, in which God is said "by horrid methods to be angry both on account of birth-sins, and on account of those also which we ourselves commit," etc. I said, two things, in these words, might admit of discussion: (1.) Whether we could correctly call it "birth-sins" in the plural number. I had scarcely made this remark, when he, without waiting for any further explanation, said, "that on one occasion, while he was explaining the Catechism to some students, he had himself begun to think whether it was a good and proper phrase; but that he had defended it by this argument—*The Catechism employs the plural number on account of original sin itself, and on account of the sin committed by Adam which was the cause of that original sin.*—But as I considered that kind of defence to be unworthy of any confutation, I said, it was better for him at once to own that these words required emendation, than to give such an explanation of them. After this conversation I added another remark: (2.) It may admit of discussion, Whether God could be angry on account of original sin which was born with us, since it seemed to be inflicted on us by God as a punishment of the actual sin which had been committed by Adam and by us in him. For, in that case, the progress would be infinite, if God, angry on account of the *actual* sin of Adam, were to punish us with this *original* sin; were He again to be angry with us for this original sin, and inflict on us another punishment; and, for a similar cause were He a third time to be angry on account of that second punishment

40. Here is an interesting testimony to the neglect of the *Belgic Confession* in Dutch churches.

which had been inflicted, *guilt* and *punishment* thus mutually and frequently succeeding each other, without the intervention of any actual sin.—When to this observation he replied, "that still it was *sin;*" I said, I did not deny that it was *sin,* but it was not *actual* sin: And I quoted the seventh chapter of *the Epistle to the Romans,* in which the Apostle treats on the sin, and says that "it produces in the unregenerate all manner of concupiscence," thus intimating that we must distinguish between actual sin, and that which was *the cause of other sins,* and which on this very account might be denominated "sin." . . .

Let the brethren recall to mind what was asked of the Professors of Divinity in our University, by the Synod of South Holland held at Gorchum, and let them compare it among themselves: We are asked diligently to read through the Confession and Catechism, and, if we find any thing in them which merits animadversion, to announce the same seasonably and in order: And this, on my own part, I promised to do. . . .

CONCLUSION.

This then is the answer which I have thought proper to make, at present, to the Thirty-one Articles that have been objected against me. If I have not given satisfaction by it to some men, I am prepared to confer in order with any of them upon these subjects and others which pertain to the Christian Religion, for this purpose,—that we may either agree in our sentiments,—or, if this result cannot be obtained by a conference, that we bear with each other, when it has become evident how far we severally proceed together in the matter of religion, and what things they are of which we approve or disapprove, and that these points of difference are not of such a description as to forbid professors of the same religion to hold different sentiments about them.

Some persons perhaps will reproach me with "appearing sometimes to answer with doubt and hesitation, when it is the duty of a Divine and a Professor of Theology to be fully persuaded about those things which he will teach to others, and not to fluctuate in his opinions."[41] To these persons I wish to reply,

1. The most learned man, and he who is most conversant with the Scriptures, is ignorant of many things, and is always but a scholar in the school of Christ and of the Scriptures. But one who is thus ignorant of all things about which an opportunity or necessity of speaking offers itself, either from adversaries, or from those who wish to ask and ascertain his sentiments by private or public conference and disputation, cannot answer without some doubt. For it is better for him to speak somewhat doubtfully, than {*affirmanter*} dogmatically, about those things of which he has no certain knowledge; and to intimate that he himself requires daily progress, and seeks for instruction as well as they. For I think no one has proceeded to such a pitch of audacity, as to style himself a master that is ignorant of nothing, and that indulges no doubts about any matter whatever.

2. It is not every thing which becomes a subject of controversy that is of equal importance. Some things are of such a nature as to render it unlawful for any man to feel a doubt concerning them, if he have any wish to be called by the name of Christian. But there are other things which are not of the same dignity, and about which those who treat on catholic sentiments [such orthodox doctrines as are held by

---

41. Arminius was accused during and after his life of hesitating on too many doctrinal matters, an epistemic humility about theology that in other eras and contexts would have been regarded as a virtue.

all Christians] have dissented from each other, without any breach of truth and Christian peace. Of what description those subjects may be which are discussed in these Articles, and about which I have appeared to answer with hesitation, and whether they be of absolute necessity, may likewise become in due time a topic of discussion.

3. My reply [to these thirty-one Articles] is not peremptory: Not that I have in them said any thing against conscience, but because I did not consider it requisite to bring forward, in the first instance, all those things which I might be able to say. I accounted my answer sufficient, and more than sufficient, for all those objections which have not the slightest foundation on any reasons whatsoever; not only because they were untruly charged against me, but because they did not impinge against the truth of the Scriptures. In the greater number of these Articles, I might have discharged the whole of my duty, in simply denying them, and in demanding proof: But I have gone further than this, that I might in some degree give satisfaction, and that I might besides challenge my brethren to a conference, if they should think it necessary: This I will never decline, provided it be lawfully instituted, and in such a manner as to inspire hopes of any benefits to be derived from it. If after that conference it be discovered, that, either because I am ignorant of necessary things which ought to be taught in the Church and in the University,—or because I hold unsound opinions about articles on which some importance is placed for obtaining salvation and for the illustration of the Divine glory,—or because I doubt concerning such things as ought to be delivered *{asseveranter}* dogmatically and inculcated with seriousness and rigour,—if for these reasons it be discovered that, according to this our unhappy condition, I am unworthy to hold any office in the Church or University, (for who is sufficient for these things?) I will without reluctance resign my situation, and give place to a man possessed of greater merit.

But I wish to advise my brethren, particularly those of them who are my juniors, and who have not "their senses so much exercised"[42] in the Scriptures as to be enabled to deliver out of those Scriptures determinate opinions about all things, that they be not too bold in asserting any thing, of which when required to give their reasons, they will be able with great difficulty to produce them; and, besides, that they be sedulously on their guard lest, after they have strenuously affirmed any thing which I call in doubt without employing the contrary affirmation, and it be discovered that the arguments which I employ in justification of my doubts are stronger than those on which they rely in that their affirmation, they incur the charge of immodesty and arrogance among men of prudence, and from this very circumstance be accounted unworthy of the place which they hold with so much presumption. For it becomes a Bishop and a Teacher of the Church, not only to hold fast the faithful word as he hath been taught, that he may be able by his sound doctrine both to exhort and to convince the gainsayers, (Titus i, 9, 7,) but likewise not to be given to self-will, arrogance, and boldness: Into which faults novices easily fall, (1 Tim. iii, 6). . . .

[*The Works of James Arminius*, 3 vols., London ed., trans. James Nichols and William Nichols (London, 1825–1875), vol. 2, 51–63]

Selection 58: Jacob Arminius, *Declaration of Sentiments* (1608)

On October 20, 1608, Arminius was summoned to The Hague by the Dutch magistrates in order to express his opinions on the

42. Cf. Heb. 5:14.

theological controversies. Ten days later, on October 30, he delivered his speech in Dutch, treating the topics of predestination, providence, free will, grace, perseverance, assurance, perfection, Christology, and justification. It was published as a pamphlet posthumously in 1610. Because this speech covers a range of topics, is addressed to laymen, and represents his mature thought less than a year before his death, the Declaration of Sentiments *functions as a good introduction to Arminius, though this document should not be mistaken for his systematic theology.*

In this excerpt on predestination, Arminius describes the view of his Reformed opponents that would later be called supralapsarianism, and he then gives twenty reasons for rejecting it (points 1, 19, and 20 selected here). He concludes the topic by describing his own opinion on predestination and twenty reasons for favoring it, in direct contrast to his points against supralapsarianism.

My Sentiments on This [Reformed] Scheme of Predestination[43]

In my opinion, if I may speak with freedom in an attempt to form a better judgment, this doctrine as formulated contains many falsehoods, inconsistencies, and contradictions, too many to recount within our time constraints. I shall therefore restrict my remarks to a global frame of reference and point out four principal points that are the most prominent and far-reaching in their implications. Once those are set out, I will endeavor to explain briefly my judgments regarding them:

I. That God has absolutely and with precision decreed to save certain human beings by his mercy and grace, but to condemn others according to his justice. God has chosen to do this without any regard for the righteousness or sinfulness, obedience or disobedience that might be present in the lives of either the elect or the reprobate.

II. That God, in order to execute this decree, determined to create Adam and all humanity in him in an upright state of original righteousness. He also ordained that they would commit sin so that they would be deprived of original righteousness, incur guilt, and deserve eternal condemnation.[44]

III. That God decreed both the decision to save some as well as the means to attain that end. He willed not only to save them, but to bring them to faith as well as to assure that they would persevere in that faith. This God accomplishes by a grace and power that is irresistible, so that it is impossible for the elect to do otherwise than believe, persevere in the faith, and be saved.

IV. That to those whom God has foreordained to perdition by his absolute will, he has also denied the grace that is necessary and sufficient for salvation. He does not confer this grace on them, and the result is that they are denied any capacity to come to faith and be saved.

In the fear of the Lord, after thorough examination and contemplation on these four points, I offer the following with regard to this doctrine of Predestination:

---

43. Arminius here lays out the principal points of the predestinarian system to which he was most vehemently opposed, but which was also being taught as Reformed orthodoxy throughout The Netherlands, including by his colleagues at Leiden University.

44. This doctrine, which is rejected by Arminius, proposes that the decree to predestine (i.e., elect and reprobate) (I.) occurred logically before the decree to create humans and permit their sin (II.). This doctrine, in placing predestination "before the fall," is thus "supralapsarian" (*supra lapsum*, above the fall).

FIRST, that this doctrine of predestination is not the foundation of Christianity, of salvation, or of the certainty of salvation.

I. Not of Christianity. (1) Because this doctrine of predestination does not correspond to the decree of God by which Christ is appointed to be the Savior, the head, and the foundation of those who will be made heirs to salvation. This decree is the sole foundation for Christianity. (2) Because the doctrine as formulated is not that doctrine by which, through faith, we as living stones are built up into Christ, the chief cornerstone, joined with him as members of the body connected to their head.

II. This doctrine is not the foundation for salvation. (1) This predestination does not correspond to that decree of the good pleasure of God in Christ Jesus on which our salvation solely rests and depends. (2) This doctrine of predestination is not the foundation of salvation, for it is not the power of God to salvation to everyone that believes [Rom 1:16], because in this plan the righteousness of God is not revealed from faith to faith [Rom. 1:17].

III. This doctrine is not a foundation for the certainty of our salvation. (1) The certainty of our salvation is: Those who believe will be saved [Mark 16:16]; and, I believe, therefore, I shall be saved. (2) For this doctrine of predestination embraces within itself neither the first nor the second part of the syllogism—a point recognized by those who say, "We do not intend to say that a knowledge of the doctrine of predestination is the foundation of Christianity, or that such knowledge is on par with knowledge of the gospel as necessary for salvation." . . .

NINETEENTH, this doctrine subverts the foundation of religion in general and the Christian religion in particular. Considered as a whole, the foundation of the Christian faith is rooted in the twofold love of God, without which there neither is nor can be any [Christian] religion. The first is a love of justice, which is the source of God's hatred of sin. The second is the love for humanity, endowed by God with reason. In the matter before us, this love acts according to the Apostle to the Hebrews, "[And without faith it is impossible to please God, for] whoever would draw near to God must believe that he exists and that he rewards those who seek him" [Heb 11:6]. God's love for justice is made known in that it is not God's will to bestow eternal life on any except on those who seek him; God's love of humanity consists in the divine willingness to bestow eternal life on those who seek him.

A mutuality exists between these two kinds of love. The love that God extends to humanity cannot come into play unless it is permitted by God's love of justice. This implies that God's love for justice is the more excellent of the two; however, love for the creature abounds, except where the love of justice would prohibit its expression. The consequence of this is demonstrated by God's condemning humanity on account of sin. God clearly demonstrates this love relationship in the original created order; however, this does not imply that God's love for the creature supersedes his love for justice. Had this been the case, God would have manifested a stronger aversion to the eternal misery of the creature than to the creature's disobedience. The abundant place for divine love is clear because God condemns no person for any reason other than sin, and God saves the multitudes of humanity who are converted from sin. In the divine dispensation, this salvation would not be possible unless it was God's will to allow an abundant scope for his love toward the creature under God's judgment, to the extent this is permitted by his justice.

The proposed doctrine inverts this order and mutual relationship in two ways: (1) This happens first when it is stated that the Lord God wills to save specific individuals without any reference to the creature's obedience. It places God's love for humanity prior to his love for justice, and as such reflects that God loves humanity more than justice. It thereby manifests a stronger aversion to human misery than to their sin and disobedience. (2) The other way in which this doctrine violates the order and mutuality [of justice and love] is the assertion that God wills to damn certain particular people without manifesting in his decree any consideration of disobedience. This detracts from God's manifest love for humanity, a love the creature is rightfully due. This doctrine implies that God hates the creature, but this hatred is not caused by or rooted in either his love of justice, nor in his hatred of iniquity. But is it not the case that sin is the primary object and the only meritorious cause of God's hate?

The powerful capacity that this teaching possesses to subvert the foundation of religion may be illustrated by the following parable: Let's suppose a son would say, "My father loves justice and fairness so much that, even though I am his beloved son, he would disinherit me if I were to be disobedient. If I desire to receive my inheritance, it is incumbent on me carefully to cultivate obedience." But suppose another son says: "My father's love for me is so great that he absolutely has resolved to make me his heir. Therefore, there is no need for me to be consistently obedient, because, according to his unchangeable will, I will remain his heir. Indeed, rather than risking my not being his heir, my father will draw me by an irresistible force to obey him." This is contrary to the words of John [the Baptist]: "Do not presume to say to yourselves, 'We have Abraham as our father'; for I tell you, God is able from these stones to raise up children to Abraham" [Matt. 3:9].

The Christian religion is anchored foundationally in this twofold love.[45] The state of humanity, created in the image of and in good favor with God, has been altered due to willful disobedience, so that humanity is by its own fault in a state of sinfulness and enmity toward God. (1) The love of justice, on which the Christian religion rests, is, first, that justice which God declared once and for all in Christ. It was God's will that sin would not be forgiven in any other way than by the blood and death of his Son, and that Christ would not come before Him in any other way as advocate and intercessor except when sprinkled by his own blood. Furthermore, God's love of justice is manifested daily in the preaching of the gospel truth that it is God's will to grant a communication of Christ and his saving work to humanity, but only to those who convert from sin and believe in Christ. (2) The second point of the twofold love, on which the Christian faith is founded, is God's love for miserable sinners, that love by which he gave his Son for them and constituted Christ as Savior of those who are obedient to him. This love for sinners and the required obedience does not rest on the rigor and severity to which God is supremely entitled, but according to his grace and mercy. To this is added the promise of forgiveness for sin, provided the fallen sinner earnestly repents.

The proposed doctrine of predestination is opposed to this foundational twofold order of love in two distinct ways: First, by asserting that God has such a great love for certain sinners that it was his will absolutely to save them before he had provided a way of forgiveness through Christ Jesus and before he had also

45. Arminius's emphasis on God's twofold love rests on the Thomistic assumption that the will of God tends toward the known good—that is, primarily toward God's own essence and secondarily toward the creature and its beatitude.

satisfied his love of justice. Prior to both of these, God willed their salvation in his own foreknowledge and according to his determinate purpose. This completely overturns the twofold order of divine love by teaching that it is God's pleasure that satisfaction should be paid to his justice because he wills specifically to save such persons. This is tantamount to making his love for justice, manifest in the saving purposes of Christ, subordinate to his love for sinful humanity, whom it is his will absolutely to save. Secondly, this logic opposes the twofold love by asserting that it is the will of God specifically to damn certain sinners without any consideration of their unrepentant state. What has become of the full and complete satisfaction in Christ that demonstrates both God's love of justice and his hatred of sin? In this full and complete satisfaction, nothing other than the condition of repentance can hinder the possibility of divine mercy to the sinner. This is the case, of course, unless some person should choose to assert (as is done in this case) that it has been God's will to act towards the greater part of humanity with the same (or even worse) severity than he exercised towards the devil and his angels. Actually, the severity toward the damned would be greater since neither Christ nor his gospel has the capacity for any greater blessing to them than to the devils, because the avenue of grace is as much closed against them due to the sin of our first parents as it is against the evil angels. Yet, each of those angels sinned freely and voluntarily, whereas humanity has sinned only in their parent Adam.

In order that we may understand more clearly the nature of this twofold order of love as the foundation of all religion, especially the manner in which mutuality exists between the two orders, it is profitable for us to pay close attention to these words of the Apostle to the Hebrews: "[And without faith it is impossible to please God, for] whoever would approach him must believe that he exists and that he rewards those who seek him" [Heb 11:6]. Herein are two foundational assumptions of religion in opposition to the two pernicious, fiery darts of Satan,[46] each of which by itself is able to overturn and destroy true religion. One is carelessness [*securitas*] and the other is despair [*desperatio*]. Carelessness is operative when one allows oneself to be persuaded that regardless of how inattentive he may be to the worship of God, he will not be damned and is certain to obtain salvation. Despair reigns when a person is persuaded that no amount of reverence toward God will lead to a positive reception from God. When either of these deadly dispositions is operative, it is impossible for true and proper worship of God to follow. Both of these, however, are overturned by the apostolic teaching that when one firmly believes that God will bestow eternal life on those who seek him—but that he will inflict eternal death on those who do not—one cannot on any account indulge himself in [the false security that leads to] carelessness. Likewise, when one believes that God is indeed the rewarder of those who diligently seek him, by applying himself to the search, he will not be in danger of falling into despair. The foundation of the former kind of faith, by which one firmly believes that God will bestow eternal life on all who seek Him, is that God loves justice more than he loves humanity. This prioritizing of justice is the only adequate protection against carelessness. At the same time, the foundation for the latter kind of faith, one that dares to believe that God will undoubtedly reward those who diligently seek Him, is that great love for humanity which neither can nor will prevent God from effecting salvation for the sinner—unless God be hindered by his

46. Cf. Eph. 6:16.

greater love for justice. Yet, this latter love is so far from operating as a hindrance to God's becoming a rewarder of those who diligently seek Him, that, on the contrary, it promotes in every possible way the bestowal of that reward. Those persons, therefore, who seek God can by no means indulge in a single doubt concerning his readiness to reward. And it is this which acts as a preservative against despair or distrust. This being the case, as we have set it out, God's twofold love, and the mutuality that each part bears toward the other, serve together to form the foundation of religion, without which no true religion can possibly exist. Any doctrine, therefore, that is in open hostility to this twofold love and to the relationship that mutually exists between them, subverts the foundation of all religion.

TWENTIETH and finally, this doctrine of predestination has been rejected by the majority of Christians in ancient as well as modern times. Passing over references to the earliest church, the facts themselves declare that the Lutherans and Anabaptists, as well as the Roman Church, hold this teaching to be false. Even though in the earliest days of the Reformation, Martin Luther and Philip Melanchthon held the doctrine in high esteem, they later moved away from this version of the doctrine. The change in Melanchthon is quite evident in his later writings, and Luther's followers contend that he refined his opinion on the subject rather than entirely abandoning his earlier position. Melanchthon himself asserted that the doctrine differs little from the concept of Fate to be found among the Stoics. His opinion may be found in many of his writings, but especially in a letter addressed to Gaspar Peucer, where he writes: "Laelius writes to me that the controversy in Geneva regarding Fate as taught by the Stoics has led to one individual being imprisoned because he happened to differ from Zeno. O unhappy times! when the doctrine of salvation is obscured by such strange disputes."

The Danish churches embrace a doctrine quite opposite to this, as may be discerned from the writings of Nicholas Hemmingius[47] in his treatise on universal grace (*de Liber Gratia universali*), in which he declares that the issue between himself and his opponents consisted in the determination of two fundamental points: "Do the elect believe?" or, "Are believers the true elect?"[48] Hemmingius is of the opinion that those who hold the former opinion are in agreement with the Manicheans and Stoics, while those who hold the latter position are in harmony with Moses and the prophets, with Christ and his Apostles.

In addition, this doctrine is viewed so negatively by many in our land that they have declared their unwillingness to continue attending our churches. A few others have joined our churches, but under protest that they cannot possibly affirm this doctrine. On account of this doctrine, our churches have been deserted by quite a few persons who agree with us on this issue. Others have threatened to leave unless they are assured that the Church holds no opinion such as is described here.

There is not a single doctrine that the Papists, Anabaptists, and Lutherans oppose with greater intensity. Each in turn places our churches in a bad light and attributes a foul odor to our doctrinal teaching, bringing into disrepute all the doctrines we profess. They likewise affirm that of all the blasphemies against God that the mind can conceive or the

47. Niels Hemmingsen (1513–1600) was a Danish Lutheran theologian and former student of Melanchthon. Arminius read and was influenced by Hemmingsen's writings.

48. In the margin, Arminius put the distinction thus: "Do we believe because we are elect, or are we elect because we believe?" He (and Hemmingsen) advocated the latter position.

tongue may express, there is no doctrine that can reasonably be deducted from our Doctors as ugly as this.

And finally, of all the difficulties and consequences that have arisen among our churches since the Reformation, there is none that has not had its origin in this doctrine to a greater or lesser degree. We recall the controversies that arose in Leiden with respect to Caspar Coolhasius (Koolhaes), at Gouda in that of Herman Herberts, at Horn with respect to Cornelius Wiggerts, and at Medemblik in the affair of Tako Sybrants—controversies in which this was a major issue. These are not the least among the motives that have led me to give my most diligent attention to this point of doctrine, especially to prevent our churches from suffering any more damage, causing Papacy to increase. The Papacy has been the benefactor. All pious teachers earnestly desire the destruction of the kingdom of the Antichrist, and we work earnestly with every available resource to that end.

Briefly stated, these are my views on this doctrine of predestination. In good faith, I have attempted to extract the teaching of the authors without adding a single word not clearly indicated in their writings. . . .

My Opinion about Predestination

Up to this point I have set out the position of others on the articles of predestination as they are being taught in our churches and the University of Leiden—positions of which I disapprove. I have also set out several reasons why I disapprove these teachings. I now proceed to declare my personal opinions, teachings that I believe are most in harmony with the Word of God.

I. The first specific and absolute divine decree regarding the salvation of sinful humanity: God decreed to appoint his Son, Jesus Christ, as Mediator, Redeemer, Savior, Priest, and King in order that he might destroy sin by his own death, so that by his own obedience he might obtain the salvation lost through disobedience, and by his power communicate this salvation.

II. In the second precise and absolute decree, God decided graciously to accept those who repent and believe in Christ, and for Christ's sake and through him to effect the final salvation of penitents and believers who persevere to the end in their faith. Simultaneously, God decreed to leave in sin under divine wrath all impenitent persons and unbelievers, damning them as alienated from Christ.

III. The third divine decree: God decided to administer in a sufficient and efficacious manner the means necessary for repentance and faith—this being accomplished according to divine wisdom, by which God knows what is proper and becoming both to his mercy and his severity. And this all proceeds according to divine justice, by which God is prepared to adopt whatever his wisdom may prescribe and carry out.

IV. From these decrees the fourth proceeds, by which God decreed to save and to damn certain particular persons. This decree has its foundation in divine foreknowledge, through which God has known from all eternity those individuals who through the established means of his prevenient grace would come to faith and believe, and through his subsequent sustaining grace would persevere in the faith.[49] Likewise, in divine foreknowledge, God knew those who would not believe and persevere.

This doctrine of predestination declares:[50]

49. The wording of this conditional decree is consistent with divine "middle knowledge" (*scientia media*), a concept that Arminius affirms in earlier writings.

50. The following twenty reasons in favor of Arminius's doctrine of conditional predestination directly correspond to his twenty reasons for opposing Reformed "supralapsarianism," of which numbers 1, 19, and 20 were included above.

1. The foundation of all Christianity, both with regard to salvation and to the certainty of that salvation.

2. The essence of the Evangel. Indeed, it declares the Gospel itself, which must be believed for salvation (as far as the first two articles above are concerned).

3. Because this predestination is a clear and explicit Scriptural teaching, it has never been examined by a general or particular Council of the Church, nor has it ever been contradicted by any orthodox divine.

4. This predestination has been consistently acknowledged and taught by all well-informed teachers.

5. It is consistent with the harmony of all the confessions of faith made by the Protestant churches.

6. The Dutch Confession and [Heidelberg] Catechism are of one accord on this doctrine. This agreement is such that if in the sixteenth article of the Confession the two expressions "those persons who" and "others" be interpreted as "believers" and "unbelievers," my position on predestination will be comprehended in that article with the utmost clarity. For this reason, when I held a public disputation at the university, I required that the article of faith under consideration be composed in the exact words of the Confession. When compared, it is evident that there is complete harmony with the [Heidelberg] Catechism, specifically questions 20 and 54.

7. Interpreted in this manner, this predestination is in full harmony with the nature of God—his wisdom, goodness, and justice, because it enshrines their primary content in the clearest possible witness to God's wisdom, goodness, and justice.

8. This predestination is in harmony with the nature of humanity at every level—in the primitive state of creation, in its fallen state, as well as in its restoration.

9. It is in complete accord with the act of creation. It affirms that creation is a genuine communication of goodness, both with regard to the intention of God as well as with regard to the actual creative act. Predestination has its origin in the goodness of God, so that whatever has reference to its being fully preserved and carried out proceeds from divine love. The act of creation is itself a perfect and appropriate divine act in which God is well pleased and through which humanity has received the requisite means to avoid falling into sin.

10. This predestination is in accord with the nature of eternal life and all the Scriptural nomenclature by which it is designated.

11. It also agrees with the nature of eternal death and all the names by which that death is described in Scripture.

12. This predestination underscores that sin is actual disobedience and therefore the meritorious cause of condemnation. For this reason predestination must be understood in the context of the fall and sin.

13. It is in every way harmonious with the nature of grace, by ascribing to grace every rightful thing and by reconciling it entirely with the righteousness of God, as well as to the nature and liberty of the human will.

14. This predestination transparently declares the glory of God, his justice, and his mercy: God is the cause of all good as well as our salvation, and humanity is the cause of sin and therefore responsible for his own damnation.

15. It contributes to the honor of Jesus Christ by rendering him the foundation of predestination, as well as the meritorious and mediating cause of salvation.

16. This predestination promotes the salvation of humanity; indeed, it is the power and the veritable means to salvation. It awakens and

creates within human consciousness a sorrow for sin, a deep concern for conversion and faith in Jesus Christ, as well as a diligence for good works and zeal in prayer—thereby causing human beings to work out their salvation with fear and trembling [Phil. 2:12-13]. Likewise, it wards off despair, as far as such prevention is necessary.

17. It confirms and establishes the order in which the gospel ought to be preached: First, by requiring repentance and faith, and then by promising the remission of sins, the grace of the Holy Spirit, and life eternal.

18. It strengthens the ministry of the gospel by making it profitable for preaching, the administration of the sacraments, and public prayers.

19. Indeed, it is the foundation of the Christian religion because in it the twofold love of God is united. God's love of justice and his love of humanity are herein reconciled to each other with the greatest consistency.

20. And finally, this doctrine of Predestination has always received the approval of the great majority of professing Christians, and even now, in these days, it enjoys the same extensive affirmation. It gives no one just cause for expressing objection, nor does it give any pretext for contention in the Christian church. . . .

[*Arminius and His* Declaration of Sentiments*: An Annotated Translation with Introduction and Theological Commentary*, trans. W. Stephen Gunter (Waco, TX: Baylor University Press, 2012), 107–8, 124–30, 135–38]

Selection 59: *Articles of Remonstrance* (1610)

On January 14, 1610, less than three months after Arminius's death, forty-three Dutch ministers sympathetic to Arminius's views signed this statement of Remonstrance. By means of this document, they hoped to carve out room for their opinions within the Dutch Reformed Church. Probably drafted by Arminius's friend Johannes Uytenbogaert, the document consists of five articles that are heavily dependent on Arminius's theology, sometimes following the* Declaration of Sentiments *verbatim (see Selection 58). The five points of Arminian (or Remonstrant) doctrine would be addressed later by the Reformed Synod of Dordt (see Selection 60).

Article 1

That God, by an eternal, unchangeable purpose in Jesus Christ his Son, before the foundation of the world, hath determined, out of the fallen, sinful race of men, to save in Christ, for Christ's sake, and through Christ, those who, through the grace of the Holy Ghost, shall believe on this his Son Jesus, and shall persevere in this faith and obedience of faith, through this grace, even to the end; and, on the other hand, to leave the incorrigible and unbelieving in sin and under wrath, and to condemn them as alienate from Christ, according to the word of the gospel in John 3:36: "He that believeth on the Son hath everlasting life: and he that believeth not the Son shall not see life; but the wrath of God abideth on him," and according to other passages of Scripture also.

Article 2

That, agreeably thereto, Jesus Christ, the Saviour of the world, died for all men and for every man, so that he has obtained for them all, by his death on the cross, redemption and the forgiveness of sins; yet that no one actually enjoys this forgiveness of sins except the believer, according to the word of the Gospel of John 3:16: "God so loved the world that he gave his only-begotten Son, that whosoever believeth in him should not perish, but have everlasting life." And in the First Epistle of John 2:2: "And he is the propitiation for our sins; and not for ours only, but also for the sins of the whole world."

Article 3

That man has not saving grace of himself, nor of the energy of his free will, inasmuch as he, in the state of apostasy and sin, can of and by himself neither think, will, nor do any thing that is truly good (such as saving Faith eminently is); but that it is needful that he be born again of God in Christ, through his Holy Spirit, and renewed in understanding, inclination, or will, and all his powers, in order that he may rightly understand, think, will, and effect what is truly good, according to the Word of Christ, John 15:5: "Without me ye can do nothing."

Article 4

That this grace of God is the beginning, continuance, and accomplishment of all good, even to this extent, that the regenerate man himself, without prevenient or assisting, awakening, following and cooperative grace, can neither think, will, nor do good, nor withstand any temptations to evil; so that all good deeds or movements, that can be conceived, must be ascribed to the grace of God in Christ. But as respects the mode of the operation of this grace, it is not irresistible, inasmuch as it is written concerning many, that they have resisted the Holy Ghost. Acts 7[:51], and elsewhere in many places.

Article 5

That those who are incorporated into Christ by a true faith, and have thereby become partakers of his life-giving Spirit, have thereby full power to strive against Satan, sin, the world, and their own flesh, and to win the victory; it being well understood that it is ever through the assisting grace of the Holy Ghost; and that Jesus Christ assists them through his Spirit in all temptations, extends to them his hand, and if only they are ready for the conflict, and desire his help, and are not inactive, keeps them from falling, so that they, by no craft or power of Satan, can be misled nor plucked out of Christ's hands, according to the Word of Christ, John 10:28: "Neither shall any man pluck them out of my hand." But whether they are capable, through negligence, of forsaking again the first beginnings of their life in Christ, of again returning to this present evil world, of turning away from the holy doctrine which was delivered them, of losing a good conscience, of becoming devoid of grace, that must be more particularly determined out of the Holy Scripture, before we ourselves can teach it with the full persuasion of our minds.[51]

These Articles, thus set forth and taught, the Remonstrants deem agreeable to the Word of God, tending to edification, and, as regards this argument, sufficient for salvation, so that it is not necessary or edifying to rise higher or to descend deeper.

[*The Creeds of Christendom*, vol. 3, ed. Philip Schaff (repr., Grand Rapids, MI: Baker, 1998), 545–49]

Selection 60: *Canons of the Synod of Dordt* (1619)

The Synod of Dordt (1618–1619) met in Dordrecht, The Netherlands, primarily for the purpose of resolving the Remonstrant (Arminian) controversy. The Reformed synod rejected the opinions of the Remonstrants and, as a result, they were deprived of their ministerial posts and exiled from their land.

51. Although there was initial hesitation on the question of whether a true believer can fall away from grace, like Arminius, most Remonstrants and Arminians later came to affirm the possibility of apostasy.

The First Main Point of Doctrine
Divine Election and Reprobation

The Judgment Concerning Divine Predestination Which the Synod Declares to Be in Agreement with the Word of God and Accepted Till Now in the Reformed Churches, Set Forth in Several Articles

Article 1: God's Right to Condemn All People

Since all people have sinned in Adam and have come under the sentence of the curse and eternal death, God would have done no one an injustice if it had been his will to leave the entire human race in sin and under the curse, and to condemn them on account of their sin. As the apostle says: "The whole world is liable to the condemnation of God" (Rom. 3:19), "All have sinned and are deprived of the glory of God" (Rom. 3:23), and "The wages of sin is death" (Rom. 6:23). . . .

Article 4: A Twofold Response to the Gospel

God's wrath remains on those who do not believe this gospel. But those who do accept it and embrace Jesus the Savior with a true and living faith are delivered through him from God's wrath and from destruction, and receive the gift of eternal life. . . .

Article 6: God's Eternal Decree

The fact that some receive from God the gift of faith within time, and that others do not, stems from his eternal decree. For "all his works are known to God from eternity" (Acts 15:18; Eph. 1:11). In accordance with this decree God graciously softens the hearts, however hard, of the elect and inclines them to believe, but by a just judgment God leaves in their wickedness and hardness of heart those who have not been chosen. And in this especially is disclosed to us God's act—unfathomable, and as merciful as it is just—of distinguishing between people equally lost. This is the well-known decree of election and reprobation revealed in God's Word.[52] The wicked, impure, and unstable distort this decree to their own ruin, but it provides holy and godly souls with comfort beyond words.

Article 7: Election

Election is God's unchangeable purpose by which he did the following:

Before the foundation of the world, by sheer grace, according to the free good pleasure of his will, God chose in Christ to salvation a definite number of particular people out of the entire human race, which had fallen by its own fault from its original innocence into sin and ruin. Those chosen were neither better nor more deserving than the others, but lay with them in the common misery. God did this in Christ, whom he also appointed from eternity to be the mediator, the head of all those chosen, and the foundation of their salvation. . . .[53]

Article 9: Election Not Based on Foreseen Faith

This same election took place, not on the basis of foreseen faith, of the obedience of faith, of holiness, or of any other good quality and disposition, as though it were based on a prerequisite cause or condition in the person to be chosen, but rather for the purpose of faith, of the obedience of faith, of holiness, and so on. Accordingly, election is the source of every saving good. Faith, holiness, and the other saving gifts, and at last eternal life itself, flow forth from election as its fruits and effects. As the apostle says, "He chose us" (not because we

---

52. The eternal decree of election and reprobation is distinct from its execution in time, which results in salvation and condemnation, respectively.

53. Dordt emphasized that Christ is the "foundation of salvation" (*salutis fundamentum*), against the Remonstrants (Arminians), who stated that Christ is the "foundation of election" (*electionis fundamentum*).

were, but) "so that we should be holy and blameless before him in love" (Eph. 1:4).

Article 10: Election Based on God's Good Pleasure

But the cause of this undeserved election is exclusively the good pleasure of God. This does not involve God's choosing certain human qualities or actions from among all those possible as a condition of salvation, but rather involves adopting certain particular persons from among the common mass of sinners as God's own possession. As Scripture says, "When the children were not yet born, and had done nothing either good or bad . . . , she (Rebecca) was told, 'The older will serve the younger.' As it is written, 'Jacob I loved, but Esau I hated' " (Rom. 9:11-13). Also, "All who were appointed for eternal life believed" (Acts 13:48).

Article 11: Election Unchangeable

Just as God is most wise, unchangeable, all-knowing, and almighty, so the election made by him can neither be suspended nor altered, revoked, or annulled; neither can God's chosen ones be cast off, nor their number reduced.

Article 12: The Assurance of Election

Assurance of their eternal and unchangeable election to salvation is given to the chosen in due time, though by various stages and in differing measure. Such assurance comes not by inquisitive searching into the hidden and deep things of God, but by noticing within themselves, with spiritual joy and holy delight, the unmistakable fruits of election pointed out in God's Word—such as a true faith in Christ, a childlike fear of God, a godly sorrow for their sins, a hunger and thirst for righteousness, and so on.

Article 13: The Fruit of This Assurance

In their awareness and assurance of this election, God's children daily find greater cause to humble themselves before God, to adore the fathomless depth of God's mercies, to cleanse themselves, and to give fervent love in return to the One who first so greatly loved them. This is far from saying that this teaching concerning election, and reflection upon it, make God's children lax in observing his commandments or carnally self-assured. By God's just judgment this does usually happen to those who casually take for granted the grace of election or engage in idle and brazen talk about it but are unwilling to walk in the ways of the chosen.

Article 14: Teaching Election Properly

By God's wise plan, this teaching concerning divine election was proclaimed through the prophets, Christ himself, and the apostles, in Old and New Testament times. It was subsequently committed to writing in the Holy Scriptures. So also today in God's church, for which it was specifically intended, this teaching must be set forth with a spirit of discretion, in a godly and holy manner, at the appropriate time and place, without inquisitive searching into the ways of the Most High. This must be done for the glory of God's most holy name, and for the lively comfort of God's people.

Article 15: Reprobation

Moreover, Holy Scripture most especially highlights this eternal and undeserved grace of our election and brings it out more clearly for us, in that it further bears witness that not all people have been chosen but that some have not been chosen or have been passed by in God's eternal election—those, that is, concerning whom God, on the basis of his entirely free, most just, irreproachable, and unchangeable good pleasure, made the following decree:

to leave them in the common misery into which, by their own fault, they have plunged themselves; not to grant them saving faith and the grace of conversion; but finally to condemn and eternally punish those who have been left in their own ways and under God's just judgment, not only for their unbelief but also for all their other sins, in order to display his justice.

And this is the decree of reprobation, which does not at all make God the author of sin (a blasphemous thought!) but rather its fearful, irreproachable, just judge and avenger.

Article 16: Responses to the Teaching of Reprobation

Those who do not yet actively experience within themselves a living faith in Christ or an assured confidence of heart, peace of conscience, a zeal for childlike obedience, and a glorying in God through Christ, but who nevertheless use the means by which God has promised to work these things in us—such people ought not to be alarmed at the mention of reprobation, nor to count themselves among the reprobate; rather they ought to continue diligently in the use of the means, to desire fervently a time of more abundant grace, and to wait for it in reverence and humility. On the other hand, those who seriously desire to turn to God, to be pleasing to God alone, and to be delivered from the body of death, but are not yet able to make such progress along the way of godliness and faith as they would like—such people ought much less to stand in fear of the teaching concerning reprobation, since our merciful God has promised not to snuff out a smoldering wick or break a bruised reed.[54] However, those who have forgotten God and their Savior Jesus Christ and have abandoned themselves wholly to the cares of the world and the pleasures of the flesh—such people have every reason to stand in fear of this teaching, as long as they do not seriously turn to God.

54. Cf. Isa. 42:3.

Article 17: The Salvation of the Infants of Believers

Since we must make judgments about God's will from his Word, which testifies that the children of believers are holy, not by nature but by virtue of the gracious covenant in which they together with their parents are included, godly parents ought not to doubt the election and salvation of their children whom God calls out of this life in infancy.

Article 18: The Proper Attitude Toward Election and Reprobation

To those who complain about this grace of an undeserved election and about the severity of a just reprobation, we reply with the words of the apostle, "Who are you, O man, to talk back to God?" (Rom. 9:20), and with the words of our Savior, "Have I no right to do what I want with my own?" (Matt. 20:15). We, however, with reverent adoration of these secret things, cry out with the apostle: "Oh, the depths of the riches both of the wisdom and the knowledge of God! How unsearchable are his judgments, and his ways beyond tracing out! For who has known the mind of the Lord? Or who has been his counselor? Or who has first given to God, that God should repay him? For from him and through him and to him are all things. To him be the glory forever! Amen" (Rom. 11:33-36).

The Second Main Point of Doctrine Christ's Death and Human Redemption Through It

Article 3: The Infinite Value of Christ's Death

This death of God's Son is the only and entirely complete sacrifice and satisfaction for sins; it is of infinite value and worth, more than sufficient to atone for the sins of the whole world. . . .[55]

55. All parties in the debate agreed that Christ's satisfaction was "sufficient" for the whole world and "efficient" or effective for the elect.

Article 6: Unbelief, a Human Responsibility

However, that many who have been called through the gospel do not repent or believe in Christ but perish in unbelief is not because the sacrifice of Christ offered on the cross is deficient or insufficient, but because they themselves are at fault. . . .

Article 8: The Saving Effectiveness of Christ's Death

For it was the entirely free plan and very gracious will and intention of God the Father that the enlivening and saving effectiveness of his Son's costly death should work itself out in all the elect, in order that God might grant justifying faith to them only and thereby lead them without fail to salvation. In other words, it was God's will that Christ through the blood of the cross (by which he confirmed the new covenant) should effectively redeem from every people, tribe, nation, and language all those and only those who were chosen from eternity to salvation and given to him by the Father; that Christ should grant them faith (which, like the Holy Spirit's other saving gifts, he acquired for them by his death). It was also God's will that Christ should cleanse them by his blood from all their sins, both original and actual, whether committed before or after their coming to faith; that he should faithfully preserve them to the very end; and that he should finally present them to himself, a glorious people, without spot or wrinkle. . . .

The Third and Fourth Main Points of Doctrine Human Corruption, Conversion to God, and the Way It Occurs

Article 1: The Effect of the Fall on Human Nature

Human beings were originally created in the image of God and were furnished in mind with a true and sound knowledge of the Creator and things spiritual, in will and heart with righteousness, and in all emotions with purity; indeed, the whole human being was holy. However, rebelling against God at the devil's instigation and by their own free will, they deprived themselves of these outstanding gifts. Rather, in their place they brought upon themselves blindness, terrible darkness, futility, and distortion of judgment in their minds; perversity, defiance, and hardness in their hearts and wills; and finally impurity in all their emotions.[56]

Article 2: The Spread of Corruption

Human beings brought forth children of the same nature as themselves after the fall. That is to say, being corrupt they brought forth corrupt children. The corruption spread, by God's just judgment, from Adam and Eve to all their descendants—except for Christ alone—not by way of imitation (as in former times the Pelagians would have it[57]) but by way of the propagation of their perverted nature.

Article 3: Total Inability

Therefore, all people are conceived in sin and are born children of wrath, unfit for any saving good, inclined to evil, dead in their sins, and slaves to sin. Without the grace of the regenerating Holy Spirit they are neither willing nor able to return to God, to reform their distorted nature, or even to dispose themselves to such reform.

Article 4: The Inadequacy of the Light of Nature

There is, to be sure, a certain light of nature remaining in all people after the fall, by virtue

56. The point is that the fall affected every part of the rational human soul—the intellect, will, and affections.

57. Against Augustine, Pelagius emphasized free choice and denied original sin, teaching that humans sin because of nurture, not by nature.

of which they retain some notions about God, natural things, and the difference between what is moral and immoral, and demonstrate a certain eagerness for virtue and for good outward behavior. But this light of nature is far from enabling humans to come to a saving knowledge of God and conversion to him—so far, in fact, that they do not use it rightly even in matters of nature and society. Instead, in various ways they completely distort this light, whatever its precise character, and suppress it in unrighteousness. In doing so all people render themselves without excuse before God.

Article 5: The Inadequacy of the Law

In this respect, what is true of the light of nature is true also of the Ten Commandments given by God through Moses specifically to the Jews. For humans cannot obtain saving grace through the Decalogue, because, although it does expose the magnitude of their sin and increasingly convict them of their guilt, yet it does not offer a remedy or enable them to escape from human misery, and, indeed, weakened as it is by the flesh, leaves the offender under the curse.

Article 6: The Saving Power of the Gospel

What, therefore, neither the light of nature nor the law can do, God accomplishes by the power of the Holy Spirit, through the Word or the ministry of reconciliation. This is the gospel about the Messiah, through which it has pleased God to save believers, in both the Old and the New Testaments.

Article 7: God's Freedom in Revealing the Gospel

In the Old Testament, God revealed this secret of his will to a small number; in the New Testament (now without any distinction between peoples) God discloses it to a large number. The reason for this difference must not be ascribed to the greater worth of one nation over another, or to a better use of the light of nature, but to the free good pleasure and undeserved love of God. Therefore, those who receive so much grace, beyond and in spite of all they deserve, ought to acknowledge it with humble and thankful hearts. On the other hand, with the apostle they ought to adore (but certainly not inquisitively search into) the severity and justice of God's judgments on the others, who do not receive this grace.

Article 8: The Earnest Call of the Gospel

Nevertheless, all who are called through the gospel are called earnestly. For urgently and most genuinely God makes known in the Word what is pleasing to him: that those who are called should come to God. God also earnestly promises rest for their souls and eternal life to all who do come and believe.

Article 9: Human Responsibility for Rejecting the Gospel

The fact that many who are called through the ministry of the gospel do not come and are not brought to conversion must not be blamed on the gospel, nor on Christ, who is offered through the gospel, nor on God, who calls them through the gospel and even bestows various gifts on them, but on the people themselves who are called. Some in self-assurance do not even entertain the Word of life; others do entertain it but do not take it to heart, and for that reason, after the fleeting joy of a temporary faith, they relapse; others choke the seed of the Word with the thorns of life's cares and with the pleasures of the world and bring forth no fruits. This our Savior teaches in the parable of the sower (Matt. 13).

Article 10: Conversion as the Work of God

The fact that others who are called through the ministry of the gospel do come and are brought to conversion must not be credited to human effort, as though one distinguishes oneself by free choice from others who are furnished with equal or sufficient grace for faith and conversion (as the proud heresy of Pelagius maintains). No, it must be credited to God: just as from eternity God chose his own in Christ, so within time God effectively calls them, grants them faith and repentance, and, having rescued them from the dominion of darkness, brings them into the kingdom of his Son, in order that they may declare the wonderful deeds of the One who called them out of darkness into this marvelous light, and may boast not in themselves, but in the Lord, as apostolic words frequently testify in Scripture.

Article 11: The Holy Spirit's Work in Conversion

Moreover, when God carries out this good pleasure in the elect, or works true conversion in them, God not only sees to it that the gospel is proclaimed to them outwardly, and enlightens their minds powerfully by the Holy Spirit so that they may rightly understand and discern the things of the Spirit of God, but, by the effective operation of the same regenerating Spirit, God also penetrates into the inmost being, opens the closed heart, softens the hard heart, and circumcises the heart that is uncircumcised. God infuses new qualities into the will, making the dead will alive, the evil one good, the unwilling one willing, and the stubborn one compliant. God activates and strengthens the will so that, like a good tree, it may be enabled to produce the fruits of good deeds.

Article 12: Regeneration a Supernatural Work

And this is the regeneration, the new creation, the raising from the dead, and the making alive so clearly proclaimed in the Scriptures, which God works in us without our help. But this certainly does not happen only by outward teaching, by moral persuasion, or by such a way of working that, after God's work is done, it remains in human power whether or not to be reborn or converted. Rather, it is an entirely supernatural work, one that is at the same time most powerful and most pleasing, a marvelous, hidden, and inexpressible work, which is not less than or inferior in power to that of creation or of raising the dead, as Scripture (inspired by the author of this work) teaches. As a result, all those in whose hearts God works in this marvelous way are certainly, unfailingly, and effectively reborn and do actually believe. And then the will, now renewed, is not only activated and motivated by God, but in being activated by God is also itself active. For this reason, people themselves, by that grace which they have received, are also rightly said to believe and to repent.

Article 13: The Incomprehensible Way of Regeneration

In this life believers cannot fully understand the way this work occurs; meanwhile, they rest content with knowing and experiencing that, by this grace of God, they do believe with the heart and love their Savior.

Article 14: The Way God Gives Faith

In this way, therefore, faith is a gift of God, not in the sense that it is offered by God for people to choose, but that it is in actual fact bestowed on them, breathed and infused into them. Nor is it a gift in the sense that God bestows only the potential to believe, but then awaits assent—the act of believing—by human choice; rather, it is a gift in the sense that God who works both willing and acting and, indeed, works all things in all people and produces in them both the will to believe and the belief itself.[58]

58. This article directly opposes Arminius, who used the analogy of a beggar in order to illustrate that faith

Article 15: Responses to God's Grace

God does not owe this grace to anyone. For what could God owe to those who have nothing to give that can be paid back? Indeed, what could God owe to those who have nothing of their own to give but sin and falsehood? Therefore those who receive this grace owe and give eternal thanks to God alone; those who do not receive it either do not care at all about these spiritual things and are satisfied with themselves in their condition, or else in self-assurance foolishly boast about having something which they lack. Furthermore, following the example of the apostles, we are to think and to speak in the most favorable way about those who outwardly profess their faith and better their lives, for the inner chambers of the heart are unknown to us. But for others who have not yet been called, we are to pray to the God who calls things that do not exist as though they did. In no way, however, are we to pride ourselves as better than they, as though we had distinguished ourselves from them.

Article 16: Regeneration's Effect

However, just as by the fall humans did not cease to be human, endowed with intellect and will, and just as sin, which has spread through the whole human race, did not abolish the nature of the human race but distorted and spiritually killed it, so also this divine grace of regeneration does not act in people as if they were blocks and stones; nor does it abolish the will and its properties or coerce a reluctant will by force, but spiritually revives, heals, reforms, and—in a manner at once pleasing and powerful—bends it back.[59]

As a result, a ready and sincere obedience of the Spirit now begins to prevail where before the rebellion and resistance of the flesh were completely dominant. In this the true and spiritual restoration and freedom of our will consists. Thus, if the marvelous Maker of every good thing were not dealing with us, we would have no hope of getting up from our fall by our own free choice, by which we plunged ourselves into ruin when still standing upright.

Article 17: God's Use of Means in Regeneration

Just as the almighty work by which God brings forth and sustains our natural life does not rule out but requires the use of means, by which God, according to his infinite wisdom and goodness, has wished to exercise that divine power, so also the aforementioned supernatural work by which God regenerates us in no way rules out or cancels the use of the gospel, which God in great wisdom has appointed to be the seed of regeneration and the food of the soul. For this reason, the apostles and the teachers who followed them taught the people in a godly manner about this grace of God, to give God the glory and to humble all pride, and yet did not neglect meanwhile to keep the people, by means of the holy admonitions of the gospel, under the administration of the Word, the sacraments, and discipline. So even today it is out of the question that the teachers or those taught in the church should presume to test God by separating what God in his good pleasure has wished to be closely joined together. For grace is bestowed through admonitions, and the more readily we perform our duty, the more lustrous the benefit of God working in us usually is, and the better that work advances. To God alone, both for the means and for their saving fruit and effectiveness, all glory is owed forever. Amen.

---

is a divine gift.

59. This article reflects how Reformed theologians generally distanced themselves from the language of "force" or "coercion" in describing God's saving grace.

The Fifth Main Point of Doctrine
The Perseverance of the Saints

Article 1: The Regenerate Not Entirely Free from Sin

Those people whom God according to his purpose calls into fellowship with his Son Jesus Christ our Lord and regenerates by the Holy Spirit, God also sets free from the dominion and slavery of sin, though not entirely from the flesh and from the body of sin as long as they are in this life.

Article 2: The Believer's Reaction to Sins of Weakness

Hence daily sins of weakness arise, and blemishes cling to even the best works of saints, giving them continual cause to humble themselves before God, to flee for refuge to Christ crucified, to put the flesh to death more and more by the Spirit of supplication and by holy exercises of godliness, and to strain toward the goal of perfection, until they are freed from this body of death and reign with the Lamb of God in heaven.

Article 3: God's Preservation of the Converted

Because of these remnants of sin dwelling in them and also because of the temptations of the world and Satan, those who have been converted could not remain standing in this grace if left to their own resources. But God is faithful, mercifully strengthening them in the grace once conferred on them and powerfully preserving them in it to the end.

Article 4: The Danger of True Believers' Falling into Serious Sins

The power of God strengthening and preserving true believers in grace is more than a match for the flesh. Yet those converted are not always so activated and motivated by God that in certain specific actions they cannot by their own fault depart from the leading of grace, be led astray by the desires of the flesh, and give in to them. For this reason they must constantly watch and pray that they may not be led into temptations. When they fail to do this, not only can they be carried away by the flesh, the world, and Satan into sins, even serious and outrageous ones, but also by God's just permission they sometimes are so carried away—witness the sad cases, described in Scripture, of David, Peter, and other saints falling into sins.

Article 5: The Effects of Such Serious Sins

By such monstrous sins, however, they greatly offend God, deserve the sentence of death, grieve the Holy Spirit, suspend the exercise of faith, severely wound the conscience, and sometimes lose the awareness of grace for a time—until, after they have returned to the right way by genuine repentance, God's fatherly face again shines upon them.

Article 6: God's Saving Intervention

For God, who is rich in mercy, according to the unchangeable purpose of election does not take the Holy Spirit from his own completely, even when they fall grievously. Neither does God let them fall down so far that they forfeit the grace of adoption and the state of justification, or commit the sin which leads to death (the sin against the Holy Spirit),[60] and plunge themselves, entirely forsaken by God, into eternal ruin.

Article 7: Renewal to Repentance

For, in the first place, God preserves in those saints when they fall the imperishable seed from which they have been born again, lest it perish or be dislodged. Secondly, by his Word and Spirit God certainly and effectively renews

60. Cf. 1 John 5:16; Mark 3:28-29, par.

them to repentance so that they have a heartfelt and godly sorrow for the sins they have committed; seek and obtain, through faith and with a contrite heart, forgiveness in the blood of the Mediator; experience again the grace of a reconciled God; through faith adore God's mercies; and from then on more eagerly work out their own salvation with fear and trembling.

Article 8: The Certainty of This Preservation

So it is not by their own merits or strength but by God's undeserved mercy that they neither forfeit faith and grace totally nor remain in their downfalls to the end and are lost. With respect to themselves this not only easily could happen, but also undoubtedly would happen; but with respect to God it cannot possibly happen. God's plan cannot be changed; God's promise cannot fail; the calling according to God's purpose cannot be revoked; the merit of Christ as well as his interceding and preserving cannot be nullified; and the sealing of the Holy Spirit can neither be invalidated nor wiped out.

Article 9: The Assurance of This Preservation

Concerning this preservation of those chosen to salvation and concerning the perseverance of true believers in faith, believers themselves can and do become assured in accordance with the measure of their faith. By this faith they firmly believe that they are and always will remain true and living members of the church, and that they have the forgiveness of sins and eternal life.

Article 10: The Ground of This Assurance

Accordingly, this assurance does not derive from some private revelation beyond or outside the Word, but from faith in the promises of God which are very plentifully revealed in the Word for our comfort, from the testimony of "the Holy Spirit testifying with our spirit that we are God's children and heirs" (Rom. 8:16-17), and finally from a serious and holy pursuit of a clear conscience and of good works. If God's chosen ones in this world did not have this well-founded comfort that the victory will be theirs and this reliable guarantee of eternal glory, they would be of all people most miserable.

Article 11: Doubts Concerning This Assurance

Meanwhile, Scripture testifies that believers have to contend in this life with various doubts of the flesh, and that under severe temptation they do not always experience this full assurance of faith and certainty of perseverance. But God, the Father of all comfort, "does not let them be tempted beyond what they can bear, but with the temptation he also provides a way out" (1 Cor. 10:13), and by the Holy Spirit revives in them the assurance of their perseverance.

Article 12: This Assurance as an Incentive to Godliness

This assurance of perseverance, however, so far from making true believers proud and carnally self-assured,[61] is rather the true root of humility, of childlike respect, of genuine godliness, of endurance in every conflict, of fervent prayers, of steadfastness in crossbearing and in confessing the truth, and of well-founded joy in God. Reflecting on this benefit provides an incentive to a serious and continual practice of thanksgiving and good works, as is evident from the testimonies of Scripture and the examples of the saints.

---

61. Arminius and all opponents of the doctrine of unconditional perseverance claimed that this teaching renders believers "self-assured" (*securus*), that is, secure or careless. Dordt denied this implication.

Article 13: Assurance No Inducement to Carelessness

Neither does the renewed confidence of perseverance produce immorality or lack of concern for godliness in those put back on their feet after a fall, but it produces a much greater concern to observe carefully the ways which the Lord prepared in advance. They observe these ways in order that by walking in them they may maintain the assurance of their perseverance, lest, by their abuse of God's fatherly goodness, the face of the gracious God (for the godly, looking upon that face is sweeter than life, but its withdrawal is more bitter than death) turn away from them again, with the result that they fall into greater anguish of spirit.

Article 14: God's Use of Means in Perseverance

And, just as it has pleased God to begin this work of grace in us by the proclamation of the gospel, so God preserves, continues, and completes this work by the hearing and reading of the gospel, by meditation on it, by its exhortations, threats, and promises, and also by the use of the sacraments.

Article 15: Contrasting Reactions to the Teaching of Perseverance

This teaching about the perseverance of true believers and saints, and about their assurance of it—a teaching which God has very richly revealed in the Word for the glory of his name and for the comfort of the godly, and which God impresses on the hearts of believers—is something which the flesh does not understand, Satan hates, the world ridicules, the ignorant and the hypocrites abuse, and the spirits of error attack. The bride of Christ, on the other hand, has always loved this teaching very tenderly and defended it steadfastly as a priceless treasure; and God, against whom no plan can avail and no strength can prevail, will ensure that the church will continue to do this. To this God alone, Father, Son, and Holy Spirit, be honor and glory forever. Amen.

Conclusion

. . . Hence it clearly appears that those of whom one could hardly expect it have shown no truth, equity, and charity at all in wishing to make the public believe:

that the teaching of the Reformed churches on predestination and on the points associated with it by its very nature and tendency draws the minds of people away from all godliness and religion, is an opiate of the flesh and the devil, and is a stronghold where Satan lies in wait for all people, wounds most of them, and fatally pierces many of them with the arrows of both despair and self-assurance;

that this teaching makes God the author of sin, unjust, a tyrant, and a hypocrite; and is nothing but a refurbished Stoicism, Manicheism, Libertinism, and Turkism[62];

that this teaching makes people carnally self-assured, since it persuades them that nothing endangers the salvation of the elect, no matter how they live, so that they may commit the most outrageous crimes with self-assurance; and that on the other hand nothing is of use to the reprobate for salvation even if they have truly performed all the works of the saints;

that this teaching means that God predestined and created, by the bare and unqualified choice of his will, without the least regard or consideration of any sin, the greatest part of the world to eternal condemnation[63]; that in the same manner in which election is the source and cause of faith and good works, reprobation is the cause of unbelief and ungodliness; that

62. That is, Islam.

63. Here and elsewhere the Canons of Dordt incline against the supralapsarian order of divine decrees in favor of infralapsarianism.

Waag-Schaal (the "Balance"), depicting Arminius's works and the coats of the magistrates outweighed by the works of Calvin and Beza, plus the sword of the Dutch prince

many infant children of believers are snatched in their innocence from their mothers' breasts and cruelly cast into hell so that neither the blood of Christ nor their baptism nor the prayers of the church at their baptism can be of any use to them; and very many other slanderous accusations of this kind which the Reformed churches not only disavow but even denounce with their whole heart. . . .

Moreover, the Synod earnestly warns the false accusers themselves to consider how heavy a judgment of God awaits those who give false testimony against so many churches and their confessions, trouble the consciences of the weak, and seek to prejudice the minds of many against the fellowship of true believers.

[*The Canons of Dort* (Grand Rapids, MI: Faith Alive, 2011), 2–6, 9–10, 12–16, 19–21, 24–25]

Further Reading

Davies, Horton. *Worship and Theology in England: From Cranmer to Baxter and Fox, 1534–1690*. Grand Rapids, MI: Eerdmans, 1996.

Kolb, Robert. *Bound Choice, Election, and Wittenberg Theological Method: From Martin Luther to the Formula of Concord*. Lutheran Quarterly Books. Grand Rapids, MI: Eerdmans, 2005.

Muller, Richard A. *After Calvin: Studies in the Development of a Theological Tradition*. Oxford Studies in Historical Theology. New York: Oxford University Press, 2003.

———. *Post-Reformation Reformed Dogmatics*. 4 vols. Grand Rapids, MI: Baker Book House, 2003.

Stanglin, Keith D., and Thomas H. McCall. *Jacob Arminius, Theologian of Grace*. New York: Oxford University Press, 2012.

Tyacke, Nicholas R. N. *Anti-Calvinists: The Rise of English Arminianism, c. 1590-1640*. Oxford: Clarendon, 1987.

Wallace, Dewey. *Puritans and Predestination: Grace in English Protestant Theology, 1525–1695*. Chapel Hill: University of North Carolina Press, 1982.

Chapter 6
Enlightenment and Skepticism

The greatest intellectual shift that occurred during the past seven hundred years of Western thought is not marked by the sixteenth-century Reformation, which in many ways was a medieval movement and schism. Rather, the rise of modernity in the seventeenth and eighteenth centuries, a development that had a long gestation and a slow birth, is the watershed in the second half of church history. For this reason, it is important to survey the social and philosophical currents that contributed to and reflected a new way of seeing God and the world, a transition that would affect every aspect of life in the West, including the future of Christian theology.

One factor that contributed to Enlightenment thought is the aftershock of the "wars of religion" between Catholics and Protestants. Attempts at toleration—the Peace of Augsburg in 1555, for instance—were fragile, limited in scope, and proved to be the exception to the rule of mutual hostility. For another example, the Dutch Revolt that began in 1568, which finally secured the position of the Protestant Church in The Netherlands, also instigated the Eighty Years War with Spain. The powder keg exploded in 1618 with the outbreak of the devastating Thirty Years War, which was effectively the first world war, and ended in 1648 with terms of toleration similar to those of 1555. Although these wars were motivated primarily by the interests of the rising, sovereign nation-state that answered to no authority higher than the state, they were often fought in the name of religion and have gone down in history as the wars of Christian religion. Therefore, theologically, the wars intensified the sentiment that attention to creeds and doctrines would result in conflict, and they introduced the idea to Europe that the Christian religion might be detrimental to society. Thus, the fine theological distinctions and debates that characterized Protestant orthodoxy were in decline from the late seventeenth century on. Toleration became an increasing demand. In England, for example, in the wake of its own Civil War, a spirit of doctrinal latitudinarianism prevailed that allowed not only Arminians but also Arians to subscribe to the Thirty-nine Articles.

Another factor in the shift to modernity is doubt about tradition. Since the beginning of the Renaissance, there was no intellectual tradition that was not subject to criticism and doubt. For example, after Christopher Columbus's discovery of the New World in 1492, received truths about geography could no longer be taken for granted. The same spirit that questioned geographical and cosmological traditions also became suspicious of historical and theological certainties. If the (alleged) fourth-century *Donation of Constantine* turned out to be an eighth-century forgery, then what about the traditional Mosaic authorship of the Pentateuch? If Protestant Reformers could defy the established church in the name of seeking truth, then what other doctrinal assumptions should be discarded? What are the true foundations and sources of religious knowledge? In fact, how can humans really know anything at all with certainty? When René Descartes (1596–1650) doubted, he had good reason for doing so. This thoroughgoing doubt accompanied the new emphasis on epistemological questions that came to characterize both philosophy and theology.

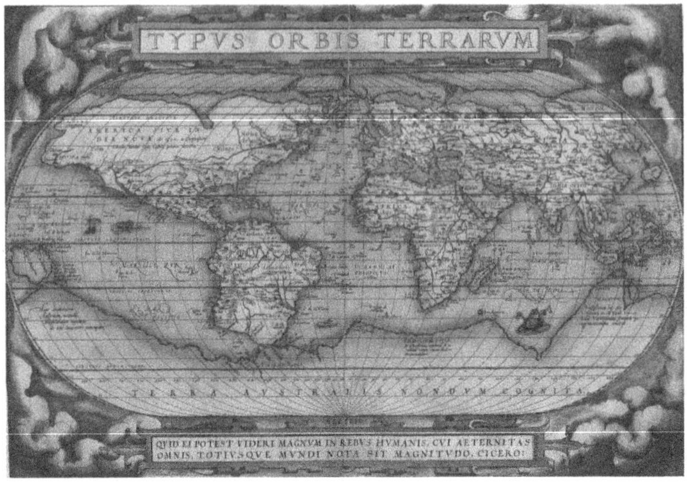

The world as it seemed to Abraham Ortelius in 1570

Since the beginning of Christian thought, theologians have offered a variety of responses to the question of how theology is to make use of secular philosophy, ranging from nearly complete rejection to nearly total embrace. With the coming of the Enlightenment, however, some streams of modern theology began to allow philosophy and science to dictate the terms of theological discourse. For example, there was general agreement that necessary knowledge of God could be attained simply through the observation of the created order—that is, a new emphasis on general revelation discerned by human reason.

Through such reason and observation, figures such as Francis Bacon (1561–1626), Galileo Galilei (1564–1642), and Isaac Newton (1642–1727) put the new scientific method to work, yielding unprecedented results and discoveries. The metaphorical description of the universe as a great machine, with God as its designer, took on a life of its own and became a literal description. The mechanistic universe came to be regarded as a self-sufficient, closed system, and God as the external force who put it into motion. Deism took this view of the cosmos for granted, positing a designer God who was universally available to human reason but did not act through special revelation or miracles. Ultimately, for deists, Christian faith was only one possibility of many legitimate religious expressions, which at their core all express—though some better than others—the religion of reason. One result was that the Bible was read and interpreted as a merely human book. This deemphasis on Scripture from a consciously Christian perspective came to full expression in the moral deism of Immanuel Kant (1724–1804) and the Spirit-infused panentheism of G. W. F. Hegel (1770–1831). Going slightly beyond deism, eighteenth-century French *philosophes* simply asserted that the cosmic machine generated itself, thus eliminating the need for the God hypothesis altogether. These self-professed atheists came to see Christian faith, and all religion, as an irrational worldview.

To be sure, not all seventeenth- and eighteenth-century philosophy was so skeptical and unorthodox, and not everyone joined with the Cartesian rationalists or the British empiricists. In their own day, thinkers such as Descartes were seen as aberrant. Many continued the orthodox line and held fast to an Aristotelian model of metaphysics. Some, such as Johann Georg Hamann (1730–1788), who lived in the midst of the Enlightenment's intellectual scene, never bought into the Enlightenment principles but instead criticized the foundations of the "Age of Reason." Despite the opposition, however, the voice of dissent was deluged by the new ways of seeing God and the world that would later affect most modern theological expressions.

A. New Philosophy and Its Theological Implications

Biographical Note: René Descartes

René Descartes (1596–1650) made his first intellectual contributions in the field of mathematics. In light of the great success of the emerging scientific method, Descartes hoped to articulate an account of reality that included both spiritual values as well as the accuracy of scientific investigation. He assumed that truth can and should enjoy mathematical certainty.

In order to achieve such certainty, and recognizing that many of the beliefs he had received were false, Descartes began his philosophical quest with the presumption of doubting everything that could possibly be doubted, so that he could build knowledge from scratch only on solid grounds. Even from within his own project, he worried that doubt can go too far, that he could simply be dreaming. Yet he pressed on, famously concluding that he cannot doubt that he is doubting and, therefore, that he exists ("I think, therefore I am"). The first indubitable certainty is this ego *("I") that thinks and thinks that it exists. From this bare foundation, Descartes attempted to demonstrate many of the propositions already taken for granted in a Christian worldview, for example, that imperfection is a kind of ontological proof of divine perfection. Descartes rooted certainty in innate ideas that served as the starting point for epistemology. Although he finds a place for sense data and perceptions in his system, according to classic Cartesian epistemological rationalism, pure reason is something ultimately disconnected from the life of the senses and emotion.*

Descartes's philosophy had only a limited impact within his own lifetime. Though he wrote in French and in an intimate, personal style not typical of philosophers, Descartes's thoughts did not appeal to the masses, whose naive realism he sought to replace with a quite complex epistemology. European universities continued to be dominated by an eclectic Aristotelianism, and very few philosophers followed Descartes to all of his conclusions. Yet the method of systematic doubt, the turn to epistemology and the ego*, and other features of Cartesianism quickly infiltrated systems of philosophy and theology, and soon the debates in these fields could not take place without reference to Descartes.*

In typical presentations of the history of philosophy that neglect premodern Christian thinkers, Descartes is often considered to represent the first major advance in Western philosophy since Aristotle. At any rate, along with Sir Isaac Newton (1642–1727), Descartes was the most original and influential thinker of the seventeenth century. He is the harbinger of the Enlightenment and, in many ways, its epitome.

Selection 61: René Descartes, *Discourse on Method* (1637)

Descartes begins the Discourse on Method *with an account of the beginning of his doubts upon completion of his childhood education. In the wake of these doubts, the epistemological method that he eventually proposed, outlined in this work, would set the tone for modern philosophy. The full title of this work,* Discourse on the Method for Rightly Conducting One's Reason and for Seeking Truth in the Sciences, *indicates the scope and ambition of Descartes's philosophical project. The content, which lacks any*

appeal to divine revelation and eschews all tradition, reflects the independence and originality of his epistemology.

Part Two

I was in Germany then, where the wars—which are still continuing there—called me;[1] and while I was returning to the army from the coronation of the emperor, the onset of winter held me up in quarters where, finding no conversation with which to be diverted and, fortunately, otherwise having no worries or passions which troubled me, I remained for a whole day by myself in a small stove-heated room, where I had complete leisure for communing with my thoughts. Among them, one of the first that I thought of considering was that often there is less perfection in works made of several pieces and in works made by the hands of several masters than in those works on which but one master has worked. Thus one sees that buildings undertaken and completed by a single architect are commonly more beautiful and better ordered than those that several architects have tried to patch up, using old walls that had been built for other purposes. Thus these ancient cities that were once merely straggling villages and have become in the course of time great cities are commonly quite poorly laid out, compared to those well-ordered towns that an engineer lays out on a vacant plain as it suits his fancy. And although, upon considering one by one buildings in the former class of towns, one finds as much art or more than one finds in buildings of the latter class of towns, still, upon seeing how the buildings are arranged—here a large one, there a small one—and how they make the streets crooked and uneven, one will say that it is chance more than the will of some men using their reason that has arranged them thus. And if one considers that there have nevertheless always been officials responsible for seeing that private buildings be made to serve as an ornament for the public, one will know that it is difficult to produce a finely executed product by laboring only on the works of others. Thus I imagined that peoples who, having once been half savages and having been civilized only gradually, have made their laws only to the extent that the inconvenience caused by crimes and quarrels forced them to do so, would not be as well ordered as those who, from the very beginning of their coming together, have followed the fundamental precepts of some prudent legislator. Thus it is quite certain that the state of the true religion, whose ordinances were fixed by God alone, ought to be incomparably better governed than all the others. And, speaking of matters human, I believe that if Sparta flourished greatly in the past, it was not because of the goodness of each of its laws taken by itself, since some of them were very strange and even contrary to good morals, but because, having been invented by only one person, they all tended toward the same goal. And thus I thought that book learning, at least the kind whose arguments are merely probable and have no demonstrations—having been built up from and enlarged gradually by the opinions of many different people—does not draw as near to the truth as the simple reasonings that can be made naturally by a man of good sense concerning what he encounters. And thus again I thought that, given the fact that we were all children before being adults and that for a long time it was our lot to be governed by our appetites and our teachers (both were often in conflict with one another, and perhaps none of them consistently gave us the best advice), it is almost impossible for our judgments to be as pure or solid as they would have been had we the full use of our reason from the moment of our birth and had we never been led by anything but our reason.

1. The Thirty Years War (1618–1648).

It is true that one does not see people pulling down all the houses in a city simply to rebuild them some other way and to make the streets more attractive; but one does see that several people do tear down their own houses in order to rebuild them, and that even in some cases they are forced to do so when their houses are in danger of collapsing and the foundations are not very steadfast. Taking this example to heart, I was persuaded that it was not really likely that a single individual might plan to reform a state by changing everything from the very foundations and by toppling it in order to set it up again; nor even also to reform all of the sciences or the order established in the schools for teaching them; but that I could not do better than to try once and for all to get all the beliefs I had accepted from birth out of my mind, so that once I have reconciled them with reason I might again set up either other, better ones or even the same ones. And I firmly believed that by this means I would succeed in conducting my life much better than were I to build only on old foundations or to lean only on the principles of which I permitted myself to be persuaded in my youth without ever having examined whether or not they were true. For although I noticed various difficulties in this operation, still they did not seem irremediable or comparable to those difficulties arising in the reformation of the least things which affect the public. These great bodies are too difficult to raise up once they have been knocked down or even to maintain once they have been shaken; and their falls can only be very violent. Now as to their imperfections, if they have any (and the mere fact of their diversity suffices to assure one that many of them are imperfect), usage has doubtlessly mitigated them and has even imperceptibly averted or corrected a great number of them, for which deliberate foresight could not have provided so well. And finally, these imperfections are almost always more tolerable than what it takes to change them; similarly, the great roads that wind around mountains become gradually so level and suitable by dint of being used frequently, that it is much better to follow these roads than to try to go by a more direct route, climbing over rocks and descending to the bottom of precipices. . . .

And for my part, I would unquestionably have been among these latter persons were I to have had only one master or had never seen the differences that have always existed among the opinions of the most learned people. But having learned since my school days that one cannot imagine anything so strange or unbelievable that it has not been said by some philosopher,[2] and since then, during my travels, having acknowledged that those who have feelings quite contrary to our own are not for that reason barbarians or savages, but that many of them use their reason as much or more than we do, and having considered how the very same man with his very own mind, having been brought up from infancy among the French or the Germans becomes different from what he would be had he always lived among the Chinese or among cannibals; and how, even to the fashions of our clothing, the same thing that pleased us ten years ago and that perhaps might again please us ten years from now seem to us extravagant and ridiculous. Thus it is more custom and example that persuades us than certain knowledge, and for all that, the majority opinion is not a proof worth anything for truths that are a bit difficult to discover, since it is more likely that only one man has found them than a whole people: I could find no one whose opinions, it seemed to me, ought to be preferred over the others, and I found myself constrained to try to lead myself on my own. . . .

2. This sentiment goes back at least to Cicero.

And since the multiplicity of laws often provides excuses for vices, so that a state is much better when, having but a few laws, its laws are strictly observed; so, in place of the large number of rules of which logic is composed, I believed that the following four rules would be sufficient, provided I made a firm and constant resolution not even once to fail to observe them:

The first was never to accept anything as true that I did not know evidently to be so; that is, carefully to avoid precipitous judgment and prejudice;[3] and to include nothing more in my judgments than what presented itself to my mind with such clarity and distinctness that I would have no occasion to put it in doubt.

The second, to divide each of the difficulties I was examining into as many parts as possible and as is required to solve them best.

The third, to conduct my thoughts in an orderly fashion, commencing with the simplest and easiest to know objects, to rise gradually, as by degrees, to the knowledge of the most composite things, and even supposing an order among those things that do not naturally precede one another.

And last, everywhere to make enumerations so complete and reviews so general that I would be sure of having omitted nothing. . . .

But what pleased me the most about this method was that by means of it I was assured of using my reason in everything, if not perfectly, then at least as best as I can. Moreover, I felt that in practicing this method my mind was gradually getting into the habit of conceiving its object more rigorously and more distinctly and that, not having subjected it to any particular matter, I promised myself to apply the method just as profitably to the problems of the other sciences, as I had done to problems in algebra.[4] Not that, on account of this, I dared immediately to undertake an examination of whatever presented itself; for even that would have been contrary to the order prescribed by the method. But having noticed that their principles must all be borrowed from philosophy, in which I still found nothing certain, I thought that I ought, above all, to try to establish therein something certain; and I thought that, this being the most important thing in the world, where precipitous judgment and prejudice were most to be feared, I ought not to have tried to succeed at doing so until I had reached a much more mature age than merely twenty-three, which I was then; and I thought that I should previously spend much time preparing myself, as much in rooting out of my mind all the wrong opinions that I had accepted before that time as in accumulating many experiences—later to be the stuff of my reasonings—and in always exercising myself in the method I had prescribed for myself so as to be stronger and stronger in its use.

Part Four

I do not know whether I ought to tell you about the first meditations I made there; for they are so metaphysical and so out of the ordinary, that perhaps they would not be to everyone's liking. Nevertheless, so that one might be able to judge whether the foundations I have laid are sufficiently firm, I am in some sense forced to speak. For a long time I have noticed that in moral matters one must sometimes follow opinions that one knows are quite uncertain, just as if they were indubitable, as has been said above; but since then I desired to attend only to the search for truth, I thought it necessary that

3. That is, prejudgment before relevant evidence has been reviewed.

4. The optimism of arriving at a method that will successfully provide epistemic certainty in every area of human knowledge is characteristic of the early Enlightenment.

I do exactly the opposite, and that I reject as absolutely false everything in which I could imagine the least doubt, so as to see whether, after this process, anything in my set of beliefs remains that is entirely indubitable. Thus, since our senses sometimes deceive us, I decided to suppose that nothing was exactly as our senses would have us imagine. And since there are men who err in reasoning, even in the simplest matters in geometry, and commit paralogisms, judging that I was just as prone to err as the next man, I rejected as false all the reasonings that I had previously taken for demonstrations. And finally, taking into account the fact that the same thoughts we have when we are awake can also come to us when we are asleep, without any of the latter thoughts being true, I resolved to pretend that everything that had ever entered my mind was no more true than the illusions of my dreams. But immediately afterward I noticed that, during the time I wanted thus to think that everything was false, it was necessary that I, who thought thus, be something. And noticing that this truth—*I think, therefore I am*—was so firm and so certain that the most extravagant suppositions of the sceptics were unable to shake it, I judged that I could accept it without scruple as the first principle of the philosophy I was seeking. . . .

[*Discourse on Method and Meditations on First Philosophy*, trans. Donald A. Cress (Indianapolis: Hackett, 1980), 6–10, 12, 17]

Selection 62: René Descartes, *Meditations on First Philosophy* (1641)

In the* Meditations on First Philosophy in Which the Existence of God and the Distinction of the Soul from the Body Are Demonstrated, *which was dedicated to the theology faculty at the University of Paris, Descartes articulates the philosophical underpinnings for his method. More fully than in the* Discourse on Method, *here Descartes guides the reader through the intimate reflections that led him to his conclusions.

Meditation One: Concerning Those Things that Can Be Called into Doubt

. . . Yet to this end it will not be necessary that I show that all my opinions are false, which perhaps I could never accomplish anyway. But because reason now persuades me that I should withhold my assent no less carefully from things which are not plainly certain and indubitable than I would to what is patently false, it will be sufficient justification for rejecting them all, if I find in each of them some reason for doubt. Nor therefore need one survey each opinion one after the other, a task of endless proportion. Rather—because undermining the foundations will cause whatever has been built upon them to fall down of its own accord—I will at once attack those principles which supported everything that I once believed. . . .

But perhaps, although the senses sometimes deceive us when it is a question of very small and distant things, still there are many other matters which one certainly cannot doubt, although they are derived from the very same senses: that I am sitting here before the fireplace wearing my dressing gown, that I feel this sheet of paper in my hands, and so on. But how could one deny that these hands and that my whole body exist? Unless perhaps I should compare myself to insane people whose brains are so impaired by a stubborn vapor from a black bile that they continually insist that they are kings when they are in utter poverty, or that they are wearing purple robes when they are naked, or that they have a head made of clay, or that they are gourds, or that they are made of glass. But they are all demented, and I would appear no less demented if I were to take their conduct as a model for myself.

All of this would be well and good, were I not a man who is accustomed to sleeping at night, and to undergoing in my sleep the very same things—or now and then even less likely ones—as do these insane people when they are awake. How often has my evening slumber persuaded me of such customary things as these: that I am here, clothed in my dressing gown, seated at the fireplace, when in fact I am lying undressed between the blankets! But right now I certainly am gazing upon this piece of paper with eyes wide awake. This head which I am moving is not heavy with sleep. I extend this hand consciously and deliberately and I feel it. These things would not be so distinct for one who is asleep. But this all seems as if I do not recall having been deceived by similar thoughts on other occasions in my dreams. As I consider these cases more intently, I see so plainly that there are no definite signs to distinguish being awake from being asleep that I am quite astonished, and this astonishment almost convinces me that I am sleeping. . . .

But it is not enough simply to have made a note of this; I must take care to keep it before my mind. For long-standing opinions keep coming back again and again, almost against my will; they seize upon my credulity, as if it were bound over to them by long use and the claims of intimacy.[5] Nor will I get out of the habit of assenting to them and believing in them, so long as I take them to be exactly what they are, namely, in some respects doubtful as by now is obvious, but nevertheless highly probable, so that it is much more consonant with reason to believe them than to deny them. Hence, it seems to me, I would do well to turn my will in the opposite direction, to deceive myself and pretend for a considerable period that they are wholly false and imaginary, until finally, as if with equal weight of prejudice on both sides, no bad habit should turn my judgment from the correct perception of things. For indeed I know that no danger or error will follow and that it is impossible for me to indulge in too much distrust, since I now am concentrating only on knowledge, not on action.

Thus I will suppose not a supremely good God, the source of truth, but rather an evil genius, as clever and deceitful as he is powerful, who has directed his entire effort to misleading me. I will regard the heavens, the air, the earth, colors, shapes, sounds, and all external things as nothing but the deceptive games of my dreams, with which he lays snares for my credulity. I will regard myself as having no hands, no eyes, no flesh, no blood, no senses, but as nevertheless falsely believing that I possess all these things. I will remain resolutely fixed in this meditation, and, even if it be out of my power to know anything true, certainly it is within my power to take care resolutely to withhold my assent to what is false, lest this deceiver, powerful and clever as he is, have an effect on me. But this undertaking is arduous, and laziness brings me back to my customary way of living. I am not unlike a prisoner who might enjoy an imaginary freedom in his sleep. When he later begins to suspect that he is sleeping, he fears being awakened and conspires slowly with these pleasant illusions. In just this way, I spontaneously fall back into my old beliefs, and dread being awakened, lest the toilsome wakefulness which follows upon a peaceful rest, have to be spent thenceforward not in the light but among the inextricable shadows of the difficulties now brought forward.

5. Descartes here reflects a first principle of Enlightenment thought: "long-standing opinions" (that is, tradition) in all fields of knowledge, including religion, are similarly to be rejected. As he goes on to write, his solution in this thought experiment is to think the opposite of that tradition.

Meditation Two: Concerning the Nature of the Human Mind: That the Mind Is More Known than the Body

Yesterday's meditation filled my mind with so many doubts that I can no longer forget about them—nor yet do I see how they are to be resolved. But, as if I had suddenly fallen into a deep whirlpool, I am so disturbed that I can neither touch my foot to the bottom, nor swim up to the top. Nevertheless I will work my way up, and I will follow the same path I took yesterday, putting aside everything which admits of the least doubt, as if I had discovered it to be absolutely false. I will go forward until I know something certain—or, if nothing else, until I at least know for certain that nothing is certain. Archimedes sought only a firm and immovable point in order to move the entire earth from one place to another.[6] Surely great things are to be hoped for if I am lucky enough to find at least one thing that is certain and indubitable.

Therefore I will suppose that all I see is false. I will believe that none of those things that my deceitful memory brings before my eyes ever existed. I thus have no senses: body, shape, extension,[7] movement, and place are all figments of my imagination. What then will count as true? Perhaps only this one thing: that nothing is certain.

But on what grounds do I know that there is nothing over and above all those which I have just reviewed, concerning which there is not even the least cause for doubt? Is there not a God (or whatever name I might call him) who instills these thoughts in me? But why should I think that, since perhaps I myself could be the author of these things? Therefore am I not at least something? But I have already denied that I have any senses and any body. Still, I hesitate; for what follows from that? Am I so tied to the body and to the senses that I cannot exist without them? But I have persuaded myself that there is nothing at all in the world: no heaven, no earth, no minds, no bodies. Is it not then true that I do not exist? But certainly I should exist, if I were to persuade myself of something. But there is a deceiver (I know not who he is) powerful and sly in the highest degree, who is always purposely deceiving me. Then there is no doubt that I exist, if he deceives me. And deceive me as he will, he can never bring it about that I am nothing so long as I shall think that I am something. Thus it must be granted that, after weighing everything carefully and sufficiently, one must come to the considered judgment that the statement "I am, I exist" is necessarily true every time it is uttered by me or conceived in my mind. . . .

But now what am I, when I suppose that some deceiver—omnipotent and, if I may be allowed to say it, malicious—takes all the pains he can in order to deceive me? Can I not affirm that I possess at least a small measure of all those traits which I already have said pertain to the nature of the body? I pay attention, I think, I deliberate—but nothing happens. I am wearied of repeating this in vain. But which of these am I to ascribe to the soul? How about eating or walking? These are surely nothing but illusions, because I do not have a body. How about sensing? Again, this also does not happen without a body, and I judge that I really did not sense those many things I seemed to have sensed in my dreams. How about thinking? Here I discover that thought is an attribute that really does belong to me. This alone cannot be detached from me. I am; I exist; this

6. Archimedes (ca. 287–ca. 212 BC) was the ancient Greek mathematician who said that, with a lever, he could move the earth from one fixed position. The Archimedean point represents a place of objective truth and certainty.

7. "Extension" is the property of something taking up space.

is certain. But for how long? For as long as I think. Because perhaps it could also come to pass that if I should cease from all thinking I would then utterly cease to exist. I now admit nothing that is not necessarily true. I am therefore precisely only a thing that thinks; that is, a mind, or soul, or intellect, or reason—words the meaning of which I was ignorant before. Now, I am a true thing, and truly existing; but what kind of thing? I have said it already: a thing that thinks.

What then? I will set my imagination going to see if I am not something more. I am not that connection of members which is called the human body. Neither am I some subtle air infused into these members, not a wind, not a fire, not a vapor, not a breath—nothing that I imagine to myself, for I have supposed all these to be nothing. The assertion stands: the fact still remains that I am something. But perhaps is it the case that, nevertheless, these very things which I take to be nothing (because I am ignorant of them) in reality do not differ from that self which I know? This I do not know. I shall not quarrel about it right now; I can make a judgment only regarding things which are known to me. I know that I exist; I ask now who is this "I" whom I know. Most certainly the knowledge of this matter, thus precisely understood, does not depend upon things that I do not yet know to exist. Therefore, it is not dependent upon any of those things that I feign in my imagination. But this word "feign" warns me of my error. For I would be feigning if I should "imagine" that I am something, because imagining is merely the contemplation of the shape or image of a corporeal thing. But I know now with certainty that I am, and at the same time it could happen that all these images—and, generally, everything that pertains to the nature of the body—are nothing but dreams. When these things are taken into account, I would speak no less foolishly were I to say: "I will imagine so that I might recognize more distinctly who I am," than were I to say: "Now I surely am awake, and I see something true, but because I do not yet see it with sufficient evidence, I will take the trouble of going to sleep so that my dreams might show this to me more truly and more evidently." Thus I know that none of what I can comprehend by means of the imagination pertains to this understanding that I have of myself. Moreover, I know that I must be most diligent about withdrawing my mind from these things so that it can perceive its nature as distinctly as possible.

But what then am I? A thing that thinks. What is that? A thing that doubts, understands, affirms, denies, wills, refuses, and which also imagines and senses. . . .

[*Discourse on Method and Meditations on First Philosophy*, trans. Donald A. Cress (Indianapolis: Hackett, 1980), 57–58, 60–63]

Selection 63: John Locke, *The Reasonableness of Christianity* (1695)

According to John Locke's (1632–1704)* Essay concerning Human Understanding, *there are two kinds of religious propositions worthy of assent. First, there are propositions acquired by human reason discerning God's natural revelation. Second, there are propositions based on reasonable faith that remain beyond the grasp of reason alone but are not contrary to it. Such faith is confirmed by reason and constitutes a form of certain knowledge. Besides these appropriate grounds, there are some religious beliefs held on improper grounds; such propositions are contrary to reason

and thus unworthy of assent.

In The Reasonableness of Christianity, as Delivered in the Scriptures, *Locke seeks to establish the existence of God (according to reason) and the truth of Christianity (above reason, but according to reasonable faith). Locke's reasonable account of Christianity grants wide latitude in the areas of doctrine that were so important to Protestant scholasticism, and it tends to neglect details of Christology, predestination, sacraments, and other issues that kept Christian Europe divided. Locke's "latitudinarianism" is evident throughout this document, and his handling of Scripture reflects the emerging historical method of modern exegesis.*

As Adam was turned out of paradise, so all his posterity were born out of it, out of the reach of the tree of life; all, like their father Adam, in a state of mortality, void of the tranquillity and bliss of paradise. Rom. v. 12, "By one man sin entered into the world, and death by sin." But here will occur the common objection, that so many stumble at: "How doth it consist with the justice and goodness of God, that the posterity of Adam should suffer for his sin; the innocent be punished for the guilty?"[8] Very well, if keeping one from what he has no right to, be called a punishment; the state of immortality, in paradise, is not due to the posterity of Adam, more than to any other creature. Nay, if God afford them a temporary, mortal life, 'tis his gift; they owe it to his bounty; they could not claim it as their right, nor does he injure them when he takes it from them. Had he taken from mankind any thing that was their right, or did he put men in a state of misery, worse than not being, without any fault or demerit of their own; this, indeed, would be hard to reconcile with the notion we have of justice; and much more with the goodness, and other attributes of the supreme Being, which he has declared of himself; and reason, as well as revelation, must acknowledge to be in him; unless we will confound good and evil, God and Satan. That such a state of extreme, irremediable torment is worse than no being at all; if every one's own sense did not determine against the vain philosophy, and foolish metaphysics of some men; yet our Saviour's peremptory decision, Matt. xxvi. 24, has put it past doubt, that one may be in such an estate, that it had been better for him not to have been born. But that such a temporary life, as we now have, with all its frailties and ordinary miseries, is better than no being, is evident, by the high value we put upon it ourselves. And therefore, though all die in Adam, yet none are truly punished, but for their own deeds. . . .

Nay, whatever God requires any-where to be done, without making any allowance for faith, that is a part of the law of works: so that forbidding Adam to eat of the tree of knowledge was part of the law of works. Only we must take notice here, that some of God's positive commands, being for peculiar ends, and suited to particular circumstances of times, places, and persons; have a limited and only temporary obligation by virtue of God's positive injunction; such as was that part of Moses's law, which concerned the outward worship or political constitution of the jews; and is called the ceremonial and judicial law, in contradistinction to the moral part of it;[9] which being conformable

8. This common question was becoming increasingly common in an age characterized by greater optimism about human ability and greater skepticism about traditional doctrines. And the increasingly common answer, which Locke basically affirms, is a denial of original sin.

9. The threefold division of Old Testament laws into ceremonial, judicial, and moral was popularized by Thomas Aquinas.

to the eternal law of right, is of eternal obligation; and therefore remains in force still, under the gospel; nor is abrogated by the law of faith, as St. Paul found some ready to infer, Rom. iii. 31, "Do we then make void the law, through faith? God forbid; yea we establish the law." . . .

What we are now required to believe to obtain eternal life, is plainly set down in the gospel. St. John tells us, John iii. 36, "He that believeth on the Son, hath eternal life; and he that believeth not the Son, shall not see life." What this believing on him is, we are also told in the next chapter: "The woman said unto him, I know that the Messiah cometh: when he is come, he will tell us all things. Jesus saith unto her, I that speak unto thee, am he. The woman then went into the city, and saith to the men, come see a man that hath told me all things that ever I did: is not this the Messiah? and many of the Samaritans believed on him for the saying of the woman, who testified, he told me all that ever I did. So when the Samaritans were come unto him, many more believed because of his words, and said to the woman, We believe not any longer, because of thy saying; for we have heard ourselves, and we know that this man is truly the Saviour of the world, the Messiah." John iv. 25, 26, 29, 39, 40, 41, 42. . . .

This was the great proposition that was then controverted, concerning Jesus of Nazareth, "Whether he was the Messiah or no?" And the assent to that was that which distinguished believers from unbelievers. When many of his disciples had forsaken him, upon his declaring that he was the bread of life, which came down from heaven, "He said to his apostles, Will ye also go away?" Then Simon Peter answered him, "Lord, to whom shall we go? Thou hast the words of eternal life. And we believe, and are sure, that thou art the Messiah, the Son of the living God," John vi. 69. This was the faith which distinguished them from apostates and unbelievers, and was sufficient to continue them in the rank of apostles: and it was upon the same proposition, "That Jesus was the Messiah, the Son of the living God," owned by St. Peter, that our Saviour said, he would build his church, Matt. xvi. 16-18.

To convince men of this, he did his miracles: and their assent to, or not assenting to this, made them to be, or not to be, of his church; believers, or not believers. . . .

. . . Though the devils believed, yet they could not be saved by the covenant of grace; because they performed not the other condition required in it, altogether as necessary to be performed as this of believing: and that is repentance. Repentance is as absolute a condition of the covenant of grace as faith; and as necessary to be performed as that. John the Baptist, who was to prepare the way for the Messiah, "Preached the baptism of repentance for the remission of sins," Mark i. 4. . . .

These two, faith and repentance, i.e. believing Jesus to be the Messiah, and a good life, are the indispensable conditions of the new covenant, to be performed by all those who would obtain eternal life. . . .[10]

He [Jesus] began his preaching with a command to repent, as St. Matthew tells us, iv. 17. "From that time Jesus began to preach, saying, Repent; for the kingdom of heaven is at hand." And Luke v. 32, he tells the scribes and pharisees, "I come not to call the righteous;" (those who were truly so, needed no help, they had a right to the tree of life), "but sinners, to repentance." In his sermon, as it is called, in the mount, Luke vi. and Matt. v. etc. he commands they should be exemplary in good works: "Let your light so shine amongst men, that they

10. The omission of grace, especially internal operating grace that precedes the faith and works, distinguishes Locke's account of salvation from that of the Augustinian tradition that dominated Protestant orthodoxy.

may see your good works, and glorify your Father which is in heaven," Matt. v. 16. And that they might know what he came for, and what he expected of them, he tells them, ver. 17-20, "Think not that I am come to dissolve," or loosen, "the law, or the prophets: I am not come to dissolve," or loosen, "but to make it full," or complete; by giving it you in its true and strict sense. Here we see he confirms, and at once re-inforces all the moral precepts in the Old Testament. "For verily I say to you, Till heaven and earth pass, one jot or one tittle, shall in nowise pass from the law, till all be done. Whosoever therefore shall break one of these least commandments, and shall teach men so, he shall be called the least (i.e. as it is interpreted, shall not be at all) in the kingdom of heaven." Ver. 21, "I say unto you, That except your righteousness," i.e. your performance of the eternal law of right, "shall exceed the righteousness of the scribes and pharisees, ye shall in no case enter into the kingdom of heaven." And then he goes on to make good what he said, ver. 17, viz. "That he was come to complete the law," viz. by giving its full and clear sense, free from the corrupt and loosening glosses of the scribes and pharisees, ver. 22-26. He tells them, That not only murder, but causeless anger, and so much as words of contempt, were forbidden. He commands them to be reconciled and kind towards their adversaries; and that upon pain of condemnation. In the following part of his sermon, which is to be read Luke vi. and more at large, Matt. v. vi. vii. he not only forbids actual uncleanness, but all irregular desires, upon pain of hell-fire; causeless divorces; swearing in conversation, as well as forswearing in judgment; revenge; retaliation; ostentation of charity, of devotion, and of fasting; repetitions in prayer, covetousness, worldly care, censoriousness: and on the other side commands loving our enemies, doing good to those that hate us, blessing those that curse us, praying for those that despitefully use us; patience and meekness under injuries, forgiveness, liberality, compassion: and closes all his particular injunctions, with this general golden rule, Matt. vii. 12, "All things whatsoever ye would that men should do to you, do you even so to them, for this is the law and the prophets." And to show how much he is in earnest, and expects obedience to these laws, he tells them, Luke vi. 35, That if they obey, "great shall be their *reward*;" they "shall be called the sons of the Highest." And to all this, in the conclusion, he adds the solemn sanction; "Why call ye me, Lord, Lord, and do not the things that I say?" It is in vain for you to take me for the Messiah your King, unless you obey me. "Not every one who calls me, Lord, Lord, shall enter into the kingdom of heaven," or be the Sons of God; "but he that doth the will of my father which is in heaven." To such disobedient subjects, though they have prophesied and done miracles in my name, I shall say at the day of judgment, "Depart from me, ye workers of iniquity; I know you not." . . .

To these I must add one advantage more by Jesus Christ, and that is the promise of assistance. If we do what we can, he will give us his Spirit to help us to do what, and how we should.[11] It will be idle for us, who know not how our own spirits move and act us, to ask in what manner the Spirit of God shall work upon us. The wisdom that accompanies that Spirit knows better than we, how we are made, and how to work upon us. If a wise man knows how to prevail on his child, to bring him to what he desires; can we suspect that the spirit and wisdom of God should fail in it; though we

11. Locke's statement here is reminiscent of the late medieval maxim, rejected by the Augustinians and the Reformers, that "God will not deny his grace to those who do what is in them."

perceive or comprehend not the ways of his operation? Christ has promised it, who is faithful and just; and we cannot doubt of the performance. It is not requisite on this occasion, for the enhancing of this benefit, to enlarge on the frailty of our minds, and weakness of our constitutions; how liable to mistakes, how apt to go astray, and how easily to be turned out of the paths of virtue. If any one needs go beyond himself, and the testimony of his own conscience in this point; if he feels not his own errours and passions always tempting, and often prevailing, against the strict rules of his duty; he need but look abroad into any stage of the world, to be convinced. To a man under the difficulties of his nature, beset with temptations, and hedged in with prevailing custom; it is no small encouragement to set himself seriously on the courses of virtue, and practice of true religion; that he is from a sure hand, and an Almighty arm, promised assistance to support and carry him through.

There remains yet something to be said to those, who will be ready to object, "If the belief of Jesus of Nazareth to be the Messiah, together with those concomitant articles of his resurrection, rule, and coming again to judge the world, be all the faith required, as necessary to justification, to what purpose were the epistles written; I say, if the belief of those many doctrines contained in them be not also necessary to salvation; and what is there delivered a christian may believe or disbelieve, and yet, nevertheless, be a member of Christ's church, and one of the faithful?"

To this I answer, that the epistles are written upon several occasions:[12] and he that will read them as he ought, must observe what it is in them, which is principally aimed at; find what is the argument in hand, and how managed; if he will understand them right, and profit by them. The observing of this will best help us to the true meaning and mind of the writer; for that is the truth which is to be received and believed; and not scattered sentences in scripture-language, accommodated to our notions and prejudices. We must look into the drift of the discourse, observe the coherence and connexion of the parts, and see how it is consistent with itself and other parts of scripture; if we will conceive it right. We must not cull out, as best suits our system, here and there a period or verse; as if they were all distinct and independent aphorisms; and make these the fundamental articles of the christian faith, and necessary to salvation; unless God has made them so. There be many truths in the bible, which a good christian may be wholly ignorant of, and so not believe: which, perhaps, some lay great stress on, and call fundamental articles, because they are the distinguishing points of their communion. The epistles, most of them, carry on a thread of argument, which, in the style they are writ, cannot every-where be observed without great attention, and to consider the texts as they stand, and bear a part in that, is to view them in their due light, and the way to get the true sense of them. They were writ to those who were in the faith, and true christians already: and so could not be designed to teach them the fundamental articles and points necessary to salvation. The epistle to the Romans was writ to all "that were at Rome, beloved of God, called to be saints, whose faith was spoken of through the world," chap. i. 7, 8. To whom St. Paul's first epistle to the Corinthians was, he shows, chap. i. 2, 4, etc. "Unto the church of God which is at Corinth, to them that are sanctified in Christ Jesus, called to be saints; with all them that in every place call upon the name of Jesus Christ our Lord, both theirs and ours. I thank my God always on your behalf, for the

12. Note Locke's hermeneutical principles that follow, all based on the occasional nature of the epistles.

grace of God which is given you by Jesus Christ; that in every thing ye are enriched by him, in all utterance, and in all knowledge: even as the testimony of Christ was confirmed in you. So that ye come behind in no gift; waiting for the coming of our Lord Jesus Christ." And so likewise the second was, "To the church of God at Corinth, with all the saints in Achaia," chap. i. 1. His next is to the churches of Galatia. That to the Ephesians was, "To the saints "that were at Ephesus, and to the faithful in Christ Jesus." So likewise, "To the saints and faithful brethren in Christ at Colosse, who had faith in Christ Jesus, and love to the saints. To the church of the Thessalonians. To Timothy his son in the faith. To Titus his own son after the common faith. To Philemon his dearly beloved, and fellow-labourer." And the author to the Hebrews calls those he writes to "Holy brethren, partakers of the heavenly calling," chap. iii. 1. From whence it is evident, that all those whom St. Paul writ to, were brethren, saints, faithful in the church, and so christians already; and therefore, wanted not the fundamental articles of the christian religion; without a belief of which they could not be saved; nor can it be supposed, that the sending of such fundamentals was the reason of the apostle's writing to any of them. To such also St. Peter writes, as is plain from the first chapter of each of his epistles. Nor is it hard to observe the like in St. James's and St. John's epistles. And St. Jude directs his thus: "To them that are sanctified by God the Father, and preserved in Jesus Christ, and called." The epistles, therefore, being all written to those who were already believers and christians, the occasion and end of writing them could not be to instruct them in that which was necessary to make them christians. This, it is plain, they knew and believed already; or else they could not have been christians and believers. And they were writ upon particular occasions; and without those occasions, had not been writ; and so cannot be thought necessary to salvation: though they resolving doubts, and reforming mistakes, are of great advantage to our knowledge and practice. I do not deny, but the great doctrines of the christian faith are dropt here and there, and scattered up and down in most of them. But it is not in the epistles we are to learn what are the fundamental articles of faith, where they are promiscuously and without distinction mixed with other truths, in discourses that were (though for edification, indeed, yet) only occasional. We shall find and discern those great and necessary points best, in the preaching of our Saviour and the apostles, to those who were yet strangers, and ignorant of the faith; to bring them in, and convert them to it. And what that was, we have seen already, out of the history of the evangelists, and the acts; where they are plainly laid down, so that nobody can mistake them.[13] The epistles to particular churches, besides the main argument of each of them, (which was some present concernment of that particular church, to which they severally were addressed,) do in many places explain the fundamentals of the christian religion, and that wisely; by proper accommodations to the apprehensions of those they were writ to; the better to make them imbibe the christian doctrine, and the more easily to comprehend the method, reasons, and grounds of the great work of salvation. Thus we see, in the epistle to the Romans, adoption (a custom well known amongst those of Rome) is much made use of, to explain to them the grace and favour of God, in giving them eternal life; to help them to conceive how they became the children of God, and to assure them of a share in the kingdom of heaven, as heirs to an inheritance. Whereas the

13. Locke thus makes the Gospels and Acts his canon within the canon.

setting out, and confirming the christian faith to the Hebrews, in the epistle to them, is by illusions and arguments, from the ceremonies, sacrifices, and economy of the jews, and references to the records of the Old Testament. And as for the general epistles, they, we may see, regard the state and exigencies, and some peculiarities of those times. These holy writers, inspired from above, writ nothing but truth; and in most places, very weighty truths to us now; for the expounding, clearing, and confirming of the christian doctrine, and establishing those in it who had embraced it. But yet every sentence of theirs must not be taken up, and looked on as a fundamental article, necessary to salvation; without an explicit belief whereof, no-body could be a member of Christ's church here, nor be admitted into his eternal kingdom hereafter. If all, or most of the truths declared in the epistles, were to be received and believed as fundamental articles, what then became of those christians who were fallen asleep (as St. Paul witnesses in his first to the Corinthians, many were) before these things in the epistles were revealed to them? Most of the epistles not being written till above twenty years after our Saviour's ascension, and some after thirty. . . .[14]

. . . The law of faith, being a covenant of free grace, God alone can appoint what shall be necessarily believed by every one whom he will justify. What is the faith which he will accept and account for righteousness, depends wholly on his good pleasure. For it is of grace, and not of right, that this faith is accepted. And therefore he alone can set the measures of it: and what he has so appointed and declared is alone necessary. No-body can add to these fundamental articles of faith; nor make any other necessary, but what God himself hath made, and declared to be so. And what these are which God requires of those who will enter into, and receive the benefits of the new covenant, has already been shown. An explicit belief of these is absolutely required of all those to whom the gospel of Jesus Christ is preached, and salvation through his name proposed. . . .

[*The Works of John Locke*, 9 vols., 12th ed. (London, 1824), vol. 6, 7–8, 13, 17–18, 103, 105, 114–16, 151–55]

Selection 64: David Hume, *Dialogues concerning Natural Religion* (1776)

In this book, David Hume (1711–1776) employed the classic form of dialogue to criticize the analogies typically used in the teleological argument (anticipating Paley, Selection 65) and to question the attributes of God in view of the reality of evil, all to underscore the severe limitations of the natural theology that had become so prevalent among Enlightenment theologians.

Part II

[Cleanthes:] . . . I shall briefly explain how I conceive this matter. Look round the world: contemplate the whole and every part of it: You will find it to be nothing but one great machine, subdivided into an infinite number of lesser machines, which again admit of subdivisions, to a degree beyond what human senses and faculties can trace and explain. All these various machines, and even their most minute parts, are adjusted to each other with an accuracy, which ravishes into admiration all men, who have ever contemplated them. The curious adapting of means to ends, throughout all

14. By this same rationale, once-fundamental doctrines such as the Trinity may be marginalized.

nature, resembles exactly, though it much exceeds, the productions of human contrivance; of human design, thought, wisdom, and intelligence. Since therefore the effects resemble each other, we are led to infer, by all the rules of analogy, that the causes also resemble; and that the Author of Nature is somewhat similar to the mind of man; though possessed of much larger faculties, proportioned to the grandeur of the work, which he has executed. By this argument *a posteriori,* and by this argument alone, do we prove at once the existence of a Deity, and his similarity to human mind and intelligence.[15]

[Demea:] I shall be so free, *Cleanthes*, said *Demea*, as to tell you, that from the beginning, I could not approve of your conclusion concerning the similarity of the Deity to men; still less can I approve of the mediums, by which you endeavour to establish it. What! No demonstration of the Being of a God! No abstract arguments! No proofs *a priori!* Are these, which have hitherto been so much insisted on by philosophers, all fallacy, all sophism? Can we reach no farther in this subject than experience and probability? I will not say, that this is betraying the cause of a deity: But surely, by this affected candour, you give advantage to Atheists, which they never could obtain, by the mere dint of argument and reasoning.

[Philo:] What I chiefly scruple in this subject, said *Philo*, is not so much, that all religious arguments are by *Cleanthes* reduced to experience, as that they appear not to be even the most certain and irrefragable of that inferior kind. That a stone will fall, that fire will burn, that the earth has solidity, we have observed a thousand and a thousand times; and when any new instance of this nature is presented, we draw without hesitation the accustomed inference. The exact similarity of the cases gives us a perfect assurance of a similar event; and a stronger evidence is never desired nor sought after. But wherever you depart, in the least, from the similarity of the cases, you diminish proportionably the evidence; and may at last bring it to a very weak *analogy,* which is confessedly liable to error and uncertainty. After having experienced the circulation of the blood in human creatures, we make no doubt that it takes place in *Titius* and *Maevius*: but from its circulation in frogs and fishes, it is only a presumption, though a strong one, from analogy, that it takes place in men and other animals. The analogical reasoning is much weaker, when we infer the circulation of the sap in vegetables from our experience, that the blood circulates in animals; and those, who hastily followed that imperfect analogy, are found, by more accurate experiments, to have been mistaken.

If we see a house, *Cleanthes*, we conclude, with the greatest certainty, that it had an architect or builder; because this is precisely that species of effect, which we have experienced to proceed from that species of cause. But surely you will not affirm, that the universe bears such a resemblance to a house, that we can with the same certainty infer a similar cause, or that the analogy is here entire and perfect. The dissimilitude is so striking, that the utmost you can here pretend to is a guess, a conjecture, a presumption concerning a similar cause; and how that pretension will be received in the world, I leave you to consider.

[Cleanthes:] It would surely be very ill received, replied *Cleanthes*; and I should be deservedly blamed and detested, did I allow, that the proofs of a Deity amounted to no more than a guess or conjecture. But is the whole adjustment of means to ends in a house and in

15. Cleanthes is here advancing a version of the so-called analogical teleological argument, which will be countered by denying the strength of the analogy.

the universe so slight a resemblance? The economy of final causes? The order, proportion, and arrangement of every part? Steps of a stair are plainly contrived, that human legs may use them in mounting; and this inference is certain and infallible. Human legs are also contrived for walking and mounting; and this inference, I allow, is not altogether so certain, because of the dissimilarity which you remark; but does it, therefore, deserve the name only of presumption or conjecture?

[Demea:] Good God! cried *Demea*, interrupting him, where are we? Zealous defenders of religion allow, that the proofs of a Deity fall short of perfect evidence! And you, *Philo*, on whose assistance I depended, in proving the adorable mysteriousness of the Divine Nature, do you assent to all these extravagant opinions of *Cleanthes*? For what other name can I give them? Or why spare my censure, when such principles are advanced, supported by such an authority, before so young a man as *Pamphilus*.[16]

[Philo:] . . . Were a man to abstract from every thing which he knows or has seen, he would be altogether incapable, merely from his own ideas, to determine what kind of scene the universe must be, or to give the preference to one state or situation of things above another. For as nothing which he clearly conceives, could be esteemed impossible or implying a contradiction, every chimera of his fancy would be upon an equal footing; nor could he assign any just reason, why he adheres to one idea or system, and rejects the others, which are equally possible. . . .

Now, according to this method of reasoning, *Demea*, it follows (and is, indeed, tacitly allowed by *Cleanthes* himself) that order, arrangement, or the adjustment of final causes, is not of itself any proof of design; but only so far as it has been experienced to proceed from that principle. For ought we can know *a priori*, matter may contain the source or spring of order originally, within itself, as well as mind does; and there is no more difficulty in conceiving, that the several elements, from an internal unknown cause, may fall into the most exquisite arrangement, than to conceive that their ideas, in the great universal mind, from a like internal, unknown cause, fall into that arrangement. The equal possibility of both these suppositions is allowed. But by experience we find (according to *Cleanthes*), that there is a difference between them. Throw several pieces of steel together, without shape or form; they will never arrange themselves so as to compose a watch: Stone, and mortar, and wood, without an architect, never erect a house. But the ideas in a human mind, we see, by an unknown, inexplicable economy, arrange themselves so as to form the plan of a watch or house. Experience, therefore, proves, that there is an original principle of order in mind, not in matter. From similar effects we infer similar causes. The adjustment of means to ends is alike in the universe, as in a machine of human contrivance. The causes, therefore, must be resembling.

I was from the beginning scandalized, I must own, with this resemblance, which is asserted, between the Deity and human creatures; and must conceive it to imply such a degradation of the Supreme Being as no sound Theist could endure. . . .

Part VII

[Philo:] But here, continued *Philo*, in examining the ancient system of the soul of the world, there strikes me, all on a sudden, a new idea, which, if just, must go near to subvert all your reasoning, and destroy even your first inferences, on which you repose such confidence. If the universe bears a greater likeness to animal

16. Pamphilus, the student of Cleanthes, is present for the discussion and only occasionally narrates.

bodies and to vegetables, than to the works of human art, it is more probable that its cause resembles the cause of the former than that of the latter, and its origin ought rather to be ascribed to generation or vegetation, than to reason or design. Your conclusion, even according to your own principles, is therefore lame and defective.

[Demea:] Pray open up this argument a little further, said *Demea*. For I do not rightly apprehend it in that concise manner in which you have expressed it.

[Philo:] Our friend *Cleanthes*, replied *Philo*, as you have heard, asserts, that since no question of fact can be proved otherwise than by experience, the existence of a Deity admits not of proof from any other medium. The world, says he, resembles the works of human contrivance; therefore its cause must also resemble that of the other. Here we may remark, that the operation of one very small part of nature, to wit man, upon another very small part, to wit that inanimate matter lying within his reach, is the rule by which *Cleanthes* judges of the origin of the whole; and he measures objects, so widely disproportioned, by the same individual standard. But to waive all objections drawn from this topic, I affirm, that there are other parts of the universe (besides the machines of human invention) which bear still a greater resemblance to the fabric of the world, and which, therefore, afford a better conjecture concerning the universal origin of this system.[17] These parts are animals and vegetables. The world plainly resembles more an animal or a vegetable, than it does a watch or a knitting-loom. Its cause, therefore, it is more probable, resembles the cause of the former. The cause of the former is generation or vegetation. The cause, therefore, of the world, we may infer to be something similar or analogous to generation or vegetation.

[Demea:] But how is it conceivable, said *Demea*, that the world can arise from any thing similar to vegetation or generation?

[Philo:] Very easily, replied Philo. In like manner as a tree sheds its seed into the neighbouring fields, and produces other trees; so the great vegetable, the world, or this planetary system, produces within itself certain seeds, which, being scattered into the surrounding chaos, vegetate into new worlds. A comet, for instance, is the seed of a world; and after it has been fully ripened, by passing from sun to sun, and star to star, it is at last tossed into the unformed elements which every where surround this universe, and immediately sprouts up into a new system. . . .

This is the topic on which I have all along insisted. I have still asserted, that we have no *data* to establish any system of cosmogony. Our experience, so imperfect in itself, and so limited both in extent and duration, can afford us no probable conjecture concerning the whole of things.[18] But if we must needs fix on some hypothesis; by what rule, pray, ought we to determine our choice? Is there any other rule than the greater similarity of the objects compared? And does not a plant or an animal, which springs from vegetation or generation, bear a stronger resemblance to the world, than does any artificial machine, which arises from reason and design?

[Demea:] But what is this vegetation and generation of which you talk? said *Demea*. Can you explain their operations, and anatomize

17. Hume, through Philo, questions the mechanistic view of the universe that had already become the dominant way of describing its operations and, by extension, its origin.

18. Note well the importance of empirical experience in the dialogue, both for Cleanthes (who finds it to be conclusive) as well as for Philo and Demea (who find it, in this regard, to be inconclusive).

that fine internal structure on which they depend?

[Philo:] As much, at least, replied *Philo*, as *Cleanthes* can explain the operations of reason, or anatomize that internal structure, on which *it* depends . . .

In reality, *Demea*, it may reasonably be expected, that the larger the views are which we take of things, the better will they conduct us in our conclusions concerning such extraordinary and such magnificent subjects. In this little corner of the world alone, there are four principles, *Reason, Instinct, Generation, Vegetation*, which are similar to each other, and are the causes of similar effects. What a number of other principles may we naturally suppose in the immense extent and variety of the universe, could we travel from planet to planet and from system to system, in order to examine each part of this mighty fabric? Any one of these four principles above mentioned (and a hundred others which lie open to our conjecture) may afford us a theory by which to judge of the origin of the world; and it is a palpable and egregious partiality to confine our view entirely to that principle by which our own minds operate. Were this principle more intelligible on that account, such a partiality might be somewhat excusable: but reason, in its internal fabric and structure, is really as little known to us as instinct or vegetation; and, perhaps, even that vague, undeterminate word, *Nature*, to which the vulgar refer every thing, is not at the bottom more inexplicable. The effects of these principles are all known to us from experience; but the principles themselves, and their manner of operation, are totally unknown; nor is it less intelligible, or less conformable to experience, to say, that the world arose by vegetation, from a seed shed by another world, than to say that it arose from a divine reason or contrivance, according to the sense in which *Cleanthes* understands it.

[Demea:] But methinks, said Demea, if the world had a vegetative quality, and could sow the seeds of new worlds into the infinite chaos, this power would be still an additional argument for design in its author. For whence could arise so wonderful a faculty but from design? Or how can order spring from any thing which perceives not that order which it bestows?

[Philo:] You need only look around you, replied *Philo*, to satisfy yourself with regard to this question. A tree bestows order and organization on that tree which springs from it, without knowing the order; an animal in the same manner on its offspring. . . .

But further, *Demea*; this objection which you urge can never be made use of by *Cleanthes*, without renouncing a defence which he has already made against one of my objections. When I enquired concerning the cause of that supreme reason and intelligence into which he resolves every thing; he told me, that the impossibility of satisfying such enquiries could never be admitted as an objection in any species of philosophy. *We must stop somewhere*, says he; *nor is it ever within the reach of human capacity to explain ultimate causes, or show the last connections of any objects. It is sufficient, if the steps, so far as we go, are supported by experience and observation.* Now, that vegetation and generation, as well as reason, are experienced to be principles of order in nature, is undeniable. If I rest my system of cosmogony on the former, preferably to the latter, it is at my choice. The matter seems entirely arbitrary. And when *Cleanthes* asks me what is the cause of my great vegetative or generative faculty, I am equally entitled to ask him the cause of his great reasoning principle.[19] These

19. The working assumption in the dialogue, typical of Enlightenment-era natural theology, is that God, rather than Being itself and the ground of all being, is

questions we have agreed to forbear on both sides; and it is chiefly his interest on the present occasion to stick to this agreement. Judging by our limited and imperfect experience, generation has some privileges above reason: for we see every day the latter arise from the former, never the former from the latter. . . .

Part X

[Demea:] It is my opinion, I own, replied *Demea*, that each man feels, in a manner, the truth of religion within his own breast; and from a consciousness of his imbecility and misery, rather than from any reasoning, is led to seek protection from that Being, on whom he and all nature is dependent. So anxious or so tedious are even the best scenes of life, that futurity is still the object of all our hopes and fears. We incessantly look forward, and endeavour, by prayers, adoration, and sacrifice, to appease those unknown powers, whom we find, by experience, so able to afflict and oppress us. Wretched creatures that we are! what resource for us amidst the innumerable ills of life, did not Religion suggest some methods of atonement, and appease those terrors with which we are incessantly agitated and tormented?

[Philo:] I am indeed persuaded, said *Philo*, that the best and indeed the only method of bringing every one to a due sense of religion, is by just representations of the misery and wickedness of men. And for that purpose a talent of eloquence and strong imagery is more requisite than that of reasoning and argument. For is it necessary to prove what every one feels within himself? 'Tis only necessary to make us feel it, if possible, more intimately and sensibly.

[Demea:] The people, indeed, replied *Demea*, are sufficiently convinced of this great and melancholy truth. The miseries of life; the unhappiness of man; the general corruptions of our nature; the unsatisfactory enjoyment of pleasures, riches, honours; these phrases have become almost proverbial in all languages. And who can doubt of what all men declare from their own immediate feeling and experience?

[Philo:] In this point, said *Philo*, the learned are perfectly agreed with the vulgar; and in all letters, *sacred* and *profane*, the topic of human misery has been insisted on with the most pathetic eloquence that sorrow and melancholy could inspire. The poets, who speak from sentiment, without a system, and whose testimony has therefore the more authority, abound in images of this nature. From *Homer* down to *Dr. Young*, the whole inspired tribe have ever been sensible, that no other representation of things would suit the feeling and observation of each individual.

[Demea:] As to authorities, replied *Demea*, you need not seek them. Look round this library of *Cleanthes*. I shall venture to affirm, that, except authors of particular sciences, such as chemistry or botany, who have no occasion to treat of human life, there is scarce one of those innumerable writers, from whom the sense of human misery has not, in some passage or other, extorted a complaint and confession of it. At least, the chance is entirely on that side; and no one author has ever, so far as I can recollect, been so extravagant as to deny it.

[Philo:] There you must excuse me, said *Philo*: *Leibnitz* has denied it; and is perhaps the first[20] who ventured upon so bold and paradoxical an opinion; at least, the first who made it essential to his philosophical system.

---

simply a discrete entity among other entities and a cause among other causes that demands an explanation.

20. [Hume] "That sentiment had been maintained by Dr [William] King and some few others, before *Leibnitz*, though by none of so great fame as that *German* philosopher."

[Demea:] . . . And why should man, added he, pretend to an exemption from the lot of all other animals? The whole earth, believe me, *Philo*, is cursed and polluted. A perpetual war is kindled amongst all living creatures. Necessity, hunger, want, stimulate the strong and courageous: fear, anxiety, terror, agitate the weak and infirm. The first entrance into life gives anguish to the new-born infant and to its wretched parent: weakness, impotence, distress, attend each stage of that life: and it is at last finished in agony and horror.

[Philo:] Observe too, says *Philo*, the curious artifices of Nature, in order to embitter the life of every living being. The stronger prey upon the weaker, and keep them in perpetual terror and anxiety. The weaker too, in their turn, often prey upon the stronger, and vex and molest them without relaxation. Consider that innumerable race of insects, which either are bred on the body of each animal, or, flying about, infix their stings in him. These insects have others still less than themselves, which torment them. And thus on each hand, before and behind, above and below, every animal is surrounded with enemies, which incessantly seek his misery and destruction.

[Demea:] Man alone, said Demea, seems to be, in part, an exception to this rule. For by combination in society, he can easily master lions, tigers, and bears, whose greater strength and agility naturally enable them to prey upon him.

[Philo:] . . . Consider, *Demea*; this very society, by which we surmount those wild beasts, our natural enemies; what new enemies does it not raise to us? What woe and misery does it not occasion? Man is the greatest enemy of man.[21] Oppression, injustice, contempt, contumely, violence, sedition, war, calumny, treachery, fraud; by these they mutually torment each other; and they would soon dissolve that society which they had formed, were it not for the dread of still greater ills, which must attend their separation.

[Demea:] . . . The disorders of the mind, continued *Demea*, though more secret, are not perhaps less dismal and vexatious. Remorse, shame, anguish, rage, disappointment, anxiety, fear, dejection, despair; who has ever passed through life without cruel inroads from these tormentors? How many have scarcely ever felt any better sensations? Labour and poverty, so abhorred by every one, are the certain lot of the far greater number; and those few privileged persons, who enjoy ease and opulence, never reach contentment or true felicity. All the goods of life united would not make a very happy man; but all the ills united would make a wretch indeed; and any one of them almost (and who can be free from every one), nay often the absence of one good (and who can possess all), is sufficient to render life ineligible. . . .

[Philo:] . . . But if they were really as unhappy as they pretend, says my antagonist, why do they remain in life? . . . .

Not satisfied with life, afraid of death.

This is the secret chain, say I, that holds us. We are terrified, not bribed to the continuance of our existence. . . .

[Cleanthes:] I can observe something like what you mention in some others, replied *Cleanthes*: but I confess I feel little or nothing of it in myself, and hope that it is not so common as you represent it.

[Demea:] If you feel not human misery yourself, cried *Demea*, I congratulate you on so happy a singularity. Others, seemingly the most prosperous, have not been ashamed to vent their complaints in the most melancholy strains. Let us attend to the great, the fortunate emperor, Charles V., when, tired with human

21. That is, whatever nature lacks in creating misery, we humans pick up the slack.

grandeur, he resigned all his extensive dominions into the hands of his son. In the last harangue which he made on that memorable occasion, he publicly avowed, *that the greatest prosperities which he had ever enjoyed, had been mixed with so many adversities, that he might truly say he had never enjoyed any satisfaction or contentment.* But did the retired life, in which he sought for shelter, afford him any greater happiness? If we may credit his son's account, his repentance commenced the very day of his resignation.

Cicero's fortune, from small beginnings, rose to the greatest lustre and renown; yet what pathetic complaints of the ills of life do his familiar letters, as well as philosophical discourses, contain? And suitably to his own experience, he introduces *Cato*, the great, the fortunate *Cato*, protesting in his old age, that, had he a new life in his offer, he would reject the present. . . .

[Philo:] And is it possible, *Cleanthes*, said *Philo*, that after all these reflections, and infinitely more, which might be suggested, you can still persevere in your Anthropomorphism, and assert the moral attributes of the Deity, his justice, benevolence, mercy, and rectitude, to be of the same nature with these virtues in human creatures? His power we allow is infinite: whatever he wills is executed: but neither man nor any other animal is happy: therefore he does not will their happiness. His wisdom is infinite: he is never mistaken in choosing the means to any end: but the course of Nature tends not to human or animal felicity: therefore it is not established for that purpose. Through the whole compass of human knowledge, there are no inferences more certain and infallible than these. In what respect, then, do his benevolence and mercy resemble the benevolence and mercy of men?

Epicurus's old questions are yet unanswered.[22]

Is he willing to prevent evil, but not able? then is he impotent. Is he able, but not willing? then is he malevolent. Is he both able and willing? whence then is evil? . . .

Our sense of music, harmony, and indeed beauty of all kinds, gives satisfaction, without being absolutely necessary to the preservation and propagation of the species. But what racking pains, on the other hand, arise from gouts, gravels, megrims, toothaches, rheumatisms, where the injury to the animal machinery is either small or incurable? Mirth, laughter, play, frolic, seem gratuitous satisfactions, which have no further tendency: spleen, melancholy, discontent, superstition, are pains of the same nature. How then does the Divine benevolence display itself, in the sense of you Anthropomorphites? None but we Mystics, as you were pleased to call us, can account for this strange mixture of phenomena, by deriving it from attributes, infinitely perfect, but incomprehensible.

[Cleanthes:] And have you at last, said *Cleanthes*, smiling, betrayed your intentions, *Philo*? Your long agreement with *Demea* did indeed a little surprise me; but I find you were all the while erecting a concealed battery against me. And I must confess, that you have now fallen upon a subject worthy of your noble spirit of opposition and controversy. If you can make out the present point, and prove mankind to be unhappy or corrupted, there is an end at once of all religion. For to what purpose establish the natural attributes of the Deity, while the moral are still doubtful and uncertain?[23]

---

22. Epicurus (341–271 BC) was a Greek philosopher and the best known advocate of the classical form of hedonism.

23. The "natural" attribute in question is omnipotence, and the "moral" is benevolence.

[Demea:] You take umbrage very easily, replied *Demea*, at opinions the most innocent, and the most generally received, even amongst the religious and devout themselves: and nothing can be more surprising than to find a topic like this, concerning the wickedness and misery of man, charged with no less than Atheism and profaneness. Have not all pious divines and preachers, who have indulged their rhetoric on so fertile a subject; have they not easily, I say, given a solution of any difficulties which may attend it? This world is but a point in comparison of the universe; this life but a moment in comparison of eternity. The present evil phenomena, therefore, are rectified in other regions, and in some future period of existence. And the eyes of men, being then opened to larger views of things, see the whole connection of general laws; and trace, with adoration, the benevolence and rectitude of the Deity, through all the mazes and intricacies of his providence.

[Cleanthes:] . . . The only method of supporting Divine benevolence (and it is what I willingly embrace) is to deny absolutely the misery and wickedness of man. Your representations are exaggerated; your melancholy views mostly fictitious; your inferences contrary to fact and experience. Health is more common than sickness; pleasure than pain; happiness than misery. And for one vexation which we meet with, we attain, upon computation, a hundred enjoyments.

[Philo:] . . . But allowing you what never will be believed, at least what you never possibly can prove, that animal, or at least human happiness, in this life, exceeds its misery, you have yet done nothing: for this is not, by any means, what we expect from infinite power, infinite wisdom, and infinite goodness. Why is there any misery at all in the world? Not by chance surely. From some cause then. Is it from the intention of the Deity? But he is perfectly benevolent. Is it contrary to his intention? But he is almighty. Nothing can shake the solidity of this reasoning, so short, so clear, so decisive; except we assert, that these subjects exceed all human capacity, and that our common measures of truth and falsehood are not applicable to them; a topic which I have all along insisted on, but which you have, from the beginning, rejected with scorn and indignation.

But I will be contented to retire still from this intrenchment, for I deny that you can ever force me in it. I will allow, that pain or misery in man is *compatible* with infinite power and goodness in the Deity, even in your sense of these attributes: what are you advanced by all these concessions? A mere possible compatibility is not sufficient. You must *prove* these pure, unmixed, and uncontrollable attributes from the present mixed and confused phenomena, and from these alone. A hopeful undertaking! Were the phenomena ever so pure and unmixed, yet being finite, they would be insufficient for that purpose. How much more, where they are also so jarring and discordant![24]

Here, *Cleanthes*, I find myself at ease in my argument. Here I triumph. Formerly, when we argued concerning the natural attributes of intelligence and design, I needed all my sceptical and metaphysical subtilty to elude your grasp. In many views of the universe and of its parts, particularly the latter, the beauty and fitness of final causes strike us with such irresistible force, that all objections appear (what I believe they really are) mere cavils and sophisms; nor can we then imagine how it was ever possible for us to repose any weight on them. But there is no view of human life, or of the condition of mankind, from which, without the greatest violence, we can infer the moral attributes, or learn that infinite benevolence,

24. This paragraph sums up well Hume's critique of natural theology.

conjoined with infinite power and infinite wisdom, which we must discover by the eyes of faith alone. It is your turn now to tug the laboring oar, and to support your philosophical subtilties against the dictates of plain reason and experience.

[David Hume, *Dialogues concerning Natural Religion* (Edinburgh: William Blackwell and Sons, 1907), 30–38, 92–100, 123–37, 139–41]

Selection 65: William Paley, *Natural Theology* (1802)

In response to philosophers who had attacked the so-called "teleological" argument for the existence of God, William Paley (1743–1805) articulated his design argument using the analogy of a watch whose "several parts are framed and put together for a purpose," that is, a* telos*. He was not the first theologian to make this argument with this analogy, but his account of it remains the most famous. The argument includes the idea that people do not recognize design in nature because they are so accustomed to seeing it, but familiarity with nature should not make the design less remarkable.

Chapter I.
State of the Argument.

In crossing a heath, suppose I pitched my foot against a *stone,* and were asked how the stone came to be there; I might possibly answer, that, for anything I knew to the contrary, it had lain there forever: nor would it perhaps be very easy to show the absurdity of this answer. But suppose I had found a *watch* upon the ground, and it should be inquired how the watch happened to be in that place; I should hardly think of the answer which I had before given, that, for anything I knew, the watch might have always been there. Yet why should not this answer serve for the watch as well as for the stone? Why is it not as admissible in the second case, as in the first? For this reason, and for no other, viz. that, when we come to inspect the watch, we perceive (what we could not discover in the stone) that its several parts are framed and put together for a purpose, *e. g.* that they are so formed and adjusted as to produce motion, and that motion so regulated as to point out the hour of the day; that if the different parts had been differently shaped from what they are, of a different size from what they are, or placed after any other manner, or in any other order, than that in which they are placed, either no motion at all would have been carried on in the machine, or none which would have answered the use that is now served by it. . . .

I. Nor would it, I apprehend, weaken the conclusion, that we had never seen a watch made: that we had never known an artist capable of making one; that we were altogether incapable of executing such a piece of workmanship ourselves, or of understanding in what manner it was performed; all this being no more than what is true of some exquisite remains of ancient art, of some lost arts, and, to the generality of mankind, of the more curious productions of modern manufacture.[25] Does one man in a million know how oval frames are turned? Ignorance of this kind exalts our opinion of the unseen and unknown artist's skill, if he be unseen and unknown, but raises no doubt in our minds of the existence and agency of such an artist, at some former time, and in some place or other. Nor can I perceive that it varies at all the inference, whether the question arise concerning a human agent, or concerning an agent of a different species, or an agent possessing, in some respects, a different nature.

25. In some ways, this point is a response to Hume, whose argument against this "proof" appeals to human ignorance both of the divine and of the created order.

II. Neither, secondly, would it invalidate our conclusion, that the watch sometimes went wrong, or that it seldom went exactly right. The purpose of the machinery, the design and the designer, might be evident, and in the case supposed would be evident, in whatever way we accounted for the irregularity of the movement, or whether we could account for it or not. It is not necessary that a machine be perfect, in order to show with what design it was made: still less necessary, where the only question is, whether it were made with any design at all.

III. Nor, thirdly, would it bring any uncertainty into the argument, if there were a few parts of the watch, concerning which we could not discover, or had not yet discovered, in what manner they conduced to the general effect; or even some parts, concerning which we could not ascertain whether they conduced to that effect in any manner whatever. For, as to the first branch of the case; if by the loss, or disorder, or decay of the parts in question, the movement of the watch were found in fact to be stopped, or disturbed, or retarded, no doubt would remain in our minds as to the utility or intention of these parts, although we should be unable to investigate the manner according to which, or the connexion by which, the ultimate effect depended upon their action or assistance; and the more complex is the machine, the more likely is this obscurity to arise. Then, as to the second thing supposed, namely, that there were parts which might be spared, without prejudice to the movement of the watch, and that we had proved this by experiment—these superfluous parts, even if we were completely assured that they were such, would not vacate the reasoning which we had instituted concerning other parts. The indication of contrivance remained, with respect to them, nearly as it was before.

IV. Nor, fourthly, would any man in his senses think the existence of the watch, with its various machinery, accounted for, by being told that it was one out of possible combinations of material forms; that whatever he had found in the place where he found the watch, must have contained some internal configuration or other; and that this configuration might be the structure now exhibited, viz. of the works of a watch, as well as a different structure.

V. Nor, fifthly, would it yield his inquiry more satisfaction to be answered, that there existed in things a principle of order, which had disposed the parts of the watch into their present form and situation. He never knew a watch made by the principle of order; nor can he even form to himself an idea of what is meant by a principle of order distinct from the intelligence of the watchmaker.

VI. Sixthly, he would be surprised to hear that the mechanism of the watch was no proof of contrivance, only a motive to induce the mind to think so.

VII. And not less surprised to be informed, that the watch in his hand was nothing more than the result of the laws of *metallic* nature. It is a perversion of language to assign any law as the efficient, operative cause of anything. A law presupposes an agent, for it is only the mode according to which an agent proceeds: it implies a power; for it is the order, according to which that power acts. Without this agent, without this power, which are both distinct from itself, the *law* does nothing; is nothing. The expression, "the law of metallic nature," may sound strange and harsh to a philosophic ear; but it seems quite as justifiable as some others which are more familiar to him, such as "the law of vegetable nature," "the law of animal nature," or indeed as "the law of nature" in general, when assigned as the cause of phenomena, in exclusion of agency and power; or when it is substituted into the place of these.

VIII. Neither, lastly, would our observer be driven out of his conclusion, or from his confidence in its truth, by being told that he knew nothing at all about the matter. He knows enough for his argument. He knows the utility of the end: he knows the subserviency and adaptation of the means to the end. These points being known, his ignorance of other points, his doubts concerning other points, affect not the certainty of his reasoning. The consciousness of knowing little need not beget a distrust of that which he does know.

Chapter II.
State of the Argument Continued.

. . . The conclusion which the *first* examination of the watch, of its works, construction, and movement, suggested, was, that it must have had, for the cause and author of that construction, an artificer, who understood its mechanism, and designed its use. This conclusion is invincible. A *second* examination presents us with a new discovery. The watch is found, in the course of its movement, to produce another watch, similar to itself: and not only so, but we perceive in it a system or organization, separately calculated for that purpose. What effect would this discovery have or ought it to have, upon our former inference? What, as hath already been said, but to increase, beyond measure, our admiration of the skill which had been employed in the formation of such a machine! Or shall it, instead of this all at once turn us round to an opposite conclusion, viz. that no art or skill whatever has been concerned in the business, although all other evidences of art and skill remain as they were, and this last and supreme piece of art be now added to the rest? Can this be maintained without absurdity? Yet this is atheism.

Chapter III.
Application of the Argument

This is atheism: for every indication of contrivance, every manifestation of design, which existed in the watch, exists in the works of nature; with the difference, on the side of nature, of being greater and more, and that in a degree which exceeds all computation. I mean, that the contrivances of nature surpass the contrivances of art, in the complexity, subtilty, and curiosity of the mechanism; and still more, if possible, do they go beyond them in number and variety: yet, in a multitude of cases, are not less evidently mechanical, not less evidently contrivances, not less evidently accommodated to their end, or suited to their office, than are the most perfect productions of human ingenuity. . . .

Chapter V.
Application of the Argument Continued.

. . . I. When we are inquiring simply after the *existence* of an intelligent Creator, imperfection, inaccuracy, liability to disorder, occasional irregularities, may subsist in a considerable degree, without inducing any doubt into the question: just as a watch may frequently go wrong, seldom perhaps exactly right, may be faulty in some parts, defective in some, without the smallest ground of suspicion from thence arising that it was not a watch; not made; or not made for the purpose ascribed to it. When faults are pointed out, and when a question is started concerning the skill of the artist, or the dexterity with which the work is executed, then, indeed, in order to defend these qualities from accusation, we must be able, either to expose some intractableness and imperfection in the materials, or point out some invincible difficulty in the execution, into which imperfection and difficulty the matter of complaint may be resolved; or if we cannot do this, we must adduce such specimens of consummate art and contrivance, proceeding from the same hand, as may convince the inquirer of the existence, in the case before him, of impediments like those which we have mentioned, although, what from the nature of the case is very likely to happen, they be unknown and unperceived by him. This we must do in order to vindicate the artist's skill, or, at least, the perfection of it; as we must also judge of his intention, and of the provision employed in fulfilling that intention, not from an instance in which they fail, but from the great plurality of instances in which they succeed. But, after all, these are different questions from the question of the artist's existence; or, which is the same, whether the thing before us be a work of art or not: and the question ought always to be kept separate in the mind. So likewise it is in the works of nature. Irregularities and imperfections are of little or no weight in the consideration, when that consideration relates simply to the existence of a Creator. When the argument respects his attributes, they are of weight; but are then to be taken in conjunction (the attention is not to rest upon them, but they are to be taken in conjunction) with the unexceptionable evidences which we possess, of skill, power, and benevolence, displayed in other instances; which evidences may, in strength, number, and variety, be such, and may so overpower apparent blemishes, as to induce us, upon the most reasonable ground, to believe, that these last ought to be referred to some cause, though we be ignorant of it, other than defect of knowledge or of benevolence in the author.

[William Paley, *Natural Theology: Or, Evidences of the Existence and Attributes of the Deity, Collected from the Appearances of Nature* (Boston: Gould and Lincoln, 1857), 5–8, 12–13, 35–36]

Selection 66: G. E. Lessing, "On the Proof of the Spirit and of Power" (1777)

From the time of the Renaissance, there was a noticeable increase of historical skepticism that accompanied the rise of modern historical criticism. By the seventeenth century, scholars such as Baruch Spinoza (1632–1677) began to turn their skepticism toward the Bible and the claims of its narratives. Gotthold Ephraim Lessing (1729–1781) epitomizes this historical skepticism in his claim that there is an "ugly, broad ditch" between the first century and ours that precludes historical certainty. The implication is that it would have been easier for a contemporary eyewitness of Jesus' miracles to believe in him than for those who have access only to the testimony of others.

Recognized as a leading Enlightenment figure in his own day, Lessing's biblical skepticism reflects a growing consensus that would come to reign in nineteenth-century German biblical and theological scholarship. The ideas expressed in his writings were formative for what is now known as classic liberal Protestant theology.

["We have to say, moreover, that the Logos has a demonstration of its own, more divine than any established by Grecian dialectics. And this more divine method is called by the apostle the 'demonstration of the Spirit and of power:'[26] on the one hand, 'of the Spirit,' because of the prophecies, which are sufficient to produce faith in any one who reads them, especially in those things which relate to Christ;] on the other hand, 'of power,' because of the wondrous miracles which we must believe to have been performed, both on many other grounds [ἐκ

26. 1 Cor. 2:4.

πολλῶν μὲν ἄλλων], and on this, that traces of them are still preserved among those who live according to the will of the Logos."[27]

To Herr Director Schumann at Hannover, Brunswick, 1777

Sir, who could be more eager to read your new work than I? I hunger for conviction so much that like Erisichthon I swallow everything that has even the appearance of nourishment. If you do the same with this pamphlet, we are the men for one another. I am, with the regard that one inquirer after truth never ceases to bear for another, Yours etc.

Fulfilled prophecies, which I myself experience, are one thing; fulfilled prophecies, of which I know only from history that others say they have experienced them, are another.

Miracles, which I see with my own eyes, and which I have the opportunity to verify for myself, are one thing; miracles, of which I know only from history that others say they have seen them and verified them, are another.

That surely, is beyond controversy? Surely there is no objection to be made against that?

If I had lived at the time of Christ, then of course the prophecies fulfilled in his person would have made me pay great attention to him. If I had actually seen him do miracles; if I had had no cause to doubt that these were true miracles; then in a worker of miracles who had been marked out so long before, I would have gained so much confidence that I would willingly have submitted my intellect to his, and I would have believed him in all things in which equally indisputable experiences did not tell against him.

Or: if I even now experienced that prophecies referring to Christ or the Christian religion, of whose priority in time I have long been certain, were fulfilled in a manner admitting no dispute; if even now miracles were done by believing Christians which I had to recognize as true miracles: what could prevent me from accepting this proof of the spirit and of power, as the apostle calls it?

In the last instance Origen was quite right in saying that in this proof of the spirit and of power the Christian religion was able to provide a proof of its own more divine than all Greek dialectic. For in his time there was still "the power to do miraculous things which still continued" among those who lived after Christ's precept; and if he had undoubted examples of this, then if he was not to deny his own senses he had of necessity to recognize that proof of the spirit and of power.

But I am no longer in Origen's position; I live in the eighteenth century, in which miracles no longer happen. If I even now hesitate to believe anything on the proof of the spirit and of power, which I can believe on other arguments more appropriate to my age: what is the problem?

The problem is that this proof of the spirit and of power no longer has any spirit or power, but has sunk to the level of human testimonies of spirit and power.

The problem is that reports of fulfilled prophecies are not fulfilled prophecies; that reports of miracles are not miracles. These, the prophecies fulfilled before my eyes, the miracles that occur before my eyes, are immediate in their effect. But those—the reports of fulfilled prophecies and miracles, have to work through a medium which takes away all their force.

To quote Origen and to cite his words that "the proof of power is so called because of the astonishing miracles which have happened to

27. Origen, *Contra Celsum* 1.2. Lessing begins his essay with this quotation in Greek. I have translated it and provided the preceding context, to which Lessing also refers, between brackets.

confirm the teaching of Christ" is of little use if one keeps from one's readers what Origen says immediately thereafter. For the readers will also turn up Origen and find with surprise that he argues for the truth of the miracles which happened with the foundation of Christianity ἐκ πολλῶν μὲν ἄλλων,[28] thus, from the narrative of the evangelists; chiefly and particularly, however, he argues their truth on the basis of miracles which were still happening.

If then this proof of the proof has now entirely lapsed; if then all historical certainty is much too weak to replace this apparent proof of the proof which has lapsed: how is it to be expected of me that the same inconceivable truths which sixteen to eighteen hundred years ago people believed on the strongest inducement, should be believed by me to be equally valid on an infinitely lesser inducement?

Or is it invariably the case, that what I read in reputable historians is just as certain for me as what I myself experience?

I do not know that anyone has ever asserted this. What is asserted is only that the reports which we have of these prophecies and miracles are as reliable as historical truths ever can be. And then it is added that historical truths cannot be demonstrated: nevertheless we must believe them as firmly as truths that have been demonstrated.

To this I answer: *First*, who will deny (not I) that the reports of these miracles and prophecies are as reliable as historical truths ever can be? But if they are only as reliable as this, why are they treated as if they were infinitely more reliable?

And in what way? In this way, that something quite different and much greater is founded upon them than it is legitimate to found upon truths historically proved.

28. That is, "on many other grounds."

If no historical truth can be demonstrated, then nothing can be demonstrated by means of historical truths.

That is: *accidental truths of history can never become the proof of necessary truths of reason.*

I do not for one moment deny that in Christ prophecies were fulfilled; I do not for one moment deny that Christ performed miracles. But since the truth of these miracles has completely ceased to be demonstrable by miracles still happening at the present time, since they are no more than reports of miracles (however incontroverted and incontrovertible they may be), I deny that they can and should bind me in the least to a faith in the other teachings of Christ. These other teachings I accept on other grounds.

Then *secondly:* What does it mean to accept an historical proposition as true? to believe an historical truth? Does it mean anything other than this: to accept this proposition, this truth as valid? to accept that there is no objection to be brought against it? to accept that one historical proposition is built on one thing, another on another, that from one historical truth another follows? to reserve to oneself the right to estimate other historical things accordingly? Does it mean anything other than this? Anything more? Examine carefully.

We all believe that an Alexander lived who in a short time conquered almost all Asia. But who, on the basis of this belief, would risk anything of great, permanent worth, the loss of which would be irreparable? Who, in consequence of this belief, would forswear for ever all knowledge that conflicted with this belief? Certainly not I. Now I have no objection to raise against Alexander and his victory: but it might still be possible that the story was founded on a mere poem of Choerilus just as the ten-year siege of Troy depends on no better authority than Homer's poetry.[29]

If on historical grounds I have no objection to the statement that Christ raised to life a dead man; must I therefore accept it as true that God has a Son who is of the same essence as himself? What is the connection between my inability to raise any significant objection to the evidence of the former and my obligation to believe something against which my reason rebels?

If on historical grounds I have no objection to the statement that this Christ himself rose from the dead, must I therefore accept it as true that this risen Christ was the Son of God?

That the Christ, against whose resurrection I can raise no important historical objection, therefore declared himself to be the Son of God; that his disciples therefore believed him to be such; this I gladly believe from my heart. For these truths, as truths of one and the same class, follow quite naturally on one another.

But to jump with that historical truth to a quite different class of truths, and to demand of me that I should form all my metaphysical and moral ideas accordingly; to expect me to alter all my fundamental ideas of the nature of the Godhead because I cannot set any credible testimony against the resurrection of Christ: if that is not a μετάβασις εἰς ἄλλο γένος,[30] then I do not know what Aristotle meant by this phrase.

It is said: "The Christ of whom on historical grounds you must allow that he raised the dead, that he himself rose from the dead, said himself that God had a Son of the same essence as himself and that he is this Son." This would be quite excellent! if only it were not the case that it is not more than historically certain that Christ said this.

If you press me still further and say: "Oh yes! this is more than historically certain. For it is asserted by inspired historians who cannot make a mistake."

But, unfortunately, that also is only historically certain, that these historians were inspired and could not err.

That, then, is the ugly, broad ditch which I cannot get across, however often and however earnestly I have tried to make the leap. If anyone can help me over it, let him do it, I beg him, I adjure him. He will deserve a divine reward from me.

And so I repeat what I have said above in the same words. I do not for one moment deny that in Christ prophecies were fulfilled. I do not for one moment deny that Christ did miracles. But since the truth of these miracles has completely ceased to be demonstrable by miracles still happening now, since they are no more than reports of miracles (even though they be narratives which have not been, and cannot be, impugned), I deny that they can and should bind me to the very least faith in the other teachings of Christ.

What then does bind me? Nothing but these teachings themselves. . . .

[*Lessing's Theological Writings* (Stanford, CA: Stanford University Press, 1957), 51–55]

B. Immanuel Kant

Biographical Note: Immanuel Kant

Immanuel Kant (1724–1804) spent his entire career as a professor of philosophy in Königsberg, Prussia (now Kaliningrad). The contemporary work of David Hume, who turned reason on its head with self-

29. Choerilus of Iasos was the poet who accompanied Alexander the Great during his conquests in Asia. Homer's *Iliad* is the earliest record of the siege of Troy.

30. That is, "shifting from one genus to another."

destructive logic, brought Kant out of his "dogmatic slumber," as he put it.

Kant's Critique of Pure Reason *(1781; 2nd ed., 1787) launched his "Copernican Revolution" in epistemology, a subjective turn which claims that external reality must conform to the human mind, not the mind to reality. The mind provides the innate categories, which are a priori "conditions of thinking in a possible experience" (234); they are "pure concepts of the understanding" (238). For example, space and time are human categories that make an object that is presented to the senses intelligible, but they do not fully apprehend an object as it exists in itself. Kant also distinguishes between the phenomenal realm (objects that appear to the senses) and the noumenal realm (objects not available empirically), the latter of which is ultimately beyond human knowing.*

Toward the end of this first Critique, *Kant discusses three traditional arguments for God's existence—the ontological, cosmological, and physico-theological (or teleological) "proofs." Like Enlightenment theologians of the previous generation, Kant ties them all to a specific version of the ontological argument. Though he respects the arguments, the difference for Kant is that he finds them all wanting, at least as a principle of theology or "foundation of religion" (582), and falling far short of proof. The arguments for God's existence cannot be refuted, but neither can they prove.*

For Kant, it is moral theology that "can make good this lack" (589), so he offers an argument for God's existence based on morality. He sought a via media *between the Enlightenment-era theistic proofs of theologians like Christian Wolff (1679–1754) and the metaphysical skepticism of philosophers like Hume. In his* Critique of Practical Reason *(1788), which treats the question of how we know what to do, he writes: "Two things fill the mind with ever new and increasing admiration and awe the more often and more enduringly reflection is occupied with them: the starry heavens above me and the moral law within me."*

The impact of Kant's project on nineteenth- and twentieth-century intellectual history is far-reaching, not least in the field of theology. The following excerpts offer a glimpse of his moral philosophy as a window into his thought.

Selection 67: Immanuel Kant, *Groundwork of the Metaphysics of Morals* (1785)

Like other moral deists in his day, Kant deemphasized dogmas peculiar to Christian faith and saw the moral life as a point of departure for theological discourse. As with most moral philosophers, what is significant for Kant is the motivation behind ethical behavior. According to Kant, an action is morally good if it is done for the sake of duty. Moral feeling may be present, but such feeling comes as a result of one's recognition of the moral law. In the following excerpts, Kant describes the so-called categorical imperative.

To assure one's own happiness is a duty (at least indirectly); for, want of satisfaction with one's condition, under pressure from many anxieties and amid unsatisfied needs, could easily become a great *temptation to transgression of duty.* But in addition, without looking to duty here, all people have already, of themselves, the strongest and deepest inclination to happiness because it is just in this idea that all inclinations unite in one sum. However, the precept of happiness is often so constituted that it greatly infringes upon some inclinations, and yet one can form no determinate and sure concept of the sum of satisfaction of all inclinations under the name of happiness. Hence it is not to be wondered at that a single inclination, determinate both as to what it promises and as to the time within which it can be satisfied, can often outweigh a fluctuating idea, and that a man—for example, one suffering from gout—can choose to enjoy what he likes and put up with what he can since, according to his calculations, on this occasion at least he has not sacrificed the enjoyment of the present moment to the perhaps groundless expectation of a happiness that is supposed to lie in health. But even in this case, when the general inclination to happiness did not determine his will; when health, at least for him, did not enter as so necessary into this calculation, there is still left over here, as in all other cases, a law, namely to promote his happiness not from inclination but from duty; and it is then that his conduct first has properly moral worth.

It is undoubtedly in this way, again, that we are to understand the passages from scripture in which we are commanded to love our neighbor, even our enemy. For, love as an inclination cannot be commanded, but beneficence from duty—even though no inclination impels us to it and, indeed, natural and unconquerable aversion opposes it—is *practical* and not *pathological*[31] love, which lies in the will and not in the propensity of feeling, in principles of action and not in melting sympathy; and it alone can be commanded.

The second proposition is this: an action from duty has its moral worth *not in the purpose* to be attained by it but in the maxim in accordance with which it is decided upon, and therefore does not depend upon the realization of the object of the action but merely upon the *principle of volition* in accordance with which the action is done without regard for any object of the faculty of desire. That the purposes we may have for our actions, and their effects as ends and incentives of the will, can give actions no unconditional and moral worth is clear from what has gone before. In what, then, can this worth lie, if it is not to be in the will in relation to the hoped for effect of the action? It can lie nowhere else *than in the principle of the will* without regard for the ends that can be brought about by such an action. . . .

The third proposition, which is a consequence of the two preceding, I would express as follows: *duty is the necessity of an action from respect for law.* For an object as the effect of my proposed action I can indeed have *inclination* but *never respect,* just because it is merely an effect and not an activity of a will. . . .

Thus the moral worth of an action does not lie in the effect expected from it and so too does not lie in any principle of action that needs to borrow its motive from this expected effect. For, all these effects (agreeableness of one's condition, indeed even promotion of others' happiness) could have been also brought about by other causes, so that there would have been no need, for this, of the will of a rational being, in which, however, the highest and unconditional good alone can be found. . . .

But what kind of law can that be, the representation of which must determine the will, even without regard for the effect expected from it, in order for the will to be called good absolutely and without limitation? Since I have deprived the will of every impulse that could arise for it from obeying some law, nothing is left but the community of actions as such with universal law, which alone is to serve the will as its principle, that is, *I ought never to act except in such a way that I could also will that my maxim should become a universal law.* Here mere

31. *Pathologische*; that is, this love is not moved by the passions or the senses.

conformity to law as such, without having as its basis some law determined for certain actions, is what serves the will as its principle, and must so serve it, if duty is not to be everywhere an empty delusion and a chimerical concept. Common human reason also agrees completely with this in its practical appraisals and always has this principle before its eyes. Let the question be, for example: may I, when hard pressed, make a promise with the intention not to keep it? Here I easily distinguish two significations the question can have: whether it is prudent or whether it is in conformity with duty to make a false promise. The first can undoubtedly often be the case. I see very well that it is not enough to get out of a present difficulty by means of this subterfuge but that I must reflect carefully whether this lie may later give rise to much greater inconvenience for me than that from which I now extricate myself; and since, with all my supposed *cunning*, the results cannot be so easily foreseen but that once confidence in me is lost this could be far more prejudicial to me than all the troubles I now think to avoid, I must reflect whether the matter might be handled *more prudently* by proceeding on a general maxim and making it a habit to promise nothing except with the intention of keeping it. But it is soon clear to me that such a maxim will still be based only on results feared. To be truthful from duty, however, is something entirely different from being truthful from anxiety about detrimental results, since in the first case the concept of the action in itself already contains a law for me while in the second I must first look about elsewhere to see what effects on me might be combined with it. For, if I deviate from the principle of duty this is quite certainly evil; but if I am unfaithful to my maxim of prudence this can sometimes be very advantageous to me, although it is certainly safer to abide by it. However, to inform myself in the shortest and yet infallible way about the answer to this problem, whether a lying promise is in conformity with duty, I ask myself: would I indeed be content that my maxim (to get myself out of difficulties by a false promise) should hold as a universal law (for myself as well as for others)? and could I indeed say to myself that every one may make a false promise when he finds himself in a difficulty he can get out of in no other way? Then I soon become aware that I could indeed will the lie, but by no means a universal law to lie; for in accordance with such a law there would properly be no promises at all, since it would be futile to avow my will with regard to my future actions to others who would not believe this avowal or, if they rashly did so, would pay me back in like coin; and thus my maxim, as soon as it were made a universal law, would have to destroy itself.

I do not, therefore, need any penetrating acuteness to see what I have to do in order that my volition be morally good. Inexperienced in the course of the world, incapable of being prepared for whatever might come to pass in it, I ask myself only: can you also will that your maxim become a universal law? If not, then it is to be repudiated, and that not because of a disadvantage to you or even to others forthcoming from it but because it cannot fit as a principle into a possible giving of universal law, for which lawgiving reason, however, forces from me immediate respect. Although I do not yet *see*[32] what this respect is based upon (this the philosopher may investigate), I at least understand this much: that it is an estimation of a worth that far outweighs any worth of what is recommended by inclination, and that the necessity of my action from *pure* respect for the practical law is what constitutes duty, to which every other motive must give way because it is

32. That is, "have insight into."

the condition of a will good *in itself*, the worth of which surpasses all else.

Thus, then, we have arrived, within the moral cognition of common human reason, at its principle, which it admittedly does not think so abstractly in a universal form but which it actually has always before its eyes and uses as the norm for its appraisals. Here it would be easy to show how common human reason, with this compass in hand, knows very well how to distinguish in every case that comes up what is good and what is evil, what is in conformity with duty or contrary to duty, if, without in the least teaching it anything new, we only, as did Socrates, make it attentive to its own principle; and that there is, accordingly, no need of science and philosophy to know what one has to do in order to be honest and good, and even wise and virtuous. We might even have assumed in advance that cognizance of what it is incumbent upon everyone to do, and so also to know, would be the affair of every human being, even the most common. Yet we cannot consider without admiration how great an advantage the practical faculty of appraising has over the theoretical in common human understanding. In the latter, if common reason ventures to depart from laws of experience and perceptions of the senses it falls into sheer incomprehensibilities and self-contradictions, at least into a chaos of uncertainty, obscurity, and instability. But in practical matters, it is just when common understanding excludes all sensible incentives from practical laws that its faculty of appraising first begins to show itself to advantage. It then becomes even subtle, whether in quibbling tricks with its own conscience or with other claims regarding what is to be called right, or in sincerely wanting to determine the worth of actions for its own instruction; and, what is most admirable, in the latter case it can even have as good a hope of hitting the mark as any philosopher can promise himself; indeed, it is almost more sure in this matter, because a philosopher, though he cannot have any other principle than that of common understanding, can easily confuse his judgment by a mass of considerations foreign and irrelevant to the matter and deflect it from the straight course. Would it not therefore be more advisable in moral matters to leave the judgment of common reason as it is and, at most, call in philosophy only to present the system of morals all the more completely and apprehensibly and to present its rules in a form more convenient for use (still more for disputation), but not to lead common human understanding, even in practical matters, away from its fortunate simplicity and to put it, by means of philosophy, on a new path of investigation and instruction? . . .

Now, all imperatives command either *hypothetically* or *categorically.* The former represent the practical necessity of a possible action as a means to achieving something else that one wills (or that it is at least possible for one to will). The categorical imperative would be that which represented an action as objectively necessary of itself, without reference to another end. . . .

We shall thus have to investigate entirely a priori the possibility of a *categorical* imperative, since we do not here have the advantage of its reality being given in experience, so that the possibility would be necessary not to establish it but merely to explain it. In the meantime, however, we can see this much: that the categorical imperative alone has the tenor of a practical law; all the others can indeed be called *principles* of the will but not laws, since what it is necessary to do merely for achieving a discretionary purpose can be regarded as in itself contingent and we can always be released from the precept if we give up the purpose; on the contrary, the unconditional command leaves the will no discretion with respect to the opposite, so that it alone brings with it that necessity which we require of a law.

Second, in the case of this categorical imperative or law of morality the ground of the difficulty (of insight into its possibility) is also very great. It is an a priori synthetic practical proposition;[33] and since it is so difficult to see the possibility of this kind of proposition in theoretical cognition, it can be readily gathered that the difficulty will be no less in practical cognition. . . .

There is, therefore, only a single categorical imperative and it is this: *act only in accordance with that maxim through which you can at the same time will that it become a universal law*. . . .

We shall now enumerate a few duties in accordance with the usual division of them into duties to ourselves and to other human beings and into perfect and imperfect duties.[34]

1) Someone feels sick of life because of a series of troubles that has grown to the point of despair, but is still so far in possession of his reason that he can ask himself whether it would not be contrary to his duty to himself to take his own life. Now he inquires whether the maxim of his action could indeed become a universal law of nature. His maxim, however, is: from self-love I make it my principle to shorten my life when its longer duration threatens more troubles than it promises agreeableness. The only further question is whether this principle of self-love could become a universal law of nature. It is then seen at once that a nature whose law it would be to destroy life itself by means of the same feeling whose destination is to impel toward the furtherance of life would contradict itself and would therefore not subsist as nature; thus that maxim could not possibly be a law of nature and, accordingly, altogether opposes the supreme principle of all duty.

2) Another finds himself urged by need to borrow money. He well knows that he will not be able to repay it but sees also that nothing will be lent him unless he promises firmly to repay it within a determinate time. He would like to make such a promise, but he still has enough conscience to ask himself: is it not forbidden and contrary to duty to help oneself out of need in such a way? Supposing that he still decided to do so, his maxim of action would go as follows: when I believe myself to be in need of money I shall borrow money and promise to repay it, even though I know that this will never happen. Now this principle of self-love or personal advantage is perhaps quite consistent with my whole future welfare, but the question now is whether it is right. I therefore turn the demand of self-love into a universal law and put the question as follows: how would it be if my maxim became a universal law? I then see at once that it could never hold as a universal law of nature and be consistent with itself, but must necessarily contradict itself. For, the universality of a law that everyone, when he

33. [Kant] "I connect the deed with the will, without a presupposed condition from any inclination, a priori and hence necessarily (though only objectively, i.e., under the idea of a reason having complete control over all subjective motives). This is, therefore, a practical proposition that does not derive the volition of an action analytically from another volition already presupposed (for we have no such perfect will), but connects it immediately with the concept of the will of a rational being as something that is not contained in it."

34. [Kant] "It must be noted here that I reserve the division of duties entirely for a future *Metaphysics of Morals*, so that the division here stands only as one adopted at my discretion (for the sake of arranging my examples). For the rest, I understand here by a perfect duty one that admits no exception in favor of inclination, and then I have not merely external but also internal *perfect duties;* although this is contrary to the use of the work adopted in the schools, I do not intend to justify it here, since for my purpose it makes no difference whether or not it is granted me."

believes himself to be in need, could promise whatever he pleases with the intention of not keeping it would make the promise and the end one might have in it itself impossible, since no one would believe what was promised him but would laugh at all such expressions as vain pretenses. . . .

For, all rational beings stand under the *law* that each of them is to treat himself and all others *never merely as means* but always *at the same time as ends in themselves.* But from this there arises a systematic union of rational beings through common objective laws, that is, a kingdom, which can be called a kingdom of ends (admittedly only an ideal) because what these laws have as their purpose is just the relation of these beings to one another as ends and means.

A rational being belongs as a *member* to the kingdom of ends when he gives universal laws in it but is also himself subject to these laws. He belongs to it *as sovereign* when, as lawgiving, he is not subject to the will of any other. . . .

Morality consists, then, in the reference of all action to the lawgiving by which alone a kingdom of ends is possible. This lawgiving must, however, be found in every rational being himself and be able to arise from his will, the principle of which is, accordingly: to do no action on any other maxim than one such that it would be consistent with it to be a universal law, and hence to act only *so that the will could regard itself as at the same time giving universal law through its maxim.* Now, if maxims are not already of their nature in agreement with this objective principle of rational beings as givers of universal law, the necessity of an action in accordance with this principle is called practical necessitation, that is, *duty.* Duty does not apply to the sovereign in the kingdom of ends, but it does apply to every member of it and indeed to all in equal measure.

The practical necessity of acting in accordance with this principle, that is, duty, does not rest at all on feelings, impulses, and inclinations but merely on the relation of rational beings to one another, in which the will of a rational being must always be regarded as at the same time *lawgiving,* since otherwise it could not be thought as an *end in itself.* Reason accordingly refers every maxim of the will as giving universal law to every other will and also to every action toward oneself, and does so not for the sake of any other practical motive or any future advantage but from the idea of the *dignity* of a rational being, who obeys no law other than that which he himself at the same time gives. . . .

Selection 68: Immanuel Kant, "On a Supposed Right to Lie from Philanthropy" (1797)

In this brief essay, Kant responds to a critic who impugned his claim that the moral duty of truth-telling is universal and always binding. The critic believes, for example, that someone seeking to harm others does not have "a right to the truth."

The πρωτον ψευδος[35] here lies in the proposition *"To tell the truth is a duty, but only to one who has a right to the truth."*[36]. . .

Now the *first question* is whether someone, in cases where he cannot evade an answer of "yes" or "no," has the *authorization* (the right) to be untruthful. The *second question* is whether he is not, indeed, bound to be untruthful in a certain statement which he is compelled to make by an unjust constraint, in order to prevent a threatened misdeed to himself or to another.

35. That is, "first lie."

36. Kant is responding to and here quoting from an essay by Benjamin Constant.

Truthfulness in statements that one cannot avoid is a human being's duty to everyone,[37] however great the disadvantage to him or to another that may result from it; and although I indeed do no wrong to him who unjustly compels me to make the statement if I falsify it, I nevertheless do wrong in the most essential part of duty *in general* by such falsification, which can therefore be called a lie (though not in a jurist's sense); that is, I bring it about, as far as I can, that statements (declarations) in general are not believed, and so too that all rights which are based on contracts come to nothing and lose their force; and this is a wrong inflicted upon humanity generally.

Thus a lie, defined merely as an intentionally untrue declaration to another, does not require what jurists insist upon adding for their definition, that it must harm another (*mendacium est falsiloquium in praeiudicium alterius*). For it always harms another, even if not another individual, nevertheless humanity generally, inasmuch as it makes the source of right unusable.

Such a well-meant lie *can*, however, also become by an *accident* (*casus*) punishable in accordance with civil laws; but what escapes being punishable merely by accident can be condemned as wrong even in accordance with external laws. That is to say, if you have *by a lie* prevented someone just now bent on murder from committing the deed, then you are legally accountable for all the consequences that might arise from it. But if you have kept strictly to the truth, then public justice can hold nothing against you, whatever the unforeseen consequences might be. It is still possible that, after you have honestly answered "yes" to the murderer's question as to whether his enemy is at home, the latter has nevertheless gone out unnoticed, so that he would not meet the murderer and the deed would not be done; but if you had lied and said that he is not at home, and he has actually gone out (though you were not aware of it), so that the murderer encounters him while going away and perpetrates his deed on him, then you can by right be prosecuted as the author of his death. For if you had told the truth to the best of your knowledge, then neighbors might have come and apprehended the murderer while he was searching the house for his enemy and the deed would have been prevented. Thus one *who tells a lie*, however well disposed he may be, must be responsible for its consequences even before a civil court and must pay the penalty for them, however unforeseen they may have been; for truthfulness is a duty that must be regarded as the basis of all duties to be grounded on contract, the law of which is made uncertain and useless if even the least exception to it is admitted.

To be *truthful* (honest) in all declarations is therefore a sacred command of reason prescribing unconditionally, one not to be restricted by any conveniences. . . .

Now, in order to progress from a *metaphysics* of right (which abstracts from all conditions of experience) to a principle of *politics* (which applies these concepts to cases of experience) and, by means of this, to the solution of a problem of politics in keeping with the universal principle of right, a philosopher will give 1) an *axiom*, that is, an apodictically certain proposition that issues immediately from the definition of external right (consistency of the *freedom* of each with the freedom of everyone in accordance with a universal law); 2) a *postulate* (of external public *law*, as the united will of all in accordance with the principle of *equality*,

---

37. [Kant] "I here prefer not to sharpen this principle to the point of saying: 'Untruthfulness is a violation of duty to oneself.' For this belongs to ethics, but what is under discussion here is a duty of right. The doctrine of virtue looks, in this transgression, only to *worthlessness*, reproach for which a liar draws upon himself."

without which there would be no freedom of everyone); 3) a *problem* of how it is to be arranged that in a society, however large, harmony in accordance with the principles of freedom and equality is maintained (namely, by means of a representative system); this will then be a principle of *politics*, the arrangement and organization of which will contain decrees, drawn from experiential cognition of human beings, that have in view only the mechanism for administering right and how this can be managed appropriately. Right must never be accommodated to politics, but politics must always be accommodated to right. . . .

All practical principles of right must contain strict truth, and here the so-called intermediary principles can contain only the closer determination of their application to cases that come up (in accordance with rules of politics), but never exceptions from those principles; for exceptions would nullify the universality on account of which alone they are called principles.

Further Reading

Allen, Diogenes, and Eric O. Springstead. *Philosophy for Understanding Theology*. 2nd ed. Louisville, KY: Westminster John Knox, 2007.

Buckley, Michael J. *At the Origins of Modern Atheism*. New Haven, CT: Yale University Press, 1987.

Dupré, Louis. *The Enlightenment and the Intellectual Foundations of Modern Culture*. New Haven: Yale University Press, 2004.

Gaukroger, Stephen. *Descartes: An Intellectual Biography*. Oxford: Clarendon, 1995.

Legaspi, Michael C. *The Death of Scripture and the Rise of Biblical Studies*. Oxford Studies in Historical Theology. New York: Oxford University Press, 2010.

Lehner, Ulrich L., and Michael Printy, eds. *A Companion to the Catholic Enlightenment in Europe*. Leiden: Brill, 2010.

Pearse, Meic. *The Age of Reason: From the Wars of Religion to the French Revolution*. The Baker History of the Church. Grand Rapids, MI: Baker Books, 2006.

Spinks, Bryan D. *Liturgy in the Age of Reason: Worship and Sacraments in England and Scotland, 1662–c. 1800*. Burlington, VT: Ashgate, 2008.

Chapter 7
Pietism and Revivalism

The period of confessionalization, in the wake of the Reformation, saw the rise of distinct denominations whose various theological emphases were codified by their new confessional documents and were defended at the highest levels by the use of scholastic method. This new theological diversity both increased the quantity of doctrinal polemic and provided another motivation for military aggression. Enlightenment reason and doctrinal latitudinarianism represent one side of the reaction to confessionalization and its immediate consequences.

Pietism and the resulting revivals represent another side of the reaction to confessionalization and the scholastic treatments of doctrine. At its simplest level, assuming a distinction between intellect (head) and affections (heart), the Pietist movement emphasized the religion of the heart in contrast to the perception of an exaggerated emphasis on head knowledge that was prevalent within scholastic theology, both Protestant and Roman Catholic. The Protestant versions of this Pietism—Reformed, Lutheran, and Anglican—influenced what would become known in the English-speaking world as evangelical Protestant churches.

As seen in previous chapters, the emphasis on piety precedes the Reformation and, in many ways, was inherent in the Reformation all along. This seems especially true within the Reformed branch, whose leaders tended to be embody greater balance between scholastic acumen and personal piety. The Reformed believed that theology is the discipline of living well. The dichotomy between head and heart seems to have been more keenly experienced in the German Lutheran churches and universities. Lutheran Pietists began meeting for Bible study outside of the regularly scheduled church services and theology lectures. In addition to Scripture, they were influenced by spiritual writers such as the early desert fathers and the later *devotio moderna*. The Pietist influence spread throughout the established Lutheran churches of Germany and northern Europe. In some cases, new denominations were formed, such as the Moravians, whose churches quickly spread west to England and sent missionaries around the world.

On the British Isles, revival spread within the Church of England. By the beginning of the eighteenth century, the Society for Promoting Christian Knowledge (SPCK) and the Society for the Propagation of the Gospel (SPG) had been established, and informal meetings for Bible study and prayer were taking place in most of the major cities. These movements soon came into contact with and were influenced by the Reformed and Lutheran Pietists on the Continent. In addition to the revival within the established church, the new denomination of Methodism was spawned in England and the United States. In the American colonies, after a period of religious stagnation and moral laxity, another independent revival grew strong in the 1720s and 1730s, which also had quick contact with the revivals in England. These first evangelical revivals in the colonies became known as the Great Awakening, and its greatest preacher, active on both sides of the Atlantic, was George Whitefield (1714–1770), who frequently preached to audiences of many thousands throughout the colonies. Whitefield reflects the predominance of Reformed theology in the Great Awakening.

Alexander Rider, "Camp Meeting" (early nineteenth century)

After the establishment of the independent American republic by means of revolution, the new sense of freedom and autonomy from old traditions—combined with a democratic optimism—set the American frontier stage for the Second Great Awakening around the turn of the nineteenth century. This movement, in contrast to the First Great Awakening, was more populist and anti-Calvinist in tone. In 1801, for example, the camp meeting at Cane Ridge, Kentucky, attracted thousands to hear open-air preaching from representatives of many denominations. Many of those in attendance, moved by the Spirit, responded with ecstatic exercises. The Second Great Awakening helped to reverse the trend of low church attendance, and it made revival, along with the subjective experience of the Holy Spirit in conversion, a permanent characteristic of American evangelicalism.

The freedom of American Christianity was reflected in the advocacy of separation of church and state, which was intended to end funding to established churches in individual states and to allow for free expression of religious views. The feeling of independence was represented especially in the proliferation of new denominations. These included some whose beliefs and practices were in line with historic orthodoxy, such as the Restoration Movement's congregations of Christian Churches and Churches of Christ; and others that were far removed from the venerable traditions of European Christianity, such as Seventh-Day Adventists, Jehovah's Witnesses, Christian Scientists, and Latter-Day Saints (Mormons).

The peculiar danger of the Pietist movements is that the heart is emphasized to the exclusion of the head; that is, it can foster an atmosphere of anti-intellectualism. In the democratized environment of the United States, where anticlericalism was one expression of a general suspicion toward professionalization, such anti-intellectualism would continue to be a prominent feature of many evangelical and revivalist groups. Despite this dominant strain, however, others sought a balance. As Charles Wesley explained the goal in a hymn that he wrote for the children at Kingswood School: "Unite the pair so long disjoined / Knowledge and vital piety."

A. Continental Pietism

Selection 69: Jean Taffin, *The Marks of God's Children* (1586)

The Dutch Reformed Pietist movement that gained strength in the seventeenth century came to be known as the Nadere Reformatie, the Further Reformation. One of the prominent slogans of this movement was* ecclesia reformata semper reformanda *("the church reformed, always to be reformed")—that is, although doctrines have been reformed, the church should continue to grow in sanctification.

Jean Taffin (1529–1602) was a minister of French-speaking Reformed churches in the northern Netherlands and a precursor to this Dutch Pietism. Taffin's first book,* The Marks of God's Children, and Their Comforts in Afflictions, *is a reflection on the question of the assurance of salvation, an issue that occupied Reformed Pietism in both its Dutch and its English forms. He does not deal with the problem of too much assurance (or carnal security) but writes primarily to bolster weak assurance by delineating the external and internal marks of the elect, as well as describing the temptations they must endure in this life.

Chapter 1: Blessedness

. . . Now this blessedness is frequently described in God's Word as eternal life. That is not without reason, since two significant aspects of this blessedness can and must be distinguished: first, the benefit itself and how great and glorious it is; then, its permanence and certainty. Both are expressed in the words "eternal life.". . .

Concerning this "life" we can distinguish three degrees, levels, or steps, and these can be applied both to the body and to the soul.

With respect to the soul, the first degree or level of life consists of the peace of conscience and the joy in the Spirit that we receive and feel when we are reconciled to God in Jesus Christ. This peace and the beginning of life exceed all understanding, as St. Paul testifies and God's children experience. . . .[1]

As for the body, the first step consists in this, that the trials it experiences are not only made lighter by the life of the soul reconciled to God and by the joy experienced from the light of God's countenance. But these physical trials themselves are transformed into salvation and glory since they become occasions of God's love toward us.

The second level of life may be seen in the separation of the soul and the body. As far as believers are concerned, this can be called death only in a figurative sense. This is true even for our bodies. Although they decay in the ground, they are delivered and freed from all diseases, from hunger, thirst, heat, cold, and from a thousand other harassments—all of which are specific forms of death—and now rest in their beds as Isaiah describes (Isa. 57:1-2). . . .

The third degree or level of life will be experienced at the glorious return of Jesus Christ, when our bodies are awakened from their sleep and will be raised perfectly renewed. They will be incorruptible, spiritual, and immortal—made in the image of the glorious body of Jesus Christ. . . .

Chapter 2: Assurance

It is certainly true that only God knows his own, those whom he has chosen before the foundation of the world to be his children. But

1. See Phil. 4:7.

that does not change the fact that there are two main ways by which he shows us who his children are. The one is external and consists of marks visible to men. The other is internal and consists of testimonies by which the believer feels within himself that he is a child of God.

The external mark consists of this, that we are members of the church of Christ. Now we call that the church of Christ the place wherever God's Word is truly preached, wherever the sacraments are purely administered, and wherever the one God is addressed in the name of his only Son, Jesus Christ. . . .

To deepen our certainty of all this, we must pay attention to the marks of the true church already mentioned.[2] The first mark is the pure preaching of God's Word. Now the Lord Jesus declares, "My sheep hear my voice; I know them, and they follow me" (John 10:27). Therefore, it is a mark of being God's child when one hears Christ's voice and follows him. In another place he says much the same: "The one who belongs to God hears what God says" (John 8:47). . . .

The second mark of the true church consists of the use of the sacraments of baptism and the Lord's Supper. With respect to baptism, it is a sign and seal that the sins of those who have received it are washed away in the blood of our Lord Jesus Christ and that as baptized people they are engrafted and incorporated into Christ's death and resurrection, that they are born again, and that they have put on Christ Jesus. Therefore, Paul says that they are God's children (Gal. 3:26). That same assurance of our adoption is given to us in the Lord's Supper. From the bread and cup handed to members of the church as a communion in the body and blood of Christ it follows that they receive nourishment and life in fellowship with Christ and as God's children shall obtain everlasting life. According to Christ's own testimony, "Whoever eats my flesh and drinks my blood has eternal life" (John 6:54).

The third mark of the true church is addressing God in the name of Jesus Christ, and in his name alone. By the term "addressing" the entire worship of God is often designated. Luke describes believers or children of God as those who call upon the name of the Lord (Acts 2:21; 9:14). But about the reprobate we read that they are the ones who do not call on the Lord's name (Ps. 14:4). Then certainly when members of the church assemble and raise their prayers to God, saying, "Our Father who art in heaven," they may be assured that God the Lord regards them as his children and will cause them to taste the fruits of their prayers. Christ promised them this when he said that all that they desire will be given to them (Matt. 18:19). Addressing God in the name of Jesus Christ only, then, makes it clear that every member of the church is and should be assured of being a child of God and should also regard the other members of the church as God's children, just as he is. . . .

Let us turn now to the internal marks.

Just as the blind and the deaf need to have their eyes and their ears opened in order to see clearly and to hear the voice of whomever is speaking, so those who by nature are spiritually blind and deaf need to have the eyes and ears of their understanding opened by the Holy Spirit. He opens our eyes and ears to comprehend the revelation of our adoption and to certify to our hearts the assurance of faith. He works in us that faith that is the hand by which we grasp this great benefit. The fruits and the activities both of the Holy Spirit and of faith are the most exceptional and the most powerful signs of our adoption as God's children. . . .

2. The three marks of the church (*notae ecclesiae*) most frequently mentioned in Reformed theology are preaching of the Word, administration of the sacraments, and church discipline.

Another fruit ripens as an internal mark to convince us more and more that we are God's children. It is this, that we love God and our neighbor for his sake, and the consequence of this, namely, that we hate evil and earnestly desire to obey God. It is true what John teaches when he says that we love God because he has loved us first. Hence, the love we have for him is a proof, a testimony, that he loves us. From the evidences of love that the woman taken in adultery showed him, Christ maintained and showed that God loved her greatly and forgave her many sins (Luke 7:47). The clarity of the moon is a clear proof that it is illuminated by the sun, for otherwise it could shed no light. In summertime the sun's heat is felt in the rocks that lie in the sun, which is a proof that the sun has been shining on them. . . .

[Jean Taffin, *The Marks of God's Children*, trans. Peter Y. De Jong (Grand Rapids, MI: Baker Academic, 2003), 26–27, 35–38, 40]

Selection 70: Blaise Pascal, *Pensées* (1669)

Blaise Pascal (1623–1662) is a prime example of a figure who held reason and piety together very effectively. A mathematician and scientist of the highest rank, he was also a philosopher and theologian who was part of the Jansenist revival in Roman Catholic France.* Pensées, *or* Thoughts, *is a collection of Pascal's ongoing reflections—most in aphoristic form—published posthumously. Together, they function as a kind of apology or defense of Christian faith, directed not primarily toward atheists but toward the upper-class society that had become indifferent to Christianity and preferred a lifestyle of diversion instead.

6 (60).[3] First part: Wretchedness of man without God. Second part: Happiness of man with God.

otherwise

First part: Nature is corrupt, proved by nature itself. Second part: There is a Redeemer, proved by Scripture.

45 (83). Man is nothing but a subject full of natural error that cannot be eradicated except through grace. Nothing shows him the truth, everything deceives him. The two principles of truth, reason and senses, are not only both not genuine, but are engaged in mutual deception. The senses deceive reason through false appearances, and, just as they trick the soul, they are tricked by it in their turn: it takes its revenge. The senses are disturbed by passions, which produce false impressions. They both compete in lies and deception.

But, apart from such accidents, error arising from the failure of these heterogeneous faculties to reach understanding . . .

(This is where the chapter on powers of deception must start.)

110 (282). We know the truth not only through our reason but also through our heart. It is through the latter that we know first principles, and reason, which has nothing to do with it, tries in vain to refute them. The sceptics have no other object than that, and they work at it to no purpose. We know that we are not dreaming, but, however unable we may be to prove it rationally, our inability proves nothing but the weakness of our reason, and not the uncertainty of all our knowledge, as they

3. Pascal scholars differ on how Pascal's various notes ought to be ordered. I have marked each excerpt with two numbers: the first number reflects the order and designation in the Penguin edition used here; the parenthetical number reflects the designation in most other editions.

maintain.[4] For knowledge of first principles, like space, time, motion, number, is as solid as any derived through reason, and it is on such knowledge, coming from the heart and instinct, that reason has to depend and base all its argument. The heart feels that there are three spatial dimensions and that demonstrate that there are no two square numbers of which one is double the other. Principles are felt, propositions proved, and both with certainty though by different means. It is just as pointless and absurd for reason to demand proof of first principles from the heart to demand an intuition of all the propositions demonstrated by reason before agreeing to accept them. . . .

183 (253). Two excesses: to exclude reason, to admit nothing but reason.

232 (566). We can understand nothing of God's works unless we accept the principle that he wished to blind some and enlighten others.

234 (581). God wishes to move the will rather than the mind. Perfect clarity would help the mind and harm the will.

Humble their pride.

235 (771). Jesus came to blind those who have clear sight and to give sight to the blind; to heal the sick and let the healthy die; to call sinners to repentance and justify them, and to leave the righteous to their sins; to fill the hungry with good things and to send the rich empty away.

236 (578). . . . There is enough light to enlighten the elect and enough obscurity to humiliate them. There is enough obscurity to blind the reprobate and enough light to condemn them and deprive them of excuse. . . .

414 (171). *Wretchedness.* The only thing that consoles us for our miseries is diversion. And yet it is the greatest of our miseries. For it is that above all which prevents us thinking about ourselves and leads us imperceptibly to destruction. But for that we should be bored, and boredom would drive us to seek some more solid means of escape, but diversion passes our time and brings us imperceptibly to our death.

418 (233). . . . We know that the infinite exists without knowing its nature, just as we know that it is untrue that numbers are finite. Thus it is true that there is an infinite number, but we do not know what it is. It is untrue that it is even, untrue that it is odd, for by adding a unit it does not change its nature. Yet it is a number, and every number is even or odd. (It is true that this applies to every finite number).

Therefore we may well know that God exists without knowing what he is. . . .

Thus we know the existence and nature of the finite, because we too are finite and extended in space.

We know the existence of the infinite without knowing its nature, because it too has extension, but unlike us no limits.

But we do not know either the existence or the nature of God, because he has neither extension nor limits.

But by faith we know his existence, through glory we shall know his nature.

Now I have already proved that it is quite possible to know that something exists without knowing its nature.

Let us now speak according to natural lights.[5]

If there is a God, he is infinitely beyond our comprehension, since, being indivisible and without limits, he bears no relation to us. We are therefore incapable of knowing either what he is or whether he is. This being so, who would

4. Descartes also addressed the possibility that life is merely a dream, but Pascal is not so disturbed about the inability to prove the contrary (see Selection 62).

5. This sentence, often excluded from excerpts of the wager that follows, lends important context to the wager. As presented by Pascal, it is not necessarily the ideal thought process of a regenerate Christian.

dare to attempt an answer to the question? Certainly not we, who bear no relation to Him.

Who then will condemn Christians for not being able to give rational grounds for their belief, professing as they do a religion for which they cannot give rational grounds? They declare that it is a folly, *stultitiam*, in expounding it to the world, and then you complain that they do not prove it. If they did prove it they would not be keeping their word. It is by being without proof that they show they are not without sense. "Yes, but although this excuses those who offer their religion as such, and absolves them from the criticism of producing it without rational grounds, it does not absolve those who accept it." Let us then examine this point, and let us say: "Either God is or he is not." But to which view shall we be inclined? Reason cannot decide this question. Infinite chaos separates us. At the far end of this infinite distance a coin is being spun which will come down heads or tails. How will you wager? Reason cannot make you choose either, reason cannot prove either wrong.

Do not then condemn as wrong those who have made a choice, for you know nothing about it. "No, but I will condemn them not for having made this particular choice, but any choice, for, although the one who calls heads and the other one [tails] are equally at fault, the fact is that they are both at fault: the right thing is not to wager at all."

Yes; but you must wager. There is no choice, you are already committed. Which will you choose then? Let us see: since a choice must be made, let us see which offers you the least interest. You have two things to lose: the true and the good; and two things to stake: your reason and your will, your knowledge and your happiness; and your nature has two things to avoid: error and wretchedness. Since you must necessarily choose, your reason is no more affronted by choosing one rather than the other. That is one point cleared up. But your happiness? Let us weigh up the gain and the loss in calling heads that God exists. Let us assess the two cases: if you win you win everything, if you lose you lose nothing. Do not hesitate then; wager that he does exist. "That is wonderful. Yes, I must wager; but perhaps I am wagering too much." Let us see; since there is an equal chance of gain and loss, if you stood to win only two lives for one you could still wager, but supposing you stood to win three?

You would have to play (since must necessarily play) and it would be unwise of you, once you are obliged to play, not to risk your life in order to win three lives at a game in which there is an equal chance of losing and winning. But there is an eternity of life and happiness. . . .

Thus our argument carries infinite weight, when the stakes are finite in a game where there are even chances of winning and losing and an infinite prize to be won.

This is conclusive and if men are capable of any truth this is it.

"I confess it, I admit it, but is there really no way of seeing what the cards are?"—"Yes, Scripture and the rest, etc." "Yes, but my hands are tied and my lips are sealed; I am being forced to wager and I am not free; I am being held fast and I am so made that I cannot believe. What do you want me to do then?" "That is true, but at least get it into your head that, if you are unable to believe, it is because of your passions, since reason impels you to believe and yet you cannot do so. Concentrate then not on convincing yourself by multiplying proofs of God's existence but by diminishing your passions. You want to find faith and you do not know the road. You want to be cured of unbelief and you ask for the remedy: learn from those who were once bound like you and who now wager all they have. These are people who know the road you wish to follow, who have been cured of the affliction of which you wish to be cured: follow the way by which they began. They behaved just as if they did believe, taking holy water, having masses said, and so on. That will make you believe quite naturally, and will make you more docile."—"But that is what I am afraid of."—"But why? What have you to lose?" . . .

423 (277). The heart has its reasons of which reason knows nothing: we know this in countless ways.

I say that it is natural for the heart to love the universal being or itself, according to its allegiance, and it hardens itself against either as it chooses. You have rejected one and kept the other. Is it reason that makes you love yourself?

424 (278). It is the heart which perceives God and not the reason. That is what faith is: God perceived by the heart, not by the reason.

434 (199). Imagine a number of men in chains, all under sentence of death, some of whom are each day butchered in the sight of the others; those remaining see their own condition in that of their fellows, and looking at each other with grief and despair await their turn. This is an image of the human condition.

444 (557). It is true then that everything teaches man his condition, but there must be no misunderstanding, for it is not true that everything reveals God, and it is not true that everything conceals God. But it true at once that he hides from those who tempt him and that he reveals himself to those who seek him, because men are at once unworthy and capable of God: unworthy through their corruption, capable through their original nature.

446 (586). If there were no obscurity man would not feel his corruption: if there were no light man could not hope for a cure. Thus it is not only right but useful for us that God should be partly concealed and partly revealed, since it is equally dangerous for man to know God without knowing his own wretchedness as to know his wretchedness without knowing God.

449 (556). . . . But let them conclude what they like against deism, their conclusions will not apply to Christianity, which properly consists in the mystery of the Redeemer, who, uniting in himself the two natures, human and divine, saved men from the corruption of sin in order to reconcile them with God in his divine person.

It teaches men then these two truths alike: that there is a God, of whom men are capable, and that there is a corruption in nature which makes them unworthy. It is of equal importance to men to know each of these points: and it is equally dangerous for man to know God without knowing his own wretchedness as to know his own wretchedness without knowing the Redeemer who can cure him. Knowing only one of these points leads either to the arrogance of the philosophers, who have known God but not their own wretchedness, or to the despair of atheists, who know their own wretchedness without knowing their Redeemer. . . .

913.[6] The year of grace 1654. Monday, 23 November . . .

From about half past ten in the evening until half past midnight.

Fire. "God of Abraham, God of Isaac, God of Jacob,"[7] not of philosophers and scholars.

6. Unlike Pascal's other excerpts presented here, this final excerpt was found not among his papers, but was found written on parchment that was sewn into his clothing. It is a reflection on a personal religious experience.

7. See Exod. 3:2, 6.

Certainty, certainty, heartfelt, joy, peace.
God of Jesus Christ.

[*Pensées*, trans. A. J. Krailsheimer (New York: Penguin, 1966), 33, 42–43, 58, 85, 101, 148–52, 154, 165, 167–68, 309]

Selection 71: Philipp Jakob Spener, *Pia Desideria* (1675)

Philipp Jakob Spener (1635–1705) was the leading figure of the German Lutheran Pietist movement. In the third section of* Pia desideria (Pious Desires)*, he offers six proposals for the more thorough reformation of the church, four of which are excerpted here. These proposals continue to resonate in Protestant evangelicalism today.

Part III
Proposals to Correct Conditions in the Church

1. Thought should be given to a *more extensive use of the Word of God among us*. We know that by nature we have no good in us. If there is to be any good in us, it must be brought about by God. To this end the Word of God is the powerful means, since faith must be enkindled through the gospel, and the law provides the rules for good works and many wonderful impulses to attain them. The more at home the Word of God is among us, the more we shall bring about faith and its fruits. . . .

It should therefore be considered whether the church would not be well advised to introduce the people to Scripture in still other ways than through the customary sermons on the appointed lessons.

This might be done, first of all, by diligent reading of the Holy Scriptures, especially of the New Testament. It would not be difficult for every housefather to keep a Bible, or at least a New Testament, handy and read from it every day or, if he cannot read, to have somebody else read. . . .

Then a second thing would be desirable in order to encourage people to read privately, namely, that where the practice can be introduced the books of the Bible be read one after another, at specified times in the public service, without further comment (unless one wished to add brief summaries). This would be intended for the edification of all, but especially of those who cannot read at all, or cannot read easily or well, or of those who do not own a copy of the Bible.

For a third thing it would perhaps not be inexpedient (and I set this down for further and more mature reflection) to reintroduce the ancient and apostolic kind of church meetings. In addition to our customary services with preaching, other assemblies would also be held in the manner in which Paul describes them in I Corinthians 14:26-40.[8] One person would not rise to preach (although this practice would be continued at other times), but others who have been blessed with gifts and knowledge would also speak and present their pious opinions on the proposed subject to the judgment of the rest, doing all this in such a way as to avoid disorder and strife. This might conveniently be done by having several ministers (in places where a number of them live in a town) meet together or by having several members of a congregation who have a fair knowledge of God or desire to increase their knowledge meet under the leadership of a minister, take up the Holy Scriptures, read aloud from them, and

8. Such meetings of *ecclesiola* (little churches) or *collegia pietatis* (societies of piety) were characteristic of the pietist and revivalist movements.

fraternally discuss each verse in order to discover its simple meaning and whatever may be useful for the edification of all. . . .

2. Our frequently mentioned Dr. Luther would suggest another means, which is altogether compatible with the first. This second proposal is *the establishment and diligent exercise of the spiritual priesthood.* Nobody can read Luther's writings with some care without observing how earnestly the sainted man advocated this spiritual priesthood, according to which not only ministers but all Christians are made priests by their Savior, are anointed by the Holy Spirit, and are dedicated to perform spiritual-priestly acts. Peter was not addressing preachers alone when he wrote, "You are a chosen race, a royal priesthood, a holy nation, God's own people, that you may declare the wonderful deeds of him who called you out of darkness into his marvelous light." Whoever wishes to understand and read at greater length what our Reformer's opinion on this was, and what the spiritual functions are, should read his treatise, addressed to the Bohemians, on how ministers of the church should be chosen and installed, which treatise appears in Volume II of the Altenburg edition of Luther's works. There one will see how splendidly it is demonstrated that all spiritual functions are open to all Christians without exception. Although the regular and public performance of them is entrusted to ministers appointed for this purpose, the functions may be performed by others in case of emergency. Especially should those things which are unrelated to public acts be done continually by all at home and in everyday life. . . .

3. Connected with these two proposals is a third: the people must have impressed upon them and must accustom themselves to believing that *it is by no means enough to have knowledge of the Christian faith, for Christianity consists rather of practice.* Our dear Savior repeatedly enjoined love as the real mark of his disciples (John 13:34-35, 15:12; I John 3:10, 18, 4:7-8, 11-13, 21). In his old age dear John (according to the testimony of Jerome in his letter to the Galatians) was accustomed to say hardly anything more to his disciples than "Children, love one another!" His disciples and auditors finally became so annoyed at this endless repetition that they asked him why he was always saying the same thing to them. He replied, "Because it is the Lord's command, and it suffices if this be done." Indeed, love is the whole life of the man who has faith and who through his faith is saved, and his fulfillment of the laws of God consists of love.

If we can therefore awaken a fervent love among our Christians, first toward one another and then toward all men (for these two, brotherly affection and general love, must supplement each other according to II Peter 1:7), and put this love into practice, practically all that we desire will be accomplished. For all the commandments are summed up in love (Rom. 13:9). Accordingly the people are not only to be told this incessantly, and they are not only to have the excellence of neighborly love and, on the other hand, the great danger and harm in the opposing self-love pictured impressively before their eyes (which is done well in the spiritually minded John Arndt's *True Christianity,*[9] IV, ii, 22 *et seq.*), but they must also practice such love. They must become accustomed not to lose sight of any opportunity in which they can render their neighbor a service of love, and yet while performing it they must diligently search their hearts to discover whether they are acting in true love or out of other motives. If they are offended, they should especially be on their guard, not only that they refrain from all

9. Johann Arndt (1555–1621) was the forerunner of Lutheran Pietism, known especially for his *Four Books on True Christianity* (1606).

vengefulness but also that they give up some of their rights and insistence on them for fear that their hearts may betray them and feelings of hostility may become involved. In fact, they should diligently seek opportunities to do good to their enemies in order that such self-control may hurt the old Adam, who is otherwise inclined to vengeance, and at the same time in order that love may be more deeply implanted in their hearts. . . .

4. Related to this is a fourth proposal: *We must beware how we conduct ourselves in religious controversies* with unbelievers and heretics. We must first take pains to strengthen and confirm ourselves, our friends, and other fellow believers in the known truth and to protect them with great care from every kind of seduction. Then we must remind ourselves of our duty toward the erring.

We owe it to the erring, first of all, to pray earnestly that the good God may enlighten them with the same light with which he blessed us, may lead them to the truth, may prepare their hearts for it or, having counteracted their dangerous errors, may reinforce what true knowledge of salvation in Christ they still have left in order that they may be saved as a brand plucked from the fire.[10] This is the meaning of the first three petitions of the Lord's Prayer, that God may hallow his name in them, bring his kingdom to them, and accomplish his gracious will in and for them.[11]

In the second place, we must give them a good example and take the greatest pains not to offend them in any way, for this would give them a bad impression of our true teaching and hence would make their conversion more difficult.

In the third place, if God has given us the gifts which are needful for it and we find the opportunity to hope to win the erring, we should be glad to do what we can to point out, with a modest but firm presentation of the truth we profess, how this is based on the simplicity of Christ's teaching. At the same time we should indicate decently but forcefully how their errors conflict with the Word of God and what dangers they carry in their wake. All of this should be done in such a way that those with whom we deal can see for themselves that everything is done out of heartfelt love toward them without carnal and unseemly feelings, and that if we ever indulge in excessive vehemence this occurs out of pure zeal for the glory of God. Especially should we beware of invectives and personal insinuations, which at once tear down all the good we have in mind to build. If we see that we have made something of a beginning in this fashion, we should be so much the more energetic in advancing what has been begun, perhaps with the assistance of others. On the other hand, if we see that they have been so captivated by their preconceived notions that, although we perceive in them a disposition to serve God gladly without being able for the present to comprehend what we have said, they are to be admonished at the very least not to slander or speak evil of the truth which they have heard from us, to reflect further on the matter in the fear of the Lord and with fervent prayer, and in the meantime to try seriously to advance in the truth and to serve their God according to the practical principles and rules of conduct which most people who call themselves Christians have to some extent in common.

To this should be added, in the fourth place, a practice of heartfelt love toward all unbelievers and heretics. While we should indicate to them that we take no pleasure in their unbelief or false belief or the practice and propagation of these, but rather are vigorously opposed to

10. See Zech. 3:2.

11. See Matt. 6:9-10.

them, yet in other things which pertain to human life we should demonstrate that we consider these people to be our neighbors (as the Samaritan was represented by Christ in Luke 10:29-37 as the Jew's neighbor), regard them as our brothers according to the right of common creation and the divine love that is extended to all (though not according to regeneration), and therefore are so disposed in our hearts toward them as the command to love all others as we love ourselves demands. To insult or wrong an unbeliever or heretic on account of his religion would be not only a carnal zeal but also a zeal that is calculated to hinder his conversion. A proper hatred of false religion should neither suspend nor weaken the love that is due the other person.

In the fifth place, if there is any prospect of a union of most of the confessions among Christians, the primary way of achieving it, and the one that God would bless most, would perhaps be this, that we do not stake everything on argumentation, for the present disposition of men's minds, which are filled by as much fleshly as spiritual zeal, makes disputations fruitless. . . .

[*Pia desideria*, trans. Theodore G. Tappert, Seminar Editions (Philadelphia: Fortress Press, 1964), 87–89, 92–93, 95–99]

B. Jonathan Edwards

Biographical Note: Jonathan Edwards

Jonathan Edwards (1703–1758) is often considered to be the greatest American theologian and philosopher, certainly before the twentieth century. Coming from a family of ministers, Edwards was not only an intellectual prodigy with broad interests but also a spiritual seeker from a young age. In 1723, at the age of nineteen (too late, he felt), he solemnly dedicated himself to the service of God. He was ordained and became minister of the Congregational Church in Northampton, Massachusetts, in 1727.

In late 1734, Edwards reported that, among the members of his church, religious matters began to dominate all conversation and there was a new and deep concern for eternal salvation. Indeed, the Northampton Church was caught up in the revival that was spreading throughout the English-speaking world and, in America, would come to be called the Great Awakening. Edwards provided an account of the work of God in his congregation and of how the conversions took place, published in 1737 as A Faithful Narrative of the Surprising Work of God in the Conversion of Many Hundred Souls in Northampton. *This work was widely read in America and England and was viewed as offering a sort of model for congregational and individual revival. Based on the influence of this* Faithful Narrative, *as well as the reputation he established through his published sermons and reflections on the revival, Edwards was the foremost preacher of the Great Awakening in the northern American colonies. In 1757, shortly before his death, he became president of the College of New Jersey (later Princeton University).*

Most of Edwards's thought is typical of English Puritan Calvinism. Even his most famous sermon, "Sinners in the Hands of an Angry God" (1741), expresses a common view of hell and condemnation. Other aspects of his theology, however, are regarded as contentious still today, especially in light of his continuing influence in modern theology. For example, like other Reformed theologians, Edwards rejected the common notion of freedom of the will understood as self-determination and instead saw

determinism as compatible with freedom. However, he went further than most Reformed theologians by advocating metaphysical determinism, thereby bequeathing to American evangelical Calvinism a pan-determinism that, according to opponents, makes God the author of sin.

Aside from his more controversial ideas, Edwards is justly known for his penetrating intellect, his prolific writings, and his emphasis on the majestic sovereignty and beauty of God.

Selection 72: Jonathan Edwards, *Miscellanies* 348 (1728)

The* Miscellanies *is a theological journal of more than 1,400 entries that Edwards made between 1722 and 1758. In this entry, he claims that creation is necessary for the display of the full range of the essential divine attributes, reflecting his panentheistic tendencies.

348. Decrees

We have shown,[12] 'tis a proper and excellent thing for infinite glory to shine forth; and for the same reason, it is proper that the shining forth of God's glory should be complete; that is, that all parts of his glory should shine forth, that every beauty should be proportionably effulgent, that the beholder might have a proper notion of God. It was not proper that one glory should be exceedingly manifested and another not at all, for then the effulgence would not answer the reality. For the same reason, it is not proper that one should be manifested exceedingly and another but very little. It is highly proper that the effulgent glory of God should answer his real excellency, that the splendor should be answerable to the real and essential glory, for the same reason that it is proper and excellent for God to glorify himself at all. Thus 'tis necessary that God's awful majesty, his authority and dreadful greatness, and justice and holiness [should be manifested]; and this could not be except sin and punishment were decreed, or at least might be decreed. So that the glory shining forth would be very imperfect, both because these parts of divine glory would not shine forth as the others do, and [because] then the glory of his goodness and love and holiness would be faint without them; nay, they could scarcely shine forth at all.

If it were not right that God should decree and permit and punish sin, there could no such thing as justice be conceived of by men or angels, neither in rewarding nor punishing, in conferring good or inflicting evil. There could be no such thing as justice in punishing, because there could be no such thing as punishing. There could be no justice in rewarding, because he that did a great deal would deserve no more than he that did little, or than he that did nothing, by the same way of arguing; because whatever anyone does is decreed, and brought about by providence. There could be no such thing as the justice of God by the justice of his law, by the same sort of reasoning still: what would a law signify, when it was impossible for men to do any evil? There could be no manifestation of God's authority; for what authority can there be without a law or without commandments? There could be no such thing as any manifestation of God's holiness in hatred of sin, or in showing any preference in his providence to godliness before it.

It would be no manifestation of God's grace or true goodness to be free from all sorts of evil, for it would be absolutely impossible that any should be any otherwise; and how much happiness soever he bestowed, his goodness would be nothing near so much prized and admired, and

12. In previous entries.

the sense of it not near so great, as we have shown elsewhere. We little consider how much the sense of good is heightened by the sense of evil, both moral and natural.

And as it [is] necessary that there should be evil, because the glory of God could not but be imperfect and incomplete without it, so it is necessary in order to the happiness of the creature, in order to the completeness of that communication of God for which he made the world; because the creature's happiness consists in the knowledge of God and the sense of his love, and if the knowledge of him be imperfect, the happiness must be proportionably imperfect. And the happiness would also be imperfect upon another account; for as we have said, the sense of good is comparatively dull and flat without the knowledge of evil.[13]

[*Works of Jonathan Edwards*, vol. 13, 419–21]

Selection 73: Jonathan Edwards, *Treatise on the Religious Affections* (1746)

In the wake of revival, controversy lingered over the signs of true revival from the Holy Spirit—many claimed genuine signs in their lives, while others saw alleged signs as positive evidence of deception or hypocrisy. Edwards wrote* Religious Affections *to deal with these controversies. In the first part, he argues that the Christian faith necessarily encompasses the soul's affective faculties. In the second part, he shows that certain affections are necessary but not sufficient signs of a genuine Christian. In other words, the alleged signs per se are not clear indications either of true Christian faith or the lack thereof. In the third and final part, he describes characteristics of the spiritual affections that truly come from God.

13. This principle expresses an assumption taken for granted in the context of conversion—that a great sinner "loves much" (see Luke 7:36-50).

Part One: Concerning the Nature of the Affections, and Their Importance in Religion

. . . There are false affections, and there are true. A man's having much affection, don't[14] prove that he has any true religion: but if he has no affection, it proves that he has no true religion.[15] The right way, is not to reject all affections, nor to approve all; but to distinguish between affections, approving some, and rejecting others; separating between the wheat and the chaff, the gold and the dross, the precious and the vile.

2. If it be so, that true religion lies much in the affections, hence we may infer, that such means are to be desired, as have much of a tendency to move the affections. Such books, and such a way of preaching the Word, and administration of ordinances, and such a way of worshiping God in prayer, and singing praises, is much to be desired, as has a tendency deeply to affect the hearts of those who attend these means.

Such a kind of means, would formerly have been highly approved of and applauded by the generality of the people of the land, as the most excellent and profitable, and having the greatest tendency to promote the ends of the means of grace. But the prevailing taste seems of late strangely to be altered: that pathetical manner of praying and preaching, which would formerly have been admired and extolled, and that for this reason, because it had such a tendency to move the affections, now, in great multitudes, immediately excites disgust, and moves

14. *Sic.* Using "don't" for third person singular was standard English before the nineteenth century. The same is true for other apparent infelicities throughout the excerpts that were composed or translated into an older English style.

15. Another standard usage that differs from today is the use of "religious" and "religion" to mean "Christian" and "Christianity" or "Christian faith."

no other affections, than those of displeasure and contempt. . . .

3. If true religion lies much in the affections, hence we may learn, what great cause we have to be ashamed and confounded before God, that we are no more affected with the great things of religion. It appears from what has been said, that this arises from our having so little true religion.

God has given to mankind affections, for the same purpose which he has given all the faculties and principles of the human soul for, viz. that they might be subservient to man's chief end, and the great business for which God has created him, that is the business of religion. And yet how common is it among mankind, that their affections are much more exercised and engaged in other matters, than in religion! In things which concern men's worldly interest, their outward delights, their honor and reputation, and their natural relations, they have their desires eager, their appetites vehement, their love warm and affectionate, their zeal ardent; in these things their hearts are tender and sensible, easily moved, deeply impressed, much concerned, very sensibly affected, and greatly engaged; much depressed with grief at worldly losses, and highly raised with joy at worldly successes and prosperity. But how insensible and unmoved are most men, about the great things of another world! How dull are their affections! How heavy and hard their hearts in these matters! Here their love is cold, their desires languid, their zeal low, and their gratitude small. How they can sit and hear of the infinite height and depth and length and breadth of the love of God in Christ Jesus, of his giving his infinitely dear Son, to be offered up a sacrifice for the sins of men, and of the unparalleled love of the innocent, holy and tender Lamb of God, manifested in his dying agonies, his bloody sweat, his loud and bitter cries, and bleeding heart, and all this for enemies, to redeem them from deserved, eternal burnings, and to bring to unspeakable and everlasting joy and glory; and yet be cold, and heavy, insensible, and regardless! Where are the exercises of our affections proper, if not here? What is it that does more require them? And what can be a fit occasion of their lively and vigorous exercise, if not such an one as this? Can anything be set in our view, greater and more important? Anything more wonderful and surprising? Or more nearly concerning our interest? Can we suppose the wise Creator implanted such principles in the human nature as the affections, to be of use to us, and to be exercised on certain proper occasions, but to lie still on such an occasion as this? Can any Christian, who believes the truth of these things, entertain such thoughts? . . .

Part Three: Showing What Are Distinguishing Signs of Truly Gracious and Holy Affections

. . . 1. I shall consider Christian practice and an holy life, as a manifestation and sign of the sincerity of a professing Christian, *to the eye of his neighbors and brethren*.

And that this is the *chief sign* of grace in this respect, is very evident from the Word of God. Christ, who knew best how to give us rules to judge of others, has repeated it and inculcated it, that we should know them by their fruits; Matthew 7:16, "Ye shall know them by their fruits." And then after arguing the point, and giving clear reasons why it must needs be, that men's fruits must be the chief evidence of what sort they are, in the following verses, he closes by repeating the assertion; v. 20, "Wherefore by their fruits ye shall know them." Again, ch. 12:33, "Either make the tree good, and his fruit good; or else make the tree corrupt, and his fruit corrupt." As much as to say, 'Tis a very absurd thing, for any to suppose that the tree is good, and yet the fruit bad, that the tree is of one sort, and the fruit of another; for the proper evidence of the nature of the tree is its fruit. Nothing else can be intended by that last clause in the verse, "for the tree is known by its fruit," than that the tree is chiefly known by its fruit, that this is the main and most proper diagnostic by which one tree is distinguished from another. So Luke 6:44, "Every tree is known by his own fruit." Christ nowhere says, Ye shall know the tree by its leaves or flowers, or ye shall know men by their talk, or ye shall know them by the good story they tell of their experiences, or ye shall know them by the manner and air of their speaking, and emphasis and pathos of expression, or by their speaking feelingly, or by making a very great show by abundance of talk, or by many tears and affectionate expressions, or by the affections ye feel in your hearts towards them: but by their fruits shall ye know them; the tree is known by its fruit; every tree is known by its own fruit. And as this is the evidence that Christ has directed us mainly to look at in others, in judging of them, so it is the evidence that Christ has mainly directed us to give to others, whereby they may judge of us; Matthew 5:16, "Let your light so shine before men, that others seeing your good works, may glorify your Father which is in heaven." Here Christ directs us to manifest our godliness to others. Godliness is as it were a light that shines in the soul: Christ directs that this light should not only shine within, but that it should shine out before men, that they may see it. But which way shall this be? 'Tis by our good works. Christ don't say, that others hearing your good words, your good story, or your pathetical expressions; but that others seeing your good works, may glorify your Father which is in heaven. Doubtless when Christ gives us a rule how to make our light shine, that others may have evidence of it, his rule is the best that is to be found. . . .

And as the Scripture plainly teaches that practice is the best evidence of the sincerity of professing Christians; so reason teaches the same thing. Reason shows that men's deeds are better and more faithful interpreters of their minds, than their words. The common sense of all mankind, through all ages and nations, teaches 'em to judge of men's hearts chiefly by their practice, in other matters: as whether a man be a loyal subject, a true lover, a dutiful child, or a faithful servant. . . . So if a man in declaring his experiences, tells how he found his heart weaned from the world, and saw the vanity of it, so that all looked as nothing to him, at such and such times, and professes that he gives up all to God, and calls heaven and earth to witness to it; but yet in his practice is violent in pursuing the world, and what he gets he keeps close, is exceeding loath to part with much of it to charitable and pious uses, it comes from him almost like his heart's blood. But there is another professing Christian, that says not a great deal, yet in his behavior appears ready at all times to forsake the world, whenever it stands in the way of his duty, and is free to part with it at any time, to promote religion and the good of his fellow creatures; reason teaches that the latter gives far the most credible manifestation of an heart weaned from the world. . . . Passing affections easily produce words; and words are cheap; and godliness is more easily feigned in words than in actions. Christian practice is a costly laborious thing. The self-denial that is required of Christians, and the narrowness of the way that leads to life, don't consist in words, but in practice. Hypocrites may much more easily be brought to talk like saints, than to act like saints.

Thus it is plain that Christian practice is the best sign or manifestation of the true godliness of a professing Christian, to the eye of his neighbors. . . .

So that in what has been said of the importance of holy practice, as the main sign of sincerity; there is nothing legal, nothing derogatory to the freedom and sovereignty of gospel grace, nothing in the least clashing with the gospel doctrine of justification by faith alone, without the works of the law, nothing in the least tending to lessen the glory of the mediator, and our dependence on his righteousness, nothing infringing on the special prerogatives of faith in the affair of our salvation, nothing in any wise detracting from the glory of God and his mercy, or exalting man, or diminishing his dependence and obligation. So that if any are against such an importance of holy practice as has been spoken of, it must be only from a senseless aversion to the letters and sound of the word "works"; when there is no reason in the world to be given for it, but what may be given with equal force, why they should have an aversion to the words "holiness," "godliness," "grace," "religion," "experience," and even "faith" itself: for to make a righteousness of any of these, is as legal, and as inconsistent with the way of the new covenant, as to make a righteousness of holy practice.

. . . But if we had got into the way of looking chiefly at those things, which Christ and his apostles and prophets chiefly insisted on, and so in judging of ourselves and others, chiefly regarding practical exercises and effects of grace, not neglecting other things; it would be of manifold happy consequence; it would above all things tend to the conviction of deluded hypocrites, and to prevent the delusion of those whose hearts were never brought to a thorough compliance with the strait and narrow way which leads to life; it would tend to deliver us from innumerable perplexities, arising from the various inconsistent schemes that are about methods and steps of experience; it would greatly tend to prevent professors[16] neglecting strictness of life, and tend to promote their engagedness and earnestness in their Christian walk; and it would become fashionable for men to shew their Christianity, more by an amiable distinguished behavior, than by an abundant and excessive declaring their experiences; and we should get into the way of appearing lively in religion, more by being lively in the service of God and our generation, than by the liveliness and forwardness of our tongues, and making a business of proclaiming on the house tops, with our mouths, the holy and eminent acts and exercises of our own hearts; and Christians that are intimate friends, would talk together of their experiences and comforts, in a manner better becoming Christian humility and modesty, and more to each other's profit; their tongues not running before, but rather going behind their hands and feet, after the prudent example of the blessed Apostle, II Corinthians 12:6; and many occasions of spiritual pride would be cut off; and so a great door shut against the devil; and a great many of the main stumbling blocks against experimental and powerful religion would be removed; and religion would be declared and manifested in such a way, that instead of hardening spectators, and exceedingly promoting infidelity and atheism, would above all things tend to convince men that there is a reality in religion, and greatly awaken them, and win them, by convincing their consciences of the importance and excellency of religion. Thus the light of professors would so shine before men, that others seeing their good works, would glorify their Father which is in heaven.[17]

[*The Works of Jonathan Edwards*, vol. 2, ed. John E. Smith (New Haven: Yale University Press, 1959), 121-23, 407-11, 458-59, 461]

---

16. That is, those who profess the Christian faith.

17. See Matt. 5:16.

C. John Wesley

John Wesley

Charles Wesley

Biographical Note: John Wesley

John Wesley (1703–1791) was born in Epworth, Lincolnshire, England, the fifteenth child of Samuel and Susanna Wesley. In 1709, at the age of five, the Wesley home burned down, and young John was rescued at the last moment from the fire. He later attended Oxford and was elected a Fellow of Lincoln College in 1726. By 1729, John Wesley and his brother Charles (1707–1788) were heavily involved in a group that became known as the "Holy Club" and later as "Methodists," which was one of many such groups throughout the university whose members were fervent in the spiritual disciplines of prayer, fasting, and Bible study, as well as works of mercy such as visiting prisoners and giving alms to the poor.

In 1738, Wesley wrote the following passage in his journal: "In the evening I went very unwillingly to a society in Aldersgate Street, where one was reading Luther's preface to the Epistle to the Romans. About a quarter before nine, while he was describing the change which God works in the heart through faith in Christ, I felt my heart strangely warmed. I felt I did trust in Christ, Christ alone, for salvation; and an assurance was given me that He had taken away my sins, even mine, and saved me from the law of sin and death." Wesley proved his new energy for the work in England by organizing the grassroots revival movements into a "connexion" for mutual faith and support. Circuits, or itinerant preaching "rounds," were eventually assigned to ensure that the Methodist message spread to new places.

Although he lived and died a "Church of England man," Wesley's evangelical revival movement within the church spawned the Methodist denomination. In addition to the significance of holy living, Methodism was characterized by an Arminian perspective on predestination and salvation, in contrast with the larger evangelical movement in England and the Great Awakening in America, which tended toward Reformed soteriology. Like all Anglican theologians, Wesley grounded his theology chiefly in Scripture, read through the lens of tradition, in accord with reason. Along with these three criteria of Scripture, tradition, and reason, Wesley emphasized the importance of experience as a confirmation of faith and practice.

Wesley did not invent the idea of heart-warming conversion and experience, the concept of open-air and itinerant preaching, or the stress on entire sanctification, but he was instrumental in popularizing these concepts that would forever be a part of evangelicalism in the English-speaking world.

Selection 74: John Wesley, *Thoughts upon Slavery* (1774)

. . . Perhaps you will say, "I do not *buy* any Negroes: I only *use* those left me by my Father." So far is well: but is it enough to satisfy your own conscience? Had your Father, have *you*, has any man living, a right to use another as a slave? It cannot be, even setting revelation aside. It cannot be that either War, or contract, can give any man such a property in another as he has in his sheep and oxen. Much less is it possible, that any child of man, should ever be *born a slave*. Liberty is the right of every human creature, as soon as he breathes the vital air.

And no human law can deprive him of that right, which he derives from the law of nature.

If therefore you have any regard to Justice, (to say nothing of Mercy, nor of the revealed Law of GOD) render unto all their due. Give Liberty to whom Liberty is due, that is to every child of man, to every partaker of human nature. Let none serve you but by his own act and deed, by his own voluntary choice. Away with all whips, all chains, all compulsion! Be gentle toward all men, and see that you invariably do unto every one, as you would he should do unto *You*.

O thou GOD of Love, thou who art loving to every man, and whose mercy is over all thy works; Thou who art the Father of the Spirits of all flesh, and who art rich in mercy unto all: Thou who hast mingled of one blood, all the nations upon earth; Have compassion upon these outcasts of men, who are trodden down as dung upon the earth! Arise and help these that have no helper, whose blood is spilt upon the ground like water! Are not these also the work of thine own hands, the purchase of thy Son's blood? Stir them up to cry unto thee in the land of their captivity; and let their complaint come up before thee; let it enter into thy ears! Make even those that lead them away captive to pity them, and turn their captivity as the rivers in the South. O burst thou all their chains in sunder; more especially the chains of their sins: Thou, Saviour of all, make them free, that they may be free indeed.

[*Thoughts upon Slavery*, 4th ed. (Dublin: for W. Whitestone, 1775), 27–28]

Selection 75: John Wesley, "The Character of a Methodist" (1742)

Because of the methodical rule keeping of John and Charles Wesley and others in the "Holy Club" at Oxford, opponents began to refer to this group as "Methodists" as early as 1732. The derisive name soon became a common designation for evangelicals within the Church of England, and by 1750 it was associated almost exclusively with the Wesleyan arm of the movement.

Outsiders, however, continued to misunderstand the beliefs of Methodism, especially in the first couple of decades. Wesley, therefore, sought to clear up the misconceptions with this tract, which is a kind of apologia. His purpose was to demonstrate that Methodism is not a novel invention, but "plain, old Christianity," nothing other than pure and authentic Christianity. If someone were to say that the allegedly distinctive elements of Methodism are common to the historic church, Wesley would agree. As mere Christianity, Methodism was intentionally ecumenical. The true Christian is one who, through faith, has knowledge of God in heart and life.

"Not as tho' I had already attained."
To the Reader

1. Since the name first came abroad into the world, many have been at a loss to know what a "Methodist" is; what are the *principles* and the *practice* of those who are commonly called by that name; and what the *distinguishing marks* of this "SECT which is everywhere spoken against."[18] . . .

3. I say "those who are called Methodists," for let it be well observed that this is not a name which they take to themselves, but one fixed upon them by way of reproach, without their approbation or consent. It was first given to three or four young men at Oxford, by Mr. John Bingham, then Student of Christ Church—either in allusion to the ancient sect

18. See Acts 28:22; cf. Acts 24:14. Wesley placed "sect" in upper case letters to emphasize that, as with "Methodist," this word is not a self-designation.

of physicians so called (from their teaching that almost all diseases might be cured by a specific *method* of diet and exercise) or from their observing a more regular *method* of study and behaviour than was usual with those of their age and station.

4. I should rejoice (so little ambitious am I to be the head of any sect or party) if the very name might never be mentioned more, might be buried in eternal oblivion. But if that cannot be, at least let those who *will* use it, know the meaning of the word they use. Let us not always be fighting in the dark. Come, and let us look one another in the face. And perhaps some of you who hate *what I am called*, may love what *I am* (by the grace of God); or rather, what "I follow after, if that I may apprehend that for which also I am apprehended of Christ Jesus." . . .

1. The *distinguishing marks* of a Methodist are not his *opinions* of any sort. . . .

2. Neither are *words* or *phrases* of any sort. We do not place our religion, or any part of it, in being attached to any peculiar mode of speaking, any quaint or uncommon set of expressions. The most obvious, easy, common words wherein our meaning can be conveyed we prefer before others, both on ordinary occasions, and when we speak of the things of God. We never therefore willingly or designedly deviate from the most usual way of speaking, unless when we express Scripture truths in Scripture words—which, we presume, no Christian will condemn. Neither do we affect to use any particular expressions of Scripture more frequently than others, unless they are such as are more frequently used by the inspired writers themselves. So that it is as gross an error to place the marks of a Methodist in his *words* as in *opinions* of any sort. . . .

5. "What then is the mark? Who is a Methodist, according to your own account?" I answer: A Methodist is one who has "the love of God shed abroad in his heart by the Holy Ghost given unto him;" one who "loves the Lord his God with all his heart, and with all his soul, and with all his mind, and with all his strength." God is the joy of his heart, and the desire of his soul, which is constantly crying out, "Whom have I in heaven but thee? and there is none upon earth that I desire beside thee! My God and my all! Thou art the strength of my heart, and my portion for ever!" . . .

17. These are the *principles* and *practices* of our SECT; these are the *marks* of a true Methodist. By these alone do those who are in derision so called desire to be distinguished from other men. If any man say, "Why, these are only the common, fundamental principles of Christianity"—"Thou hast said." So I mean. This is the very truth. I know they are no other, and I would to God both thou and all men knew that I, and all who follow my judgment, do vehemently refuse to be distinguished from other men by any but the common principles of Christianity—the plain, old Christianity that I teach, renouncing and detesting all other marks of distinction. And whosoever *is* what I *preach* (let him be *called* what he will; for names change not the nature of things) he is a Christian, not in *name* only, but in *heart* and in *life*. He is inwardly and outwardly conformed to the will of God, as revealed in the written Word. *He thinks, speaks, and lives according to the* "method" *laid down in the revelation of Jesus Christ*. His soul is "renewed after the image of God," "in righteousness and in all true holiness." And "having the mind that was in Christ" he "so walks as" Christ "also walked."

18. By these *marks*, by these fruits of a living faith, do we labour to *distinguish* ourselves from the unbelieving world, from all those whose minds or lives are not according to the gospel of Christ. But from real Christians, of whatsoever denomination they be, we earnestly desire not

to be distinguished at all. Nor from any who sincerely follow after what they know they have not yet attained. No: "Whosoever doth the will of my Father which is in heaven, the same is my brother and sister and mother." And I beseech you, brethren, by the mercies of God, that we be in no wise divided among ourselves. "Is thy heart right, as my heart is with thine?" I ask no farther question. "If it be, give me thy hand."[19] For opinions, or terms, let us "not destroy the work of God." Dost thou love and serve God? It is enough. I give thee the right hand of fellowship. "If there be any consolation in Christ, if any comfort of love, if any fellowship of the Spirit, if any bowels and mercies," let us "strive together for the faith of the gospel"; "walking worthy of the vocation wherewith we are called, with all lowliness and meekness, with longsuffering, forbearing one another in love, endeavouring to keep the unity of the Spirit in the bond of peace"; remembering, "there is one body and one Spirit, even as we are called with one hope of our calling; one Lord, one faith, one baptism; one God and Father of all, who is above all, and through all, and in you all!"

[*The Works of John Wesley*, bicentennial ed., vol. 9 (Nashville, TN: Abingdon, 1989), 32–35, 41–42]

Selection 76: John Wesley, "Christian Perfection" (Sermon 40) (1741)

The Wesleyan emphasis on holiness and Christian perfection was the most distinctive—and in some ways central—element of early Methodism. The language of "perfection" and the affirmation of its possibility in this life were controversial in Protestant England, and Wesley was frequently misunderstood. Although his views on perfection gradually changed and the criteria softened over the course of his long ministry, John Wesley maintained the belief that entire sanctification is the goal of the Christian life, a perfect love experienced most often in the face of physical death.

Philippians 3:12

"Not as though I had already attained, either were already perfect."

1. There is scarce any expression in Holy Writ which has given more offence than this. The word "perfect" is what many cannot bear. The very sound of it is an abomination to them. And whosoever "preaches perfection" (as the phrase is), i.e. asserts that it is attainable in this life, runs great hazard of being accounted by them worse than a heathen man or a publican.

2. And hence some have advised, wholly to lay aside the use of those expressions, "because they have given so great offence." But are they not found in the oracles of God? If so, by what authority can any messenger of God lay them aside, even though all men should be offended? We have not so learned Christ; neither may we thus give place to the devil. Whatsoever God hath spoken, that will we speak, whether men will hear or whether they will forbear: knowing that then alone can any minister of Christ be "pure from the blood of all men," when he hath "not shunned to declare unto them all the counsel of God". . . .

4. . . . I shall endeavour to show,

First, in what sense Christians are *not*, and

Secondly, in what sense they *are*, perfect.

I.1. In the first place I shall endeavour to show in what sense Christians are *not perfect.* And both from experience and Scripture it appears,[20] first, that they are not perfect in

19. See 2 Kgs. 10:15. This text will become the point of departure for Wesley's sermon on the "catholic spirit" (see Selection 78).

20. Wesley's frequent appeal to "experience" is added to the typical Anglican appeal to Scripture, tradition, and

knowledge: they are not *so* perfect in this life as to be free from ignorance. They know, it may be, in common with other men, many things relating to the present world; and they know, with regard to the world to come, the general truths which God hath revealed. They know likewise (what "the natural man receiveth not," for these things "are spiritually discerned") "what manner of love it is wherewith the Father hath loved them, that they should be called the sons of God." They know "the mighty working of his Spirit" in their hearts, and the wisdom of his providence directing all their paths, and causing all things to work together for their good. Yea, they know in every circumstance of life what the Lord requireth of them, and how "to keep a conscience void of offence both toward God and toward man". . . .

3. They know not the reasons even of many of his present dispensations with the sons of men; but are constrained to rest here, though "clouds and darkness are round about him, righteousness and judgment are the habitation of his seat." Yea, often with regard to his dealings with themselves doth their Lord say unto them, "What I do, thou knowest not now; but thou shalt know hereafter." And how little do they know of what is ever before them, of even the visible works of his hands! How "he spreadeth the north over the empty place, and hangeth the earth upon nothing." How he unites all the parts of this vast machine by a secret chain which cannot be broken. So great is the ignorance, so very little the knowledge of even the best of men.

4. No one then is so perfect in this life as to be free from ignorance. Nor, secondly, from mistake, which indeed is almost an unavoidable consequence of it; seeing those who "know but in part" are ever liable to err touching the things which they know not. 'Tis true the children of God do not mistake as to the things essential to salvation. They do not "put darkness for light, or light for darkness," neither "seek death in the error of their life." For they are "taught of God," and the way which he teaches them, the way of holiness, is so plain that "the wayfaring man, though a fool, need not err therein." But in things unessential to salvation they do err, and that frequently. The best and wisest of men are frequently mistaken even with regard to facts; believing those things not to have been which really were, or those to have been done which were not. Or suppose they are not mistaken as to the fact itself, they may be with regard to its circumstances; believing them, or many of them, to have been quite different from what in truth they were. And hence cannot but arise many farther mistakes. Hence they may believe either past or present actions which were or are evil to be good; and such as were or are good to be evil. Hence also they may judge not according to truth with regard to the characters of men; and that not only by supposing good men to be better, or wicked men to be worse, than they are, but by believing them to have been or to be good men who were or are very wicked; or perhaps those to have been or to be wicked men who were or are holy and unreprovable. . . .

6. If it be objected to what has been observed under this and the preceding head that St. John speaking to his brethren in the faith says, "Ye have an unction from the Holy One, and know all things" (1 John 2:20), the answer is plain—"Ye know all things that are needful for your soul's health." That the Apostle never designed to extend this farther, that he could not speak it in an absolute sense, is clear first from hence: that otherwise he would describe the disciple as

reason, thus forming the so-called "Wesleyan quadrilateral." In many cases, though, what Wesley means by experience was often included in what previous theologians meant by reason.

"above his Master"; seeing Christ himself, as man, knew not all things.[21] "Of that hour," saith he, "knoweth no man, no, not the Son, but the Father only." It is clear, secondly, from the Apostle's own words that follow: "These things have I written unto you concerning them that deceive you," as well as from his frequently repeated caution, "Let no man deceive you," which had been altogether needless had not those very persons who had that unction from the Holy One been liable not to ignorance only but to mistake also.

7. Even Christians therefore are not *so* perfect as to be free either from ignorance or error. We may, thirdly, add: nor from infirmities. Only let us take care to understand this word aright. Let us not give that soft title to known sins, as the manner of some is. So, one man tells us, "Every man has his infirmity, and mine is drunkenness." Another has the infirmity of uncleanness; another of taking God's holy name in vain; and yet another has the infirmity of calling his brother, "Thou fool," or returning "railing for railing." It is plain that all you who thus speak, if ye repent not, shall with your infirmities go quick into hell. But I mean hereby not only those which are properly termed "bodily infirmities," but all those inward or outward imperfections which are not of a moral nature. Such are weakness or slowness of understanding, dullness or confusedness of apprehension, incoherency of thought, irregular quickness or heaviness of imagination. Such (to mention no more of this kind) is the want of a ready or of a retentive memory. Such in another kind are those which are commonly in some measure consequent upon these: namely slowness of speech, impropriety of language, ungracefulness of pronunciation—to which one might add a thousand nameless defects either in conversation or behaviour. These are the infirmities which are found in the best of men in a larger or smaller proportion. And from these none can hope to be perfectly freed till the spirit returns to God that gave it.

8. Nor can we expect till then to be wholly free from temptation. Such perfection belongeth not to this life. It is true, there are those who, being given up to work all uncleanness with greediness, scarce perceive the temptations which they resist not, and so seem to be without temptation. There are also many whom the wise enemy of souls, seeing [them] to be fast asleep in the dead form of godliness, will not tempt to gross sin, lest they should awake before they drop into everlasting burnings. I know there are also children of God who, being now "justified freely," having found "redemption in the blood of Christ," for the present feel no temptation. God hath said to their enemies, "Touch not mine anointed, and do my children no harm." And for this season, it may be for weeks or months, he causeth them to "ride on high places"; he beareth them as on eagles' wings, above all the fiery darts of the wicked one.[22] But this state will not last always, as we may learn from that single consideration that the Son of God himself, in the days of his flesh, was tempted even to the end of his life. Therefore so let his servant expect to be; for "it is enough that he be as his Master."

9. Christian perfection therefore does not imply (as some men seem to have imagined) an exemption either from ignorance or mistake, or infirmities or temptations. Indeed, it is only another term for holiness. They are two names for the same thing. . . .

21. Although this point has been frequently misunderstood, the belief that Jesus' human limitations extended also to his intellect—as expressed here by Wesley—is historically orthodox.

22. See Exod. 19:4; Eph. 6:16.

II.1. In what sense then are Christians perfect? This is what I shall endeavour, in the second place, to show. . . .

3. Now the Word of God plainly declares that even those who are justified, who are born again in the lowest sense, do not "continue in sin"; that they cannot "live any longer therein" (Rom. 6:1, 2); that they are "planted together in the likeness of the death of Christ" (Rom. 6:5); that their "old man is crucified with him, the body of sin being destroyed, so that thenceforth they do not serve sin"; that "being dead with Christ, they are freed from sin" (Rom. 6:6, 7); that they are "dead unto sin," and "alive unto God" (Rom. 6:11); that "sin hath not dominion over them," who are "not under the law, but under grace"; but that these, "being made free from sin, are become the servants of righteousness" (Rom. 6:15, 18).

4. The very least which can be implied in these words is that the persons spoken of therein, namely all real Christians or believers in Christ, are made free from outward sin. And the same freedom which St. Paul here expresses in such variety of phrases St. Peter expresses in that one: "He that hath suffered in the flesh hath ceased from sin; that he no longer should live . . . to the desires of men, but to the will of God" (1 Pet. 4:1-2). For this "ceasing from sin," if it be interpreted in the lowest sense, as regarding only the outward behaviour, must denote the ceasing from the outward act, from any outward transgression of the law.[23]

[*The Works of John Wesley*, bicentennial ed., vol. 2 (Nashville, TN: Abingdon, 1985), 99–106]

23. In the course of Wesley's long career, he had many occasions to address this controversial topic of Christian perfection. His concept developed in subsequent decades, with his description generally becoming more inclusive as more people claimed perfection.

Selection 77: John Wesley, "The Scripture Way of Salvation" (Sermon 43) (1765)

Wesley has been called a "folk theologian" because of his insistence on communicating the content of the gospel to the common people. He achieved this goal not by writing academic theology but by means of popular-level publications, especially the preaching and publishing of sermons.

"The Scripture Way of Salvation" is a sermon that Wesley preached frequently throughout his career. It is a perfect example of Wesley attempting to boil down an issue of absolute importance—and one that could be burdened by a number of complexities—into a simple presentation. For Wesley, salvation through faith is "the substance of all the Bible." This salvation is a process that begins with "preventing" (that is, prevenient) grace, the grace that "precedes" saving faith, and then continues through the new birth and the life of sanctification. Consistent with Protestant soteriology, and against those who worried that Wesley taught works righteousness, he stresses that faith is the only condition for salvation.

Ephesians 2:8
"Ye are saved through faith."

1. Nothing can be more intricate, complex, and hard to be understood, than religion as it has been often described. And this is not only true concerning the religion of the heathens, even many of the wisest of them, but concerning the religion of those also who were in some sense Christians; yea, and men of great name in the Christian world, men "who seemed to be pillars" thereof. Yet how easy to be understood, how plain and simple a thing, is the genuine religion of Jesus Christ! Provided only that we take it in its native form, just as it is described in the oracles of God. It is exactly suited by the

wise Creator and Governor of the world to the weak understanding and narrow capacity of man in his present state. How observable is this both with regard to the end it proposes and the means to attain that end! The end is, in one word, salvation: the means to attain it, faith. . . .

Let us then seriously inquire,

I. What is salvation?

II. What is that faith whereby we are saved? And

III. How we are saved by it.

I.1. And first let us inquire, What is *salvation?* The salvation which is here spoken of is not what is frequently understood by that word, the going to heaven, eternal happiness. It is not the soul's going to paradise, termed by our Lord "Abraham's bosom." It is not a blessing which lies on the other side [of] death, or (as we usually speak) in the other world. The very words of the text itself put this beyond all question. "Ye *are* saved." It is not something at a distance: it is a present thing, a blessing which, through the free mercy of God, ye are now in possession of. Nay, the words may be rendered, and that with equal propriety, "Ye *have been* saved." So that the salvation which is here spoken of might be extended to the entire work of God, from the first dawning of grace in the soul till it is consummated in glory. . . .

3. But we are at present concerned only with that salvation which the Apostle is directly speaking of.[24] And this consists of two general parts, justification and sanctification.

Justification is another word for pardon. It is the forgiveness of all our sins, and (what is necessarily implied therein) our acceptance with God. . . .

4. And at the same time that we are justified, yea, in that very moment, *sanctification* begins. In that instant we are "born again," "born from above," "born of the Spirit." There is a *real* as well as a *relative* change. We are inwardly renewed by the power of God. We feel the "love of God shed abroad in our heart by the Holy Ghost which is given unto us," producing love to all mankind, and more especially to the children of God; expelling the love of the world, the love of pleasure, of ease, of honour, of money; together with pride, anger, self-will, and every other evil temper—in a word, changing the "earthly, sensual, devilish" mind into "the mind which was in Christ Jesus."

5. How naturally do those who experience such a change imagine that all sin is gone! That it is utterly rooted out of their heart, and has no more any place therein! How easily do they draw that inference, "I *feel* no sin; therefore I *have* none." . . .

6. But it is seldom long before they are undeceived, finding sin was only suspended, not destroyed. Temptations return and sin revives, showing it was but stunned before, not dead. They now feel two principles in themselves, plainly contrary to each other: "the flesh lusting against the spirit," nature opposing the grace of God. They cannot deny that although they still feel power to believe in Christ and to love God, and although his "Spirit" still "witnesses with" their "spirits that" they "are the children of God"; yet they feel in themselves, sometimes pride or self-will, sometimes anger or unbelief. They find one or more of these frequently *stirring* in their heart, though not *conquering*; yea, perhaps "thrusting sore at them, that they" may "fall; but the Lord is" their "help". . . .

8. From the time of our being "born again" the gradual work of sanctification takes place. We are enabled "by the Spirit" to "mortify the deeds of the body," of our evil nature. And as we are more and more dead to sin, we are more and more alive to God. We go on from grace to grace, while we are careful to "abstain from all

24. That is, Paul in Eph. 2:8.

appearance of evil," and are "zealous of good works," "as we have opportunity, doing good to all men"; while we walk in all his ordinances blameless, therein worshipping him in spirit and in truth; while we take up our cross and deny ourselves every pleasure that does not lead us to God.

9. It is thus that we wait for entire sanctification, for a full salvation from all our sins, from pride, self-will, anger, unbelief, or, as the Apostle expresses it, "Go on to perfection." But what is perfection? The word has various senses: here it means perfect love.[25] It is love excluding sin; love filling the heart, taking up the whole capacity of the soul. It is love "rejoicing evermore, praying without ceasing, in everything giving thanks."

II. But what is that "faith through which we are saved"? This is the second point to be considered.

1. Faith in general is defined by the Apostle, ἔλεγκος πραγμάτων οὐ βλεπομένων—"an evidence," a divine "evidence and conviction" (the word means both), "of things not seen"—not visible, not perceivable either by sight or by any other of the external senses. It implies both a supernatural *evidence* of God and of the things of God, a kind of spiritual *light* exhibited to the soul, and a supernatural *sight* or perception thereof. Accordingly the Scripture speaks sometimes of God's giving light, sometimes a power of discerning it. So St. Paul: "God, who commanded light to shine out of darkness, hath shined in our hearts, to give us the light of the knowledge of the glory of God in the face of Jesus Christ." And elsewhere the same Apostle speaks "of the eyes of" our "understanding being opened." By this twofold operation of the Holy Spirit—having the eyes of our soul both *opened* and *enlightened*—we see the things which the natural "eye hath not seen, neither the ear heard." We have a prospect of the invisible things of God. We see the *spiritual world*, which is all round about us, and yet no more discerned by our natural faculties than if it had no being; and we see the *eternal world*, piercing through the veil which hangs between time and eternity. Clouds and darkness then rest upon it no more, but we already see the glory which shall be revealed.

2. Taking the word in a more particular sense, faith is a divine evidence and conviction, not only that "God was in Christ, reconciling the world unto himself," but also that Christ "loved *me*, and gave himself for *me*." It is by this faith (whether we term it the *essence*, or rather a *property* thereof) that we "receive Christ"; that we receive him in all his offices, as our Prophet, Priest, and King.[26] It is by this that he "is made of God unto us wisdom, and righteousness, and sanctification, and redemption."

3. "But is this the 'faith of assurance' or 'faith of adherence'?" The Scripture mentions no such distinction. The Apostle says: "There is one faith, and one hope of our calling," one Christian, saving faith, as "there is one Lord" in whom we believe, and "one God and Father of us all." And it is certain this faith necessarily implies an *assurance* (which is here only another word for *evidence*, it being hard to tell the difference between them) that "Christ loved *me*, and gave himself for *me*." For "he that believeth" with the true, living faith, "hath the witness in himself." "The Spirit witnesseth with his spirit that he is a child of God." "Because he is a son, God hath sent forth the Spirit of his Son into his heart, crying, Abba, Father;" giving him an assurance that he is so, and a childlike

25. These three phrases used interchangeably here—entire sanctification, perfection, and perfect love—are distinct emphases of the Wesleyan movement.

26. The concept of the threefold office of Christ goes back to the early church, but it was codified and popularized by John Calvin.

confidence in him. But let it be observed that, in the very nature of the thing, the assurance goes before the confidence. For a man cannot have a childlike confidence in God till he knows he is a child of God. Therefore confidence, trust, reliance, adherence, or whatever else it be called, is not the first, as some have supposed, but the second branch or act of faith.

4. It is by this faith we "are saved," justified and sanctified, taking that word in its highest sense. But how are we justified and sanctified by faith? This is our third head of inquiry. And this being the main point in question, and a point of no ordinary importance, it will not be improper to give it a more distinct and particular consideration.

III.1. And first, how are we justified by faith? In what sense is this to be understood? I answer, faith is the condition, and the only condition, of justification. It is the condition: none is justified but he that believes; without faith no man is justified. And it is the only condition: this alone is sufficient for justification.[27] Everyone that believes is justified, whatever else he has or has not. In other words: no man is justified till he believes; every man when he believes is justified.

2. "But does not God command us to *repent* also? Yea, and to 'bring forth fruits meet for repentance'? To 'cease,' for instance, 'from doing evil,' and 'learn to do well'? And is not both the one and the other of the utmost necessity? Insomuch that if we willingly neglect either we cannot reasonably expect to be justified at all? But if this be so, how can it be said that faith is the only condition of justification?"

God does undoubtedly command us both to repent and to bring forth fruits meet for repentance; which if we willingly neglect we cannot reasonably expect to be justified at all. Therefore both repentance and fruits meet for repentance are in some sense necessary to justification. But they are not necessary in the *same sense* with faith, nor in the *same degree*. Not in the *same degree*; for those fruits are only necessary *conditionally*, if there be time and opportunity for them. Otherwise a man may be justified without them, as was the "thief" upon the cross (if we may call him so; for a late writer has discovered that he was no thief, but a very honest and respectable person!). But he cannot be justified without faith: this is impossible. Likewise let a man have ever so much repentance, or ever so many of the fruits meet for repentance, yet all this does not at all avail: he is not justified till he believes. But the moment he believes, with or without those fruits, yea, with more or less repentance, he is justified. Not in the *same sense*: for repentance and its fruits are only *remotely* necessary, necessary in order to faith; whereas faith is *immediately* and *directly* necessary to justification. It remains that faith is the only condition which is *immediately* and *proximately* necessary to justification.

3. "But do you believe we are sanctified by faith? We know you believe that we are justified by faith; but do not you believe, and accordingly teach, that we are sanctified by our works?"

So it has been roundly and vehemently affirmed for these five and twenty years. But I have constantly declared just the contrary, and that in all manner of ways. I have continually testified in private and in public that we are sanctified, as well as justified, by faith. And indeed the one of these great truths does exceedingly illustrate the other. Exactly as we are justified by faith, so are we sanctified by faith. Faith is the condition, and the only condition of sanctification, exactly as it is of justification.

27. Although he states his position unequivocally here, Wesley later came into controversy for allegedly undermining justification through faith alone. Indeed, he qualifies it slightly in the subsequent sections.

It is the condition: none is sanctified but he that believes; without faith no man is sanctified. And it is the only condition: this alone is sufficient for sanctification. Everyone that believes is sanctified, whatever else he has or has not. In other words: no man is sanctified till he believes; every man when he believes is sanctified. . . .

6. I say "repentance rightly understood"; for this must not be confounded with the former repentance. The repentance consequent upon justification is widely different from that which is antecedent to it. This implies no guilt, no sense of condemnation, no consciousness of the wrath of God. It does not suppose any doubt of the favour of God, or any "fear that hath torment." It is properly a conviction wrought by the Holy Ghost of the "sin" which still "remains" in our heart, of the φρόνημα σαρκός, "the carnal mind," which "does still *remain*," as our Church speaks, "even in them that are regenerate"[28]—although it does no longer *reign*, it has not now dominion over them. It is a conviction of our proneness to evil, of an heart "bent to backsliding," of the still continuing tendency of the "flesh" to "lust against the Spirit." Sometimes, unless we continually watch and pray, it lusteth to pride, sometimes to anger, sometimes to love of the world, love of ease, love of honour, or love of pleasure more than of God. It is a conviction of the tendency of our heart to self-will, to atheism, or idolatry; and above all to unbelief, whereby in a thousand ways, and under a thousand pretences, we are ever "departing" more or less "from the living God". . . .

18. "But does God work this great work in the soul *gradually* or *instantaneously*?" Perhaps it may be gradually wrought in some. I mean in this sense—they do not advert to the particular moment wherein sin ceases to be. But it is infinitely desirable, were it the will of God, that it should be done instantaneously; that the Lord should destroy sin "by the breath of his mouth" in a moment, in the twinkling of an eye. And so he generally does, a plain fact of which there is evidence enough to satisfy any unprejudiced person. *Thou* therefore look for it every moment. Look for it in the way above described; in all those "good works" whereunto thou art "created anew in Christ Jesus." There is then no danger. You can be no worse, if you are no better for that expectation. For were you to be disappointed of your hope, still you lose nothing. But you shall not be disappointed of your hope: it will come, and will not tarry. Look for it then every day, every hour, every moment. Why not this hour, this moment? Certainly you may look for it *now*, if you believe it is by faith. And by this token may you surely know whether you seek it by faith or by works. If by works, you want something to be done *first*, *before* you are sanctified. You think, "I must first *be* or *do* thus or thus." Then you are seeking it by works unto this day. If you seek it by faith, you may expect it *as you are*: and if as you are, then expect it *now*. It is of importance to observe that there is an inseparable connection between these three points—expect it *by faith*, expect it *as you are*, and expect it *now*! To deny one of them is to deny them all: to allow one is to allow them all. Do *you* believe we are sanctified by faith? Be true then to your principle, and look for this blessing just as you are, neither better, nor worse; as a poor sinner that has still nothing to pay, nothing to plead but "Christ died." And if you look for it as you are, then expect it *now*. Stay for nothing. Why should you? Christ is ready. And he is all you want. He is waiting for you. He is at the door! Let your inmost soul cry out,

Come in, come in, thou heavenly Guest!

28. See article 9 of the *Thirty-Nine Articles* (Selection 51).

Nor hence again remove:
But sup with me, and let the feast
Be everlasting love.[29]

[*The Works of John Wesley*, bicentennial ed., vol. 2 (Nashville, TN: Abingdon, 1985), 155–65, 168–69]

Selection 78: John Wesley, "Catholic Spirit" (Sermon 39) (1750)

This sermon captures Wesley's ecumenical spirit and the common love he urged among all those who love God. He encouraged unity in diversity, an attitude increasingly typical in the wake of more than two centuries of Western Christian divisions.

2 Kings 10:15

"And when he was departed thence, he lighted on Jehonadab the son of Rechab coming to meet him. And he saluted him and said, Is thine heart right, as my heart is with thy heart? And Jehonadab answered, It is. If it be, give me thine hand."

. . . 2. But it is sure, there is a peculiar love which we owe to those that love God. So David: "All my delight is upon the saints that are in the earth, and upon such as excel in virtue." And so a greater than he: "A new commandment I give unto you, that ye love one another: as I have loved you, that ye also love one another. By this shall all men know that ye are my disciples, if ye have love one to another" (John 13:34-35). This is that love on which the Apostle John so frequently and strongly insists. "This," said he, "is the message that ye heard from the beginning, that we should love one another" (1 John 3:11). "Hereby perceive we the love of God, because he laid down his life for us. And we ought," if love should call us thereto, "to lay down our lives for the brethren" (1 John 3:16). And again, "Beloved, let us love one another; for love is of God. He that loveth not, knoweth not God; for God is love" (1 John 4:7-8). "Not that we loved God, but that he loved us, and sent his Son to be the propitiation for our sins. Beloved, if God so loved us, we ought also to love one another" (1 John 4:10-11).

3. All men approve of this. But do all men practise it? Daily experience shows the contrary. Where are even the Christians who "love one another, as he hath given us commandment"? How many hindrances lie in the way! The two grand, general hindrances are, first, that they can't all think alike; and in consequence of this, secondly, they can't all walk alike; but in several smaller points their practice must differ in proportion to the difference of their sentiments. . . .

I.1. And, first, let us consider the question proposed by Jehu to Jehonadab, "Is thine heart right, as my heart is with thy heart?" . . .

2. And yet Jehu (although it seems to have been his manner, both in things secular and religious, to "drive furiously"[30]) does not concern himself at all with any of these things, but lets Jehonadab abound in his own sense. And neither of them appears to have given the other the least disturbance touching the opinions which he maintained.

3. 'Tis very possible that many good men now also may entertain peculiar opinions; and some of them may be as singular herein as even Jehonadab was. And 'tis certain, so long as "we know" but "in part," that all men will not see all things alike. It is an unavoidable consequence of the present weakness and shortness of human understanding that several men will be of several minds, in religion as well as in common life. So it has been from the beginning of the world, and so it will be "till the restitution of all things."

29. This is taken from the final verse of a hymn by Charles Wesley published in 1741.

30. See 2 Kgs. 9:20.

4. Nay farther: although every man necessarily believes that every particular opinion which he holds is true (for to believe any opinion is not true is the same thing as not to hold it) yet can no man be assured that all his own opinions taken together are true. Nay, every thinking man is assured they are not, seeing *humanum est errare et nescire*[31]—to be ignorant of many things, and to mistake in some, is the necessary condition of humanity. This therefore, he is sensible, is his own case. He knows in the general that he himself is mistaken; although in what particulars he mistakes he does not, perhaps cannot, know. . . .

6. Every wise man therefore will allow others the same liberty of thinking which he desires they should allow him; and will no more insist on their embracing his opinions than he would have them to insist on his embracing theirs. He bears with those who differ from him, and only asks him with whom he desires to unite in love that single question. "Is thine heart right, as my heart is with thy heart?" . . .

9. And how shall we choose among so much variety? No man can choose for or prescribe to another. But everyone must follow the dictates of his own conscience in simplicity and godly sincerity. He must be fully persuaded in his own mind, and then act according to the best light he has. Nor has any creature power to constrain another to walk by his own rule. God has given no right to any of the children of men thus to lord it over the conscience of his brethren. But every man must judge for himself, as every man must give an account of himself to God.

10. Although therefore every follower of Christ is obliged by the very nature of the Christian institution to be a member of some particular congregation or other, some church, as it is usually termed (which implies a particular manner of worshipping God; for "two cannot walk together unless they be agreed"); yet none can be obliged by any power on earth but that of his own conscience to prefer this or that congregation to another, this or that particular manner of worship. I know it is commonly supposed that the place of our birth fixes the church to which we ought to belong; that one, for instance, who is born in England ought to be a member of that which is styled "the Church of England," and consequently to worship God in the particular manner which is prescribed by that church. I was once a zealous maintainer of this, but I find many reasons to abate of this zeal. I fear it is attended with such difficulties as no reasonable man can get over. Not the least of which is that if this rule had took place, there could have been no Reformation from popery, seeing it entirely destroys the right of private judgment on which that whole Reformation stands.

11. I dare not therefore presume to impose my mode of worship on any other. I believe it is truly primitive and apostolical. But my belief is no rule for another. I ask not therefore of him with whom I would unite in love, "Are you of my Church? Of my congregation? Do you receive the same form of church government and allow the same church officers with me? Do you join in the same form of prayer wherein I worship God?" I inquire not, "Do you receive the Supper of the Lord in the same posture and manner that I do?" Nor whether, in the administration of baptism, you agree with me in admitting sureties for the baptized, in the manner of administering it, or the age of those to whom it should be administered. Nay, I ask not of you (as clear as I am in my own mind) whether you allow baptism and the Lord's Supper at all. Let all these things stand by: we will talk of them, if need be, at a more convenient season. My only question at present is this, "Is

31. That is, "it is human to err and not to know."

thine heart right, as my heart is with thy heart?"[32] . . .

II.1. "If it be, give me thine hand." I do not mean, "Be of my opinion." You need not. I do not expect nor desire it. Neither do I mean, "I will be of your opinion." I cannot. It does not depend on my choice. I can no more think than I can see or hear as I will. Keep you your opinion, I mine; and that as steadily as ever. . . .

3. I mean, first, love me. And that not only as thou lovest all mankind; not only as thou lovest thine enemies or the enemies of God, those that hate thee, that "despitefully use thee and persecute thee"; not only as a stranger, as one of whom thou knowest neither good nor evil. I am not satisfied with this. No; "If thine heart be right, as mine with thy heart," then love me with a very tender affection, as a friend that is closer than a brother; as a brother in Christ, a fellow-citizen of the new Jerusalem, a fellow-soldier engaged in the same warfare, under the same Captain of our salvation. Love me as a companion in the kingdom and patience of Jesus, and a joint-heir of his glory.

4. Love me (but in an higher degree than thou dost the bulk of mankind) with the love that is "long-suffering and kind"; that is patient if I am ignorant or out of the way, bearing and not increasing my burden; and is tender, soft, and compassionate still; that "envieth not" if at any time it please God to prosper me in his work even more than thee. Love me with the love that "is not provoked" either at my follies or infirmities, or even at my acting (if it should sometimes so appear to thee) not according to the will of God. Love me so as to "think no evil" of me, to put away all jealousy and evil surmising. Love me with the love that "covereth all things," that never reveals either my faults or infirmities; that "believeth all things," is always willing to think the best, to put the fairest construction on all my words and actions; that "hopeth all things," either that the thing related was never done, or not done with such circumstances as are related, or, at least, that it was done with a good intention, or in sudden stress of temptation. And hope to the end that whatever is amiss will, by the grace of God, be corrected, and whatever is wanting supplied, through the riches of his mercy in Christ Jesus.

5. I mean, secondly, commend me to God in all thy prayers; wrestle with him in my behalf, that he would speedily correct what he sees amiss and supply what is wanting in me. In thy nearest access to the throne of grace beg of him who is then very present with thee that my heart may be more as thy heart, more right both toward God and toward man; that I may have a fuller conviction of things not seen, and a stronger view of the love of God in Christ Jesus; may more steadily walk by faith, not by sight, and more earnestly grasp eternal life. Pray that the love of God and of all mankind may be more largely poured into my heart; that I may be more fervent and active in doing the will of my Father which is in heaven, more zealous of good works, and more careful to abstain from all appearance of evil.

6. I mean, thirdly, provoke me to love and to good works. Second thy prayer as thou hast opportunity by speaking to me in love whatsoever thou believest to be for my soul's health. Quicken me in the work which God has given me to do, and instruct me how to do it more perfectly. Yea, "smite me friendly and reprove me"[33] whereinsoever I appear to thee to be doing rather my own will than the will of him

32. It is also relevant to this topic to note that Methodists were often persecuted in England because of their divergent practices. Wesley would certainly have hoped for the same courtesy and toleration toward Methodists that he here extends to other groups.

33. Ps. 141:5 (Prayer Book Version).

that sent me. O speak and spare not, whatever thou believest may conduce either to the amending my faults, the strengthening my weakness, the building me up in love, or the making me more fit in any kind for the Master's use.

7. I mean, lastly, love me not in word only, but in deed and in truth. So far as in conscience thou canst (retaining still thy own opinions and thy own manner of worshipping God), join with me in the work of God, and let us go on hand in hand. And thus far, it is certain, thou mayst go. Speak honourably, wherever thou art, of the work of God, by whomsoever he works, and kindly of his messengers. And if it be in thy power, not only sympathize with them when they are in any difficulty or distress, but give them a cheerful and effectual assistance, that they may glorify God on thy behalf.

8. Two things should be observed with regard to what has been spoken under this last head. The one, that whatsoever love, whatsoever offices of love, whatsoever spiritual or temporal assistance, I claim from him whose heart is right, as my heart is with his, the same I am ready, by the grace of God, according to my measure, to give him. The other, that I have not made this claim in behalf of myself only, but of all whose heart is right toward God and man, that we may all love one another as Christ hath loved us.

III.1. One inference we may make from what has been said. We may learn from hence what is a "catholic spirit". . . .

For from hence we may learn, first, that a catholic spirit is not *speculative latitudinarianism*.[34] It is not an indifference to all opinions. This is the spawn of hell, not the offspring of heaven. This unsettledness of thought, this being "driven to and fro, and tossed about with every wind of doctrine," is a great curse, not a blessing; an irreconcilable enemy, not a friend, to true catholicism. A man of a truly catholic spirit has not now his religion to seek. He is fixed as the sun in his judgment concerning the main branches of Christian doctrine. 'Tis true he is always ready to hear and weigh whatsoever can be offered against his principles. But as this does not show any wavering in his own mind, so neither does it occasion any. He does not halt between two opinions, nor vainly endeavour to blend them into one. Observe this, you who know not what spirit ye are of, who call yourselves men of a catholic spirit only because you are of a muddy understanding; because your mind is all in a mist; because you have no settled, consistent principles, but are for jumbling all opinions together. Be convinced that you have quite missed your way: you know not where you are. You think you are got into the very spirit of Christ, when in truth you are nearer the spirit of antichrist. Go first and learn the first elements of the gospel of Christ, and then shall you learn to be of a truly catholic spirit.

2. From what has been said we may learn, secondly, that a catholic spirit is not any kind of *practical latitudinarianism*. It is not indifference as to public worship or as to the outward manner of performing it. This likewise would not be a blessing but a curse. Far from being an help thereto it would, so long as it remained, be an unspeakable hindrance to the worshipping

34. Latitudinarianism describes the English theology, common after the Restoration of the monarchy, that deemphasized doctrine in favor of practical morality, thus granting wide "latitude" in doctrinal matters. Up through the nineteenth century, advocates of ecumenism frequently faced the charge of latitudinarianism. As a pejorative accusation, it was taken as synonymous with "indifference," as Wesley indicates.

of God in spirit and in truth.[35] But the man of a truly catholic spirit, having weighed all things in the balance of the sanctuary, has no doubt, no scruple at all concerning that particular mode of worship wherein he joins. He is clearly convinced that *this* manner of worshipping God is both scriptural and rational. He knows none in the world which is more scriptural, none which is more rational. Therefore without rambling hither and thither he cleaves close thereto, and praises God for the opportunity of so doing.

3. Hence we may, thirdly, learn that a catholic spirit is not indifference to all congregations. This is another sort of latitudinarianism, no less absurd and unscriptural than the former. But it is far from a man of a truly catholic spirit. He is fixed in his congregation as well as his principles. He is united to one, not only in spirit, but by all the outward ties of Christian fellowship. There he partakes of all the ordinances of God. There he receives the Supper of the Lord. There he pours out his soul in public prayer, and joins in public praise and thanksgiving. There he rejoices to hear the word of reconciliation, the gospel of the grace of God. With these his nearest, his best beloved brethren, on solemn occasions he seeks God by fasting. These particularly he watches over in love, as they do over his soul, admonishing, exhorting, comforting, reproving, and every way building up each other in the faith. These he regards as his own household, and therefore according to the ability God has given him naturally cares for them, and provides that they may have all the things that are needful for life and godliness.

[*The Works of John Wesley*, bicentennial ed., vol. 2 (Nashville, TN: Abingdon, 1985), 81–87, 89–94]

35. John 4:24.

D. English and American Results

Selection 79: William Carey, *An Enquiry into the Obligations of Christians, to Use Means* (1792)

Although foreign missions had long been a concern of early modern Roman Catholicism, and Protestants had also engaged in mission and written on the topic, nevertheless Protestant missionary activity blossomed in conjunction with the Pietist and evangelical movements of the late seventeenth and early eighteenth centuries. The work of the Baptist missionary William Carey (1761–1834) in India, along with his publication of the* Enquiry, *was a significant inspiration in the explosion of missionary societies and activity in the nineteenth century.

Introduction

As our blessed Lord has required us to pray that his kingdom may come, and his will be done on earth as it is in heaven,[36] it becomes us not only to express our desires of that event by words, but to use every lawful method to spread the knowledge of his name. In order to this, it is necessary that we should become, in some measure acquainted with the religious state of the world; and as this is an object we should be prompted to pursue, not only by the gospel of our Redeemer, but even by the feelings of humanity, so an inclination to conscientious activity therein would form one of the strongest proofs that we are the subjects of grace, and partakers of that spirit of universal benevolence and genuine philanthropy, which appears so eminent in the character of God himself. . . .

36. See Matt. 6:10.

Section IV

The Practicability of something being done, more than what is done, for the Conversion of the Heathen.

The impediments in the way of carrying the gospel among the heathen must arise, I think, from one or other of the following things;—either their distance from us, their barbarous and savage manner of living, the danger of being killed by them, the difficulty of procuring the necessaries of life, or the unintelligibleness of their languages.

FIRST, As to their distance from us, whatever objections might have been made on that account before the invention of the mariner's compass, nothing can be alleged for it, with any colour of plausibility in the present age. Men can now sail with as much certainty through the Great South Sea, as they can through the Mediterranean, or any lesser Sea. Yea, and providence seems in a manner to invite us to the trial, as there are to our knowledge trading companies, whose commerce lies in many of the places where these barbarians dwell. At one time or other ships are sent to visit places of more recent discovery, and to explore parts the most unknown; and every fresh account of their ignorance, or cruelty, should call forth our pity, and excite us to concur with providence in seeking their eternal good. Scripture likewise seems to point out this method, *Surely the Isles shall wait for me; the ships of Tarshish first, to bring my sons from far, their silver, and their gold with them, unto the name of the Lord, thy God.* Isai. lx. 9. This seems to imply that in the time of the glorious increase of the church, in the latter days, (of which the whole chapter is undoubtedly a prophecy,) commerce shall subserve the spread of the gospel. The ships of Tarshish were trading vessels, which made voyages for traffic to various parts; thus much therefore must be meant by it, that *navigation*, especially that which is *commercial*, shall be one great mean of carrying on the work of God; and perhaps it may imply that there shall be a very considerable appropriation of wealth to that purpose.

SECONDLY, As to their uncivilized, and barbarous way of living, this can be no objection to any, except those whose love of ease renders them unwilling to expose themselves to inconveniences for the good of others.

It was no objection to the apostles and their successors, who went among the barbarous *Germans* and *Gauls*, and still more barbarous *Britons!* They did not wait for the ancient inhabitants of these countries, to be civilized, before they could be christianized, but went simply with the doctrine of the cross; and *Tertullian* could boast that "those parts of Britain which were proof against the Roman armies, were conquered by the gospel of Christ."—It was no objection to an *Elliot*, or a *Brainerd*, in later times.[37] They went forth, and encountered every difficulty of the kind, and found that a cordial reception of the gospel produced those happy effects which the longest intercourse with Europeans, without it could never accomplish. It *is* no objection to commercial men. It only requires that we should have as much love to the souls of our fellow-creatures, and fellow sinners, as they have for the profits arising from a few otter-skins, and all these difficulties would be easily surmounted.

After all, the uncivilized state of the heathen, instead of affording an objection *against* preaching the gospel to them, ought to furnish an argument *for* it. Can we as men, or as christians, hear that a great part of our fellow

---

37. John Eliot (1604–1690), the "apostle to the Indians," ministered to Native Americans and translated the Bible into their language. David Brainerd (1718–1747) was also a famous missionary to the Native Americans. Jonathan Edwards published a biography of Brainerd, and John Wesley abridged Edwards's account for a subsequent publication.

creatures, whose souls are as immortal as ours, and who are as capable as ourselves, of adorning the gospel, and contributing by their preaching, writings, or practices to the glory of our Redeemer's name, and the good of his church, are inveloped in ignorance and barbarism? Can we hear that they are without the gospel, without government, without laws, and without arts, and sciences; and not exert ourselves to introduce amongst them the sentiments of men, and of Christians? Would not the spread of the gospel be the most effectual mean of their civilization? Would not that make them useful members of society? We know that such effects did in a measure follow the afore-mentioned efforts of *Elliot*, *Brainerd*, and others amongst the American Indians; and if similar attempts were made in other parts of the world, and succeeded with a divine blessing (which we have every reason to think they would) might we not expect to see able Divines, or read well-conducted treatises in defence of the truth, even amongst those who at present seem to be scarcely human?

THIRDLY, *In respect to the danger of being killed by them*, it is true that whoever does go must put his life in his hand, and not consult with flesh and blood; but do not the goodness of the cause, the duties incumbent on us as the creatures of God, and Christians, and the perishing state of our fellow men, loudly call upon us to venture all and use every warrantable exertion for their benefit? *Paul* and *Barnabas*, who *hazarded their lives for the name of our Lord Jesus Christ*, were not blamed as being rash, but commended for so doing, while *John Mark* who through timidity of mind deserted them in their perilous undertaking, was branded with censure.[38] After all, as has been already observed, I greatly question whether most of the barbarities practiced by the savages upon those who have visited them, have not originated in some real or supposed affront, and were therefore, more properly, acts of self-defence, than proofs of ferocious dispositions. No wonder if the imprudence of sailors should prompt them to offend the simple savage, and the offence be resented; but *Elliot*, *Brainerd*, and the *Moravian missionaries*, have been very seldom molested. Nay, in general the heathen have shewed a willingness to hear the word; and have principally expressed their hatred of Christianity on account of the vices of nominal Christians.

FOURTHLY, *As to the difficulty of procuring the necessaries of life*, this would not be so great as may appear at first sight; for though we could not procure European food, yet we might procure such as the natives of those countries which we visit, subsist upon themselves. And this would only be passing through what we have virtually engaged in by entering on the ministerial office. A Christian minister is a person who in a peculiar sense is *not his own*; he is the *servant* of God, and therefore ought to be wholly devoted to him. By entering on that sacred office he solemnly undertakes to be always engaged, as much as possible, in the Lord's work, and not to chuse his own pleasure, or employment, or pursue the ministry as a something that is to subserve his own ends, or interests, or as a kind of bye-work. He engages to go where God pleases, and to do, or endure what he sees fit to command, or call him to, in the exercise of his function. He virtually bids farewell to friends, pleasures, and comforts, and stands in readiness to endure the greatest sufferings in the work of his Lord, and Master. It is inconsistent for ministers to please themselves with thoughts of a numerous auditory, cordial friends, a civilized country, legal protection, affluence, splendour, or even a competency. The flights, and hatred of men, and even

38. See Acts 15:25-26, 37-38.

pretended friends, gloomy prisons, and tortures, the society of barbarians of uncouth speech, miserable accommodations in wretched wildernesses, hunger, and thirst, nakedness, weariness, and painfulness, hard work, and but little worldly encouragement, should rather be the objects of their expectation. Thus the apostles acted, in the primitive times, and endured hardness, as good soldiers of Jesus Christ; and though we living in a civilized country where Christianity is protected by law, are not called to suffer these things while we continue here, yet I question whether all are justified in staying here, while so many are perishing without means of grace in other lands. Sure I am that it is entirely contrary to the spirit of the gospel, for its ministers to enter upon it from interested motives, or with great worldly expectations. On the contrary the commission is a sufficient call to them to venture all, and, like the primitive Christians, go everywhere preaching the gospel.

It might be necessary, however, for two, at least, to go together, and in general I should think it best that they should be married men, and to prevent their time from being employed in procuring necessaries, two, or more, other persons, with their wives and families, might also accompany them, who should be wholly employed in providing for them. In most countries it would be necessary for them to cultivate a little spot of ground just for their support, which would be a resource to them, whenever their supplies failed. Not to mention the advantages they would reap from each others company, it would take off the enormous expense which has always attended undertakings of this kind, the first expense being the whole; for though a large colony needs support for a considerable time, yet so small a number would, upon receiving the first crop, maintain themselves. They would have the advantage of choosing their situation, their wants would be few; the women, and even the children, would be necessary for domestic purposes; and a few articles of stock, as a cow or two, and a bull, and a few other cattle of both sexes, a very few utensils of husbandry, and some corn to sow their land, would be sufficient. Those who attend the missionaries should understand husbandry, fishing, fowling, etc. and be provided with the necessary implements for these purposes. Indeed a variety of methods may be thought of, and when once the work is undertaken, many things will suggest themselves to us, of which we at present can form no idea.

FIFTHLY, As to *learning their languages*, the same means would be found necessary here as in trade between different nations. In some cases interpreters might be obtained, who might be employed for a time; and where these were not to be found, the missionaries must have patience, and mingle with the people, till they have learned so much of their language as to be able to communicate their ideas to them in it. It is well known to require no very extraordinary talents to learn, in the space of a year, or two at most, the language of any people upon earth, so much of it at least, as to be able to convey any sentiments we wish to their understandings.[39]

The Missionaries must be of great piety, prudence, courage, and forbearance; of undoubted orthodoxy in their sentiments, and must enter with all their hearts into the spirit of their mission; they must be willing to leave all the comforts of life behind them, and to encounter all the hardships of a torrid, or a

---

39. Although this claim is probably true, it is coming from a man who translated the whole Bible into Bengali, Oriya, Hindi, Marathi, and Sanskrit, and portions of the Bible into nearly thirty other languages and dialects.

frigid climate, an uncomfortable manner of living, and every other inconvenience that can attend this undertaking. Clothing, a few knives, powder and shot, fishing-tackle, and the articles of husbandry above-mentioned, must be provided for them; and when arrived at the place of their destination, their first business must be to gain some acquaintance with the language of the natives, (for which purpose two would be better than one,) and by all lawful means to endeavour to cultivate a friendship with them, and as soon as possible let them know the errand for which they were sent. They must endeavour to convince them that it was their good alone, which induced them to forsake their friends, and all the comforts of their native country. They must be very careful not to resent injuries which may be offered to them, nor to think highly of themselves, so as to despise the poor heathens, and by those means lay a foundation for their resentment, or rejection of the gospel. They must take every opportunity of doing them good, and labouring, and travelling, night and day, they must instruct, exhort, and rebuke, with all long suffering, and anxious desire for them, and, above all, must be instant in prayer for the effusion of the Holy Spirit upon the people of their charge. Let but missionaries of the above description engage in the work, and we shall see that it is not impracticable.

It might likewise be of importance, if God should bless their labours, for them to encourage any appearances of gifts amongst the people of their charge; if such should be raised up many advantages would be derived from their knowledge of the language, and customs of their countrymen; and their change of conduct would give great weight to their ministrations.

Section V
An Enquiry into the Duty of Christians in general, and what Means ought to be used, in order to promote this Work.

If the prophecies concerning the increase of Christ's kingdom be true, and if what has been advanced, concerning the commission given by him to his disciples being obligatory on us, be just, it must be inferred that all Christians ought heartily to concur with God in promoting his glorious designs, for *he that is joined to the Lord is one spirit*.

One of the first, and most important of those duties which are incumbent upon us, is *fervent and united prayer*. However the influence of the Holy Spirit may be set at nought, and run down by many, it will be found upon trial, that all means which we can use, without it, will be ineffectual. If a temple is raised for God in the heathen world, it will not be *by might, nor by power*, nor by the authority of the magistrate, or the eloquence of the orator; *but by my Spirit, saith the Lord of Hosts*. We must therefore be in real earnest in supplicating his blessing upon our labours. . . .

Suppose a company of serious Christians, ministers and private persons, were to form themselves into a society, and make a number of rules respecting the regulation of the plan, and the persons who are to be employed as missionaries, the means of defraying the expense, etc. etc. . . .

If there is any reason for me to hope that I shall have any influence upon any of my brethren, and fellow Christians, probably it may be more especially amongst them of my own denomination. I would therefore propose that such a society and committee should be formed amongst the *particular baptist denomination*.[40]

40. The Particular Baptists held to a Reformed view of predestination and "particular" (not general) redemption.

I do not mean by this, in any wise to confine it to one denomination of Christians. I wish with all my heart, that everyone who loves our Lord Jesus Christ in sincerity, would in some way or other engage in it. But in the present divided state of Christendom, it would be more likely for good to be done by each denomination engaging separately in the work, than if they were to embark in it conjointly. There is room enough for us all, without interfering with each other; and if no unfriendly interference took place, each denomination would bear good will to the other, and wish, and pray for its success, considering it as upon the whole friendly to the great cause of true religion; but if all were intermingled, it is likely their private discords might throw a damp upon their spirits, and much retard their public usefulness.

[*An Enquiry into the Obligations of Christians, to Use Means for the Conversion of the Heathens* (Leicester, 1792), 3, 67–77, 82, 84]

Selection 80: Thomas Campbell, *Declaration and Address* (1809)

Thomas Campbell (1763–1854) here expresses his desire to unite all Christians on the basis of the Bible alone. Thomas, his son Alexander Campbell (1788–1866), and Barton Stone (1772–1844) became the leaders of the Restoration Movement, represented today by Churches of Christ, Christian Churches, and the Disciples of Christ.

ADDRESS

To all that love our Lord Jesus Christ, in sincerity, throughout all the Churches, the following Address is most respectfully submitted.[41]

41. This address is the main body of the document and follows an introductory declaration.

DEARLY BELOVED BRETHREN,

THAT it is the grand design, and native tendency, of our holy religion, to reconcile and unite men to God, and to each other, in truth and love, to the glory of God, and their own present and eternal good, will not, we presume, be denied, by any of the genuine subjects of christianity. The nativity of its Divine Author was announced from heaven, by an host of angels, with high acclamations of "glory to God in the highest, and, on earth, peace and good will towards men." The whole tenor of that divine book which contains its institutes, in all its gracious declarations, precepts, ordinances, and holy examples, most expressly and powerfully inculcates this. In so far, then, as this holy unity and unanimity in faith and love is attained; just in the same degree, is the glory of God, and the happiness of men, promoted and secured. Impressed with those sentiments, and at the same time grievously affected with those sad divisions which have so awfully interfered with the benign and gracious intention of our holy religion, by exciting its professed subjects to bite and devour one another; we cannot suppose ourselves justifiable, in withholding the mite of our sincere and humble endeavours, to heal and remove them. . . .

The cause that we advocate is not our own peculiar, nor the cause of any party, considered as such; it is a common cause, the cause of Christ and our brethren of all denominations. All that we presume, then, is to do, what we humbly conceive to be *our* duty, in connexion with our brethren; to each of whom it equally belongs, as to us, to exert themselves for this blessed purpose. And as we have no just reason to doubt the concurrence of our brethren, to accomplish an object so desirable in itself, and fraught with such happy consequences, so neither can we look forward to that happy event, which will forever put an end to our hapless divisions, and restore to the church its primitive unity, purity and prosperity; but, in the pleasing prospect of their hearty and dutiful concurrence. . . .

Let none imagine that the subjoined propositions are at all intended as an overture towards a new creed, or standard, for the church; or, as in any wise designed to be made a term of communion;—nothing can be farther from our intention. They are merely designed for opening up the way, that we may come fairly and firmly to original ground: upon clear and certain premises: and take up things just as the Apostles left them.[42]—That thus disentangled from the accruing embarrassments of intervening ages, we may stand with evidence upon the same ground on which the church stood at the beginning—Having said so much to solicit attention and prevent mistake, we submit as follows.

PROP[OSITION] 1. THAT the church of Christ upon earth is essentially, intentionally, and constitutionally one; consisting of all those in every place that profess their faith in Christ and obedience to him in all things according to the scriptures, and that manifest the same by their tempers and conduct, and of none else, as none else can be truly and properly called christians.

2. That although the church of Christ upon earth must necessarily exist in particular and distinct societies, locally separate one from another; yet there ought to be no schisms, no uncharitable divisions among them. They ought to receive each other as Christ Jesus hath also received them to the glory of God. And for this purpose, they ought all to walk by the same rule, to mind and speak the same thing; and to be perfectly joined together in the same mind, and in the same judgment.

3. That in order to this, nothing ought to be inculcated upon christians as articles of faith; nor required of them as terms of communion; but what is expressly taught, and enjoined upon them, in the word of God. Nor ought any thing be admitted, as of divine obligation, in their church constitution and managements, but what is expressly enjoined by the authority of our Lord Jesus Christ and his Apostles upon the New Testament church; either in express terms, or by approven precedent.

4. That although the scriptures of the Old and New Testament are inseparably connected, making together but one perfect and entire revelation of the Divine will, for the edification and salvation of the church; and therefore in that respect cannot be separated; yet as to what directly and properly belongs to their immediate object, the New Testament is as perfect a constitution for the worship, discipline and government of the New Testament church, and as perfect a rule for the particular duties of its members; as the Old Testament was for the worship discipline and government of the Old Testament church, and the particular duties of its members.

5. That with respect to the commands and ordinances of our Lord Jesus Christ, where the scriptures are silent, as to the express time or manner of performance, if any such there be; no human authority has power to interfere, in order to supply the supposed deficiency, by making laws for the church; nor can any thing more be required of christians in such cases, but only that they so observe these commands and ordinances, as will evidently answer the declared and obvious end of their institution. Much less has any human authority power to impose new commands or ordinances upon the church, which our Lord Jesus Christ has not

42. This desire, expressed throughout this document, to return to the faith and practice not merely of the ancient church, but specifically of the first-century apostolic church, is sometimes labeled "restorationism."

enjoined. Nothing ought to be received into the faith or worship of the church; or be made a term of communion amongst christians, that is not as old as the New Testament.

6. That although inferences and deductions from scripture premises, when fairly inferred, may be truly called the doctrine of God's holy word: yet are they not formally binding upon the consciences of christians farther than they perceive the connection, and evidently see that they are so; for their faith must not stand in the wisdom of men; but in the power and veracity of God—therefore no such deductions can be made terms of communion, but do properly belong to the after and progressive edification of the church. Hence it is evident that no such deductions or inferential truths ought to have any place in the church's confession.

7. That although doctrinal exhibitions of the great system of divine truths, and defensive testimonies in opposition to prevailing errors, be highly expedient; and the more full and explicit they be, for those purposes, the better; yet, as these must be in a great measure the effect of human reasoning, and of course must contain many inferential truths, they ought not to be made terms of christian communion: unless we suppose, what is contrary to fact, that none have a right to the communion of the church, but such as possess a very clear and decisive judgment; or are come to a very high degree of doctrinal information; whereas the church from the beginning did, and ever will, consist of little children and young men, as well as fathers.

8. That as it is not necessary that persons should have a particular knowledge or distinct apprehension of all divinely revealed truths in order to entitle them to a place in the church; neither should they, for this purpose, be required to make a profession more extensive than their knowledge: but that, on the contrary, their having a due measure of scriptural self-knowledge respecting their lost and perishing condition by nature and practice; and of the way of salvation thro' Jesus Christ, accompanied with a profession of their faith in, and obedience to him, in all things according to his word, is all that is absolutely necessary to qualify them for admission into his church.

9. That all that are enabled, thro' grace, to make such a profession, and to manifest the reality of it in their tempers and conduct, should consider each other as the precious saints of God, should love each other as brethren, children of the same family and father, temples of the same spirit, members of the same body, subjects of the same grace, objects of the same divine love, bought with the same price, and joint heirs of the same inheritance. Whom God hath thus joined together no man should dare to put asunder.[43]

10. That division among christians is a horrid evil, fraught with many evils. It is anti-christian, as it destroys the visible unity of the body of Christ; as if he were divided against himself, excluding and excommunicating a part of himself. It is anti-scriptural, as being strictly prohibited by his sovereign authority; a direct violation of his express command. It is anti-natural, as it excites christians to contemn, to hate and oppose one another, who are bound by the highest and most endearing obligations to love each other as brethren, even as Christ has loved them. In a word, it is productive of confusion, and of every evil work.

11. That, (in some instances,) a partial neglect of the expressly revealed will of God; and, (in others,) an assumed authority for making the approbation of human opinions, and human inventions, a term of communion, by introducing them into the constitution, faith, or worship, of the church; are, and have been, the

43. Cf. Matt. 19:6.

immediate, obvious, and universally acknowledged causes, of all the corruptions and divisions that ever have taken place in the church of God.

12. That all that is necessary to the highest state of perfection and purity of the church upon earth is, first, that none be received as members, but such as having that due measure of scriptural self-knowledge described above, do profess their faith in Christ and obedience to him in all things according to the scriptures; nor, 2dly, that any be retained in her communion longer than they continue to manifest the reality of their profession by their tempers and conduct. 3dly, that her ministers, duly and scripturally qualified, inculcate none other things than those very articles of faith and holiness expressly revealed and enjoined in the word of God. Lastly, that in all their administrations they keep close by the observance of all divine ordinances, after the example of the primitive church, exhibited in the New Testament; without any additions whatsoever of human opinions or inventions of men.

13. Lastly. That if any circumstantials indispensably necessary to the observance of divine ordinances be not found upon the page of express revelation, such, and such only, as are absolutely necessary for this purpose, should be adopted, under the title of human expedients, without any pretence to a more sacred origin—so that any subsequent alteration or difference in the observance of these things might produce no contention nor division in the church. . . .[44]

Appendix

TO prevent mistakes, we beg leave to subjoin the following explanations. As to what we have done—our reasons for so doing—and the grand object we would desire to see accomplished—all these, we presume, are sufficiently declared in the foregoing pages. As to what we intend to do in our associate capacity, and the ground we have taken in that capacity, tho' expressly and definitely declared; yet, these, perhaps, might be liable to some misconstruction.—First, then, we beg leave to assure our brethren, that we have no intention to interfere, either directly, or indirectly, with the peace and order of the settled churches, by directing any ministerial assistance, with which the Lord may please to favour us, to make inroads upon such; or, by endeavouring to erect churches out of churches—to distract and divide congregations. We have no nostrum, no peculiar discovery of our own to propose to fellow-christians, for the fancied importance of which, they should become followers of us. We propose to patronize nothing but the inculcation of the express word of God—either as to matter of faith or practice;—but every one that has a Bible, and can read it, can read this for himself.—Therefore we have nothing new. Neither do we pretend to acknowledge persons to be ministers of Christ, and, at the same time, consider it our duty to forbid, or discourage people to go to hear them, merely because they may hold some things disagreeable to us; much less to encourage their people to leave them on that account;—and such do we esteem all, who preach a free unconstitutional salvation through the blood of Jesus to perishing sinners of every description; and who manifestly connect with this a life of holiness, and pastoral diligence in the performance of all the duties of their sacred office according to the scriptures; even all, of whom, as to all appearance, it may be truly said to the objects of their charge, "they seek not *yours*, but *you*." May the good Lord prosper all such, by whatever name they are called; and fast hasten that happy period, when Zion's watchmen shall see eye to eye, and all be called by the same name. . . .

44. It is clear that Campbell's primary concern is anything that undermines or threatens the unity of the church.

Thus have we briefly endeavored to shew our brethren, what evidently appears to us to be the heinous nature and dreadful consequences of that truly latitudinarian principle and practice, which is the bitter root of almost all our divisions; namely, the imposing of our private opinions upon each other, as articles of faith or duty; introducing them into the public profession and practice of the church, and acting upon them, as if they were the express law of Christ, by judging and rejecting our brethren that differ with us in those things; or, at least, by *so* retaining them in our public profession and practice, that our brethren cannot join with us, or we with them, without becoming actually partakers in those things, which they, or we, cannot, in conscience approve; and which the word of God no where expressly enjoins upon us. To cease from all such things, by simply returning to the original standard of christianity—the profession and practice of the primitive church, as expressly exhibited upon the sacred page of New Testament scripture, is the only possible way, that we can perceive, to get rid of those evils. And we humbly think that a uniform agreement in *that* for the preservation of charity would be infinitely preferable to our contentions and divisions: nay, that such a uniformity is the very thing that the Lord requires, if the New Testament be a perfect model—a sufficient formula for the worship discipline and government of the christian church. Let *us* do, as we are there expressly told *they* did, say as *they* said: that is, profess and practise as therein expressly enjoined by precept and precedent, in every possible instance, after *their* approved example; and in so doing we shall realize, and exhibit, all that unity and uniformity, that the primitive church possessed, or that the law of Christ requires. But if after all, our brethren can point out a better way to regain and preserve that christian unity and charity expressly enjoined upon the church of God, we shall thank them for the discovery, and cheerfully embrace it. . . .[45]

[*The Quest for Christian Unity, Peace, and Purity in Thomas Campbell's* Declaration and Address, ed. Thomas H. Olbricht and Hans Rollmann (Lanham, MD: Scarecrow, 2000), 8, 12, 17–20, 26, 37]

Selection 81: Charles G. Finney, *Lectures on Revivals of Religion* (1835)

Charles Grandison Finney (1792–1875) was the most influential revival preacher in the mid-nineteenth century. He experienced a conversion in 1821, eventually abandoned his law practice, and was ordained in the Presbyterian Church in 1824, but he soon left it for the Congregational Church. He was a professor of theology and later president of Oberlin College in Ohio.

In 1835, Finney delivered a series of weekly lectures in New York, published as **Lectures on Revivals of Religion.** ***Beginning with the text Habakkuk 3:2 ("O Lord, revive thy work"), he argued that revivals and conversions are not the results of divine miracles but require human cooperation to provide the occasion for revival. Thus, in response to criticism of his methods, Finney defended his use of "New Measures" such as "anxious seats" and other high-pressure techniques that later became commonplace in American evangelicalism. Finney's message was staunchly anti-Calvinist and fit in well with the optimistic spirit of the nineteenth century in general and the independent individualism of the young American republic in particular.***

45. The fact that Campbell is open to "a better way" indicates that restoring the New Testament model is simply a proposed means to a greater end (unity) but not the end itself.

Lecture 1: What a Revival of Religion Is

I. A Revival of Religion Is Not a Miracle.

1. A miracle has been generally defined to be, a Divine interference, setting aside or suspending the laws of nature. It is not a miracle in this sense. All the laws of matter and mind, remain in force. They are neither suspended nor set aside in a revival.

2. It is not a miracle according to another definition of the term miracle—*something above the powers of nature*. There is nothing in religion beyond the ordinary powers of nature. It consists entirely in the *right exercise* of the powers of nature. It is just that, and nothing else . . .

III. I Am to Consider the Agencies Employed in Carrying Forward a Revival of Religion.

Ordinarily, there are three agents employed in the work of conversion, and one instrument. The agents are God,—some person who brings the truth to bear on the mind,—and the sinner himself. The instrument is the truth. There are *always two* agents, God and the sinner, employed and active in every case of genuine conversion.[46]

1. The agency of God is two-fold; by his Providence and by his Spirit.

(1.) By his providential government, he so arranges events as to bring the sinner's mind and the truth in contact. He brings the sinner where the truth reaches his ears or his eyes. It is often interesting to trace the manner in which God arranges events so as to bring this about, and how he sometimes makes every thing seem to favor a revival. The state of the weather, and of the public health, and other circumstances concur to make every thing just right to favor the application of truth with the greatest possible efficacy. How he sometimes sends a minister along, just at the time he is wanted! How he brings out a particular truth, just at the particular time when the individual it is fitted to reach is in the way to hear!

(2.) God's special agency by his Holy Spirit. Having direct access to the mind, and knowing infinitely well the whole history and state of each individual sinner, he employs that truth which is best adapted to his particular case, and then sets it home with Divine power. He gives it such vividness, strength, and power, that the sinner quails, and throws down his weapons of rebellion, and turns to the Lord. Under his influence, the truth burns and cuts its way like fire. He makes the truth stand out in such aspects, that it crushes the proudest man down with the weight of a mountain. If men were *disposed* to obey God, the truth is given with sufficient clearness in the Bible; and from preaching they could learn all that is necessary for them to know. But because they are wholly *disinclined* to obey it, God clears it up before their minds, and pours in a blaze of convincing light upon their souls, which they cannot withstand, and they yield to it, and obey God, and are saved.

2. The agency of men is commonly employed. Men are not mere *instruments* in the hands of God. Truth is the instrument. The preacher is a moral agent in the work; he acts; he is not a mere passive instrument; he is voluntary in promoting the conversion of sinners.

3. The agency of the sinner himself. The conversion of a sinner consists in his obeying the truth. It is therefore impossible it should take place without his agency, for it consists in *his* acting right. He is influenced to this by the agency of God, and by the agency of men. Men act on their fellow-men, not only by language, but by their looks, their tears, their daily deportment. See that impenitent man there, who has a pious wife. Her very looks, her tenderness, her solemn, compassionate dignity,

46. Finney is making the point, common in older theology, that conversion happens ordinarily through the proclamation of the Word but in extraordinary cases may occur by direct, divine intervention.

softened and moulded into the image of Christ are a sermon to him all the time. He has to turn his mind away, because it is such a reproach to him. He feels a sermon ringing in his ears all day long. . . .

Lecture 7: Be Filled with the Spirit

. . . Remarks

1. Christians are as guilty for not having the Spirit, as sinners are for not repenting.

2. They are even more so. As they have more light, they are so much the more guilty.

3. All beings have a right to complain of Christians who are not filled with the Spirit. You are not doing work for God, and he has a right to complain. He has placed his Spirit at your disposal, and if you have it not, he has a right to look to you and to hold you responsible for all the good you might do, did you possess it. You are sinning against all heaven, for you ought to be adding to their happy ranks. Sinners, the church, ministers, have a right to complain.

4. You are right in the way of the work of the Lord. It is in vain for a minister to try to work over your head. Ministers often groan and struggle, and wear themselves out in vain, trying to do good where there is a church who live so that they do not have the Spirit of God. If the Spirit is poured out at any time, the church will grieve him right away.[47] Thus you may tie the hands and break the heart of your minister, and break him down, and perhaps kill him, because you will not be filled with the Spirit.

5. You see the reason why Christians need the Spirit, and the degree of their dependence. This cannot be too strongly exhibited.

6. Do not tempt God, by waiting for his Spirit, while using no means to procure his presence.

7. If you mean to have the Spirit, you must be childlike, and yield to his influences—just as yielding as air. If he is drawing you to prayer, you must quit everything to yield to his gentle strivings. No doubt you have sometimes felt a desire to pray for some object, and you have put it off and resisted, and God left you. If you wish him to remain, you must yield to his softest and gentlest motions, and watch to learn what he would have you do, and yield yourself up to his guidance.

8. Christians ought to be willing to make any sacrifice to enjoy the presence of the Spirit. Said a woman in high life, a professor of religion, "I must either give up hearing such a minister (naming him) preach, or I must give up my gay company." She gave up the preaching and staid away. How different from another case!

A woman in the same rank of life heard the same minister preach, and went home resolved to abandon her gay and worldly manner of life—dismissed most of her attendants—changed her whole mode of dress, of equipage, of living, and of conversation; so that her gay and worldly friends were soon willing to leave her to the enjoyment of communion with God, and free to spend her time in doing good.

9. You see from this, that it must be very difficult for those in fashionable life to go to heaven. What a calamity to be in such circles! Who can enjoy the presence of God in them?

10. See how crazy those are who are scrambling to get up to these circles, enlarging their houses, changing their style of living, furniture, etc. It is like climbing up mast-head to be thrown off into the ocean. To enjoy God, you must come down, not go up there. God is not there, among all the starch and flattery of hell.

11. Many professors of religion are as ignorant of spirituality as Nicodemus was of the new birth.[48] They are ignorant, and I fear unconverted. If any body talks to them about the spirit of prayer, it is all algebra to them.

47. See Eph. 4:30.

48. See John 3:3-8.

The case of such professors is awful. How different was the character of the apostles! Read the history of their lives, read their letters, and you will see that they were always spiritual, and walked daily with God. But now how little is there of such religion! "When the Son of Man cometh, will he find faith on the earth?"[49] Set some of these professors to work in a revival, and they do not know what to do, have no energy, no skill, and make no impression. When will professors of religion set themselves to work, filled with the Spirit? If I could see this church filled with the Spirit, I would ask nothing more to move this whole mighty mass of minds. Not two weeks would pass before the revival would spread all over this city.

Lecture 14: Measures to Promote Revivals

. . . *In the present generation*, many things have been introduced which have proved useful, but have been opposed on the ground *that they were innovations*. And as many are still unsettled in regard to them, I have thought it best to make some remarks concerning them. There are three things in particular which have chiefly attracted remark, and therefore I shall speak of them. They are *Anxious Meetings*, *Protracted Meetings*, and the *Anxious Seat*. These are all opposed, and are called new measures. . . .

(3.) *The Anxious Seat.*

By this I mean the appointment of some particular seat in the place of meeting, where the anxious may come and be addressed particularly, and be made subjects of prayer, and sometimes be conversed with individually. Of late this measure has met with more opposition than any of the others. What is the great objection? I cannot see it. The *design* of the anxious seat is undoubtedly philosophical, and according to the laws of mind. It has two bearings:

1. When a person is seriously troubled in mind, everybody knows that there is a powerful tendency to try to keep it private that he is so, and it is a great thing to get the individual willing to have the fact known to others. And as soon as you can get him willing to make known his feelings, you have accomplished a great deal. When a person is borne down with a sense of his condition, if you can get him willing to have it known, if you can get him to break away from the chains of pride, you have gained an important point towards his conversion. This is agreeable to the philosophy of the human mind. How many thousands are there who will bless God to eternity, that when pressed by the truth they were ever brought to take this step, by which they threw off the idea that it was a dreadful thing to have anybody know that they were serious about their souls.

2. Another bearing of the anxious seat, is to detect deception and delusion, and thus prevent false hopes. It has been opposed on this ground, that it was calculated to create delusion and false hopes. But this objection is unreasonable. The truth is the other way. Suppose I were preaching on the subject of Temperance, and that I should first show the evils of intemperance, and bring up the drunkard and his family, and show the various evils produced, till every heart is beating with emotion. Then I portray the great danger of moderate drinking, and show how it leads to intoxication and ruin, and that there is no safety but in TOTAL ABSTINENCE, till a hundred hearts are ready to say, "I will never drink another drop of ardent spirit in the world; if I do, I shall expect to find a drunkard's grave." Now, I stop short, and let the pledge be circulated, and everyone that is fully resolved is ready to sign it. But how many will begin to draw back and hesitate, when you begin to call on them to *sign a pledge* of total abstinence. One says to himself

49. Luke 18:8.

"Shall I sign it, or not? I thought my mind was made up, but this signing a pledge *never* to drink again, I do not know about that." Thus you see that when a person is called upon to give a pledge, if he is found not to be decided, he makes it manifest that he was not sincere. That is, he never came to that resolution on the subject, which could be relied on to control his future life. Just so with the awakened sinner. Preach to him, and at the moment he thinks he is willing to do anything; he thinks he is determined to serve the Lord; but bring him to the test, call on him to do one thing, to take one step that shall identify him with the people of God, or cross his pride—his pride comes up, and he refuses; his delusion is brought out, and he finds himself a lost sinner still; whereas, if you had not done it, he might have gone away flattering himself that he was a Christian. If you say to him, "There is the anxious seat, come out and avow your determination to be on the Lord's side," and if he is not willing to do so small a thing as that, then he is not willing to do *anything*, and there he is, brought out before his own conscience. It uncovers the delusion of the human heart, and prevents a great many spurious conversions, by showing those who might otherwise imagine themselves willing to do anything for Christ, that in fact they are willing to do *nothing*.

The church has always felt it necessary to have something of the kind to answer this very purpose. In the days of the apostles *baptism* answered this purpose.[50] The Gospel was preached to the people, and then all those who were willing to be on the side of Christ were called on to be *baptized*. It held the precise place that the anxious seat does now, as a public manifestation of their determination to be Christians. And in modern times, those who have been violently opposed to the anxious seat have been obliged to adopt some substitute, or they could not get along in promoting a revival. Some have adopted the expedient of inviting the people who were anxious for their souls to stay for conversation after the rest of the congregation had retired. But what is the difference? This is as much setting up a test as the other. Others, who would be much ashamed to employ the anxious seat, have asked those who have any feeling on the subject to sit still in their seats when the rest retire. Others have called the anxious to retire into the lecture room. The object of all these is the same, and the principle is the same, to bring people out from the refuge of false shame. One man I heard of who was very far gone in his opposition to new measures, in one of his meetings requested all those who were willing to submit to God, or desired to be made subjects of prayer, to signify it by leaning forward and putting their heads down upon the pew before them. Who does not see that this was a mere evasion of the anxious seat, and that it was designed to answer the purpose in its place, and he adopted this because he felt that something of the kind was important?

Now what objection is there against taking a particular seat, or rising up, or going into the lecture-room? They all mean the same thing, when properly conducted. And they are not novelties in principle at all. The thing has always been done in substance. In Joshua's day, he called on the people to decide what they would do, and they spoke right out in the meeting, "We will serve the Lord; the Lord our God will we serve, and his voice will we obey."[51]

50. Here is an interesting admission about the anxious seat replacing baptism in evangelism. In evangelicalism, the historic initiation rite of the church came to have little or no place in conversion.

51. Josh. 24:21, 24.

Remarks

. . . 5. Without new measures it is impossible that the church should succeed in gaining the attention of the world to religion. There are so many exciting subjects constantly brought before the public mind, such a running to and fro, so many that cry "Lo here," and "Lo there," that the church cannot maintain her ground, cannot command attention, without very exciting preaching, and sufficient novelty in measures, to get the public ear. The measures of politicians, of infidels and heretics, the scrambling after wealth, the increase of luxury, and the ten thousand exciting and counteracting influences that bear upon the church and upon the world, will gain their attention and turn all men away from the sanctuary and from the altars of the Lord, unless we increase in wisdom and piety, and wisely adopt such new measures as are calculated to get the attention of men to the Gospel of Christ. I have already said, in the course of these lectures, that novelties should be introduced no faster than they are really called for. They should be introduced with the greatest wisdom, and caution, and prayerfulness, and in a manner calculated to excite as little opposition as possible. But new measures we *must have*. And may God prevent the church from settling down in any *set* of forms, and getting the present or any other edition of her measures *stereotyped*.

6. It is evident that we must have more exciting preaching, to meet the character and wants of the age. Ministers are generally beginning to find this out. And some of them complain of it, and suppose it to be owing to new measures, as they call them. They say that such ministers as our fathers would have been glad to hear, now cannot be heard, cannot get a settlement, nor collect an audience. And they think that new measures have perverted the taste of the people. But this is not the difficulty. The character of the age is changed, and these men have not conformed to it, but retain the same stiff, dry, prosing style of preaching that answered half a century ago.

Look at the Methodists. Many of their ministers are unlearned, in the common sense of the term, many of them taken right from the shop or the farm, and yet they have gathered congregations, and pushed their way, and won souls everywhere. Wherever the Methodists have gone, their plain, pointed and simple, but warm and animated mode of preaching has always gathered congregations. Few Presbyterian ministers have gathered so large assemblies, or won so many souls. Now are we to be told that we must pursue the same old, formal mode of doing things, amidst all these changes? As well might the North River be rolled back, as the world converted under such preaching. Those who adopt a different style of preaching, as the Methodists have done, will run away from us. The world will escape from under the influence of this old fashioned or rather new fashioned ministry. It is impossible that the public mind should be held by such preaching. We must have exciting, powerful preaching, or the devil will have the people, except what the Methodists can save. It is impossible that our ministers should continue to do good, unless we have innovations in regard to the style of preaching. Many ministers are finding it out already, that a Methodist preacher, without the advantages of a liberal education, will draw a congregation around him which a Presbyterian minister, with perhaps ten times as much learning, cannot equal, because he has not the earnest manner of the other, and does not pour out fire upon his hearers when he preaches.[52]

[***Lectures on Revivals of Religion*** **(New York: Leavitt, Lord, and Co., 1835), 12, 15–16, 111–13, 242, 246–49, 251–53]**

---

52. In these remarks, Finney is influenced by a long line of pietistic reaction to scholastic doctrine, but he also partakes of the antiprofessionalism and anticlericalism that ran deep in antebellum America.

Selection 82: Joseph Smith, "The King Follett Sermon" (1844)

Joseph Smith (1805–1844) was the founder and original prophet of the Church of Jesus Christ of Latter-day Saints (LDS). In many ways, Smith and his followers represent the quintessentially American faith. Within a Christian context, yet with no regard for historic Christian doctrine or its intellectual tradition, the LDS sought to restore true religion, but based primarily on an additional revelation from Christ to the natives on North American soil. In this sermon, preached at the funeral of a respected church leader, Smith discusses the dead and several related topics, including the nature of God. Smith delivered this discourse on April 6, 1844, only two months before he was murdered in a prison in Carthage, Illinois, on June 27.

Beloved Saints, I will call [for] the attention of this congregation while I address you on the subject of the dead. The decease of our beloved brother, Elder King Follett, who was crushed in a well by the falling of a tub of rock, has more immediately led me to this subject. I have been requested to speak by his friends and relatives; but inasmuch as there are a great many in this congregation who live in this city, as well as elsewhere, who have lost friends, I feel disposed to speak on the subject in general, and offer you my ideas so far as I have ability and so far as I shall be inspired by the Holy Spirit to dwell on this subject. . . .

There are but a very few beings in the world who understand rightly the character of God. The great majority of mankind do not comprehend anything, either that which is past or that which is to come, as it respects their relationship to God. They do not know, neither do they understand the nature of that relationship; and, consequently, they know but little above the brute beast, or more than to eat, drink, and sleep. This is all man knows about God or his existence, unless it is given by the inspiration of the Almighty. . . .

My first object is to find out the character of the only wise and true God, and what kind of a being he is; and if I am so fortunate as to be the man to comprehend God, and explain or convey the principles to your hearts, so that the Spirit seals them upon you, then let every man and woman henceforth sit in silence, put their hands on their mouths, and never lift their hands or voices or say anything against the man of God or the servants of God again. But if I fail to do it, it becomes my duty to renounce all further pretensions to revelations, inspirations, or to be a Prophet; and I should be like the rest of the world—a false teacher, be hailed as a friend, and no man would seek my life. But if all religious teachers were honest enough to renounce their pretensions to godliness when their ignorance of the knowledge of God is made manifest, they will all be as badly off as I am, at any rate; and you might just as well take the lives of other false teachers as that of mine. If any man is authorized to take away my life because he thinks and says I am a false teacher, then, upon the same principle, we should be justified in taking away the life of every false teacher; and where would be the end of blood? And who would not be the sufferer?

But meddle not with any man for his religion; and all governments ought to permit every man to enjoy his religion unmolested. No man is authorized to take away life in consequence of difference of religion, which all laws and governments ought to tolerate and protect, right or wrong. Every man has a natural and, in our country, a constitutional right to be a false prophet as well as a true prophet. If I show, verily, that I have the truth of God, and show that ninety-nine out of every hundred professing religious ministers are false teachers, having no authority, while they pretend to hold the keys of God's kingdom on earth, and was to kill them because they are false teachers, it would deluge the whole world with blood. . . .

God himself was once as we are now, and is an exalted Man, and sits enthroned in yonder heavens. That is the great secret. If the veil were rent today, and the great God who holds this world in its orbit, and who upholds all worlds and all things by his power, was to make himself visible—I say, if you were to see him today, you would see him like a man in form—like yourselves, in all the person, image, and very form as a man; for Adam was created in the very fashion, image and likeness of God, and received instruction from, and walked, talked and conversed with him, as one man talks and communes with another. . . .

I wish I was in a suitable place to tell it, and that I had the trump of an archangel, so that I could tell the story in such a manner that persecution would cease forever. What did Jesus say? (Mark it, Elder Rigdon.[53]) The scriptures inform us that Jesus said, as the Father hath power in himself, even so hath the Son power—to do what? Why, what the Father did. The answer is obvious—in a manner to lay down his body and take it up again. Jesus, what are you going to do? To lay down my life as my Father did, and take it up again. Do you believe it? If you do not believe it you do not believe the Bible. The Scriptures say it, and I defy all the learning and wisdom and all the combined powers of earth and hell together to refute it. . . .

I shall comment on the very first Hebrew word in the Bible. I will make a comment on the very first sentence of the history of creation in the Bible—*Berosheit.* I want to analyze the word. *Baith*—in, by, through, and everything else. *Rosh*—the head, *Sheit*—grammatical termination. When the inspired man wrote it, he did not put the baith there. An old Jew without any authority added the word; he thought it too bad to begin to talk about the head! It read first, "The head one of the Gods brought forth the Gods." That is the true meaning of the words. *Baurau* signifies to bring forth. If you do not believe it, you do not believe the learned man of God. Learned men can teach you no more than what I have told you. Thus, the head God brought forth the Gods in the grand council.

I will transpose and simplify it in the English language. Oh, ye lawyers, ye doctors, and ye priests, who have persecuted me, I want to let you know that the Holy Ghost knows something as well as you do. The head God called together the Gods and sat in grand council to bring forth the world. The grand counsellors sat at the head in yonder heavens, and contemplated the creation of the worlds which were created at the time. When I say doctors and lawyers, I mean the doctors and lawyers of the Scriptures. I have done so hitherto without explanation, to let the lawyers flutter, and everybody laugh at them. Some learned doctor might take a notion to say the scriptures say thus and so; and we must believe the Scriptures; they are not to be altered. But I am going to show you an error in them.

I have an old edition of the New Testament in the Hebrew, Latin, German, and Greek languages. I have been reading the German, and find it to be the most correct translation, and to correspond nearest to the revelations which God has given to me for the last fourteen years. It tells about Jachoboy, the son of Zebedee. It means Jacob. In the English New Testament it

53. Sidney Rigdon (1793–1876) was a prominent preacher for the LDS until his excommunication after Smith's death.

is translated James. Now, if Jacob had the keys, you might talk about James through all eternity, and never get the keys. In the 21st [verse] of the fourth chapter of Matthew, my old German edition gives the word Jacob instead of James.[54]

The doctors (I mean doctors of law, not of physic) say, "If you preach anything not according to the Bible, we will cry treason." How can we escape the damnation of hell, except God be with us and reveal to us? Men bind us with chains. The Latin says Jachabod, which means Jacob; the Hebrew says Jacob, the Greek says Jacob, and the German says Jacob. Here we have the testimony of four against one. I thank God I have got this old book; but I thank him more for the gift of the Holy Ghost. I have got the oldest book in the world; but I have got the oldest book in my heart, even the gift of the Holy Ghost. I have all the four Testaments. Come here, ye learned men, and read, if you can. I should not have introduced this testimony, were it not to back up the word *Rosh*—the head, the father of the Gods. I should not have brought it up, only to show that I am right. . . .

You ask the learned doctors why they say the world was made out of nothing; and they will answer, "Don't the Bible say he *created* the world?" And they infer, from the word *create*, that it must have been made out of nothing. Now, the word *create* came from the word *baurau,* which does not mean to *create out of nothing*; it means to *organize*—the same as a man would organize materials and build a ship.[55] Hence we infer that God had materials to organize the world out of chaos—chaotic matter, which is element, and in which dwells all the glory. Element had an existence from the time He had. The pure principles of element are principles which can never be destroyed; they may be organized and re-organized, but not destroyed. They had no beginning, and can have no end. . . .

I want to talk more of the relation of man to God. I will open your eyes in relation to your dead. All things whatsoever God of his infinite wisdom has seen fit and proper to reveal to us, while we are dwelling in mortality, in regard to our mortal bodies, are revealed to us in the abstract and independent of affinity of this mortal tabernacle, but are revealed to our spirits precisely as though we had no bodies at all; and those revelations which will save our spirits will save our bodies. God reveals them to us in view of no eternal dissolution of the body, or tabernacle. Hence the responsibility, the awful responsibility, that rests upon us in relation to our dead; for all the spirits who have not obeyed the Gospel in the flesh must either obey it in the spirit or be damned. Solemn thought!—dreadful thought! Is there nothing to be done?—no preparation—no salvation for our fathers and friends who have died without having had the opportunity to obey the decrees of the Son of Man? Would to God that I had forty days and nights in which to tell you all! I would let you know that I am not a "fallen prophet." . . .

The contention in heaven was—Jesus said there would be certain souls that would not be saved; and the Devil said he could save them all, and laid his plans before the grand council, who gave their vote in favor of Jesus Christ. So the Devil rose up in rebellion against God, and was cast down, with all who put up their heads for him. . . .

I will leave this subject here, and make a few remarks on the subject of baptism. The baptism of water, without the baptism of fire and the Holy Ghost attending it, is of no use: they are necessarily and inseparably connected. An

54. Smith seems not to understand that "James" is simply an English translation of the Latin "Iacobus."

55. Unlike his exercise in Hebrew philology above, Smith's explanation here is more plausible.

individual must be born of water and the spirit in order to get into the kingdom of God. In the German, the text bears me out the same as the revelations which I have given and taught for the past fourteen years on that subject. I have the testimony to put in their teeth. My testimony has been true all the time. You will find it in the declaration of John the Baptist. (Reads from the German.) John says, "I baptize you with water, but when Jesus comes, who has the power (or keys) He shall administer the baptism of fire and the Holy Ghost." Great God! Where is now all the sectarian world? And if this testimony is true, they are all damned as clearly as anathema can do it. *I know the text is true.* I call upon all you Germans who know that it is true to say aye. (Loud shouts of aye.)

Alexander Campbell, how are you going to save people with water alone?[56] For John said his baptism was good for nothing without the baptism of Jesus Christ. . . .

[*Journal of Discourses Delivered by President Brigham Young, His Two Counsellors, the Twelve Apostles, and Others*, vol. 6 (Liverpool: Asa Calkin, 1859), 1–8, 10]

Selection 83: Phoebe Palmer, *The Promise of the Father* (1859)

Phoebe Worrall Palmer (1807–1874) was an influential lay leader in the Wesleyan holiness movement. Although she did not press for the full ordination of women, in* The Promise of the Father *she advocated the right of women to speak and teach in the church.

Do not be startled, dear reader. We do not intend to discuss the question of "Women's Rights" or of "Women's Preaching," technically so called. We leave this for those whose ability and tastes may better fit them for discussions of this sort. We believe woman has her legitimate sphere of action, which differs in most cases materially from that of man; and in this legitimate sphere she is both happy and useful. Yet we do not doubt that some reforms contemplated in recent movements may, in various respects, be decidedly advantageous. But we have never conceived that it would be subservient to the happiness, usefulness, or true dignity of woman, were she permitted to occupy a prominent part in legislative halls, or take a leading position in the orderings of church conventions. Ordinarily, these are not the circumstances where woman can best serve her generation according to the will of God. Yet facts show that it is in the order of God that woman may occasionally be brought out of the ordinary sphere of action, and occupy in either church or state positions of high responsibility; and if, in the orderings of providence, it so occur, the God of providence will enable her to meet the emergency with becoming dignity, wisdom, and womanly grace.

Examples of modern and ancient days might be furnished of women who have been called to fill positions involving large responsibilities, both civil and ecclesiastical. It was thus that Deborah, a prophetess, the wife of Lapidoth, was called to judge Israel—not because there were no men in Israel who might fill the position, but because God, in his wisdom, had so ordained; and it was also by the direction of Providence she was compelled to take the lead in the orderings of the battle—not because there were not men in Israel to do this, for she sent and called Barak, who might, as captain of the host, have led forth the people to conquest, but his faith and courage were insufficient to lead out Israel. . . .

56. Alexander Campbell, certainly not present at this sermon, is being invoked for his alleged advocacy of baptismal regeneration.

And when Josiah the King of Israel and his officers of state saw, from the reading of a book found in the house of the Lord, that great wrath was impending, they did not go to Huldah the prophetess for advice, because there was not a male prophet who might have been consulted; for it was in the days of Jeremiah the prophet, that this official deputation went from the king to Huldah. And when, in the order of God, woman has from time to time been called to sustain positions of momentous trust, involving the destinies of her country, facts show that she has not been wanting in ability to meet the demands of her station in such a manner, as to command the respect of her constituents or the homage of her subjects. . . .

And is it in religion alone that woman is prone to overstep the bounds of propriety, when the impellings of her Heaven-baptized soul would lead her to come out from the cloister, and take positions of usefulness for God? Whence has the idea obtained that she may not even open her lips for God in the assembly of the pious, without being looked upon repulsively, as though she were unwomanly in her aims and predilections?

And where is the beloved female disciple of any denomination, truly baptized of the Holy Ghost, but feels the Spirit's urgings to open her mouth for God? We do not now speak of that cold, worldly conformed professor, who has never, in obedience to the command of the Saviour, tarried at Jerusalem, as did Mary and the other women, on the day of Pentecost. We speak of that consistently pious, earnest, Christian woman, whose every-day life is an ever-speaking testimony of an indwelling Saviour, and on whose head the tongue of fire has descended. . . .

And here we come to the point, and are forced to an answer to which in the name of the Head of the church we claim a rejoinder. Our answer is this: The Christian churches of the present day, with but few exceptions, have imposed silence on Christian woman, so that her voice may but seldom be heard in Christian assemblies. And why do the churches impose it? The answer comes from a thousand lips, and from every point. The Head of the church forbids it, and the churches only join in the authoritative prohibition, "Let your women keep silence in the churches."[57] . . .

But if Paul's prohibition, "Let your women keep silence in the churches," is to be carried out to the letter in relation to the prophesying of women,—that is, her speaking "to edification, exhortation, and comfort,"—regardless of explanatory connections and contradictory passages, why should it not be carried out to the letter in other respects? If the apostle intended to enjoin silence in an absolute sense, then our Episcopalian friends trespass against this prohibition at every church service, in calling out the responses of women in company with the men in their beautiful Church Liturgy, and when they repeat our Lord's Prayer in concert with their brethren. And thus also do they trespass against this prohibition every time they break silence and unite in holy song in the church of God of any or every denomination. And in fact, we doubt not but it were less displeasing to the Head of the church that his female disciples were forbidden to open their lips in singing, or in church responses, than that they should be forbidden to open their lips in fulfilment of the "Promise of the Father,"[58] when the spirit of prophecy has been poured out upon them, moving them to well nigh irrepressible utterances of God's great goodness.

Under what circumstances was this prohibition given? Was it not by way of reproving

57. 1 Cor. 14:34.

58. The "promise of the Father" is the pouring out of the Holy Spirit. Cf. Luke 24:49; Acts 1:4; 2:33, 39.

some unseemly practices which had been introduced into the Corinthian church, and which, in fact, seem to have been peculiar to that church, for it is in connection with this and kindred disorders which had been introduced among the Corinthian believers, in connection with the exercise of the gift of prophecy, that Paul says, "We have no such custom, *neither the churches of God;*" that is, the other churches of God over which the Holy Ghost had made them overseers. . . .

It is not our aim in this Work to suggest, in behalf of woman, a change in the social or domestic relation. We are not disposed to feel that she is burdened with wrong in this direction. But we feel that there is a wrong, a serious wrong, affectingly cruel in its influences, which has long been depressing the hearts of the most devotedly pious women. And this wrong is inflicted by pious men, many of whom, we presume, imagine that they are doing God service in putting a seal upon lips which God has commanded to speak.

It is not our intention to chide those who have thus kept the Christian female in bondage, as we believe in ignorance they have done it. But we feel that the time has now come when ignorance will involve guilt; and the Head of the church imperatively demands a consideration of the question proposed in the following pages. . . .

Christian ministers, of every name and order, we ask you, in the name of thousands of your Christian sisters, upon whom God has poured out his Spirit, and who, in the social, prayer, and conference circle, would fain open their lips for God, will you not take this matter with you, as you enter into the inner sanctuary of the divine presence? Will you not, in prayerful waiting before the Head of the church, and in the light of the Holy Scriptures, investigate the subject, in view of bringing out a speedy answer, which may bear the light of eternity, and which, when reviewed in the day of reckoning, will meet your responsibilities? . . .

No one would regret more deeply than ourselves the error of writing one line that might seem to diminish the influence of an officially ordained ministry; yet it has for many years been our belief, that the modern ideas of preaching, and apostolic preaching, differ greatly.

What is meant by preaching the gospel? Says the devoted Dr. Wayland, "The word *preach* in the New Testament has a different meaning from that which at present commonly attaches to it. We understand by it the delivery of an oration, or discourse on a particular theme, connected more or less closely with religion. It may be the discussion of a doctrine, an exegetical essay, a dissertation on social virtues or vices, as well as a persuasive unfolding of the teaching of the Holy Ghost. No such general idea was intended by the word, as it is used by the writers of the New Testament. The words translated *preach* in our version are two. The one signifies, simply, to herald, to announce, to proclaim, to publish. The other, with this general idea, combines the notion of good tidings, and means to publish, or be the messenger of good news."[59] And in this exposition of the word, we believe most, and perhaps all other Bible expositors agree. And if this be the scriptural meaning of the word *preach,* then where is the Christian, either of the clergy or laity, but would have every man, woman, or child, who had an experimental knowledge of the saving power of Christ, herald far and near the tidings of a Saviour willing and able to save? . . .

If this be the true scriptural idea of *preaching,* to this we believe *every* individual called, whether male or female, who has been brought

59. Francis Wayland (1796–1865) was a preacher and the president of Brown University.

to an experimental knowledge of the grace of Christ, as the Saviour of sinners. And it is thus only that the command *can* be obeyed, and the gospel preached to every creature. How varied are the processes of grace on the human heart, in leading it from sin to holiness! And just so diversified, and correspondingly varied in interest, would be the proclamation of the healing, saving power of Christ, in the assemblies of the saints, if the same ideas of preaching now prevailed as in the primitive days of Christianity. . . .

But here is a witness prepared with a class of varied, well-digested, religious truth. So closely has she followed the Saviour, and listened to his teachings, and so rich, and deep, and diversified is her experience of the grace of God, that she is prepared from this personal experience to bring out of the treasury things new and old. She is a mother in Israel, and has learned with Deborah, the ancient mother in Israel, to be valiant for God. . . .

But who can conceive the result? "Tell it not in Gath; publish it not in the streets of Askelon!"[60] Our hearts are indeed pained when we think of the crucifying results which have, from time to time, come to our knowledge. Were we to tell some particulars in connection with restrainings, which have occurred on the part of church communities and individuals, we fear that we might tarnish our page. But the well-known fact, that earnestly-pious and intelligent women are ever withstood, and the testimony of their lips ruled out, with but few exceptions, in the presence of the men, in nearly all church communities, seems of itself more like a return to barbarism than a perpetuation of Christianity. And the reader will, in this connection, excuse us for saying, that we have been informed, from a source which we know to be true, of a member of a church session who actually advised a brother member to resort to corporal punishment, if he could not otherwise restrain his wife, who felt that Christ would have her testify of his grace.

The lady was a deeply-experienced Christian, and we presume none doubted her blessed experience in the divine life. And we could bring up more than one case similar to this. Our heart sickens and our pen falters over such recordings, and we could not consent to the task but from the hope that these revelations, so suited to the darker ages, may have a tendency to arouse the brethren of other church communities who are withstanding in woman the testimony of Jesus, which is the spirit of prophecy, to the danger of receding from the enlightening and ennobling principles of Christianity, and going back to the dark ages. . . .

[*The Promise of the Father; Or, a Neglected Speciality of the Last Days. Addressed to the Clergy and Laity of All Christian Communities* (repr., Shoals, IN: Old Paths Tract Society, n.d.), 1–6, 13, 68, 329–30, 333–34]

60. This is a quotation from 2 Sam. 1:20 regarding the proclamation of bad news.

Further Reading

Davies, Horton. *Worship and Theology in England: From Watts and Wesley to Martineau, 1690–1900*. Grand Rapids, MI: Eerdmans, 1996.

Hatch, Nathan O. *The Democratization of American Christianity*. New Haven, CT: Yale University Press, 1989.

Heitzenrater, Richard P. *Wesley and the People Called Methodists*. 2nd ed. Nashville, TN: Abingdon, 2012.

Kilde, Jeanne Halgren. *When Church Became Theatre: The Transformation of Evangelical Architecture and Worship in Nineteenth-Century America*. New York: Oxford University Press, 2002.

Marsden, George M. *Jonathan Edwards: A Life*. New Haven, CT: Yale University Press, 2004.

Noll, Mark A. *A History of Christianity in the United States and Canada*. Grand Rapids, MI: Eerdmans, 1992.

———. *The Rise of Evangelicalism: The Age of Edwards, Whitefield and the Wesleys*. A History of Evangelicalism, vol. 1. Downers Grove, IL: IVP Academic, 2003.

Shantz, Douglas H. *An Introduction to German Pietism: Protestant Renewal at the Dawn of Modern Europe*. Baltimore: Johns Hopkins University Press, 2013.

Chapter 8

Liberal Protestantism and Responses

The rational approach to religion that characterized the Enlightenment and was epitomized in deism continued to influence theology in the nineteenth century. Deism proper was on the decline, but its vision of God who stood above the cosmos as chief designer, its emphasis on morality, and its deemphasis on the historically distinct doctrines of Christianity lived on in varying degrees within what became known as classic "liberal Protestant theology."

The challenges of modernity to Christian orthodoxy came in various forms, many of which arose out of the Christian intellectual tradition itself. For instance, the rise of historical criticism could become a problem for a faith that regards historical knowledge as significant because it is the means of special revelation. The historical criticism that began in the Renaissance and was applied to secular and some church documents moved quickly to biblical documents such as the Pentateuch and eventually the Gospels. For various reasons, the narratives came to be viewed as later reconstructions that were historically unreliable, therefore casting doubt on the central acts of redemption.

Another challenge came from natural science, which, again, was a Christian enterprise that took for granted God's general revelation in the cosmos along with its orderly, teleological nature. However, once science became autonomous and methodologically removed God's immanent being and action from the cosmos, discoveries that supported an old earth and universe, the long extinction of species, and the evolution of higher forms of life from lower forms were commonly viewed as difficulties for Christian theism rather than as means through which God created.

As the Enlightenment project in general advanced knowledge in many disciplines, by the turn of the nineteenth century, it also had introduced other challenges to traditional, premodern Christian anthropology. Rather than seeing humanity as the center and pinnacle of creation, humans were increasingly regarded merely as creatures of blind nature, like all other animals. This cosmic marginalization was anticipated by the Copernican revolution and came to full bloom with Darwinism, especially when interpreted in an atheistic context. Along with this decentralization, reason was no longer seen as the objective instrument that many in the early Enlightenment assumed it to be. The worry of Descartes, brought to completion in Hume, is that what humans take to be rational thought is really subject to unproved traditions and passions. Thus Kant's Copernican revolution in epistemology codified the concept of subjectivity in human knowledge. Although reason as such did not suffer an immediate or fatal blow, and indeed continued to thrive in every realm of scholarship, nevertheless the nineteenth century would see definite reactions to the exaltation of reason in movements that found ultimate value in the

Charles Darwin

nonrational, such as Romanticism (with its celebration of nature and emotion), Marxism (emphasis on economic and social forces), and nihilism (valuing the absurd, the nothing).

The chief concern of all modern, post-Enlightenment theology, extending into the present day, may be summed up in the dual quest to preserve the benefits of the Enlightenment and, simultaneously, to maintain the validity of the Christian faith. As was the case in every period, the debates came down to the search for proper religious authority and foundations of theological certainty. Nancey Murphy proposes that modern theology may be summarized by looking for answers to three questions: (1) What proposals have been made regarding foundations for religious knowledge? (2) What are the problems with each of these proposals? and (3) Given the difficulty of finding a problem-free foundation, what moves have been made to sidestep the whole issue?[1]

In answer to the first question, at least three camps can be distinguished. One approach sought the foundation in reason and experience and has become known as liberal Protestant theology. This group tended to begin with anthropology and the immediate self-conscious awareness or feeling (*Gefühl*) of the divine. Liberal theology tended to accommodate Christian faith to modern culture and deny direct divine action in miracles such as the virgin birth and the bodily resurrection of Jesus Christ.

The second and third approaches may each be characterized as more or less resistant to modernity. The second group affirmed the priority of ecclesiastical authority. The church's infallibility was a long-held belief, and claims of papal infallibility go back to the medieval period. In response to competing claims of authority and the increasing influence of liberal theology, the Oxford Movement of Anglo-Catholics represents a mild form of the appeal to church tradition. In a bolder move, the Roman Catholic Church pressed these claims of authority to new levels in its dogmatizing of the infallible teaching of the pope.

The third group consisted of Protestant evangelicals who, on the one hand, resisted the emerging liberal theology with its alleged dismissal of divine revelation in favor of science and experience, and, on the other hand, rejected the claims of ecclesiastical authority and papal infallibility. These evangelicals instead maintained the principle of *sola Scriptura* and, like most premodern theologians, understood Scripture to be infallible. But again, in the atmosphere of competing options and increasing doubt, the doctrine of verbal inerrancy became a central identification mark of what would become evangelical fundamentalism.

1. Nancey Murphy, "What Has Theology to Learn from Scientific Methodology?" in *Science and Theology: Questions at the Interface*, ed. Murray Rae, et al. (Grand Rapids, MI: Eerdmans, 1994), 103.

A. Reshaping Christianity

Selection 84: William Ellery Channing, "Unitarian Christianity" (1819)

Antitrinitarianism had been a feature of certain Protestant groups since the sixteenth century, most notably the Socinians and those under their influence (see Selection 39). Around the turn of the nineteenth century, Unitarians rose to prominence in the United States, especially in Boston and through the influence of Harvard Divinity School. Infiltrating Congregationalist churches at first, Unitarianism was institutionalized with the founding of the American Unitarian Association in 1825. The basic Unitarian impulse was rational, biblical, and antitraditional—that is, typically American and restorationist. In connection with its optimistic view of human nature and reason, however, Unitarianism quickly became a modernizing, rationalistic movement that equally embraced non-Christian religions.

William Ellery Channing (1780–1842) lays out the fundamental principles of "Unitarian Christianity" in this speech delivered for an ordination ceremony in Baltimore. Channing himself disapproved of Unitarianism establishing a new sect, but he is regarded as the foremost theologian of early American Unitarian thought.

There are two natural divisions under which my thoughts will be arranged. I shall endeavor to unfold, 1st, The principles which we adopt in interpreting the Scriptures; and 2dly, Some of the doctrines which the Scriptures, so interpreted, seem to us clearly to express.

I. We regard the Scriptures as the records of God's successive revelations to mankind, and particularly of the last and most perfect revelation of his will by Jesus Christ. Whatever doctrines seem to us to be clearly taught in the Scriptures, we receive without reserve or exception. We do not, however, attach equal importance to all the books in this collection. Our religion, we believe, lies chiefly in the New Testament. The dispensation of Moses, compared with that of Jesus, we consider as adapted to the childhood of the human race, a preparation for a nobler system, and chiefly useful now as serving to confirm and illustrate the Christian Scriptures. Jesus Christ is the only master of Christians, and whatever he taught, either during his personal ministry or by his inspired Apostles, we regard as of divine authority, and profess to make the rule of our lives.

This authority which we give to the Scriptures is a reason, we conceive, for studying them with peculiar care, and for inquiring anxiously into the principles of interpretation by which their true meaning may be ascertained. The principles adopted by the class of Christians in whose name I speak need to be explained, because they are often misunderstood. We are particularly accused of making an unwarrantable use of reason in the interpretation of Scripture. We are said to exalt reason above revelation, to prefer our own wisdom to God's. Loose and undefined charges of this kind are circulated so freely, that we think it due to ourselves, and to the cause of truth, to express our views with some particularity.

Our leading principle in interpreting Scripture is this, that the Bible is a book written for men, in the language of men, and that its meaning is to be sought in the same manner as that of other books.[2] We believe that God,

2. The hermeneutical principle of interpreting the Bible like any other book became increasingly common

when he speaks to the human race, conforms, if we may so say, to the established rules of speaking and writing. . . .

Were the Bible written in a language and style of its own, did it consist of words which admit but a single sense, and of sentences wholly detached from each other, there would be no place for the principles now laid down. We could not reason about it as about other writings. But such a book would be of little worth; and perhaps, of all books, the Scriptures correspond least to this description. The word of God bears the stamp of the same hand which we see in his works. It has infinite connections and dependences. Every proposition is linked with others, and is to be compared with others, that its full and precise import may he understood. Nothing stands alone. The New Testament is built on the Old. The Christian dispensation is a continuation of the Jewish, the completion of a vast scheme of providence, requiring great extent of view in the reader. Still more, the Bible treats of subjects on which we receive ideas from other sources besides itself—such subjects as the nature, passions, relations, and duties of man; and it expects us to restrain and modify its language by the known truths which observation and experience furnish on these topics. . . .

Need I descend to particulars to prove that the Scriptures demand the exercise of reason? Take, for example, the style in which they generally speak of God, and observe how habitually they apply to him human passions and organs. Recollect the declarations of Christ, that he came not to send peace but a sword; that unless we eat his flesh and drink his blood we have no life in us; that we must hate father and mother, and pluck out the right eye; and a vast number of passages equally bold and unlimited. Recollect the unqualified manner in which it is said of Christians that they possess all things, know all things, and can do all things. Recollect the verbal contradiction between Paul and James and the apparent clashing of some parts of Paul's writings with the general doctrines and end of Christianity. I might extend the enumeration indefinitely; and who does not see that we must limit all these passages by the known attributes of God, of Jesus Christ, and of human nature, and by the circumstances under which they were written, so as to give the language a quite different import from what it would require had it been applied to different beings, or used in different connections.

Enough has been said to show in what sense we make use of reason in interpreting Scripture. From a variety of possible interpretations we select that which accords with the nature of the subject and the state of the writer, with the connection of the passage, with the general strain of Scripture, with the known character and will of God, and with the obvious and acknowledged laws of nature. In other words, we believe that God never contradicts in one part of Scripture what He teaches in another; and never contradicts in revelation what He teaches in his works and providence. And we therefore distrust every interpretation which, after deliberate attention, seems repugnant to any established truth. We reason about the Bible precisely as civilians do about the constitution under which we live; who, you know, are accustomed to limit one provision of that venerable instrument by others, and to fix the precise import of its parts by inquiring into its general spirit, into the intentions of its authors, and into the prevalent feelings, impressions, and circumstances of the time when it was framed. Without these principles of interpretation, we frankly acknowledge that we cannot defend the divine authority of the Scriptures. Deny us this latitude, and we must abandon this book to its enemies.

---

since the seventeenth century.

We do not announce these principles as original, or peculiar to ourselves. All Christians occasionally adopt them, not excepting those who most vehemently decry them when they happen to menace some favorite article of their creed. All Christians are compelled to use them in their controversies with infidels. All sects employ them in their warfare with one another. All willingly avail themselves of reason when it can be pressed into the service of their own party, and only complain of it when its weapons wound themselves. None reason more frequently than those from whom we differ. It is astonishing what a fabric they rear from a few slight hints about the fall of our first parents; and how ingeniously they extract from detached passages mysterious doctrines about the divine nature. We do not blame them for reasoning so abundantly, but for violating the fundamental rules of reasoning, for sacrificing the plain to the obscure, and the general strain of Scripture to a scanty number of insulated texts.

We object strongly to the contemptuous manner in which human reason is often spoken of by our adversaries, because it leads, we believe, to universal skepticism. If reason be so dreadfully darkened by the fall that its most decisive judgments on religion are unworthy of trust, then Christianity, and even natural theology, must be abandoned; for the existence and veracity of God, and the divine original of Christianity, are conclusions of reason, and must stand or fall with it.[3] If revelation be at war with this faculty, it subverts itself, for the great question of its truth is left by God to be decided at the bar of reason. It is worthy of remark, how nearly the bigot and the skeptic approach. Both would annihilate our confidence in our faculties, and both throw doubt and confusion over every truth. We honor revelation too highly to make it the antagonist of reason, or to believe that it calls us to renounce our highest powers.

We indeed grant that the use of reason in religion is accompanied with danger. But we ask any honest man to look back on the history of the church and say whether the renunciation of it be not still more dangerous. Besides, it is a plain fact that men reason as erroneously on all subjects as on religion. Who does not know the wild and groundless theories which have been framed in physical and political science? But who ever supposed that we must cease to exercise reason on nature and society because men have erred for ages in explaining them? We grant that the passions continually, and sometimes fatally, disturb the rational faculty in its inquiries into revelation. The ambitious contrive to find doctrines in the Bible which favor their love of dominion. The timid and dejected discover there a gloomy system, and the mystical and fanatical a visionary theology. The vicious can find examples or assertions on which to build the hope of a late repentance, or of acceptance on easy terms. The falsely refined contrive to light on doctrines which have not been soiled by vulgar handling. But the passions do not distract the reason in religious any more than in other inquiries which excite strong and general interest; and this faculty, of consequence, is not to be renounced in religion, unless we are prepared to discard it universally. The true inference from the almost endless errors which have darkened theology is, not that we are to neglect and disparage our powers, but to exert them more patiently, circumspectly, uprightly: the worst errors, after all, having sprung up in that church which proscribes reason, and demands from its members implicit faith. The most pernicious doctrines have been the growth of the darkest times,

3. Channing's rhetoric reflects the high regard in this period for natural theology and the deliverances of human reason.

when the general credulity encouraged bad men and enthusiasts to broach their dreams and inventions, and to stifle the faint remonstrances of reasons, by the menaces of everlasting perdition. Say what we may, God has given us a rational nature, and will call us to account for it. We may let it sleep, but we do so at our peril. Revelation is addressed to us as rational beings. We may wish, in our sloth, that God had given us a system demanding no labor of comparing, limiting, and inferring. But such a system would be at variance with the whole character of our present existence; and it is the part of wisdom to take revelation as it is given to us, and to interpret it by the help of the faculties which it everywhere supposes, and on which it is founded. . . .[4]

II. Having thus stated the principles according to which we interpret Scripture, I now proceed to the second great head of this discourse, which is, to state some of the views which we derive from that sacred book, particularly those which distinguish us from other Christians.

1. In the first place, we believe in the doctrine of God's UNITY, or that there is one God, and one only. To this truth we give infinite importance, and we feel ourselves bound to take heed lest any man spoil us of it by vain philosophy. The proposition that there is one God seems to us exceedingly plain. We understand by it that there is one being, one mind, one person, one intelligent agent, and one only, to whom underived and infinite perfection and dominion belong. We conceive that these words could have conveyed no other meaning to the simple and uncultivated people who were set apart to be the depositaries of this great truth, and who were utterly incapable of understanding those hair-breadth distinctions between being and person which the sagacity of later ages has discovered. We find no intimation that this language was to be taken in an unusual sense, or that God's unity was a quite different thing from the oneness of other intelligent beings.

We object to the doctrine of the Trinity, that, whilst acknowledging in words, it subverts in effect, the unity of God. According to this doctrine, there are three infinite and equal persons, possessing supreme divinity, called the Father, Son, and Holy Ghost. Each of these persons, as described by theologians, has his own particular consciousness, will, and perceptions. They love each other, converse with each other, and delight in each other's society. They perform different parts in man's redemption, each having his appropriate office, and neither doing the work of the other. The Son is mediator, and not the Father. The Father sends the Son, and is not himself sent; nor is he conscious, like the Son, of taking flesh. Here, then, we have three intelligent agents, possessed of different consciousnesses, different wills, and different perceptions, performing different acts, and sustaining different relations; and if these things do not imply and constitute three minds or beings, we are utterly at a loss to know how three minds or beings are to be formed. It is difference of properties, and acts, and consciousness, which leads us to the belief of different intelligent beings, and, if this mark fails us, our whole knowledge falls; we have no proof that all the agents and persons in the universe are not one and the same mind. When we attempt to conceive of three Gods, we can do nothing more than represent to ourselves three agents, distinguished from each other by similar marks and peculiarities to those which separate the persons of the Trinity; and when common Christians hear these persons spoken of as conversing with each other, loving each other, and performing different acts, how can

4. In short, reason and Scripture are the sources of theology; there is no room for church tradition.

they help regarding them as different beings, different minds?

We do, then, with all earnestness, though without reproaching our brethren, protest against the irrational and unscriptural doctrine of the Trinity. . . .

2. Having thus given our views of the unity of God, I proceed, in the second place, to observe that we believe in the unity of Jesus Christ. We believe that Jesus is one mind, one soul, one being, as truly one as we are, and equally distinct from the one God. We complain of the doctrine of the Trinity, that, not satisfied with making God three beings, it makes Jesus Christ two beings, and thus introduces infinite confusion into our conceptions of his character. This corruption of Christianity, alike repugnant to common sense and to the general strain of Scripture, is a remarkable proof of the power of a false philosophy in disfiguring the simple truth of Jesus. . . .

We say that if a doctrine [of Christ's two natures] so strange, so difficult, so remote from all the previous conceptions of men, be indeed a part, and an essential part, of revelation, it must be taught with great distinctness, and we ask our brethren to point to some plain, direct passage, where Christ is said to be composed of two minds infinitely different, yet constituting one person. We find none. Other Christians, indeed, tell us that this doctrine is necessary to the harmony of the Scriptures, that some texts ascribe to Jesus Christ human, and others divine properties, and that to reconcile these, we must suppose two minds, to which these properties may be referred. In other words, for the purpose of reconciling certain difficult passages, which a just criticism can in a great degree, if not wholly, explain, we must invent an hypothesis vastly more difficult, and involving gross absurdity. We are to find our way out of a labyrinth by a clue which conducts us into mazes infinitely more inextricable. . . .[5]

3. Having thus given our belief on two great points, namely, that there is one God, and that Jesus Christ is a being distinct from and inferior to God, I now proceed to another point on which we lay still greater stress. We believe in the *moral perfection of God*. We consider no part of theology so important as that which treats of God's moral character; and we value our views of Christianity chiefly as they assert his amiable and venerable attributes. . . .

We believe that God is infinitely good, kind, benevolent, in the proper sense of these words—good in disposition as well as in act; good not to a few, but to all; good to every individual, as well as to the general system. . . .[6]

To give our views of God in one word, we believe in his parental character. We ascribe to him not only the name, but the dispositions and principles of a father. We believe that he has a father's concern for his creatures, a father's desire for their improvement, a father's equity in proportioning his commands to their powers, a father's joy in their progress, a father's readiness to receive the penitent, and a father's justice for the incorrigible. We look upon this world as a place of education, in which he is training men by prosperity and adversity, by aids and obstructions, by conflicts of reason and passion, by motives to duty and temptations to sin, by a various discipline suited to free and moral beings, for union with himself, and for a sublime and ever-growing virtue in heaven. . . .

4. Having thus spoken of the unity of God; of the unity of Jesus, and his inferiority to God; and of the perfections of the divine character; I

5. The point is not made explicitly, but Channing implies that Jesus was a mere man, rather than a preexistent creature (as in Arianism).

6. Channing is emphasizing these (and many other) points against Reformed theology in particular.

now proceed to give our views of the mediation of Christ, and of the purposes of his mission. With regard to the great object which Jesus came to accomplish, there seems to be no possibility of mistake. We believe that he was sent by the Father to effect a moral or spiritual deliverance of mankind; that is, to rescue men from sin and its consequences, and to bring them to a state of everlasting purity and happiness. We believe, too, that he accomplishes this sublime purpose by a variety of methods—by his instructions respecting God's unity, parental character, and moral government, which are admirably fitted to reclaim the world from idolatry and impiety, to the knowledge, love, and obedience of the Creator; by his promises of pardon to the penitent, and of divine assistance to those who labor for progress in moral excellence; by the light which he has thrown on the path of duty; by his own spotless example, in which the loveliness and sublimity of virtue shine forth to warm and quicken as well as guide us to perfection; by his threatenings against incorrigible guilt; by his glorious discoveries of immortality; by his sufferings and death; by that signal event, the resurrection, which powerfully bore witness to his divine mission, and brought down to men's senses a future life; by his continual intercession, which obtains for us spiritual aid and blessings; and by the power with which he is invested of raising the dead, judging the world, and conferring the everlasting rewards promised to the faithful. . . .

We farther agree in rejecting, as unscriptural and absurd, the explanation given by the popular system, of the manner in which Christ's death procures forgiveness for men. . . .[7]

We believe, too, that this system is unfavorable to the character. It naturally leads men to think that Christ came to change God's mind rather than their own; that the highest object of his mission was to avert punishment rather than to communicate holiness; and that a large part of religion consists in disparaging good works and human virtue, for the purpose of magnifying the value of Christ's vicarious sufferings. In this way a sense of the infinite importance and indispensable necessity of personal improvement is weakened, and high-sounding praises of Christ's cross seem often to be substituted for obedience to his precepts. For ourselves, we have not so learned Jesus. Whilst we gratefully acknowledge that he came to rescue us from punishment, we believe that he was sent on a still nobler errand, namely, to deliver us from sin itself, and to form us to a sublime and heavenly virtue. We regard him as a Saviour, chiefly as he is the light, physician, and guide of the dark, diseased, and wandering mind. No influence in the universe seems to us so glorious, as that over the character; and no redemption so worthy of thankfulness, as the restoration of the soul to purity. Without this, pardon, were it possible, would be of little value. Why pluck the sinner from hell, if a hell be left to burn in his own breast? Why raise him to heaven, if he remain a stranger to its sanctity and love? With these impressions, we are accustomed to value the gospel chiefly as it abounds in effectual aids, motives, excitements to a generous and divine virtue. In this virtue, as in a common centre, we see all its doctrines, precepts, promises meet; and we believe that faith in this religion is of no worth, and contributes nothing to salvation any farther than as it uses these doctrines, precepts, promises, and the whole life, character, sufferings, and triumphs of Jesus, as the means of purifying the

7. Channing goes on to describe what he rejects—the satisfaction and penal substitution theory of atonement.

mind, of changing it into the likeness of his celestial excellence.[8]

5. Having thus stated our views of the highest object of Christ's mission that it is the recovery of men to virtue, or holiness, I shall now, in the last place, give our views of the nature of Christian virtue, or true holiness. We believe that all virtue has its foundation in the moral nature of man that is, in conscience, or his sense of duty, and in the power of forming his temper and life according to conscience. We believe that these moral faculties are the grounds of responsibility, and the highest distinctions of human nature, and that no act is praiseworthy any farther than it springs from their exertion. We believe that no dispositions infused into us without our own moral activity are of the nature of virtue, and therefore we reject the doctrine of irresistible divine influence on the human mind, moulding it into goodness as marble is hewn into a statue. Such goodness, if this word may be used, would not be the object of moral approbation, any more than the instinctive affections of inferior animals, or the constitutional amiableness of human beings. . . .

We would not, by these remarks, be understood as wishing to exclude from religion warmth, and even transport. We honor and highly value true religious sensibility. We believe that Christianity is intended to act powerfully on our whole nature, on the heart as well as the understanding and the conscience. We conceive of heaven as a state where the love of God will be exalted into an unbounded fervor and joy; and we desire, in our pilgrimage here, to drink into the spirit of that better world. But we think that religious warmth is only to be valued when it springs naturally from an improved character, when it comes unforced, when it is the recompense of obedience, when it is the warmth of a mind which understands God by being like him, and when, instead of disordering, it exalts the understanding, invigorates conscience, gives a pleasure to common duties, and is seen to exist in connection with cheerfulness, judiciousness, and a reasonable frame of mind. When we observe a fervor called religious in men whose general character expresses little refinement and elevation, and whose piety seems at war with reason, we pay it little respect. We honor religion too much to give its sacred name to a feverish, forced, fluctuating zeal, which has little power over the life. . . .[9]

[*The Works of William E. Channing* (Boston: American Unitarian Association, 1890), 367–70, 371, 373–74, 376, 377, 378, 379–80, 381]

Selection 85: Ralph Waldo Emerson, "Divinity School Address" (1838)

The son of a Unitarian minister and deeply affected by Unitarian thought, Ralph Waldo Emerson (1803–1882) was an ordained minister and preached until 1847, after which he lectured on literature and philosophy. Moving beyond Unitarianism, he became associated with the movement known as Transcendentalism, characterized by the belief that God is in every person. This speech, delivered to Harvard Divinity School students, reflects the Transcendentalist ideas of optimistic individualism and religious protest against organized religion, as well as the principles of Romanticism and exaltation of created nature.

A more secret, sweet, and overpowering beauty appears to man when his heart and mind open to the sentiment of virtue. Then instantly he is

8. Channing here advocates the moral exemplar theory of atonement.

9. Note the thinly veiled contempt for the excesses of the First and Second Great Awakenings.

instructed in what is above him. He learns that his being is without bound; that, to the good, to the perfect, he is born, low as he now lies in evil and weakness. That which he venerates is still his own, though he has not realized it yet. *He ought*. . . .

The sentiment of virtue is a reverence and delight in the presence of certain divine laws. It perceives that this homely game of life we play, covers, under what seem foolish details, principles that astonish. The child amidst his baubles, is learning the action of light, motion, gravity, muscular force; and in the game of human life, love, fear, justice, appetite, man, and God, interact. These laws refuse to be adequately stated. They will not by us or for us be written out on paper, or spoken by the tongue. They elude, evade our persevering thought, and yet we read them hourly in each other's faces, in each other's actions, in our own remorse. The moral traits which are all globed into every virtuous act and thought,—in speech, we must sever, and describe or suggest by painful enumeration of many particulars. Yet, as this sentiment is the essence of all religion, let me guide your eye to the precise objects of the sentiment, by an enumeration of some of those classes of facts in which this element is conspicuous. . . .

Meantime, whilst the doors of the temple stand open, night and day, before every man, and the oracles of this truth cease never, it is guarded by one stern condition; this, namely; it is an intuition.[10] It cannot be received at second hand. Truly speaking, it is not instruction, but provocation, that I can receive from another soul. What he announces, I must find true in me, or wholly reject; and on his word, or as his second, be he who he may, I can accept nothing. On the contrary, the absence of this primary faith is the presence of degradation. As is the flood so is the ebb. Let this faith depart, and the very words it spake, and the things it made, become false and hurtful. Then falls the church, the state, art, letters, life. The doctrine of the divine nature being forgotten, a sickness infects and dwarfs the constitution. Once man was all; now he is an appendage, a nuisance. And because the indwelling Supreme Spirit cannot wholly be got rid of, the doctrine of it suffers this perversion, that the divine nature is attributed to one or two persons, and denied to all the rest, and denied with fury. The doctrine of inspiration is lost; the base doctrine of the majority of voices, usurps the place of the doctrine of the soul. Miracles, prophecy, poetry, the ideal life, the holy life, exist as ancient history merely; they are not in the belief, nor in the aspiration of society; but, when suggested, seem ridiculous. Life is comic or pitiful, as soon as the high ends of being fade out of sight, and man becomes near-sighted, and can only attend to what addresses the senses. . . .

1. In thus contemplating Jesus, we become very sensible of the first defect of historical Christianity. Historical Christianity has fallen into the error that corrupts all attempts to communicate religion. As it appears to us, and as it has appeared for ages, it is not the doctrine of the soul, but an exaggeration of the personal, the positive, the ritual. It has dwelt, it dwells, with noxious exaggeration about the *person* of Jesus. The soul knows no persons. It invites every man to expand to the full circle of the universe, and will have no preferences but those of spontaneous love. But by this eastern monarchy of a Christianity, which indolence and fear have built, the friend of man is made the injurer of man. . . .

2. The second defect of the traditionary and limited way of using the mind of Christ is a consequence of the first; this, namely; that the

10. The influence of Romanticism, which is itself a result of Enlightenment thought, is evident especially here. The subjective intuition that Emerson describes is the proper basis of institutional religion.

Moral Nature, that Law of laws, whose revelations introduce greatness,—yea, God himself, into the open soul, is not explored as the fountain of the established teaching in society. Men have come to speak of the revelation as somewhat long ago given and done, as if God were dead. The injury to faith throttles the preacher; and the goodliest of institutions becomes an uncertain and inarticulate voice.

It is very certain that it is the effect of conversation with the beauty of the soul, to beget a desire and need to impart to others the same knowledge and love. If utterance is denied, the thought lies like a burden on the man. Always the seer is a sayer. Somehow his dream is told. Somehow he publishes it with solemn joy. . . .

Whenever the pulpit is usurped by a formalist, then is the worshipper defrauded and disconsolate.[11] We shrink as soon as the prayers begin, which do not uplift, but smite and offend us. We are fain to wrap our cloaks about us, and secure, as best we can, a solitude that hears not. I once heard a preacher who sorely tempted me to say, I would go to church no more. Men go, thought I, where they are wont to go, else had no soul entered the temple in the afternoon. A snow storm was falling around us. The snow storm was real; the preacher merely spectral; and the eye felt the sad contrast in looking at him, and then out of the window behind him, into the beautiful meteor of the snow. He had lived in vain. He had no one word intimating that he had laughed or wept, was married or in love, had been commended, or cheated, or chagrined. If he had ever lived and acted, we were none the wiser for it. The capital secret of his profession, namely, to convert life into truth, he had not learned. Not one fact in all his experience, had he yet imported into his doctrine. This man had ploughed, and planted, and talked, and bought, and sold; he had read books; he had eaten and drunken; his head aches; his heart throbs; he smiles and suffers; yet was there not a surmise, a hint, in all the discourse, that he had ever lived at all. Not a line did he draw out of real history. The true preacher can be known by this, that he deals out to the people his life,—life passed through the fire of thought. But of the bad preacher, it could not be told from his sermon, what age of the world he fell in; whether he had a father or a child; whether he was a freeholder or a pauper; whether he was a citizen or a countryman; or any other fact of his biography.

It seemed strange that the people should come to church. It seemed as if their houses were very unentertaining, that they should prefer this thoughtless clamor. It shows that there is a commanding attraction in the moral sentiment, that can lend a faint tint of light to dulness and ignorance, coming in its name and place. The good hearer is sure he has been touched sometimes; is sure there is somewhat to be reached, and some word that can reach it. When he listens to these vain words, he comforts himself by their relation to his remembrance of better hours, and so they clatter and echo unchallenged. . . .

My friends, in these two errors, I think, I find the causes of that calamity of a decaying church and a wasting unbelief, which are casting malignant influences around us, and making the hearts of good men sad. And what greater calamity can fall upon a nation, than the loss of worship? Then all things go to decay. Genius leaves the temple, to haunt the senate, or the market. Literature becomes frivolous. Science is cold. The eye of youth is not lighted by the hope of other worlds, and age is without honor. Society lives to trifles, and when men die, we do not mention them.

11. That is, only when that prime intuition is abandoned and replaced by the institutional church does religion become stale.

And now, my brothers, you will ask, What in these desponding days can be done by us? The remedy is already declared in the ground of our complaint of the Church. We have contrasted the Church with the Soul. In the soul, then, let the redemption be sought. In one soul, in your soul, there are resources for the world. Wherever a man comes, there comes revolution. The old is for slaves. When a man comes, all books are legible, all things transparent, all religions are forms. He is religious. Man is the wonderworker. He is seen amid miracles. All men bless and curse. He saith yea and nay, only. The stationariness of religion; the assumption that the age of inspiration is past, that the Bible is closed; the fear of degrading the character of Jesus by representing him as a man; indicate with sufficient clearness the falsehood of our theology. It is the office of a true teacher to show us that God is, not was; that He speaketh, not spake. . . .

Let me admonish you, first of all, to go alone; to refuse the good models, even those most sacred in the imagination of men, and dare to love God without mediator or veil. Friends enough you shall find who will hold up to your emulation Wesleys and Oberlins,[12] Saints and Prophets. Thank God for these good men, but say, "I also am a man." Imitation cannot go above its model. The imitator dooms himself to hopeless mediocrity. The inventor did it, because it was natural to him, and so in him it has a charm. In the imitator, something else is natural, and he bereaves himself of his own beauty, to come short of another man's.

[Ralph Waldo Emerson, *An Address Delivered before the Senior Class in Divinity College, Cambridge* (Boston: James Munroe and Company, 1838), 4–6, 10–11, 13, 16, 19–20, 24–26]

12. That is, Jean Frédéric Oberlin (1740–1826), a Protestant minister known for his piety and good works, and for whom Oberlin College (Ohio) is named.

B. Friedrich D. E. Schleiermacher

Biographical Note: Friedrich D. E. Schleiermacher

Friedrich Daniel Ernst Schleiermacher (1768–1834) was born in Breslau, Prussia, and received his seminary education in the Pietist tradition of the Moravians. He later studied at the University of Halle. He was ordained to the ministry of the German Reformed Church in 1794 and became a preacher in Berlin. He was instrumental in the founding of the university in Berlin, and he was appointed as the dean of its theology faculty in 1810. Schleiermacher also advocated the union of the Reformed and Lutheran Churches in Prussia, which was ordered by King Frederick of Prussia in 1817.

*Schleiermacher's thought is, in part, a mixture of the older Continental Pietism, the emerging Romanticism of the post-Enlightenment period, and liberalism. Romanticism in particular inclined toward a pantheistic or panentheistic theology, emphasizing the world spirit, along with naturalistic explanations of reality. It was also characterized by an appreciation for the universal brotherhood of humanity in all its diverse forms. Thus, for Schleiermacher, the finite world is a manifestation of the infinite, living God, and the vast multiplicity of individual humanity finds its unity in the God-world relation. A person's deepest dimension of existence lies in recognizing this relationship to the Absolute or the Whole by a feeling (*Gefühl*) of complete dependence on the Whole, recognized also through subordinate relationships of dependence with other creatures. Each individual is a valid, if only partial, manifestation of the Absolute.*

Schleiermacher took the Pietist and Romantic emphasis on feeling to new theological heights, arguing that religion is really nothing other than feeling at its core. As morality was primary for Kant, Romantic intuition, innate and universally available, was the chief religious category for Schleiermacher. According to Schleiermacher, religion has had many valid expressions throughout human history, though some expressions are more complete and integrated than others. Christianity is the highest form of religion because it takes seriously the relation between humanity and the Absolute.

Schleiermacher also embodied the ideals of modern biblical criticism and influenced modern hermeneutics. He stressed the proper use of historical and exegetical techniques, inherited especially from the Renaissance and developed after the Reformation. The goal of reading Scripture is to experience the original human author's own experience of divine revelation.

Especially for his influence on Ernst Troeltsch (1865–1923), Adolf von Harnack (1851–1930), and other German theologians at the pinnacle of classic liberal Protestantism, Schleiermacher has justly become known as the father of modern (that is, liberal Protestant) theology. At the same time, for his accommodation of theology to modern culture, his marginalizing of distinctive Christian doctrines, and his location of God-consciousness within humanity, Schleiermacher later became the whipping boy for Karl Barth and the neo-orthodox movement.

Selection 86: Friedrich D. E. Schleiermacher, *On Religion: Speeches to Its Cultured Despisers* (1799)

Given the obsolescence of deism and Enlightenment rationalism, Schleiermacher attempts to provide a new foundation for Christian theology. Thus, in apologetic mode, he argues that religion is essentially a human intuition that the cultured critics of religion both experience and value.

First Speech: Apology

It may be an unexpected undertaking, and you might rightly be surprised that someone can demand from just those persons who have raised themselves above the herd, and are saturated by the wisdom of the century, a hearing for a subject so completely neglected by them. I confess that I do not know how to indicate anything that presages a fortunate outcome for me, not even the one of winning your approval of my efforts, much less the one of communicating my meaning and enthusiasm to you. From time immemorial faith has not been everyone's affair, for at all times only a few have understood something of religion while millions have variously played with its trappings with which it has willingly let itself be draped out of condescension.

Especially now, the life of cultivated persons is removed from everything that would in the least way resemble religion. I know that you worship the deity in holy silence just as little as you visit the forsaken temples, that in your tasteful dwellings there are no other household gods than the maxims of the sages and the songs of the poets, and that humanity and fatherland, art and science (for you imagine yourselves capable of all of this) have taken possession of your minds so completely that no room is left over for the eternal and holy being that for you lies beyond the world, and that you have no feelings for and with it.[13] You have succeeded in making your earthly lives so rich and many-sided that you no longer need the

13. *Gefühl(e)*, here translated as "feeling(s)," will prove to be a central concept in Schleiermacher's theology and religious epistemology.

eternal, and after having created a universe for yourselves, you are spared from thinking of that which created you. You are agreed, I know, that nothing new and nothing convincing can be said anymore about this matter, which has been sufficiently belabored in all directions by philosophers and prophets and, if only I might not add, by scoffers and priests. Least of all—something that can escape no one—are you inclined to listen to something on this subject from the last mentioned, who have long since made themselves unworthy of your trust, as the kind of people who best like to dwell only in the dilapidated ruins of the sanctuary and who cannot live even there without disfiguring and damaging it still more.[14] All this I know and am nevertheless convinced to speak by an inner and irresistible necessity that divinely rules me, and cannot retract my invitation that you especially should listen to me.

With regard to this last point I could probably ask you, How does it happen that on every subject, be it important or insignificant, you most desire to be instructed by persons who have dedicated their lives and their intellectual powers to it, and your thirst for knowledge does not shun even the huts of peasants and the workshops of humble artisans, and yet in matters of religion you consider everything more suspicious that comes from those who claim to be experts on the subject and are considered to be such by the state and people? You will surely not be able to show that they are not that and that they rather hold and preach everything else but religion. Thus reasonably disdaining such an unfounded judgment, I confess before you that I also am a member of this order and I do so at the risk, if you do not listen to me attentively, of being thrown into the same category with the same bunch.

14. These opening lines are striking testimony to the widespread loss of religion in cultured European society already by the end of the eighteenth century.

It is at least a voluntary confession, for my speech would not have betrayed me, and the eulogies of my fellow guildmembers would not either. What I intend lies almost completely outside their sphere and would hardly resemble what they want to see and hear. I do not chime in with the cry for help of most of them concerning the demise of religion, for I would not know what other age may have accommodated it better than the present; and I have nothing to do with the old-fashioned and barbaric lamentation with which they would like to clamor for the caved-in walls of their Jewish Zion and its Gothic pillars. . . .

Can you seriously expect me to believe that those who daily torment themselves most tiresomely with earthly things are most preeminently suited to become intimate with heaven? That those who brood anxiously over the next moment and are firmly chained to the nearest objects can raise their eyes the furthest to the universe? And that persons who have not yet found themselves in the uniform succession of a dead industriousness will most clearly discover the living deity? Therefore, I can call only you to me, you who are capable of raising yourselves above the common standpoint of humanity, you who do not shrink from the burdensome way into the depths of human nature in order to find the ground of its action and thought. . . .

Without doubt, you are familiar with the history of human follies and have perused the different edifices of religion, from the meaningless fables of barbarous nations to the most refined deism, from the crude superstition of our people to the poorly stitched together fragments of metaphysics and morals that are called rational Christianity, and you have found them all without rhyme or reason. I am far from wishing to contradict you in that. On the contrary, if you but honestly mean that the most developed religious systems bear these characteristics no less than the crudest, if you would only realize that the divine cannot lie in a series that terminates on both sides in something common and despicable, then I shall gladly spare you the trouble of evaluating more closely all those that lie between. They all appear as transitions to and approximations of the former; each comes from the hand of its age somewhat more honed until finally art has ascended to that perfected plaything with which our century has until now whiled away the time.

But this consummation is almost anything but an approximation of religion. I cannot speak of it without indignation. For everyone who has a feeling for all that issues from the depths of the heart and who takes it seriously that every side of human nature should be formed and exhibited must bewail how the high and noble has strayed from its vocation and has lost its freedom in order to be held in a despicable slavery by the scholastic and metaphysical spirit of barbaric and cold times. Where it is present and effective it must so reveal itself that it moves the mind in a peculiar manner, mingling or rather removing all functions of the human soul and resolving all activity in an astonishing intuition of the infinite. Do you feel this way about these systems of theology, about these theories of the origin and end of the world, about these analyses of the nature of an incomprehensible being, where everything amounts to cold argumentation and nothing can be treated except in the tone of an ordinary didactic controversy?[15] In all these systems you despise, you have accordingly not found religion and cannot find it because it is not there, and if it were shown to you that it were elsewhere, you would still not be capable of finding and honoring it. . . .

The injunction to seek the true and the right, which you have not found in the great multitude, in the first apparently unformed rudiments cannot seem strange to any of you, who are more or less concerned about philosophy and are familiar with its fortunes. Recall how few of those who have descended on their own path into the inner side of human nature and the world, and who have intuited and portrayed their mutual relationship and inner harmony in a unique light, have formed their own system of philosophy. Have not all communicated their discoveries in a more delicate—be it also more fragile—form? . . .

Consider by whom these artificial edifices are raised? Consider whose changeableness you mock, whose disproportion offends you, and whose inadequacy on account of their petty tendencies is so ludicrous to you? By chance one of the heroes of religion? Name me one individual among all those who have brought down to us some new revelation, from whoever first conceived the one universal God—certainly the most systematic thought in the whole field of religion—to the most recent mystic in whom perhaps an original beam of the inner light still gleams. (You will not blame me if I do not include the literalistic theologians who believe the salvation of the world and the light of knowledge is to be found in the new garb of their formulas or in the new arrangements of their calculating proofs.) Name me a single individual among all of these who would have thought it worth the effort to be occupied with this Sisyphean labor. Only single sublime thoughts flash through their soul that ignited from an ethereal fire, and the magic thunder of a charmed speech accompanied the lofty appearance and proclaimed to a worshiping mortal that the deity had spoken.

15. Schleiermacher's aversion to theological discourse seems to have softened somewhat over the next decades.

An atom impregnated by a celestial power fell into their mind, assimilated everything there, expanded it mightily, and then burst, as if by divine decree, in a world whose atmosphere offered too little resistance and brought forth in its final moments one of those heavenly meteors, one of those significant signs of the times whose origin no one mistakes and which fills all mortals with awe. . . .

I ask, therefore, that turning from all that is usually called religion you aim your attention only at these individual intimations and moods that you will find in all expressions and noble deeds of God-inspired persons. If you then discover nothing new and pertinent even in the particular, as I hope may occur despite your learning and your knowledge, if your narrow concept that is produced only by superficial observation does not expand and transform itself, if you could then still despise this bent of the mind toward the eternal—if all that is important to humanity can still seem ludicrous to you even from this point of view, then I shall believe that your disdain of religion is in conformity with your nature and shall have nothing further to say to you.[16] Only do not worry that I still might, in the end, resort after all to those common measures of demonstrating to you how necessary religion is for maintaining right and order in the world and for coming to the aid of the shortsightedness of human perspective and the narrow limits of human power with the reminder of an all-seeing and infinite power. Nor shall I say that religion would be a true friend and a saving support of morality, since its holy feelings and its brilliant prospects make the struggle with the self and the accomplishment of good very much easier for a weak humanity. Thus indeed do those speak who pretend to be the best friends and most zealous defenders of religion. But I shall not decide for whom the most contempt is due in this chain of ideas, whether it be right and morality, which are represented as in need of support, or religion, which is supposed to undergird them, or you, to whom this is addressed. . . .

Yet those who thus proceed from utility, for whom, in the end, even ethical life and law are there for the sake of another advantage, might themselves better founder in this eternal cycle of general utility in which they allow everything good to perish and of which no person who even wishes to be something for himself understands a sound word. Better that than to set themselves up as defenders of religion whose cause they are truly the most inept to lead. A lovely fame for heavenly religion, if it were now able to provide so passably for the earthly affairs of humanity! Much honor to this free and carefree one, if it were only somewhat more vigilant and active than the conscience! Religion does not descend to you from heaven for such purpose. What is loved and esteemed only for an advantage that lies outside may well be needed, but it is not in itself necessary; it can always remain a pious wish that never comes into existence, and a reasonable person places no extraordinary value on it, but merely the value that is appropriate to the other thing. And this would be little enough in the case of religion. I, at least, would bid for it stingily, for I must only confess that I do not believe that the unjust actions it hinders and the ethical deeds it is supposed to have produced are so serious. If that should be the only thing that can command respect for it, I want to have nothing to do with its cause. To recommend it merely as an aside is too insignificant. An imagined praise that disappears when one observes it more closely cannot assist something that deals in higher claims. What I assert and what I should

16. Schleiermacher turns the tables on common modern sensibilities, arguing that those who dismiss religion are the truly closed-minded.

like to establish for religion include the following: It springs necessarily and by itself from the interior of every better soul, it has its own province in the mind in which it reigns sovereign, and it is worthy of moving the noblest and the most excellent by means of its innermost power and by having its innermost essence known by them. Now it is up to you to decide whether it is worth your while to listen to me before you become still more entrenched in your contempt.

Fifth Speech: On the Religions

. . . However, you must not grope about by chance in this infinite chaos—although I must forgo leading you around in it in systematic and complete fashion, for that would be the study of a lifetime and not the task of an address. So that you are not misled by vulgar concepts, you should survey the true content and the actual essence of the individual religions according to a correct standard, and should learn to distinguish the inner from the outer, the native from the borrowed and foreign, the holy from the profane according to the determinate and firm ideas. In order to do this, forget for the present each individual religion and what is taken to be its individual characteristic and first seek from inside out to attain a general idea of what actually makes up the essence of a determinate form of religion. You will find that precisely the positive religions are these determinate forms in which infinite religion manifests itself in the finite, and that natural religion cannot claim to be something similar inasmuch as it is merely an indefinite, insufficient, and paltry idea that can never really exist by itself. You will find that in these positive religions alone a true, individual development of the religious capacity is possible and that by their very essence they do no injury at all to the freedom of their confessors.

Why have I assumed that religion cannot be completely given except in an unending multitude of thoroughly determinate forms? Only on grounds that were explained when I spoke about the essence of religion. These are that every intuition of the infinite exists wholly for itself, is dependent on no other, and has no other as a necessary consequence; they are infinitely many and have no reason in themselves why they should be related to one another in one way and not is some other, and yet each appears completely different if it is viewed from another point or related to another intuition; thus the whole of religion cannot possibly exist otherwise than when all these different views of each intuition that can arise in such a manner are really given. This is not possible except in an infinite multitude of various forms, each of which is thoroughly determined by the different principle of relation in it and in each of which the same object is quite differently modified; that is to say, that are all true individuals.

[*On Religion: Speeches to Its Cultured Despisers* (1799), ed. Richard Crouter, 2nd ed. (Cambridge: Cambridge University Press, 1996), 77–79, 87, 89–92, 94–95, 194–95]

Selection 87: Friedrich D. E. Schleiermacher, *The Christian Faith* (1821–1822; 2nd ed., 1830–1831)

Schleiermacher intended his magnum opus, entitled* The Christian Faith according to the Principles of the Evangelical Church, *to be an articulation of theology in support of the new union of Lutheran and Reformed Churches in Prussia. In it, he examines Christian theology more through the lens of the phenomenology of religion than through traditional Christian dogma or Enlightenment reason. By his definition, the feeling of absolute dependence is not something that

originates in Scripture or any other revelation specific to Christianity.

In his effort to establish a new foundation for Christian theology and to communicate it effectively to the educated society, Schleiermacher reinterpreted many traditional doctrines. He famously marginalized the once-central doctrine of the Trinity by relegating his discussion to a brief appendix at the end of his book. For its innovation and subsequent influence,* The Christian Faith *is widely regarded to be, after Calvin's* Institutes *(see Selection 30), the most important statement of Protestant systematic theology written before the twentieth century.

Chapter 1: The Definition of Dogmatics

§ 4. *The common element in all howsoever diverse expressions of piety, by which these are conjointly distinguished from all other feelings, or, in other words, the self-identical essence of piety, is this: the consciousness of being absolutely dependent, or, which is the same thing, of being in relation with God. . . .*

§ 8. *Those forms of piety in which all religious affections express the dependence of everything finite upon one Supreme and Infinite Being, i.e. the monotheistic forms, occupy the highest level; and all others are related to them as subordinate forms, from which men are destined to pass to those higher ones.*[17]

2. As for this difference, of believing in one God on whom the religious man regards himself as being (along with the world of which he is a part) absolutely dependent, or in a group of gods to whom he stands in different relations according as they divide the government of the world among them, or finally in particular idols which belong to the family or the locality or the particular occupation in which he lives: it seems at first, indeed, to be only a difference in the mode of representation, and therefore, from our point of view, only a derivative difference. And only a difference in the immediate self-consciousness can for us be a fit measure of the development of religion. But it is also very easy to show that these different representations depend on different states of self-consciousness. Idol-worship proper is based upon a confused state of the self-consciousness which marks the lowest condition of man, since in it the higher and the lower are so little distinguished that even the feeling of absolute dependence is reflected as arising from a particular object to be apprehended by the senses. So, too, with Polytheism: in its combination of the religious susceptibility with diverse affections of the sensible self- consciousness, it exhibits this diversity in such a very preponderant degree that the feeling of absolute dependence cannot appear in its complete unity and indifference to all that the sensible self-consciousness may contain; but, instead, a plurality is posited as its source. But when the higher self-consciousness, in distinction from the sensible, has been fully developed, then, in so far as we are open in general to sensible stimulation, i.e. in so far as we are constituent parts of the world, and therefore in so far as we take up the world into our self-consciousness and expand the latter into a general consciousness of finitude, we are conscious of ourselves as absolutely dependent. Now this self-consciousness can only be described in terms of Monotheism, and indeed only as we have expressed it in our proposition. For if we are conscious of ourselves, as such and in our finitude, as absolutely dependent, the same holds true of all finite existence, and in this connexion we take up the whole world along with ourselves into the unity of our self-consciousness. Thus the different ways of representing that existence outside of us to which the consciousness of absolute dependence refers, depend partly on the different degrees of

17. The influence of Pietism is evident in Schleiermacher's language and in his emphasis on the feeling of absolute dependence on God.

extensiveness of the self-consciousness (for as long as a man identifies himself only with a small part of finite existence, his god will remain a fetich[18]); and partly on the degree of clearness with which the higher self-consciousness is distinguished from the lower. Polytheism naturally represents in both respects an indeterminate middle stage, which sometimes is very little different from Idol-worship, but sometimes, when in the handling of the plurality there appears a secret striving after unity, may border very closely on Monotheism; whether it be that the gods rather represent the forces of Nature, or that they symbolize the human qualities which are operative in social relationships, or that both these tendencies are united in the same cult. Otherwise it could not in itself be explained how the correlative term in the feeling of absolute dependence could be reflected as a plurality of beings. But if the higher consciousness has not become quite distinct from the lower, then the correlative can only be conceived in a sensible way, and then for that very reason it contains the germs of plurality. Thus it is only when the religious consciousness expresses itself as capable of being combined with all the states of the sensible self-consciousness without discrimination, but also as clearly distinct from the latter, in such a way that in the religious emotions themselves no sharper distinction appears than that between the joyful and the depressing tone—it is only then that man has successfully passed beyond those two stages, and can refer his feeling of absolute dependence solely to one Supreme Being. . . .

4. On this highest plane, of Monotheism, history exhibits only three great communions—the Jewish, the Christian, and the Mohammedan; the first being almost in process of extinction, the other two still contending for the mastery of the human race. Judaism, by its limitation of the love of Jehovah to the race of Abraham, betrays a lingering affinity with Fetichism; and the numerous vacillations towards idol-worship prove that during the political heyday of the nation the monotheistic faith had not yet taken fast root, and was not fully and purely developed until after the Babylonian Exile. Islam, on the other hand, with its passionate character, and the strongly sensuous content of its ideas, betrays, in spite of its strict Monotheism, a large measure of that influence of the sensible upon the character of the religious emotions which elsewhere keeps men on the level of Polytheism. Thus Christianity, because it remains free from both these weaknesses, stands higher than either of those other two forms, and takes its place as the purest form of Monotheism which has appeared in history. Hence there is strictly no such thing as a wholesale relapse from Christianity to either Judaism or Mohammedanism, any more than there is from any monotheistic religion to Polytheism or idol-worship. Individual exceptions will always be connected with pathological states of mind; or, instead of religion, it will prove to be simply one form of irreligion that is exchanged for another, which indeed is what always happens in the case of renegades. And so this comparison of Christianity with other similar religions is in itself a sufficient warrant for saying that Christianity is, in fact, the most perfect of the most highly developed forms of religion. . . .

Postscript 2.—But for the assonance of the names there would scarcely be any occasion for us expressly to remark that it is not at all our present business to say anything about that way of thinking which is called Pantheism. For it has never been the confession of a religious communion which actually appeared in history,

18. A fetish (or fetich) is properly an object believed to possess supernatural powers.

and it is only with these that we are concerned. Moreover, this name was not originally used even by individuals to designate their own views, but crept in as a taunt and nickname; and in such cases it always remains difficult to hold consistently to any one meaning. The one thing concerning the subject which can be discussed in this place (and indeed *only* in such a place as this) is the question of the relation of this way of thinking to piety. It is admitted that it does not, like the three above-described theories, spring from the religious emotions, by direct reflection upon them. But it may be asked whether, having once arisen in some other way—by the way of speculation or simply of reasoning—it is yet compatible with piety. To this question an affirmative answer may be given without hesitation, provided that Pantheism is taken as expressing some variety or form of Theism, and that the word is not simply and solely a disguise for a materialistic negation of Theism. If we look at idol-worship, and consider how it is always conjoined with a very limited knowledge of the world, and is also full of magic and sorcery of every sort, it is very easy to see that in very few cases can one speak of a clear distinction on this level between what is assigned to God and what is assigned to the world. And why could not a Hellenic polytheist, embarrassed by the entirely human shapes of the gods, have identified his great gods with the evolved gods of Plato, leaving out the God whom Plato represents as addressing them, and positing only the enthroned Necessity? This would not imply any change in his piety, yet his representation of it would have become pantheistic. But let us think of the highest stage of religion, and let us accordingly hold Pantheism fast to the usual formula of One and All: then God and world will remain distinct at least as regards function, and thus such a man, since he reckons himself as belonging to the world, can feel himself, along with this All, to be dependent on that which is the corresponding One. Such states of mind can scarcely be distinguished from the religious emotions of many a Monotheist. At any rate, the distinction (always rather a curious one, and, if I may say so, roughly drawn) between a God who is outside of and above the world, and a God who is in the world, does not particularly meet the point, for nothing can strictly be said about God in terms of the antithesis between internal and external without imperilling in some way the divine omnipotence and omnipresence.

Conclusion: The Divine Trinity

§ 170. *All that is essential in this Second Aspect of the Second Part of our exposition is also posited in what is essential in the doctrine of the Trinity; but this doctrine itself, as ecclesiastically framed, is not an immediate utterance concerning the Christian self-consciousness, but only a combination of several such utterances.*

1. An essential element of our exposition in this Part has been the doctrine of the union of the Divine Essence with human nature, both in the personality of Christ and in the common Spirit of the Church; therewith the whole view of Christianity set forth in our Church teaching stands and falls. For unless the being of God in Christ is assumed, the idea of redemption could not be thus concentrated in His Person. And unless there were such a union also in the common Spirit of the Church, the Church could not thus be the Bearer and Perpetuator of the redemption through Christ. Now these exactly are the essential elements in the doctrine of the Trinity, which, it is clear, only established itself in defence of the position that in Christ there was present nothing less than the Divine Essence, which also indwells the Christian Church as its common Spirit, and that we take

these expressions in no reduced or sheerly artificial sense, and know nothing of any special higher essences, subordinate deities (as it were) present in Christ and the Holy Spirit. The doctrine of the Trinity has no origin but this; and at first it had no other aim than to equate as definitely as possible the Divine Essence considered as thus united to human nature with the Divine Essence in itself. This is the less doubtful that those Christian sects which interpret the doctrine of redemption differently are also necessarily without the doctrine of the Trinity—they have no point of belief to which it could be attached—which could not possibly be the case if even in Catholic doctrine there existed at least some other points than this to which the attachment could be made. It is equally clear from this why those divergent sects which are chiefly distinguishable by their denial of the Trinity are not thereby forced into still other divergences in the doctrine of God and the divine attributes, as must have been the case if the doctrine of the Trinity were rooted in a special view of the nature of the Supreme Being as such. But on the other hand, they *are* forced to set up a different theory of the Person of Christ, and hence also of man's need for redemption and of the value of redemption. In virtue of this connexion, we rightly regard the doctrine of the Trinity, in so far as it is a deposit of these elements, as the coping-stone of Christian doctrine, and this equating with each other of the divine in each of these two unions, as also of both with the Divine Essence in itself, as what is essential in the doctrine of the Trinity.

2. But at this point we would call a halt; we cannot attach the same value to the further elaboration of the dogma, which alone justifies the ordinary term. For the term "Trinity" is really based on the fact that each of the two above-mentioned unions is traced back to a separate distinction posited independently of such union, and eternally, in the Supreme Being as such; further, after the member of this plurality destined to union with Jesus had been designated by the name "Son," it was felt necessary to posit the Father in accordance therewith as a special distinction. The result was the familiar dualism—unity of Essence and trinity of Persons. But the assumption of an eternal distinction in the Supreme Being is not an utterance concerning the religious consciousness, for there it never could emerge.[19] Who would venture to say that the impression made by the divine in Christ obliges us to conceive such an eternal distinction as its basis? Anyone who were to find this task set us in the Johannine conception of the Logos, as if that conception definitely included one element of the doctrine of the Trinity and the completion of the doctrine were called for by that simple fact, would be in so difficult a position that he could hardly maintain his ground. For one thing, it is in this very passage that Arianism sought a foothold; and the exegesis of both sides in that controversy is so exposed to equal though opposite objections that we cannot help saying that if either of the two antagonistic views was in John's mind as fundamental to the passage, it must be confessed that he went to work to express it in a highly unsatisfactory and ineffective manner. On the other hand, if the Trinity had been in the Apostle's mind, his exposition would very easily have lent itself to a similar introduction of the Holy Spirit, whose name occurs so often in Christ's discourses as reported by John; nor would he have lacked opportunity elsewhere to bring in this other member, and to speak of the place of the Spirit as that which

19. The assumption is that only beliefs that arise directly from the human religious self-consciousness are of prime importance. Belief in the Trinity is rather a conclusion derived from prior perceptions of distinction within God.

was in the beginning with God and was God. Assuming, however, that John here declares of the divine united in Christ with human nature that it existed in God from all eternity in a distinct form, it does not follow by any means that this was meant in the sense of the doctrine of the Trinity, and that that doctrine is therefore the true and the only natural completion of the Johannine statements. For underlying the elaboration of the doctrine is not merely a desire to reproduce very exactly our Christian consciousness that the Divine Essence in both forms of union is the same, and also is equal to the being of God *per se*; rather, it was only after the distinction had been eternalized and made antecedent to the union that there arose a need to guard against the semblance of polytheism, and to secure that this, in a sense separated, being of God was none the less embraced within the unity of the Divine Essence. But of such a need there is in John no trace whatever, which means that he was not on the way to the doctrine of the Trinity as we have it.

3. Hence the second part of our paragraph must not be understood as meaning that the orthodox doctrine of the Trinity is to be regarded as an immediate or even a necessary combination of utterances concerning the Christian self-consciousness. On the contrary, the intermediate step has been taken of eternalizing, in separation, the being of God in itself, and the being of God which makes union with human nature possible. Now if this arose so definitely out of the utterances of Christ Himself and of the Apostles concerning Him that we had to accept it on their testimony, the doctrine of the Trinity in that case would be a fully elaborated doctrine of this type, and we should accept it as a combination of testimonies regarding a supersensible fact; but it would no more be a "doctrine of faith" in the really original and proper sense of that phrase than the doctrines of the resurrection and ascension of Christ; and it would resemble these last also in this respect that our faith in Christ and our living fellowship with Him would be the same although we had no knowledge of any such transcendent fact, or although the fact itself were different.[20] But the exegesis meant to establish the position just mentioned has never been able to entrench itself so strongly as to escape constant attacks upon it. Hence it is important to make the point that the main pivots of the ecclesiastical doctrine—the being of God in Christ and in the Christian Church—are independent of the doctrine of the Trinity.

Let it be supposed that we further elaborate our knowledge of this supersensible fact and—to avoid the idea that the said distinction within the Supreme Being led to nothing up to the beginning of the union—teach besides that both the Second and the Third Person in the Trinity were implicated even in the creation of the world, while the Second Person was also the subject thereafter of all the Old Testament theophanies, and it was from the Third Person that the whole prophetic movement of the Old Testament received its impulse. Then these statements are still further removed from being utterances about our Christian consciousness. And we can wait all the more calmly to see whether the exegetical results on which these expansions of the doctrine rest are any more fully confirmed by the latest work on the subject than has hitherto been the case.

Postscript.—If success ever had attended, or ever could attend, the attempt to exhibit or prove a trinity in God from general conceptions or *a priori* (an effort perhaps stimulated by Church doctrine, apart from which it would hardly occur to anyone, but yet without any

20. Schleiermacher here emphasizes his belief that belief in the Trinity makes no practical difference in one's practical piety.

relation to the facts of redemption or any appeal to Scripture), still such a doctrine of the Trinity even though worked out with much greater elaboration than the ecclesiastical doctrine (bound up as it is with the basal facts of Christianity) has ever obtained or ever could obtain, could find no place in a Christian Dogmatic. Even although it kept strictly to the use of the same terms in denoting both the trinity and the unity as are employed in the ecclesiastical doctrine, we should firmly maintain that as a doctrine it was different. For deductions of that kind, standing in no connexion with those basal facts, do not merely show it to be quite different from the other in origin; on that very account they are of no sort of use in Christian doctrine. Therefore we must simply put them aside as "philosophemes";[21] nor are we in any way called upon to submit them to criticism, whether they originate with ancient or modern Church teachers.

§ 171. *The ecclesiastical doctrine of the Trinity demands that we think of each of the three Persons as equal to the Divine Essence, and vice versa, and each of the three Persons as equal to the others. Yet we cannot do either the one or the other, but can only represent the Persons in a gradation, and thus either represent the unity of the Essence as less real than the three Persons, or* vice versa.

1. There can be no doubt that from this assumption of eternal distinctions in the Divine Essence, there necessarily follows the implication of the double equality of the divine in all three Persons, and of the divine in each Person with the Supreme Being as a unity. If divinity or power and glory were less in all the three Persons together than in the Supreme Being conceived as a unity, the three Persons would not be in but under the Supreme Being. In that case, the divine in them would only improperly be called divine, and our living fellowship with Christ as well as our participation in the Holy Spirit would not be fellowship with God. The result would be the same if the divine in the Persons themselves were not the same, only the divine in (say) the Father being truly and properly divine, but the divine in Christ and the Holy Spirit unreal and subordinate. In that case our indwelling sense of need for redemption would necessarily take a different form of expression, if indeed as a hindrance to fellowship to God it would in any way be met by a redemption which did not bring us to fellowship with God. In short, everything most important in Christianity would be changed. On those assumptions, no other definition can be reached than that posited by the ecclesiastical doctrine, and the ever-renewed zeal shown in its defence is perfectly intelligible.

21. A philosopheme is a principle of reasoning considered to be based on self-evident premises. It has the connotation, however, of an assertion rather than a valid argument.

[*The Christian Faith* (New York: T and T Clark, 1989), 12, 34, 35–36, 37–39, 738–43]

Selection 88: Friedrich D. E. Schleiermacher, "Sermon at Nathanael's Grave" (1829)

On November 1, 1829, Schleiermacher delivered a sermon at the graveside of his nine-year-old son, Nathanael, who died after a three-day bout with scarlet fever. Not only the theology but especially the piety, pathos, and pain of the father of modern theology are on unique display here.

My dear friends, come here to grieve with this stooped father at the grave of his beloved child, I know you are not come with the intention of seeing a reed shaken by the wind.[22] But what you find is in truth only an old stalk, which yet

22. See Matt. 11:7.

does not break even from this gust of wind that has suddenly struck him from on high, out of the blue. Thus it is! For a happy household, cared for and spared by Heaven for twenty years, I have God to thank; for a much longer pursuit of my vocation, accompanied by undeserved blessings; for a great abundance of joys and sorrows, which, in my calling and as a sympathetic friend, I have lived through with others. Many a heavy cloud has passed over my life; yet what has come from without, faith has surmounted, and what from within, love has recompensed. But now, this one blow, the first of its kind, has shaken my life to its roots.

Ah, children are not only dear pledges entrusted to us from God, for whom we must give account; not only inexhaustible subjects of concern and duty, of love and prayer: they are also an immediate blessing upon the house; they give easily as much as they receive; they freshen life and gladden the heart. Just such a blessing was this boy for our house. As the Redeemer said that the angels of the little ones see the face of this Father in heaven, so with this child it appeared to us as if such an angel beamed out from his countenance the kindness of our God. When God gave him to me, my first prayer was that fatherly love would never mislead me to expect more of the boy than was right; and I believe the Lord has granted me this. I know very well that there are children far more outstanding in gifts of mind, in eager alertness, and upon whom far greater expectations concerning what they will accomplish in the world could be raised, and I would rejoice should there be many of them. When I gave him the name he bore, not only did I want thereby to greet him as a precious and welcome gift of God.[23] I wanted at the same time to express my earnest wish that he might become like his biblical namesake, a soul in which there is no falsehood; and this too the Lord has granted me. Honest and frank as our boy was, he looked everyone in the eye full of trust, doing only good to all, and we have never found anything false in him. And for this reason, my dear children whom I see around me here—because he was truthful—he also remained free from many sorrows which otherwise come even upon those of your age. A selfish nature was also something far from him, and he bore love and goodwill for all humanity. So he lived among us as the joy of the whole house.

. . . And so I believe that perhaps no one passes on, concerning whom those who lived most closely with him are completely satisfied when they examine themselves before God—even if the allotment of life has been as short as this one. Therefore let us all truly love one another as persons who could soon—alas, how soon!—be snatched away. . . . Ah yes, let us all love one another as persons who could soon be separated!

Now, thou God who are love, let me not only resign myself to thy omnipotence, not only submit to thy impenetrable wisdom, but also know thy fatherly love! Make even this grievous trial a new blessing for me in my vocation! For me and all of mine let this communal pain become wherever possible a new bond of still more intimate love, and let it issue in a new apprehension of thy Spirit in all my household! Grant that even this grave hour may become a blessing for all who are gathered here. Let us all more and more mature to that wisdom which, looking beyond the void, sees and loves only the eternal in all things earthly and perishable, and in all thy decrees finds thy peace as well, and eternal life, to which through faith we are delivered out of death. Amen.

[*Journal of Religion* 57, no. 1 (1977): 72–75]

23. "Nathanael" comes from the Hebrew for "gift of God."

C. Søren Kierkegaard

Biographical Note: Søren Kierkegaard

Søren Aabye Kierkegaard (1813–1855) was a Danish philosopher and theologian. Living off his inherited wealth, he was a prolific writer known for his wit and humor. He was a gregarious man about town, though he was not well liked by the religious and political establishment of Copenhagen. Several events in his life contributed to his becoming gradually more despondent and reclusive.

Apparently, when Kierkegaard's father was a child he cursed God, which he believed brought a curse from God on his own life and family. That melancholy, combined with a Lutheran Pietism, influenced young Søren and stayed with him throughout his life. He later fell in love with Regine Olsen and was engaged to marry her, when he suddenly broke off the engagement so that he could pursue his vocation of writing. This act confirmed Kierkegaard's marginalization from Copenhagen's respectable elites. For several months in 1846, the satirical journal The Corsair *lampooned Kierkegaard on a personal level, especially his clothing and hunched frame. He exacerbated the situation by responding. In 1854, at the funeral of the Bishop Mynster, his successor praised him as a "truth witness" of the Christian faith. This strong language angered Kierkegaard, who later responded with a series of papers published in* The Moment. *He attacked the concept of "Christendom," the European (in his case, Danish) state church that promoted an innocuous, liberalizing Christian faith, including the idea that being a Dane made one a Christian.*

Kierkegaard was a creative writer, and perhaps in order to focus on the ideas and not on himself, he wrote most of his books under various pseudonyms. Nevertheless, his personal struggles are latent in his authorship. As Kierkegaard's writing evolved from ostensibly philosophical works criticizing Hegelianism and Romanticism to more overtly Christian treatises, all of these biographical events illuminate the themes in his own writing, especially the themes of suffering, the importance of the solitary individual before God, the deception of the crowd, and the challenge of being a true Christian in the midst of a worldly Christendom.

Kierkegaard is also known for his emphasis on faith as opposed to reason, and, because of his insistence on individual choice, is regarded as the father of existentialism, both theistic and atheistic. Theologically, Kierkegaard stressed the infinite gulf and moral separation between humanity and God, the wholly other, a point that would become foundational for Karl Barth's theology in the next century.

Selection 89: Søren Kierkegaard, *Concluding Unscientific Postscript to Philosophical Fragments* (1846)

Kierkegaard wrote this book as a follow-up to his Philosophical Fragments *(1844), both of which he wrote under the pseudonym Johannes Climacus. In this excerpt, Kierkegaard challenges the objective account of truth and claims that good living entails more than merely holding to an objectively true set of beliefs.*

. . . When the question about truth is asked objectively, truth is reflected upon objectively as an object to which the knower relates himself. What is reflected upon is not the relation but that what he relates himself to is the truth, the true. If only that to which he relates himself is the truth, the true, then the subject is in the truth. When the question about truth is asked subjectively, the individual's relation is reflected upon subjectively. If only the how of this relation is in truth, the individual is in truth, even if he in this way were to relate himself to untruth.[24]. . .

The existing person who chooses the objective way now enters upon all approximating deliberation intended to bring forth God objectively, which is not achieved in all eternity, because God is a subject and hence only for subjectivity in inwardness. The existing person who chooses the subjective way instantly comprehends the whole dialectical difficulty because he must use some time, perhaps a long time, to find God objectively. He comprehends this dialectical difficulty in all its pain, because he must resort to God at that very moment, because every moment in which he does not have God is wasted.[25] At that very moment he has God, not by virtue of any objective deliberation but by virtue of the infinite passion of inwardness. The objective person is not bothered by dialectical difficulties such as what it means to put a whole research period into finding God, since it is indeed possible that the researcher would die tomorrow, and if he goes on living, he cannot very well regard God as something to be taken along at his convenience, since God is something one takes along *a tout prix* [at any price], which, in passion's understanding, is the true relationship of inwardness with God. . . .

Now, if the problem is to calculate where there is more truth (and, as stated, simultaneously to be on both sides equally is not granted to an existing person but is only a beatifying delusion for a deluded *I-I),* whether on the side of the person who only objectively seeks the true God and the approximating truth of the God-idea or on the side of the person who is infinitely concerned that he in truth relate himself to God with the infinite passion of need—then there can be no doubt about the answer for anyone who is not totally botched by scholarship and science. If someone who lives in the midst of Christianity enters, with knowledge of the true idea of God, the house of God, the house of the true God, and prays, but prays in untruth, and if someone lives in an idolatrous land but prays with all the passion of infinity, although his eyes are resting upon the image of an idol—where, then, is there more truth? The one prays in truth to God although he is worshiping an idol; the other prays in untruth to the true God and is therefore in truth worshiping an idol. . . .

Let us consider Socrates. These days everyone is dabbling in a few proofs or demonstrations—one has many, another fewer. But Socrates! He poses the question objectively, problematically: if there is an immortality. So, compared with one of the modern thinkers with the three demonstrations, was he a doubter? Not at all. He stakes his whole life on this "if"; he dares to die, and with the passion of the infinite he has so ordered his whole life that it might be acceptable—*if* there is an immortality. Is there any better demonstration for the immortality of the

24. [Kierkegaard:] "The reader will note that what is being discussed here is essential truth, or the truth that is related essentially to existence, and that it is specifically in order to clarify it as inwardness or as subjectivity that the contrast is pointed out."

25. [Kierkegaard:] "In this way God is indeed a postulate, but not in the loose sense in which it is ordinarily taken. Instead, it becomes clear that this is the only way an existing person enters into a relationship with God: when the dialectical contradiction brings passion to despair and assists him in grasping God with 'the category of despair' (faith), so that the postulate, far from being the arbitrary, is in fact *necessary* defense, self-defense; in this way God is not a postulate, but the existing person's postulating of God is—a necessity."

soul? But those who have the three demonstrations do not order their lives accordingly. If there is an immortality, it must be nauseated by their way of living—is there any better counter-demonstration to the three demonstrations? The "fragment" of uncertainty helped Socrates, because he himself helped with the passion of infinity. The three demonstrations are of no benefit whatever to those others, because they are and remain slugs and, failing to demonstrate anything else, have demonstrated it by their three demonstrations. . . .

Objectively the emphasis is on WHAT is said; subjectively the emphasis is on HOW it is said. This distinction applies even esthetically and is specifically expressed when we say that in the mouth of this or that person something that is truth can become untruth. Particular attention should be paid to this distinction in our day, for if one were to express in a single sentence the difference between ancient times and our time, one would no doubt have to say: In ancient times there were only a few individuals who knew the truth; now everyone knows it, but inwardness has an inverse relation to it. Viewed esthetically, the contradiction that emerges when truth becomes untruth in this and that person's mouth is best interpreted comically. Ethically-religiously, the emphasis is again on: *how.* But this is not to be understood as manner, modulation of voice, oral delivery, etc., but it is to be understood as the relation of the existing person, in his very existence, to what is said. Objectively, the question is only about categories of thought; subjectively, about inwardness. At its maximum, this "how" is the passion of the infinite, and the passion of the infinite is the very truth. But the passion of the infinite is precisely subjectivity, and thus subjectivity is truth. From the objective point of view, there is no infinite decision, and thus it is objectively correct that the distinction between good and evil is canceled, along with the principle of contradiction, and thereby also the infinite distinction between truth and falsehood. Only in subjectivity is there decision, whereas wanting to become objective is untruth. The passion of the infinite, not its content, is the deciding factor, for its content is precisely itself. In this way the subjective "how" and subjectivity are the truth. . . .

When subjectivity is truth, the definition of truth must also contain in itself an expression of the antithesis to objectivity, a memento of that fork in the road, and this expression will at the same time indicate the resilience of the inwardness. Here is such a definition of truth: *An objective uncertainty, held last through appropriation with the most passionate inwardness, is the truth,* the highest truth there is for an *existing* person. At the point where the road swings off (and where that is cannot be stated objectively, since it is precisely subjectivity), objective knowledge is suspended. Objectively he then has only uncertainty, but this is precisely what intensifies the infinite passion of inwardness, and truth is precisely the daring venture of choosing the objective uncertainty with the passion of the infinite. I observe nature in order to find God, and I do indeed see omnipotence and wisdom, but I also see much that troubles and disturbs. The *summa summarum* [sum total] of this is an objective uncertainty, but the inwardness is so very great, precisely because it grasps this objective uncertainty with all the passion of the infinite. In a mathematical proposition, for example, the objectivity is given, but therefore its truth is also an indifferent truth.

But the definition of truth stated above is a paraphrasing of faith. Without risk, no faith. Faith is the contradiction between the infinite passion of inwardness and the objective uncertainty. If I am able to apprehend God objectively, I do not have faith; but because I cannot do this, I must have faith. If I want to keep myself in faith, I must continually see to it that I hold fast the objective uncertainty, see to it that in the objective uncertainty I am "out on 70,000 fathoms of water" and still have faith.[26]

The thesis that subjectivity, inwardness, is truth contains the Socratic wisdom, the undying merit of which is to have paid attention to the essential meaning of existing, of the knower's being an existing person. That is why, in his ignorance, Socrates was in the truth in the highest sense within paganism. To comprehend this, that the misfortune of speculative thought is simply that it forgets again and again that the knower is an existing person, can already be rather difficult in our objective age. "But to go beyond Socrates when one has not even comprehended the Socratic—that, at least, is not Socratic."[27]. . .

[*Concluding Unscientific Postscript to Philosophical Fragments, vol. 1*, trans. Howard and Edna Hong, Kierkegaard's Writings 12 (Princeton: Princeton University Press, 1992), 199–204]

Selection 90: Søren Kierkegaard, *Practice in Christianity* (1850)

Practice in Christianity ***was written in 1848 under the pseudonym Anti-Climacus, whom Kierkegaard described as "a Christian on an extraordinary level." Kierkegaard referred to this book as "the most perfect and the truest thing I have written." Among the many prominent themes of this book, he reflects on the concept of God incarnate and incognito and the difficulty of faith, especially for Christ's own contemporaries.***

Kierkegaard in the coffee-house

G. E. Lessing had said that he would like to believe in Jesus, but there is an "ugly, broad ditch" of eighteen hundred years standing in the way (see Selection 66). The implication is that it would be much easier to believe if one were contemporary with Jesus. Kierkegaard challenges this common notion in this excerpt, which is part of an extended meditation on the invitation of Jesus recorded in Matt. 11:28: "Come to me, all who are weary and burdened, and I will give you rest." What would the historical contemporaries of Jesus have thought of him and his invitation?

It is indeed eighteen hundred years since Jesus Christ walked here on earth, but this is certainly not an event just like other events, which once they are over pass into history and then, as the distant past, pass into oblivion. No, his presence here on earth never becomes a thing of the past, thus does not become more and more distant—that is, if faith is at all to be found upon the earth; if not, well, then in that very instant it is a long time since he lived. But as long as there is a believer, this person, in order to have become that, must have been and as a believer must be just as contemporary with Christ's presence as his contemporaries were. This contemporaneity is the condition of faith, and, more sharply defined, it is faith. Lord Jesus Christ, would that we, too, might become contemporary with you in this way, might see you in your true form and in the surroundings of actuality as you walked here on earth, not in the

26. The image of someone floating over "70,000 fathoms of water" comes from another of Kierkegaard's pseudonyms, Frater Taciturnus, in the previously published *Stages on Life's Way*.

27. This is an allusion to a statement in an earlier book, *Philosophical Fragments* (Princeton: Princeton University Press, 1985), 111, also written by the pseudonym Johannes Climacus.

form in which an empty and meaningless or a thoughtless-romantic or a historical-talkative remembrance has distorted you, since it is not the form of humility in which the believer sees you, and it cannot possibly be the form of glory in which no one as yet has seen you. Would that we might see you as you are and were and will be until your second coming in glory, as the sign of stumbling and the object of faith, the lowly man, yet the Savior and Redeemer of the human race, who out of love came to earth to seek the lost, to suffer and die, and yet, alas, every step you took on earth, every time you called to the straying, every time you reached out your hand to do signs and wonders, and every time you defenselessly suffered the opposition of people without raising a hand—again and again in concern you had to repeat, "Blessed is the one who is not offended at me" [Matt. 11:6]. Would that we might see you in this way and that we then might not be offended at you! . . .

The First Period of His Life

Let us talk about him quite frankly, just as his contemporaries talked about him and as we talk about a contemporary, a person just like ourselves, whom we see in passing on the street; we know where he lives, on what floor, what he is, what he does for a living, who his parents are, his kinfolk, what he looks like, what he wears, with whom he associates, and "there is really nothing extraordinary about him, he looks just like everyone else." In short, let us talk about him as we talk about a contemporary about whom we do not make a lot of fuss, for in the situation of contemporaneity with all these thousands and thousands of *actual* people there can be no room for a distinction between perhaps being remembered for centuries and being an *actual* store clerk "just as good as he is."—So let us talk about him as contemporaries talk about a contemporary. I know very well what I am doing, and, believe me, the acquired, drilled, dull, world-historical custom whereby we always speak with a certain veneration about Christ since, after all, we have learned suchlike from history and have heard so much of that sort of thing, about his supposedly having been something great—this veneration is not worth a pickled herring; it is thoughtlessness, hypocrisy, to that extent blasphemy, because it is blasphemy to have a thoughtless veneration for the one whom we must either believe in or be offended at.

It is the abased Jesus Christ, a lowly man, born of a despised virgin, his father a carpenter. But he does make his appearance, it is true, under circumstances that must draw attention to him in a very special way. The little nation in which he makes his appearance, God's chosen people, as it calls itself, is anticipating an expected one who will bring in a golden age to the country and people. Of course, the form in which he appears is as different as possible from what the majority expect. However, it does more or less correspond to the ancient prophecy with which the people must be assumed to be familiar. So he makes his appearance; a predecessor[28] has called attention to him, and he himself decidedly attracts attention to himself by wonders and signs that become the talk of the whole country—and he is the hero of the moment; wherever he goes he is surrounded by a countless throng of people. The sensation he creates is enormous. All eyes are upon him; everyone who can walk, indeed, even those who can only crawl, must go and see this prodigy—and everyone must have a judgment, an opinion of him; thus the suppliers of opinions and judgments almost have to close shop because business is so rushed and the opinions so conflicting. Yet he, the miracle worker, is still the lowly

28. That is, John the Baptist.

man who literally does not have a place to lay his head.—And let us not forget: in the situation of contemporaneity signs and wonders have an entirely different elasticity to repel and to attract than this tame, this, as warmed up by the preachers, even tamer bit about signs and wonders eighteen hundred years ago. In the situation of contemporaneity signs and wonders are something exasperatingly annoying, something that in a very embarrassing way almost forces one to have an opinion, something that, if one does not happen to feel like believing, can be a burdensome thing to be contemporary with, especially since it makes existence far too strenuous, especially the more intelligent, developed, and cultured one is. It is a very awkward matter to have to assume in connection with a contemporary that he actually does do signs and wonders—when we have him at a distance, when the outcome of his life encourages one in delusions, then it is easy to delude oneself into thinking that one believes it.

Thus the crowd is enraptured with him; it follows him enthusiastically, sees signs and wonders, both those he does and those he does not do, happy in the hope that the golden age will commence when he becomes king. But the crowd can rarely account for its judgment, has one opinion today, another tomorrow. That is why the sagacious and sensible do not participate as a matter of course. Let us now see what a sagacious and sensible person is bound to think as soon as he has recovered from the impact of surprise and astonishment.

The sagacious and sensible person might say, "Assuming that this man is what he purports to be, the extraordinary—for this business about his supposedly being God I can regard only as an exaggeration, which I would be willing to make allowances for and to forgive if I actually regarded him as the extraordinary, for I do not quibble about words—on the assumption that it is miracles he is doing, although I have my doubts about this and in any case suspend my judgment, is it not, then, an inexplicable riddle that this very same man can be so foolish, so narrow, so totally ignorant of human nature, so weak or so amiably conceited or whatever you may want to call it, to behave in this way, almost to force his good deeds upon people! Instead of haughtily and domineeringly keeping people from himself at the distance of profoundest servility and accepting their adoration on the rare occasions when he is seen, instead of that to be accessible to all or, more correctly, to go himself to everyone, to associate with everyone, almost as if being the extraordinary meant to be the servant of all;[29] as if being the extraordinary, as he himself claims to be, meant to be concerned whether people will have benefit from him or not—in short, as if being the extraordinary meant to be more concerned than anybody else. The whole thing is inexplicable to me—what he wants, what his purpose is, what he is trying to do, what he wants to achieve, what it all means. He who by many a statement betrays such a deep insight into the human heart, which I cannot deny him, he certainly must very well know what I with less than half of my sagacity can tell him in advance, that this is no way to get ahead in the world—unless, disdaining sagacity, one honestly aspires to become a fool or perhaps even goes so far in honesty that one prefers to be put to death, but then one must indeed be really insane to want that. To repeat, as a knower of human nature he very likely must know that what one has to do is to deceive people and then give one's deception the appearance of benefactions one is doing for the whole human race. Then one harvests all the advantages, even the one giving the most precious enjoyment of all, that of being called by one's contemporaries the benefactor of the human

29. See Mark 9:35; 10:44.

race—and as soon as one is in one's grave, who cares a hang about what posterity says about one. But to sacrifice himself as he is doing, not to assert himself in the least, almost to beg people to accept these benefactions—no, it could never occur to me to join him. And, of course, he does not invite me anyway; for he invites only those who labor and are burdened."

Or: "His life is just downright fantasticality, and yet that is the mildest expression we can use about it. If one judges in that way, one is kind enough to forget completely this sheer madness that he considers himself to be God. It is fantasticality. One can live that way for at most a few years in one's youth. But he is already past thirty. And he is literally a nobody. Furthermore, in a very short time he is bound to lose all esteem and standing among the people, the only thing one can say he has managed to gain for himself up to now. If one wishes to be assured of popular favor in the long run, which I readily admit is the most insecure thing that one can choose at all, one must behave differently. It will not be many months before the crowd is tired of someone who is at its service in this way; he will be regarded as dead and done for, a kind of *mauvais sujet* [black sheep] who can rejoice if he ends up in in some remote corner of the world, forgetting the world and forgotten, unless by remaining on the spot he should, in a continuation of his previous activity, be fantastic enough to want to be put to death, the inescapable result of remaining on the spot. What has he done about his future? Nothing. Does he have a permanent job? No. What are his prospects? None. To mention only this simple matter, how will he pass the time when he becomes old, the long winter evenings—with what will he fill them—he cannot even play cards. He enjoys a bit of popular favor—truly the most movable of all movable property—in a turn of the hand it can become enormous popular disfavor.—To join him—no, thanks, thank God I certainly have not gone crazy yet."

Or: "That there is something extraordinary about the man, of that there really is no doubt (provided one reserves one's right and the right of sound human understanding to refrain from any opinion with respect to his claim to be God). One could rather become almost indignant with Governance for having entrusted to such a person what has been entrusted to him, a person like that who does the opposite of what he himself says: that one should not cast one's pearls before swine—which is why it will surely end with their quite rightly turning around and trampling him underfoot.[30] Such behavior can always be expected of swine—but we would not expect someone who himself is aware of this to do the opposite of what he knows should not be done. Yes, if only one could deftly trick his wisdom out of him—for that extremely singular idea upon which he himself seems to place so much value, that he is God, I am happy to leave to him alone as his exclusive property—if only one could trick his wisdom out of him—without becoming his follower! If only one could secretly visit him at night and get it out of him—for I am quite capable of editing and publishing it, *und zwar* [but] in a quite different way. To the astonishment of the whole world, something totally different will come of it, I promise you, for this much I certainly do perceive, that there is something very profound in what he says—the only trouble is that he is the person he is. But perhaps, who knows, perhaps *am Ende* [in the end] it may be possible to trick it out of him; perhaps in this respect he is such a good-natured fool as to communicate quite openly. That would not be impossible, for it seems to me that the wisdom he obviously possesses, by

30. See Matt. 7:6.

being entrusted to him, has been entrusted to a fool: his life is such a contradiction.—But to join him, to become a follower—no, that would be making oneself a fool."

Or: "If what this man wants is the good and the true, something I leave undecided, then he is at least doing good so far, especially for the youth and the inexperienced young, for whom because of the earnestness of life it is so beneficial to understand this properly, the earlier the better. He makes it obvious even to the most infatuated that this high-flown talk about living for the good and the true has a considerable admixture of the ludicrous in it; he demonstrates how our contemporary writers have hit the nail on the head when they always have the good and the true represented by a half-witted character or by someone who is so obtuse that he is a dunderpate. To exert oneself as strenuously as this man does, to renounce everything but toil and trouble, to be at everybody's beck and call every hour of the day, more zealous than the busiest practicing physician—and why? Is it because this is his livelihood? No, not in the remotest way. As far as we can perceive, it just never occurred to him to want to have any. Then is it because he wants to earn money thereby? No, not a penny—he does not have a penny, and if he did he would promptly give it away. Then is it to gain honor and prestige in the state? The very opposite—he disdains all worldly prestige. And he who, since he has now renounced all worldly prestige and is practicing the art of being able to live on nothing, he who more than anyone else could be counted on to pass his life in the most pleasant loafing (and there could be some sense in that)—he is the one who lives more strenuously than any public servant who is rewarded with honor and prestige, more strenuously than any businessman who makes money to burn. Why, then, does he exert himself in this way, or (to what end this question about something about which there can be no question!): to exert himself in this way, in order to achieve the success of being ridiculed, scoffed at, etc.!—this is surely a queer kind of pleasure. That someone pushes his way through the crowd to reach the place where money, glory, and honor are dished out—that is understandable. But to push oneself to the front in order to be whipped publicly—how sublime, how Christian, how stupid!"[31]

Or: "So many rash and hasty judgments are heard about this person from people who understand nothing—and idolize him—and so many severe judgments from those who perhaps misunderstand him. But no one can rightly charge me with any rash and hasty judgment; I keep perfectly cool and calm. Indeed, what is more, I fully realize that I am as accommodating and moderate toward him as possible. Let us suppose, something I admit only to a certain degree, that even the understanding is impressed by this man. What judgment must be formed of him now? The judgment is; in the first place, I can have no opinion about him. I do not mean about his claim to be God, for in all eternity I shall never be able to have any opinion about that; no, I mean about him as a human being. Only the outcome of his life will be able to decide whether he actually was the extraordinary or whether he, deceived by his powers of imagination, set a much too high criterion not only for himself but for what it means to be a human being at all. Even with the best will in the world I can do no more for him; even if he were my one and only friend, my own child, I could not judge more leniently, and not otherwise, either. But from this it in all likelihood follows that for good reasons I cannot come to have an

31. It is clear that modern Danes who despise the weakness of Christianity are the imagined speakers and Kierkegaard's ultimate audience.

opinion about him. For in order to have an opinion I must first see the outcome of his life, and to the very end—that is, he must be dead. Then I can, and yet only perhaps, have an opinion about him; and even assuming this, it is still only an opinion of him in an improper sense, for then, of course, he is no more. It follows, then, that I cannot join him as long as he is living. The *authority* with which he is said to teach cannot have any decisive meaning for me. It is indeed rather easy to see that he is going in a circle; so he appeals to what he is to demonstrate, which in turn can be demonstrated only by the outcome, provided that it is not connected to his fixed idea that he is God, for if *that is the reason* he has authority, because he is God, then the answer is: Yes—*if.* But I will concede this much to him—that if I imagined myself living in a later generation, and if by then the outcome of his life, its results in history, had made it clear that he was the extraordinary: then I just might come very near to, very close to, becoming his follower."

The clergyman might say: "For an impostor and demagogue there is really something unusually honest about him, and therefore he cannot become absolutely dangerous, even if it does appear to be rather dangerous as long as the rain shower lasts, looks rather dangerous with his enormous popularity, until the rain shower is over and the people—the very same people—throw him down again. The honesty is this claiming to be the expected one and then to resemble him as little as he does—this is honest, just as when someone planning to pass counterfeit paper money makes it so crudely that anyone with any knowledge promptly can detect it.—It is true that we all look forward to an expected one, but that it is God in person who is to come is not the expectation of any rational person, and every religious person shudders at the blasphemy of which this person is guilty. Yet we do look forward to an expected one; in that we are all agreed. But the government of the world does not advance tumultuously by leaps, world development is not—and this is indeed already implicit in its being a development—*revolutionair* but *evolutionair.* Therefore the authentic expected one will look entirely different, will come as the most glorious flowering and the highest unfolding of the established order. That is how the authentic expected one will come, and he will conduct himself quite differently; he will recognize the established order as the authority, will summon all the clergy to a convention, present to it his achievements, together with his credentials—and then if in balloting he has the majority he will be accepted and hailed as the extraordinary that he is: the expected one.

"But there is a duplicity in this person's conduct; he is too much of a judge; it seems as if he simultaneously wants to be the judge who judges the established order and yet also the expected one himself. If he does not want to be the former, then why his absolute isolation, his distance from everything that is called the established order! If he does not want to be the judge, then why his fantastic flight beyond actuality out into association with ignorant commoners, why his arrogant, revolutionary disdain of all the intelligence and competence of the established order, just to begin all over again from the beginning with the help of—fishermen and tradespeople—thus with regard to the established order it seems as if the motto for his whole existence is that he is illegitimate! If he simply wants to be the expected one, then why does he talk about not putting a new piece of cloth on an old garment, words that are the very slogan of any revolution, for they do not imply a willingness to recognize the established order but wanting to do away with it, instead of joining the established order and, if one is a reformer, improving it and, if one is the expected one, developing it to its highest level. This is a duplicity, and this cannot be done—to be both judge and the expected one. And this duplicity will be his downfall, which I have already calculated. A judge's catastrophe is properly depicted as meeting a violent death, but the expected one's catastrophe certainly cannot possibly be a downfall, in that case he of course *eo ipso*[32] is not the expected one, is not the one for whom the established order is waiting in order to deify him. The people still do not perceive this duplicity, they see in him the expected one—something the established order cannot possibly see and something that only the people, the idle and unemployed crowd, can see, since they are anything but the established order. But as soon as the duplicity becomes manifest, it is his downfall. No, then his predecessor was a more definitely distinct figure; he was only one thing—the judge. What confusion and derangement, to want to be both, and what further confusion, himself to acknowledge the predecessor as the one who should sit in judgment, consequently to make the established order receptive to the expected one and entirely able to accept him, and then want to be himself the expected one who succeeds the judge—and then still not to be willing to join the established order!"

And the philosopher might say, "A conceit so dreadful, or rather so insane, that an individual human being presumes to be God, has never been heard of before; such an extreme form of pure subjectivity and sheer negativity has never been seen. He has no doctrine, no system; basically he knows nothing; there are a few aphorisms, some maxims, and a couple of parables, which he goes on repeating or revising, whereby he blinds the masses, for whom he also does signs and wonders, so that instead of coming to know something or gaining some sound instruction, they come to believe in him, he who as calamitously as possible incessantly imposes his subjectivity upon one. There is absolutely no objectivity or positivity in what he says. As a matter of fact, he does not need to succumb; *philosophically* he has already succumbed; after all, it is the qualification of pure subjectivity to fall to the ground.[33] One may concede that he is a remarkable subjectivity, and that as a teacher, no matter how you judge his signs and wonders, he does continually repeat the miracle with the five small loaves and sets the whole country in motion with only some lyrics and aphorisms. But even if the madness that *he* considers himself to be God is disregarded, it is an incomprehensible mistake, which indeed only betrays little philosophic training, to think that God could reveal himself at all in the form of an individual human being. The human race, the universal, the totality, is God, but the race certainly is not any particular individual. That the single individual wants to be something is the very presumptuousness that lies in subjectivity, but of course it is madness for the single individual to want to be God. If this madness were possible, that an individual human being was God, then to be consistent one would have to worship this particular human being; a greater philosophical brutishness cannot be imagined."

The sagacious statesman might say: "That this man is a power at the moment cannot be denied—apart, of course, from the delusion he has that he is God. Such a thing one cancels out once and for all as a private hobby that will amount to nothing and is of no concern to anybody, least of all a statesman. A statesman looks only at what power a person has, and that he at this moment is a power cannot, as said before, be denied. But what he wants, what he is

32. That is, "by that very fact."

33. The "philosopher" here alludes to Hegel.

aiming at is hard to make out; if this is sagacity, it must be a totally new and unique kind, not entirely unlike what is otherwise called madness. He has considerable powers, but he seems to destroy them, instead of using them; he expends them, but *he* receives nothing in return. I regard him as a phenomenon with whom it is wise not to become involved—and this one never does with a phenomenon—since it is altogether impossible to calculate him or the catastrophe of his life. It is possible that he can become king, it is possible—but it is not impossible or, more correctly, it is just as possible that he can end up on the scaffold. He lacks earnestness in his whole endeavor. With an enormous wingspan, he floats—no more than that; he fixes no end, charts no course—he floats. Is he fighting for nationality, or is he aiming at a communist revolution, does he want a republic or a monarchy, which party will he join and which oppose, or does he want to be in favor with all parties, or does he want to contend with all parties? I become involved with him? No, that would be the last thing I would do; I do even more—I take every precaution against him. I keep absolutely quiet; I do nothing. I am as if I did not exist; for if one were to undertake the least little thing, one cannot calculate how he might intrude disturbingly or how it might be twisted in with his affairs. The man is dangerous, in a certain sense, extremely dangerous. But my scheme is to trap him simply by doing nothing at all. For he must be overthrown—and the safest way is by himself, by tripping over himself. I do not have, at least at the moment, the power to overthrow him, and I do not know anyone who has. To do the least little thing against him at present would only mean to be crushed oneself. No, always nothing but negative opposition, nothing, then he will very likely become entangled in the enormous consequences he draws after him; he will trip on his cloak—and then he will fall."

And the solid citizen might say what the opinion would be in his family. "No, let us be human. In moderation everything is good; too little and too much spoil everything. According to a French proverb I heard from a traveling salesman: Any power carried to excess is toppled—and this man, his downfall, I am sure, is certain. I have also earnestly taken my son to task, warned and impressed upon him that he should not go and mess up his life by joining this man, and why?—because they are all running after him. Well, who are these 'all'? Idle and unemployed people, street loafers and tramps, who find it easy to run around. But not many of the property owners and well-to-do and not a one of the sagacious and reputable people by whom I always set my watch, not Councilor Jeppesen nor Chief Magistrate Marcus nor the wealthy Commissioner Christophersen—no, no, these people know well enough what's what. And if we look at the clergy, who must understand such things best—they decline with thanks. As Pastor Grønwald said last evening at the club: 'That life will have a horrible ending.' And that fellow can more than just preach; one should not hear him on Sunday in church but on Monday at the club; I just wish I had half of his understanding of the world. He was absolutely correct when he said—and it was as if spoken from my own heart—'It is only the idle and the unemployed who run after him.' And why do they run after him? Because he can do a few miracles. But who says that it is a miracle or that he gives his followers the same power? And in any case a miracle is something very uncertain, whereas what is certain is certain.[34] Every earnest father with grown-up children must

34. The "solid citizen" here sounds very much like Hume and Lessing (see Selection 66).

really be concerned lest his sons let themselves be beguiled and carried away and then take up with him along with these desperate people who follow him, desperate people who have nothing to lose. And even these people—how does he help them? One must be crazy to want to be helped in that way. As a matter of fact, he helps even the poorest beggar out of the frying pan into the fire, helps him into a new misery that the beggar could have avoided by remaining what he was, an out-and-out beggar."

And the scoffer, not the scoffer despised by all for his malice but the one admired by all for his wit, also liked for his good nature, might say: "It is fundamentally a priceless idea, one that as a matter of course must benefit all of us—that an individual human being just like the rest of us says that he is God. If that is not doing good to mankind, then I do not know what good- and well-doing or well- and good-doing are. Assuming that the distinctive mark of being God is (indeed, who in the whole world would have thought of this; how true that such a thing did not arise in any human heart!) to look exactly like everybody else, neither more nor less: then we are all gods. *Quod erat demonstrandum* [Which was to be demonstrated]. Long may he live, the inventor of this very extraordinary discovery for mankind! Tomorrow I shall announce that I, the undersigned, am God—and the inventor at least cannot deny it without contradicting himself. In the dark all cats are gray—and if to be God is to look like everyone else, just exactly like everyone else: then it is dark and we are all . . . or, what I wanted to say, we are all, each one individually, God, and then one person is no better than another. It is the most ludicrous thing one can imagine. The contradiction (the comic always lies in contradiction) is enormous—but the merit is not mine, it is solely and only and exclusively the inventor's: that a human being just like the rest of us, but not as well-dressed as the average person, therefore that a poorly dressed person who most likely belongs (at least seems to belong there considerably more than under the rubric 'God') under the welfare department—that he is God. It is really worst for the welfare director, that with this general advancement of the human race he does not improve his position."

Ah, my friend, I really do know what I am doing, I know my responsibility, and my soul is eternally convinced of the rightness of what I am doing. So imagine yourself contemporary with him, the inviter. Imagine that you were a sufferer—but bear in mind the risk you are running by becoming his disciple, by following him. In the eyes of all the sagacious, sensible, and reputable people, you are running the risk of unconditionally losing almost everything. He, the inviter, demands that you shall give up everything, let everything go—but the commonsensicality of the contemporary age does not let you go; it judges that to join him is madness. And mockery will cruelly overwhelm you. Whereas it almost treats him with leniency out of sympathy, it finds it totally insane to become his follower. It says, "A romantic visionary is a romantic visionary, that is all right; but to become his follower in earnest is the greatest possible lunacy. There is always only one possibility of becoming more lunatic than a lunatic: the higher lunacy, in earnest to join a madman and regard him as wise."

Do not say that this whole account is an exaggeration. You do know, of course (but you perhaps have not paid close attention to it), that of all the esteemed, all the enlightened and sensible contemporaries—while it certainly is possible that one or two of them, perhaps several, had something to do with him out of curiosity—there was only one, just one, who in earnest sought him out, and he came to him—at night.[35] And you know very well that at night one walks the forbidden paths; one chooses the nighttime to go where one does not wish it to be known that one is a regular visitor—bear in mind the judgment on the inviter that this implies: to visit him was a disgrace, something no reputable person, no man of honor could be known to do—no more than (this, too, is concealed by the night) going to—but, no, I would rather not follow this up, this "no more than."

Come here *to me now* all you who labor and are burdened, and I will give you rest.

[*Practice in Christianity*, trans. Howard and Edna Hong, Kierkegaard's Writings 20 (Princeton: Princeton University Press, 1991), 9–10, 40–53]

D. Social Implications

Selection 91: Harriet Beecher Stowe, *Uncle Tom's Cabin* (1852)

Harriet Beecher Stowe (1811–1896)—daughter of revivalist Lyman Beecher, sister of the preacher Henry Ward Beecher, and wife of a Congregationalist minister—was a staunch abolitionist. Her novel,* Uncle Tom's Cabin; Or, Life among the Lowly, *was one of the greatest documents of the antislavery movement in the United States. As the narrative itself reflects deep Christian faith and revivalism, Stowe's preface and conclusion, excerpted here, rally the American churches to take their Christian faith seriously and to stand up against slavery.

Preface

The scenes of this story, as its title indicates, lie among a race hitherto ignored by the associations of polite and refined society; an exotic race, whose ancestors, born beneath a tropic sun, brought with them, and perpetuated to their descendants, a character so essentially unlike the hard and dominant Anglo-Saxon race, as for many years to have won from it only misunderstanding and contempt.

But, another and better day is dawning; every influence of literature, of poetry and of art, in our times, is becoming more and more in unison with the great master chord of Christianity, "good will to man."

The poet, the painter, and the artist, now seek out and embellish the common and gentler humanities of life, and, under the allurements of fiction, breathe a humanizing and subduing influence, favorable to the development of the great principles of Christian brotherhood.

The hand of benevolence is everywhere stretched out, searching into abuses, righting wrongs, alleviating distresses, and bringing to the knowledge and sympathies of the world the lowly, the oppressed, and the forgotten.

In this general movement, unhappy Africa at last is remembered; Africa, who began the race of civilization and human progress in the dim, gray dawn of early time, but who, for centuries, has lain bound and bleeding at the foot of civilized arid Christianized humanity, imploring compassion in vain.

But the heart of the dominant race, who have been her conquerors, her hard masters, has at length been turned towards her in mercy; and it has been seen how far nobler it is in nations to protect the feeble than to oppress them. Thanks be to God, the world has at last outlived the slave-trade![36]. . .

When an enlightened and Christianized community shall have, on the shores of Africa,

35. That is, Nicodemus (John 3:1-2).

36. The Atlantic slave trade was outlawed earlier in the nineteenth century, though emancipation in the United States would not occur until the 1860s.

laws, language and literature, drawn from among us, may then the scenes of the house of bondage be to them like the remembrance of Egypt to the Israelite,—a motive of thankfulness to Him who hath redeemed them! . . .

Chapter 45: Concluding Remarks

. . . Northern men, northern mothers, northern Christians, have something more to do than denounce their brethren at the South; they have to look to the evil among themselves.

But, what can any individual do? Of that, every individual can judge. There is one thing that every individual can do,—they can see to it that *they feel right*. An atmosphere of sympathetic influence encircles every human being; and the man or woman who *feels* strongly, healthily and justly, on the great interests of humanity, is a constant benefactor to the human race. See, then, to your sympathies in this matter! Are they in harmony with the sympathies of Christ? or are they swayed and perverted by the sophistries of worldly policy?

Christian men and women of the North! still further,—you have another power; you can *pray*! Do you believe in prayer? or has it become an indistinct apostolic tradition? You pray for the heathen abroad; pray also for the heathen at home. And pray for those distressed Christians whose whole chance of religious improvement is an accident of trade and sale; from whom any adherence to the morals of Christianity is, in many cases, an impossibility, unless they have given them, from above, the courage and grace of martyrdom.

But, still more. On the shores of our free states are emerging the poor, shattered, broken remnants of families,—men and women, escaped, by miraculous providences, from the surges of slavery,—feeble in knowledge, and, in many cases, infirm in moral constitution, from a system which confounds and confuses every principle of Christianity and morality. They come to seek a refuge among you; they come to seek education, knowledge, Christianity.

What do you owe to these poor unfortunates, oh Christians? Does not every American Christian owe to the African race some effort at reparation for the wrongs that the American nation has brought upon them? Shall the doors of churches and school-houses be shut upon them? Shall states arise and shake them out? Shall the church of Christ hear in silence the taunt that is thrown at them, and shrink away from the helpless hand that they stretch out; and, by her silence, encourage the cruelty that would chase them from our borders? If it must be so, it will be a mournful spectacle. If it must be so, the country will have reason to tremble, when it remembers that the fate of nations is in the hands of One who is very pitiful, and of tender compassion.

Do you say, "We don't want them here; let them go to Africa"?

That the providence of God has provided a refuge in Africa, is, indeed, a great and noticeable fact; but that is no reason why the church of Christ should throw off that responsibility to this outcast race which her profession demands of her.

To fill up Liberia with an ignorant, inexperienced, half-barbarized race, just escaped from the chains of slavery, would be only to prolong, for ages, the period of struggle and conflict which attends the inception of new enterprises. Let the church of the north receive these poor sufferers in the spirit of Christ; receive them to the educating advantages of Christian republican society and schools, until they have attained to somewhat of a moral and intellectual maturity, and then assist them in their passage to those shores, where they may put in practice the lessons they have learned in America. . . .[37]

37. Stowe clearly regarded abolition as a specifically Christian movement and the care of former slaves as a Christian responsibility.

O, Church of Christ, read the signs of the times! Is not this power the spirit of Him whose kingdom is yet to come, and whose will to be done on earth as it is in heaven?

But who may abide the day of his appearing? "for that day shall burn as an oven: and he shall appear as a swift witness against those that oppress the hireling in his wages, the widow and the fatherless, and that *turn aside the stranger in his right*: and he shall break in pieces the oppressor."

Are not these dread words for a nation bearing in her bosom so mighty an injustice? Christians! every time that you pray that the kingdom of Christ may come, can you forget that prophecy associates, in dread fellowship, the *day of vengeance* with the year of his redeemed?

A day of grace is yet held out to us. Both North and South have been guilty before God; and the *Christian church* has a heavy account to answer. Not by combining together, to protect injustice and cruelty, and making a common capital of sin, is this Union to be saved,—but by repentance, justice and mercy; for, not surer is the eternal law by which the millstone sinks in the ocean, than that stronger law, by which injustice and cruelty shall bring on nations the wrath of Almighty God![38]

[*Uncle Tom's Cabin; Or, Life among the Lowly*, 2 vols. (Boston: John P. Jewett, 1852), 1:v–vi, viii; 2:317–18, 322]

Selection 92: Walter Rauschenbusch, *A Theology for the Social Gospel* (1917)

In the wake of the Industrial Revolution and the influx of immigrants to the United States, late-nineteenth-century American cities were increasingly overcrowded with an underprivileged population that was impoverished and frequently plagued by vices such as drunkenness. Christian movements inspired social action that sought to improve these urban conditions, resulting in the establishment of institutions such as the Young Men's and Young Women's Christian Associations (YMCA/YWCA). The actions of and message behind such movements became known as "the social gospel."

Walter Rauschenbusch (1861–1918) was the pastor of Second German Baptist Church in Manhattan, professor at Rochester Seminary, and the foremost theologian of the social gospel. To its critics, the social gospel emphasized good works to the exclusion of traditional doctrine and bore too many of the hallmarks of liberal Protestantism. In this book, a publication of his 1917 Taylor Lectures at Yale, Rauschenbusch, claiming that theology must change with the times, intended to lay a substantive theological foundation for the social gospel and respond to its critics.

Chapter I
The Challenge of the Social Gospel to Theology

We have a social gospel. We need a systematic theology large enough to match it and vital enough to back it.

This is the main proposition of this book. The first three chapters are to show that a readjustment and expansion of theology, so that it will furnish an adequate intellectual basis for the social gospel, is necessary, feasible, desirable, and legitimate. The remainder of the book offers concrete suggestions how some of the most important sections of doctrinal theology may be expanded and readjusted to make room for the religious convictions summed up in "the social gospel."

Some of my readers, who know the age, the tenacity, and the monumental character of theology well, will smile at the audacity of this

38. There was a common sentiment that the sin of slavery would merit an impending divine judgment. The Civil War later confirmed this interpretation.

proposal. Others, who know theology still better, will treat this venture very seriously. If theology stops growing or is unable to adjust itself to its modern environment and to meet its present tasks, it will die. Many now regard it as dead. The social gospel needs a theology to make it effective; but theology needs the social gospel to vitalize it. The work attempted in this book is doomed to futility if it has only the personal ideas of the author behind it. It is worthy of consideration only if the needs of a new epoch are seeking expression in it, and in that case its personal defects are of slight importance.

The argument of this book is built on the conviction that the social gospel is a permanent addition to our spiritual outlook and that its arrival constitutes a stage in the development of the Christian religion.

We need not waste words to prove that the social gospel is being preached. It is no longer a prophetic and occasional note. It is a novelty only in backward social or religious communities. The social gospel has become orthodox. . . .[39]

The social gospel is the old message of salvation, but enlarged and intensified. The individualistic gospel has taught us to see the sinfulness of every human heart and has inspired us with faith in the willingness and power of God to save every soul that comes to him. But it has not given us an adequate understanding of the sinfulness of the social order and its share in the sins of all individuals within it. It has not evoked faith in the will and power of God to redeem the permanent institutions of human society from their inherited guilt of oppression and extortion. Both our sense of sin and our faith in salvation have fallen short of the realities under its teaching. The social gospel seeks to bring men under repentance for their collective sins and to create a more sensitive and more modern conscience. It calls on us for the faith of the old prophets who believed in the salvation of nations. . . .

The adjustment of the Christian message to the regeneration of the social order is plainly one of the most difficult tasks ever laid on the intellect of religious leaders. The pioneers of the social gospel have had a hard time trying to consolidate their old faith and their new aim. Some have lost their faith; others have come out of the struggle with crippled formulations of truth. Does not our traditional theology deserve some of the blame for this spiritual wastage because it left these men without spiritual support and allowed them to become the vicarious victims of our theological inefficiency? If our theology is silent on social salvation, we compel college men and women, workingmen, and theological students, to choose between an unsocial system of theology and an irreligious system of social salvation. It is not hard to predict the outcome. If we seek to keep Christian doctrine unchanged, we shall ensure its abandonment. . . .

In short, we need a theology large enough to contain the social gospel, and alive and productive enough not to hamper it.

Chapter IV
The Consciousness of Sin

It remains now to pass in review the doctrines which would be affected by the social gospel and which ought to give more adequate expression to it. On some of the more speculative doctrines the social gospel has no contribution to make. Its interests lie on earth, within the social relations of the life that now is. It is concerned with the eradication of sin and the fulfilment of the mission of redemption. The sections of theology which ought to express it effectively,

39. Rauschenbusch acknowledges the ubiquity of the social gospel and chides those communities that have not already embraced it.

therefore, are the doctrines of sin and redemption. . . .

Any religious tendency or school of theology must be tested by the question whether it does justice to the religious consciousness of sin. Now, one cause of distrust against the social gospel is that its exponents often fail to show an adequate appreciation of the power and guilt of sin. Its teachings seem to put the blame for wrongdoing on the environment, and instead of stiffening and awakening the sense of responsibility in the individual, it teaches him to unload it on society.

There is doubtless truth in this accusation. The emphasis on environment and on the contributory guilt of the community, does offer a chance to unload responsibility, and human nature is quick to seize the chance. But the old theology has had its equivalents for environment. Men unloaded on original sin, on the devil, and on the decrees of God. Adam began soon after the fall to shift the blame. This shiftiness seems to be one of the clearest and most universal effects of original sin. . . .

The delinquencies of a new movement are keenly observed because they are new; the shortcomings of an old system are part of the accepted scheme of life. If the exponents of the old theology have taught humanity an adequate consciousness of sin, how is it that they themselves have been blind and dumb on the master iniquities of human history? During all the ages while they were the theological keepers of the conscience of Christendom, the peasants in the country and the working class in the cities were being sucked dry by the parasitic classes of society, and war was damning poor humanity. Yet what traces are there in traditional theology that the minds of old-line theologians were awake to these magnificent manifestations of the wickedness of the human heart? How is it that only in the modern era, since the moral insight of mankind has to some extent escaped from the tuition of the old theology, has a world-wide social movement arisen to put a stop to the exploitation of the poor, and that only in the last three years has war been realized as the supreme moral evil? One of the culminating accusations of Jesus against the theological teachers of his time was that they strained out gnats and swallowed camels,[40] judiciously laying the emphasis on the minor sins and keeping silence on the profitable major wrongs. It is possible to hold the orthodox doctrine on the devil and not recognize him when we meet him in a real estate office or at the stock exchange. . . .

Chapter X
The Social Gospel and Personal Salvation

We take up now the doctrine of salvation. All that has been said about sin will have to be kept in mind in discussing salvation, for the conceptions of sin and salvation are always closely correlated in every theological or religious system.

The new thing in the social gospel is the clearness and insistence with which it sets forth the necessity and the possibility of redeeming the historical life of humanity from the social wrongs which now pervade it and which act as temptations and incitements to evil and as forces of resistance to the powers of redemption. Its chief interest is concentrated on those manifestations of sin and redemption which lie beyond the individual soul.[41] If our exposition of the superpersonal agents of sin and of the Kingdom of Evil is true, then evidently a salvation confined to the soul and its personal

40. Matt. 23:24.

41. Opponents of the social gospel worried that its emphasis on salvation here and now marginalized the traditional view of eternal salvation of the soul.

interests is an imperfect and only partly effective salvation.

Yet the salvation of the individual is, of course, an essential part of salvation. Every new being is a new problem of salvation. It is always a great and wonderful thing when a young spirit enters into voluntary obedience to God and feels the higher freedom with which Christ makes us free. It is one of the miracles of life. The burden of the individual is as heavy now as ever. The consciousness of wrong-doing, of imperfection, of a wasted life lies on many and they need forgiveness and strength for a new beginning. Modern pessimism drains the finer minds of their confidence in the world and the value of life itself. At present we gasp for air in a crushing and monstrous world. Any return of faith is an experience of salvation.

Therefore our discussion can not pass personal salvation by. We might possibly begin where the old gospel leaves off, and ask our readers to take all the familiar experiences and truths of personal evangelism and religious nurture for granted in what follows. But our understanding of personal salvation itself is deeply affected by the new solidaristic comprehension furnished by the social gospel.

[*A Theology for the Social Gospel* (New York: Macmillan, 1917), 1–2, 5–7, 9, 31–35, 95–96]

E. Orthodoxies Restated

Selection 93: John Henry Newman, *An Essay on the Development of Christian Doctrine* (1845; new ed., 1878)

John Henry Newman (1801–1890) was an Anglican clergyman and a leading figure in the Oxford Movement. He converted to Roman Catholicism in 1845 and was made a cardinal in 1879. He wrote **An Essay on the Development of Christian Doctrine** ***partially in defense of his conversion. The following excerpts come from the second chapter of the book.***

Section I: Developments of Doctrine to be Expected

. . . 3. 2. Again, if Christianity be an universal religion, suited not simply to one locality or period, but to all times and places, it cannot but vary in its relations and dealings towards the world around it, that is, it will develope. Principles require a very various application according as persons and circumstances vary, and must be thrown into new shapes according to the form of society which they are to influence. Hence all bodies of Christians, orthodox or not, develope the doctrines of Scripture. Few but will grant that Luther's view of justification had never been stated in words before his time: that his phraseology and his positions were novel, whether called for by circumstances or not. It is equally certain that the doctrine of justification defined at Trent was, in some sense, new also. The refutation and remedy of errors cannot precede their rise; and thus the fact of false developments or corruptions involves the correspondent manifestation of true ones. Moreover, all parties appeal to Scripture, that is, argue from Scripture; but argument implies deduction, that is, development. Here there is no difference between early times and late, between a Pope *ex cathedrâ*[42] and an individual Protestant, except that their authority is not on a par. On either side the claim of authority is the same, and the process of development.

Accordingly, the common complaint of Protestants against the Church of Rome is, not

42. That is, "from the chair," the authoritative teaching of the pope for the church. This would later be defined as "infallible" teaching. See Selection 96.

simply that she has added to the primitive or the Scriptural doctrine, (for this they do themselves,) but that she contradicts it, and moreover imposes her additions as fundamental truths under sanction of an anathema. For themselves they deduce by quite as subtle a method, and act upon doctrines as implicit and on reasons as little analyzed in time past, as Catholic schoolmen. What prominence has the Royal Supremacy in the New Testament, or the lawfulness of bearing arms, or the duty of public worship, or the substitution of the first day of the week for the seventh, or infant baptism, to say nothing of the fundamental principle that the Bible and the Bible only is the religion of Protestants? These doctrines and usages, true or not, which is not the question here, are surely not gained by the direct use and immediate application of Scripture, nor by a mere exercise of argument upon words and sentences placed before the eyes, but by the unconscious growth of ideas suggested by the letter and habitual to the mind.

4. 3. And, indeed, when we turn to the consideration of particular doctrines on which Scripture lays the greatest stress, we shall see that it is absolutely impossible for them to remain in the mere letter of Scripture, if they are to be more than mere words, and to convey a definite idea to the recipient. When it is declared that "the Word became flesh," three wide questions open upon us on the very announcement. What is meant by "the Word," what by "flesh," what by "became"? The answers to these involve a process of investigation, and are developments. Moreover, when they have been made, they will suggest a series of secondary questions; and thus at length a multitude of propositions is the result, which gather round the inspired sentence of which they come, giving it externally the form of a doctrine, and creating or deepening the idea of it in the mind.

It is true that, so far as such statements of Scripture are mysteries, they are relatively to us but words, and cannot be developed. But as a mystery implies in part what is incomprehensible or at least unknown, so does it in part imply what is not so; it implies a partial manifestation, or a representation by economy. Because then it is in a measure understood, it can so far be developed, though each result in the process will partake of the dimness and confusion of the original impression.

5. 4. This moreover should be considered,—that great questions exist in the subject-matter of which Scripture treats, which Scripture does not solve; questions too so real, so practical, that they must be answered, and, unless we suppose a new revelation, answered by means of the revelation which we have, that is, by development. Such is the question of the Canon of Scripture and its inspiration: that is, whether Christianity depends upon a written document as Judaism;—if so, on what writings and how many;—whether that document is self-interpreting, or requires a comment, and whether any authoritative comment or commentator is provided;—whether the revelation and the document are commensurate, or the one outruns the other;—all these questions surely find no solution on the surface of Scripture, nor indeed under the surface in the case of most men, however long and diligent might be their study of it. Nor were these difficulties settled by authority, as far as we know, at the commencement of the religion; yet surely it is quite conceivable that an Apostle might have dissipated them all in a few words, had Divine Wisdom thought fit. But in matter of fact the decision has been left to time, to the slow process of thought, to the influence of mind upon mind, the issues of controversy, and the growth of opinion. . . .

Section II: An Infallible Developing Authority to be Expected

. . . 11. 5. Moreover, it must be borne in mind that, as the essence of all religion is authority and obedience, so the distinction between natural religion and revealed lies in this, that the one has a subjective authority, and the other an objective. Revelation consists in the manifestation of the Invisible Divine Power, or in the substitution of the voice of a Lawgiver for the voice of conscience. The supremacy of conscience is the essence of natural religion; the supremacy of Apostle, or Pope, or Church, or Bishop, is the essence of revealed; and when such external authority is taken away, the mind falls back again of necessity upon that inward guide which it possessed even before Revelation was vouchsafed. Thus, what conscience is in the system of nature, such is the voice of Scripture, or of the Church, or of the Holy See, as we may determine it, in the system of Revelation. It may be objected, in deed, that conscience is not infallible; it is true, but still it is ever to be obeyed. And this is just the prerogative which controversialists assign to the See of St. Peter; it is not in all cases infallible, it may err beyond its special province, but it has in all cases a claim on our obedience. "All Catholics and heretics," says Bellarmine, "agree in two things: first, that it is possible for the Pope, even as pope, and with his own assembly of councillors, or with General Council, to err in particular controversies of fact, which chiefly depend on human information and testimony; secondly, that it is possible for him to err as a private Doctor, even in universal questions of right, whether of faith or of morals, and that from ignorance, as sometimes happens to other doctors. Next, all Catholics agree in other two points, not, however, with heretics, but solely with each other: first, that the Pope with General Council cannot err, either in framing decrees of faith or general precepts of morality; secondly, that the Pope when determining anything in a doubtful matter, whether by himself or with his own particular Council, *whether it is possible for him to err or not, is to be obeyed* by all the faithful."[43] And as obedience to conscience, even supposing conscience ill-informed, tends to the improvement of our moral nature, and ultimately of our knowledge, so obedience to our ecclesiastical superior may subserve our growth in illumination and sanctity, even though he should command what is extreme or inexpedient, or teach what is external to his legitimate province.

12. 6. The common sense of mankind does but support a conclusion thus forced upon us by analogical considerations. It feels that the very idea of revelation implies a present informant and guide, and that an infallible one; not a mere abstract declaration of Truths unknown before to man, or a record of history, or the result of an antiquarian research, but a message and a lesson speaking to this man and that. This is shown by the popular notion which has prevailed among us since the Reformation, that the Bible itself is such a guide; and which succeeded in overthrowing the supremacy of Church and Pope, for the very reason that it was a rival authority, not resisting merely, but supplanting it. In proportion, then, as we find, in matter of fact, that the inspired volume is not adapted or intended to subserve that purpose, are we forced to revert to that living and present Guide, who, at the era of our rejection of her, had been so long recognized as the dispenser of Scripture, according to times and circumstances, and the arbiter of all true doctrine and holy practice to her children. We feel a need, and she alone of all things under heaven supplies it. We are told that God has spoken.

---

43. Robert Bellarmine, *De Romano Pontifice* iv.2.

Where? In a book? We have tried it and it disappoints; it disappoints us, that most holy and blessed gift, not from fault of its own, but because it is used for a purpose for which it was not given. The Ethiopian's reply, when St. Philip asked him if he understood what he was reading, is the voice of nature: "How can I, unless some man shall guide me?" The Church undertakes that office; she does what none else can do, and this is the secret of her power. "The human mind," it has been said, "wishes to be rid of doubt in religion; and a teacher who claims infallibility is readily believed on his simple word. We see this constantly exemplified in the case of individual pretenders among ourselves. In Romanism the Church pretends to it; she rids herself of competitors by forestalling them. And probably, in the eyes of her children, this is not the least persuasive argument for her infallibility, that she alone of all Churches dares claim it, as if a secret instinct and involuntary misgivings restrained those rival communions which go so far towards affecting it."[44] These sentences, whatever be the errors of their wording, surely express a great truth. The most obvious answer, then, to the question, why we yield to the authority of the Church in the questions and developments of faith, is, that some authority there must be if there is a revelation given, and other authority there is none but she. A revelation is not given, if there be no authority to decide what it is that is given. In the words of St. Peter, to her Divine Master and Lord, "To whom shall we go?" Nor must it be forgotten in confirmation, that Scripture expressly calls the Church "the pillar and ground of the Truth," and promises her as by covenant that "the Spirit of the Lord that is upon her, and His words which He has put in her mouth shall not depart out of her mouth, nor out of the mouth of her seed, nor out of the mouth of her seed's seed, from henceforth and for ever."[45]

44. John Henry Newman, *The Via Media of the Anglican Church*, vol. 1:117. Newman wrote these quoted words before his conversion to Roman Catholicism.

[*An Essay on the Development of Christian Doctrine*, new ed. (London, 1878), 58–60, 86–89]

Selection 94: Pope Pius IX, *Ineffabilis Deus* (Decree on the Immaculate Conception) (1854)

Pope Pius IX (1792–1878) issued this papal bull (or encyclical) on December 8, 1854, that defined the doctrine of the immaculate conception. Contrary to popular misunderstandings, the "immaculate conception" does not refer to the virgin birth of Jesus but, rather, states that his mother was conceived without the stain of original sin. Stated in this way, not only does this doctrine safeguard Jesus from receiving original sin, but it also preserves Mary from what is otherwise common to the fallen human experience.

The immaculate conception defined what had been believed by many Roman Catholics for centuries and further bolstered the developing Mariology. Although Eastern Orthodox Churches similarly venerate Mary, they never accepted the strong Augustinian formulation of original sin and thus did not require the kind of explanation embodied in this definition. In addition to the significance of the doctrine itself, the papal pronouncement of this dogma, independent of the council of bishops, anticipates the later codification of the infallibility of papal teaching (see Selection 96).

45. 1 Tim. 3:16; Isa. 59:21.

Since we have never ceased in humility and fasting to offer up our prayers and those of the Church to God the Father through his Son, that he might deign to direct and confirm our mind by the power of the Holy Ghost, after imploring the protection of the whole celestial court, and after invoking on our knees the Holy Ghost the Paraclete, under his inspiration we pronounce, declare, and define, unto the glory of the Holy and Indivisible Trinity, the honor and ornament of the holy Virgin the Mother of God, for the exaltation of the Catholic faith and the increase of the Christian religion, by the authority of our Lord Jesus Christ and the blessed Apostles Peter and Paul, and in our own authority, that the doctrine which holds the Blessed Virgin Mary to have been, from the first instant of her conception, by a singular grace and privilege of Almighty God, in view of the merits of Christ Jesus the Saviour of mankind, preserved free from all stain of original sin, was revealed by God, and is, therefore, to be firmly and constantly believed by all the faithful.

Therefore, if some should presume to think in their hearts otherwise than we have defined (which God forbid), they shall know and thoroughly understand that they are by their own judgment condemned, have made shipwreck concerning the faith, and fallen away from the unity of the Church; and, moreover, that they, by this very act, subject themselves to the penalties ordained by law, if, by word or writing, or any other external means, they dare to signify what they think in their hearts.

[*The Creeds of Christendom*, vol. 2, ed. Philip Schaff (repr., Grand Rapids: Baker, 1998), 211–12]

Selection 95: Pope Pius IX, *Syllabus of Errors* (1864)

On December 8 (the Feast of the Immaculate Conception), 1864, Pope Pius IX published this syllabus (or collection) of alleged errors that were becoming increasingly prominent in Western Christianity. The eighty errors are listed as brief propositions, each of which had been dealt with in previous papal documents by Pius IX. Each proposition is stated in its positive form, and the Roman Catholic Church by implication was to emphasize their contraries. Together with other formulations of Pius IX (see Selections 94 and 96), this document reflects the Roman Catholic Church's strong stand against the liberal Protestant views of authority and society contained in these propositions.

1. There exists no supreme, most wise, and most provident divine being distinct from the universe, and God is none other than nature, and is therefore subject to change. In effect, God is produced in man and in the world, and all things are God, and have the very substance of God. God is therefore one and the same thing with the world, and thence spirit is the same thing with matter, necessity with liberty, true with false, good with evil, justice with injustice. . . .

8. As human reason is placed on a level with religion, so theological matters must be treated in the same manner as philosophical ones. . . .

15. Every man is free to embrace and profess the religion he shall believe true, guided by the light of reason. . . .

17. We may entertain at least a well-founded hope for the eternal salvation of all those who are in no manner in the true Church of Christ.

18. Protestantism is nothing more than another form of the same true Christian religion, in which it is possible to be equally pleasing to God as in the Catholic Church. . . .

23. The Roman Pontiffs and œcumenical Councils have exceeded the limits of their power, have usurped the rights of princes, and have even committed errors in defining matters of faith and morals. . . .

42. In the case of conflicting laws between the two powers, the civil law ought to prevail. . . .[46]

55. The Church ought to be separated from the State, and the State from the Church. . . .

58. No other forces are to be recognized than those which reside in matter; and all moral teaching and moral excellence ought to be made to consist in the accumulation and increase of riches by every possible means, and in the enjoyment of pleasure. . . .

60. Authority is nothing else but the result of numerical superiority and material force. . . .

76. The abolition of the temporal power, of which the Apostolic See is possessed, would contribute in the greatest degree to the liberty and prosperity of the Church.

77. In the present day, it is no longer expedient that the Catholic religion shall be held as the only religion of the State, to the exclusion of all other modes of worship.

78. Whence it has been wisely provided by law, in some countries called Catholic, that persons coming to reside therein shall enjoy the public exercise of their own worship.

[*The Creeds of Christendom*, vol. 2, ed. Philip Schaff (repr., Grand Rapids: Baker, 1998), 213, 215, 217-19, 223, 227-28, 232]

Selection 96: Council of Vatican I (1869–1870)

Pope Pius IX convoked the first Vatican Council (1869–1870), and its fourth session met on July 18, 1870. This excerpt from the "First Dogmatic Constitution of the Church of Christ," also known as* Pastor aeternus, *defines "the infallible teaching office of the Roman pontiff."

Session 4 (18 July 1870)
First Dogmatic Constitution on the Church of Christ

. . . The eternal shepherd and guardian of our souls, in order to render permanent the saving work of redemption, determined to build a church in which, as in the house of the living God, all the faithful should be linked by the bond of one faith and charity. Therefore, before he was glorified, he besought his Father, not for the apostles only, but also *for those who were to believe in him through their word, that they all might be one as the Son himself and the Father are one.* So then, just as he sent apostles, whom he chose out of the world, even as he had been sent by the Father, in like manner it was his will that in his church there should be shepherds and teachers until the end of time. In order, then, that the episcopal office should be one and undivided and that, by the union of the clergy, the whole multitude of believers should be held together in the unity of faith and communion, he set blessed Peter over the rest of the apostles and instituted in him the permanent principle of both unities and their visible foundation. Upon the strength of this foundation was to be built the eternal temple, and the church whose topmost part reaches heaven was to rise upon the firmness of this foundation. And since the gates of hell trying, if they can, to overthrow the church, make their assault with a hatred that increases day by day against its divinely laid foundation, we judge it necessary, with the approbation of the sacred council, and for the protection, defence and growth of the catholic flock, to propound the doctrine

46. This and other propositions reflect the church's rejection of the increasing independence of the modern nation-state from the influence of the church.

concerning the institution, permanence and nature of the sacred and apostolic primacy, upon which the strength and coherence of the whole church depends. This doctrine is to be believed and held by all the faithful in accordance with the ancient and unchanging faith of the whole church. Furthermore, we shall proscribe and condemn the contrary errors which are so harmful to the Lord's flock.

Chapter 1. On the institution of the apostolic primacy in blessed Peter

We teach and declare that, according to the gospel evidence, a primacy of jurisdiction over the whole church of God was immediately and directly promised to the blessed apostle Peter and conferred on him by Christ the lord. It was to Simon alone, to whom he had already said *You shall be called Cephas*, that the Lord, after his confession, *You are the Christ, the son of the living God*, spoke these words: *Blessed are you, Simon Bar-Jona. For flesh and blood has not revealed this to you, but my Father who is in heaven. And I tell you, you are Peter, and on this rock I will build my church, and the gates of the underworld shall not prevail against it. I will give you the keys of the kingdom of heaven, and whatever you bind on earth shall be bound in heaven, and whatever you loose on earth shall be loosed in heaven.*[47] And it was to Peter alone that Jesus, after his resurrection, confided the jurisdiction of supreme pastor and ruler of his whole fold, saying: *Feed my lambs, feed my sheep.*[48] To this absolutely manifest teaching of the sacred scriptures, as it has always been understood by the catholic church, are clearly opposed the distorted opinions of those who misrepresent the form of government which Christ the lord established in his church, and deny that Peter, in preference to the rest of the apostles, taken singly or collectively, was endowed by Christ with a true and proper primacy of jurisdiction. The same may be said of those who assert that this primacy was not conferred immediately and directly on blessed Peter himself, but rather on the church, and that it was through the church that it was transmitted to him in his capacity as her minister.

Therefore, if anyone says that blessed Peter the apostle was not appointed by Christ the lord as prince of all the apostles and visible head of the whole church militant; or that it was a primacy of honour only and not one of true and proper jurisdiction that he directly and immediately received from our lord Jesus Christ himself: let him be anathema.

Chapter 2. On the permanence of the primacy of blessed Peter in the Roman pontiffs

That which our lord Jesus Christ, the prince of shepherds and great shepherd of the sheep, established in the blessed apostle Peter, for the continual salvation and permanent benefit of the church, must of necessity remain for ever, by Christ's authority, in the church which, founded as it is upon a rock, will stand firm until the end of time. For no one can be in doubt, indeed it was known in every age, that the holy and most blessed Peter, prince and head of the apostles, the pillar of faith and the foundation of the catholic church, received the keys of the kingdom from our lord Jesus Christ, the saviour and redeemer of the human race; and that to this day and for ever he lives and presides and exercises judgment in his successors the bishops of the holy Roman see, which he founded and consecrated with his blood. Therefore whoever succeeds to the chair of Peter obtains, by the institution of Christ himself, the primacy of Peter over the whole church.

47. Matt. 16:16-19 is the primary biblical text cited to support papal primacy.

48. After Matthew 16 (quoted above), this passage from John 21:15-17 is perhaps the most frequently cited Scripture in support of the papal office.

So what the truth has ordained stands firm, and blessed Peter perseveres in the rock-like strength he was granted, and does not abandon that guidance of the church which he once received. For this reason it has always been necessary for every church—that is to say the faithful throughout the world—to be in agreement with the Roman church because of its more effective leadership. In consequence of being joined, as members to head, with that see, from which the rights of sacred communion flow to all, they will grow together into the structure of a single body. . . .

Chapter 3. On the power and character of the primacy of the Roman pontiff

. . . Wherefore we teach and declare that, by divine ordinance, the Roman church possesses a pre-eminence of ordinary power over every other church, and that this jurisdictional power of the Roman pontiff is both episcopal and immediate. Both clergy and faithful, of whatever rite and dignity, both singly and collectively, are bound to submit to this power by the duty of hierarchical subordination and true obedience, and this not only in matters concerning faith and morals, but also in those which regard the discipline and government of the church throughout the world. In this way, by unity with the Roman pontiff in communion and in profession of the same faith, the church of Christ becomes one flock under one supreme shepherd. This is the teaching of the catholic truth, and no one can depart from it without endangering his faith and salvation. . . .

Since the Roman pontiff, by the divine right of the apostolic primacy, governs the whole church, we likewise teach and declare that he is the supreme judge of the faithful, and that in all cases which fall under ecclesiastical jurisdiction recourse may be had to his judgment. The sentence of the apostolic see (than which there is no higher authority) is not subject to revision by anyone, nor may anyone lawfully pass judgment thereupon. And so they stray from the genuine path of truth who maintain that it is lawful to appeal from the judgments of the Roman pontiffs to an ecumenical council as if this were an authority superior to the Roman pontiff. . . .

Chapter 4. On the infallible teaching authority of the Roman pontiff

To satisfy this pastoral office, our predecessors strove unwearyingly that the saving teaching of Christ should be spread among all the peoples of the world; and with equal care they made sure that it should be kept pure and uncontaminated wherever it was received. It was for this reason that the bishops of the whole world, sometimes individually, sometimes gathered in synods, according to the long established custom of the churches and the pattern of ancient usage, referred to this apostolic see those dangers especially which arose in matters concerning the faith. This was to ensure that any damage suffered by the faith should be repaired in that place above all where the faith can know no failing. The Roman pontiffs, too, as the circumstances of the time or the state of affairs suggested, sometimes by summoning ecumenical councils or consulting the opinion of the churches scattered throughout the world, sometimes by special synods, sometimes by taking advantage of other useful means afforded by divine providence, defined as doctrines to be held those things which, by God's help, they knew to be in keeping with sacred scripture and the apostolic traditions. For the holy Spirit was promised to the successors of Peter not so that they might, by his revelation, make known some new doctrine, but that, by his assistance, they might religiously guard and faithfully expound the revelation or deposit of faith transmitted by the apostles. Indeed, their apostolic teaching was embraced by all the venerable fathers and reverenced and followed by all the holy orthodox doctors, for they knew very well that this see of St. Peter always remains unblemished by any error, in accordance with the divine promise of our Lord and Saviour to the prince of his disciples: *I have prayed for you that your faith may not fail; and when you have turned again, strengthen your brethren.*[49]

This gift of truth and never-failing faith was therefore divinely conferred on Peter and his successors in this see so that they might discharge their exalted office for the salvation of all, and so that the whole flock of Christ might be kept away by them from the poisonous food of error and be nourished with the sustenance of heavenly doctrine. Thus the tendency to schism is removed and the whole church is preserved in unity, and, resting on its foundation, can stand firm against the gates of hell. . . .

Therefore, faithfully adhering to the tradition received from the beginning of the christian faith, to the glory of God our saviour, for the exaltation of the catholic religion and for the salvation of the christian people, with the approval of the sacred council, we teach and define as a divinely revealed dogma that when the Roman pontiff speaks *ex cathedra*,[50] that is, when, in the exercise of his office as shepherd and teacher of all Christians, in virtue of his supreme apostolic authority, he defines a doctrine concerning faith or morals to be held by the whole church, he possesses, by the divine assistance promised to him in blessed Peter, that infallibility which the divine Redeemer willed his church to enjoy in defining doctrine concerning faith or morals. Therefore, such definitions of the Roman pontiff are of themselves, and not by the consent of the church, irreformable.

So then, should anyone, which God forbid, have the temerity to reject this definition of ours: let him be anathema.

[*Decrees of the Ecumenical Councils*, ed. Norman Tanner, 2:811–16]

Selection 97: B. B. Warfield, "The Deity of Christ" (1910)

The Fundamentals: A Testimony to the Truth ***was a series of twelve multiauthored, paperback booklets containing a variety of articles that covered a range of theological topics. They were published from 1910 to 1915 and were meant to reiterate the fundamental, or foundational, points of Christian faith in response to liberal theology, emphasizing such doctrines as biblical inerrancy, the deity of Christ, his virgin birth, his bodily resurrection, and the historicity of the biblical miracles. Benjamin Breckinridge Warfield (1851–1921), professor of theology at Princeton Seminary, contributed this article on Christ's deity in the first volume of the series.***

A recent writer has remarked that our assured conviction of the deity of Christ rests, not upon "proof-texts or passages, nor upon old arguments drawn from these, but upon the general fact of the whole manifestation of Jesus Christ, and of the whole impression left by Him upon the world." The antithesis is too absolute, and possibly betrays an unwarranted distrust of the evidence of Scripture. To make it just, we should read the statement rather thus: Our conviction of the deity of Christ rests not alone on the scriptural passages which assert it, but also on His entire impression on the world; or

49. This passage from Luke 22:32 is cited as the primary biblical basis for the infallibility of papal teaching.

50. That is, "from the chair."

perhaps thus: Our conviction rests not more on the scriptural assertions than upon His entire manifestation. Both lines of evidence are valid; and when twisted together form an unbreakable cord. The proof-texts and passages do prove that Jesus was esteemed divine by those who companied with Him; that He esteemed Himself divine; that He was recognized as divine by those who were taught by the Spirit; that, in fine, He was divine. But over and above this Biblical evidence the impression Jesus has left upon the world bears independent testimony to His deity, and it may well be that to many minds this will seem the most conclusive of all its evidences. It certainly is very cogent and impressive.

Experience as Proof

The justification which the author we have just quoted gives of his neglecting the scriptural evidence in favor of that borne by Jesus' impression on the world is also open to criticism. "Jesus Christ," he tells us, "is one of those essential truths which are too great to be proved, like God, or freedom, or immortality." Such things rest, it seems, not on proofs but on experience. We need not stop to point out that this experience is itself a proof. We wish rather to point out that some confusion seems to have been fallen into here between our ability to marshal the proof by which we are convinced and our accessibility to its force. It is quite true that "the most essential conclusions of the human mind are much wiser and stronger than the arguments by which they are supported;" that the proofs "are always changing but the beliefs persist."[51] But this is not because the conclusions in question rest on no sound proofs; but because we have not had the skill to adduce, in our argumentative presentations of them, the really fundamental proofs on which they rest.

Unconscious Rationality

. . . We do not need to wait to analyse the grounds of our convictions before they operate to produce convictions, any more than we need to wait to analyse our food before it nourishes us; and we can soundly believe on evidence much mixed with error, just as we can thrive on food far from pure. The alchemy of the mind, as of the digestive tract, knows how to separate out from the mass what it requires for its support; and as we may live without any knowledge of chemistry, so we may possess earnest convictions, solidly founded in right reason, without the slightest knowledge of logic. The Christian's conviction of the deity of his Lord does not depend for its soundness on the Christian's ability convincingly to state the grounds of his conviction. The evidence he offers for it may be wholly inadequate, while the evidence on which it rests may be absolutely compelling.

Testimony in Solution

The very abundance and persuasiveness of the evidence of the deity of Christ greatly increases the difficulty of adequately stating it. This is true even of the scriptural evidence, as precise and definite as much of it is. . . .

A Saturated Gospel

. . . In three passages of Matthew, reporting words of Jesus, He is represented as speaking familiarly and in the most natural manner in the world, of "*His* angels" (13:41; 16:27; 24:31). In all three He designates Himself as the "Son of man"; and in all three there are additional suggestions of His majesty. . . .

51. The quotations in this and the preceding paragraph come from William Porcher DuBose, *The Gospel in the Gospels* (New York: Longmans, Green, 1908), 206–7.

Heaven Come to Earth

There are three parables recorded in the fifteenth chapter of Luke as spoken by our Lord in His defence against the murmurs of the Pharisees at His receiving sinners and eating with them. The essence of the defence which our Lord offers for Himself is, that there is joy *in heaven* over repentant sinners! Why "in heaven," "before the throne of God"? Is He merely setting the judgment of heaven over against that of earth, or pointing forward to His future vindication? By no means. He is representing His action in receiving sinners, in seeking the lost, as His proper action, because it is the normal conduct of heaven, manifested in Him. He is heaven come to earth. His defence is thus simply the unveiling of what the real nature of the transaction is. The lost when they come to Him are received because this is heaven's way; and *He* cannot act otherwise than in heaven's way. He tacitly assumes the good Shepherd's part as His own.

The Unique Position

All the great designations are not so much asserted as assumed by Him for Himself. He does not call Himself a prophet, though He accepts this designation from others: He places Himself above all the prophets, even above John the greatest of the prophets, as Him to whom all the prophets look forward. . . . Indeed, all that God has and is He asserts Himself to have and be; omnipotence, omniscience, perfection belong as to the one so to the other. Not only does He perform all divine acts; His self-consciousness coalesces with the divine consciousness. If His followers lagged in recognizing His deity, this was not because He was not God or did not sufficiently manifest His deity. It was because they were foolish and slow of heart to believe what lay patently before their eyes.

The Great Proof

. . . Take it objectively. Read such a book as Harnack's "The Expansion of Christianity," or such an one as Von Dobschütz's "Christian Life in the Primitive Church"—neither of which allows the deity of Christ—and then ask, Could these things have been wrought by power less than divine? And then remember that these things were not only wrought in that heathen world two thousand years ago, but have been wrought over again every generation since; for Christianity has reconquered the world to itself each generation. Think of how the Christian proclamation spread, eating its way over the world like fire in the grass of a prairie. Think how, as it spread, it transformed lives. The thing, whether in its objective or in its subjective aspect, were incredible, had it not actually occurred. "Should a voyager," says Charles Darwin, "chance to be on the point of shipwreck on some unknown coast, he will most devoutly pray that the lesson of the missionary may have reached thus far. The lesson of the missionary is the enchanter's wand."[52] Could this transforming influence, undiminished after two millenniums, have proceeded from a mere man? It is historically impossible that the great movement which we call Christianity, which remains unspent after all these years, could have originated in a merely human impulse; or could represent today the working of a merely human force.

The Proof Within

Or take it subjectively. Every Christian has within himself the proof of the transforming power of Christ, and can repeat the blind man's syllogism: Why herein is the marvel that ye

52. See Charles Darwin, *Journal of Researches into the Natural History and Geology of the Countries Visited during the Voyage of H.M.S. Beagle round the World*, new ed. (New York: Appleton, 1896), 414.

know not whence He is, and yet He opened my eyes. "Spirits are not touched to fine issues who are not finely touched." "Shall we trust," demands an eloquent reasoner, "the touch of our fingers, the sight of our eyes, the hearing of our ears, and not trust our deepest consciousness of our higher nature—the answer of conscience, the flower of spiritual gladness, the glow of spiritual love? To deny that spiritual experience is as real as physical experience is to slander the noblest faculties of our nature. It is to say that one half of our nature tells the truth, and the other half utters lies. The proposition that facts in the spiritual region are less real than facts in the physical realm contradicts all philosophy." The transformed hearts of Christians, registering themselves "in gentle tempers, in noble motives, in lives visibly lived under the empire of great aspirations"[53]—these are the ever-present proofs of the divinity of the Person from whom their inspiration is drawn.

The supreme proof to every Christian of the deity of his Lord is then his own inner experience of the transforming power of his Lord upon the heart and life. Not more surely does he who feels the present warmth of the sun know that the sun exists, than he who has experienced the re-creative power of the Lord know Him to be his Lord and his God. Here is, perhaps we may say the proper, certainly we must say the most convincing, proof to every Christian of the deity of Christ; a proof which he cannot escape, and to which, whether he is capable of analyzing it or drawing it out in logical statement or not, he cannot fail to yield his sincere and unassailable conviction. Whatever else he may or may not be assured of, he knows that his Redeemer lives. Because He lives, we shall live also—that was the Lord's own assurance. Because we live, He lives also—that is the ineradicable conviction of every Christian heart.

[*The Fundamentals: A Testimony to the Truth, Volume I* (Chicago: Testimony Publishing, 1910), 21–28]

53. W. H. Fitchett, *The Unrealized Logic of Religion: A Study in Credibilities* (London: Charles H. Kelly, 1906), 93–94.

Further Reading

Evans, C. Stephen. *Kierkegaard on Faith and the Self: Collected Essays*. Waco, TX: Baylor University Press, 2006.

Faught, C. Brad. *The Oxford Movement: A Thematic History of the Tractarians and Their Times*. University Park: Pennsylvania State University Press, 2003.

Livingston, James C. *Modern Christian Thought: The Enlightenment and the Nineteenth Century*. 2nd ed. Minneapolis: Fortress Press, 2006.

Mariña, Jacqueline, ed. *The Cambridge Companion to Friedrich Schleiermacher*. Cambridge: Cambridge University Press, 2005.

Marsden, George M. *Fundamentalism and American Culture*. 2nd ed. New York: Oxford University Press, 2006.

Porterfield, Amanda, ed. *Modern Christianity to 1900*. A People's History of Christianity, vol. 6. Minneapolis: Fortress Press, 2007.

Chapter 9
Late Modern Fragmentation and Ecumenism

The twentieth century began with a continuation of the optimism of the nineteenth century. The gospel had now been spread around the world to an unprecedented extent. As scientific knowledge, technology, and industry were progressing and spreading "civilization," theologians were working to adapt the faith to the new cultural realities. In 1900, the editor of the Disciples of Christ magazine *The Christian Oracle* renamed it *The Christian Century*, reflecting the widespread optimism for the coming century. Much of this optimism would be crushed in the second decade of the new century.

It has been said that the twentieth century—and, along with it, twentieth-century theology—really began with the outbreak of the Great War in 1914. Whereas many liberal Protestant theologians of the state church in Germany supported the war and united the church with the aggressive goals of the state, others became disillusioned by the war and disenchanted with the theology that supported it. "Neo-orthodox" theologians reacted against what they perceived to be an anthropocentric theology that did not take the doctrines of the fall and of divine grace seriously enough. An even starker crisis occurred in the 1930s with the rise of Nazism leading up to the Second World War. Neo-orthodox thinkers again asserted that the mission of the church cannot be subjected to the worldly goals of the state. Neo-orthodoxy would come to dominate the theological scene in Europe and North America from the 1930s to the 1960s.

The Roman Catholic Church experienced a number of renewal movements. Just before the turn of the twentieth century, there was a revival of interest in scholastic theology, especially that of Thomas Aquinas. A few decades into the century, there was renewed interest in patristic theology, led in part by the *Nouvelle Théologie* of French Catholics. In the 1960s, the Roman Catholic Church convened the Second Vatican Council, which brought many changes and greater openness to the Church. A catechism was published in 1994 for the purpose of popularizing post–Vatican II Catholicism. Eastern Orthodox churches had greater visibility than ever before in the West, particularly due to immigration. Many such immigrants came westward from the Soviet Union, whose official policy of atheistic communism was hostile to the world's largest Orthodox communion, the Russian Orthodox Church.

Evangelical and fundamentalist churches remained the dominant force in North America in the early part of the century. Some of these churches remained sectarian, but others embraced a more open stance to modern culture and other churches. In the latter half of the century, evangelical Protestant churches grew through campaigns like those of Billy Graham (1918–), and many such churches increased exposure through mass media and marketing enterprises. Evangelical mega-churches and parachurch organizations also contributed to the growth and cultural exposure of "born again" Christians.

After midcentury, fragmentation in society and in theological approaches increased. Theologians began interpreting and applying the Christian message from new contexts and perspectives, reflecting the growing pluralism in the Western world. This pluralism has led not only to a greater variety of theological approaches but also to increased interaction with other religions and philosophies, including more aggressive attacks from secular atheism.

Along with fragmentation, the twentieth-century ecumenical movement has brought various denominations into official doctrinal conversations with one another. The first general assembly of the World Council of Churches (WCC) in Amsterdam (1948) had the theme "Man's Disorder and God's Design." The social agenda of the WCC has been its most controversial aspect since 1968 (Uppsala). But the most common form of ecumenism still occurs not formally but as grassroots, interdenominational cooperation.

After World War II, especially in North America, there was renewed optimism for growth in the mainline Protestant churches. In the latter half of the century, however, these same mainline churches began to lose members while more conservative churches grew. Throughout the century in Europe, the churches saw a rapid decline in membership. In the global South, by contrast, Christianity has spread, especially in parts of Africa and Asia. The neo-Pentecostal, "charismatic" Christianity is the fastest-growing form.

A. Neo-orthodoxy

Biographical Note: Karl Barth

Karl Barth (1886–1968) was the greatest theologian of the twentieth century. He was born in Basel, Switzerland, the son and grandson of pastors. After receiving his theological education under the brightest lights of liberal Protestant theology, he became a pastor in the small town of Safenwil, Switzerland, serving from 1911 until 1921. It was here that he wrote his epoch-making commentary on Romans. He then moved to Germany and taught theology first at Göttingen, then at Münster, and later at Bonn, where he began writing his Church Dogmatics. *In 1934, Barth helped pen the Barmen Declaration and he joined the Confessing Church. When he refused to sign an oath of allegiance to the Führer (Adolf Hitler), he was removed from his teaching position. Barth then returned to his native Switzerland and taught at Basel from 1935 until his retirement in 1962.*

Barth's theology has been categorized under a number of different labels. For instance, "dialectical theology" points to his method of seeking the truth by exploring statements and their antitheses, whereas "theology of crisis" points to his social and theological contexts in the wake of the First World War and the dominance of liberal theology. But Barth's thought and the movement he inspired have become more frequently known as neo-orthodoxy. This movement was led by Barth and other German-speaking theologians, and, in addition to Barth, the label has been applied to Emil Brunner (1889–1966), Rudolf Bultmann (1884–1976), Dietrich Bonhoeffer (1906–1945), H. Richard Niebuhr (1894–1962), and Reinhold Niebuhr (1892–1971), among others. Although these figures represent a variety of theological perspectives, they are unified in their reaction against the classic liberal theology in which they had been educated, which they came to see as overly optimistic in its anthropology, resulting in the marginalization of special divine revelation. In his rejection of liberal theology, Barth moved closer to the older Protestant orthodoxy, although he never embraced anything like the fundamentalism becoming more prevalent in British and North American circles.

The direction of Barth's theology may be described as "from above to below," deliberately beginning with God, not humanity, as the primary topic and reality. With this emphasis, Barth meant to turn Schleiermacher's theology—and along with him, liberal theology—on its head. According to Barth, true theology cannot begin with human feeling and consciousness about God, which is nothing but anthropology; rather, it must begin with a word from God to humanity.

Selection 98: Karl Barth, *Epistle to the Romans* (1919; 2nd ed., 1922)

The first edition of Barth's commentary on Romans (1919) did not receive much publicity, but the completely revised second edition (1922) had a wide impact. In his exposition of Romans, Barth set the tone for his theological challenge to the hegemony of liberal Protestant theology in the academy.

[On Rom. 1:18] . . . But what does "apart from and without Christ" mean? "The wrath of God is revealed against all ungodliness and unrighteousness of men" [Rom. 1:18]. These are the characteristic features of our relation to God, as it takes shape on this side [of] resurrection. Our relation to God is *ungodly*. We suppose that we know what we are saying when we say "God." . . . We dare to deck ourselves out as His companions, patrons, advisers, and commissioners. We confound time with eternity. This is the *ungodliness* of our relation to God. And our relation to God is *unrighteous*. Secretly we are ourselves the masters in this relationship. . . . And so, when we set God upon the throne of the world, we mean by "God" ourselves. . . . Under the banners of humility and emotion we rise in rebellion against God. We confound time with eternity. That is our *unrighteousness*.—Such is our relation to God apart from and without Christ, on this side [of] resurrection, and before we are called to order. God Himself is not acknowledged as God and what is called "God" is in fact Man. By living to ourselves, we serve the "No-God." . . .

[On Rom. 1:21] . . . And so the light has become in us darkness, and the wrath of God is inevitable—"They became vain in their reasonings, and their senseless heart was darkened" [Rom. 1:21]. The barrier is now indeed a barrier, and the "No" of God is now indeed negation. . . . Unbroken thought thereby divests itself of any true relation to the concrete world, and, contrariwise, the unbroken heart, that is to say, that sensitiveness to things which is guarded by no final insight, divests itself of the control of thought. Dark, blind, uncritical, capricious, mankind becomes a thing in itself. Heartless, perceiving without observing and therefore empty, is our thought: thoughtless, observing without perceiving and therefore blind, is our heart. Fugitive is the soul in this world and soulless is the world, when men do not find themselves within the sphere of the knowledge of the unknown God, when they avoid the true God in whom they and the world must lose themselves in order that both may find themselves again.

This is the Cause of the Night in which we are wandering: this also is the Cause of the Wrath of God which has been manifested over our heads.

[On Rom. 1:22] "Professing themselves to be wise, they became fools."

The picture of a world without paradox and without eternity, of knowing without the background of not-knowing, of a religion without the unknown God, of a view of life without the memory of the "No" by which we are encountered, has much to be said in its favour. It evokes confidence, for it is simple and straightforward and uncramped; it provides considerable security and has few ragged edges; it corresponds, generally speaking, with what is required by the practical experiences of life; its standards and general principles are conveniently vague and flexible; and it possesses, moreover, a liberal prospect of vast future possibilities. . . .[1] That God is not known as God is due not merely to some error of thought or to some gap in experience, but to a fundamentally wrong attitude to life. . . . The more the unbroken man marches along his road secure of himself, the more surely does he make a fool of himself, the more certainly do that morality and that manner of life which are built up upon a forgetting of the abyss, upon a forgetting of men's true home, turn out to be a lie. It is indeed not difficult to show that this is so. . . .

[On Rom. 9:20] "Nay but, O man, who art thou that repliest against God?" All that must be said about the objection is comprehended in the words—*O man*. The objector overlooks the infinite qualitative distinction between God and man. He proceeds as though God and man were two things. He speaks of men as though they were God's partners, junior partners

1. Barth is here describing the apparent advantages of liberal Protestant theology, to which he was formerly attracted.

perhaps, but nevertheless competent to conduct an argument with Him. . . . It is precisely the man who respects God as God who will have no occasion to object, for he will neither fear nor desire the dissolution of his responsibility: such a man will become NOT insane, NOT immoral, NOT a criminal, NOT a suicide. . . . If, on the other hand, the tribulation be accepted, men will discover that their relative sense of responsibility is thereby guaranteed—"These things have not been said in order that we might by our lethargy checkmate the Holy Spirit, who hath given us a spark of His brightness, but in order that we might perceive that what we have comes from Him, and in order that we may learn to hope in Him, to surrender ourselves to Him, and to pursue our salvation with fear and trembling" (Calvin). . . .

[On Rom. 9:32b, 33] "They stumbled at the stone of stumbling; even as it is written, Behold, I lay in Sion a stone of stumbling and a rock of offence: and *only* he that believeth on it shall not be put to shame."

This admirable Biblical citation is composed by bringing together Isa. viii. 14 and xxviii. 16. The stone of stumbling, the rock of offence, which is, however, at the same time the precious corner-stone laid in Sion, is—Jesus Christ. In Him God reveals Himself inexorably as the hidden God who can be apprehended only indirectly. In Him He conceals Himself utterly, in order that He may manifest Himself to faith only. . . .[2] He that is of the truth heareth His voice. And yet, who is *of the truth*? Who sees God as He is? Who does not advance a thousand excuses for keeping out of His way? We do not endure the truth. . . . When this offence and scandal is encountered, only the believer will not be put to shame. He that *follows after* (ix. 31) but does not believe will inevitably gather nothing but empty nuts; he will run like a man who charges up a blind alley. And so there breaks forth the KRISIS of knowledge and the catastrophe of religion. There is no avoiding the shame and nakedness which accompany an impracticable undertaking. The Church of Esau is, and remains, what it is. It must nail Christ, its only hope, to the Cross. . . . Were the Church to appear before men as a Church under judgement; did it know of no other justification save that which is in judgement; did it believe in the stone of stumbling and rock of offence, instead of being offended and scandalized at it; then, with all its failings and offences—and certainly one day purified of some of them—it would be the Church of God. The Church, however, which sings its triumphs and trims and popularizes and modernizes itself, in order to minister to and satisfy every need except the one!; the Church which, in spite of many exposures, is still satisfied with itself, and, like quicksilver, still seeks and finds its own level; such a Church can never succeed, be it never so zealous, never so active in ridding itself of its failings and blemishes. With or without offences, it can never be the Church of God, because it is ignorant of the meaning of repentance. . . .

[On Rom. 12:1] I beseech you—"by the mercies of God." We are not now starting a new book or even a new chapter of the same book. Paul is not here turning his attention to practical religion, as though it were a second thing side by side with the theory of religion.[3] On the contrary, the theory, with which we have hitherto been concerned, is the theory of the practice of religion. We have spoken of the *mercies of*

2. In this section, as in many others, Barth reflects the influence of Kierkegaard.

3. Romans 12 is normally seen by commentators as a new, practical section that follows doctrinal instruction. Barth challenges the dichotomy to which this point about literary structure often leads.

God, of grace and resurrection, of forgiveness and Spirit, of election and faith, of the varied refractions of the uncreated light. But the ethical problem has nowhere been left out of account. The questions "What shall we do?"—"How are we to live?" have nowhere been excluded. We have not been searching out hidden things for the mere joy of so doing. . . . We have found the world one great, unsolved enigma; an enigma to which Christ, the mercy of God, provides the answer. . . . Once again, then, we are confronted by the problem of the "This-sidedness" of the whole course of our concrete existence. Once again—and now quite unavoidably—our life and will and acts are brought in question. For the freedom of God, the "Other-sidedness" of His mercies, means that there is a relationship between God and man, that there is a dissolution of human "This-sidedness," and that a radical assault is made upon every contrasted, second, other, thing. . . . This means that very great reserve is necessary when judgements concerning human capacity of will and action, whether they be positive or negative, have to be made—not for fear lest the criticism should be too sweeping, but lest it should not be sweeping enough. . . . The decisive word about ethics must disclose their full ambiguity, an ambiguity covering every aspect of human behaviour. The decisive word must be the word which cuts down to the roots. . . . EXHORTATION lets what is be as it is, because of what it is not. Grace means not judging, because the judgement has already taken place. Grace means the recognition that a bad conscience must be assumed in the daily routine of an evil world. . . .

[On Rom. 13:5] "Wherefore ye must needs be in subjection, not only because of the wrath, but also for conscience sake." To experience the wrath of God as wrath only would be eternal death. It is, however, our *conscience* that understands the "Halt"! of the drawn sword, and recognizes God in His wrath. Our *conscience* prevents us from supposing that the evil we encounter is merely obstruction and fate. It reminds us that we are evil; but it also recognizes in the sword that is drawn upon us the righteousness of the hand of God. Conscience sees in the evil that is done against us the *minister* of good. It interprets our judgement, not to our advantage, but to our salvation. It makes of the injury done to us, not our justification, but our hope. Conscience, therefore, does not allow us to rise up from the severity of our lives—embittered and ready to revolt; rather, it pronounces the end of the grim cycle of evil unto evil. Conscience leads us out of the turmoil of human suffering back to our Primal Origin, back to God—*Wherefore ye must needs be in subjection.* Revolution provides the great opportunity of willing to do what God does. And yet, such an intention is impossible; for we have to understand that our "new" is not THE "new." We have therefore to return to the source of our rebellion, to the apprehension of the evil in the existing order before there had issued from it revolutionary thought and action, before ever revolution was born. Our terror then was a guiltless terror, for we were then terrified with God at the misery of the creature. Then we knew also—and this knowledge was our deepest, most assured knowledge—the hope of the creation. Then was the "Moment" when our most simple perception of the relation between God and man was identical with the doing *that which is good.* But this pure "Moment" was no moment in time; and therefore being *in subjection* is also no temporal human action. And yet, to know that we have no Right, even when we are in the right, is a knowledge in time. It is this knowledge which reveals that we have a hope—the hope of the

Coming World where Revolution and Order are one. . . .

[*Epistle to the Romans*, 6th ed. (Oxford: Oxford University Press, 1933), 44, 48–49, 355–56, 369–70, 426–28, 490–91]

Selection 99: Karl Barth, *Church Dogmatics* (1932–1967)

Barth's* Church Dogmatics *is the most comprehensive and influential systematic theology of the twentieth century. He intended five large volumes, but he died before completing the fourth. The four volumes were published in thirteen discrete "parts." He published the first part of volume 1 during his tenure at Bonn, and the remainder was written in Basel; the last fragment of volume 4 was published posthumously. In broad outline, volume 1 deals with the doctrine of the Word of God and divine revelation; volume 2, the doctrine of God as Trinity; volume 3, the doctrine of creation as the work of God the Father; and volume 4, the doctrine of reconciliation as the work of God the Son, specifically treating in its four parts the doctrines of Christ, sin, salvation, and the church. The fifth volume on the doctrine of redemption as the work of God the Spirit was never begun.

This excerpt from volume 2, part 1, reflects on the knowledge about God and God's readiness to be known.

The Knowability of God

The possibility of the knowledge of God springs from God, in that He is Himself the truth and He gives Himself to man in His Word by the Holy Spirit to be known as the truth. It springs from man, in that, in the Son of God by the Holy Spirit, he becomes an object of the divine good-pleasure and therefore participates in the truth of God.

1. The Readiness of God

To ask about the "knowability" of God is to ask about the possibility on the basis of which God is known. It is to look back from the knowledge of God and to ask about the presuppositions and conditions on the basis of which it comes about that God is known. Only in this way, only with this backward look, is it possible to ask about the knowability of God in the Church's doctrine of God. We come to it from "the knowledge of God in its fulfilment." It is from there that we go on to ask about the knowability of God. The type of thinking which wants to begin with the question of the knowability of God and then to pass on from that point to the question of the fulfilment of the knowledge of God is not grateful but grasping, not obedient but self-autonomous. It is not theological thinking. It does not arise from the Church, or rather, from the Church's basis, and it does not serve the Church. What it affirms to be knowable and then to be actually known—whatever else it may be—is certainly not God the Father, the Son and the Holy Spirit whose revelation and work is attested by the Holy Scriptures and proclaimed by the Church. If this God is God—and there is no other God—there is no way from the question of the knowability of God to that of the actual knowledge of Him. There is only the descending way in the opposite direction. . . .

If this is to become quite clear, we must first go back to the decision which is prior to all our questions about the knowledge and knowability of God (and is therefore their origin and at the same time their answer). This decision was made from eternity and in eternity by the fact that God is who He is. . . . In this way and for this reason the power of what He is among us and for us is distinguished from all other powers by the fact that it is the divine power. . . . How can there be opposition, how can there be doubt and difficulty, when we have to do with the actualisation of an eternal possibility, God's own possibility? . . . If there is any encroachment here, it is the encroachment which God Himself has made in His revelation in Jesus Christ by the Holy Spirit. Of course, we accept the fact of this encroachment. We think of it when we look back to the fulfilment of the knowledge of God. There is real knowledge of God in the power of His self-demonstration. But this self-demonstration is His revelation as the triune God. We know God in consequence of God knowing Himself—the Father knowing the Son and the Son the Father by the Holy Spirit of the Father and the Son. Because He is first and foremost knowable to Himself as the triune God, He is knowable to us as well. We cannot speak of the knowability of God as an abstract possibility. For it is concretely realised by God Himself, in the Father and in the Son by the Holy Spirit. And by God's revelation we, too, receive and have a part both in His self-knowledge and also in His self-knowability. Though mediated and not immediate, it is nevertheless a real part. . . .[4]

One would think there was nothing simpler and more obvious than this. God—the God in whom we believe as the Head and Shepherd of the Church—is the Lord, the Creator, the Reconciler and Redeemer. Therefore we can find His knowability only in the readiness of God Himself, which is to be understood as His free good-pleasure. . . . Therefore, we can only give thanks for His knowability. Therefore, we can find it, not in a place where to some degree we already have and take it for ourselves, not in an already existent analogy, but only in an analogy to be created by God's grace, the analogy of grace and faith to which we say Yes as to the inaccessible which is made accessible to us in incomprehensible reality.[5] One would think that nothing could be simpler or more obvious than the insight that a theology which makes a great show of guaranteeing the knowability of God apart from grace and therefore from faith, or which thinks and promises that it is able to give such a guarantee—in other words, a "natural" theology—is quite impossible within the Church, and indeed, in such a way that it cannot even be discussed in principle. . . .

Why is it, then, that our statement on the knowability of God is not so simple and self-evident that the question of a basis of our knowledge of God in ourselves and our relationship to the world cannot be settled once and for all, but seems as though it must continually arise again in different forms and phases?

1. It may perhaps be pointed out that the establishment of our knowledge of God in this way is in fact possible and practicable, and that it vouches for its own legitimacy and necessity by its actual fulfilment. But what does it mean to be possible and practicable? And what does it mean that it vouches for itself? We have to do here with the attempt of man to answer the riddle of his own existence and of that of the world, and in that way to master himself and the world; with his attempt to strike a balance between himself and the world; even with his attempt to put these questions in the belief that he can regard the supposed goal of his answers or even the supposed origin of his questions as a first and final thing and therefore as God. This attempt is, of course, possible and practicable. This attempt does really exist, of course, in an

4. Human knowledge of God begins not with humanity, but with God's self-knowledge and his willingness to be known.

5. For Barth, there is no analogy by which humans can get to God, but only an analogy made possible by God's grace. Barth's critique of the *analogia entis* (analogy of being) is unusual in the history of Christian theology.

infinite variety of forms. . . . Does this attempt succeed? Certainly it succeeds. How can it fail to succeed, although not always so obviously and happily? With all the failures, the history of mankind and the history of the individual will always be in part and even in very large part a history of the success of this attempt. Our whole existence bears witness to the fact that we can know "God." But for what does this witness vouch? For the knowability of God? In other words, is that which we can know (as, of course our whole existence bears witness) really God? that final goal of our answers, that origin of our questions? Do we really know a first and last thing which can even be measured or compared with what Holy Scripture calls "God," let alone identified with Him in such a way that, from the starting-point of Holy Scripture and hence of the basis and essence of the Church, we can and must say that God is known here and therefore that God is knowable? What is "God" to the natural man, and what he also certainly calls his "God," is a false god. This false god is known by him and is therefore knowable to him. But as a false god it will not lead him in any sense to a knowledge of the real God. It will not in any way prepare him for it. On the contrary, it will keep him from it. Its knowledge and knowability will make him an enemy of the real God. Therefore, there can be no question of either a knowledge or a knowability of God. It is simply that the contradiction is ignored which Holy Scripture sets up against the identification of God with idols. Holy Scripture and therefore the basis and essence of the Church are abandoned. A general—and from the scriptural standpoint limited—concept of "God" is arbitrarily adopted as a criterion, and—measuring by this criterion—there is ascribed to the natural man, or to the witness of his life's endeavour, a competence and trustworthiness which Holy Scripture at any rate does not ascribe to him. . . .

Now all this is in its own way very important and interesting. But it all boils down to the question whether in this sphere there exists as a possibility somehow attainable within the life-endeavour of natural man the knowability of a god whose disclosure will bear the character of an outstanding decision, of a decision which is previous to the decision of faith or unbelief, and for the sake of which theology must betake itself to this preliminary field of operation with at least a preliminary seriousness simply because this god is identical with the real God whom the Christian Church must proclaim, so that the establishing of his knowability in the natural sphere, in the sphere of the human life-endeavour, will in fact mean a preparation for the establishing of His knowability in His revelation. If this question has to be affirmed, the pedagogic necessity of a "natural" theology as a prelude to real theology will obviously force itself upon us. Man will have to be incited and instructed to make the right use of this position of his, i.e., to make a general survey of his different possibilities and perhaps their gradation, in order finally to discover the possibility from which he can be told that it is not only his, but that as his it is the divine possibility attested in God's revelation. . . .

In the light of the recognised main line of the biblical statements, and of the biblical witness to revelation as such, how is it possible for man in the cosmos, and his witness, to arrive at this dependent position?[6] On this main line the whole relationship of God and man is effected on the presupposition that God is holy but man a sinner fallen from Him and therefore lost;

6. Barth is here wrestling with why "natural theology" is so strong in the Christian tradition and, specifically, why it seems to appear in Scripture. He thus distinguishes between a "main line" and a "side line."

that God is eternally living in Himself, but man lies in death; that God is in light unapproachable,[7] but man in darkness. According to the statements which follow on the main biblical line, what takes place between God and man takes place in the free election, calling and illumination, in the undeserved justification and sanctification of man by God! What unites man with God on this main line is, from God's side, His grace, in which, before all, there is disclosed to man the judgment under which he stands—and from man's side, the faith in which he bows beneath this judgment, and in so doing grasps the grace of God. If we look at the matter from the point of view of this main line, how can there possibly be this side line on which man in the cosmos can have another relationship with God, i.e., a relationship not founded by God's election and therefore not determined by the grace of God in judgment? From this point of view, how can he be in a position where we can appeal to him as an independent witness—independent of the order of revelation? . . .

Revelation is indeed the truth: the truth of God, but necessarily, therefore, the truth of man in the cosmos as well. The biblical witnesses cannot bear witness to the one without also bearing witness to the other, which is included in it. How can they proclaim the revelation of God as what it is, namely as God's seizure of power in relation to man, if at the same time they do not first bear witness to God as the One to whose power man is already subjected as it is proclaimed to him; if they do not testify to man that he is not concerned with a foreign Lord but with his own, not with a man but with his eternal Lord, i.e., his Lord who holds and rules his whole time in and with His hands. As they proclaim God's revelation to man they must claim man himself as the man already objectively changed by the event of revelation. It is because this last takes place that the side line of the Bible arises. Hence our answer to this question is: The biblical witnesses point also to man in the cosmos in order to interpret the revelation of God in its necessary and compulsive direction and relation to the one to whom it is addressed; in order to characterise his existence and all that it involves, including the whole place in which he exists, as one which cannot legitimately be withdrawn from the claim of revelation, because the most real and original right under which it stands is the right which the God has over it who claims it in His revelation, and because this very fact that God is its Lord, that it belongs to God and lives in His service, is its truth and its unveiled reality. Because this fact, too, must always be attested, this side line of the Bible exists. Our contention is that it is not drawn from any other point than revelation itself. And how can it be drawn to any other place than back to this main line? Everything that can be said on this line means the objective otherness of man in the cosmos, which becomes audible as the echo of the Word of God, and visible as the reflection of His light. In Holy Scripture man in the cosmos is addressed upon this echo and reflection, and starting from revelation he is referred back all the more surely to revelation itself. . . .

2. The Readiness of Man

. . . The very existence of man considered in its reality, i.e., its reality as disclosed by the grace of God, shows us man in himself and as such not at peace but at war with grace. If it is otherwise, we are definitely not thinking only of this reality, of this reality in itself and as such. . . . Man can bear this, and what is more, he does bear it. Through it all, he can uphold and assert himself. . . . He endures this reality far rather and far more easily than the grace of

7. See 1 Tim. 6:16.

God by which he might be expected finally to let himself be carried instead of trying to bear his own life. The reality is that man does not want to be carried. But this picture is not altered when we consider him in the light of the Word of God. On the contrary, in the light of the Word of God it simply emerges in all its clarity and necessity. . . . So far as all this is still no more than his own reality, the light of divine truth in the prism of his own existence, what this reality has to show us will, as far as the eye can reach, be, not his peace with grace, but his war against it, and therefore his wretchedness. He will believe in grace; he will affirm that he feels it and rejoices over it; he will perhaps appraise it, perhaps teach it, perhaps defend it; and he will do all this in sincerity. But through it all, he will not live by grace; perhaps by his faith, perhaps by his zeal for grace, or his knowledge of grace and his willingness for it; but not by grace itself—only against it. He will know how to uphold and affirm himself even on this side. He will rebel against any questioning of the richness which he thinks he can secure in this way. . . .

This openness is, therefore, lacking. Considered even in its reality, all the supposed need and knowledge and willingness in which this openness must consist is obviously the very opposite of this openness. It follows, then, that even when we put the question in this deeper form we have still not caught a glimpse of the readiness of man which we can equate with his readiness for God's grace, and in which we can also rediscover the knowability of God for man which follows and is enclosed in God's readiness. We are indeed pressed forward from a possibility to a reality: to the last reality attainable by us, even to the deepest human reality; for is there deeper human reality than that of the man addressed by God's Word and therefore awakened to his real existence? But even our deepest reality is still separated by an abyss from our openness for God's grace and therefore from the knowability of God for us. . . .

For this reason, when and because we are concerned with Jesus Christ, we stand in the mystery and at the same time in the revelation of God, in His own innermost reality. God is knowable to Himself; the Son to the Father, but also the Father to the Son. This is the first and last thing which is to be said about the knowability of God even from the point of view of the readiness of man. Of course, at this point man still seems to stand outside. Everything still seems to be invalid for him. For we are not God. Indeed we are not. But God is man. For Jesus Christ, the Lord attested in the Old and New Testaments, is as little God in Himself and as such as He is man in himself and as such. He is God who is man. This is Jesus Christ. In Him we do not stand outside but inside; we participate in this first and last. In Him the fact that God is knowable is true not only for God Himself, not only between the Father and Son, but for man, for us. For in Him man is ready for God. But what does this mean? . . . It means that the only begotten Son of God and therefore God Himself, who is knowable to Himself from eternity to eternity, has come in our flesh, has taken our flesh, has become the bearer of our flesh, and does not exist as God's Son from eternity to eternity except in our flesh.[8] Our flesh is therefore present when He knows God as the Son the Father, when God knows Himself. In our flesh God knows Himself. Therefore in Him it is a fact that our flesh knows God Himself. . . .

[*Church Dogmatics* II/1 (Edinburgh: T & T Clark, 1957), 63, 67–68, 85–86, 89–90, 103, 110–11, 133–34, 151]

8. Barth seems to imply that the Son is incarnate, or always considered as such, even in eternity past.

Selection 100: Reinhold Niebuhr, *Moral Man and Immoral Society* (1932)

Reinhold Niebuhr (1892–1971), like the neo-orthodox, rejected the optimistic view of human potential advanced by Protestant liberalism. In this book,* Moral Man and Immoral Society, *he argued that societal evil is greater than the sum of its individual evil persons. He later admitted that a more fitting title would have been "immoral man and even more immoral society."

Introduction

The thesis to be elaborated in these pages is that a sharp distinction must be drawn between the moral and social behavior of individuals and of social groups, national, racial, and economic; and that this distinction justifies and necessitates political policies which a purely individualistic ethic must always find embarrassing. The title "Moral Man and Immoral Society" suggests the intended distinction too unqualifiedly, but it is nevertheless a fair indication of the argument to which the following pages are devoted. Individual men may be moral in the sense that they are able to consider interests other than their own in determining problems of conduct, and are capable, on occasion, of preferring the advantages of others to their own. They are endowed by nature with a measure of sympathy and consideration for their kind, the breadth of which may be extended by an astute social pedagogy. Their rational faculty prompts them to a sense of justice which educational discipline may refine and purge of egoistic elements until they are able to view a social situation, in which their own interests are involved, with a fair measure of objectivity. But all these achievements are more difficult, if not impossible, for human societies and social groups. In every human group there is less reason to guide and to check impulse, less capacity for self-transcendence, less ability to comprehend the needs of others and therefore more unrestrained egoism than the individuals, who compose the group, reveal in their personal relationships. . . .

Chapter One
Man and Society: The Art of Living Together

Though human society has roots which lie deeper in history than the beginning of human life, men have made comparatively but little progress in solving the problem of their aggregate existence. Each century originates a new complexity and each new generation faces a new vexation in it. For all the centuries of experience, men have not yet learned how to live together without compounding their vices and covering each other "with mud and with blood." The society in which each man lives is at once the basis for, and the nemesis of, that fulness of life which each man seeks. However much human ingenuity may increase the treasures which nature provides for the satisfaction of human needs, they can never be sufficient to satisfy all human wants; for man, unlike other creatures, is gifted and cursed with an imagination which extends his appetites beyond the requirements of subsistence. Human society will never escape the problem of the equitable distribution of the physical and cultural goods which provide for the preservation and fulfillment of human life.

Unfortunately the conquest of nature, and the consequent increase in nature's beneficences to man, have not eased, but rather accentuated, the problem of justice. The same technology, which drew the fangs of nature's enmity of man, also created a society in which the intensity and extent of social cohesion has been greatly increased, and in which power is so unevenly distributed, that justice has become a more difficult achievement. Perhaps it is man's sorry fate, suffering from ills which have their source in the inadequacies of both nature and human society, that the tools by which he eliminates the former should become the means of increasing the latter. That, at least, has been his fate up to the present hour; and it may be that there will be no salvation for the human spirit from the more and more painful burdens of social injustice until the ominous tendency in human history has resulted in perfect tragedy.

Human nature is not wanting in certain endowments for the solution of the problem of human society. Man is endowed by nature with organic relations to his fellow-men; and natural impulse prompts him to consider the needs of others even when they compete with his own. With the higher mammals man shares concern for his offspring; and the long infancy of the child created the basis for an organic social group in the earliest period of human history. Gradually intelligence, imagination, and the necessities of social conflict increased the size of this group. Natural impulse was refined and extended until a less obvious type of consanguinity than an immediate family relationship could be made the basis of social solidarity. Since those early days the units of human cooperation have constantly grown in size, and the areas of significant relationships between the units have likewise increased. Nevertheless conflict between the national units remains as a permanent rather than a passing characteristic of their relations to each other; and each national unit finds it increasingly difficult to maintain either peace or justice within its common life.

While it is possible for intelligence to increase the range of benevolent impulse, and thus prompt a human being to consider the needs and rights of other than those to whom he is bound by organic and physical relationship, there are definite limits in the capacity of ordinary mortals which makes it impossible for them to grant to others what they claim for themselves. Though educators ever since the eighteenth century have given themselves to the fond illusion that justice through voluntary co-operation waited only upon a more universal or a more adequate educational enterprise, there is good reason to believe that the sentiments of benevolence and social goodwill will never be so pure or powerful, and the rational capacity to consider the rights and needs of others in fair competition with our own will never be so fully developed as to create the possibility for the anarchistic millennium which is the social utopia, either explicit or implicit, of all intellectual or religious moralists.

All social cooperation on a larger scale than the most intimate social group requires a measure of coercion. While no state can maintain its unity purely by coercion neither can it preserve itself without coercion. Where the factor of mutual consent is strongly developed, and where standardised and approximately fair methods of adjudicating and resolving conflicting interests within an organised group have been established, the coercive factor in social life is frequently covert, and becomes apparent only in moments of crisis and in the group's policy toward recalcitrant individuals. Yet it is never absent. . . .

Chapter Four
The Morality of Nations

The difference between the attitudes of individuals and those of groups has been frequently alluded to, the thesis being that group relations can never be as ethical as those which characterise individual relations. In dealing with the problem of social justice, it may be found that the relation of economic classes within a state is more important than international relations. But from the standpoint of analysing the ethics of group behavior, it is feasible to study the ethical attitudes of nations first; because the modern nation is the human group of strongest social cohesion, of most undisputed central authority and of most clearly defined membership. The church may have challenged its preeminence in the Middle Ages, and the economic class may compete with it for the loyalty of men in our own day; yet it remains, as it has been since the seventeenth century, the most absolute of all human associations. . . .

The social ignorance of the private citizen of the nation has thus far been assumed. It may be reasonable to hope that the general level of intelligence will greatly increase in the next decades and centuries and that growing social intelligence will modify national attitudes. It is doubtful whether it will ever increase sufficiently to eliminate all the moral hazards of international relations. There is an ethical paradox in patriotism which defies every but the most astute and sophisticated analysis. The paradox is that patriotism transmutes individual unselfishness into national egoism. Loyalty to the nation is a high form of altruism when compared with lesser loyalties and more parochial interests. It therefore becomes the vehicle of all the altruistic impulses and expresses itself, on occasion, with such fervor that the critical attitude of the individual toward the nation and its enterprises is almost completely destroyed. The unqualified character of this devotion is the very basis of the nation's power and of the freedom to use the power without moral restraint. Thus the unselfishness of individuals makes for the selfishness of nations. That is why the hope of solving the larger social problems of mankind, merely by extending the social sympathies of individuals, is so vain. Altruistic passion is sluiced into the reservoirs of nationalism with great ease, and is made to flow beyond them with great difficulty. What lies beyond the nation, the community of mankind is too vague to inspire devotion. The lesser communities within the nation, religious, economic, racial and cultural, have equal difficulty in competing with the nation for the loyalty of its citizens. The church was able to do so when it had the prestige of a universality it no longer possesses. Future developments may make the class rather than the nation the community of primary loyalty. But for the present the nation is still supreme. It not only possesses a police power, which other communities lack, but it is able to avail itself of the most potent and vivid symbols to impress its claims upon the consciousness of the individual. Since it is impossible to become conscious of a large social group without adequate symbolism this factor is extremely important. The nation possesses in its organs of government, in the panoply and ritual of the state, in the impressive display of its fighting services, and, very frequently, in the splendors of a royal house, the symbols of unity and greatness, which inspire awe and reverence in the citizen. Furthermore the love and pious attachment of a man to his countryside, to familiar scenes, sights, and experiences, around which the memories of youth have cast a halo of sanctity, all this flows into the sentiment of patriotism; for a simple imagination transmutes the universal beneficences of nature into symbols of the peculiar blessings which a benevolent nation bestows upon its citizens. Thus the sentiment of patriotism achieves a potency in the modern soul, so unqualified, that the nation is given *carte blanche* to use the power, compounded of the devotion of individuals, for any purpose it desires. Thus, to choose an example among hundreds, Mr. Lloyd George during the famous Agadir Crisis in 1911 in which a European war became imminent,[9]

9. David Lloyd George (1863–1945) was a British politician and later prime minister (1916–1922). The Agadir Crisis in Morocco heightened tensions between

because marauding nations would not allow a new robber to touch their spoils in Africa, could declare in his Mansion House speech: "If a situation were to be forced upon us in which peace could only be preserved by the surrender of the great and beneficent position Britain has won by centuries of heroism and achievement, by allowing Britain to be treated, when her interests were vitally affected, as if she were of no account in the cabinet of nations, then I say emphatically that peace at that price would be a humiliation intolerable for a great country like ours to endure." The very sensitive "honor" of nations can always be appeased by the blood of its citizens and no national ambition seems too base or petty to claim and to receive the support of a majority of its patriots. . . .

Perhaps the most significant moral characteristic of a nation is its hypocrisy. We have noted that self-deception and hypocrisy is an unvarying element in the moral life of all human beings. It is the tribute which morality pays to immorality; or rather the device by which the lesser self gains the consent of the larger self to indulge in impulses and ventures which the rational self can approve only when they are disguised. One can never be quite certain whether the disguise is meant only for the eye of the external observer or whether, as may be usually the case, it deceives the self. Naturally this defect in individuals becomes more apparent in the less moral life of nations. Yet it might be supposed that nations, of whom so much less is expected, would not be under the necessity of making moral pretensions for their actions. There was probably a time when they were under no such necessity. Their hypocrisy is both a tribute to the growing rationality of man and a proof of the ease with which rational demands may be circumvented.

Germany and France, which also promised to involve Great Britain.

The dishonesty of nations is a necessity of political policy if the nation is to gain the full benefit of its double claim upon the loyalty and devotion of the individual, as his own special and unique community and as a community which embodies universal values and ideals. The two claims, the one touching the individual's emotions and the other appealing to his mind, are incompatible with each other, and can be resolved only through dishonesty. This is particularly evident in war-time. Nations do not really arrive at full self-consciousness until they stand in vivid, usually bellicose, juxtaposition to other nations. The social reality, comprehended in the existence of a nation, is too large to make a vivid impression upon the imagination of the citizen. He vaguely identifies it with his own little community and fireside and usually accepts the mythos which attributes personality to his national group. But the impression is not so vivid as to arouse him to any particular fervor of devotion. This fervor is the unique product of the times of crisis, when his nation is in conflict with other nations. It springs from the new vividness with which the reality and the unity of his nation's discreet existence is comprehended. In other words, it is just in the moments when the nation is engaged in aggression or defense (and it is always able to interpret the former in terms of the latter) that the reality of the nation's existence becomes so sharply outlined as to arouse the citizen to the most passionate and uncritical devotion toward it. But at such a time the nation's claim to uniqueness also comes in sharpest conflict with the generally accepted impression that the nation is the incarnation of universal values. This conflict can be resolved only by deception. In the imagination of the simple patriot the nation is not a society but Society. Though its values are relative they appear, from his naive perspective, to be absolute. The religious instinct for the absolute is no less potent in patriotic religion than in any other. The nation is always endowed with an aura of the sacred, which is one reason why religions, which claim universality, are so easily captured and tamed by national sentiment, religion and patriotism merging in the process. The spirit of the nationally established churches and the cult of "Christentum und Deutschtum"[10] of pre-war Germany are interesting examples. The best means of harmonising the claim to universality with the unique and relative life of the nation, as revealed in moments of crisis, is to claim general and universally valid objectives for the nation. It is alleged to be fighting for civilisation and for culture; and the whole enterprise of humanity is supposedly involved in its struggles. In the life of the simple citizen this hypocrisy exists as a naïve and unstudied self-deception. The politician practices it consciously (though he may become the victim of his own arts), in order to secure the highest devotion from the citizen for his enterprises. The men of culture give themselves to it with less conscious design than the statesmen because their own inner necessities demand the deceptions, even more than do those of the simple citizens. The religious or the rational culture to which they are devoted helps them to realise that moral values must be universal, if they are to be real; and they cannot therefore give themselves to national aspirations, unless they clothe them in the attributes of universality. A few of them recognise the impossibility of such a procedure. Among most, the force of reason operates only to give the hysterias of war and the imbecilities of national politics more plausible excuses than an average man is capable of inventing. So they become the worst liars of war-time. "England," declared Professor Adolf Harnack, most eminent of German war-period theologians, "cuts the dyke which has preserved western Europe and its civilisation from the encroaching desert of Russia and Pan-Slavism. We must hold out for we must defend the work of fifteen hundred years for Europe and for England itself." The great philosopher Rudolf Eucken was even more unequivocal in identifying his nation's cause with ultimate values. "In this sense," he said, "we have a right to say that we form the soul of humanity and that the destruction of German nature would rob world history of its deepest meaning." M. Paul Sabatier could declare, "No doubt we are fighting for ourselves but we are fighting, too, for all peoples. The France of today is fighting religiously. . . . We all feel that our sorrows continue and fulfill those of the innocent victim of Calvary."[11] The literature of the war period teems with similar examples of the self-deception of intellectuals. There is always the possibility that some of it was prompted by dishonest truckling to the hysteria of the populace and the pressure of governments. But most of it was not as dishonest as that. . . .

[*Moral Man and Immoral Society: A Study in Ethics and Politics* (New York: Simon and Schuster, 1960), xi–xii, 1–4, 83, 90–93, 95–98]

Selection 101: Dietrich Bonhoeffer, *Ethics* (1949)

Dietrich Bonhoeffer (1906–1945) was a German theologian and a leading figure of the Confessing Church, which was formed in opposition to the state church's support of Adolf Hitler's National Socialist Third Reich. For his resistance and association with a plot to assassinate Hitler in 1943, Bonhoeffer was imprisoned at Tegel and

10. That is, "Christendom and Germanness."

11. Niebuhr cites these three examples from Kirby Page, *National Defense.*

later hanged in the concentration camp at Flossenbürg on April 9, 1945, just before the camp's liberation by Allied troops.

Ethics, *Bonhoeffer's magnum opus, is an unfinished collection of essays written between 1940 and 1943 and published posthumously in 1949. This excerpt is from the essay entitled, "Christ, Reality, and Good: Christ, Church, and World."*

Those who wish even to focus on the problem of a Christian ethic are faced with an outrageous demand—from the outset they must give up, as inappropriate to this topic, the very two questions that led them to deal with the ethical problem: "How can I be good?" and "How can I do something good?" Instead they must ask the wholly other, completely different question: what is the will of God? This demand is radical precisely because it presupposes a decision about ultimate reality, that is, a decision of faith. . . .

The source of a Christian ethic is not the reality of one's own self, not the reality of the world, nor is it the reality of norms and values. It is the reality of God that is revealed in Jesus Christ. This is the demand, before all others, that must honestly be made of anyone who wishes to be concerned with the problem of a Christian ethic. It places us before the ultimate and decisive question: With what reality will we reckon in our life? With the reality of God's revelatory word or with the so-called realities of life? With divine grace or with earthly inadequacies? With the resurrection or with death? . . .

The *subject matter of a Christian ethic is God's reality revealed in Christ becoming real {Wirklichwerden} among God's creatures,* just as the subject matter of doctrinal theology is the truth of God's reality revealed in Christ. The place that in all other ethics is marked by the antithesis between ought and is, idea and realization, motive and work, is occupied in Christian ethics by the relation between reality and becoming real, between past and present, between history and event (faith) or, to replace the many concepts with the simple name of the thing itself, the relation between Jesus Christ and the Holy Spirit. The question of the good becomes the question of participating in God's reality revealed in Christ. . . .

The same is true of the distinction that the American philosopher of religion Reinhold Niebuhr has made with the concepts moral man and immoral society.[12] The split between individual and society that is expressed here is just as abstract as that between person and work. What is inseparable is here torn apart, and each part, which by itself is dead, is examined separately. The result is the complete ethical aporia that goes by the name "social ethics." Of course, if good is seen as an existing entity's conformity to what ought to be, then the more massive resistance that society sets against what ought to be must lead to an ethical preference for the individual over society. (And conversely, precisely this result should warn us to detect in this concept of the ethical its sociological origin in the age of individualism.) The question of good must not be narrowed to investigating the relation of actions to their motives, or to their consequences, measuring them by a ready-made ethical standard. An ethic of disposition or intention is just as superficial as an ethic of consequences. For what right do we have to stay with inner motivation as the ultimate phenomenon of ethics, ignoring that "good" intentions can grow out of very dark backgrounds in human consciousness and subconsciousness, and that often the worst things happen as a result of "good intentions"? As the question of the motives of action finally disappears in the tangled web of the past, so the question of its

12. See Selection 100.

consequences gets lost in the mists of the future. There are no clear boundaries on either side. Nothing justifies us in stopping at any arbitrary point we choose in order to make a definitive judgment. In practice, we ever and again stop to make such an arbitrary determination, whether along the lines of an ethic of motives [Motivethik] or an ethic of consequences [Erfolgsethik]. Whatever we do will depend on the different needs of the changing times. Neither has any fundamental advantage over the other, because in both cases the question of good is posed abstractly, severed from reality. Good is not the agreement of some way of existence that I describe as reality with some standard placed at our disposal by nature or grace. Rather, good is reality, reality itself seen and recognized in God. Human beings, with their motives and their works, with their fellow humans, with the creation that surrounds them, in other words, reality as a whole held in the hands of God—that is what is embraced by the question of good. The divine "behold, it was very good"[13] meant the whole of creation. The good desires the whole, not only of motives but also of works; it desires whole persons along with the human companions with whom they are given to live. What could it mean anyway that only a part be named good, motives for instance, while works are bad, or vice versa? *Human beings are indivisible wholes, not only as individuals in both their person and work,* but *also as members of the human and created community* to which they belong. It is this indivisible whole, that is, this reality grounded and recognized in God, that the question of good has in view. "Creation" is the name of this indivisible whole according to its origin. According to its goal it is called the kingdom of God. Both are equally far from us and yet near to us, because God's creation and God's kingdom are present in us only in God's self-revelation in Jesus Christ.

To participate in the indivisible whole of God's reality is the meaning of the Christian question about the good. To avoid misunderstanding, we need at this point a further clarification of what is meant here by reality.

There is a way of grounding ethics in a concept of reality that is completely different from the Christian way, namely, the positivist-empiricist approach. It attempts to remove the concept of norms from ethics completely, and sees in them only the idealizing of actual ways of behavior that are useful in life; good is seen as basically nothing but that which serves reality usefully and purposefully. . . .

Christian ethics speaks otherwise of the reality that is the origin of the good. It means thereby the reality of God as the ultimate realm beyond and in all that exists. It means also the reality of the existing world that is real only through the reality of God. The reality of God is not just another idea. Christian faith perceives this in the fact that the reality of God has revealed itself and witnessed to itself in the middle of the real world. *In Jesus Christ the reality of God has entered into the reality of this world.* The place where the questions about the reality of God and about the reality of the world are answered at the same time is characterized solely by the name: Jesus Christ. God and the world are enclosed in this name. In Christ all things exist (Col. 1:17). From now on we cannot speak rightly of either God or the world without speaking of Jesus Christ. . . .

In Christ we are invited to participate in the reality of God and the reality of the world at the same time, the one not without the other. The reality of God is disclosed only as it places me completely into the reality of the world. But I find the reality of the world always already borne, accepted, and reconciled in the reality of

13. Gen. 1:31.

God. That is the mystery of the revelation of God in the human being Jesus Christ. The Christian ethic asks, then, how this reality of God and of the world that is given in Christ becomes real in our world. It is not as if "our world" were something outside this God-world reality that is in Christ, as if it did not already belong to the world borne, accepted, and reconciled in Christ; it is not, therefore, as if some "principle" must first be applied to our circumstances and our time. Rather, the question is how the reality in Christ—which has long embraced us and our world within itself—works here and now or, in other words, how life is to be lived in it. What matters is *participating in the reality of God and the world in Jesus Christ today*, and doing so in such a way that I never experience the reality of God without the reality of the world, nor the reality of the world without the reality of God.

As we travel further along this road, a large part of traditional Christian ethical thought stands like a Colossus obstructing our way. Since the beginnings of Christian ethics after New Testament times, the dominant basic conception, consciously or unconsciously determining all ethical thought, has been that two realms [Räume] bump against each other: one divine, holy, supernatural, and Christian; the other worldly, profane, natural, and unchristian. This view reached its first peak in the High Middle Ages, and its second in the pseudo-Reformation thought of the post-Reformation period. Reality as a whole splits into two parts, and the concern of ethics becomes the right relation of both parts to each other. In the high scholastic period the natural realm was subordinated to the realm of grace. In pseudo-Lutheranism the autonomy of the orders of this world is proclaimed against the law of Christ. . . .

This division of the whole of reality into sacred and profane, or Christian and worldly, sectors creates the possibility of existence in only one of these sectors: for instance, a spiritual existence that takes no part in worldly existence, and a worldly existence that can make good its claim to autonomy over against the sacred sector. The monk and the cultural Protestant[14] of the nineteenth century represent these two possibilities. . . .

As hard as it may now seem to break the spell of this conceptual framework of realms, it is just as certain that this perspective deeply contradicts both biblical and Reformation thought, therefore bypassing reality. There are not two realities, but *only one reality,* and that is God's reality revealed in Christ in the reality of the world. Partaking in Christ, we stand at the same time in the reality of God and in the reality of the world. The reality of Christ embraces the reality of the world in itself. The world has no reality of its own independent of God's revelation in Christ. It is a denial of God's revelation in Jesus Christ to wish to be "Christian" without being "worldly," or [to] wish to be worldly without seeing and recognizing the world in Christ. Hence there are not two realms, but only *the one realm of the Christ-reality [Christuswirklichkeit],* in which the reality of God and the reality of the world are united. . . .

When one therefore wants to speak of the space of the church, one must be aware that this space has already been broken through, abolished, and overcome in every moment by the witness of the church to Jesus Christ. Thus all false thinking in terms of realms is ruled out as endangering the understanding of the church. . . .

[*Ethics*, Bonhoeffer Works, vol. 6 (Minneapolis: Fortress Press, 2009), 47, 49–58, 64]

14. "Cultural Protestantism" refers to the liberal theology in the mode of Schleiermacher that sought cultural accommodation with modern post-Enlightenment society.

B. Roman Catholic, Eastern Orthodox, and Evangelical Approaches

Selection 102: G. K. Chesterton, *Orthodoxy* (1908)

Gilbert Keith Chesterton (1874–1936) was a British writer, journalist, and cultural critic, an adult convert from the Church of England to Roman Catholicism. He became a popular apologist celebrated for his down-to-earth style and wit. These excerpts from* Orthodoxy *come from the chapter entitled, "The Ethics of Elfland."

When the business man rebukes the idealism of his office-boy, it is commonly in some such speech as this: "Ah, yes, when one is young, one has these ideals in the abstract and these castles in the air; but in middle age they all break up like clouds, and one comes down to a belief in practical politics, to using the machinery one has and getting on with the world as it is." Thus, at least, venerable and philanthropic old men now in their honoured graves used to talk to me when I was a boy. But since then I have grown up and have discovered that these philanthropic old men were telling lies. What has really happened is exactly the opposite of what they said would happen. They said that I should lose my ideals and begin to believe in the methods of practical politicians. Now, I have not lost my ideals in the least; my faith in fundamentals is exactly what it always was. What I have lost is my old childlike faith in practical politics. I am still as much concerned as ever about the Battle of Armageddon;[15] but I am not so much concerned about the General Election. As a babe I leapt up on my mother's knee at the mere mention of it. No; the vision is always solid and reliable. The vision is always a fact. It is the reality that is often a fraud. As much as I ever did, more than I ever did, I believe in Liberalism. But there was a rosy time of innocence when I believed in Liberals. . . .

This is the first principle of democracy: that the essential things in men are the things they hold in common, not the things they hold separately. And the second principle is merely this: that the political instinct or desire is one of these things which they hold in common. Falling in love is more poetical than dropping into poetry. The democratic contention is that government (helping to rule the tribe) is a thing like falling in love, and not a thing like dropping into poetry. It is not something analogous to playing the church organ, painting on vellum, discovering the North Pole (that insidious habit), looping the loop, being Astronomer Royal, and so on. For these things we do not wish a man to do at all unless he does them well. It is, on the contrary, a thing analogous to writing one's own love-letters or blowing one's own nose. These things we want a man to do for himself, even if he does them badly. I am not here arguing the truth of any of these conceptions; I know that some moderns are asking to have their wives chosen by scientists, and they may soon be asking, for all I know, to have their noses blown by nurses. I merely say that mankind does recognize these universal human functions, and that democracy classes government among them. In short, the democratic faith is this: that the most terribly important things must be left to ordinary men themselves—the mating of the sexes, the rearing of the young, the laws of the state. This is democracy; and in this I have always believed.

But there is one thing that I have never from my youth up been able to understand. I have

15. See Rev. 16:16.

never been able to understand where people got the idea that democracy was in some way opposed to tradition. It is obvious that tradition is only democracy extended through time. It is trusting to a consensus of common human voices rather than to some isolated or arbitrary record. The man who quotes some German historian against the tradition of the Catholic Church, for instance, is strictly appealing to aristocracy. He is appealing to the superiority of one expert against the awful authority of a mob. It is quite easy to see why a legend is treated, and ought to be treated, more respectfully than a book of history. The legend is generally made by the majority of people in the village, who are sane. The book is generally written by the one man in the village who is mad. Those who urge against tradition that men in the past were ignorant may go and urge it at the Carlton Club,[16] along with the statement that voters in the slums are ignorant. It will not do for us. If we attach great importance to the opinion of ordinary men in great unanimity when we are dealing with daily matters, there is no reason why we should disregard it when we are dealing with history or fable. Tradition may be defined as an extension of the franchise. Tradition means giving votes to the most obscure of all classes, our ancestors. It is the democracy of the dead. Tradition refuses to submit to the small and arrogant oligarchy of those who merely happen to be walking about. All democrats object to men being disqualified by the accident of birth; tradition objects to their being disqualified by the accident of death. Democracy tells us not to neglect a good man's opinion, even if he is our groom; tradition asks us not to neglect a good man's opinion, even if he is our father. I, at any rate, cannot separate the two ideas of democracy and tradition; it seems evident to me that they are the same idea. We will have the dead at our councils. The ancient Greeks voted by stones; these shall vote by tombstones. . . .

My first and last philosophy, that which I believe in with unbroken certainty, I learnt in the nursery. I generally learnt it from a nurse; that is, from the solemn and star-appointed priestess at once of democracy and tradition. The things I believed most then, the things I believe most now, are the things called fairy tales. They seem to me to be the entirely reasonable things. They are not fantasies: compared with them other things are fantastic. . . .

There were, then, these two first feelings, indefensible and indisputable. The world was a shock, but it was not merely shocking; existence was a surprise, but it was a pleasant surprise. In fact, all my first views were exactly uttered in a riddle that stuck in my brain from boyhood. The question was, "What did the first frog say?" And the answer was, "Lord, how you made me jump!" That says succinctly all that I am saying. God made the frog jump; but the frog prefers jumping. But when these things are settled there enters the second great principle of the fairy philosophy.

Any one can see it who will simply read "Grimm's Fairy Tales" or the fine collections of Mr. Andrew Lang. For the pleasure of pedantry I will call it the Doctrine of Conditional Joy. Touchstone talked of much virtue in an "if";[17] according to elfin ethics all virtue is in an "if." The note of the fairy utterance always is, "You may live in a palace of gold and sapphire, *if* you do not say the word 'cow'"; or "You may live happily with the King's daughter, *if* you do not

16. The Carlton Club is an exclusive club in London for men, in which new members must be nominated and elected.

17. Jacob and Wilhelm Grimm are famous for their collections of tales. Andrew Lang published a series of "Fairy Books" from 1889 to 1910. Touchstone is a character in Shakespeare's *As You Like It*.

show her an onion." The vision always hangs upon a veto. All the dizzy and colossal things conceded depend upon one small thing withheld. All the wild and whirling things that are let loose depend upon one thing that is forbidden. . . .

Thus ends, in unavoidable inadequacy, the attempt to utter the unutterable things. These are my ultimate attitudes towards life; the soils for the seeds of doctrine. These in some dark way I thought before I could write, and felt before I could think: that we may proceed more easily afterwards, I will roughly recapitulate them now. I felt in my bones; first, that world does not explain itself. It may be miracle with a supernatural explanation; it may be a conjuring trick, with a natural explanation. But the explanation of the conjuring trick, if it is to satisfy me, will have to be better than the natural explanations I have heard. The thing is magic, true or false. Second, I came to feel as if magic must have a meaning, and meaning must have some one to mean it. There was something personal in the world, as in a work of art; whatever it meant it meant violently. Third, I thought this purpose beautiful in its old design, in spite of its defects, such as dragons. Fourth, that the proper form of thanks to it is some form of humility and restraint: we should thank God for beer and Burgundy by not drinking too much of them. We owed, also, an obedience to whatever made us. And last, and strangest, there had come into my mind a vague and vast impression that in some way all good was a remnant to be stored and held sacred out of some primordial ruin. Man had saved his good as Crusoe saved his goods: he had saved them from a wreck. All this I felt and the age gave me no encouragement to feel it. And all this time I had not even thought of Christian theology.

[*Orthodoxy* (New York: John Lane, 1909), 81–87, 98–99, 117–18]

Selection 103: Pope Pius XII, *Munificentissimus Deus* (1950)

In this rare exercise of papal infallibility, Pope Pius XII (1876–1958) argues on the basis of tradition and liturgy that Mary was bodily assumed into heaven. This excerpt includes the appeal to Scripture, followed by the definition of the dogma.

24. Among the scholastic theologians there have not been lacking those who, wishing to inquire more profoundly into divinely revealed truths and desirous of showing the harmony that exists between what is termed the theological demonstration and the Catholic faith, have always considered it worthy of note that this privilege of the Virgin Mary's Assumption is in wonderful accord with those divine truths given us in Holy Scripture.

25. When they go on to explain this point, they adduce various proofs to throw light on this privilege of Mary. As the first element of these demonstrations, they insist upon the fact that, out of filial love for his mother, Jesus Christ has willed that she be assumed into heaven. They base the strength of their proofs on the incomparable dignity of her divine motherhood and of all those prerogatives which follow from it. These include her exalted holiness, entirely surpassing the sanctity of all men and of the angels, the intimate union of Mary with her Son, and the affection of preeminent love which the Son has for his most worthy Mother.

26. Often there are theologians and preachers who, following in the footsteps of the holy Fathers,[18] have been rather free in their use of events and expressions taken from Sacred Scripture to explain their belief in the Assumption. Thus, to mention only a few of the texts

18. Here the text cites John of Damascus (ca. 655–ca. 750) and (Pseudo-)Modestus of Jerusalem (d. ca. 634).

rather frequently cited in this fashion, some have employed the words of the psalmist: "Arise, O Lord, into your resting place: you and the ark, which you have sanctified" [Ps. 131:8]; and have looked upon the Ark of the Covenant, built of incorruptible wood and placed in the Lord's temple, as a type of the most pure body of the Virgin Mary, preserved and exempt from all the corruption of the tomb and raised up to such glory in heaven. Treating of this subject, they also describe her as the Queen entering triumphantly into the royal halls of heaven and sitting at the right hand of the divine Redeemer. Likewise they mention the Spouse of the Canticles "that goes up by the desert, as a pillar of smoke of aromatical spices, of myrrh and frankincense" to be crowned [Song 3:6]. These are proposed as depicting that heavenly Queen and heavenly Spouse who has been lifted up to the courts of heaven with the divine Bridegroom. . . .

38. All these proofs and considerations of the holy Fathers and the theologians are based upon the Sacred Writings as their ultimate foundation. These set the loving Mother of God as it were before our very eyes as most intimately joined to her divine Son and as always sharing his lot. Consequently it seems impossible to think of her, the one who conceived Christ, brought him forth, nursed him with her milk, held him in her arms, and clasped him to her breast, as being apart from him in body, even though not in soul, after this earthly life. Since our Redeemer is the Son of Mary, he could not do otherwise, as the perfect observer of God's law, than to honor, not only his eternal Father, but also his most beloved Mother. And, since it was within his power to grant her this great honor, to preserve her from the corruption of the tomb, we must believe that he really acted in this way. . . .

40. Hence the revered Mother of God, from all eternity joined in a hidden way with Jesus Christ in one and the same decree of predestination, immaculate in her conception,[19] a most perfect virgin in her divine motherhood, the noble associate of the divine Redeemer who has won a complete triumph over sin and its consequences, finally obtained, as the supreme culmination of her privileges, that she should be preserved free from the corruption of the tomb and that, like her own Son, having overcome death, she might be taken up body and soul to the glory of heaven where, as queen, she sits in splendor at the right hand of her Son, the immortal King of the ages. . . .

45. Hence if anyone, which God forbid, should dare willfully to deny or to call into doubt that which we have defined, let him know that he has fallen away completely from the divine and Catholic faith.

Pope John XXIII

Selection 104: Council of Vatican II (1962–1965)

When John XXIII (1881–1963) became pope in 1958, he surprised the establishment by emphasizing "modernization" as the theme of his papacy. He paved the way for the Second Vatican Council, which is reckoned by the Roman Catholic Church as the twenty-first ecumenical council, and he lived to preside over its first session. Pope Paul VI (1897–1978) continued the council and presided over its remaining sessions.

Vatican II is justly known for the extensive changes it introduced to Roman Catholicism, many of which open the church to ecumenical dialogue and soften the strong anti-Protestant stance of the Council of

19. See *Ineffabilis Deus* (Selection 94).

Trent (see Selection 45). Indeed, some of the modifications echo Protestant emphases that were rejected four centuries earlier, such as greater encouragement of lay Bible study and conducting liturgy in the vernacular. These and other shifts were resisted by some Roman Catholics, although the majority embraced the new direction. The following excerpts from various sessions of the council give a taste of this new direction.

Session 3 (4 December 1963) Constitution on the Sacred Liturgy, *Sacrosanctum Concilium*

36. 1. Particular law remaining in force, the use of the Latin language is to be preserved in the Latin rites.

2. But since the use of the mother tongue, whether in the Mass, the administration of the sacraments, or other parts of the liturgy, frequently may be of great advantage to the people, the limits of its employment may be extended. This will apply in the first place to the readings and directives, and to some of the prayers and chants, according to the regulations on this matter to be laid down separately in subsequent chapters.

3. These norms being observed, it is for the competent territorial ecclesiastical authority (mentioned in Art. 22, 2[20]) to decide whether, and to what extent, the vernacular language is to be used; their decrees are to be approved, that is, confirmed, by the Apostolic See. And, whenever it seems to be called for, this authority is to consult with bishops of neighboring regions which have the same language.

4. Translations from the Latin text into the mother tongue intended for use in the liturgy must be approved by the competent territorial ecclesiastical authority mentioned above. . . .

55. That more perfect form of participation in the Mass whereby the faithful, after the priest's communion, receive the Lord's body from the same sacrifice, is strongly commended.

The dogmatic principles which were laid down by the Council of Trent remaining intact, communion under both kinds may be granted when the bishops think fit, not only to clerics and religious, but also to the laity, in cases to be determined by the Apostolic See, as, for instance, to the newly ordained in the Mass of their sacred ordination, to the newly professed in the Mass of their religious profession, and to the newly baptized in the Mass which follows their baptism. . . .

73. "Extreme unction," which may also and more fittingly be called "anointing of the sick," is not a sacrament for those only who are at the point of death. Hence, as soon as any one of the faithful begins to be in danger of death from sickness or old age, the fitting time for him to receive this sacrament has certainly already arrived.

Session 5 (21 November 1964) Dogmatic Constitution on the Church, *Lumen Gentium*

Chapter 1: The Mystery of the Church

1. Christ is the Light of nations. Because this is so, this Sacred Synod gathered together in the Holy Spirit eagerly desires, by proclaiming the Gospel to every creature, to bring the light of Christ to all men, a light brightly visible on the countenance of the Church. Since the Church is in Christ like a sacrament or as a sign and instrument both of a very closely knit union with God and of the unity of the whole human race, it desires now to unfold more fully to the faithful of the Church and to the whole world its own inner nature and universal mission. This it intends to do following faithfully the

20. 22.2 reads: "In virtue of power conceded by the law, the regulation of the liturgy within certain defined limits belongs also to various kinds of competent territorial bodies of bishops legitimately established."

teaching of previous councils. The present-day conditions of the world add greater urgency to this work of the Church so that all men, joined more closely today by various social, technical and cultural ties, might also attain fuller unity in Christ. . . .

5. The mystery of the holy Church is manifest in its very foundation. The Lord Jesus set it on its course by preaching the Good News, that is, the coming of the Kingdom of God, which, for centuries, had been promised in the Scriptures: "The time is fulfilled, and the kingdom of God is at hand." In the word, in the works, and in the presence of Christ, this kingdom was clearly open to the view of men. . . .

7. . . . The Head of this Body is Christ. He is the image of the invisible God and in Him all things came into being. He is before all creatures and in Him all things hold together. He is the head of the Body which is the Church. He is the beginning, the firstborn from the dead, that in all things He might have the first place. By the greatness of His power He rules the things in heaven and the things on earth, and with His all-surpassing perfection and way of acting He fills the whole body with the riches of His glory.

All the members ought to be molded in the likeness of Him, until Christ be formed in them. For this reason we, who have been made to conform with Him, who have died with Him and risen with Him, are taken up into the mysteries of His life, until we will reign together with Him. On earth, still as pilgrims in a strange land, tracing in trial and in oppression the paths He trod, we are made one with His sufferings like the body is one with the Head, suffering with Him, that with Him we may be glorified. . . .

8. . . . This is the one Church of Christ which in the Creed is professed as one, holy, catholic and apostolic,[21] which our Saviour, after His Resurrection, commissioned Peter to shepherd, and him and the other apostles to extend and direct with authority, which He erected for all ages as "the pillar and mainstay of the truth." This Church constituted and organized in the world as a society, subsists in the Catholic Church, which is governed by the successor of Peter and by the Bishops in communion with him, although many elements of sanctification and of truth are found outside of its visible structure. These elements, as gifts belonging to the Church of Christ, are forces impelling toward catholic unity. . . .

Chapter 8: The Blessed Virgin Mary, Mother of God, in the Mystery of Christ and the Church

56. The Father of mercies willed that the incarnation should be preceded by the acceptance of her who was predestined to be the mother of His Son, so that just as a woman contributed to death, so also a woman should contribute to life. That is true in outstanding fashion of the mother of Jesus, who gave to the world Him who is Life itself and who renews all things, and who was enriched by God with the gifts which befit such a role. It is no wonder therefore that the usage prevailed among the Fathers whereby they called the mother of God entirely holy and free from all stain of sin, as though fashioned by the Holy Spirit and formed as a new creature. Adorned from the first instant of her conception with the radiance of an entirely unique holiness, the Virgin of Nazareth is greeted, on God's command, by an angel messenger as "full of grace," and to the heavenly messenger she replies: "Behold the handmaid of the Lord, be it done unto me according to thy word." Thus Mary, a daughter of Adam, consenting to the divine Word, became the mother of Jesus, the one and only Mediator. Embracing God's

21. In the Nicene-Constantinopolitan Creed of 381.

salvific will with a full heart and impeded by no sin, she devoted herself totally as a handmaid of the Lord to the person and work of her Son, under Him and with Him, by the grace of almighty God, serving the mystery of redemption. Rightly therefore the holy Fathers see her as used by God not merely in a passive way, but as freely cooperating in the work of human salvation through faith and obedience. For, as St. Irenaeus says, she "being obedient, became the cause of salvation for herself and for the whole human race." Hence not a few of the early Fathers gladly assert in their preaching, "The knot of Eve's disobedience was untied by Mary's obedience; what the virgin Eve bound through her unbelief, the Virgin Mary loosened by her faith." Comparing Mary with Eve, they call her "the Mother of the living," and still more often they say: "death through Eve, life through Mary."[22] . . .

58. In the public life of Jesus, Mary makes significant appearances. This is so even at the very beginning, when at the marriage feast of Cana, moved with pity, she brought about by her intercession the beginning of miracles of Jesus the Messiah. In the course of her Son's preaching she received the words whereby in extolling a kingdom beyond the calculations and bonds of flesh and blood, He declared blessed those who heard and kept the word of God, as she was faithfully doing. After this manner the Blessed Virgin advanced in her pilgrimage of faith, and faithfully persevered in her union with her Son unto the cross, where she stood, in keeping with the divine plan, grieving exceedingly with her only begotten Son, uniting herself with a maternal heart with His sacrifice, and lovingly consenting to the immolation of this Victim which she herself had brought forth. Finally, she was given by the same Christ Jesus dying on the cross as a mother to His disciple with these words: "Woman, behold thy son." . . .

62. This maternity of Mary in the order of grace began with the consent which she gave in faith at the Annunciation and which she sustained without wavering beneath the cross, and lasts until the eternal fulfillment of all the elect. Taken up to heaven she did not lay aside this salvific duty, but by her constant intercession continued to bring us the gifts of eternal salvation. By her maternal charity, she cares for the brethren of her Son, who still journey on earth surrounded by dangers and difficulties, until they are led into the happiness of their true home. Therefore the Blessed Virgin is invoked by the Church under the titles of Advocate, Auxiliatrix, Adjutrix, and Mediatrix. This, however, is to be so understood that it neither takes away from nor adds anything to the dignity and efficaciousness of Christ the one Mediator. . . .

Session 5 (21 November 1964) Decree on Ecumenism, *Unitatis Redintegratio*

Chapter 3: Churches and Ecclesial Communities Separated from the Roman Apostolic See

19. In the great upheaval which began in the West toward the end of the Middle Ages, and in later times too, Churches and ecclesial Communities came to be separated from the Apostolic See of Rome.[23] Yet they have retained a particularly close affinity with the Catholic Church as a result of the long centuries in

22. The church fathers cited here include Irenaeus, Epiphanius, Jerome, Augustine, Cyril of Jerusalem, John Chrysostom, and John of Damascus.

23. Although Vatican II softened the Tridentine Roman Catholic language about Protestant churches, nevertheless this decree on ecumenism insisted on referring to them as "ecclesial communities" rather than "churches." The term "church" is reserved for those communions that retain apostolic succession.

which all Christendom lived together in ecclesiastical communion.

However, since these Churches and ecclesial Communities, on account of their different origins, and different teachings in matters of doctrine on the spiritual life, vary considerably not only with us, but also among themselves, the task of describing them at all adequately is extremely difficult; and we have no intention of making such an attempt here.

Although the ecumenical movement and the desire for peace with the Catholic Church have not yet taken hold everywhere, it is our hope that ecumenical feeling and mutual esteem may gradually increase among all men.

It must however be admitted that in these Churches and ecclesial Communities there exist important differences from the Catholic Church, not only of a historical, sociological, psychological and cultural character, but especially in the interpretation of revealed truth. To make easier the ecumenical dialogue in spite of these differences, we wish to set down some considerations which can, and indeed should, serve as a basis and encouragement for such dialogue.

20. Our thoughts turn first to those Christians who make open confession of Jesus Christ as God and Lord and as the sole Mediator between God and men, to the glory of the one God, Father, Son and Holy Spirit. We are aware indeed that there exist considerable divergences from the doctrine of the Catholic Church concerning Christ Himself, the Word of God made flesh, the work of redemption, and consequently, concerning the mystery and ministry of the Church, and the role of Mary in the plan of salvation. But we rejoice to see that our separated brethren look to Christ as the source and center of Church unity. Their longing for union with Christ inspires them to seek an ever closer unity, and also to bear witness to their faith among the peoples of the earth.

21. A love and reverence of Sacred Scripture which might be described as devotion, leads our brethren to a constant meditative study of the sacred text. For the Gospel "is the power of God for salvation to every one who has faith, to the Jew first and then to the Greek."

While invoking the Holy Spirit, they seek in these very Scriptures God as it were speaking to them in Christ, Whom the prophets foretold, Who is the Word of God made flesh for us. They contemplate in the Scriptures the life of Christ and what the Divine Master taught and did for our salvation, especially the mysteries of His death and resurrection.

But while the Christians who are separated from us hold the divine authority of the Sacred Books, they differ from ours—some in one way, some in another—regarding the relationship between Scripture and the Church. For, according to Catholic belief, the authentic teaching authority of the Church has a special place in the interpretation and preaching of the written word of God.

But Sacred Scriptures provide for the work of dialogue an instrument of the highest value in the mighty hand of God for the attainment of that unity which the Saviour holds out to all.

22. Whenever the Sacrament of Baptism is duly administered as Our Lord instituted it, and is received with the right dispositions, a person is truly incorporated into the crucified and glorified Christ, and reborn to a sharing of the divine life, as the Apostle says: "You were buried together with Him in Baptism, and in Him also rose again—through faith in the working of God, who raised Him from the dead."[24]

Baptism therefore establishes a sacramental bond of unity which links all who have been

24. Col. 2:12.

reborn by it. But of itself Baptism is only a beginning, an inauguration wholly directed toward the fullness of life in Christ. . . .

Though the ecclesial Communities which are separated from us lack the fullness of unity with us flowing from Baptism, and though we believe they have not retained the proper reality of the eucharistic mystery in its fullness, especially because of the absence of the sacrament of Orders, nevertheless when they commemorate His death and resurrection in the Lord's Supper, they profess that it signifies life in communion with Christ and look forward to His coming in glory. Therefore the teaching concerning the Lord's Supper, the other sacraments, worship, the ministry of the Church, must be the subject of the dialogue.

23. The daily Christian life of these brethren is nourished by their faith in Christ and strengthened by the grace of Baptism and by hearing the word of God. This shows itself in their private prayer, their meditation on the Bible, in their Christian family life, and in the worship of a community gathered together to praise God. Moreover, their form of worship sometimes displays notable features of the liturgy which they shared with us of old.

Their faith in Christ bears fruit in praise and thanksgiving for the blessings received from the hands of God. Among them, too, is a strong sense of justice and a true charity toward their neighbor. This active faith has been responsible for many organizations for the relief of spiritual and material distress, the furtherance of the education of youth, the improvement of the social conditions of life, and the promotion of peace throughout the world.

While it is true that many Christians understand the moral teaching of the Gospel differently from Catholics, and do not accept the same solutions to the more difficult problems of modern society, nevertheless they share our desire to stand by the words of Christ as the source of Christian virtue, and to obey the command of the Apostle: "And whatever you do, in word or in work, do all in the name of the Lord Jesus Christ, giving thanks to God the Father through Him."[25] For that reason an ecumenical dialogue might start with discussion of the application of the Gospel to moral conduct.

24. Now that we have briefly set out the conditions for ecumenical action and the principles by which it is to be directed, we look with confidence to the future. This Sacred Council exhorts the faithful to refrain from superficiality and imprudent zeal, which can hinder real progress toward unity. . . .

It is the urgent wish of this Holy Council that the measures undertaken by the sons of the Catholic Church should develop in conjunction with those of our separated brethren so that no obstacle be put in the ways of divine Providence and no preconceived judgments impair the future inspirations of the Holy Spirit. The Council moreover professes its awareness that human powers and capacities cannot achieve this holy objective—the reconciling of all Christians in the unity of the one and only Church of Christ. It is because of this that the Council rests all its hope on the prayer of Christ for the Church, on our Father's love for us, and on the power of the Holy Spirit.

Session 8 (18 November 1965) Dogmatic Constitution on Divine Revelation, *Dei Verbum*

Chapter 2: Handing on Divine Revelation

7. In His gracious goodness, God has seen to it that what He had revealed for the salvation of all nations would abide perpetually in its full integrity and be handed on to all generations. Therefore Christ the Lord in whom the full revelation of the supreme God is brought to

25. Col. 3:17.

completion (see 2 Cor. 1:20; 3:16; 4:6), commissioned the Apostles to preach to all men that Gospel which is the source of all saving truth and moral teaching, and to impart to them heavenly gifts. This Gospel had been promised in former times through the prophets, and Christ Himself had fulfilled it and promulgated it with His lips. This commission was faithfully fulfilled by the Apostles who, by their oral preaching, by example, and by observances handed on what they had received from the lips of Christ, from living with Him, and from what He did, or what they had learned through the prompting of the Holy Spirit. The commission was fulfilled, too, by those Apostles and apostolic men who under the inspiration of the same Holy Spirit committed the message of salvation to writing.

But in order to keep the Gospel forever whole and alive within the Church, the Apostles left bishops as their successors, "handing over" to them "the authority to teach in their own place."[26] This sacred tradition, therefore, and Sacred Scripture of both the Old and New Testaments are like a mirror in which the pilgrim Church on earth looks at God, from whom she has received everything, until she is brought finally to see Him as He is, face to face (see 1 John 3:2).

8. And so the apostolic preaching, which is expressed in a special way in the inspired books, was to be preserved by an unending succession of preachers until the end of time. Therefore the Apostles, handing on what they themselves had received, warn the faithful to hold fast to the traditions which they have learned either by word of mouth or by letter (see 2 Thess. 2:15), and to fight in defense of the faith handed on once and for all (see Jude 1:3). Now what was handed on by the Apostles includes everything which contributes toward the holiness of life and increase in faith of the peoples of God; and so the Church, in her teaching, life and worship, perpetuates and hands on to all generations all that she herself is, all that she believes.

This tradition which comes from the Apostles develops in the Church with the help of the Holy Spirit. For there is a growth in the understanding of the realities and the words which have been handed down. This happens through the contemplation and study made by believers, who treasure these things in their hearts (see Luke, 2:19, 51) through a penetrating understanding of the spiritual realities which they experience, and through the preaching of those who have received through Episcopal succession the sure gift of truth. For as the centuries succeed one another, the Church constantly moves forward toward the fullness of divine truth until the words of God reach their complete fulfillment in her.

The words of the holy fathers witness to the presence of this living tradition, whose wealth is poured into the practice and life of the believing and praying Church. Through the same tradition the Church's full canon of the sacred books is known, and the sacred writings themselves are more profoundly understood and unceasingly made active in her; and thus God, who spoke of old, uninterruptedly converses with the bride of His beloved Son; and the Holy Spirit, through whom the living voice of the Gospel resounds in the Church, and through her, in the world, leads unto all truth those who believe and makes the word of Christ dwell abundantly in them (see Col. 3:16).

9. Hence there exists a close connection and communication between sacred tradition and Sacred Scripture. For both of them, flowing from the same divine wellspring, in a certain way merge into a unity and tend toward the same end. For Sacred Scripture is the word of

26. Irenaeus is cited here.

God inasmuch as it is consigned to writing under the inspiration of the divine Spirit, while sacred tradition takes the word of God entrusted by Christ the Lord and the Holy Spirit to the Apostles, and hands it on to their successors in its full purity, so that led by the light of the Spirit of truth, they may in proclaiming it preserve this word of God faithfully, explain it, and make it more widely known. Consequently it is not from Sacred Scripture alone that the Church draws her certainty about everything which has been revealed. Therefore both sacred tradition and Sacred Scripture are to be accepted and venerated with the same sense of loyalty and reverence.

10. Sacred tradition and Sacred Scripture form one sacred deposit of the word of God, committed to the Church. Holding fast to this deposit the entire holy people united with their shepherds remain always steadfast in the teaching of the Apostles, in the common life, in the breaking of the bread and in prayers (see Acts 2, 42, Greek text), so that holding to, practicing and professing the heritage of the faith, it becomes on the part of the bishops and faithful a single common effort.

But the task of authentically interpreting the word of God, whether written or handed on, has been entrusted exclusively to the living teaching office of the Church, whose authority is exercised in the name of Jesus Christ. This teaching office is not above the word of God, but serves it, teaching only what has been handed on, listening to it devoutly, guarding it scrupulously and explaining it faithfully in accord with a divine commission and with the help of the Holy Spirit, it draws from this one deposit of faith everything which it presents for belief as divinely revealed.

It is clear, therefore, that sacred tradition, Sacred Scripture and the teaching authority of the Church, in accord with God's most wise design, are so linked and joined together that one cannot stand without the others, and that all together and each in its own way under the action of the one Holy Spirit contribute effectively to the salvation of souls.

Chapter 6: Sacred Scripture in the Life of the Church

21. The Church has always venerated the divine Scriptures just as she venerates the body of the Lord, since, especially in the sacred liturgy, she unceasingly receives and offers to the faithful the bread of life from the table both of God's word and of Christ's body. She has always maintained them, and continues to do so, together with sacred tradition, as the supreme rule of faith, since, as inspired by God and committed once and for all to writing, they impart the word of God Himself without change, and make the voice of the Holy Spirit resound in the words of the prophets and Apostles. Therefore, like the Christian religion itself, all the preaching of the Church must be nourished and regulated by Sacred Scripture. For in the sacred books, the Father who is in heaven meets His children with great love and speaks with them; and the force and power in the word of God is so great that it stands as the support and energy of the Church, the strength of faith for her sons, the food of the soul, the pure and everlasting source of spiritual life. Consequently these words are perfectly applicable to Sacred Scripture: "For the word of God is living and active" (Heb. 4:12) and "it has power to build you up and give you your heritage among all those who are sanctified" (Acts 20:32; see 1 Thess. 2:13).

22. Easy access to Sacred Scripture should be provided for all the Christian faithful. That is why the Church from the very beginning accepted as her own that very ancient Greek translation of the Old Testament which is called the septuagint; and she has always given

a place of honor to other Eastern translations and Latin ones, especially the Latin translation known as the vulgate. But since the word of God should be accessible at all times, the Church by her authority and with maternal concern sees to it that suitable and correct translations are made into different languages, especially from the original texts of the sacred books. And should the opportunity arise and the Church authorities approve, if these translations are produced in cooperation with the separated brethren as well, all Christians will be able to use them.

23. The bride of the incarnate Word, the Church taught by the Holy Spirit, is concerned to move ahead toward a deeper understanding of the Sacred Scriptures so that she may increasingly feed her sons with the divine words. Therefore, she also encourages the study of the holy Fathers of both East and West and of sacred liturgies. Catholic exegetes then and other students of sacred theology, working diligently together and using appropriate means, should devote their energies, under the watchful care of the sacred teaching office of the Church, to an exploration and exposition of the divine writings. This should be so done that as many ministers of the divine word as possible will be able effectively to provide the nourishment of the Scriptures for the people of God, to enlighten their minds, strengthen their wills, and set men's hearts on fire with the love of God. The sacred synod encourages the sons of the Church and Biblical scholars to continue energetically, following the mind of the Church, with the work they have so well begun, with a constant renewal of vigor.[27]

24. Sacred theology rests on the written word of God, together with sacred tradition, as its primary and perpetual foundation. By scrutinizing in the light of faith all truth stored up in the mystery of Christ, theology is most powerfully strengthened and constantly rejuvenated by that word. For the Sacred Scriptures contain the word of God and since they are inspired, really are the word of God; and so the study of the sacred page is, as it were, the soul of sacred theology. By the same word of Scripture the ministry of the word also, that is, pastoral preaching, catechetics and all Christian instruction, in which the liturgical homily must hold the foremost place, is nourished in a healthy way and flourishes in a holy way.

25. Therefore, all the clergy must hold fast to the Sacred Scriptures through diligent sacred reading and careful study, especially the priests of Christ and others, such as deacons and catechists who are legitimately active in the ministry of the word. This is to be done so that none of them will become "an empty preacher of the word of God outwardly, who is not a listener to it inwardly"[28] since they must share the abundant wealth of the divine word with the faithful committed to them, especially in the sacred liturgy. . . .

It devolves on sacred bishops "who have the apostolic teaching"[29] to give the faithful entrusted to them suitable instruction in the right use of the divine books, especially the New Testament and above all the Gospels. This can be done through translations of the sacred texts, which are to be provided with the necessary and really adequate explanations so that the children of the Church may safely and profitably become conversant with the Sacred Scriptures and be penetrated with their spirit.

Furthermore, editions of the Sacred Scriptures, provided with suitable footnotes, should be prepared also for the use of non-Christians and adapted to their situation. Both pastors of

27. Pope Pius XII is cited in these last two sentences.

28. A sermon of Augustine is cited here.

29. Irenaeus, *Against Heresies* IV.xxxii.1.

souls and Christians generally should see to the wise distribution of these in one way or another.

26. In this way, therefore, through the reading and study of the sacred books "the word of God may spread rapidly and be glorified" (2 Thess. 3:1) and the treasure of revelation, entrusted to the Church, may more and more fill the hearts of men. Just as the life of the Church is strengthened through more frequent celebration of the Eucharistic mystery, similar we may hope for a new stimulus for the life of the Spirit from a growing reverence for the word of God, which "lasts forever" (Is. 40:8; see 1 Peter 1:23-25).

Selection 105: Georges Florovsky, "The Function of Tradition in the Ancient Church" (1964)

Especially since the Great Schism of 1054, Eastern Orthodoxy has exerted relatively little influence on the Western Church. Since the mid-twentieth century, however, Eastern Orthodox churches have increasingly flourished in the West, due not only to immigration from countries such as Russia but also to the attraction and conversion of evangelical Protestants to Eastern Orthodoxy. Georges Florovsky (1893–1979), a Russian immigrant to France and later to the United States, was an Orthodox priest and theology professor. Through his teaching and writing on the basics of Eastern Orthodoxy, he in turn introduced this tradition to many in the West.

Christ Pantocrator, Hagia Sophia, Istanbul

The famous dictum of St. Vincent of Lérins was characteristic of the attitude of the Ancient Church in the matters of faith: . . . *teneamus quod ubique, quod semper, quod ab omnibus creditum est* [let us hold what has been believed everywhere, always, and by all].[30] This was at once the criterion and the norm. The crucial emphasis was here on the permanence of Christian teaching. St. Vincent was actually appealing to the double "ecumenicity" of Christian faith—in space and in time. . . . These two aspects of faith, or rather—the two dimensions, could never be separated from each other. *Universitas* and *antiquitas*, as well as *consensio*,[31] belonged together. Neither was an adequate criterion by itself. . . . This did not imply, however, that there were two sources of Christian doctrine. Indeed, the rule, or canon, of Scripture was "perfect" and "self-sufficient"—*ad omnia satis superque sufficiat* [it suffices and is more than enough for all things]. Why then should it be supplemented by any other "authority"? Why was it imperative to invoke also the authority of "ecclesiastical understanding"—*ecclesiasticae intelligentiae auctoritas*? The reason was obvious: Scriptures were differently interpreted by individuals: *ut paene quot homines tot illinc sententiae erui posse videantur* [so that one might almost gain the impression that it can yield as many different meanings as there are men]. To this variety of "private" opinions St. Vincent opposes the "common" mind of the Church, the mind of the Church Catholic: *ut propheticae et apostolicae interpretationis linea secundum ecclesiastici et catholici sensus normam dirigatur* [that the trend of the prophetic and apostolic interpretation is directed according to the norm of the ecclesiastical and catholic meaning]. Tradition was not, according to St. Vincent, an independent instance, nor was it a complementary source of faith. "Ecclesiastical understanding" could not add anything to the Scripture. But it

30. This statement, sometimes known as the Vincentian Canon, comes from Vincent of Lérins, *Commonitorium* 2, written in 434.

31. That is, the totality, antiquity, and consensus.

was the only means to ascertain and to disclose the true meaning of Scripture. Tradition was, in fact, the authentic interpretation of Scripture. And in this sense it was co-extensive with Scripture. Tradition was actually "Scripture rightly understood." And Scripture was for St. Vincent the only, primary and ultimate, *canon* of Christian truth. . . .

The problem of right exegesis was still a burning issue in the Fourth century, in the contest of the Church with the Arians, no less than it has been in the Second century, in the struggle against Gnostics, Sabellians, and Montanists. All parties in the dispute used to appeal to Scripture. Heretics, even Gnostics and Manichees, used to quote Scriptural texts and passages and to invoke the authority of the Holy Writ. . . . It was in this historical situation that the authority of Tradition was first invoked. Scripture belonged to the Church, and it was only in the Church, within the community of right faith, that Scripture could be adequately understood and correctly interpreted. Heretics, that is—those outside of the Church, had no key to the mind of the Scripture. It was not enough just to read and to quote Scriptural words—the true meaning, or intent, of Scripture, taken as an integrated whole, had to be elicited. . . . Emphatically did Tertullian insist on the priority of the "rule of faith," *regula fidei*.[32] It was the only key to the meaning of the Scripture. And this "rule" was Apostolic, was rooted in, and derived from, the Apostolic preaching. . . .

Denouncing the Gnostic mishandling of Scriptures, St. Irenaeus introduced a picturesque simile.[33] A skillful artist has made a beautiful image of a king, composed of many precious jewels. Now, another man takes this mosaic image to pieces, re-arranges the stones on another pattern so as to produce the image of a dog or of a fox. Then he starts claiming that this was the original picture, by the first master, under the pretext that the gems (the *psêphides*) were authentic. In fact, however, the original design had been destroyed—*lysas tên hypokeimenên tou anthrôpou idean* [having destroyed the man's prescribed form]. This is precisely what the heretics do with the Scripture. . . . Thus, for St. Irenaeus, the reading of Scripture must be guided by the "rule" of faith—to which believers are committed (and into which they are initiated) by their baptismal profession, and by which only the basic message, or "the truth," of the Scripture can be adequately assessed and identified. The favorite phrase of St. Irenaeus was "the rule of truth," *kanon tês alêtheias*, *regula veritatis*. Now, this "rule" was, in fact, nothing else than the witness and preaching of the Apostles, their *kêrygma* and *praedicatio* (or *praeconium*) [proclamation], which was "deposited" in the Church and entrusted to her by the Apostles, and then was faithfully kept and handed down, with complete unanimity in all places, by the succession of accredited pastors: *qui cum episcopatus successione charisma veritatis certum acceperunt* [those who, together with the succession of the episcopacy, have received the firm charisma of truth] (*Against Heresies* IV. 26. 2). . . .

Tradition was in the Early Church, first of all, an hermeneutical principle and method. Scripture could be rightly and fully assessed and understood only in the light and in the context of the living Apostolic Tradition, which was an integral factor of Christian existence. It was so, of course, not because Tradition could add anything to what has been manifested in the Scripture, but because it

32. Tertullian of Carthage (ca. 160–ca. 225) was the first major Christian theologian to write in Latin. He invoked the rule of faith against the Gnostics and Marcion.

33. Irenaeus of Lyons (ca. 130–ca. 200) was an Eastern church father who studied in Rome and ministered in Gaul. His principal writing is *Against Heresies*.

provided that living context, the comprehensive perspective, in which only the true "intention" and the total "design" of the Holy Writ, of the Divine Revelation itself, could be detected and grasped. . . .

The situation did not change in the Fourth century. . . . It was imperative for the Orthodox to appeal to the mind of the Church, to that "Faith" which had been once delivered and then faithfully kept. This was the main concern, and the usual method, of St. Athanasius.[34] The Arians quoted various passages from the Scripture to substantiate their contention that the Saviour was a creature. In reply St. Athanasius invoked the "rule of faith." This was his usual argument. "Let us, who possess *ton skopon tês pisteôs* [the scope of faith], restore the correct meaning (*orthên tên dianoian*) of what they had wrongly interpreted" (*c. Arian.* III. 35). St. Athanasius contended that the "correct" interpretation of particular texts was only possible in the total perspective of faith. . . .

It would be proper to recall at this point the famous passage from the *Indiculus de gratia Dei*, which was mistakenly attributed to Pope Celestine and was in fact composed by St. Prosper of Aquitania: . . . *ut legem credendi lex statuat supplicandi* [so that the law of prayer might establish the law of faith].[35] It is true, of course, that this phrase in its immediate context was not a formulation of a general principle, and its direct intention was limited to one particular point: Infant Baptism as an instance pointing to the reality of an inherited or original sin. Indeed, it was not an authoritative proclamation of a Pope, but a private opinion of an individual theologian, expressed in the context of a heated controversy. Yet, it was not just an accident, and not a misunderstanding, that the phrase had been taken out of its immediate context and slightly changed in order to express the principle: *ut legem credendi statuat lex orandi* [so that the law of worship might establish the law of faith].[36] "Faith" found its first expression precisely in the liturgical, sacramental, rites and formulas—and "Creeds" first emerged as an integral part of the rite of initiation. . . .

There are many other "unwritten mysteries of the Church," says St. Basil: *ta agrapha tês ekklêsias mystêria* (c. 66 and 67).[37] They are not mentioned in the Scripture. But they are of great authority and significance. They are indispensable for the preservation of right faith. They are effective means of witness and communication. . . .

The Church had the authority to interpret the Scripture, since she was the only authentic depository of Apostolic *kerygma*. This *kerygma* was unfailingly kept alive in the Church, as she was endowed with the Spirit. The Church was still teaching *viva voce* [with the living voice], commending and furthering the Word of God. And *viva vox Evangelii* [the living voice of the Gospel] was indeed not just a recitation of the words of the Scripture. It was a proclamation of the Word of God, as it was heard and preserved in the Church, by the ever abiding power of the quickening Spirit. . . .

In the same sense we have to interpret the well known, and justly startling, statement of St. Augustine: *Ego vero Evangelio non crederem, nisi me catholicae Ecclesiae commoveret auctoritas* [Indeed, I would not have believed the Gospel, unless the authority of the catholic Church had moved me] (*c. epistolam Fundamenti,* v.6). The phrase must be read in its context. First of all,

34. Athanasius of Alexandria (ca. 296–373) was the chief defender of Nicene orthodoxy against the Arians.

35. Prosper of Aquitaine (ca. 390–ca. 463) was an influential Augustinian theologian.

36. This principle, so important to liturgical theology, is often condensed as *lex orandi lex credendi*.

37. Basil (the Great) of Caesarea (ca. 330–379) was one of the three Cappadocian Fathers.

St. Augustine did not utter this sentence on his own behalf. He spoke of the attitude which a simple believer had to take, when confronted with the heretical claim for authority. . . . St. Augustine had no intention "to subordinate" the Gospel to the Church. He only wanted to emphasize that "Gospel" is actually received always in the context of the Church's catholic preaching and simply cannot be separated from the Church. Only in this context it can be assessed and properly understood. . . .

["The Function of Tradition in the Ancient Church," *Greek Orthodox Theological Review* 9, no. 2 (1964): 181–88, 192, 195, 197, 199]

Selection 106: *Chicago Statement on Biblical Inerrancy* (1978)

The belief that Scripture infallibly functions to reveal God to humanity has been a foundational doctrine throughout Christian history. But in the face of Post-Enlightenment doubt, the rise of higher criticism, new claims about history and science, and the assertion of papal infallibility, Protestant fundamentalists emphasized the literal inerrancy of Scripture in all matters theological as well as historical and scientific. By the 1970s, there were mounting concerns among fundamentalists and evangelicals that too many scholars were drifting from a strict inerrantist position. This document, signed by about three hundred evangelicals, upholds biblical inerrancy and still serves as a touchstone for many evangelical institutions today.

Preface

The authority of Scripture is a key issue for the Christian church in this and every age. Those who profess faith in Jesus Christ as Lord and Savior are called to show the reality of their discipleship by humbly and faithfully obeying God's written Word. To stray from Scripture in faith or conduct is disloyalty to our Master. Recognition of the total truth and trustworthiness of Holy Scripture is essential to a full grasp and adequate confession of its authority.

The following Statement affirms this inerrancy of Scripture afresh, making clear our understanding of it and warning against its denial. We are persuaded that to deny it is to set aside the witness of Jesus Christ and of the Holy Spirit and to refuse that submission to the claims of God's own Word which marks true Christian faith. We see it as our timely duty to make this affirmation in the face of current lapses from the truth of inerrancy among our fellow Christians and misunderstandings of this doctrine in the world at large.

This Statement consists of three parts: a Summary Statement, Articles of Affirmation and Denial, and an accompanying Exposition. It has been prepared in the course of a three-day consultation in Chicago.[38] Those who have signed the Summary Statement and the Articles wish to affirm their own conviction as to the inerrancy of Scripture and to encourage and challenge one another and all Christians to growing appreciation and understanding of this doctrine. We acknowledge the limitations of a document prepared in a brief, intensive conference and do not propose that this Statement be given creedal weight. Yet we rejoice in the deepening of our own convictions through our discussions together, and we pray that the Statement we have signed may be used to the glory of our God toward a new reformation of the Church in its faith, life and mission. . . .

I. Summary Statement

1. God, who is Himself Truth and speaks truth only, has inspired Holy Scripture in order thereby to reveal Himself to lost mankind

38. On October 26–28, 1978.

through Jesus Christ as Creator and Lord, Redeemer and Judge. Holy Scripture is God's witness to Himself.

2. Holy Scripture, being God's own Word, written by men prepared and superintended by His Spirit, is of infallible divine authority in all matters upon which it touches: It is to be believed, as God's instruction, in all that it affirms; obeyed, as God's command, in all that it requires; embraced, as God's pledge, in all that it promises.

3. The Holy Spirit, Scripture's divine Author, both authenticates it to us by His inward witness and opens our minds to understand its meaning.

4. Being wholly and verbally God-given, Scripture is without error or fault in all its teaching, no less in what it states about God's acts in creation, about the events of world history, and about its own literary origins under God, than in its witness to God's saving grace in individual lives.

5. The authority of Scripture is inescapably impaired if this total divine inerrancy is in any way limited or disregarded, or made relative to a view of truth contrary to the Bible's own; and such lapses bring serious loss to both the individual and the Church.

II. Articles of Affirmation and Denial

Article II.

We affirm that the Scriptures are the supreme written norm by which God binds the conscience, and that the authority of the Church is subordinate to that of Scripture.

We deny that Church creeds, councils, or declarations have authority greater than or equal to the authority of the Bible. . . .[39]

Article IV.

We affirm that God who made mankind in His image has used language as a means of revelation.

We deny that human language is so limited by our creatureliness that it is rendered inadequate as a vehicle for divine revelation. We further deny that the corruption of human culture and language through sin has thwarted God's work of inspiration. . . .

Article X.

We affirm that inspiration, strictly speaking, applies only to the autographic text of Scripture, which in the providence of God can be ascertained from available manuscripts with great accuracy. We further affirm that copies and translations of Scripture are the Word of God to the extent that they faithfully represent the original.

We deny that any essential element of the Christian faith is affected by the absence of the autographs. We further deny that this absence renders the assertion of Biblical inerrancy invalid or irrelevant. . . .

Article XII.

We affirm that Scripture in its entirety is inerrant, being free from all falsehood, fraud, or deceit.

We deny that Biblical infallibility and inerrancy are limited to spiritual, religious, or redemptive themes, exclusive of assertions in the fields of history and science. We further deny that scientific hypotheses about earth history may properly be used to overturn the teaching of Scripture on creation and the flood. . . .[40]

---

39. This article is a direct challenge to what is affirmed in *Dei Verbum* from the Second Vatican Council (Selection 104).

40. This article represents what is perhaps the point most contested by opponents of inerrancy.

III. Exposition

Our understanding of the doctrine of inerrancy must be set in the context of the broader teachings of the Scripture concerning itself. This exposition gives an account of the outline of doctrine from which our summary statement and articles are drawn. . . .

Infallibility, Inerrancy, Interpretation

. . . *Infallible* signifies the quality of neither misleading nor being misled and so safeguards in categorical terms the truth that Holy Scripture is a sure, safe and reliable rule and guide in all matters.

Similarly, *inerrant* signifies the quality of being free from all falsehood or mistake and so safeguards the truth that Holy Scripture is entirely true and trustworthy in all its assertions.[41]

We affirm that the canonical Scripture should always be interpreted on the basis that it is infallible and inerrant. However, in determining what the God-taught writer is asserting in each passage, we must pay the most careful attention to its claims and character as a human production. In inspiration, God utilized the culture and conventions of His penman's milieu, a milieu that God controls in His sovereign providence; it is misinterpretation to imagine otherwise.

So history must be treated as history, poetry as poetry, hyperbole and metaphor as hyperbole and metaphor, generalization and approximation as what they are, and so forth. Differences between literary conventions in Bible times and in our time must also be observed: Since, for instance, nonchronological narration and imprecise citation were conventional and acceptable and violated no expectations in those days, we must not regard these things as faults when we find them in Bible writers. When total precision of a particular kind was not expected nor aimed at, it is no error not to have achieved it. Scripture is inerrant, not in the sense of being absolutely precise by modern standards, but in the sense of making good its claims and achieving that measure of focused truth at which its authors aimed. . . .

Transmission and Translation

Since God has nowhere promised an inerrant transmission of Scripture, it is necessary to affirm that only the autographic text of the original documents was inspired and to maintain the need of textual criticism as a means of detecting any slips that may have crept into the text in the course of its transmission. The verdict of this science, however, is that the Hebrew and Greek text appears to be amazingly well preserved, so that we are amply justified in affirming, with the Westminster Confession, a singular providence of God in this matter and in declaring that the authority of Scripture is in no way jeopardized by the fact that the copies we possess are not entirely error-free.

Similarly, no translation is or can be perfect, and all translations are an additional step away from the *autographa*. Yet the verdict of linguistic science is that English-speaking Christians, at least, are exceedingly well served in these days with a host of excellent translations and have no cause for hesitating to conclude that the true Word of God is within their reach. . . .

[*Journal of the Evangelical Theological Society* 21, no. 4 (1978): 289–93, 295–96]

41. These two terms, *infallible* and *inerrant*, are often used interchangeably. At other times, when a distinction is drawn, inerrancy is usually considered the stricter of the two.

C. Liberation Theologies

Selection 107: Gustavo Gutiérrez, *A Theology of Liberation: History, Politics, and Salvation* (1971; rev. ed., 1988)

Broadly speaking, liberation theology is concerned with enfranchising the disenfranchised through the message of the gospel, which is seen to privilege the marginalized and outcast. Depending on the social context, such marginalization may be based on such categories as economics (the poor), gender (women), race (Black), and region (Latin America). Liberation theology has been carried out from all of these (and other) perspectives, seeking to give voice not simply to the concerns of church doctrine and eschatological salvation but especially to social change and salvation in the midst of this world. In addition to Scripture and tradition, some forms of liberation theology exhibit undercurrents of Marxist thought.

Gustavo Gutiérrez (1928–) is a Peruvian theologian of the Dominican order, and he is considered the father of liberation theology. In* A Theology of Liberation, *first published in Spanish, Gutiérrez writes that the goal of liberation is to construct a just and fraternal society in which persons can live in dignity and be the agents of their own destiny.

For the Latin American Church, it is becoming increasingly clearer that to be in the world without being of the world means concretely to be *in* the system without being of the system.[42] It is evident that only a break with the unjust order and a frank commitment to a new society can make the message of love which the Christian community bears credible to Latin Americans. These demands should lead the Church to a profound revision of its manner of preaching the Word and of living and celebrating its faith.

Closely connected with this problem is another very controversial question: Should *the Church put its social weight* behind social transformation in Latin America? Some are worried that it would be a mistake for the Church to attempt to achieve the necessary and urgent changes. The fear is that the Church will become linked to the future established order, albeit a more just one. There is also a fear that an effort in this direction will end in a noisy failure: the Latin American bishops are not all of one mind and do not have the necessary means at their disposal to orientate Christians as a whole toward social progress.

The relevance of these fears cannot be denied. There is indeed great risk. But the social influence of the Church is a fact. Not to exercise this influence in favor of the oppressed of Latin America is really to exercise it against them, and it is difficult to determine beforehand the consequences of this action. Not to speak is in fact to become another kind of Church of silence, silence in the face of the despoliation and exploitation of the weak by the powerful. On the other hand, would not the best way for the Church to break its links with the existing order—and in the process lose its ambiguous social prestige—be precisely to denounce the fundamental injustice upon which this order is based? Often the Church alone is in a position publicly to raise its voice and its protest. When some churches have attempted to do this, they have been harassed by the dominant groups and repressed by political power. In order to reflect on what action the Latin American Church should take and to act accordingly, it is necessary to consider its historical and social coordinates, its here and now.

42. See John 17:14-18.

To neglect doing this is to remain on an abstract and ahistorical theological level; or, perhaps more subtly, it is to remain on the level of a theology more concerned with avoiding past errors than with discovering the originality of the present situation and committing itself to tomorrow. . . .

What is the relationship between salvation and the process of human liberation throughout history? Or more precisely, what is the meaning of the struggle against an unjust society and the creation of a new humanity in the light of the Word? A response to these questions presupposes an attempt to define what is meant by salvation, a concept central to the Christian mystery. This is a complex and difficult task which leads to reflection on the meaning of the saving action of the Lord in history. The salvation of the whole man is centered upon Christ the Liberator. . . .

From this point of view the notion of salvation appears in a different light. Salvation is not something otherworldly, in regard to which the present life is merely a test. Salvation—the communion of human beings with God and among themselves—is something which embraces all human reality, transforms it, and leads it to its fullness in Christ. . . .

The approach we have been considering opens up for us—and this is of utmost importance—unforeseen vistas on the problem of sin. An unjust situation does not happen by chance; it is not something branded by a fatal destiny: there is human responsibility behind it. The prophets said it clearly and energetically and we are rediscovering their words now. This is the reason why the Medellín Conference refers to the state of things in Latin America as a "sinful situation," as a "rejection of the Lord."[43] This characterization, in all its breadth and depth, not only criticizes the individual abuses on the part of those who enjoy great power in this social order; it challenges all their practices, that is to say, it is a repudiation of the whole existing system—to which the Church itself belongs. . . .

The human person is destined to total communion with God and to the fullest fellowship with all other persons. "Dear friends, let us love one another, because love is from God. Everyone who loves is a child of God and knows God, but the unloving know nothing of God. For God is love" (1 John 4:7-8). This was Christ's revelation. To be saved is to reach the fullness of love; it is to enter into the circle of charity which unites the three Persons of the Trinity; it is to love as God loves. The way to this fullness of love can be no other than love itself, the way of participation in this charity, the way of accepting, explicitly or implicitly, to say with the Spirit: "Abba, Father" (Gal. 4:6). Acceptance is the foundation of all communion among human persons. To sin is to refuse to love, to reject communion and fellowship, to reject even now the very meaning of human existence. Matthew's text is demanding: "Anything you did not do for one of these, however humble, you did not do for me" (25:45). To abstain from serving is to refuse to love; to fail to act for another is as culpable as expressly refusing to do it. This same idea is found later in John: "The man who does not love is still in the realm of death" (1 John 3:14). The parable of the Good Samaritan ends with the famous inversion which Christ makes of the original question. They asked him, "Who is my neighbor?" and when everything seemed to point to the wounded man in the ditch on the side of the road, Christ asked, "Which of these three do you think was neighbor to the man who fell

43. The Conference of Latin American Bishops met in Medellín, Colombia, in 1968. Their discussions and documents were in some ways a precursor to Latin American liberation theology.

into the hands of the robbers?" (Luke 10:29, 36). The neighbor was the Samaritan who *approached* the wounded man and *made him his neighbor.* The neighbor, as has been said, is not the one whom I find in my path, but rather the one in whose path I place myself, the one whom I approach and actively seek. The other aspects of the Christian life become meaningful if they are animated by charity; otherwise, in Paul's words, they simply are empty actions (cf. 1 Cor. 13). This is why Matthew's text says we will be definitively judged by our love for others, by our capacity to create comradely conditions of life. From a prophetic viewpoint, the judgment ("crisis") will be based, according to Matthew, on the new ethic arising from this universal principle of love. . . .

Earlier in this book I said that awareness of the conflict going on in history does not mean acceptance of it and that the important thing is to struggle "for the establishment of peace and justice amid all humankind." The connection of peace with justice is an important theme in the Bible. Peace is promised along with the gift of the kingdom, and it requires the establishment of just social relationships. Drawing inspiration from some words of Paul VI, which it cites, Medellín begins its document on peace by saying: "'If development is the new name for peace,' Latin American underdevelopment, with its own characteristics in its different countries, is an unjust situation promoting tensions that conspire against peace" ("Peace," 1).

These tensions, which can develop into very sharp conflicts, are part of everyday life in Latin America. Moreover, they often place us in disconcerting situations in which theological reflection can advance only gropingly and in an exploratory way. But the trickiness of the subject does not justify an approach that forgets the universalist demands of Christian love and ecclesial communion. On the other hand, these demands must be shown to have a necessary connection with the concrete situations mentioned above if we are to give adequate and effective answers to the Christians who face them.

The gospel proclaims God's love for every human being and calls us to love as God loves. Yet recognition of the fact of class struggle means taking a position, opposing certain groups of persons, rejecting certain activities, and facing hostilities. For if we are convinced that peace indeed supposes the establishment of justice, we cannot remain passive or indifferent when the most basic human rights are at risk. That kind of behavior would not be ethical or Christian. Conversely, our active participation on the side of justice and in defense of the weakest members of society does not mean that we are encouraging conflict; it means rather that we are trying to eliminate its deepest root, which is the absence of love. . . .

[*A Theology of Liberation: History, Politics, and Salvation*, rev. ed., trans. Caridad Inda and John Eagleson (Maryknoll, NY: Orbis, 1988), 76, 83, 85, 102, 113, 159]

Selection 108: Elisabeth Schüssler Fiorenza, *In Memory of Her: A Feminist Theological Reconstruction of Christian Origins* (1983)

The work of Elisabeth Schüssler Fiorenza (1938–), professor at Harvard Divinity School, exemplifies a liberation approach from a feminist perspective. Unlike some other feminist theologians whose thought is only loosely tied to Christianity, she seeks to ground her theology in the Scripture and history of Christianity, though not without challenging traditional interpretations. In these excerpts, Schüssler Fiorenza articulates her approach to biblical interpretation and the goals of her method.

Chapter 1
Toward a Feminist Critical Hermeneutics

To discuss the relationship between biblical-historical interpretation and feminist reconstruction of women's history in biblical times is to enter an intellectual and emotional minefield. One has to trace and lay bare the contradictions and tensions between historical exegesis and systematic-theological tenets, the reactions and emotions elicited by the prospect of "historical-critical" exegesis of the Bible, the relationship between academic work and political-societal forces and conditions, between so-called value-neutral scientific investigation and "advocacy" scholarship. . . .

To raise this complex set of historical, theoretical, and theological questions from a feminist theological perspective is to expose oneself to double intellectual jeopardy. While women as a group share a common experience and while feminists are committed to the struggle for the liberation of women, the individual perception and interpretation of women's experience of oppression, as well as the concrete formulation of the values and goals for women's liberation, vary considerably. . . .

Models of Biblical Interpretation

The formulation of a feminist historical hermeneutics must not only trace the overall cultural shift from an androcentric to a feminist paradigm of reality construction and change, but must also discuss the theoretical models of biblical hermeneutics and their implications for the feminist cultural paradigm. Since the Bible as Holy Scripture is not only a historical book but also claims significance and authority for Christians today, theological scholarship has developed different theoretical approaches and models in order to do justice to this theoretical tension between the theological and historical claims of the Bible. The same theoretical tension is also given in a feminist historical reconstruction insofar as it is not antiquarian but committed to contemporary women and their struggle for liberation. It is necessary therefore to review the various theoretical models developed by biblical historical scholarship.

The first model, which I will call the *doctrinal approach,* understands the Bible in terms of divine revelation and canonical authority. However, it conceives of biblical revelation and authority in a-historical, dogmatic terms. In its most consistent forms it insists on the verbal inspiration and literal-historical inerrancy of the Bible. . . .[44]

The second model, that of *positivist historical exegesis,* was developed in confrontation with the dogmatic claims of Scripture and the doctrinal authority of the church. Its attack on the revelatory authority of Scripture is linked with an understanding of exegesis and historiography that is positivist, factual, objective, and value-free. . . .

Although historical-critical scholarship has moved away from such an objectivist-factual understanding of biblical texts, it still adheres to the dogma of value-neutral, detached interpretation. It often avoids articulating the implications and significance of its research because it does not want to be accused of pressing the biblical texts and "data" into a preestablished ideological mold. Although this scholarly detachment is historically understandable it is theoretically impossible.

That latter insight was developed by the third model, that of *dialogical-hermeneutical interpretation.* This model takes seriously the historical methods developed by the second model, while at the same time reflecting on the interaction between text and community, or text and interpreter. . . .

44. This approach is exemplified in the *Chicago Statement on Biblical Inerrancy* (Selection 106).

Hermeneutical discussion is concerned with establishing the meaning of biblical texts. Although the interpreter always approaches a historical text with specific contemporary experiences and questions, the scholar must attempt to become as free from preconceived understanding of the texts as possible, even though it is impossible to detach oneself completely from any preunderstanding. . . .

The fourth and last model of biblical interpretation is that of *liberation theology.* The various forms of liberation theology have challenged the so-called objectivity and value-neutrality of academic theology. The basic insight of all liberation theologies, including feminist theology, is the recognition that all theology, willingly or not, is by definition always engaged for or against the oppressed. Intellectual neutrality is not possible in a world of exploitation and oppression. . . .

At this point it becomes necessary to inquire after the commitment of academic historical, theological scholarship. After freeing itself from the doctrinal infringements of ecclesiastical authority, it is in danger of falling prey to the interest of academic institutions that justify the status quo of the dominant political power structures. . . .

The Woman's Bible

No one who is even remotely aware of the history of feminist biblical interpretation can deny that the scholarly discussion of "Women in the Bible" can be abstracted from its apologetic-political setting and function of legitimization. Whether the Bible is used in the trial of Anne Hutchinson (1637) or in the Vatican statement against the ordination of women (1977),[45] its function is the same, namely, the legitimization of societal and ecclesiastical patriarchy and of women's "divinely ordained place" in it. From the outset of the women's movement and even today, the Bible has played a key role in the argument against women's emancipation. . . .

Epilogue
Toward a Feminist Biblical Spirituality: The Ekklesia of Women

In the first part of the book I have argued that only in and through a critical evaluative process of feminist hermeneutics can Scripture be used as a resource in the liberation struggle of women and other "subordinated" people. The vision and praxis of our foresisters who heard the call to coequal discipleship and who acted in the power of the Spirit must be allowed to become a transformative power that can open up a feminist future for women in biblical religion. We have, therefore, moved from a reading of androcentric texts to the reconstruction of the history of women in early Christianity. . . .

The image and vision of the people of God, of my people, who are women, theologically sums up my own spiritual feminist experiences and that of my sisters who have celebrated our bonding in sisterhood for empowerment and reclaimed our baptismal call to the discipleship of equals. This image and self-understanding allows us to build a feminist movement not on the fringes of church but as the central embodiment and incarnation of the vision of church that lives in solidarity with the oppressed and the impoverished, the majority of whom are women and children dependent on women.

Ekklesia—the term for church in the New Testament—is not so much a religious as a civil-political concept. It means the actual assembly of free citizens gathering for deciding

45. Anne Hutchinson (1591–1643) was a Puritan banished from Massachusetts Bay Colony for her views on grace. The Vatican statement is no doubt *Inter insigniores* from 1976.

their own spiritual-political affairs. Since women in a patriarchal church cannot decide their own theological-religious affairs and that of their own people—women—the *ekklesia* of women is as much a future hope as it is a reality today. . . .

It is usually assumed that spirituality has something to do with the life of the "soul," prayer life and worship, meditation and mystical union, with the "waiting" for God's will to come to pass and the religious experience of the divine. In this understanding spirituality concentrates above all on prayer and meditation, on "spiritual" direction and Christ's indwelling in the soul, on ascetic and religious exercises as the precondition for progress on the spiritual journey of the soul from one level to another. In a similar fashion feminist spirituality can be occupied with meditation and incantations, spells and incense, womb chant and candle gazing, feminine symbols for the divine and trance induction. Such an understanding of spirituality, of religious rituals and exercises, is found in all religions and not limited to Christianity. Therefore, it does not capture the specific new vision of Jesus and the movement initiated by him.

The gospel is not a matter of the individual soul; it is the communal proclamation of the life-giving power of Spirit-Sophia[46] and of God's vision of an alternative community and world. The experience of the Spirit's creative power releases us from the life-destroying powers of sin and sets us free to choose an alternative life for ourselves and for each other. . . .

Like Jesus' own ministry, the ministry of the community called forth by Jesus, the messenger of divine wisdom, is not an end in itself. In the power of the Spirit the disciples are sent to do what he did: to feed the hungry, heal the sick, liberate the oppressed, and to announce the inbreaking of God's new world and humanity here and now. In every generation Divine Wisdom commissions prophets—women and men—and makes them friends and children of God. To embrace the gospel means to enter into a movement, to become a member of God's people who are on the road that stretches from Christ's death to Her return in glory. . . .

In the Greek Old Testament *ekklesia* means the "assembly of the people of Israel before God." In the New Testament *ekklesia* comes through the agency of the Spirit to visible, tangible expression in and through the gathering of God's people around the table, eating together a meal, breaking the bread, and sharing the cup in memory of Christ's passion and resurrection. *Christian* spirituality means eating together, sharing together, drinking together, talking with each other, receiving each other, experiencing God s presence through each other, and, in doing so, proclaiming the gospel as God's alternative vision for everyone, especially for those who are poor, outcast, and battered. . . .

A feminist Christian spirituality, therefore, calls us to gather together the *ekklesia of women* who, in the angry power of the Spirit, are sent forth to feed, heal, and liberate our own people who are women. It unmasks and sets us free from the structural sin and alienation of sexism and propels us to become children and spokeswomen of God. It rejects the idolatrous worship of maleness and articulates the divine image in female human existence and language. . . .

[***In Memory of Her: A Feminist Theological Reconstruction of Christian Origins*** **(New York: Crossroad, 1983), 3–7, 343–46]**

46. Sophia here refers to (divine) Wisdom personified.

D. Pluralism and Ecumenism

Selection 109: Karl Rahner, "Christianity and the Non-Christian Religions" (1966)

Karl Rahner (1904–1984) was a Jesuit and German theologian who taught at Innsbruck, Munich, and Münster. He was an expert advisor at the Second Vatican Council and was one of the most influential Roman Catholic theologians of the twentieth century. He is known for his contributions to the revival of the doctrine of the Trinity in Western theology.

Rahner is also well known for his work on the issue of religious diversity, an issue that became more prominent for Roman Catholics in the wake of Vatican II's greater openness to dialogue with other faiths. Indeed, as the late modern world has become smaller and the world's cultures and religions less isolated from one another, no Christian can afford to ignore the questions raised by such interaction. When it comes to the question of salvation for those who have never heard the gospel, in this essay Rahner opts for inclusivism and discusses the category of "anonymous Christians."

"Open Catholicism" involves two things. It signifies the fact that the Catholic Church is opposed by historical forces which she herself cannot disregard as if they were purely "worldly" forces and a matter of indifference to her but which, on the contrary, although they do not stand in a positive relationship of peace and mutual recognition to the Church, do have a significance for her. "Open Catholicism" means also the task of becoming related to these forces in order to understand their existence (since this cannot be simply acknowledged), in order to bear with and overcome the annoyance of their opposition and in order to form the Church in such a way that she will be able to overcome as much of this pluralism as should not exist, by understanding herself as the higher unity of this opposition. "Open Catholicism" means therefore a certain attitude towards the present-day pluralism of powers with different outlooks on the world. We do not, of course, refer to pluralism merely as a fact which one simply acknowledges without explaining it. Pluralism is meant here as a fact which ought to be thought about and one which, without denying that—in part at least—it should not exist at all, should be incorporated once more from a more elevated viewpoint into the totality and unity of the Christian understanding of human existence. For Christianity, one of the gravest elements of this pluralism in which we live and with which we must come to terms, and indeed the element most difficult to incorporate, is the pluralism of religions. We do not refer by this to the pluralism of Christian denominations. This pluralism too is a fact, and a challenge and task for Christians. But we are not concerned with it here. . . .

1st Thesis: We must begin with the thesis which follows, because it certainly represents the basis in the Christian faith of the theological understanding of other religions. This thesis states that Christianity understands itself as the absolute religion, intended for all men, which cannot recognize any other religion beside itself as of equal right. This proposition is self-evident and basic for Christianity's understanding of itself. There is no need here to prove it or to develop its meaning. . . .

2nd Thesis: Until the moment when the Gospel really enters into the historical situation of an individual, a non-Christian religion (even outside the Mosaic religion) does not merely contain elements of a natural knowledge of

God, elements, moreover, mixed up with human depravity which is the result of original sin and later aberrations. It contains also supernatural elements arising out of the grace which is given to men as a gratuitous gift on account of Christ. For this reason a non-Christian religion can be recognized as a *lawful* religion (although only in different degrees) without thereby denying the error and depravity contained in it. . . .

The thesis itself is divided into two parts. It means first of all that it is *a priori* quite possible to suppose that there are supernatural, grace-filled elements in non-Christian religions. . . .

Our second thesis goes even further than this, however, and states in its second part that, from what has been said, the actual religions of "pre-Christian" humanity too must not be regarded as simply illegitimate from the very start, but must be seen as quite capable of having a positive significance. This statement must naturally be taken in a very different sense which we cannot examine here for the various particular religions. This means that the different religions will be able to lay claim to being lawful religions only in very different senses and to very different degrees. But precisely this variability is not at all excluded by the notion of a "lawful religion," as we will have to show in a moment. A lawful religion means here an institutional religion whose "use" by man at a certain period can be regarded on the whole as a positive means of gaining the right relationship to God and thus for the attaining of salvation, a means which is therefore positively included in God's plan of salvation. . . .

3rd Thesis: If the second thesis is correct, then Christianity does not simply confront the member of an extra-Christian religion as a mere non-Christian but as someone who can and must already be regarded in this or that respect as an anonymous Christian. It would be wrong to regard the pagan as someone who has not yet been touched in any way by God's grace and truth. . . .

4th Thesis: It is possibly too much to hope, on the one hand, that the religious pluralism which exists in the concrete situation of Christians will disappear in the foreseeable future. On the other hand, it is nevertheless absolutely permissible for the Christian himself to interpret this non-Christianity as Christianity of an anonymous kind which he does always still go out to meet as a missionary, seeing it as a world which is to be brought to the explicit consciousness of what already belongs to it as a divine offer or already pertains to it also over and above this as a divine gift of grace accepted unreflectedly and implicitly.[47] If both these statements are true, then the Church will not so much regard herself today as the exclusive community of those who have a claim to salvation but rather as the historically tangible vanguard and the historically and socially constituted explicit expression of what the Christian hopes is present as a hidden reality even outside the visible Church.

To begin with, however much we must always work, suffer and pray anew and indefatigably for the unification of the whole human race, in the one Church of Christ, we must nevertheless expect, for theological reasons and not merely by reason of a profane historical analysis, that the religious pluralism existing in the world and in our own historical sphere of existence will not disappear in the foreseeable future. We know from the gospel that the opposition to Christ and to the Church will not disappear until the end of time. If anything, we must even be prepared for a heightening of this antagonism to Christian existence. If, however, this opposition to the Church cannot confine

47. It is a genuine challenge for Rahner's viewpoint of anonymous Christianity to articulate the necessity of missions, which he attempts here.

itself merely to the purely private sphere of the individual but must also be of a public, historical character, and if this opposition is said to be present in a history which today, in contrast to previous ages, possesses a worldwide unity, then the continuing opposition to the Church can no longer exist merely locally and outside a certain limited sector of history such as that of the West. It must be found in our vicinity and everywhere else. And this is part of what the Christian must expect and must learn to endure. The Church, which is at the same time the homogeneous characterization of an in itself homogeneous culture (i.e. the medieval Church), will no longer exist if history can no longer find any way to escape from or go back on the period of its planetary unity. In a unified world history in which everything enters into the life of everyone, the "necessary" public opposition to Christianity is a factor in the existential sphere of all Christianity. If this Christianity, thus always faced with opposition and unable to expect seriously that this will ever cease, nevertheless believes in God's universal salvific will—in other words, believes that God can be victorious by his secret grace even where the Church does not win the victory but is contradicted—then this Church cannot feel herself to be just *one* dialectic moment in the whole of history but has already overcome this opposition by her faith, hope and charity. In other words, the others who oppose her are merely those who have not yet recognized what they nevertheless really already are (or can be) even when, on the surface of existence, they are in opposition; they are already anonymous Christians, and the Church is not the communion of those who possess God's grace as opposed to those who lack it, but is the communion of those who can explicitly confess what they *and* the others hope to be.[48] Non-Christians may think it presumption for the Christian to judge everything which is sound or restored (by being sanctified) to be the fruit in every man of the grace of his Christ, and to interpret it as anonymous Christianity; they may think it presumption for the Christian to regard the non-Christian as a Christian who has not yet come to himself reflectively. But the Christian cannot renounce this "presumption" which is really the source of the greatest humility both for himself and for the Church. For it is a profound admission of the fact that God is greater than man and the Church. The Church will go out to meet the non-Christian of tomorrow with the attitude expressed by St Paul when he said: What therefore you do not know and yet worship (and yet *worship*!) that I proclaim to you (Acts 17:23). On such a basis one can be tolerant, humble and yet firm towards all non-Christian religions.

[*Christianity and Other Religions*, ed. John Hick and Brian Hebblethwaite (Philadelphia: Fortress Press, 1980), 52–53, 56, 60–61, 66–67, 75, 77–79]

Selection 110: John Hick, *Problems of Religious Pluralism* (1985)

John Hick (1922–2012) was a British philosopher of religion who taught at the University of Birmingham and at Claremont Graduate University. His contributions to theology include **Evil and the God of Love** ***(1966), a defense of an "Irenaean" approach to theodicy in contrast to an Augustinian approach. He has also argued for a metaphorical view of the incarnation that relativizes the traditional understanding of the uniqueness of the Christ event. In this essay, Hick outlines three major options for thinking about religious diversity, and he makes his case for "pluralism."***

48. This perspective is somewhat analogous to the Muslim concept of "reversion" rather than conversion to Islam.

This way of seeing the religious life of humanity, as organised in a number of communities based upon rival sets of religious beliefs, leads to the posing of questions about religion in a certain way. For the beliefs which a religion professes are beliefs about God, or the Ultimate, and as such they define a way of human salvation or liberation and are accordingly a matter of spiritual life and death. Looking at the religions of the world, then, in the plural we are presented with competing claims to possess the saving truth. For each community believes that its own gospel is true and that other gospels are false in so far as they differ from it. Each believes that the way of salvation to which it witnesses is the authentic way, the only sure path to eternal blessedness. And so the proper question in face of this plurality of claims is, which is the true religion? . . .

Both because of the fullness of this discussion within Christianity, and because I am myself a Christian and am concerned with the problem from a Christian point of view, I propose to describe the main options in Christian terms. They are three in number.

The first, which we may call "exclusivism," relates salvation/liberation exclusively to one particular tradition, so that it is an article of faith that salvation is restricted to this one group, the rest of mankind being either left out of account or explicitly excluded from the sphere of salvation. The most emphatic and influential expression of such a faith occurred in the Catholic dogma *Extra ecclesiam nulla salus* (outside the Church, no salvation)[49] and the corresponding assumption of the nineteenth-century Protestant missionary movement: outside Christianity, no salvation. . . .

Christian exclusivism has now largely faded out from the "mainline" churches, but is still powerful in many of the "marginal" fundamentalistic sects; and it should be added that the "margins" of Christianity are probably more extensive today than ever before.

However, we may now turn to a second Christian answer to our question, which can be labelled "inclusivism." This can be expressed in terms either of a juridical or of a transformation-of-human-existence conception of salvation. In the former terms it is the view that God's forgiveness and acceptance of humanity have been made possible by Christ's death, but that the benefits of this sacrifice are not confined to those who respond to it with an explicit act of faith. The juridical transaction of Christ's atonement covered *all* human sin, so that all human beings are now open to God's mercy, even though they may never have heard of Jesus Christ and why he died on the cross of Calvary. I take it that it is this form of inclusivism that the present Pope was endorsing in his first encyclical when he said that "man—every man without any exception whatever—has been redeemed by Christ, and because with man—with each man without any exception whatever—Christ is in a way united, even when man is unaware of it." . . .

How are they [forms of inclusivism] to be combined with the traditional *Extra ecclesiam* dogma? The best known attempt is that of Karl Rahner, with his concept of the "anonymous Christian."[50] Those who do not have an explicit Christian faith but who nevertheless seek, consciously or unconsciously, to do God's will can be regarded as, so to speak, honorary Christians—and this even though they do not so regard themselves and even though they may insist that they are not Christians but Muslims, Jews, Hindus, or whatever. Rahner's is a brave attempt to attain an inclusivist position which is in principle universal but which does not thereby renounce the old exclusivist dogma.

49. This saying is credited to Cyprian of Carthage.

50. See Selection 109.

But the question is whether in this new context the old dogma has not been so emptied of content as no longer to be worth affirming. When salvation is acknowledged to be taking place without any connection with the Christian Church or Gospel, in people who are living on the basis of quite other faiths, is it not a somewhat empty gesture to insist upon affixing a Christian label to them? Further, having thus labelled them, why persist in the aim of gathering all humankind into the Christian Church? Once it is accepted that salvation does not depend upon this, the conversion of the people of the other great world faiths to Christianity hardly seems the best way of spending one's energies.

The third possible answer to the question of the relation between salvation/liberation and the cumulative religious traditions can best be called pluralism. As a Christian position this can be seen as an acceptance of the further conclusion to which inclusivism points. If we accept that salvation/liberation is taking place within all the great religious traditions, why not frankly acknowledge that there is a plurality of saving human responses to the ultimate divine Reality? Pluralism, then, is the view that the transformation of human existence from self-centredness to Reality-centredness is taking place in different ways within the contexts of all the great religious traditions. There is not merely one way but a plurality of ways of salvation or liberation. In Christian theological terms, there is a plurality of divine revelations, making possible a plurality of forms of saving human response.

What however makes it difficult for Christians to move from inclusivism to pluralism, holding the majority of Christian theologians today in the inclusivist position despite its evident logical instability, is of course the traditional doctrine of the Incarnation, together with its protective envelope, the doctrine of the Trinity. For in its orthodox form, as classically expressed at the Councils of Nicaea and Chalcedon, the incarnational doctrine claims that Jesus was God incarnate, the Second Person of the Triune God living a human life. It is integral to this faith that there has been (and will be) no other divine incarnation. This makes Christianity unique in that it, alone among the religions of the world, was founded by God in person. Such a uniqueness would seem to demand Christian exclusivism—for must God not want all human beings to enter the way of salvation which he has provided for them? However, since such exclusivism seems so unrealistic in the light of our knowledge of the wider religious life of mankind, many theologians have moved to some form of inclusivism, but now feel unable to go further and follow the argument to its conclusion in the frank acceptance of pluralism. The break with traditional missionary attitudes and long-established ecclesiastical and liturgical language would, for many, be so great as to be prohibitive. . . .

There is however the possibility of an acceptable Christian route to religious pluralism in work which has already been done, and which is being done, in the field of Christology with motivations quite other than to facilitate pluralism, and on grounds which are internal to the intellectual development of Christianity. For there is a decisive watershed between what might be called all-or-nothing Christologies and degree Christologies. The all-or-nothing principle is classically expressed in the Chalcedonian Definition, according to which Christ is "to be acknowledged in Two Natures," "Consubstantial with the Father according to his Deity, Consubstantial with us according to his Humanity."[51]. . . Degree Christologies, on the

51. These are quotations from the definition codified at the Council of Chalcedon (451).

other hand, apply the term "incarnation" to the activity of God's Spirit or of God's grace in human lives, so that the divine will is done on earth. . . .

These modern degree Christologies were not in fact for the most part developed in order to facilitate a Christian acceptance of religious pluralism. They were developed as alternatives to the old substance Christology, in which so many difficulties, both historical and philosophical, had become apparent. They claim to be compatible with the teachings of Jesus and of the very early Church, and to avoid the intractable problem, generated by a substance Christology, of the relation between Jesus's two natures. But, as an unintended consequence, degree Christologies open up the possibility of seeing God's activity in Jesus as being of the same kind as God's activity in other great human mediators of the divine. . . .

I think, then, that a path exists along which Christians can, if they feel so drawn, move to an acceptance of religious pluralism. Stated philosophically such a pluralism is the view that the great world faiths embody different perceptions and conceptions of, and correspondingly different responses to, the Real or the Ultimate from within the major variant cultural ways of being human; and that within each of them the transformation of human existence from self-centredness to Reality-centredness is manifestly taking place—and taking place, so far as human observation can tell, to much the same extent. Thus the great religious traditions are to be regarded as alternative soteriological "spaces" within which, or "ways" along which, men and women can find salvation/liberation/enlightenment/fulfilment.

But how can such a view be arrived at? Are we not proposing a picture reminiscent of the ancient allegory of the blind men and the elephant, in which each runs his hands over a different part of the animal, and identifies it differently, a leg as a tree, the trunk as a snake, the tail as a rope, and so on? Clearly, in the story the situation is being described from the point of view of someone who can observe both elephant and blind men. But where is the vantage-point from which one can observe both the divine Reality and the different limited human standpoints from which that Reality is being variously perceived? The advocate of the pluralist understanding cannot pretend to any such cosmic vision. How then does he profess to know that the situation is indeed as he depicts it? The answer is that he does not profess to *know* this, if by knowledge we mean infallible cognition. Nor indeed can anyone else properly claim to have knowledge, in this sense, of either the exclusivist or the inclusivist picture. All of them are, strictly speaking, hypotheses. The pluralist hypothesis is arrived at inductively. One starts from the fact that many human beings experience life in relation to a limitlessly greater transcendent Reality—whether the direction of transcendence be beyond our present existence or within its hidden depths. . . . In other words, besides one's own religion, sustained by its distinctive form of religious experience, there are also other religions, through each of which flows the life blood of a different form of religious experience. . . .

Does this epistemological pattern of the schematisation of a basic religious concept into a range of particular correlates of religious experience apply also to the non-theistic traditions? I suggest that it does. Here the general concept, the Absolute, is schematised in actual religious experience to form the range of divine *impersonae*—Brahman, the Dharma, the Tao, *nirvana, sunyata,* and so on—which are experienced within the Eastern traditions. The structure of these *impersonae* is however importantly different from that of the *personae.* A divine *persona* is concrete, implicitly finite, sometimes visualisable and even capable of being pictured. A divine *impersona,* on the other hand, is not a "thing" in contrast to a person. It is the infinite being-consciousness-bliss (*saccidananda*) of Brahman; or the beginningless and endless process of cosmic change *(pratitya samutpada)* of Buddhist teaching; or again the ineffable "further shore" of *nirvana,* or the eternal Buddha-nature (*dharmakaya*); or the ultimate Emptiness *(sunyata)* which is also the fullness or suchness of the world; or the eternal principle of the Tao. It is thus not so much an entity as a field of spiritual force, or the ultimate reality of everything, that which gives final meaning and joy. . . . In other words the Real is experienced not *an sich*,[52] but in terms of the various non-personal images or concepts that have been generated at the interface between the Real and different patterns of human consciousness. . . .

[***Problems of Religious Pluralism*** **(London: Macmillan, 1985), 28, 31–38, 42–44**]

Selection 111: Lesslie Newbigin, *The Gospel in a Pluralist Society* (1989)

James Edward Lesslie Newbigin (1909–1998) was a British minister, theologian, and missionary to India, and one of the leading missiologists of the twentieth century. In this book and other writings, he articulates his vision of the uniqueness of the Christian gospel in the midst of a pluralistic world.

52. The "Real an sich," or reality in itself, corresponds to the Kantian noumenal realm that is unknown apart from phenomena. Hick claims that this ultimate reality is unknown and unknowable in itself but is experienced in both personal manifestations (*personae*), such as distinct deities, and nonpersonal manifestations (*impersonae*), such as the idea of the Absolute.

Chapter 10: The Logic of Mission

. . . The mission of the Church is to be understood, can only be rightly understood, in terms of the trinitarian model. It is the Father who holds all things in his hand, whose providence upholds all things, whose tender mercies are over all his works, where he is acknowledged and where he is denied, and who has never left himself without witness to the heart and conscience and reason of any human being. In the incarnation of the Son he has made known his nature and purpose fully and completely, for in Jesus "all the fullness of God was pleased to dwell" (Col. 1:19). But this presence was a veiled presence in order that there might be the possibility of repentance and freely given faith. In the Church the mission of Jesus is continued in the same veiled form. It is continued through the presence and active working of the Holy Spirit, who is the presence of the reign of God in foretaste. . . .

It is impossible to stress too strongly that the beginning of mission is not an action of ours, but the presence of a new reality, the presence of the Spirit of God in power. The whole New Testament bears witness to this, and so does the missionary experience of the Church through the ages. . . . The world's questions are not the questions which lead to life. What really needs to be said is that where the Church is faithful to its Lord, there the powers of the kingdom are present and people begin to ask the question to which the gospel is the answer. And that, I suppose, is why the letters of St. Paul contain so many exhortations to faithfulness but no exhortations to be active in mission. . . .

So the logic of mission is this: the true meaning of the human story has been disclosed. Because it is the truth, it must be shared universally. It cannot be private opinion. When we share it with all peoples, we give them the opportunity to know the truth about themselves, to know who they are because they can know the true story of which their lives are a part. . . .

Chapter 20: Confidence in the Gospel

Churches, at least in Britain, have been eager to avoid the charge of arrogance. They have been eloquent in their efforts to distance themselves from what is now judged to have been the arrogance of missionaries who talked of the evangelization of the world in their generation. They are eager to repent of the arrogance of their predecessors. In reaction to this arrogance, two moods are widely discernible. One is timidity. This is, I think, the most obvious feature of much contemporary English theology. Most theology in this country is carried on within the universities whose curricula are governed by the assumptions of "modernity." It is difficult for theologians to step outside these boundaries. Literary, historical, and phenomenological studies in religious history and practice can be carried on without transgressing these boundaries. "Religious studies" can flourish, since they are—in general—descriptive rather than normative. They do not pass judgment on the truth or otherwise of the religious beliefs studied, much less on what is taught as truth in other faculties. But Christian dogmatics, the teaching as truth of beliefs which run counter to the accepted assumptions of our culture, is much more difficult. Academic theology tends to live within the frontiers which the reigning "plausibility structure" dictates. The resulting tension between academic theology and the beliefs of ordinary churchgoers is a familiar matter of comment.

The other mood is one of anxiety. Christianity is perceived to be a good cause which is in danger of collapsing through lack of support. Or—in a quite different manifestation of the same fundamental attitude—there is a strident summons to more energetic efforts in evangelism and social action. I do not mean by speaking in this way that it is not very important for Christians to be active in both evangelism and social action. But I do sense an underlying Pelagianism which lays too much stress on our own activities and is too little controlled by the sense of the greatness and majesty and sufficiency of God. I am saying that there can be a kind of Christian activity which only thinly masks a lack of confidence in the sufficiency of God.

I want to suggest the word "confidence" as the one which designates the proper attitude. In a pluralist society, any confident affirmation of the truth is met by the response, "Why should I believe this rather than that?" Every statement of ultimate belief is liable to be met by this criticism, and—of course—if it is indeed an ultimate belief then it cannot be validated by something more ultimate. Our ultimate commitments are (as I have argued in an earlier chapter) always circular in structure. Having been brought (not by our own action but by the action of God) to the point of believing in Jesus as Lord and Savior, we seek to understand and cope with every kind of experience and every evidence of truth in the light of this faith. We are constantly called upon to rethink our faith in the light of these new experiences and evidences. We are prepared to recognize (as every human being has to recognize) that there are areas of mystery and that there are puzzles which are not solved for a long time. But we expect to find, and we do find, that the initial faith is confirmed, strengthened, and enlarged as we go on through life. And if, as always happens in a pluralist society, we are asked: "But why start with Jesus? Why not start somewhere else?" we have to answer that no rational thought is possible except by starting with something which is already given in some human tradition of rational thought and discourse. Our immediate answer may well be, "Why not?" For the ultimate answer we have to wait for the end of all things. That expectant waiting is part of what it is to live a full human life.

I therefore believe that a Christian must welcome some measure of plurality but reject pluralism. We can and must welcome a plural society because it provides us with a wider range of experience and a wider diversity of human responses to experience, and therefore richer opportunities for testing the sufficiency of our faith than are available in a monochrome society. As we confess Jesus as Lord in a plural society, and as the Church grows through the coming of people from many different cultural and religious traditions to faith in Christ, we are enabled to learn more of the length and breadth and height and depth of the love of God (Eph. 3:14-19) than we can in a monochrome society. But we must reject the ideology of pluralism. We must reject the invitation to live in a society where everything is subjective and relative, a society which has abandoned the belief that truth can be known and has settled for a purely subjective view of truth—"truth for you" but not truth for all. For one thing, I doubt whether such a society can long sustain its integrity in the face of the claims of those who have a firm commitment to some vision of truth. As I write, the press is full of the cries of outrage from Western liberal writers and critics in face of the Muslim reaction to Salman Rushdie's book *The Satanic Verses*.[53] But it is doubtful whether these cries have behind them anything that can withstand the determined onslaught of those who hold firm beliefs about the truth. Freedom to think and say what you like will not provide the resources for a resolute grappling with false beliefs. The demand for freedom of thought and expression must itself rest on some firmly held belief about the origin, nature, and destiny of human life. If it has no such foundation it will prove powerless in the face of those who have firm beliefs about the truth.

In a pluralist society there is always a temptation to judge the importance of any statement of the truth by the number of people who believe it. Truth, for practical purposes, is what most people believe. Christians can fall into this trap. It may well be that for some decades, while churches grow rapidly in other parts of the world, Christians in Europe may continue to be a small and even shrinking minority. If this should be so, it must be seen as an example of that pruning which is promised to the Church in order that it may bear more fruit (John 15:1ff.). When that happens it is painful. But Jesus assures us, "My Father is the gardener." He knows what he is doing, and we can trust him. Such experience is a summons to self-searching, to repentance, and to fresh commitment. It is not an occasion for anxiety. God is faithful, and he will complete what he has begun.

[*The Gospel in a Pluralist Society* (Grand Rapids, MI: Eerdmans, 1989), 118–19, 125–26, 242–44]

Selection 112: *Baptism, Eucharist and Ministry* (1982)

The World Council of Churches (WCC) is a group dedicated to the unity of all Christians. This ecumenical body formed at a meeting in Amsterdam in 1948 and included 147 Protestant churches; by 2012, there were 345 member churches. WCC's Constitution opens with the following "basis," revised in 1961: "The World Council of Churches is

53. The "Muslim reaction" consisted of public book burnings, condemnation of Rushdie, and the leader of Iran calling for Rushdie's death and placing a bounty on his head.

a fellowship of churches which confess the Lord Jesus Christ as God and Savior according to the Scriptures and therefore seek to fulfill together their common calling to the glory of the one God, Father, Son, and Holy Spirit."

Baptism, Eucharist and Ministry *was adopted by the Faith and Order Commission of the World Council at its plenary meeting in Lima, Peru, in 1982, and is the most widely distributed and studied document of the WCC. The document provides succinct description, analysis, and evaluation of—and commentary on—the various interpretations and practices of baptism, eucharist, and ordained ministry. It thus models ecumenical dialogue on these historically divisive issues of ecclesiology.*

Baptism
II. The Meaning of Baptism

C. The Gift of the Spirit

5. The Holy Spirit is at work in the lives of people before, in and after their baptism. It is the same Spirit who revealed Jesus as the Son (Mark 1:10–11) and who empowered and united the disciples at Pentecost (Acts 2). God bestows upon all baptized persons the anointing and the promise of the Holy Spirit, marks them with a seal and implants in their hearts the first instalment of their inheritance as sons and daughters of God. The Holy Spirit nurtures the life of faith in their hearts until the final deliverance when they will enter into its full possession, to the praise of the glory of God (II Cor. 1:21-22; Eph. 1:13-14).

D. Incorporation into the Body of Christ

6. Administered in obedience to our Lord, baptism is a sign and seal of our common discipleship. Through baptism, Christians are brought into union with Christ, with each other and with the Church of every time and place. Our common baptism, which unites us to Christ in faith, is thus a basic bond of unity. . . .[54]

Commentary: *The inability of the churches mutually to recognize their various practices of baptism as sharing in the one baptism, and their actual dividedness in spite of mutual baptismal recognition, have given dramatic visibility to the broken witness of the Church. . . . The need to recover baptismal unity is at the heart of the ecumenical task as it is central for the realization of genuine partnership within the Christian communities. . . .*

III. Baptism and Faith

8. Baptism is both God's gift and our human response to that gift. It looks towards a growth into the measure of the stature of the fullness of Christ (Eph. 4:13). The necessity of faith for the reception of the salvation embodied and set forth in baptism is acknowledged by all churches. Personal commitment is necessary for responsible membership in the body of Christ. . . .[55]

IV. Baptismal Practice

A. Baptism of Believers and Infants

11. While the possibility that infant baptism was also practised in the apostolic age cannot be excluded, baptism upon personal profession of faith is the most clearly attested pattern in the New Testament documents. . . .

12. Both the baptism of believers and the baptism of infants take place in the Church as the community of faith. When one who can answer for himself or herself is baptized, a personal confession of faith will be an integral part of the baptismal service. When an infant is

54. See Eph. 4:3-6.

55. The intimate connection between baptism and faith, exhibited in this brief excerpt, is affirmed throughout this section.

baptized, the personal response will be offered at a later moment in life. In both cases, the baptized person will have to grow in the understanding of faith. . . .

13. Baptism is an unrepeatable act. Any practice which might be interpreted as "re-baptism" must be avoided.

Commentary: *Churches which have insisted on a particular form of baptism or which have had serious questions about the authenticity of other churches' sacraments and ministries have at times required persons coming from other church traditions to be baptized before being received into full communicant membership. As the churches come to fuller mutual understanding and acceptance of one another and enter into closer relationships in witness and service, they will want to refrain from any practice which might call into question the sacramental integrity of other churches or which might diminish the unrepeatability of the sacrament of baptism.*

B. Baptism—Chrismation—Confirmation

14. In God's work of salvation, the paschal mystery of Christ's death and resurrection is inseparably linked with the pentecostal gift of the Holy Spirit. Similarly, participation in Christ's death and resurrection is inseparably linked with the receiving of the Spirit. Baptism in its full meaning signifies and effects both.

Christians differ in their understanding as to where the sign of the gift of the Spirit is to be found. Different actions have become associated with the giving of the Spirit. For some it is the water rite itself. For others, it is the anointing with chrism and/or the imposition of hands, which many churches call confirmation. For still others it is all three, as they see the Spirit operative throughout the rite. All agree that Christian baptism is in water and the Holy Spirit.

Commentary: *(a) Within some traditions it is explained that as baptism conforms us to Christ crucified, buried and risen, so through chrismation Christians receive the gift of the pentecostal Spirit from the anointed Son.*

(b) If baptism, as incorporation into the body of Christ, points by its very nature to the eucharistic sharing of Christ's body and blood, the question arises as to how a further and separate rite can be interposed between baptism and admission to communion. Those churches which baptize children but refuse them a share in the eucharist before such a rite may wish to ponder whether they have fully appreciated and accepted the consequences of baptism.

(c) Baptism needs to be constantly reaffirmed. The most obvious form of such reaffirmation is the celebration of the eucharist. . . .

C. Towards Mutual Recognition of Baptism

16. In order to overcome their differences, believer baptists and those who practice infant baptism should reconsider certain aspects of their practices. The first may seek to express more visibly the fact that children are placed under the protection of God's grace. The latter must guard themselves against the practice of apparently indiscriminate baptism and take more seriously their responsibility for the nurture of baptized children to mature commitment to Christ.

V. The Celebration of Baptism

18. In the celebration of baptism the symbolic dimension of water should be taken seriously and not minimalized. The act of immersion can vividly express the reality that in baptism the Christian participates in the death, burial and resurrection of Christ.[56]

56. See Rom. 6:3-4; Col. 2:12.

20. Within any comprehensive order of baptism at least the following elements should find a place: the proclamation of the scriptures referring to baptism; an invocation of the Holy Spirit; a renunciation of evil; a profession of faith in Christ and the Holy Trinity; the use of water; a declaration that the persons baptized have acquired a new identity as sons and daughters of God, and as members of the Church, called to be witnesses of the Gospel. Some churches consider that Christian initiation is not complete without the sealing of the baptized with the gift of the Holy Spirit and participation in holy communion.

21. It is appropriate to explain in the context of the baptismal service the meaning of baptism as it appears from scriptures (i.e. the participation in Christ's death and resurrection, conversion, pardoning and cleansing, gift of the Spirit, incorporation into the body of Christ and sign of the Kingdom). . . .

23. Since baptism is intimately connected with the corporate life and worship of the Church, it should normally be administered during public worship, so that the members of the congregation may be reminded of their own baptism and may welcome into their fellowship those who are baptized and whom they are committed to nurture in the Christian faith. The sacrament is appropriate to great festival occasions such as Easter, Pentecost and Epiphany, as was the practice in the early Church.

Eucharist
II. The Meaning of the Eucharist

A. The Eucharist as Thanksgiving to the Father

3. The eucharist, which always includes both word and sacrament, is a proclamation and a celebration of the work of God. It is the great thanksgiving to the Father for everything accomplished in creation, redemption and sanctification, for everything accomplished by God now in the Church and in the world in spite of the sins of human beings, for everything that God will accomplish in bringing the Kingdom to fulfilment. . . .

B. The Eucharist as Anamnesis or Memorial of Christ

6. Christ himself with all that he has accomplished for us and for all creation (in his incarnation, servant-hood, ministry, teaching, suffering, sacrifice, resurrection, ascension and sending of the Spirit) is present in this *anamnesis*,[57] granting us communion with himself. The eucharist is also the foretaste of his *parousia*[58] and of the final kingdom.

7. The *anamnesis* in which Christ acts through the joyful celebration of his Church is thus both representation and anticipation. It is not only a calling to mind of what is past and of its significance.

8. Representation and anticipation are expressed in thanksgiving and intercession. The Church, gratefully recalling God's mighty acts of redemption, beseeches God to give the benefits of these acts to every human being. . . .

Commentary: *It is in the light of the significance of the eucharist as intercession that references to the eucharist in Catholic theology as "propitiatory sacrifice" may be understood. The understanding is that there is only one expiation, that of the unique sacrifice of the cross, made actual in the eucharist and presented before the Father in the intercession of Christ and of the Church for all humanity.*

12. Since the *anamnesis* of Christ is the very content of the preached Word as it is of the eucharistic meal, each reinforces the other. The

57. That is, "remembrance."

58. That is, "presence" or "coming."

celebration of the eucharist properly includes the proclamation of the Word. . . .

C. The Eucharist as Invocation of the Spirit

15. It is in virtue of the living word of Christ and by the power of the Holy Spirit that the bread and wine become the sacramental signs of Christ's body and blood. They remain so for the purpose of communion. . . .

D. The Eucharist as Communion of the Faithful

19. The eucharistic communion with Christ who nourishes the life of the Church is at the same time communion within the body of Christ which is the Church. The sharing in one bread and the common cup in a given place demonstrates and effects the oneness of the sharers with Christ and with their fellow sharers in all times and places. It is in the eucharist that the community of God's people is fully manifested. Eucharistic celebrations always have to do with the whole Church, and the whole Church is involved in each local eucharistic celebration. . . .

III. The Celebration of the Eucharist

28. The best way towards unity in eucharistic celebration and communion is the renewal of the eucharist itself in the different churches in regard to teaching and liturgy. The churches should test their liturgies in the light of the eucharistic agreement now in the process of attainment. . . .

31. As the eucharist celebrates the resurrection of Christ, it is appropriate that it should take place at least every Sunday. As it is the new sacramental meal of the people of God, every Christian should be encouraged to receive communion frequently. . . .

Ministry

I. The Calling of the Whole People of God

3. The Church lives through the liberating and renewing power of the Holy Spirit. That the Holy Spirit was upon Jesus is evidenced in his baptism, and after the resurrection that same Spirit was given to those who believed in the Risen Lord in order to recreate them as the body of Christ. . . .

IV. Succession in the Apostolic Tradition

B. Succession of the Apostolic Ministry

35. The primary manifestation of apostolic succession is to be found in the apostolic tradition of the Church as a whole. The succession is an expression of the permanence and, therefore, of the continuity of Christ's own mission in which the Church participates. . . . The orderly transmission of the ordained ministry is therefore a powerful expression of the continuity of the Church throughout history; it also underlines the calling of the ordained minister as guardian of the faith. Where churches see little importance in orderly transmission, they should ask themselves whether they have not to change their conception of continuity in the apostolic tradition. On the other hand, where the ordained ministry does not adequately serve the proclamation of the apostolic faith, churches must ask themselves whether their ministerial structures are not in need of reform.[59]

[*Baptism, Eucharist and Ministry*, Faith and Order Paper No. 111 (Geneva: World Council of Churches, 1982), 2–14, 16, 20, 28]

59. This statement confirms that ministry structure is a means of passing on the faith, not an end in itself or a constitutive part of the *kerygma*.

Selection 113: David Bentley Hart, "Christ and Nothing (No Other God)" (2003)

By the late twentieth and early twenty-first century, Christians have witnessed a rising ecumenism, the numerical decline of mainline Protestantism, and the numerical explosion of global Christianity. Christians have also witnessed a progressive secularization of Western society increasingly infused with militant atheism, as well as a growing worldwide tension and persecution in the face of militant Islam. As a reflection of these and other realities, there has been a strong collective voice in Western theology that has become ever more eclectic and ecumenical, historically sensitive in its retrieval of the Christian past, and critical of the principal themes of the modernist project.

Many of these concerns resonate in the work of David Bentley Hart (1965–), an American writer and Eastern Orthodox theologian. His books have primarily focused on the history of the church and the nature of God and being, but his many essays delve into a wide range of topics. In this essay, Hart reflects on the first commandment ("You will have no other gods before me") and contrasts Christian truth with the nihilism of modernity.

As modern men and women—to the degree that we are modern—we believe in nothing. This is not to say, I should add, that we do not believe in anything; I mean, rather, that we hold an unshakable, if often unconscious, faith in *the* nothing, or in nothingness as such. It is this in which we place our trust, upon which we venture our souls, and onto which we project the values by which we measure the meaningfulness of our lives. Or, to phrase the matter more simply and starkly, our religion is one of very comfortable nihilism. . . .

"I am the Lord thy God," says the first commandment. "Thou shalt have no other gods before me." For Israel this was first and foremost a demand of fidelity, by which God bound his people to himself, even if in later years it became also a proclamation to the nations. To Christians, however, the commandment came through—and so was indissolubly bound to—Christ. As such, it was not simply a prohibition of foreign cults, but an assault upon the antique order of the heavens—a declaration of war upon the gods. All the world was to be evangelized and baptized, all idols overturned, all worship turned towards the one God who, in these latter days, had sent his Son into the world for our salvation. It was a long and sometimes terrible conflict, occasionally exacting a fearful price in martyrs' blood, but it was, by any just estimate, a victory: the temples of Zeus and Isis alike were finally deserted, both the paean and the dithyramb ceased to be sung, altars were bereft of sacrifices, the sibyls fell silent, and ultimately all the glory, nobility, and cruelty of the ancient world lay supine under the foot of Christ the conqueror. . . .

How, though, to make war on nothingness, on the abyss itself, denuded of its mythic allure? It seems to me much easier to convince a man that he is in thrall to demons and offer him manumission than to convince him that he is a slave to himself and prisoner to his own will. Surely this is a god more elusive, protean, and indomitable than either Apollo or Dionysus; and whether he manifests himself in some demonic titanism of the will, like the mass delirium of the Third Reich, or simply in the mesmerizing banality of consumer culture, his throne has been set in the very hearts of those he enslaves. And it is this god, in all likelihood, against whom the first commandment obliges modern Christians to struggle most tirelessly. . . .

The word "nihilism" has a complex history in modern philosophy, but I use it in a sense largely determined by Nietzsche and Heidegger,[60] both of whom not only diagnosed modernity as nihilism, but saw Christianity as complicit in its genesis; both, it seems to me, were penetratingly correct in some respects, if disastrously wrong in others, and both raised questions that Christians ignore at their peril. . . . Heidegger's tale is not as catastrophist, and so emphasizes less Christianity's novelty than its continuity with a nihilism implicit in all Western thought, from at least the time of Plato (something that Nietzsche, in his way, also acknowledged). Nihilism, says Heidegger, is born in a forgetfulness of the mystery of being, and in the attempt to capture and master being in artifacts of reason (the chief example—and indeed the prototype of every subsequent apostasy from true "ontology"—being Plato's ideas). Scandalously to oversimplify his argument, it is, says Heidegger, the history of this nihilistic impulse to reduce being to an object of the intellect, subject to the will, that has brought us at last to the age of technology, for which reality is just so many quanta of power, the world a representation of consciousness, and the earth a mere reserve awaiting exploitation; technological mastery has become our highest ideal, and our only real model of truth. Christianity, for its part, is not so much a new thing as a prolonged episode within the greater history of nihilism, notable chiefly for having brought part of this history's logic to its consummation by having invented the metaphysical God, the form of all forms, who grounds all of being in himself as absolute efficient cause, and who personifies that cause as total power and will. From this God, in the fullness of time, would be born the modern subject who has usurped God's place. . . .

60. Friedrich Nietzsche (1844–1900) was a German philosopher, classicist, and bold opponent of Christianity. Martin Heidegger (1889–1976) was a German existentialist philosopher.

The word "tragic," incidentally, is especially apt here. A sacrificial mythos need not always express itself in slaughter, after all. Attic tragedy, for instance, began as a kind of sacrificial rite. It was performed during the festival of Dionysus, which was a fertility festival, of course, but only because it was also an apotropaic celebration of delirium and death: the *Dionysia* was a sacred negotiation with the wild, antinomian cruelty of the god whose violent orgiastic cult had once, so it was believed, gravely imperiled the city; and the hope that prompted the feast was that, if this devastating force could be contained within bright Apollonian forms and propitiated through a ritual carnival of controlled disorder, the polis could survive for another year, its precarious peace intact. . . .

Nor does one require extraordinarily penetrating insight to see how the shadow of this mythos falls across the philosophical schools of antiquity. To risk a generalization even more reckless than those I have already ventured: from the time of the pre-Socratics, all the great speculative and moral systems of the pagan world were, in varying degrees, confined to this totality, to either its innermost mechanisms or outermost boundaries; rarely did any of them catch even a glimpse of what might lie beyond such a world; and none could conceive of reality except as a kind of strife between order and disorder, within which a sacrificial economy held all forces in tension. This is true even of original Platonism, at least in its more dualistic moments, with its dialectic of change and the changeless (or of limit and the infinite) and its equation of truth with eidetic abstraction; the world, for all its beauty, is the realm of fallen vision, separated by a great *chorismos*[61] from the

61. That is, "separation."

realm of immutable reality. It is true of Aristotle too: the dialectic of act and potency that, for sublunary beings, is inseparable from decay and death, or the scale of essences by which all things—especially various classes of persons—are assigned their places in the natural and social order. Stoicism offers an obvious example: a vision of the universe as a fated, eternally repeated divine and cosmic history, a world in which finite forms must constantly perish simply in order to make room for others, and which in its entirety is always consumed in a final *ecpyrosis*[62] (which makes a sacrificial pyre, so to speak, of the whole universe). And Neoplatonism furnishes the most poignant example, inasmuch as its monism merely inverts earlier Platonism's dualism, and only magnifies the melancholy: the mutable world is separated from its divine principle—the One—by intervals of emanation that descend in ever greater alienation from their source, and so—inasmuch as the highest truth is the secret identity between the human mind and the One—the labor of philosophy is one of escape: all multiplicity, change, particularity, every feature of the living world, is not only accidental to this formless identity, but a kind of falsehood, and to recover the truth that dwells within, one must detach oneself from what lies without, including the sundry incidentals of one's individual existence; truth is oblivion of the flesh, a pure nothingness, to attain which one must sacrifice the world.

In any event, the purpose behind these indefensibly broad pronouncements—however elliptically pursued—is to aid in recalling how shatteringly subversive Christianity was of so many of the certitudes of the world it entered, and how profoundly its exclusive fidelity to the God of Christ transformed that world. This is, of course, entirely in keeping with the New Testament's Paschal triumphalism: "Now is the judgment of this world, now will the prince of this world be cast out" (John 12:31); "I have overcome the world" (John 16:33); he is "far above all principality, and power, and might, and dominion" and all things are put "under his feet" (Ephesians 1:21-22); "having spoiled principalities and powers, he made a show of them openly, triumphing over them in it" (Colossians 2:15); "he led captivity captive" (Ephesians 4:8); and so on. Still we can largely absorb scripture's talk of the defeat of the devil, the angels of the nations, and the powers of the air, and yet fail to recognize how radically the Gospels reinterpreted (or, as Nietzsche would say, "transvalued") everything in the light of Easter.

Read in the context of its time, for example, what could be more seditious than the account John's Gospel gives of the dialogue between Christ and Pilate (John 18:28–19:12)? . . . This slave is the Father's eternal Word, whom God has vindicated with victory, and so ten thousand immemorial certainties are unveiled as lies: the first become last, the mighty are put down from their seats and the lowly exalted, the hungry are filled with good things while the rich are sent empty away. Nietzsche was quite right to be appalled. Almost as striking, for me, is the tale of Peter, at the cock's crow, going apart to weep. Nowhere in the literature of pagan antiquity, I assure you, had the tears of a rustic been regarded as worthy of anything but ridicule; to treat them with reverence, as meaningful expressions of real human sorrow, would have seemed grotesque from the perspective of all the classical canons of good taste. Those wretchedly subversive tears, and the dangerous philistinism of a narrator so incorrigibly vulgar as to treat them with anything but contempt, were most definitely signs of a

62. That is, the "conflagration" that terminates this universe.

slave-revolt in morality, if not quite the one against which Nietzsche inveighed—a revolt moreover that all the ancient powers proved impotent to resist.

In a narrow sense, then, one might say that the chief offense of the Gospels is their defiance of the insights of tragedy—and not only because Christ does not fit the model of the well-born tragic hero. More important is the incontestable truth that, in the Gospels, the destruction of the protagonist emphatically does not restore or affirm the order of city or cosmos. Were the Gospels to end with Christ's sepulture, in good tragic style, it would exculpate all parties, including Pilate and the Sanhedrin, whose judgments would be shown to have been fated by the exigencies of the crisis and the burdens of their offices; the story would then reconcile us to the tragic necessity of all such judgments. But instead comes Easter, which rudely interrupts all the minatory and sententious moralisms of the tragic chorus, just as they are about to be uttered to full effect, and which cavalierly violates the central tenet of sound economics: rather than trading the sacrificial victim for some supernatural benefit, and so the particular for the universal, Easter restores the slain hero in his particularity again, as the only truth the Gospels have to offer. This is more than a dramatic peripety. The empty tomb overturns all the "responsible" and "necessary" verdicts of Christ's judges, and so grants them neither legitimacy nor pardon. . . .

I am tempted to say, then, that the cross of Christ is not simply *a* sacrifice, but the place where two opposed understandings of sacrifice clashed. Christ's whole life was a reconciling *qurban*:[63] an approach to the Father, a real indwelling of God's glory in the temple of Christ's body, and an atonement made for a people enslaved to death; in pouring himself out in the form of a servant, and in living his humanity as an offering up of everything to God in love, the shape of the eternal Son's life was already sacrificial in this special sense; and it was this absolute giving, as God and man, that was made complete on Golgotha. While, from a pagan perspective (on the other hand), the crucifixion itself could be viewed as a sacrifice in the most proper sense—destruction of the agent of social instability for the sake of peace, which is always a profitable exchange—Christ's life of charity, service, forgiveness, and righteous judgment could not; indeed, it would have to seem the very opposite of sacrifice, an aneconomic and indiscriminate inversion of rank and order. Yet, at Easter, it is the latter God accepts and the former He rejects; what then of all the hard-won tragic wisdom of the ages?

Naturally, also, with the death of the old mythos, metaphysics too was transformed. For one thing, while every ancient system of philosophy had to presume an economy of necessity binding the world of becoming to its inmost or highest principles, Christian theology taught from the first that the world was God's creature in the most radically ontological sense: that it is called from nothingness, not out of any need on God's part, but by grace. The world adds nothing to the being of God, and so nothing need be sacrificed for his glory or sustenance. In a sense, God and world alike were liberated from the fetters of necessity; God could be accorded his true transcendence and the world its true character as divine gift. The full implications of this probably became visible to Christian philosophers only with the resolution of the fourth-century Trinitarian controversies, when the subordinationist schemes of Alexandrian Trinitarianism were abandoned, and with them the last residue

63. A Semitic (Hebrew, Syriac, Arabic) word for "offering."

within theology of the late antique metaphysical vision of a descending scale of divinity mediating between God and world—the both of them comprised in a single totality. That is a technical and disputable point, though; one more general, and uncontroversial, is that theology rejected nothing good in the metaphysics, ethics, or method of antique philosophy, but—with a kind of omnivorous glee—assimilated such elements as served its ends, and always improved them in the process. Stoic morality, Plato's language of the Good, Aristotle's metaphysics of act and potency—all became richer and more coherent when emancipated from the morbid myths of sacrificial economy and tragic necessity. In truth, Christian theology nowhere more wantonly celebrated its triumph over the old gods than in the use it made of the so-called *spolia Aegyptorum*;[64] and, by despoiling pagan philosophy of its most splendid achievements, and integrating them into a vision of reality more complete than philosophy could attain on its own, theology took to itself irrevocably all the intellectual glories of antiquity. The temples were stripped of their gold and precious ornaments, the sacred vessels were carried away into the precincts of the Church and turned to better uses, and nothing was left behind but a few grim, gaunt ruins to lure back the occasional disenchanted convert and to shelter a few atavistic ghosts. . . .

But what is the consequence, then, when Christianity, as a living historical force, recedes? We have no need to speculate, as it happens; modernity speaks for itself: with the withdrawal of Christian culture, all the glories of the ancient world that it baptized and redeemed have perished with it in the general cataclysm. Christianity is the midwife of nihilism, not because it is itself nihilistic, but because it is too powerful in its embrace of the world and all of the world's mystery and beauty; and so to reject Christianity now is, of necessity, to reject everything except the barren anonymity of spontaneous subjectivity. As Ivan Karamazov's Grand Inquisitor tells Christ, the freedom that the gospel brings is too terrible to be borne indefinitely. Sin makes us feeble and craven, and we long to flee from the liberty of the sons of God; but where now can we go? Everything is Christ's.

It is tempting to take the history of modern philosophy—at least in its continental (and, so to speak, proper) form—as a particularly vivid illustration of this point. There is something of a theological fashion at present of attempting precise genealogies of modernity, which would be a task far too ambitious for this essay; but it does seem clear to me that the special preoccupations and perversities of modern philosophy were incubated in the age of late scholasticism, with the rise of nominalism and voluntarism: whereas earlier theology spoke of God as Goodness as such, whose every act (by virtue of divine simplicity) expresses his nature, the specter that haunts much of late scholastic thought is a God whose will precedes his nature, and whose acts then are feats of pure spontaneity. It is a logically incoherent way of conceiving of God, as it happens, but it is a powerful idea, elevating as it does will over all else and redefining freedom—for God and, by extension, for us—not as the unhindered realization of a nature (the liberty to "become what you are"), but as the absolute liberty of the will in determining even what its nature is. Thus when modern philosophy established itself anew as a discipline autonomous from theology, it did so naturally by falling back upon an ever

64. That is, "the spoils of the Egyptians" that Israel took from Egypt in their exodus (Exod. 11:2-3; 12:36). In the early church, this event became a metaphor for Christianity's appropriation of pagan learning and culture.

more abyssal subjectivity. Real autonomy could not be gained by turning back to the wonder of being or to the transcendental perfections of the world, for to do so would be to slip again into a sphere long colonized by theology; and so the new point of departure for reason had to be the perceiving subject rather than the world perceived. Descartes, for instance, explicitly forbade himself any recourse to the world's testimony of itself; in his third Meditation, he seals all his senses against nature, so that he can undertake his rational reconstruction of reality from a position pure of any certitude save that of the ego's own existence. The world is recovered thereafter only insofar as it is posited, as an act of will. And while God appears in that reconstruction, he does so only as a logical postulate following from the idea of the infinite. From there, it is a short step to Kant's transcendental ego, for whom the world is the representation of its own irreducible "I think," and which (inasmuch as it is its own infinity) requires God as a postulate only in the realm of ethics, and merely as a regulative idea in the realm of epistemology. And the passage from transcendental idealism to absolute idealism, however much it involved an attempt to escape egoistic subjectivity, had no world to which to return; even Hegel's system, for all that it sought to have done with petty subjectivism, could do so only by way of a massive metaphysical myth of the self-positing of the Concept, and of a more terrible economy of necessity than any pagan antiquity had imagined. This project was, in every sense, incredible, and its collapse inevitably brought philosophy, by way of Nietzsche and Heidegger, to its "postmodern condition"—a "heap of broken images." If Heidegger was right—and he was—in saying that there was always a nihilistic core to the Western philosophical tradition, the withdrawal of Christianity leaves nothing but that core behind, for the gospel long ago stripped away both the deceits and the glories that had concealed it; and so philosophy becomes, almost by force of habit, explicit nihilism.

Modern philosophy, however, merely reflects the state of modern culture and modern cult. And here, I should admit, I feel a certain sympathy for Nietzsche's melancholy plaint, "Nearly two-thousand years and no new god"; and for Heidegger's mournful, twilight oracle: "Only a god can save us." No new gods, of course, will come. The Christian God has taken up everything into himself; all the treasures of ancient wisdom, all the splendor of creation, every good thing has been assumed into the story of the incarnate God, and every stirring towards transcendence is soon recognized by the modern mind—weary of God—as leading back towards faith. Antique pieties cannot be restored, for we moderns know that the hungers they excite can be sated only by the gospel of Christ crucified. To be a Stoic today, for instance, is simply to be a soul *in via*[65] to the Church; a Platonist, most of us understand, is only a Christian *manqué*;[66] and a polytheist is merely a truant from the one God he hates and loves. The only cult that can truly thrive in the aftermath of Christianity is a narrow service of the self, of the impulses of the will, of the nothingness that is all that the withdrawal of Christianity leaves behind. The only futures open to post-Christian culture are conscious nihilism, with its inevitable devotion to death, or the narcotic banality of the Last Men, which is a kind of death in life. Surveying the desert of modernity, it would be a kind of moral dereliction for Christians to fail to acknowledge that Nietzsche was right in holding Christianity responsible (even if he misunderstood why) for

65. That is, "on the way."
66. That is, one who has not quite lived up to his potential.

the catastrophe around us. Christians should be willing to confess that the failure of Christian culture to live up to its victory over the old gods has allowed the dark power that once hid behind them to step forward *in propria persona*.[67] And everyone with some consciousness of cultural history should certainly dread whatever rough beast it is that is being bred in our ever coarser, crueler, more inarticulate, more vacuous popular culture; because, cloaked in its anodyne insipience, lies a world increasingly devoid of merit, wit, kindness, imagination, or charity.

These are, I admit, extreme formulations; but I do not intend them simply as provocations. When recently I made these very remarks from a speaker's podium, two theologians (neither of whom I would consider a champion of modernity) raised objections to them. From one quarter, I was chided for forgetting the selflessness of which modern persons are capable; on 11 September 2001, I was reminded, we had seen plenteous demonstrations of that selflessness; and those of us who teach undergraduates must be aware that, for all the cultural privations they suffer, they are often decent and admirable. From the other quarter I was cautioned that so starkly stated an alternative as "Christianity or nihilism" amounted to a denial of the goodness of natural wisdom and virtue, and seemed to suggest that *gratia non perficit, sed destruit naturam*.[68] As fair, however, as such remarks may be, they are not apposite to the argument I mean to advance.

To the former objection, I would wish to reply by making clear that I do not intend to suggest that, because modernity has lost the organic integrity of Christianity's moral grammar, every person living in modern society must therefore become heartless, violent, or unprincipled. My observations are directed at the dominant language and ethos of a culture, not at the souls of individuals. Many among us retain some loyalty to ancient principles, most of us are in some degree pre-modern, and there are always and everywhere to be found examples of natural virtue, innate nobility, congenital charity, and so on; if Christian teaching is correct, the light of God is ubiquitous and the image of God is impressed upon our nature. The issue for me is whether, within the moral grammar of modernity, any of these good souls could give an account of his or her virtue. I wish, that is, to make a point not conspicuously different from Alasdair MacIntyre's in the first chapter of his *After Virtue*: that is, what an odd *bricolage* ethics has become in the wake of a morality of the Good. As far as I can tell, *homo nihilisticus* may often be in several notable respects a far more amiable rogue than *homo religiosus*, exhibiting a far smaller propensity for breaking the crockery, destroying sacred statuary, or slaying the nearest available infidel. But, love, let us be true to one another: even when all of this is granted, it would be a willful and culpable blindness for us to refuse to recognize how culturally and spiritually impoverished our society has become—which any unprejudiced survey of the artifacts of popular culture will effortlessly confirm. How, after all, should Christians regard the present age when, in America alone, more than 40 million babies have been killed in the womb since the Supreme Court invented the right to abortion, and when there arc many who see these deaths not just as tragic necessities, but as blameless consequences of a moral social triumph? When the Carthaginians were prevailed upon to cease sacrificing their babies, at least the place vacated

67. That is, "in its own (or proper) person."

68. That is, "grace does not perfect, but destroys nature." This criticism expresses the opposite of Thomas Aquinas's claim that "grace does not destroy, but perfects nature."

by Baal reminded them that they should seek the divine above themselves; but our culture offers up its babies to "my" freedom of choice, to "me." Surely a Christian must doubt that any other society's moral vision has ever shown itself to be more degenerate.

To the latter objection, I would make three responses. First, my remarks here do not concern the entirety of human experience, nature, or culture; they concern one particular location in time and space: late Western modernity. Nor have I anything to say about cultures or peoples who have not suffered the history of faith and disenchantment we have, or who do not share our particular relation to European antiquity or the heritage of ancient Christendom. "Nihilism" is simply a name for post-Christian sensibility and conviction (and not even an especially opprobrious one). Second, the alternative between Christianity and nihilism is never, in actual practice, a kind of Kierkegaardian either/or posed between two absolute antinomies, incapable of alloy or medium; it is an antagonism that occurs along a continuum, whose extremes are rarely perfectly expressed in any single life (else the world were all saints and satanists). Third, and most important, my observations do not concern nature at all, which is inextinguishable and which, at some level, always longs for God; they concern culture, which has the power to purge itself of the natural in some considerable degree. Indeed, much of the discourse of late modernity—speculative, critical, moral, and political—consists precisely in an attempt to deny the authority, or even the reality, of any general order of nature or natures. Nature is good, I readily affirm, and is itself the first gift of grace. But that is rather the point at issue: modernity is profoundly unnatural.

Which is why I repeat that our age is not one in danger of reverting to paganism (would that we were so fortunate). If we turn from Christ today, we turn only towards the god of absolute will, and embrace him under either his most monstrous or his most vapid aspect. A somewhat more ennobling retreat to the old gods is not possible for us; we can find no shelter there, nor can we sink away gently into those old illusions and tragic consolations that Christ has exposed as falsehoods. To love or be nourished by the gods, we would have to fear them; but the ruin of their glory is so complete that they have been reduced—like everything else—to commodities. . . .

This commandment has always been a hard discipline: it destroys, it breaks in order to bind; like a cautery, it wounds in order to heal. In practical terms, I suspect that this means that Christians must make an ever more concerted effort to recall and recover the wisdom and centrality of the ascetic tradition. It takes formidable faith and devotion to resist the evils of one's age, and it is to the history of Christian asceticism—especially, perhaps, the apophthegms of the Desert Fathers—that all Christians, whether married or not, should turn for guidance. To have no god but the God of Christ, after all, means today that we must endure the Lenten privations of what is most certainly a dark age, and strive to resist the bland solace, inane charms, brute viciousness, and dazed passivity of post-Christian culture—all of which are so tempting precisely because they enjoin us to believe in and adore ourselves. It means also to remain aloof from many of the moral languages of our time, which are—even at their most sentimental, tender, and tolerant—usually as decadent and egoistic as the currently most fashionable vices. It means, in short, self-abnegation, contrarianism, a willingness not only to welcome but to condemn, and a refusal of secularization as fierce as the refusal of the ancient Christians to burn incense to the genius of the emperor. This is not an especially grim prescription, I should add: Christian asceticism is not, after all, a cruel disfigurement of the will, contaminated by the world-weariness or malice towards creation; it is a different kind of detachment, the cultivation of the pure heart and pure eye, which allows one to receive the world, and rejoice in it, not as a possession of the will or an occasion for the exercise of power, but as the good gift of God. It is, so to speak, a kind of Marian waiting upon the Word of God and its fruitfulness. Paradoxical as it may seem to modern temperaments, Christian asceticism is the practice of love, what Maximus the Confessor calls learning to see the logos of each thing within the Logos of God, and it leads most properly in the grateful reverence of a Bonaventure or the lyrical ecstasy of a Thomas Traherne.

Still, it is a discipline for all that; and for modern Christians it must involve the painful acknowledgement that neither they nor their distant progeny will live to see a new Christian culture rise in the Western world, and to accept this with both charity and faith. After all, in the mystery of God's providence, all of this has followed from the work of the Holy Spirit in time. Modern persons will never find rest for their restless hearts without Christ, for modern culture is nothing but the wasteland from which the gods have departed, and so this restlessness has become its own deity; and, deprived of the shelter of the sacred and the consoling myths of sacrifice, the modern person must wander or drift, vainly attempting one or another accommodation with death, never escaping anxiety or *ennui*, and driven as a result to a ceaseless labor of distraction, or acquisition, or willful idiocy. And, where it works its sublimest magic, our culture of empty spectacle can so stupefy the intellect as to blind it to its own disquiet, and induce a spiritual torpor more deplorable than mere despair. But perhaps Christians—while not ignoring how appalling such a condition may be—should actually rejoice that modernity offers no religious comforts to those who seek them. If this is a time of waiting, marked most deeply by the absence of faith in Christ, it is perhaps good that the modern soul should lack repose, piety, peace, or nobility, and should often find the world outside the Church barren of spiritual rapture or mystery, and should go about vainly looking for beautiful or terrible or merciful gods to adore. With Christ came judgment into the world, a light of discrimination from which there is neither retreat nor sanctuary. And this means that, as a quite concrete historical condition, the only choice that remains for the children of post-Christian culture is not whom to serve, but whether to serve the God Christ has revealed or to serve nothing—*the* nothing. No third way lies open now, because—as all of us now know, whether we acknowledge it consciously or not—all things have been made subject to him, all the thrones and dominions of the high places have been put beneath his feet, until the very end of the world, and—simply said—there *is* no other god.

["Christ and Nothing," *First Things* 136 (2003): 47–57]

Further Reading

Busch, Eberhard. *Karl Barth: His Life from Letters and Autobiographical Texts*. Trans. John Bowden. 1976; repr., Grand Rapids, MI: Eerdmans, 1994.

Grenz, Stanley J., and Roger E. Olson. *Twentieth-Century Theology: God and World in a Transitional Age*. Downers Grove, IL: IVP Academic, 1992.

Livingston, James C., and Francis Schüssler Fiorenza. *Modern Christian Thought: The Twentieth Century*. 2nd ed. Minneapolis: Fortress Press, 2006.

Metaxas, Eric. *Bonhoeffer: Pastor, Martyr, Prophet, Spy*. Nashville, TN: Thomas Nelson, 2010.

Murphy, Nancey. *Beyond Liberalism and Fundamentalism: How Modern and Postmodern Philosophy Set the Theological Agenda*. New York: Trinity Press International, 1996.

O'Malley, John W. *What Happened at Vatican II*. Cambridge, MA: Belknap Press of Harvard University Press, 2008.

Rowland, Christopher, ed. *The Cambridge Companion to Liberation Theology*. 2nd ed. Cambridge, UK: Cambridge University Press, 2007.

Sources and Acknowledgments

Sources

Selection 1: Boniface VIII, *Unam Sanctam,* from *Documents of the Christian Church 4th Edition*, Bettenson and Maunder, eds. Copyright © Oxford University Press. Reprinted by permission of the publisher.

Selection 2: *Propositions of Wycliffe Condemned* and *The Twelve Conclusions of the Lollards* from *Documents of the Christian Church*, 4th ed., Bettenson and Maunder, eds. eprinted by permission of the publisher.

Selection 3: "Decrees of Council of Constance, Sessions 5 and 12," in Norman P. Tanner, *Decrees of the Ecumenical Councils*, vol. 1 (London: Sheed & Ward), copyright © 1990. Used by permission of Bloomsbury Publishing PLC.

Selection 4: Excerpts from *Julian of Norwich: Showings*, Classics of Western Spirituality, trans. Edmund Colledge and James Walsh. Copyright © 1978 by Paulist Press, Inc. All rights reserved.

Selection 5: "Beinecke 757," *Worship in Medieval and Early Modern Europe: Change and Continuity in Religious Practice*, trans. Margot Fassler, ed. Karin Maag and John D. Witvliet. Copyright © 2004 University of Notre Dame Press. Used by permission.

Selection 7: Desiderius Erasmus, "Some New Prayers," in *Collected Works of Erasmus*, vol. 69, ed. John W. O'Malley and Louis A. Perraud, trans. and annotated by Stephen Ryle. Copyright © 1999 University of Toronto Press. Used by permission of the publisher.

Selection 8: Desiderius Erasmus, "To the Reader," in *Collected Works of Erasmus*, vol. 3, ed. R. A. B. Mynors and D. F. S. Thomson, annotated by James J. McConica. Copyright © 1976 University of Toronto Press. Used by permission of the publisher.

Selection 9: Desiderius Erasmus, "The Handbook of the Christian Soldier," *in Collected Works of Erasmus*, vol. 66, ed., trans., and annotated by Charles Fantazzi. Copyright © 1988 University of Toronto Press. Used by permission of the publisher.

Selection 10: Desiderius Erasmus, "Julius Exclusus," in *Collected Works of Erasmus*, vol. 27, ed. A.H.T. Levi, trans. and annotated by Michael J. Heath. Copyright © 1986 University of Toronto Press. Used by permission of the publisher.

Selection 11: Desiderius Erasmus, Freedom of the Will, in *Luther and Erasmus: Free Will and Salvation, Library of Christian Classics*, vol. 17, trans. and ed. E. Gordon Rupp. © 1969 Wesminster Press. Reprinted here with permission of Westminster John Knox Press. All rights reserved.

Selection 12: Excerpt from *Luther's Works*, vol. 30, copyright © 1967 Concordia Pubilshing House (www.cph.org). All rights reserved.

Selection 13: Excerpts from *Luther's Works*, vol. 31, copyright © 1957 Fortress Press.

Selection 14: Excerpts from *Luther's Works*, vol. 31, copyright © 1957 Fortress Press.

Selection 15: Excerpts from *Luther's Works*, vol. 34, copyright © 1960 Fortress Press.

Selection 16: Excerpts from *Luther's Works*, vol. 44, copyright © 1960 Fortress Press.

Selection 17: Excerpts from *Luther's Works*, vol. 36, copyright © 1959 Fortress Press.

Selection 18: Excerpts from *Luther's Works*, vol. 46, copyright © 1967 Fortress Press.

Selection 19: Excerpts from *Luther's Works*, vol. 35, copyright © 1960 Fortress Press.

Selection 20: Excerpts from *Luther's Works*, vol. 53, copyright © 1965 Fortress Press.

Selection 21: Excerpts from *Luther's Works*, vol. 54, copyright © 1967 Fortress Press.

Selection 22: Ulrich Zwingli, *Of Baptism,* in *Zwingli and Bullinger*, The Library of Christian Classics, vol. 24, copyright © 1953 Westminster Press. Reprinted here with permission of Westminster John Knox Press. All rights reserved.

Selection 23: Ulrich Zwingli, *Exposition of the Faith,* in *Zwingli and Bullinger*, The Library of Christian Classics, vol. 24, copyright © 1953 Westminster Press. Reprinted here with permission of Westminster John Knox Press. All rights reserved.

Selection 24: Excerpts from *Luther's Works*, vol. 38, Helmut Lehman, ed. Copyright © 1971 Fortress Press.

Selection 25: Katharina Schütz Zell, *Apologia for Master Matthew Zell (1524)*, in *Church Mother*, trans. and ed. Elsie A. McKee. Copyright © 2006 University of Chicago Press. Used by permission of the publisher.

Selection 29: John Calvin, *Calvin: Theological Treatises,* ed. J. K. S. Reid, Library of Christian Classics, vol 22 © 1954 The Westminster Press. Used by permission of Westminster John Knox Press. All rights reserved.

Selection 30: John Calvin, *Institutes of the Christian Religion*, ed. John T. McNeill and trans. Ford Lewis Battles, Library of Christian Classics, vol. 20, © 1960 The Westminster Press. Used by permission of Westminster John Knox Press. All rights reserved.

Selection 31: Andreas Bodenstein von Karlstadt, *Whether One Should Proceed Slowly*, in *The Radical Reformation*, ed. Michael Baylor. Copyright © 1991 Cambridge University Press. Used by permission.

Selection 32: Thomas Müntzer, *A Sermon to the Princes* (1524), in *Spiritual and Anabaptist Writers*, ed. George H. Williams and Angel Mergal. © 1957 Westminster Press. Reprinted here with permission of Westminster John Knox Press. All rights reserved.

Selection 33: Conrad Grebel, *Letter to Thomas Müntzer* (1524), in *Spiritual and Anabaptist Writers*, ed. George H. Williams and Angel Mergal. © 1957 Westminster Press. Reprinted here with permission of Westminster John Knox Press. All rights reserved.

Selection 34: "Freedom of Will" (1527), in *Balthasar Hubmaier: Theologian of Anabaptism*, trans. and ed. H. Wayne Pipkin and John H. Yoder. Copyright © 1989 Herald Press, Scottdale, PA. Used by permission.

Selection 35: "Schleitheim Confession" (1527), in *The Legacy of Michael Sattler*, trans. and ed. by John H. Yoder. Copyright © 1973 Herald Press, Scottdale, PA. Used by permission.

Selection 36: "Christian baptism" (1539), in *The Complete Writings of Menno Simons*, trans. Leonard Verduin, ed. J. C. Wenger. Copyright © 1956, 1984 by Mennonite Publishing House, Scottdale, PA. Used by permission.

Selection 37: "The Trial and Martyrdom of Michael Sattler," in *Spiritual and Anabaptist Writers*, ed. George H. Williams and Angel Mergal. © 1957 Westminster Press. Reprinted here with permission of Westminster John Knox Press. All rights reserved.

Selection 40: Johann Tetzel, *Rebuttal to Luther's Sermon on Indulgences*, trans. Dewey Weiss Kramer (Atlanta: Pitts Theology Library, 2012). Reprinted here with permission of the Pitts Theological Library (www.pitts.emory.edu).

Selection 41: *Leo X, Exsurge Domine* from *Martin Luther* by E.G. Rupp and Benjamin Drewery, copyright © 1970 Macmillan Press Ltd. Reprinted here by permission of Palgrave Macmillan.

Selection 42: Ignatius of Loyola, *The Autobiography of St. Ignatius Loyola with Related Documents*, trans. Joseph F. O'Callaghan. © 1992 Fordham University Press, all rights reserved. Used by permission.

Selection 43: Excerpt from *The Spiritual Exercises of St. Ignatius of Loyola*, by Louis J. Puhl, S.J. (Newman Press 1951). Reprinted with permission of Loyola Press. (For more information call 1-800-621-1008 or visit www.loyolapress.com).

Selection 44: From *The Collected Works of St. Teresa of Avila*, vol. 1, trans. Kieran Kavanaugh and Otilio Rodriguez. Copyright © 1976 by Washington Province of Discalced Carmelites. Used by permission of ICS Publications (www.icspublications.org).

Selection 47: Guido de Brès, *Belgic Confession,* from www.crcna.org. Used by permission of Faith Alive Resources.

Selection 48: *Heidelberg Catechism* (Q & A 1-2, 75-85) from www.crcna.org. Used by permission of Faith Alive Resources.

Selection 50: Heinrich Bullinger, "Second Helvetic Confession" (1566), in *Creeds and Confessions of Faith in the Christian Tradition*, vol. 2, ed. Jaroslav Pelikan and Valerie Hotchkiss © 2003 Yale University Press. Used by permission of the publisher. All rights reserved.

Selection 54: Excerpts from *Book of Concord*, ed. Robert Kolb and Timothy Wengert, copyright © 2000 Augsburg Fortress.

Selection 58: Jacob Arminius, *Declaration of Sentiments*, *Arminius and His Declaration of Sentiments: An Annotated Translation with Introduction and Theological Commentary*, ed. W. Stephen Gunter (Waco, TX: Baylor University Press, 2012). Reprinted here with permission of the publisher. All rights reserved.

Selection 60: *Canons of the Synod of Dordt* (1619) from www.crcna.org. Used by permission of Faith Alive Resources.

Selections 61 and 62: René Descartes, *Discourse on Method and Meditations on First Philosophy*, 1st ed., trans. Donald A. Cress, copyright © 1980 by Hackett Publishing Company, Inc. All rights reserved. Used by permission of the publisher.

Selection 66: G. E. Lessing. "On the Proof of the Spirit and of Power" (1777), in *Theological Writings* (Stanford: Stanford University Press, 1957). Copyright © 1956 by A & C Black, Ltd. All rights reserved.

Selection 67: Immanuel Kant, *Groundwork of the Metaphysics of Morals (1785)*, in *Practical Philosophy*, trans. Mary J. Grego. Copyright © 1996 Cambridge University Press. Used by permission.

Selection 68: Immanuel Kant, "On a Supposed Right to Lie from Philanthropy," in *Practical Philosophy*, trans. Mary J. Grego. Copyright © 1996 Cambridge University Press. Used by permission.

Selection 69: Jean Taffin, *The Marks of God's Children* (1586), trans. Peter Y. De Jong. Translation © 2003. Reprinted by permission of Reformation Heritage Books.

Selection 70: Excerpts from Blaise Pascal, *Pensées*, trans. A. J. Krailsheimer (Penguin Books, 1966). Copyright © A.J. Krailsheimer, 1966, 1995. All rights reserved. Used by permission of the publisher (www.penguin.co.uk).

Selection 71: Philipp Jakob Spener, *Pia desideria*, trans. Theodore G. Tappert, Seminar Editions (Philadelphia: Fortress Press). Copyright © 1964 Fortress Press.

Selection 72: Jonathan Edwards, *Miscellanies*, number 348, in *Works of Jonathan Edwards*, vol. 13, © 1994 Yale University Press. Used by permission of the publisher. All rights reserved.

Selection 73: Jonathan Edwards, *Treatise on Religious Affections* (1746) © 1959 Yale University Press. Used by permission of the publisher. All rights reserved.

Selection 75: "The Character of a Methodist," from *The Works of John Wesley*, Vol. 9 © 1989 Abingdon Press. Used by permission. All rights reserved.

Selection 76: "Christian Perfection," from *The Works of John Wesley*, vol. 2 © 1985 Abingdon Press. Used by permission. All rights reserved.

Selection 77: "The Scripture Way of Salvation," from *The Works of John Wesley*, vol. 2 © 1985 Abingdon Press. Used by permission. All rights reserved.

Selection 78: "Catholic Spirit," from *The Works of John Wesley*, vol. 2 © 1985 Abingdon Press. Used by permission. All rights reserved.

Selection 80: Thomas Campbell, *Declaration and Address (1809)*, in *The Quest for Christian Unity, Peace, and Purity in Thomas Campbell's Declaration and Address*, ed. Thomas H. Olbricht and Hans Rollmann. Copyright © 2000 Scarecrow Press. Used by permission. (www.rowman.com/scarecrow)

Selection 86: From Friedrich D. E. Schleiermacher, *On Religion: Speeches to Its Cultured Despisers*, 2nd ed., ed. Richard Crouter. Copyright © 1988, 1996 Cambridge University Press. Used by permission.

Selection 87: From Friedrich D. E. Schleiermacher, *The Christian Faith*, 2nd ed., copyright © 1976 T&T Clark. Used by permission of Bloomsbury Publishing PLC.

Selection 88: Friedrich D. E. Schleiermacher, "Sermon at Nathanael's Grave," trans. Albert L. Blackwell, from the *Journal of Religion* 57, © 1977 by the University of Chicago Press. Reprinted by permission.

Selection 89: *The Collected Writings of Søren Kierkegaard*, trans. Howard and Edna Hong, vol. 12; Copyright © 1992. Reprinted by permission of Princeton University Press.

Selection 90: *The Collected Writings of Søren Kierkegaard*, trans. Howard and Edna Hong, vol. 20; Copyright © 1991. Reprinted by permission of Princeton University Press. All rights reserved.

Selection 96: "First Dogmatic Constitution on the Church of Christ," in Norman P. Tanner, *Decrees of the Ecumenical Councils*, vol. 2 (London: Sheed & Ward), copyright © 1990. Used by permission of Bloomsbury Publishing PLC.

Selection 98: From Karl Barth, *The Epistle to the Romans*, trans. Edwyn C. Hoskyns, © Oxford University Press. Used by permission of the publisher.

Selection 99: Karl Barth, *Church Dogmatics* II (no 1), copyright © 1957 T&T Clark. Used by permission of Bloomsbury Publishing PLC.

Selection 100: Excerpt from Reinhold Niebuhr, *Moral Man and Immoral Society: A Study in Ethics and Politics* (Charles Scribner & Sons, 1932). Copyright © The Estate of Reinhold Niebuhr. All rights reserved. Reprinted here with permission from The Estate of Reinhold Niebuhr.

Selection 101: Excerpts from *Ethics*, Dietrich Bonhoeffer Works, vol. 6. Copyright © 2005 Augsburg Fortress. All rights reserved.

Selections 103 and 104: http://w2.vatican.va/content/vatican/en.html. Copyright © Libreria Editrie Vaticana. All rights reserved.

Selection 105: Georges Florovsky, "The Function of Tradition in the Ancient Church," in *Greek Orthodox Theological Review* 9, no. 2 (1964). Copyright © Hellenic College, Inc. Reprinted here with permission from Holy Cross Orthodox Press.

Selection 106: "Chicago Statement on Biblical Inerrancy" from the International Council on Biblical Inerrancy (1978).

Selection 107: Excerpt from Gustavo Gutiérrez, *A Theology of Liberation* (Maryknoll, NY: Orbis Books). Copyright © 1988 by Orbis Books. All rights reserved. Reprinted by permission of the publisher.

Selection 108: Elisabeth Schüssler Fiorenza, *In Memory of Her* (Crossroad, 1994). Used with permission by The Crossroad Publishing Company.

Selection 109: Karl Rahner, "Christianity and the Non-Christian Religions," in *Christianity and Other Religions*, ed. John Hick and Brian Hebblethwaite (Philadelphia: Fortress Press, 1980). Copyright © John Hick and Brian Hebblethwaite. All rights reserved.

Selection 110: Excerpts from John Hick, *Problems of Religious Pluralism*, copyright © 1985 Macmillan Press Ltd., London. Used by permission of Palgrave Macmillan.

Selection 111: Lesslie Newbigin, *The Gospel in a Pluralist Society* © 1989 Wm. B. Eerdmans Publishing Company, Grand Rapids, MI. Reprinted by permission of the publisher; all rights reserved.

Selection 112: Lima Report, *Baptism, Eucharist, and Ministry*; copyright © 1982 World Council of Chuches (http://www.oikoumene.org/en).

Selection 113: "Christ and Nothing" is reprinted with permission from the October 2003 issue of *First Things* (www.firstthings.com).

Illustrations

Chapter 1 introduction: http://commons.wikimedia.org/wiki/File:FraMauroMap.jpg

Selection 3: http://commons.wikimedia.org/wiki/File:Brozik,_Vaclav_-_Jan_Hus_souzen_na_snemu_Kostnickem_r._1415.jpg

Selection 4: http://commons.wikimedia.org/wiki/File:Statue_of_Dame_Julian.JPG

Selection 6: http://commons.wikimedia.org/wiki/File:Rembrandt%27s_Son_Titus_in_a_Monk%27s_Habit.jpg

Selection 7: http://commons.wikimedia.org/wiki/File:Holbein-erasmus.jpg

Selection 10: http://commons.wikimedia.org/wiki/File:Raffaello_Sanzio_-_Portrait_of_Julius_II_-_WGA18798.jpg

Selection 12: http://commons.wikimedia.org/wiki/File:Portrait_of_Martin_Luther_as_an_Augustinian_Monk.jpg

Selection 14: http://commons.wikimedia.org/wiki/File:95Thesen.jpg

Selection 22: http://commons.wikimedia.org/wiki/File:Ulrich_Zwingli_03.jpg

Selection 26: http://commons.wikimedia.org/wiki/File:John_Calvin_21.jpg

Selection 30: http://commons.wikimedia.org/wiki/File:Reformatoren_Gruppenportrait.jpg

Selection 31: http://commons.wikimedia.org/wiki/File:Frans_Hogenberg_-_The_Calvinist_Iconoclastic_Riot_of_August_20,_1566_-_WGA11470.jpg

Selection 32: http://commons.wikimedia.org/wiki/File:ThomasM%C3%BCntzerDDR5Mark.jpg

Selection 34: http://commons.wikimedia.org/wiki/File:Balthasar_Hubmaier.png

Selection 36: http://commons.wikimedia.org/wiki/File:Menno_Simons_by_Jacob_Burghart.jpg

Selection 37: http://commons.wikimedia.org/wiki/File:Anneke_jans.jpg

Selection 38: http://commons.wikimedia.org/wiki/File:Witch-scene4.JPG

Selection 40: "Unused Indulgence" Courtesy of the Richard C. Kessler Reformation Collection, Pitts Theology Library, Candler School of Theology, Emory University

Selection 41: http://commons.wikimedia.org/wiki/File:Raphael_-_Pope_Leo_X_with_two_cardinals.jpg

Selection 43: http://commons.wikimedia.org/wiki/File:Gesu6.jpg

Selection 44: http://commons.wikimedia.org/wiki/File:Teresa_of_%C3%81vila.jpg

Selection 45: http://commons.wikimedia.org/wiki/File:Pasquale_Cati_Da_Iesi_-_The_Council_of_Trent_-_WGA04574.jpg and http://upload.wikimedia.org/wikipedia/commons/7/71/Landshut_prozession_Dreifaltigkeitsplatz_1733.png

Selection 49: http://commons.wikimedia.org/wiki/File:Zacharias_Ursinus.png

Selection 54: http://commons.wikimedia.org/wiki/File:Concordia,_Dresden_1580_-_fba.jpg

Biographical note, Jacob Arminius: David Bailly, "James Arminius, Pastor, Professor, and Theologian" Courtesy of Remonstrantse Gemeente Rotterdam.

Selection 57: "Great king protect us . . ." Amsterdam, 1628.

Selection 60: "Op de Waag-Schaal" Courtesy of Jeremy Bangs

Chapter 6 introduction: http://commons.wikimedia.org/wiki/File:OrteliusWorldMap1570.jpg

Selection 61: http://commons.wikimedia.org/wiki/File:Frans_Hals_111_WGA_version.jpg
Selection 63: http://commons.wikimedia.org/wiki/File:Locke-John-LOC.jpg
Selection 64: http://commons.wikimedia.org/wiki/File:David_Hume.jpg
Selection 66: http://commons.wikimedia.org/wiki/File:Gotthold_Ephraim_Lessing.jpg
Selection 67: http://commons.wikimedia.org/wiki/File:Immanuel_Kant_2.jpg
Chapter 7 introduction: http://commons.wikimedia.org/wiki/File:Camp_meeting.jpg
Selection 70: http://commons.wikimedia.org/wiki/File:Blaise_Pascal_Versailles.JPG
Selection 71: http://commons.wikimedia.org/wiki/File:Philipp_Jakob_Spener.jpg
Selection 73: http://commons.wikimedia.org/wiki/File:Jonathan_Edwards.jpg
John Wesley biographical note (John Wesley): http://en.wikipedia.org/wiki/File:John_Wesley_by_George_Romney.jpg
John Wesley biographical note (Charles Wesley): http://uploads6.wikiart.org/images/john-russell/reverend-charles-wesley-1707-1788-ma-1771.jpg
Selection 82: http://commons.wikimedia.org/wiki/File:Joseph_Smith,_Jr._profile_by_Bathsheba_Smith_circa_1843.jpg
Chapter 8 introduction: http://commons.wikimedia.org/wiki/File:1878_Darwin_photo_by_Leonard_from_Woodall_1884.jpg
Selection 84: http://commons.wikimedia.org/wiki/File:William_Ellery_Channing_engraved_by_Cheney.jpg
Selection 86: http://commons.wikimedia.org/wiki/File:Friedrich_Daniel_Ernst_Schleiermacher.jpg
Selection 89: http://commons.wikimedia.org/wiki/File:Kierkegaard_portrait.jpg
Selection 90: http://commons.wikimedia.org/wiki/File:Kierkegaard_olavius.jpg
Selection 94: http://upload.wikimedia.org/wikipedia/commons/thumb/a/ae/Pius_ix.jpg/412px-Pius_ix.jpg
Selection 104: http://commons.wikimedia.org/wiki/File:Hist1.jpg
Selection 105: http://commons.wikimedia.org/wiki/File:Santa_Sofia_-_Crist_Pantocrator.JPG